ADOBE INDESIGN CS5

CS5

REVEALED

ADOBE
INDESIGN CS5

Adobe Approved Certification Courseware™

REVEALED

CHRIS BOTELLO

DELMAR
CENGAGE Learning™

Australia • Brazil • Japan • Korea • Mexico • Singapore • Spain • United Kingdom • United States

Adobe InDesign CS5 Revealed
Chris Botello

Vice President, Career and Professional Editorial:
   Dave Garza

Director of Learning Solutions: Sandy Clark

Senior Acquisitions Editor: Jim Gish

Managing Editor: Larry Main

Product Managers: Jane Hosie-Bounar, Meaghan O'Brien

Editorial Assistant: Sarah Timm

Vice President Marketing, Career and Professional:
   Jennifer Baker

Executive Marketing Manager: Deborah S. Yarnell

Marketing Manager: Erin Brennan

Marketing Coordinator: Jonathan Sheehan

Production Director: Wendy Troeger

Senior Content Project Manager: Kathryn B. Kucharek

Developmental Editor: Sandra Kruse

Technical Editor: Tara Botelho

Senior Art Director: Joy Kocsis

Cover Design: Joe Villanova

Cover Art: Spitting Images

Cover Photo: Panda: © istockphoto.com/Life on White;
   Beauty Salon: © Cat Gwynn/Corbis

Text Designer: Liz Kingslein

Production House: Integra Software Services Pvt. Ltd.

Proofreader: Harold Johnson

Indexer: Alexandra Nickerson

Technology Project Manager: Christopher Catalina

For product information and technology assistance, contact us at **Cengage Learning Customer & Sales Support, 1-800-354-9706**

For permission to use material from this text or product, submit all requests online at **www.cengage.com/permissions**

Further permissions questions can be emailed to **permissionrequest@cengage.com**

Adobe® Photoshop®, Adobe® InDesign®, Adobe® Illustrator®, Adobe® Flash®, Adobe® Dreamweaver®, Adobe® Fireworks®, and Adobe® Creative Suite® are trademarks or registered trademarks of Adobe Systems, Inc. in the United States and/or other countries. Third party products, services, company names, logos, design, titles, words, or phrases within these materials may be trademarks of their respective owners.

Adobe product screenshot(s) reprinted with permission from Adobe Systems Incorporated.

The Adobe Approved Certification Courseware logo is a proprietary trademark of Adobe. All rights reserved. Cengage Learning and Adobe InDesign CS5––Revealed are independent from ProCert Labs, LLC and Adobe Systems Incorporated, and are not affiliated with ProCert Labs and Adobe in any manner. This publication may asssist students to prepare for an Adobe Certified Expert exam, however, neither ProCert Labs nor Adobe warrant that use of this material will ensure success in connection with any exam.

Library of Congress Control Number: 2010921376

Hardcover edition:
ISBN-13: 978-1-111-13051-0
ISBN-10: 1-111-13051-5

Soft cover edition:
ISBN-13: 978-1-111-13049-7
ISBN-10: 1-111-13049-3

Delmar
5 Maxwell Drive
Clifton Park, NY 12065-2919
USA

Cengage Learning is a leading provider of customized learning solutions with office locations around the globe, including Singapore, the United Kingdom, Australia, Mexico, Brazil, and Japan. Locate your local office at: **international.cengage.com/region**

Cengage Learning products are represented in Canada by Nelson Education, Ltd.

To learn more about Delmar, visit **www.cengage.com/delmar**

Purchase any of our products at your local college store or at our preferred online store **www.cengagebrain.com**

Notice to the Reader
Publisher does not warrant or guarantee any of the products described herein or perform any independent analysis in connection with any of the product information contained herein. Publisher does not assume, and expressly disclaims, any obligation to obtain and include information other than that provided to it by the manufacturer. The reader is expressly warned to consider and adopt all safety precautions that might be indicated by the activities described herein and to avoid all potential hazards. By following the instructions contained herein, the reader willingly assumes all risks in connection with such instructions. The publisher makes no representations or warranties of any kind, including but not limited to, the warranties of fitness for particular purpose or merchantability, nor are any such representations implied with respect to the material set forth herein, and the publisher takes no responsibility with respect to such material. The publisher shall not be liable for any special, consequential, or exemplary damages resulting, in whole or part, from the readers' use of, or reliance upon, this material.

Printed in the United States of America
1 2 3 4 5 6 7 14 13 12 11 10

Revealed Series Vision

The Revealed Series is your guide to today's hottest multimedia applications. These comprehensive books teach the skills behind the application, showing you how to apply smart design principles to multimedia products such as dynamic graphics, animation, websites, software authoring tools, and digital video.

A team of design professionals including multimedia instructors, students, authors, and editors worked together to create this series. We recognized the unique learning environment of the multimedia classroom and created a series that:

- Gives you comprehensive step-by-step instructions
- Offers in-depth explanation of the "Why" behind a skill
- Includes creative projects for additional practice
- Explains concepts clearly using full-color visuals
- Keeps you up to date with the latest software upgrades so you can always work with cutting edge technology

It was our goal to create a book that speaks directly to the multimedia and design community—one of the most rapidly growing computer fields today. We think we've done just that, with a sophisticated and instructive book design.

—The Revealed Series

New to This Edition!

The latest edition of Adobe InDesign CS5 Revealed includes many exciting new features, including:

- Coverage of the Gap Tool, Live Distribute, Content Indicator, and multiple page sizes, all designed to make creating professional-looking layouts even easier.
- Coverage of Path and Point Highlighting, Live Corner Effects, and Super Step-and-Repeat.
- A brand new chapter (Chapter 12) about the online interactive features of InDesign.

Author's Vision

I am thrilled to have written this book on Adobe InDesign CS5. For me, it's been a pleasure to watch InDesign evolve into the smart, strategic layout package that it is today. And it's exciting to see that Adobe is developing the software both for print and interactive uses. As new media evolves, InDesign remains positioned with a central role in that evolution, and that's exciting.

Thank you to Sandra Kruse for her intelligence and dedication as the developmental editor on this title. Many thanks to Jane Hosie-Bounar, the Product Manager. Jane shepherded this book through to completion with her combination of patience, persistence, and clarity of vision. I also want to acknowledge Technical Editor Tara Botelho for her input.

Last but not least, many thanks to my two dogs, Blake and Rex. Their movie star good looks made them the perfect models for the photos you'll see in the book. Most times, at least one of them was sleeping on my lap as I was writing.

—Chris Botello

Introduction to Adobe InDesign CS5

Welcome to *Adobe InDesign CS5—Revealed*. This book offers creative projects, concise instructions, and complete coverage of basic to advanced InDesign skills, helping you to create polished, professional-looking layouts. Use this book both in the classroom and as your own reference guide.

This text is organized into 12 chapters. These chapters cover basic to intermediate InDesign skills, and let you work with many of the newest features, including multiple page sizes, path and point highlighting, Presentation view, Live Corner Effects, and Super Step-and-Repeat. In these chapters, you will explore the many options InDesign provides for creating comprehensive layouts, including formatting text and body copy, designing display headlines, setting up a document, working with

process and non-process colors, placing graphics from Adobe Illustrator and Adobe Photoshop, working with tabs and tables, and preparing an InDesign layout for output. You'll also explore the brand new Animation panel and interactive features of InDesign in a completely new Chapter 12. By the end of the book, you'll be able to create professional-looking layouts that incorporate illustrations and bitmap graphics as well as sophisticated presentations of text and typography.

What You'll Do

A What You'll Do figure begins every lesson. This figure gives you an at-a-glance look at what you'll do in the chapter, either by showing you a page or pages from the current project or a tool you'll be using.

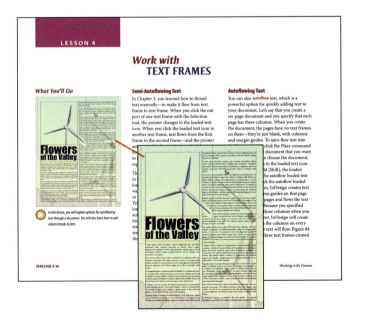

Comprehensive Conceptual Lessons

Before jumping into instructions, in-depth conceptual information tells you "why" skills are applied. This book provides the "how" and "why" through the use of professional examples. Also included in the text are tips and sidebars to help you work more efficiently and creatively, or to teach you a bit about the history or design philosophy behind the skill you are using.

Step-by-Step Instructions

This book combines in-depth conceptual information with concise steps to help you learn InDesign CS5. Each set of steps guides you through a lesson where you will create, modify, or enhance an InDesign CS5 file. Step references to large colorful images and quick step summaries round out the lessons. The Data Files for the steps are provided on the CD at the back of this book.

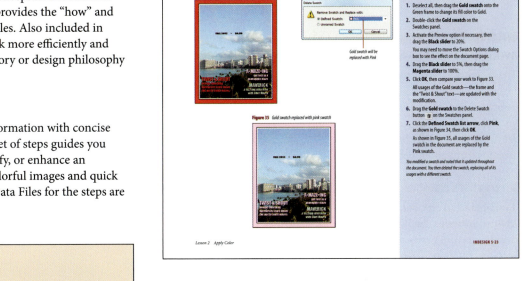

Projects

This book contains a variety of end-of-chapter materials for additional practice and reinforcement. The Skills Review contains hands-on practice exercises that mirror the progressive nature of the lesson material. The chapter concludes with four projects: two Project Builders, one Design Project, and one Portfolio Project. The Project Builders and the Design Project require you to apply the skills you've learned in the chapter. Portfolio Projects encourage you to address and solve challenges based on the content explored in the chapter, and to develop your own portfolio of work.

What Instructor Resources Are Available with This Book?

The Instructor Resources CD-ROM is Delmar's way of putting the resources and information needed to teach and learn effectively into your hands. All the resources are available for both Macintosh and Windows operating systems.

Instructor's Manual

Available as an electronic file, the Instructor's Manual includes chapter overviews and detailed lecture topics for each chapter, with teaching tips. The Instructor's Manual is available on the Instructor Resources CD-ROM.

Sample Syllabus

Available as an electronic file, the Sample Syllabus includes a suggested syllabus for any course that uses this book. The syllabus is available on the Instructor Resources CD-ROM.

PowerPoint Presentations

Each chapter has a corresponding PowerPoint presentation that you can use in lectures, distribute to your students, or customize to suit your course.

Data Files for Students

To complete most of the chapters in this book, your students will need Data Files. The Data Files are available on the CD at the back of this text book. Instruct students to use the Data Files List at the end of this book. This list gives instructions on organizing files.

Solutions to Exercises

Solution Files are Data Files completed with comprehensive sample answers. Use these files to evaluate your students' work. Or distribute them electronically so students can verify their work. Sample solutions to lessons and end-of-chapter material are provided with the exception of some portfolio projects.

Test Bank and Test Engine

ExamView is a powerful testing software package that allows instructors to create and administer printed and computer (LAN-based) exams. ExamView includes hundreds of questions that correspond to the topics covered in this text, enabling students to generate detailed study guides that include page references for further review. The computer-based and LAN-based/online testing component allows students to take exams using the EV Player, and also saves the instructor time by grading each exam automatically.

BRIEF CONTENTS

CONTENTS

CHAPTER 1: GETTING TO KNOW INDESIGN

CHAPTER 3: SETTING UP A DOCUMENT

CHAPTER 4: WORKING WITH FRAMES

CHAPTER 5: WORKING WITH COLOR

CHAPTER 7: CREATING GRAPHICS

CHAPTER 9: WORKING WITH TABS AND TABLES

CHAPTER 10: MAKING BOOKS, TABLES OF CONTENTS, AND INDEXES

CHAPTER 11: PREPARING, PACKAGING, AND EXPORTING DOCUMENTS FOR PRINT

CHAPTER 12: CREATING AN INTERACTIVE DOCUMENT

READ THIS BEFORE YOU BEGIN

Units and Increments

The page layout measurements for the documents in this book are given in inches, not points or picas. In order to follow these exercises, it is important that the horizontal and vertical ruler units are set to inches. To verify this, click Edit (Win) or InDesign (Mac) on the Application bar, point to Preferences, then click Units & Increments.

All text sizes and rule weights are expressed in points.

You may or may not prefer to work with rulers showing. You can make rulers visible by clicking View on the Application bar, then clicking Show Rulers. You can make rulers invisible by clicking View on the Application bar, then clicking Hide Rulers. Having rulers visible or invisible will not affect your ability to follow the exercises in this book in any way, unless a step specifically refers to a measurement on the ruler.

Fonts

Because InDesign is a page layout program, text is involved in almost every exercise in the book, even those that focus on placed graphics. The fonts used in the exercises in this book were chosen from a set of very common typefaces that you are likely to have available on your computer. In most cases, the fonts used are either Impact or Garamond.

If any of the fonts in use is not available on your computer, please make a substitution with another typeface that has a similar look. Also, please note that because Garamond is such a common typeface, it is possible that the Garamond font on your computer will be that of a different manufacturer than the Garamond used in the exercises, particularly if you are using a Macintosh computer. If that is the case, simply replace the "missing" Garamond in the exercises with the Garamond font on your computer. The following tip, which explains how to substitute fonts, appears in Chapter 1.

Quicktip

If you see the Missing Fonts dialog box, you can use the font chosen by InDesign by clicking OK, or click Find Font and choose another font in the Find Font dialog box. If you see a Missing Links dialog box, click Fix Links Automatically.

When you open an InDesign Data File, if any fonts used in the file are not available on your computer, the usages of that font will be highlighted in pink. Once you substitute the missing font with an available font, the pink highlight disappears.

Working with Guides

Chapter 3 focuses on creating and setting up a new document, which includes a thorough exploration of creating and positioning guides and changing the color of guides. Throughout the remainder of the book, the steps in the lessons will direct you to make guides visible or invisible when necessary. However, when guides are inconsequential to the lesson, the steps do not instruct you to make guides visible or not. Therefore, your document may differ from the figures in the book in terms of guides. For example, your document may have guides visible, whereas the figures in the book may not show guides.

Panels

Chapter 1 explains panels in depth. You are shown how to group, ungroup, dock, and undock panels. Like guides, the way that you choose to display panels may differ from the figures in the book.

Hiding and Showing Frame Edges / Normal View Mode and Preview Mode

Objects on an InDesign page appear with frame edges. When an object is selected, the frame edges are more prominent, but even when the object is not selected, the frame edges are visible. Sometimes the frame edges can be distracting, especially at the end of a lesson when you want to view the final result of your work. You can choose to hide frame edges, so that an object's frame is visible only when the object is selected. An alternative to hiding frame edges is to switch from Normal view to Preview using the appropriate buttons on the Tools panel. In Preview, all guides and frame edges are hidden.

The lessons in the book offer specific instruction for hiding and showing frame edges and for switching between Normal view and Preview. Once you learn these commands, you can work with the settings that are most comfortable. Because this is a personal choice, you may find that your work differs from the figures in the book. For example, you may be working in Preview, whereas the figures in the book may be in Normal view.

File Formats for Placed Graphics

Because InDesign is an Adobe product, it interfaces naturally with Adobe Photoshop and Adobe Illustrator. Therefore, Photoshop and Illustrator files can be placed in InDesign as "native" Photoshop and Illustrator files—it is not necessary to save them as TIFF or EPS files. For this reason, in the exercises that include placed images, the placed images are sometimes native Photoshop files, sometimes native Illustrator files, sometimes Photoshop TIFF files, and sometimes they are EPS files from Photoshop or Illustrator. The point is to understand that InDesign works with a variety of file formats, including native Photoshop and Illustrator files.

Working with Process Colors and Spot Colors

Chapter 5 focuses on creating colors in the Swatches panel. Some of these colors will be process colors, some will be spot colors. The narrative in this chapter provides substantial information on the offset printing process and the role of CMYK inks vs. non-process inks. Nevertheless, comprehensive coverage of the myriad concepts involved in offset printing is beyond the scope of this book. The author presumes that readers already have some familiarity with the basic concepts of 4-color process printing and/or can consult a resource specifically devoted to covering that topic in detail.

Updating Placed Graphics

You will be working with Data Files that contain placed graphics throughout the book. These support files are stored in the same folder as the InDesign Data File they are placed in. Normally, there are no issues for opening files with placed graphics; nevertheless, for a number of reasons, a warning dialog box may appear stating that the placed graphics have been modified and the link needs to be updated. In most cases, the placed graphics themselves have not been modified—only their location has been modified. Because the placed graphics are now on a new computer, InDesign may determine that the link needs to be updated. When this occurs, click the button that says Fix Links Automatically.

After clicking the Fix Links Automatically button, an additional warning dialog box may appear stating that "Edits have been made to this object. You will lose these edits by updating. Update anyway?" This dialog box refers to a handful of text documents used throughout the book. Make sure you click No in this dialog box so that the text file is not updated. Otherwise, the formatting applied to the text will be lost.

In Chapter 6, which focuses on managing links to placed graphics, links from the InDesign document to the placed graphics have been modified or are missing intentionally to teach you how to react to those situations. Read the narrative in Chapter 6 thoroughly to become familiar with the issues involved in updating modified and missing links. Should you encounter a linking problem before Chapter 6, Chapter 6 might very well have the information you need to fix it.

Quick Keys

Quick keys are keyboard shortcuts that you can use in place of clicking a command in a pull-down menu. [Ctrl][X] (Win) or ⌘ [X] (Mac), for example, are basic quick keys for the Cut command. After you become familiar with InDesign basics, you will find that learning and using quick keys will speed up your work considerably.

Certification

This book covers the objectives necessary for Adobe InDesign ACE certification. Use the Certification Grid at the back of the book to find out where an objective is covered.

CHAPTER 1

GETTING TO KNOW
INDESIGN

1. Explore the InDesign workspace

2. View and modify page elements

3. Navigate through a document

4. Work with objects and Smart Guides

CHAPTER 1

GETTING TO KNOW
INDESIGN

Welcome to Adobe InDesign! InDesign is a comprehensive software program that allows you to create output-ready layouts for anything from a simple coupon to a 120-page full-color magazine and an interactive PDF to a splash page for a web site. What's even better is that, with InDesign, Adobe Systems has created a layout program that interfaces seamlessly with Adobe Photoshop and Illustrator.

If you love those two applications, you'll love InDesign too. In terms of its concept and its intuitive design, InDesign is pure Adobe. You'll feel right at home. In fact, at times, you may need to remind yourself that you're working in InDesign, not Photoshop or Illustrator.

The key word to keep in mind is "layout." It's InDesign's primary function. Everything you need is there—along with some pleasant surprises. With InDesign, you can build tables quickly and easily. The table of contents and index features are fun and easy to learn. And try to remember that you're not using Illustrator when you're positioning that text on a curved path!

Best of all, you'll never have to leave the world of Adobe. InDesign, Photoshop, and Illustrator together form a formidable trifecta of design, with InDesign emerging as the best and most powerful layout utility ever devised.

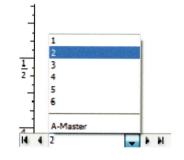

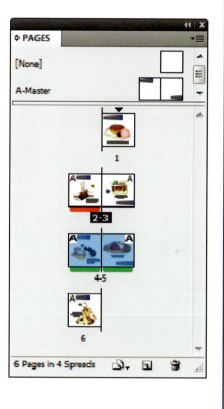

Explore the
INDESIGN WORKSPACE

What You'll Do

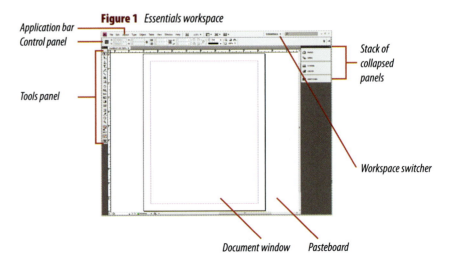

In this lesson, you will start Adobe InDesign and explore the workspace.

Looking at the InDesign Workspace

The arrangement of windows and panels that you see on your monitor is called the **workspace**. The InDesign workspace features the following areas: the document window, pasteboard, Application bar, Control panel, Tools panel, and a stack of collapsed panels along the right side of the pasteboard. Figure 1 shows the default workspace, which is called Essentials.

InDesign CS5 offers a number of pre-defined workspaces that are customized for different types of tasks. Each workspace is designed so that panels with similar functions are grouped together. For example, the Typography workspace shows the many type- and typography-based panels that are useful for working with type. You can switch from one workspace to another by clicking Window on the application bar, pointing to Workspace, and then choosing a workspace.

Figure 1 *Essentials workspace*

Application bar

Control panel

Tools panel

Stack of collapsed panels

Workspace switcher

Document window   Pasteboard

Or you can use the workspace switcher on the Application bar.

You can customize the workspace, including predefined workspaces, to suit your working preferences. For example, you can open and close whatever panels you want and change the location of any panel. You can save a customized workspace by clicking Window on the Application bar, pointing to Workspace, then clicking New Workspace. Once the new workspace is named, it will appear in the Workspace menu.

The **pasteboard** is the area surrounding the document. The pasteboard provides space for extending objects past the edge of the page (known as "creating a bleed"), and it also provides space for storing objects that you may or may not use in the document. Objects that are positioned wholly on the pasteboard, as shown in Figure 2, do not print.

Exploring the Tools Panel

As its name implies, the Tools panel houses all the tools that you will work with in InDesign. The first thing that you should note about the Tools panel is that not all tools are visible; many are hidden. Look closely and you will see that some tools have small black triangles beside them. These triangles indicate that other tools are hidden behind them. To access hidden tools, point to the visible tool on the Tools panel, then press and hold the mouse button; this will reveal a menu of hidden tools. The small black square to the left of a tool name in the menu indicates the tool that is currently visible on the Tools panel, as shown in Figure 3.

Figure 2 *Using the pasteboard*

Object that "bleeds" onto the pasteboard on two sides

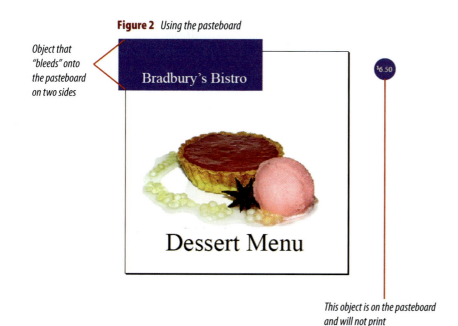

This object is on the pasteboard and will not print

Figure 3 *Hidden tools on the Tools panel*

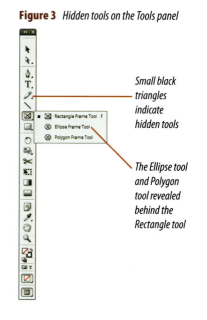

Small black triangles indicate hidden tools

The Ellipse tool and Polygon tool revealed behind the Rectangle tool

As shown in Figure 4, you can view the Tools panel as a single column, a double column, or even a horizontal row of tools. Simply click the Collapse to Icons button at the top of the Tools panel to toggle between the different setups.

Horizontal lines divide the Tools panel into eight sections. The top section contains the selection tools. The section beneath that contains item creation tools, such as the drawing, shape, and type tools. Next is a section that contains transform tools, such as the Rotate and Scale tools. The next section

contains navigation tools. Here you can find the Hand tool—used to scroll through a document, and the Zoom tool, used to magnify your view of a document.

The bottom-most sections of the Tools panel contain functions for applying colors and gradients to objects and choosing different modes for viewing documents, such as the commonly used Preview mode.

To choose a tool, simply click it; you can also press a shortcut key to access a tool. For example, pressing [p] selects the Pen

tool. To learn the shortcut key for each tool, point to a tool until a tooltip appears with the tool's name and its shortcut key in parentheses. Figure 5 shows the tooltip for the Type tool.

QUICK TIP

Shortcut keys are not case-sensitive. In other words, if you press [P], you'll switch to the Pen tool regardless of whether or not Caps Lock is on.

Figure 4 *Three different setups for the Tools panel*

Figure 5 *Viewing a tool name and shortcut key*

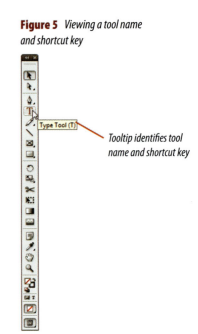

Tooltip identifies tool name and shortcut key

Working with Panels

Many InDesign functions are grouped into panels. For example, the Paragraph panel contains paragraph editing functions such as text alignment and paragraph indents. The Character panel, shown in Figure 6, offers controls for changing the font, font size, and leading.

All panels can be accessed from the Window menu. Some panels are placed within categories on the Window menu. For example, all of the text and table-related panels, such as the Character panel and the Table panel, are listed in the Type & Tables category. When you choose a panel from the Window menu, the panel appears in its expanded view. You can close any panel by clicking the Close button in the top-right corner of the panel, and you can display panel options by clicking the Panel options button. To reduce the size of a panel, click the Collapse to Icons button, which collapses the panel to a named icon in a stack along the right side of the pasteboard. These three buttons are identified in Figure 6.

Figure 7 shows three panels grouped together. The Paragraph panel is the active panel—it is in front of the others in the group and available for use. To better manage available workspace, it's a good idea to minimize or "collapse" panels to make them smaller but still available in the workspace. Clicking a panel icon in the stack of collapsed panels expands the panel as well as any other panels with which it is grouped. Click the thumbnail in the stack again, and it will collapse the panel you just expanded.

Figure 6 *Character panel*

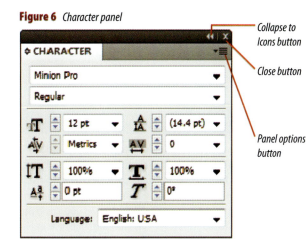

Collapse to Icons button

Close button

Panel options button

Figure 7 *Three grouped panels*

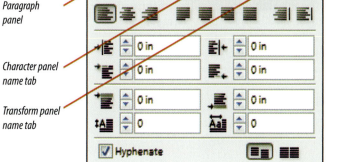

Paragraph panel

Character panel name tab

Transform panel name tab

When you have expanded a panel, the other panels grouped with it appear as tabs on the panel. You can activate these other panels by clicking their tabs. You can ungroup panels by dragging a panel's name tab away from the other panels in the group. To add a panel to a group, simply drag a panel by its name tab next to another panel name tab.

QUICK TIP

You can restore the default arrangement of a given workspace by clicking Window on the Application bar, pointing to Workspace, then clicking the Reset command for that workspace's name.

Don't confuse grouping panels with docking panels. **Docking** panels is a different function. When you dock panels, you connect the bottom edge of one panel to the top edge of another panel, so that both move together. To dock panels, first drag a panel's name tab to the bottom edge of another panel. When the bottom edge of the other panel is highlighted in bright blue, release the mouse button and the two panels will be docked. Figure 8 shows docked panels. To undock a panel, simply drag it away from its group.

QUICK TIP

You can temporarily hide all open panels, including the Tools panel, by pressing [Tab]. Press [Tab] again to show the panels.

Figure 8 *Docked panels*

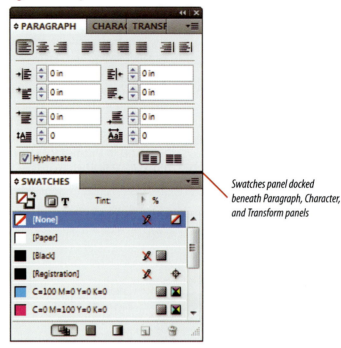

Swatches panel docked beneath Paragraph, Character, and Transform panels

Responding to Links and Font Warnings

InDesign documents often contain support files, such as graphics created in other programs like Photoshop and Illustrator. In creating this book, we included all such support files in the same folder as the InDesign data files, with which you will be working. By doing so, InDesign will be able to locate those files and update the InDesign document when you open it. When you open a document, however, you will often see a warning about missing or modified links. Unless you are instructed otherwise, you should always click Update Links when you see this warning. Likewise, we have used common fonts in the data files to minimize missing font warnings. However, should you encounter a layout that uses a font not currently loaded on your computer, you can accept the replacement font InDesign offers as an automatic replacement, or you can use the Find Font command on the Type menu to choose another font if you prefer.

Figure 9 *Tools that contain hidden tools*

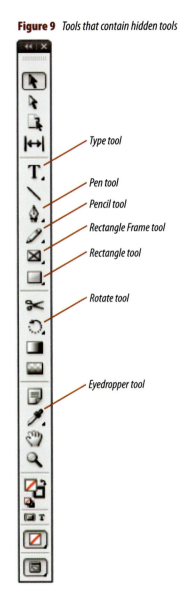

Type tool

Pen tool

Pencil tool

Rectangle Frame tool

Rectangle tool

Rotate tool

Eyedropper tool

Explore the Tools panel

1. Launch Adobe InDesign CS5.

2. Click **File** on the Application bar, click **Open**, navigate to the drive and folder where your Chapter 1 Data Files are stored, click **ID 1-1.indd**, then click **Open**.

TIP If you see a warning about missing links, click Update Links. If you see the Missing Fonts dialog box, you can use the font chosen by InDesign by clicking OK, or click Find Font and choose another font in the Find Font dialog box. For more information, see the Sidebar on Page 1-8.

3. Click **Window** on the Application bar, point to **Workspace**, then click **[Typography]**.

TIP If you are already working in the Typography workspace, click Window on the Application bar, point to Workspace, then click Reset Typography to return to the default Typography workspace settings.

4. Point to the **Type tool** T , then press and hold the mouse button to see the Type on a Path tool.

5. Using the same method, view the hidden tools behind the other tools with small black triangles, shown in Figure 9.

   Your visible tools may differ from the figure.

6. Position your mouse pointer over the **Selection tool** , until its tooltip appears.

7. Press the following keys and note which tools are selected with each key: **[a]**, **[p]**, **[v]**, **[t]**, **[i]**, **[h]**, **[z]**.

(continued)

8. Press **[Tab]** to temporarily hide all open panels, then press **[Tab]** again. The panels reappear.

You explored the Tools panel, revealed hidden tools, used shortcut keys to access tools quickly, hid the panels, then displayed them again.

Work with panels

1. Click the **Paragraph panel icon** in the stack of collapsed panels to the right of the pasteboard to expand the Paragraph panel.

   The Paragraph panel is grouped with the Paragraph Styles panel in this Typography workspace. The panel expands, but does not detach from the stack of collapsed icons.

2. Click the **Collapse to Icons button** 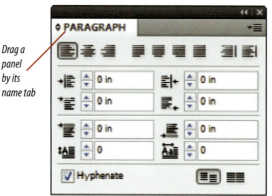 at the top of the panel to collapse it, then click the **Paragraph** panel icon again to expand it.

3. Drag the **Paragraph panel name tab** to the left so it is ungrouped, as shown in Figure 10.

4. Drag the **Character panel icon** to the blank space next to the **Paragraph panel name tab**, then release the mouse.

   The Character panel is grouped with the Paragraph panel, as shown in Figure 11.

5. Click **Window** on the Application bar, point to **Object and Layout**, then click **Transform**.

   The Transform panel appears expanded on the document.

   (continued)

Figure 10 *Removing the Paragraph panel from the group*

Drag a panel by its name tab

Figure 11 *Grouping the Character panel with the Paragraph panel*

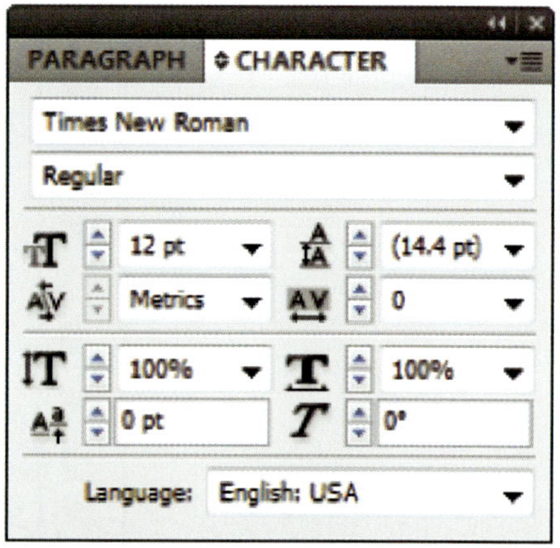

Opening InDesign CS5 Files in InDesign CS4

InDesign CS4 cannot open InDesign CS5 documents. To open an InDesign CS5 document in InDesign CS4, you must export the CS5 document in the InDesign Markup Language (IDML) format. Click File on the Application bar, click Export, then choose InDesign Markup (IDML) as the file format. The exported document can be opened in InDesign CS4. Note, however, that any new CS5 features applied to your document will be lost when the file is converted to the older version. If you want to go even farther back, you can export the file as an InDesign Interchange (INX) format from InDesign CS4 and then open the file in InDesign CS3.

Figure 12 *Docking the Transform panel*

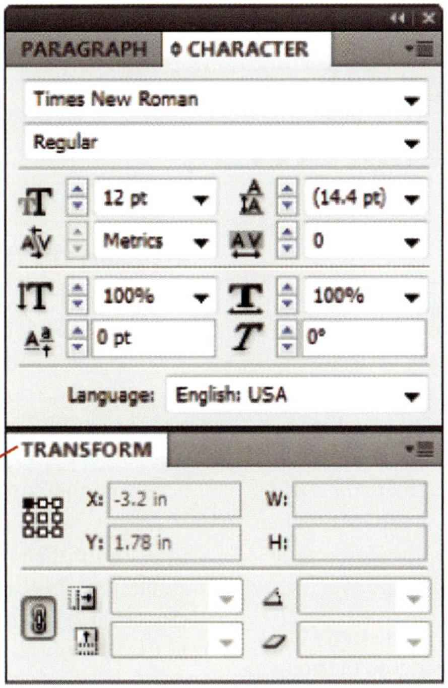

Drag a panel to
the bottom edge of
another to dock it

6. Drag the **Transform panel name tab** to the bottom edge of the Character and Paragraph panels group, then, when a blue horizontal bar appears, release the mouse.

   The Transform panel is docked, as shown in Figure 12.

7. Click and drag the **dark gray bar at the top of the panel group**, found above the Paragraph and Character panel name tabs, in different directions.

   The Transform panel moves with the Character and Paragraph panels because it is docked.

8. Click the **Transform panel name tab**, then drag it away from the other two panels.

   The Transform panel is undocked.

9. Click **Window** on the Application bar, point to **Workspace**, then **click Reset Typography**.

You explored methods for grouping and ungrouping panels, and you docked and undocked a panel.

Creating Custom Workspaces

With InDesign CS5, you can customize the workspace as you like it, opening and dragging panels wherever they help make your workflow most efficient. When you are happy with the way that you have customized your workspace, click Window on the Application bar, point to Workspace, then click New Workspace. Assign a descriptive name to your workspace, verify that the Panel Locations check box is checked, then click OK. With this option checked, the workspace will be saved with all panels in their current positions. Once you've saved a workspace, you load it by clicking Window on the Application bar, then pointing to Workspace. You'll see your custom-named workspace in the list of workspaces.

View and Modify
PAGE ELEMENTS

What You'll Do

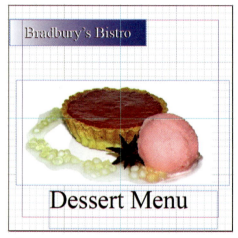

In this lesson, you will explore various methods for viewing the document and document elements like rulers, guides, grids and frame edges.

Using the Zoom Tool

Imagine creating a layout on a traditional pasteboard—not on your computer. For precise work, you would bring your nose closer to the pasteboard so that you could better see what you were doing. At other times, you would hold the pasteboard away from you, at arms' length, so that you could get a larger perspective of the artwork. When you're working in InDesign, the Zoom tool performs these functions for you.

When you click the Zoom tool and move the pointer over the document window, the pointer becomes the Zoom pointer with a plus sign; when you click the document with the Zoom pointer, the document area you clicked is enlarged. To reduce the view of the document, press and hold [Alt] (Win) or [option] (Mac). When the plus sign changes to a minus sign, click the document with this Zoom pointer, and the document size is reduced.

Using the Zoom tool, you can reduce or enlarge the view of the document from 5% to 4000%. Note that the current magnification level appears in the document tab and in the Zoom Level text box on the Application bar, as shown in Figure 13.

Accessing the Zoom Tool

As you work, you can expect to zoom in and out of the document more times than you can count. The most basic way of accessing the Zoom tool is simply to click its icon on the Tools panel, however this can get very tiring. A better method for accessing the Zoom tool is to use keyboard shortcuts. When you are using the Selection tool, for example, don't switch to the Zoom tool. Instead, press and hold [Ctrl] [Spacebar] (Win) or [⌘] [Spacebar] (Mac) to temporarily change the Selection tool into the Zoom tool. Click the document to zoom in. When you release the keys, the Zoom tool changes back to the Selection tool.

To Zoom out using keyboard shortcuts, press and hold [Ctrl][Alt][Spacebar] (Win) or [⌘] [option][Spacebar] (Mac).

> **QUICK TIP**
> Double-clicking the Zoom tool on the Tools panel changes the document view to 100% (actual size).

In addition to the Zoom tool, InDesign offers a number of other ways to zoom in and out of your document. One of the quickest and easiest is to press [Ctrl][+] (Win) or ⌘ [+] (Mac) to enlarge the view and [Ctrl][-] (Win) or ⌘ [-] (Mac) to reduce the view. You can also use the Zoom In and Zoom Out commands on the View menu.

Using the Hand Tool

When you zoom in on a document—when you make it appear larger—eventually the document will be too large to fit in the window. Therefore, you will need to scroll to see other areas of it. You can use the scroll bars along the bottom and the right sides of the document window or you can use the Hand tool to scroll through the document, as shown in Figure 14.

The best way to understand the concept of the Hand tool is to think of it as your own hand. Imagine that you could put your hand up to the document on your monitor, then move the document left, right, up, or down, like a paper on a table or against a wall. This is analogous to how the Hand tool works.

QUICK TIP

Double-clicking the Hand tool on the Tools panel changes the document view to fit the page (or the spread) in the document window.

Figure 13 *A reduced view of the document*

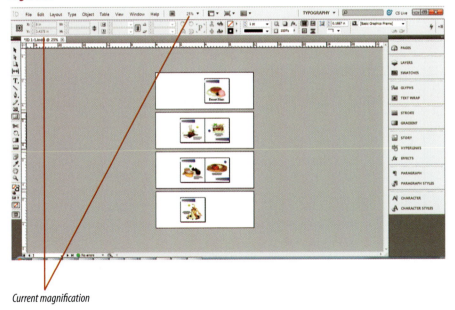

Current magnification

Figure 14 *Scrolling through a document*

Scrolling with the Hand tool

The Hand tool is often a better choice for scrolling than the scroll bars. Why? Because you can access the Hand tool using a keyboard shortcut. Simply press and hold [Spacebar] to access the Hand tool. Release [Spacebar] to return to the tool you were using, without having to choose it again.

Working with Rulers, Grids, and Guides

Designing and working with page layouts involves using measurements to position and align elements in your documents. You'll find that InDesign is well-equipped with a number of features that help you with these tasks.

Figure 15 shows various measurement utilities. **Rulers** are positioned at the top and left side of the pasteboard to help you align objects. Simply click Show Rulers/Hide Rulers on the View menu. Rulers (and all other measurement utilities in the document) can display measurements in different units, such as inches, picas, or points. You determine the units and increments with which you want to work in the Preferences dialog box. On the Edit menu, point to Preferences, then click Units & Increments to display the dialog box shown in Figure 16.

Ruler guides are horizontal and vertical rules that you can position anywhere in a layout as a reference for positioning elements. **Margin guides** are guides that you specify to appear at a given distance within the page, usually to maintain visual consistency from page to page or as a reminder to keep text or other

Figure 15 *Various measurement utilities*

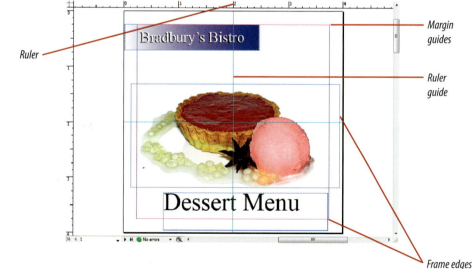

Ruler

Margin guides

Ruler guide

Frame edges

Figure 16 *Units & Increments preferences dialog box*

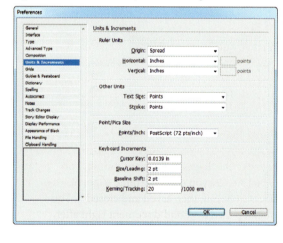

important elements from getting too close to the edge of the page. In addition to guides, InDesign offers a **document grid** for precise alignment. With the 'snap' options on, objects that you move around on the page automatically align themselves with guides or with the grid quickly and easily.

Hiding and Showing Frame Edges

InDesign is a frame-based application. **Frames** are rectangular, oval, or polygonal shapes that you use for a variety of purposes, such as creating a colored area on the document or placing text and graphics. All frames have visible **frame edges**, and when a frame is selected, those edges automatically highlight.

While you're working on designing your layout, you'll often want to have frame edges visible; but once you're done designing, you'll want to see your layout without the frame edges in the way. To hide or show frame edges, click the Hide/Show Edges command on the View menu.

Keep in mind that when you hide or show guides, grids or frame edges in a document, none of these settings is saved with it. For example, say you showed frame edges in Dessert Menu, then saved and closed it. You then opened a second document right after, and hid the frame edges while you worked. If you were to open Dessert Menu again, its frame edges would be hidden too, because that is the most current display status in the InDesign window.

Choosing Screen Modes

Screen Modes are options for viewing your documents. The two basic screen modes in InDesign CS5 are Normal and Preview. You'll work in **Normal mode** most of the time. In Normal mode, you can see any and all page elements, including margin guides, ruler guides, frame edges, and the pasteboard.

Preview mode shows you what your page would look like with all non-printing elements removed. When you switch to Preview mode, all guides, grids, and frame edges become invisible to give you an idea of what your document would look like printed or as a PDF file. Even the pasteboard is hidden and becomes gray; thus, any objects on the pasteboard—or any objects that extend off of your document page—become invisible. You can think of Preview mode as showing you a "cropped" view of your page—only that which is on the page is visible.

QUICK TIP

Preview mode doesn't hide panels or the Application bar.

The View menu offers commands for switching between Normal and Preview modes, but it's much faster and easier to press the [W] key on your keypad to toggle between the two modes.

Presentation mode presents a view of your document as though it were being showcased on your computer monitor. In Presentation mode, your document goes full screen against a black background and is centered and sized so that the entire document fits in your monitor window. All other InDesign elements, including panels and the Application bar, disappear.

When would you use Presentation mode? When you are giving a presentation! Let's say you have a multi-page document and your client is coming to your office to view it. Rather than show her the document in Normal or Preview modes with distracting menu bars and panels, show it to her in Presentation mode for a cleaner and more professional look.

To toggle Presentation Mode on and off, press [Shift] [W] on your keypad.

When in Presentation mode, you'll have no tools or menus whatsoever to navigate through a multi-page document, but you can use the following keys in Table 1 to move around in it:

TABLE 1: PRESENTATION MODE NAVIGATION KEYS	
→ or [Pg Dn]	Next Spread
← or [Pg Up]	Previous Spread
[Home]	First Spread
[End]	Last Spread
[Esc]	Exit Presentation Mode

Understanding Preferences

All Adobe products come loaded with preferences. Preferences are options you have for specifying how certain features of the application behave. The Preferences dialog box houses the multitude of InDesign preferences available. Figure 17 shows the Interface preferences for InDesign. Note the long list of other preference categories on the left. Getting to know available preferences is a smart approach to mastering InDesign. Many preferences offer important choices that will have significant impact on how you work.

Working with Multiple Open Documents

On many occasions, you'll find yourself working with multiple open documents. For example, let's say you're into scrapbooking. If you were designing a new document to showcase a recent trip to Italy, you might also have the file open for the scrapbook you created last year when you went to Hawaii. Why? For any number of reasons. You might want to copy and paste layout elements from the Hawaii document into the new document. Or, you might want the Hawaii document open simply as a reference for typefaces, type sizes, image sizes, and effects like drop shadows that you used. When you're working with multiple open documents, you can switch from one to the other simply by clicking on the title bar of each document.

InDesign offers a preference for having multiple open documents available as tabs in the document window. With this preference selected, a tab will appear for each open document showing the name of

the document. Simply click the tab and the document becomes active. This can be useful for keeping your workspace uncluttered, though at times it might be inhibiting, because when working with multiple documents, the tabbed option allows you to view only one document at a time.

You indicate in the Interface Preferences dialog box whether or not you want open documents to appear as tabs. Click Edit on the Application bar, point to Preferences, then click Interface. Click the Open Documents as Tabs check box to select it, as shown in Figure 17, then click OK.

Figure 17 *Interface preferences dialog box*

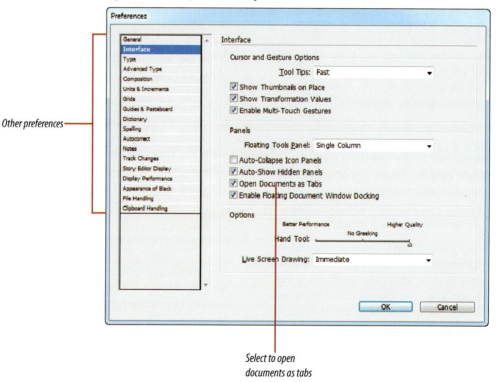

Other preferences

Select to open documents as tabs

Figure 18 *Scrolling with the Hand tool*

The Hand tool will become a fist when you click and drag

Use the Zoom tool and the Hand tool

1. Press **[z]** to access the Zoom tool.
2. Position the Zoom tool over the document window, click twice to enlarge the document, press **[Alt]** (Win) or **[option]** (Mac), then click twice to reduce the document.
3. Click the **Zoom Level list arrow** on the Application bar, then click **800%**.

   Note that 800% is now listed in the document tab.
4. Double-click **800%** in the Zoom Level text box, type **300**, then press **[Enter]** (Win) or **[return]** (Mac).
5. Click the **Hand tool** on the Tools panel, then click and drag the **document window** so that the image in the window appears as shown in Figure 18.
6. Double-click the **Zoom tool button** on the Tools panel. The magnification changes to 100% (actual size).
7. Click the **Selection tool**, point to the center of the document window, then press and hold **[Ctrl][Spacebar]** (Win) or [⌘] **[Spacebar]** (Mac).

   The Selection tool changes to the Zoom tool.
8. Click three times, then release [Ctrl][Spacebar] (Win) or [⌘] [Spacebar] (Mac).
9. Press and hold **[Spacebar]** to access the Hand tool, then scroll around the image.

(continued)

10. Press and hold **[Ctrl][Alt][Spacebar]** (Win) or ⌘ **[option][Spacebar]** (Mac), then click the mouse multiple times to reduce the view to 25%.

11. Your document window should resemble Figure 19.

You explored various methods for accessing and using the Zoom tool for enlarging and reducing the document. You also used the Hand tool to scroll around an enlarged document.

Hide and show rulers and set units and increments preferences

1. Click **View** on the Application bar, note the shortcut key on the Fit Page in Window command, then click **Fit Page in Window**.

   Most commonly used commands in InDesign list a shortcut key beside the command name. Shortcut keys are useful for quickly accessing commands without stopping work to go to the menu. Make a mental note of helpful shortcut keys and incorporate them into your work. You'll find that using them becomes second nature.

2. Click **View** on the Application bar, then note the Rulers command and its shortcut key.

   The Rulers command says Hide Rulers or Show Rulers, depending on your current status.

3. Click the **pasteboard** to escape the View menu, then press **[Ctrl] [R]**(Win) or ⌘ **[R]** (Mac) several times to hide and show rulers, finishing with rulers showing.

4. Note the units on the rulers.

   Depending on the preference you have set, your rulers might be showing inches, picas, or another unit of measure.

(continued)

Figure 19 *A reduced view of the document*

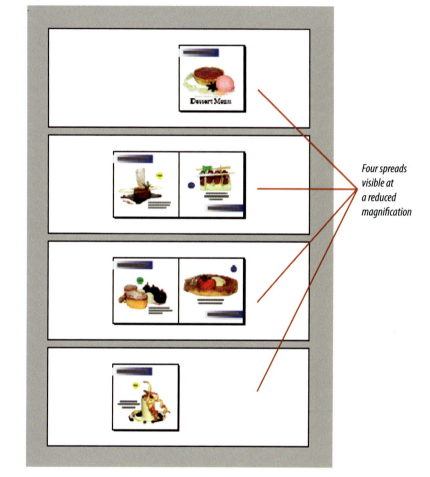

Four spreads visible at a reduced magnification

Figure 20 *Setting the Units & Increments ruler units to Picas*

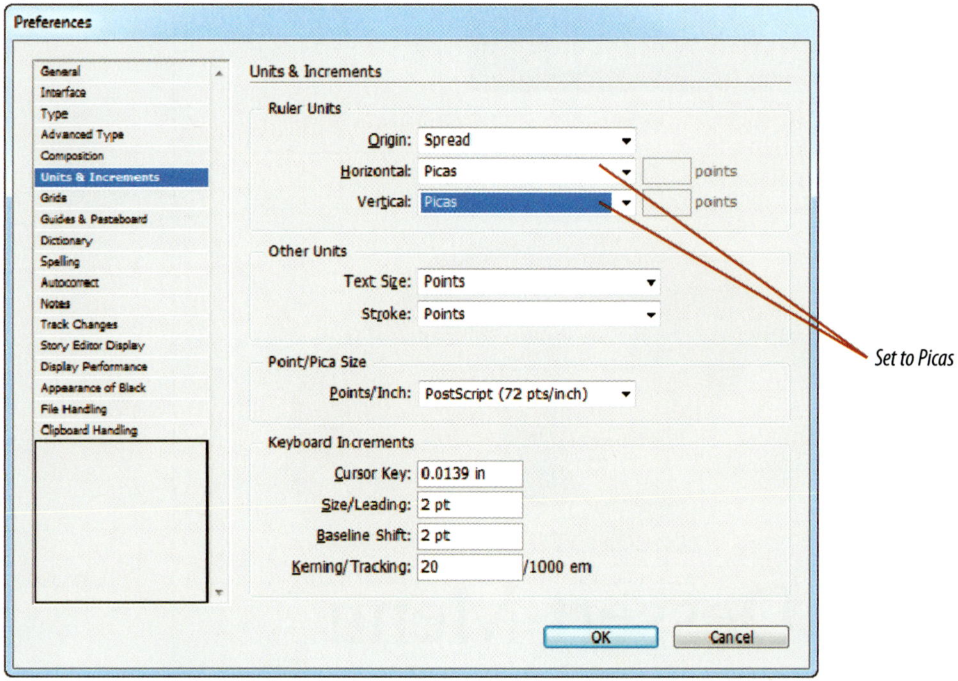

Preferences

General
Interface
Type
Advanced Type
Composition
Units & Increments
Grids
Guides & Pasteboard
Dictionary
Spelling
Autocorrect
Notes
Track Changes
Story Editor Display
Display Performance
Appearance of Black
File Handling
Clipboard Handling

Units & Increments

Ruler Units

Origin: Spread
Horizontal: Picas ___ points
Vertical: Picas ___ points

Other Units

Text Size: Points
Stroke: Points

Point/Pica Size

Points/Inch: PostScript (72 pts/inch)

Keyboard Increments

Cursor Key: 0.0139 in
Size/Leading: 2 pt
Baseline Shift: 2 pt
Kerning/Tracking: 20 /1000 em

Set to Picas

OK   Cancel

5. Click **Edit** (Win) or **InDesign** (Mac) on the Application bar, point to **Preferences**, then click **Units & Increments**.

6. In the Ruler Units section, click the **Horizontal list arrow** to see the available measurement options.

7. Set the Horizontal and Vertical fields to Picas so that your dialog box resembles Figure 20, then click **OK**.

   The horizontal and vertical rulers change to pica measurements. Picas are a unit of measure used in layout design long before the advent of computerized layouts. One pica is equal to 1/6 an inch. It's important you understand that the unit of measure you set in the preferences dialog box is a global choice. It will affect all measurement utilities in the application, such as those on the Transform panel, in addition to the ruler increments.

8. Reopen the Units & Increments preferences dialog box, change the Horizontal and Vertical fields to Inches, then click **OK**.

You used shortcut keys to hide and show rulers in the document. You used the Units & Increments preferences dialog box to change the unit of measure for the document.

Hide and show ruler guides, frame edges, and the document grid

1. Click **View** on the Application bar, point to **Extras**, then note the Show/Hide Frame Edges command and its shortcut key.

   The Frame Edges command says either Hide Frame Edges or Show Frame Edges depending on your current status.

(continued)

2. Click the **pasteboard** to escape the View menu, then press **[Ctrl][H]** (Win) or [Ctrl] ⌘ **[H]** (Mac) several times to toggle between hiding and showing frame edges, finishing with frame edges showing.

TIP The Hide Frames shortcut key is easy to remember if you think of H for Hide. Remember though, that this shortcut key only hides and shows frame edges, not other elements, like ruler guides, which use different shortcut keys.

3. Click **View** on the Application bar, point to **Grids & Guides**, then note the Show/Hide Guides command and its shortcut key.

   The Guides command says either Hide Guides or Show Guides depending on your current status.

4. Click the **pasteboard** to escape the View menu, then press **[Ctrl][;]** (Win) or ⌘ **[;]** (Mac) several times to toggle between hiding and showing guides, finishing with guides showing.

   Horizontal and vertical ruler guides alternately hide and show. In addition, purple margin guides hide and show .25" within the perimeter of the page, as shown in Figure 21.

TIP Make note of the difference between the Hide/Show guides shortcut key and the Hide/Show Frame Edges shortcut key.

5. Click **View** on the Application bar, point to **Grids & Guides**, then note the Show/Hide Document Grid command and its shortcut key.

(continued)

Figure 21 *Viewing frame edges and guides*

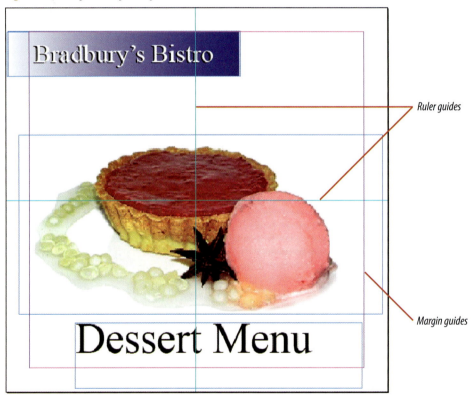

Ruler guides

Margin guides

TABLE 2: SHORTCUT KEYS FOR VIEWING COMMANDS

	Windows	Mac
Hide/Show Guides	Ctrl+;	⌘+;
Hide/Show Edges	Ctrl+H	[Ctrl] ⌘+H
Hide/Show Rulers	Ctrl+R	⌘+R
Activate/Deactivate Smart Guides	Ctrl+U	⌘+U
Fit Page in Window	Ctrl+0	⌘+0
Fit Spread in Window	Alt+Ctrl+0	Option+⌘+0
Toggle Normal and Preview Screen Modes	W	W
Toggle Presentation Mode On/Off	Shift+W	Shift+W

Setting up Document and Frame-Based Grids

Sometimes ruler guides just aren't enough, so designers choose to work with grids. Grids are multiple guides positioned to create a grid pattern across the layout. Grids help you align objects quickly and precisely. Every InDesign file you create has a default Document Grid, which you can hide or show using the Hide or Show Document Grid command in the Guides & Grids options on the View menu. You can modify the color and spacing increments of the default document grid using the Grids command in the Preferences options on the Edit menu. Choose Snap to Document Grid in the Grids and Guides options on the View menu to force objects to align to the Document Grid.

Sometimes you'll want to use a grid in a specific text frame as opposed to across the entire document. You can set up a grid for a text frame in the Text Frame Options dialog box. Select the frame, click the Object menu, then click Text Frame Options. Click the Baseline Options tab at the top of the dialog box, then enter specifications for the frame-based grid.

The Document Grid command says either Hide Document Grid or Show Document Grid depending on your current status.

6. Click the **pasteboard** to escape the View menu, then press **[Ctrl][']**(Win) or ⌘ **[']** (Mac) several times to toggle between hiding and showing the document grid.

   Table 2 includes frequently used Viewing command shortcut keys.

TIP Make note of the difference between the Hide/Show Guides shortcut key and the Hide/Show Document Grid shortcut key—they're just one key away from each other.

7. Click **View** on the Application bar, point to **Grids & Guides**, then note the Snap to Guides and Snap to Document Grid commands.

   The Snap to Guides and Snap to Document Grid commands are on/off commands. When they're active, a check mark is visible to the left of the command.

8. Click the **pasteboard** to escape the View menu.

You used shortcut keys to hide and show frame edges, ruler guides, and the document grid. You noted the location of the Snap to Guides and Snap to Document Grid commands in the View menu.

Toggle between screen modes

1. Click the **View** menu, point to **Screen Mode**, then click **Preview**.

   All guides and frame edges are hidden and the pasteboard is now gray. The Application bar and panels remain visible.

2. Press **[W]** on your keypad several times to toggle between Preview and Normal modes, finishing with your document in Normal mode.

(continued)

3. Click **View** on the Application bar, point to **Screen Mode**, then click **Presentation**.

   As shown in Figure 22, the window goes full-screen, and the full document appears against a black background. Guides, grids, frame edges, panels, and the Application bar are no longer visible.

4. Press the ↓ on your keypad to scroll through the document to the last page.

5. Press the ↑ on your keypad to scroll up to the first page.

6. Press **[Esc]** to leave Presentation mode.

7. Press **[Shift][W]** to switch to Presentation mode.

8. Press **[Shift][W]** again to return to Normal mode.

You used menu commands and keyboard keys to toggle among Normal, Preview, and Presentation modes. When in Presentation mode, you used keyboard keys to navigate through the document.

Work with multiple documents

1. Click **Edit** (Win) or **InDesign** (Mac) on the Application bar, point to **Preferences**, click **Interface**, click the **Open Documents as Tabs check box** to select it if it is unchecked, then click **OK**.

2. Save ID 1-1.indd as **Dessert Menu**.

3. Open ID 1-2.indd, then click the **tabs** of each document several times to toggle between them, finishing with Dessert Menu as the active document.

4. Position your mouse pointer over the bottom-right corner of the document, then click and drag downward and to the right to try to resize it.

   Because it is a tabbed document, the window is "fixed" and can't be resized.

(continued)

Figure 22 *Viewing the document in Presentation mode*

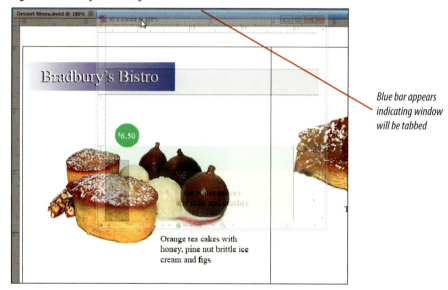

Figure 23 *"Tabbing" the floating document*

Blue bar appears indicating window will be tabbed

5. Drag the **Dessert Menu tab** straight down approximately 1/2 inch.

   When you drag a tabbed document down, it becomes "untabbed" and becomes a "floating" document.

6. Position your mouse pointer over the bottom-right corner of the document window, then click and drag towards the center of the monitor window to reduce the window to approximately half its size.

7. Position your mouse pointer over the title bar of the document, then click and drag to move Dessert Menu half way down towards the bottom of your monitor screen.

   A "floating" document window can be positioned so that part of it is off-screen.

8. Position your mouse pointer over the title bar of Dessert Menu, click and drag to position it at the top of the window beside the ID 1-2.indd tab, then release your mouse when you see a horizontal blue bar, as shown in Figure 23.

   The document is tabbed once again.

9. Close ID 1-2.indd without saving changes if you are prompted.

You selected the Open Documents as Tabs option in the Preferences dialog box. You opened a second document and noted that it was tabbed and couldn't be resized. You removed the document from its tabbed position, resized it, moved it around, then returned it to its tabbed status.

Navigate Through
A DOCUMENT

What You'll Do

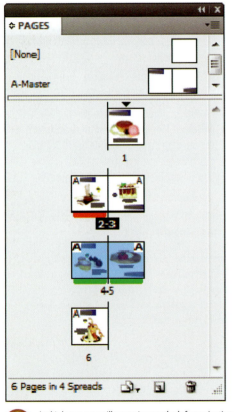

In this lesson, you will use various methods for navigating through a multiple page document.

Navigating to Pages in a Document

When you create a layout for a magazine, book, or brochure, you create a document that has multiple pages. **Spreads** are two pages that face each other; a left page and a right page in a multi-page document.

You have a variety of methods at your disposal for navigating to pages or spreads in your document. The Go to Page command in the Layout menu offers you the option to enter the page to which you want to go. You can also use the scroll bars on the bottom and right sides of the document window or choose a page from the Page menu in the lower-left corner of the document window. There are also First Spread, Previous Spread, Next Spread and Last Spread buttons at the bottom of the document window, which you can click to navigate to designated spreads, as shown in Figure 24. These navigation buttons have corresponding menu commands on the Layout menu.

Figure 24 *Page buttons and the Page menu*

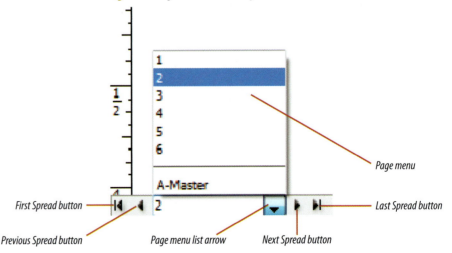

First Spread button

Previous Spread button

Page menu list arrow

Next Spread button

Last Spread button

Page menu

Getting to Know InDesign

The Pages panel, shown in Figure 25, is a comprehensive solution for moving from page to page in your document. The Pages panel shows icons for all of the pages in the document. Double-clicking a single page icon brings that page into view. The icon representing the currently visible page appears in blue on the panel. Click the Pages panel options button to display the Pages panel options menu. This menu contains a number of powerful commands that you can use to control all of your page navigation in InDesign.

Double-clicking the numbers under the page icons representing a spread, as shown in Figure 26, centers the spread in the document window. In this case, both icons representing the spread appear blue on the Pages panel.

Applying Color Labels to Thumbnails in the Pages Panel

You can apply one of 15 color labels to a page thumbnail in the Pages panel. Color labels can be useful for organizing your own work or for working with others on a document. For your own work, you might want to

assign color labels to different types of pages. For example, you might want to assign a color label to pages in a document that contain imported Photoshop graphics. Or you might want to assign a specific color to pages that have been approved by your client. When working with others, color labels can be effective as status codes. For example, you can apply a specific color to all pages that are

proofed and approved. This way, at a glance, your whole team can see what's done and what needs to be done.

To apply color labels, simply click the Pages panel options button, then point to Color Label and choose a color. The color that you choose will appear as a small solid rectangle beneath the thumbnail.

Figure 25 *Pages panel*

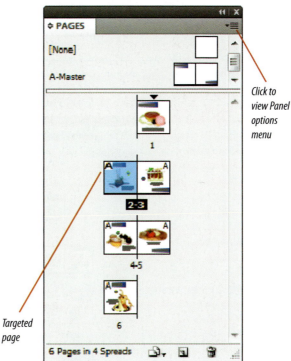

Click to view Panel options menu

Targeted page

Figure 26 *A selected two-page spread*

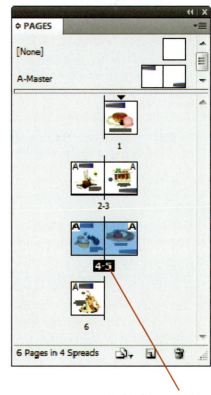

Double-click page numbers to target a spread

Navigate to pages in a document

1. Click the **Page menu list arrow** at the bottom-left of the document window, then click **3**.

   The document view changes to page 3.

2. Click **View** on the Application bar, then click **Fit Spread in Window**.

3. Click the **Next Spread button** ▶.

   Your screen should resemble Figure 27.

4. Click the **Previous Spread button** ◀ twice.

5. Click the **Pages panel icon** to display the Pages panel, if necessary.

   TIP If you do not see the Pages panel icon in the stack of collapsed panels, click Window on the Application bar, then click Pages.

6. Double-click the **page 6 icon** on the Pages panel.

   The document view changes to page 6, and the page 6 icon on the Pages panel changes to blue, as shown in Figure 28.

7. Double-click the **page 3 icon** on the Pages panel.

   The right half of the spread—page 3—is centered in the document window.

8. Double-click the numbers **2-3** beneath the page 2 and page 3 icons on the Pages panel.

   TIP Double-clicking numbers below the icons on the Pages panel centers the full spread in the document window.

   (continued)

Figure 27 *Spread 4-5*

Figure 28 *Targeting page 6 on the Pages panel*

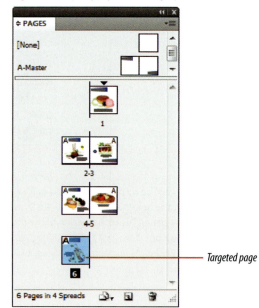

Targeted page

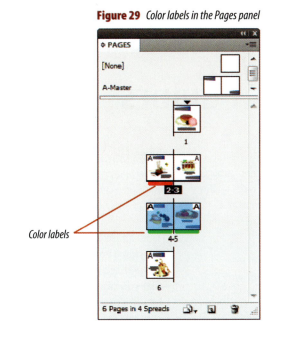

Figure 29 *Color labels in the Pages panel*

Color labels

Pages Panel Options

To customize the Pages panel, click the Pages Panel options button, then click Panel Options. This opens the Panel Options dialog box. In the Pages and Masters sections of the dialog box, you can choose a size for page and master icons by clicking the Size list arrow, then clicking a size ranging from Extra Small to Extra Large. The Show Vertically and Show Thumbnails check boxes in the Pages and Masters sections control how the icons on the panel are displayed. If you remove the Show Vertically check mark, the page icons on the Pages panel will be displayed horizontally and you will only be able to resize the width of the Pages panel, not the height. If you remove the Show Thumbnails check mark, the page icons will be blank on the Pages panel. The Icons section of the dialog box defines which additional icons appear next to the page icons. For example, if the Transparency check box is checked, a small transparency icon that looks like a checkerboard appears next to the page icon where transparency has been applied to master items. Finally, in the Panel Layout section, you can choose whether you want masters on top or document pages on top of the Pages panel.

9. Click **Layout** on the Application bar, then click **First Page**.

10. Enter **[Ctrl] [J]**(Win) or ⌘ **[J]** (Mac) to open the Go to Page dialog box, enter **5**, then press **[Enter]**(Win) or **[Return]** (Mac).

TIP Make a point of remembering this command—*J for Jump*. It is one of the fastest ways to jump to a specific page, especially in long documents with lots of pages in the Pages panel.

You navigated to pages using the Page menu, the Next Spread and Previous Spread buttons, page icons on the Pages panel, the Layout menu, and the Go to Page dialog box.

Apply color labels to page thumbnails

1. Click the **Page 2 thumbnail** in the Pages panel.

2. Click the **Pages panel options button** ▾≡ , point to **Color Label**, then click **Red**.

   A red bar appears beneath the page thumbnail.

3. Click the **page numbers 4-5** in the Pages panel to select both thumbnails.

4. Click the **Pages panel options button** ▾≡ , point to **Color Label**, then click **Green**.

   Your Pages panel should resemble Figure 29.

5. Save the file, then close Dessert Menu.indd.

You applied a color label to a single page thumbnail and a spread thumbnail.

Work with Objects
AND SMART GUIDES

What You'll Do

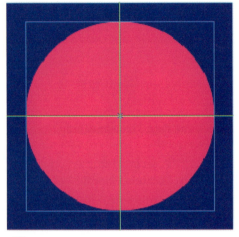

In this lesson, you will work with objects with Smart Guides.

Resizing Objects

Objects are text or graphic elements—images, blocks of color and even simple lines—that are placed in an InDesign document. As mentioned earlier, all objects in InDesign are in frames.

When you select an object's frame, its handles become highlighted, as shown in Figure 30.

Figure 30 *Viewing frame handles on a text frame*

You can click and drag the handles to change the shape and size of the frame. InDesign offers three basic keyboard combinations that you can use when dragging frame handles to affect how the frame and its contents are affected, as shown in Table 3.

TABLE 3: DRAGGING FRAME HANDLES WITH KEYBOARD COMBINATIONS		
Windows	**Mac**	**Result**
Shift-drag a handle	Shift-drag a handle	The frame is resized in proportion; its shape doesn't change; contents of the frame are not scaled
Alt-drag a handle	Option-drag a handle	Resizes the object from its center point
Ctrl-drag a handle	Command-drag a handle	Resizes the object and its contents

These keyboard combinations can themselves be combined. For example, if you hold [Shift] and [Ctrl], then drag a handle, you can resize an object and its contents, while ensuring that you retain the proportions of the object's shape.

You can resize multiple objects just as easily. Simply select multiple objects and handles will appear around all the selected objects, as shown in Figure 31. You can then drag those handles to affect all the objects simultaneously.

Copying Objects

At any time, you can copy and paste an object. That's pretty standard program functionality. InDesign also offers the Paste in Place command on the Edit menu. This is useful for placing a copy of an object exactly in front of the original object. Simply select an object, copy it, then click the Paste in Place command.

You can also copy objects while dragging them. Press and hold [Alt] (Win) or [Option] (Mac), then drag to create a copy of the object.

Hiding, Locking, Grouping, and Ungrouping Objects

The Hide, Lock, Group, and Ungroup commands on the Object menu are essential for working effectively with layouts, especially complex layouts with many objects. Hide objects to get them out of your way. They won't print, and nothing you do changes the location of them as long as they are hidden. Lock an object to make it immovable—you will not even be able to select it. Lock your objects when you have them in a specific location and you don't

Figure 31 *Viewing frame handles around two objects*

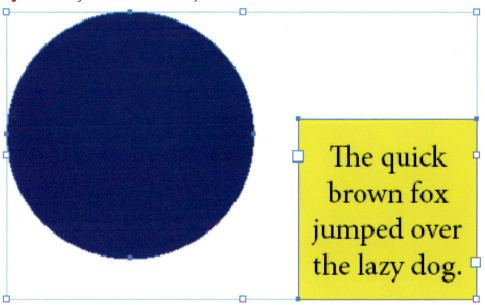

The quick brown fox jumped over the lazy dog.

want them accidentally moved or deleted. Don't think this is being overly cautious; accidentally moving or deleting objects—and being unaware that you did so—happens all the time in complex layouts.

You group multiple objects with the Group command under the Object menu. Grouping objects is a smart and important strategy for protecting the relationships between multiple objects. When you click on grouped objects with the Selection Tool, all the objects are selected. Thus, you can't accidentally select a single object and move or otherwise alter it independently from the group. However, you *can* select individual objects within a group with the Direct Selection Tool—that's how the tool got its name. Even if you select and alter a single object within a group, the objects are not ungrouped. If you click on any of them with the Selection tool, all members of the group will be selected.

Working with Smart Guides

When aligning objects, you will find **Smart Guides** to be really effective and, well, really smart. When the Smart Guides feature is activated, Smart Guides appear automatically when you move objects in the document. Smart Guides give you visual information for positioning objects precisely—in relation to the page or in relation to other objects. For example, you can use Smart Guides to align objects to the edges and centers of other objects and to the horizontal and vertical centers of the page.

You enable Smart Guide options as a preference. You use the View menu to turn them on and off. Figure 32 shows Smart Guides at work.

Figure 32 *Smart Guides aligning the top edges of two objects*

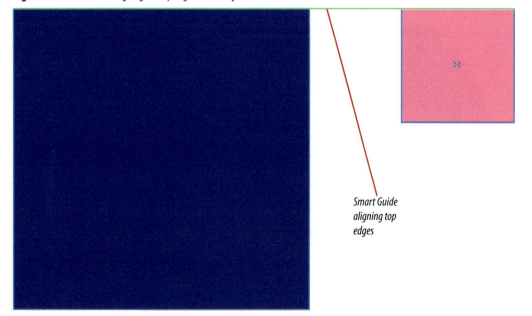

Smart Guide aligning top edges

Getting to Know InDesign

Figure 33 *Resized object and contents*

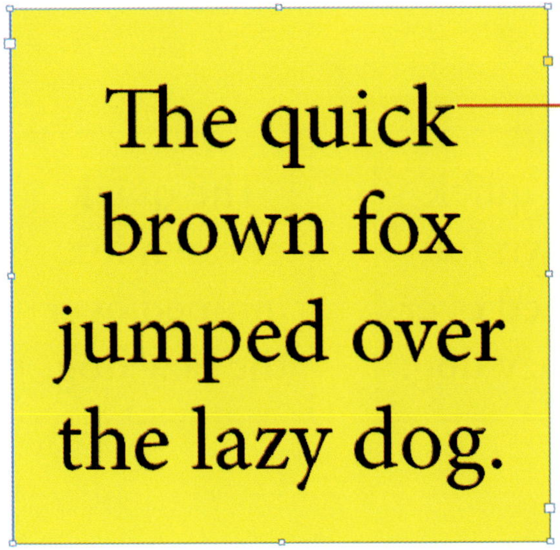

The quick brown fox jumped over the lazy dog.

Text resized
with object

Resize a text object

1. Open ID 1-1.indd, then save it as **Objects**.
2. Click the **Selection Tool** 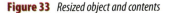 , then click the **yellow text box** to select it.
3. Click and drag **various handles** and note how the object is resized.
4. When you are done experimenting, undo all of the moves you made.

   The Undo command is at the top of the Edit menu.
5. Press and hold **[Shift]**, then drag the **top left corner handle** to the left edge of the document.

   The object is resized proportionately. The text reflows within the resized object, but the text itself is not enlarged.
6. Undo the move.
7. Press and hold **[Alt]**(Win) or **[Option]**(Mac), then click and drag **any corner handle**.

   The object is resized from its center. The text is not resized.
8. Undo the move.
9. Press and hold **[Ctrl]** (Win) or ⌘ (Mac), then click and drag **any corner handle**.

   The object and the text are resized.

TIP If this were a picture frame containing an image, the image would be resized.

10. Undo the move.
11. Press and hold **[Shift][Ctrl][Alt]**(Win) or **[Shift]** ⌘ **[Option]** (Mac), then drag **any corner handle**.

    As shown in Figure 33, the object and the text in the object are resized proportionately from the object's center.

(continued)

12. Click **File** on the Application bar, click **Revert**, then click **Yes** if you are prompted to confirm.

Reverting a file returns it to its status when you last saved it.

You explored various options for resizing an object and its contents, then you reverted the file.

Copy and duplicate objects

1. Select the **text frame**, then copy it, using the [Ctrl][C] (Win) or ⌘ [C] (Mac) shortcut keys.

2. Click **Edit** on the Application bar, then click **Paste in Place**.

A copy of the text frame is placed in front of the original in the exact location.

3. Drag the **copy** of the object to the right so that your screen resembles Figure 34.

4. Select the left object.

(continued)

Figure 34 *Repositioning the pasted copy*

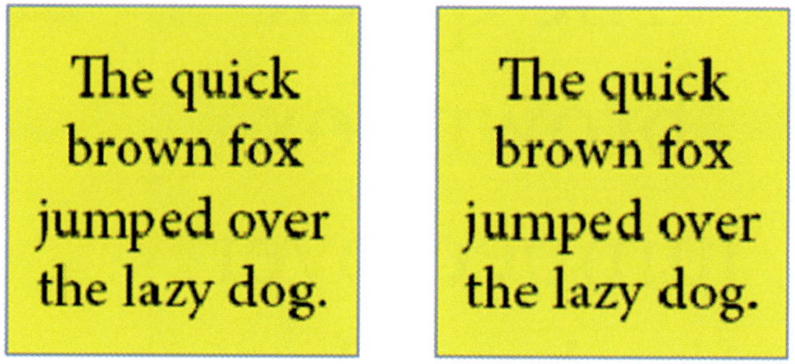

The quick brown fox jumped over the lazy dog.

The quick brown fox jumped over the lazy dog.

Figure 35 *Dragging a copy*

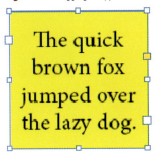

5. Press and hold **[Alt]** (Win) or **[Option]** (Mac), then drag a **copy of the object** to the left so that your screen resembles Figure 35.

TIP This method for creating a copy is referred to as "drag-and-drop" a copy.

6. Select all three objects.

Handles appear around all three objects.

7. Click and drag **various handles** to resize all three objects.

8. Click **Edit** on the Application bar, then click **Cut**.

9. Save the file.

You duplicated an object in two different ways, first with the Copy and Paste in Place command combination, then with the drag-and-drop technique. You resized multiple objects, and cut them from the document.

NEW Hide, lock, and group objects

1. Click **Object** on the Application bar, then click **Show All on Spread**.

This document was originally saved with hidden objects. Three objects appear. They are unselected.

2. Select all three objects, click **Object** on the Application bar, then click **Group**.

3. Click the **Selection tool**, click the **pasteboard** to deselect all, then click the **pink circle**.

(continued)

As shown in Figure 36, all three objects are selected because they are grouped. The dotted line around the objects is a visual indication that they are grouped.

4. Click the **pasteboard** to deselect all, click the **Direct Selection tool** 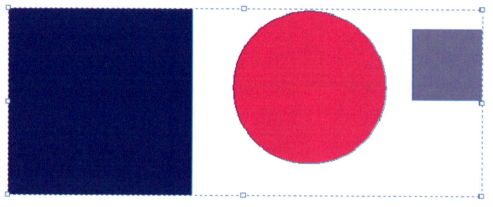, then click the **pink circle.**

   Only the circle is selected, because the Direct Selection tool selects individual objects within a group.

5. Select all, click **Object** on the Application bar, click **Ungroup**, then click the **pasteboard** to deselect all.

   Click the **Selection tool** , select the small square, click **Object** on the Application bar, then click **Lock**.

   The object's handles disappear and it can no longer be selected.

6. Click **Object** on the Application bar, then click **Unlock All on Spread**.

   The small blue square is unlocked.

7. Select **all**, click **Object** on the Application bar, then click **Hide**.

   All selected objects disappear.

8. Click **Object** on the Application bar, then click **Show All on Spread**.

   The three objects reappear in the same location that they were in when they were hidden.

TIP Memorize the shortcut keys for Hide/Show, Group/Ungroup, and Lock/Unlock. They are fairly easy to remember and extremely useful. You will be using these commands over and over again when you work in InDesign.

(continued)

Figure 36 *Three grouped objects*

Getting to Know InDesign

Figure 37 *Guides & Pasteboard preferences dialog box*

9. Hide the pink circle and the small blue square.
10. Save the file.

You revealed hidden objects, grouped them, then used the Direct Selection tool to select individual objects within the group. You ungrouped the objects, locked them, unlocked them, and hid them.

Work with Smart Guides

1. Click **Edit** on the Application bar, point to **Preferences** (Win) or **InDesign** (Mac), then click **Guides and Pasteboard**.
2. Verify that your Smart Guide Options section resembles Figure 37, then click OK.
3. Click **View** on the Application bar, point to **Grids & Guides**, then click **Smart Guides** if necessary, to activate it.
4. Click the **blue rectangle**, then try to center it visually on the page.

(continued)

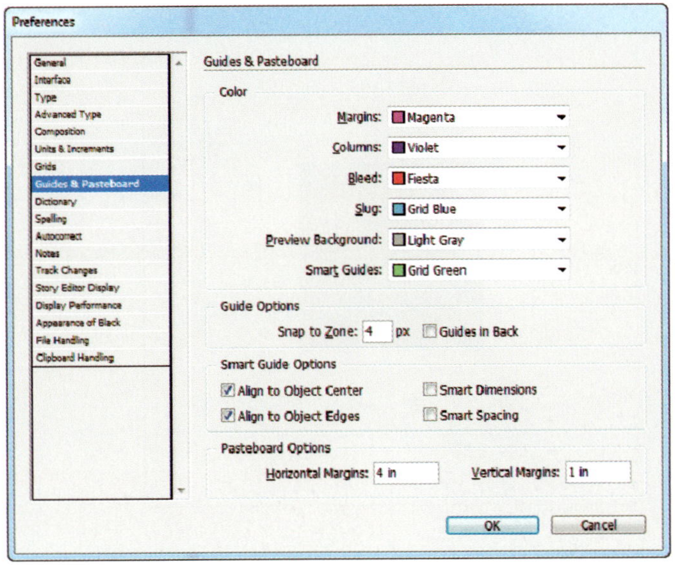

Using the Smart Cursor

One of the Smart Guides options is the Smart Cursor. With the Smart Cursor activated, a small gray window appears beside your cursor and displays the X/Y coordinates of an object you're moving, resizing, rotating, or otherwise manipulating. To turn the Smart Cursor on and off, activate or deactivate the Show Transformation Values option in the Interface preferences dialog box.

5. Release your mouse when both the horizontal and vertical Smart Guides appear, as shown in Figure 38.

   Both the horizontal and the vertical pink Smart Guides appear when the object's center point is aligned with the center point of the document. By default, Smart Guides that show the relationship between objects and the document are pink.

TIP The gray box beside the cursor shows the location coordinates of the object on the page. You will learn a lot more about location coordinates in Chapter 3.

6. Show the hidden objects, then hide the small light blue square.

7. Using the same method, align the center of the pink circle with the center of the large blue square.

   When the center points of the two object are aligned, your Smart Guides will resemble Figure 39.

(continued)

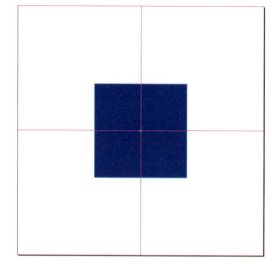

Figure 38 *Centering the square on the page*

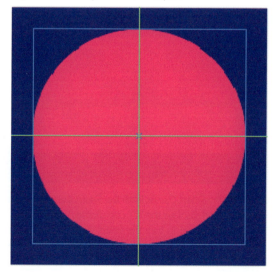

Figure 39 *Centering the circle on the square*

Figure 40 *Aligning the top edges of the two squares*

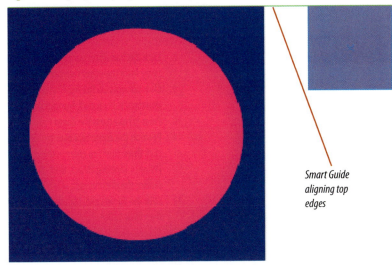

Smart Guide
aligning top
edges

Figure 41 *Aligning the bottom edges of the two squares*

8. Show the hidden small blue square.

9. Use Smart Guides to align the top of the small square with the top of the large square, as shown in Figure 40.

10. "Snap" the left edge of the small square to the right edge of the large square.

11. Position the small square as shown in Figure 41.

12. Save, then close the file.

You aligned an object at the center of the document and created precise relationships between three objects, using Smart Guides.

Explore the InDesign Workspace

1. Launch Adobe InDesign CS5.
2. Click File on the Application bar, click Open, navigate to the drive and folder where your Chapter 1 Data Files are stored, click ID 1-3.indd, then click Open.
3. Save the File as **Hana.indd**.
4. Click Window on the Application bar, point to Workspace, then click [Essentials].

TIP If you are already working in the Essentials workspace, click Window on the Application bar, then click Reset Essentials to return to the default Essentials workspace settings.

5. Point to the Type tool, then press and hold the mouse button to see the Type on a Path tool.
6. Using the same method, view the hidden tools behind the other tools with small black triangles.
7. Position your mouse pointer over the Selection tool until its tooltip appears.
8. Press the following keys and note which tools are selected with each key: [a], [p], [v], [t], [i], [h], [z].
9. Press [Tab] to temporarily hide all open panels, then press [Tab] again. The panels reappear.

View and Modify Page Elements

1. Click the Color panel icon in the stack of collapsed panels in the right of the workspace to expand the Color panel.
2. Click the Collapse to Icons button at the top of the Color panel to minimize the panel, then click the Color panel icon again to expand the panel again.
3. Drag the Color panel name tab to the left so it is ungrouped from the Stroke panel.
4. Drag the Swatches panel name tab to the blank space next to the Color panel name tab, then release the mouse.
5. Click Window on the Application bar, point to Object and Layout, then click Transform. The Transform panel appears expanded on the document.
6. Drag the Transform panel name tab to the bottom edge of the Swatches and Color panels group, then release the mouse a blue horizontal bar appears.
7. Click and drag the dark gray bar at the top of the panel group, above the Color and Swatches panel tabs. All three panels move together. The Transform panel moves with the two panels above because they are docked.

8. Click the Transform panel name tab, then drag it away from the other two panels.
9. Click Window on the Application bar, point to Workspace, then click Typography.
10. Press [z] to access the Zoom tool.
11. Position the Zoom tool over the document window, click three times to enlarge the document, press [Alt] (Win) or [option] (Mac), then click three times to reduce the document.
12. Click the Zoom Level list arrow on the Application bar, then click 1200%.
13. Double-click 1200% in the Zoom Level text box, type 350, then press [Enter] (Win) or [return] (Mac).
14. Click the Hand tool on the Tools panel, then click and drag the document window to scroll around the page.
15. Double-click the Zoom tool.
16. Click the Selection tool, point to the center of the document window, then press and hold [Ctrl][Spacebar] (Win) or ⌘ [Spacebar] (Mac).
17. Click three times, then release [Ctrl][Spacebar] (Win) or ⌘ [Spacebar] (Mac).
18. Press and hold [Spacebar] to access the Hand tool, then scroll around the image.

19. Press and hold [Ctrl][Alt][Spacebar] (Win) or ⌘ [option][Spacebar] (Mac), then click the mouse multiple times to reduce the view to 25%.

20. Click View on the Application bar, note the shortcut key on the Fit Page in Window command, then click Fit Page in Window.

21. Click View on the application bar, then note the Rulers command and its shortcut key.

22. Click the pasteboard to escape the View menu, then press [Ctrl] [R](Win) or ⌘ [R] (Mac) several times to hide and show rulers, finishing with rulers showing.

23. Note the units on the rulers.

24. Click Edit on the Application bar, point to Preferences, then click Units & Increments.

25. In the Ruler Units section, click the Horizontal list arrow to see the available measurement options.

26. Set the Horizontal and Vertical fields to Picas.

27. Reopen the Units & Increments preferences dialog box, change the Horizontal and Vertical fields to Inches, then click OK.

28. Click View on the application bar, point to Extras, then note the Frame Edges command and its shortcut key.

29. Click the pasteboard to escape the View menu, then enter [Ctrl][H] (Win) or [Ctrl] ⌘ [H] (Mac) several times to hide and show frame edges, finishing with frame edges showing.

30. Click View on the Application bar, point to Grids & Guides, then note the Guides command and its shortcut key.

31. Click the pasteboard to escape the View menu, then enter [Ctrl] [;] (Win) or ⌘ [;] (Mac) several times to hide and show guides, finishing with guides showing.

32. Click View on the application bar, point to Grids & Guides, then note the Document Grid command and its shortcut key.

33. Click the pasteboard to escape the View menu, then enter [Ctrl]['](Win) or ⌘ ['] (Mac) repeatedly to hide and show the document grid.
Click View on the Application bar, point to Grids & Guides, then note the Snap to Guides and Snap to Document Grid commands.
In the same menu, note the Delete All Guides on Spread command.
Click the pasteboard to escape the View menu.

34. Click the View menu, point to Screen Mode, then click Preview.

35. Press the [W] on your keypad to toggle between Preview and Normal modes, finishing in Normal mode.

36. Click View on the Application bar, point to Screen Mode, then click Presentation.

37. Press the ↓ on your keypad to scroll through the document to the last page.

38. Press the ↑ on your keypad to scroll up to the first page.

39. Press [Esc] to leave Presentation mode.

40. Press and hold [Shift], then press [W] to switch to Presentation mode.

41. Still holding [Shift], press [W] again to return to Normal mode.

42. Click Edit (Win) or InDesign (Mac) on the Application bar, point to Preferences, click Interface, click the Open Documents as Tabs check box if it is unchecked, then click OK.

43. Open ID 1-2.indd, then click the tabs to toggle between viewing both documents, finishing with Hana as the active document.

44. Position your mouse pointer over the right edge or the bottom-right corner of the document, then click and drag to try to resize it. Because it is a tabbed document, the window is "fixed" and can't be resized.

45. Drag the Hana tab straight down approximately 1/2 inch.

46. Position your mouse pointer over the bottom-right corner, then click and drag towards the center of the monitor window to reduce the window to approximately half its size.

47. Position your mouse pointer over the title bar of the document, then click and drag to move Hana half way down towards the bottom of your monitor screen.

48. Float your mouse pointer over the title bar of Hana, click and drag to position it at the top of the window beside ID 1-2.indd tab, then release your mouse when you see a horizontal blue bar. The document is tabbed once again.

49. Close ID 1-2.indd without saving changes if you are prompted.

Navigate through a document

1. Click the Page menu list arrow at the bottom-left of the document window, then click 3.
2. Click View on the Application bar, then click Fit Spread in Window.
3. Click the Next Spread button.
4. Click the Previous Spread button twice.
5. Click the Pages icon in the stack of collapses panel to expand the Pages panel if it is not already expanded.
6. Double-click the page 6 icon on the Pages panel.
7. Double-click the page 3 icon on the Pages panel.
8. Double-click the numbers 2-3 beneath the page 2 and page 3 icons on the Pages panel.
9. Click Layout on the Application bar, then click First Page.
10. Enter [Ctrl][J] (Win) or ⌘ [J] (Mac) to open the Go to Page dialog box, enter 5, then press [Enter] (Win) or [Return] (Mac).
11. Save the file.
12. Click the Page 5 thumbnail in the Pages panel.
13. Click the Pages panel option button, point to Color Label, then click Blue.
14. Click the page numbers 2-3 in the Pages panel to select both thumbnails.
15. Click the Pages panel option button, point to Color Label, then click Orange. Your Pages panel should resemble Figure 42.
16. Save the file.

Work with objects and Smart Guides

1. Open ID 1-4.indd, then save it as **Skills Objects**.
2. Click the Selection Tool, then click to select the object.
3. Click and drag various handles and note how the object is resized.
4. Undo all of the moves you made.
5. Press and hold [Shift], then drag the top left corner handle towards the left edge of the document.
6. Undo the move.
7. Press and hold [Alt] (Win) or [Option] (Mac), then click and drag any corner handle.
8. Undo the move.

Figure 42 *Color labels applied to pages*

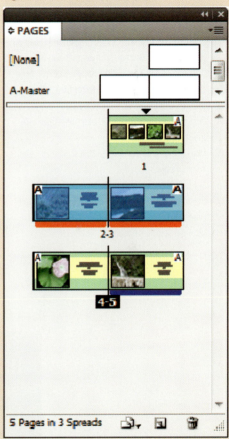

9. Press and hold [Ctrl] (Win) or ⌘ (Mac), then click and drag any corner handle.
10. Undo the move.
11. Press and hold [Shift][Ctrl][Alt] (Win) or [Shift] ⌘ [Option] (Mac), then drag any corner handle.
12. Click File on the Application bar, click Revert, then click Yes if you are prompted to confirm.
13. Select the text frame, then copy it.
14. Click Edit on the Application bar, then click Paste in Place.
15. Drag the copy to the right so that it is beside the original object.
16. Select the left object.
17. Press and hold [Alt] (Win) or [Option] (Mac), then drag a copy of the object to the left so that your screen resembles Figure 43.

18. Select all three objects.
19. Click and drag various handles to resize all three objects.
20. Click Edit on the application bar, then click Cut.
21. Save the file.
22. Click Object on the Application bar, then click Show All on Spread.
23. Select all three objects, click Object on the Application bar, then click Group.
24. Click the Selection tool, click anywhere on the pasteboard to deselect all, then click the green diamond.
25. Click the pasteboard to deselect all, click the Direct Selection tool, then click the green diamond.
26. Select all, click Object on the Application bar, then click Ungroup.

27. Click the Selection tool, select the small circle, click Object on the Application bar, then click Lock.
28. Click Object on the Application bar, then click Unlock All on Spread.
29. Select all, click Object on the Application bar, then click Hide.
30. Click Object on the Application bar, then click Show All on Spread.
31. Hide the green diamond and the small blue circle.
32. Save the file.
33. Click Edit (Win) or (InDesign) Mac on the Application bar, point to Preferences, then click Guides & Pasteboard.
34. Verify that your Smart Guide Options section shows the two left options checked and the two right objects unchecked, then click OK.

Figure 43 *Text frame copied and duplicated*

35. Click View on the Application bar, point to Grids & Guides, then click Smart Guides, if necessary, to activate it.
36. Click the yellow circle, then try to center it visually on the page.

37. Release your mouse when both the horizontal and vertical Smart Guides appear, as shown in Figure 44.
38. Show the hidden objects, then hide the small circle.
39. Using the same method, align the center of the green diamond with the center of the yellow circle.

40. Show the hidden small circle.
41. Referring to Figure 45, align the vertical center of the small circle with the right point of the green diamond.
42. Save, then close the file.

Figure 44 *Horizontal and vertical Smart Guides*

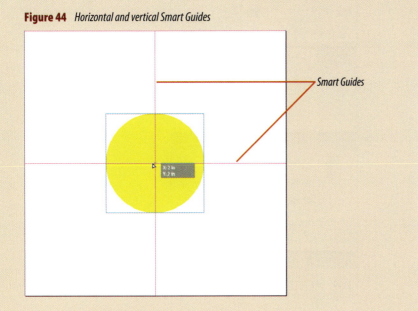

Smart Guides

Figure 45 *Completed Skills Review*

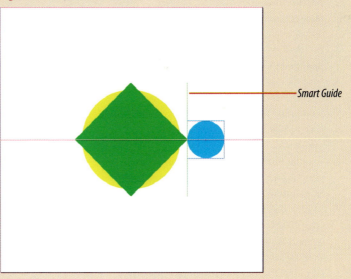

Smart Guide

You work at a local design studio. Your boss has informed you that the studio will be switching to Adobe InDesign for its layout software. She tells you that she wants you to spend the day investigating the software and creating simple layouts. You decide first to group and dock panels in a way that you think will be best for working with type and simple layouts.

1. Start Adobe InDesign.
2. Without creating a new document, group the Paragraph and Character panels together, then click the Paragraph panel name tab so that it is the active panel.
3. Dock the Pages panel to the bottom of the Paragraph panel group.
4. Group the Layers panel with the Pages panel, then click the Layers panel name tab so that it is the active panel.
5. Dock the Swatches panel below the Layers panel group.
6. Group the Color, Stroke, and Gradient panels with the Swatches panel, then click the Gradient panel name tab so that it is the active panel.
7. Dock the Align panel below the Gradient panel group. (*Hint*: The Align panel is in the Object & Layout section of the Window menu.)
8. Group the Transform and the Effects panels with the Align panel, then click the Transform panel name tab so that it is the active panel. (*Hint*: The Transform panel is in the Object & Layout section of the Window menu.)
9. Compare your panels with Figure 46.

Figure 46 *Completed Project Builder 1*

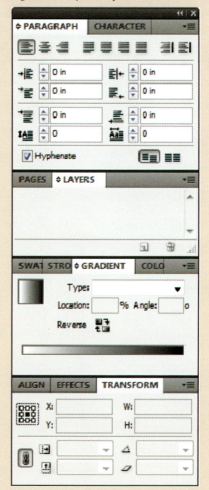

Getting to Know InDesign

You are the creative director at a design studio. The studio has recently switched to Adobe InDesign for its layout software. You will be conducting a series of in-house classes to teach the junior designers how to use InDesign. Before your first class, you decide to practice some basic skills for viewing a document.

1. Open ID 1-5.indd.
2. Click the Selection tool if it is not active, then press [Ctrl][Spacebar] (Win) or ⌘ [Spacebar] (Mac) to access the Zoom tool.
3. Position the Zoom tool slightly above and to the left of the left eye, click and drag the Zoom tool pointer to draw a dotted rectangle around the eye, then release the mouse button.
4. Press [Spacebar], then scroll with the Hand tool to the right eye.
5. Press [Ctrl][Alt][Spacebar] (Win) or [Option] ⌘ [Spacebar] (Mac), then click the Zoom tool five times on the dog's right eye.
6. Move the image with the Hand tool so that both of the dog's eyes and his snout are visible in the window and your screen resembles Figure 47. (Your magnification may differ from that shown in the figure.)
7. Close ID 1-5.indd without saving any changes.

Figure 47 *Completed Project Builder 2*

You will be teaching a small, in-house class on InDesign and making grids and targets. You decide to set up a test exercise for your students to practice duplicating objects and aligning them with one another and with the document.

1. Open ID 1- 6.indd, then save it as **Squares and Targets**.
2. Use the techniques you learned in this chapter to recreate the layout in Figure 48. Try it on your own, then go through the following steps and compare your results with those in the figure.
3. Verify that Smart Guides are activated.
4. Align the large yellow circle to the center of the page.
5. Center the large green circle in the large yellow circle.
6. Center the remaining three circles.
7. Copy the smallest yellow circle, then apply the Paste in Place command.
8. Center the pasted circle in the blue square.
9. Group the yellow circle and the blue square.
10. Click the Selection tool.
11. Drag and drop three copies of the group at the four corners of the document.
12. Save your work, then close the file.

Figure 48 *Completed Design Project*

In this project, you will examine the layout that you worked with in the lessons of this chapter. You are encouraged to critique the layout from a design perspective, to comment on the elements that you think are effective, and to suggest ways that the presentation may be improved.

1. Open ID 1-7.indd.
2. Click View on the Application bar, point to Display Performance, then click High Quality Display.
3. Use the Pages panel to move from page to page, viewing each page at least one time. (*Hint*: You can refer to Figure 49.)
4. What do you think of the photographs? Are they effective? Does the fact that they are "silhouetted" against a white background make them more effective, or do you think it would be better if they were photographed in context, such as on a plate or on a table in a restaurant setting?
5. How does the clean white background affect the look and feel of the piece, given that this is a layout about food?
6. Move through all the pages again. The layout changes from page to page. Though the restaurant's name doesn't move from one spread to another and the desserts are all positioned at the center of the page, the location of the menu descriptions changes, as does the location of the prices. Also, the circle behind the prices changes color. What do you think about these changes from page to page? Would the layout be improved if all items were consistent from page to page?
7. Should the prices be in a bold typeface?

8. None of the pages features a title of the food item; the food is described only in the menu description. Do you think it would be better if a title appeared on every page? If so, would you be willing to discard the restaurant's name in the upper-left corner in favor of a title?

9. Submit your answers to these three questions in a document called Design Critique.
10. Close ID 1-7.indd without saving any changes.

Figure 49 *ID 1-7.indd*

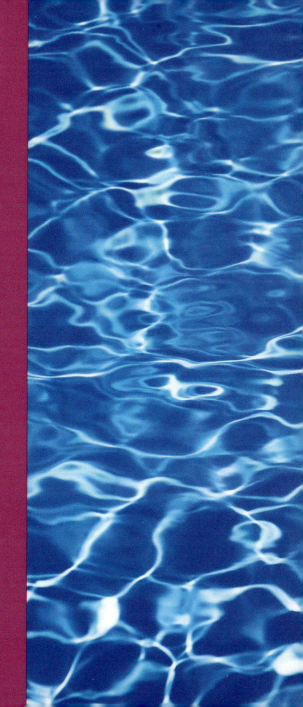

CHAPTER  WORKING WITH
TEXT

1. Format text

2. Format paragraphs

3. Create and apply styles

4. Edit text

5. Create bulleted and numbered lists

CHAPTER 2 WORKING WITH TEXT

Earth, air, fire, and water were considered the four essential elements of our world by the ancients. Another quartet—text, color, illustration, and imagery—are considered the four essential elements of layout by designers. Take a moment to read them again and make a mental note. We will use these four elements as categories throughout this book to approach the myriad features InDesign offers.

In this chapter, we will focus on working with text. Like Proteus, the mythological figure who could change his outer form at will, text in a layout can appear in a variety of ways. It is *protean*, or, versatile. As display text it can be a bold, dramatic headline at the center of a page or a miniscule footnote tucked away unobtrusively. As paragraphs of text, it can be flowed as body copy, or it can appear as simple page numbers at the lower corner of a page.

You will be pleased to find that InDesign is a first-rate application for generating and editing text. Everything you want to do can be done. With InDesign, your ability to generate functional, readable text and beautiful typographic artwork is without limitation.

TOOLS YOU'LL USE

CHARACTER

Times New Roman

Regular

12 pt   (14.4 p

Metric: AV 0

100%   100%

0 pt   0°

Language: English: USA

Find/Change

Query: [Custom]

Text GREP Glyph Object

Find what:
Miniature Pinscher

Change to:
Min-Pin

Search: Document

Aa

Find Format:

Change Format:

Done
Find
Change
Change All
Change/Find
Fewer Options

Check Spelling

Not in Dictionary:
refered

Change To:
refered

Suggested Corrections:
referred
refereed
refired
referee
revered
referees
refreshed
referral

Add To: User Dictionary

Case Sensitive

Language: English: USA

Search: Document

Done
Skip
Change
Ignore All
Change All
Dictionary...

Add

Format
TEXT

What You'll Do

Introducing the Min-Pin
by Christopher Smith

In this lesson, you will use the Character panel and various keyboard commands to modify text attributes.

Using the Character Panel

The Character panel, shown in Figure 1, is the command center for modifying text. The Character panel works hand-in-hand with the Paragraph panel, which is why it's wise to keep them grouped together. While the Paragraph panel, as its name implies, focuses on manipulating paragraphs or blocks of text, the Character panel focuses on more specific modifications, such as font, font style, and font size.

In addition to these basic modifications, the Character panel offers other controls for manipulating text. You use the panel to modify leading, track and kern text, apply a horizontal scale or a vertical scale to text, perform a baseline shift, or skew text. To select text quickly for editing, you can use the methods shown in Table 1: Keyboard Commands for Selecting Text, on the next page.

QUICK TIP

You can set the font list on the Character panel to show font names or font names and samples of each font. To enable or disable this feature, click Edit on the Application bar, point to Preferences, click Type on the left, then add or remove a check mark in the Font Preview Size check box. Notice also that you can click the Font Preview Size list arrow and choose Small, Medium, or Large.

Understanding Leading

Leading is the term used to describe the vertical space between lines of text. This space is measured from the baseline of one line of text to the baseline of the next line of text. As shown in Figure 2, the **baseline** is the invisible line on which a line of text sits. Leading, like font size, is measured in points.

Pasting Text Without Formatting

When you copy text, then paste it, it is, by default, pasted with all of its formatting—its typeface, type style, type size, and any other formatting that has been applied. Sometimes, this can be undesirable. This is where the Paste without Formatting command comes into play. It strips the copied text of all its original formatting, then reformats it to match the formatting of the text frame where it is pasted.

Figure 1 *Character panel*

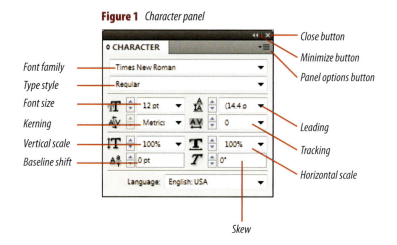

Font family
Type style
Font size
Kerning
Vertical scale
Baseline shift

Close button
Minimize button
Panel options button
Leading
Tracking
Horizontal scale

Skew

Figure 2 *Examples of leading*

12 pt text with
14 pt leading

As soon as the Min-Pin climbs onto the bed, he usually slips under the covers like a mole, all the way to the very foot of the bed.

12 pt text with
24 pt leading

As soon as the Min-Pin climbs onto the

bed, he usually slips under the covers

like a mole, all the way to the very foot

of the bed.

As soon as the Min-Pin climbs onto the
bed, he usually slips under the covers
like a mole, all the way to the very foot
of the bed.

12 pt text with
8 pt leading

TABLE 1: KEYBOARD COMMANDS FOR SELECTING TEXT	
To select:	**Do the following:**
One word	Double-click word
One line	Triple-click any word in the line
One paragraph	Click any word in the paragraph four times
Entire story	Click any word in the story five times
Entire story	[Ctrl][A] (Win) or ⌘[A] (Mac)
One character to the right of insertion point	[Shift]→
One character to the left of insertion point	[Shift]←
One line up from insertion point	[Shift]↑
One line down from insertion point	[Shift]↓
One word to the right of insertion point	[Shift][Ctrl] → (Win) or [Shift] ⌘ → (Mac)
One word to the left of insertion point	[Shift][Ctrl] ← (Win) or [Shift] ⌘ ← (Mac)
One paragraph above insertion point	[Shift][Ctrl] ↑ (Win) or [Shift] ⌘ ↑ (Mac)
One paragraph below insertion point	[Shift][Ctrl] ↓ (Win) or [Shift] ⌘ ↓ (Mac)

Scaling Text Horizontally and Vertically

When you format text, your most basic choice is which font you want to use and at what size you want to use it. Once you've chosen a font and a font size, you can further manipulate the appearance of the text with a horizontal or vertical scale.

On the Character panel, horizontal and vertical scales are expressed as percentages. By default, text is generated at a 100% horizontal and 100% vertical scale, meaning that the text is not scaled at all. Decreasing the horizontal scale only, for example, maintains the height of the characters but decreases the width—on the horizontal axis. Conversely, increasing the horizontal scale again maintains the height but increases the width of the characters on the horizontal axis. Figure 3 shows four examples of horizontal and vertical scales.

QUICK TIP

You can also control the vertical alignment of text inside a text box by selecting the text box, clicking Object on the Application bar, then clicking Text Frame Options. Click the Align list arrow, then click Top, Center, Bottom, or Justify.

Kerning and Tracking Text

Though your computer is a magnificent instrument for generating text in myriad fonts and font sizes, you will often want to manipulate the appearance of text after you have created it—especially if you have the meticulous eye of a designer. **Kerning** is a long-standing process of increasing or decreasing space between a pair of characters. **Tracking** is more global. Like kerning, tracking affects the spaces between letters, but it is applied globally to an entire word or paragraph.

Kerning and tracking are standard features in most word processing applications, but they are more about typography than word processing—that is, they are used for setting text in a way that is pleasing to the eye. Spacing problems with text are usually more prominent with large size headlines than with smaller body copy—this is why many designers will spend great amounts of time tracking and kerning a headline. Figures 4 and 5 show examples of kerning and tracking applied to a headline. Note, though, that kerning and tracking are also used often on body copy as a simple solution for fitting text within an allotted space.

InDesign measures both kerning and tracking in increments of 1/1000 em—a unit of measure that is determined by the current type size. In a 6-point font, 1 em equals 6 points; in a 12-point font, 1 em equals

Figure 3 *Scaling text horizontally and vertically*

original text
50% horizontal scale
150% horizontal scale
50% vertical scale
150% vertical scale

Figure 4 *Kerning text*

Wonderful —— No kerning

Wonderful

With kerning

Figure 5 *Tracking text*

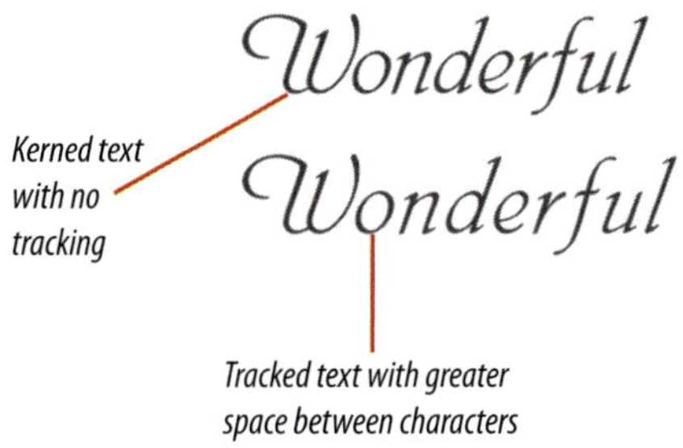

Wonderful

Kerned text with no tracking

Wonderful

Tracked text with greater space between characters

12 points. It's good to know this, but you don't need to have this information in mind when kerning and tracking text. Just remember that the increments are small enough to provide you with the specificity that you desire for creating eye-pleasing text.

Creating Superscript Characters

You are already familiar with superscript characters, even if you don't know them by that term. When you see a footnote in a book or document, the superscripted character is the footnote itself, the small number positioned to the upper-right of a word. Figure 6 shows a superscripted character.

The only tricky thing about applying a superscript is remembering how to do it.

The Superscript command, as shown in Figure 7, is listed in the Character panel options. Wait—there's one more tricky thing you need to remember about superscripts. If you select a 12-point character, for example, and then apply the Superscript command, the size of the character will decrease; however, its point size will still be identified on the Character panel as 12 points.

Creating Subscript Characters

The Character panel menu also offers a command for Subscript. You can think of Subscript as the opposite of Superscript. Instead of raising the baseline of the selected text, the Subscript command positions the text below its original baseline. As with

Superscript, the Subscript command makes the selected text appear smaller.

Of the two, Subscript is used less often. Though it is seldom used for footnotes, many designers use Subscript for trademarks and registration marks.

Underlining Text

InDesign offers different methods for underlining text and for creating **rules**, which are horizontal, vertical, or diagonal lines. When you simply want to underline selected text, the most basic method is to use the Underline command on the Character panel menu. With this command, the weight of the underline is determined by the point size of the selected text. The greater the point size, the greater the weight of the line.

Figure 6 *Identifying a superscripted character*

Superscripted character

Figure 7 *Locating the Superscript command*

Superscript command

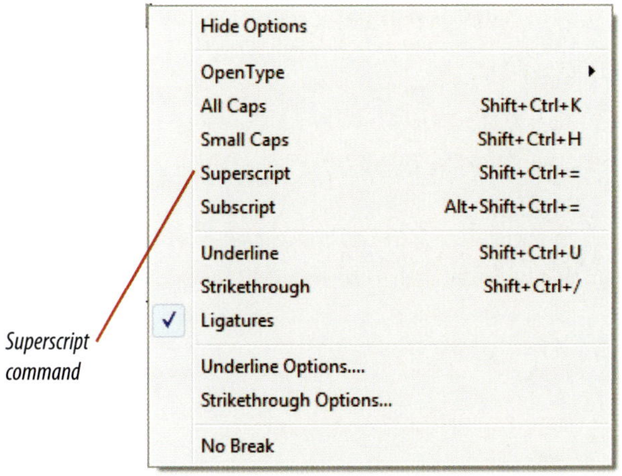

Modify text attributes

1. Open ID 2-1.indd, then save it as **Min-Pin Intro**.

2. Click **Edit** (Win) or **InDesign** (Mac) on the Application bar, point to **Preferences**, then click **Units & Increments**.

3. Verify that your Preferences dialog box has the same settings shown in Figure 8, then click **OK**.

4. Click **Window** on the Application bar, point to **Workspace**, then click [**Typography**] or **Reset Typography** if [Typography] is already checked.

5. Click the **Type tool** T, then double-click the word **Introducing** at the top of the page.

6. Open the Character panel.

   The Character panel displays the formatting of the selected text.

7. Triple-click **Introducing** to select the entire line.

8. On the Character panel, click the **Font Family list arrow**, click **Impact**, click the **Font Size list arrow**, click **48 pt**, then verify that the Leading text box contains **57.6** pt, as shown in Figure 9.

9. Press and hold [**Shift**][**Ctrl**] (Win) or [**Shift**] [⌘] (Mac), then press [**<**] 10 times.

   The point size is reduced by one point size every time you press [**<**].

10. Press and hold [**Shift**][**Ctrl**] (Win) or [**Shift**] [⌘] (Mac), then press [**>**] two times.

    The point size is increased by two points.

11. Triple-click **by** on the second line, change the font to Garamond or a similar font, click the **Type Style list arrow**, click **Italic**, click the **Font Size list arrow**, then click **18 pt**.

TIP If the Garamond font is not available to you, use a similar font.

(continued)

Figure 8 *Units & Increments section of the Preferences dialog box*

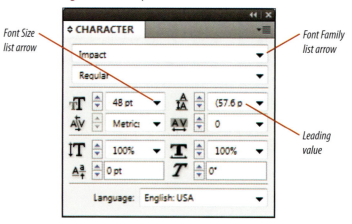

Size/Leading value

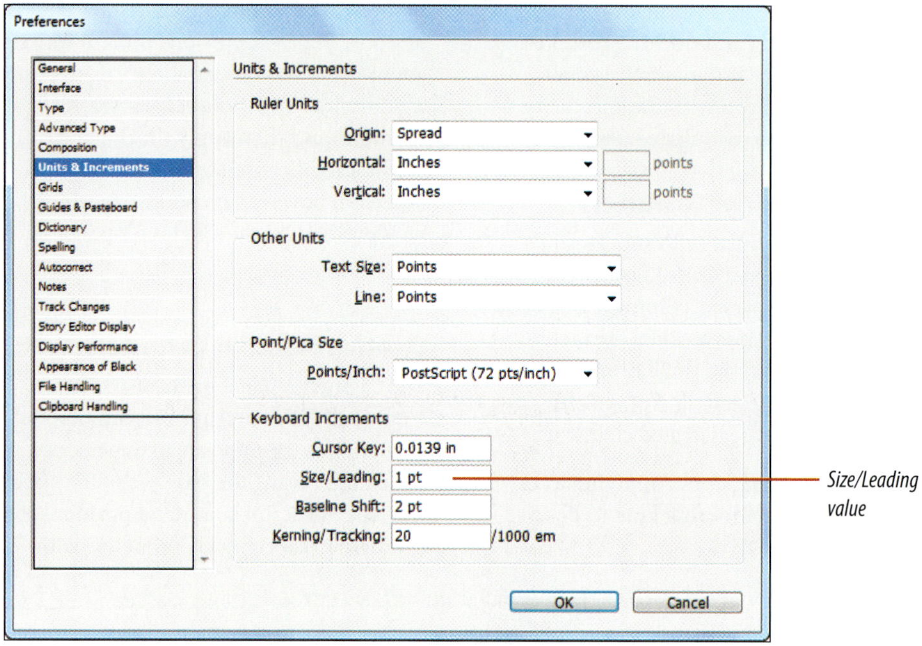

Figure 9 *Character panel*

Font Size list arrow

Font Family list arrow

Leading value

Figure 10 *Selected text box*

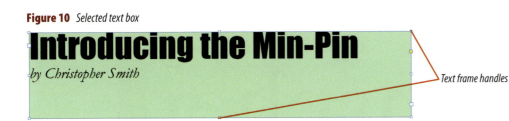

Text frame handles

Figure 11 *Increasing the tracking value of selected text*

Figure 12 *Decreasing the kerning value between two letters*

Decreased kerning

12. Click the **Selection tool** , then note that the text frame is highlighted, as shown in Figure 10.
13. Click **Object** on the Application bar, click **Text Frame Options**, click the **Align list arrow** in the Vertical Justification section, click **Center**, then click **OK**.

You used keyboard commands and the Character panel to modify text.

Track and kern text

1. Click the **Zoom tool** , click and drag the **Zoom tool pointer** around the light green text frame, then release the mouse button.

   When you drag the Zoom tool pointer, a dotted-lined selection rectangle appears. When you release the mouse, the contents within the rectangle are magnified.

2. Click the **Type tool** , then triple-click the word **Introducing**.

3. Click the **Tracking list arrow** on the Character panel, then click **200**.

   The horizontal width of each word increases, and a consistent amount of space is applied between each letter, as shown in Figure 11.

4. Reduce the tracking value to **25**.

5. Click between the letters h and e in the word the, click the **Kerning list arrow**, then click **-50**.

   The space between the two letters decreases.

6. Click the **Kerning up arrow** twice to decrease the kerning value to **-30**.

7. Click the **Selection tool** .

   Your headline should resemble Figure 12.

You used the Character panel to modify tracking and kerning values applied to text.

Create superscript characters

1. Click **View** on the Application bar, click **Fit Page in Window**, click the **Zoom** 🔍 , then drag a selection box that encompasses all of the body copy on the page.

2. Click the **Type tool** T. , then select the number **1** after the words Doberman Pinscher at the end of the fourth paragraph.

3. Click the **Character panel options button** ▼≣ , then click **Superscript**.

   The character's size is reduced and it is positioned higher than the characters that precede it, as shown in an enlarged view in Figure 13.

4. Select the number **2** after the word cows in the last paragraph, then apply the Superscript command.

TIP When the Superscript command is applied to text, its designated font size remains the same.

5. Select the number **1** beside the footnote at the bottom of the page, apply the Superscript command, select the number **2** below, apply the Superscript command again, then deselect the text.

   Your footnotes should resemble Figure 14.

You applied the Superscript command to format selected text as footnotes.

Figure 13 *Applying the Superscript command*

Superscript character

Figure 14 *Using the Superscript command to format footnotes*

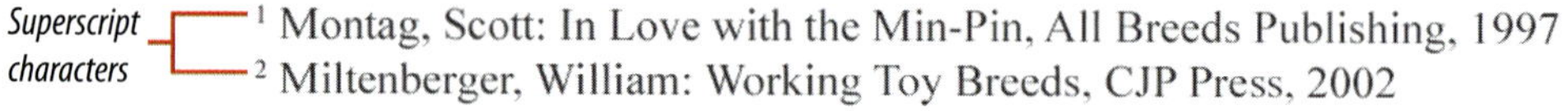

Superscript characters

[1] Montag, Scott: In Love with the Min-Pin, All Breeds Publishing, 1997
[2] Miltenberger, William: Working Toy Breeds, CJP Press, 2002

Inserting Footnotes Automatically

While you can insert footnotes using the techniques in this lesson, if you have many footnotes in a document, you can use the InDesign CS5 enhanced footnote feature to insert them quickly and easily. In InDesign, a footnote consists of a reference number that appears in document text, and the footnote text that appears at the bottom of the page or column. To add a footnote, place the insertion point in the document location where you want the reference number to appear. Click Type on the Application bar, then click Insert Footnote. The insertion point moves to the footnote area at the bottom of the page or column. Type the footnote text; the footnote area expands as you type. If the text containing a footnote moves to another page, its footnote moves with it.

Figure 15 *Underlining text*

¹ Montag, Scott: <u>In Love with the Min-Pin</u>, All Breeds
² Miltenberger, William: Working Toy Breeds, CJP Pre

Figure 16 *Formatting footnotes*

¹ Montag, Scott: <u>In Love with the Min-Pin</u>, All Breeds Publishing, 1997

² Miltenberger, William: <u>Working Toy Breeds</u>, CJP Press, 2002

8 pt text

Formatting Footnotes

If you use the Insert Footnote command to enter footnotes in a document, you can specify a number of formatting attributes. Click Type on the Application bar, then click Document Footnote Options. On the Numbering and Formatting tab, you can select the numbering style, starting number, prefix, position, character style, or separator. The Layout tab lets you set the spacing above and between footnotes, as well as the rule that appears above them. Formatting changes you make to footnotes affect all existing and new footnotes.

Underline text

1. Click **View** on the Application bar, click **Fit Page in Window**, click the **Zoom tool** 🔍, then drag a selection box that encompasses both footnotes at the bottom of the page.

2. Click the **Type tool** T, then select **In Love with the Min-Pin** in the first footnote.

3. Click the **Character panel options button** ▾☰, then click **Underline**.

   Only the selected text is underlined, as shown in Figure 15.

TIP The weight of the line is automatically determined, based on the point size of the selected text.

4. Select **Working Toy Breeds** in the second footnote, then apply the Underline command.

5. Select the **entire first footnote** except the number 1, double-click **12** in the Font Size text box, type **8**, then press **[Enter]** (Win) or **[return]** (Mac).

6. Select the **entire second footnote** except the number 2, change its font size to 8 pt, then click to deselect the text.

   Your footnotes should resemble Figure 16.

TIP To specify how far below the baseline the underline is positioned, click the Underline Options command on the Character panel options menu, then increase or decrease the Offset value.

You selected text, then applied the Underline command from the Character panel options menu.

Format
PARAGRAPHS

What You'll Do

Introducing the Min-Pin
by Christopher Smith

The Miniature Pinscher is a smooth coated dog in the Toy Group. He is frequently - and incorrectly - referred to as a Miniature Doberman. The characteristics that distinguish the Miniature Pinscher are his size (ten to twelve and a half inches), his racy elegance, and the gait which he exhibits in a self-possessed, animated and cocky manner.

The Miniature Pinscher is part of the larger German Pinscher family, which belonged to a prehistoric group that dates back to 3000 B.C. One of the clear-cut traits present in the ancient Pinschers was that of the two opposing size tendencies: one toward the medium to larger size and the other toward the smaller "dwarf" of miniature size. This ancient miniature-sized Pinscher was the forerunner of today's Miniature pinscher.

"Is the Miniature Pinscher bred down from the Doberman Pinscher?"

The answer is a definite "No." Since ancient times, the Min Pin was developing with its natrual tendency to smallness in stature. In fact, as a recognized breed, the Miniature Pinscher predates the development of the well-known Doberman Pinscher².

The Min Pin is an excellent choice as a family pet. The breed tends to attach itself very quickly to children and really delights in joining a youngster in bed. As soon as the Min-Pin climbs onto the bed, he usually slips under the covers like a mole, all the way to the foot of the bed.

The Min Pin is intelligent and easily trained. He has a tendency to be clean in all respects, the shedding of the short coat constitutes minimal, if any, problems to the apartment dweller. On the other hand, the Miniature Pinscher certainly is not out of his element on the farm and has been trained to tree squirrels, chase rabbits, and even help herd cows². It is not unusual for the Miniature Pinscher on a farm to catch a rabbit that is equal to or larger than the size of the dog.

¹ Missing, Scott: In Love with the Min-Pin, All Breeds Publishing, 1997
² Miltensberger, William: Working Toy Breeds, CJP Press, 2002

In this lesson, you will use the Paragraph panel and various keyboard commands to modify paragraph attributes.

Using the Paragraph Panel

The Paragraph panel, shown in Figure 17, is the command center for modifying paragraphs or blocks of text also known as body copy.

The Paragraph panel is divided into three main sections. The top section controls alignment. Of the nine icons offering options for aligning text, the first four—Align left, Align center, Align right, and Justify with last line aligned left—are the most common. The remaining five options include subtle modifications of justified text and two options for aligning text towards or away from the spine of a book.

The next section offers controls for indents. Use an indent when you want the first line of each paragraph to start further to the right than the other lines of text, as shown in Figure 18. This figure also shows what is commonly referred to as a **pull quote**. You have probably seen pull quotes in most magazines. They are a typographical design solution in which text is used at a larger point size and positioned prominently on the page.

Figure 17 *Paragraph panel*

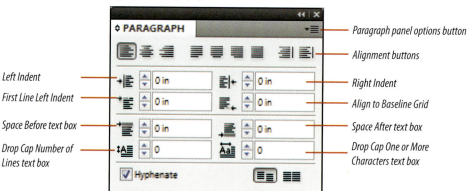

Paragraph panel options button

Alignment buttons

Left Indent

First Line Left Indent

Space Before text box

Drop Cap Number of Lines text box

Right Indent

Align to Baseline Grid

Space After text box

Drop Cap One or More Characters text box

Note the left and right indents applied to the pull quote in Figure 18. They were created using the Left Indent and Right Indent buttons on the Paragraph panel.

The third section of the Paragraph panel controls vertical spacing between paragraphs and applying drop caps. For large blocks of text, it is often most pleasing to the eye to create either a subtle or distinct space after every paragraph. In InDesign, you create these by entering values in the Space After or the Space Before text boxes on the Paragraph panel. Of the two, the Space After text box is more commonly used. The Space Before text box, when it is used, is often used in conjunction with the Space After text box to offset special page elements, such as a pull quote.

A **drop cap** is a design element in which the first letter or letters of a paragraph are increased in size to create a visual effect. In the figure, the drop cap is measured as being three text lines in height. If you click to place the cursor to the right of the drop cap then increase the kerning value on the Character panel, the space between the drop cap and all three lines of text will be increased. Figure 19 shows a document with a drop cap and a .25 inch space after every paragraph.

Figure 18 *First line indent and left and right indents*

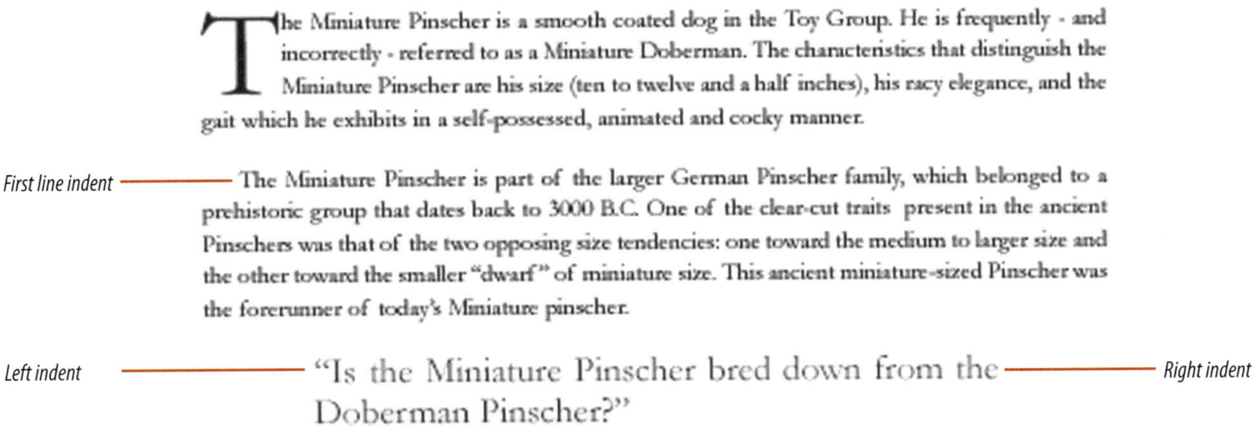

The Miniature Pinscher is a smooth coated dog in the Toy Group. He is frequently - and incorrectly - referred to as a Miniature Doberman. The characteristics that distinguish the Miniature Pinscher are his size (ten to twelve and a half inches), his racy elegance, and the gait which he exhibits in a self-possessed, animated and cocky manner.

First line indent ————————— The Miniature Pinscher is part of the larger German Pinscher family, which belonged to a prehistoric group that dates back to 3000 B.C. One of the clear-cut traits present in the ancient Pinschers was that of the two opposing size tendencies: one toward the medium to larger size and the other toward the smaller "dwarf" of miniature size. This ancient miniature-sized Pinscher was the forerunner of today's Miniature pinscher.

Left indent ————————— "Is the Miniature Pinscher bred down from the ————————— Right indent
Doberman Pinscher?"

Using Optical Margin Alignment

Optical Margin Alignment is a great feature that controls the alignment of punctuation marks for all paragraphs within a block of type. Optical Margin Alignment forces punctuation marks, as well as the edges of some letters, to hang outside the text margins so that the type appears aligned. To override this feature, click the text box or type object, click the Paragraph panel options button, then click Ignore Optical Margin. You can also click the Paragraph Styles panel options button, click Style Options, click the Indents and Spacing category, then click the Ignore Optical Margin check box.

Avoiding Typographic Problems with the Paragraph Panel

Widows and **orphans** are words or single lines of text that become separated from the other lines in a paragraph. Orphans are left alone at the bottom of a page and widows at the top. The Paragraph panel options menu has a number of commands that allow you to control how text appears and flows, specifically at the end of a column or page, avoiding unsightly widows and orphans. The Keep Options command lets you highlight text that should always stay together instead of being split over two pages. The Keep Options dialog box lets you choose to keep the selected text together or choose how many lines to keep with the selected text. The Justification command opens the Justification dialog box in which you can define the percentages assigned to minimum, desired and maximum word spacing, letter spacing, and glyph scaling. You can also change the Auto Leading value and tell InDesign how to justify a one-word line. The Hyphenation Settings dialog box, which opens by clicking Hyphenation on the Paragraph panel options menu, allows you to define how words should be hyphenated. You can turn hyphenation off completely by removing the check mark in the Hyphenation check box.

Understanding Returns and Soft Returns

Most people think of a paragraph as a block of text, but, in design language, a paragraph can be a block of text, a line of text, or even a single word, followed by a paragraph return. A **paragraph return**, also called a **hard return**, is inserted into the text formatting by pressing [Enter] (Win) or [return] (Mac).

Figure 19 *A drop cap and paragraphs with vertical space applied after every paragraph*

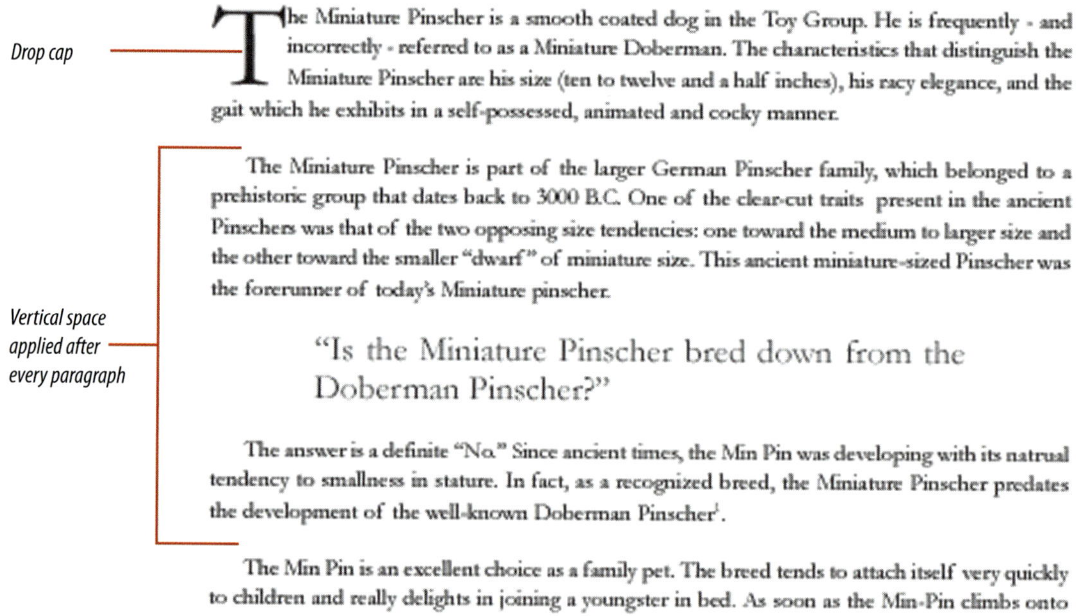

Drop cap ———

The Miniature Pinscher is a smooth coated dog in the Toy Group. He is frequently - and incorrectly - referred to as a Miniature Doberman. The characteristics that distinguish the Miniature Pinscher are his size (ten to twelve and a half inches), his racy elegance, and the gait which he exhibits in a self-possessed, animated and cocky manner.

The Miniature Pinscher is part of the larger German Pinscher family, which belonged to a prehistoric group that dates back to 3000 B.C. One of the clear-cut traits present in the ancient Pinschers was that of the two opposing size tendencies: one toward the medium to larger size and the other toward the smaller "dwarf" of miniature size. This ancient miniature-sized Pinscher was the forerunner of today's Miniature pinscher.

Vertical space
applied after ———
every paragraph

"Is the Miniature Pinscher bred down from the Doberman Pinscher?"

The answer is a definite "No." Since ancient times, the Min Pin was developing with its natrual tendency to smallness in stature. In fact, as a recognized breed, the Miniature Pinscher predates the development of the well-known Doberman Pinscher[1].

The Min Pin is an excellent choice as a family pet. The breed tends to attach itself very quickly to children and really delights in joining a youngster in bed. As soon as the Min-Pin climbs onto

For example, if I type my first name and then enter a paragraph return, that one word—my first name—is a paragraph. When working with body copy, paragraphs appear as blocks of text, each separated by a single paragraph return.

When typing body copy, designers will often want a space after each paragraph because it is visually pleasing and helps to keep paragraphs distinct. The mistake many designers make is pressing [Enter] (Win) or [return] (Mac) twice to create that space after the paragraph. Wrong! What they've done is created two paragraphs. The correct way to insert space between paragraphs is to enter a value in the Space After text box on the Paragraph panel.

As you edit text, you may encounter a "bad line break" at the end of a line, such as an oddly hyphenated word or a phrase that is split from one line to the next. In many of these cases, you will want to move a word or phrase to the next line. You can do this by entering a **soft return**. A soft return moves words down to the next baseline but does not create a new paragraph. You enter a soft return by pressing and holding [Shift], then pressing [Enter] (Win) or [return] (Mac).

You can avoid untold numbers of formatting problems by using correct typesetting behaviors, especially those regarding Space After and First Line Indent.

Using the Type on a Path tool

Hidden behind the Type tool in the Tools panel is the Type on a Path tool. The Type on a Path tool allows you to position text on any closed or open InDesign path. For example, you could draw a closed path, such as a circle, then position text on the circular path. Or you could draw a simple curved path across the page, then flow text along the path. Simply click the Type on a Path tool on the path. A blinking cursor will appear, and you can then begin typing on the path. The path itself remains visible and selectable; you can apply stroke colors and various widths to the path. You can format the size, typeface, and type style of type on a path as well. Give it a try!

Use the Paragraph panel and Character panel to modify leading and alignment

1. Click **View** on the Application bar, click **Fit Page in Window**, then click the first instance of **The** in the first paragraph four times.

TIP Clicking a word four times selects the entire paragraph.

2. Click the same word five times.

TIP Clicking a word five times selects all the text in the text frame.

3. Click the **Leading list arrow** on the Character panel, then click **30 pt**.

   The vertical space between each line of text is increased, as shown in Figure 20.

TIP Because leading can be applied to a single selected word as well as to an entire paragraph, the Leading setting is on the Character panel (as opposed to the Paragraph panel).

4. Double-click **30** in the Leading text box, type **16**, then press **[Enter]** (Win) or **[return]** (Mac).

5. Display the Paragraph panel, then click the **Justify with last line aligned left button** ▤.

6. Click **Introducing** at the top of the document three times, then click the **Align center button** ▤ on the Paragraph panel.

7. Click **Edit** on the Application bar, then click **Deselect All**.

   Your document should resemble Figure 21.

You modified the leading and alignment of a block of selected text.

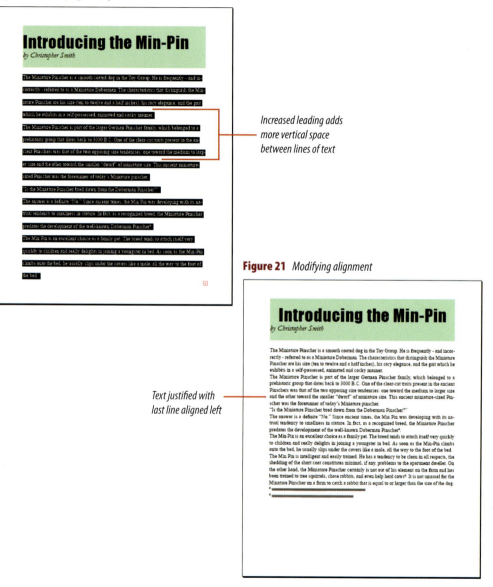

Figure 20 *Modifying leading*

Increased leading adds more vertical space between lines of text

Figure 21 *Modifying alignment*

Text justified with last line aligned left

Figure 22 *Increasing the Space After value*

Figure 23 *Increasing Space Before value to move footnotes down*

Space before value increased

Apply vertical spacing between paragraphs

1. Click the **Type tool** T., click anywhere in the body copy, click **Edit** on the Application bar, then click **Select All**.

TIP The keyboard shortcut for Select All is [Ctrl][A] (Win) or ⌘ [A] (Mac).

2. Click the **Space After up arrow** on the Paragraph panel three times, so that the value reads .1875 in, then deselect all.

   .1875 inches of vertical space is applied after every paragraph, as shown in Figure 22.

TIP You may need to click the Paragraph panel options button, then click Show Options to expand the panel.

3. Click and drag to select the **two footnotes** at the bottom of the document, double-click the **Space After text box** on the Paragraph panel, type **0**, then press **[Enter]** (Win) or **[return]** (Mac).

4. Select only the first footnote, double-click the **0** in the Space Before text box on the Paragraph panel, type **.25**, then press **[Enter]** (Win) or **[return]** (Mac).

   .25 inches of vertical space is positioned above the first footnote.

5. Click **Edit** on the Application bar, then click **Deselect All**.

   Your document should resemble Figure 23.

You used the Space After and Space Before text boxes on the Paragraph panel to apply vertical spacing between paragraphs.

Apply paragraph indents

1. Click **Type** on the Application bar, then click **Show Hidden Characters**.

   As shown in Figure 24, hidden characters appear in blue, showing blue dots for spaces, created by pressing [Spacebar], and paragraph marks for paragraph returns.

   Be sure to memorize the keyboard command (listed beside each menu item in the menu) for hiding and showing hidden characters.

2. Select all the body copy on the page except the two footnotes, then click the **First Line Left Indent up arrow** on the Paragraph panel four times to change the value to .25 in, as shown in Figure 25.

   The first line of each paragraph is indented .25 in.

3. Select **by Christopher Smith**, then click the **Left Indent up arrow** until the value is changed to .5.

4. Click anywhere in the third paragraph, change the First Line Left Indent value to **0 in**, change the Left Indent value to **.75 in**, then change the Right Indent value to **.75 in**.

5. Click **any word in the third paragraph** three times to select the entire line, click the **Character panel name tab**, change the font size to **18 pt**, change the leading to **20 pt**, then deselect the paragraph.

   Your document should resemble Figure 26.

You showed hidden characters so that you could better identify each paragraph. You indented the first lines of every paragraph, and then you added substantial left and right indents to a paragraph and increased its point size to create a "pull quote."

Figure 24 *Showing hidden characters*

The·characteristics·that ——— Space symbol

lf·inches),·his·racy·elegan

ocky·manner.¶ ——— Paragraph return symbol

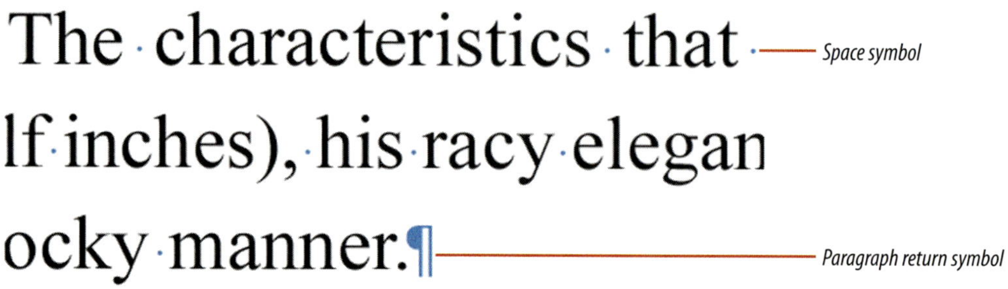

Figure 25 *Applying a first line left indent*

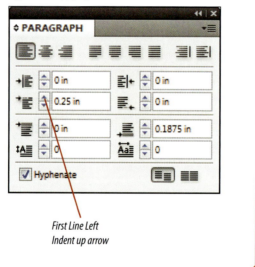

First Line Left
Indent up arrow

Figure 26 *Using indents to format text as a pull quote*

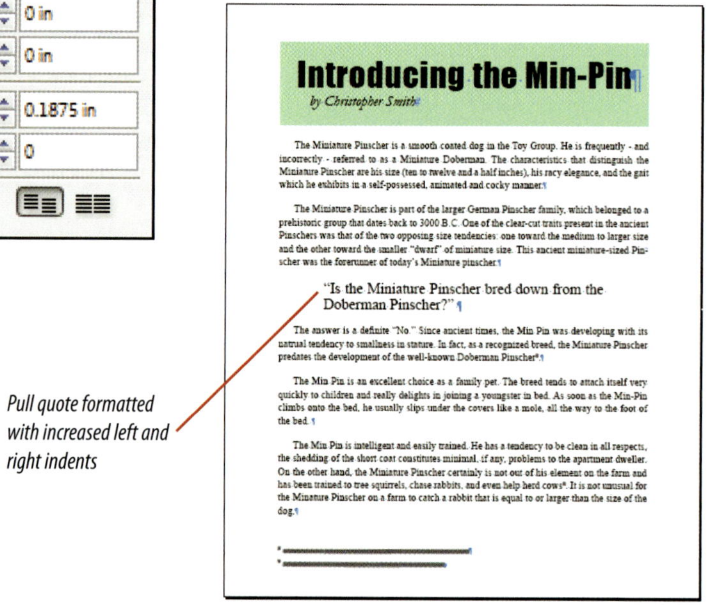

Pull quote formatted
with increased left and
right indents

Working with Text

Figure 27 *Creating a drop cap*

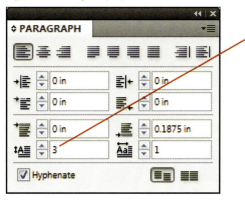

Drop Cap Number
of Lines value

Figure 28 *Viewing the finished document*

No new
paragraph

Apply drop caps and soft returns

1. Click the **Paragraph panel name tab**, click anywhere in the first paragraph, then change the First Line Left Indent value to **0**.

2. Click the **Drop Cap Number of Lines up arrow** three times, so that the text box displays a 3, as shown in Figure 27.

   A drop cap with the height of three text lines is added to the first paragraph.

3. Select all the body copy text, including the two footnotes, then change the font to **Garamond** or a similar font.

4. Click the **Zoom tool** 🔍, then drag a selection box around the entire last paragraph.

5. Click the **Type tool** T, then click to insert the cursor immediately before the capital letter O of the word On in the third sentence of the last paragraph.

6. Press and hold **[Shift]**, then press **[Enter]** (Win) or **[return]** (Mac) to create a soft return.

TIP Note that a new paragraph is not created.

7. Use the keyboard command to hide hidden characters.

8. Click **View** on the Application bar, then click **Fit Page in Window**.

   Your document should resemble Figure 28.

9. Click **File** on the Application bar, click **Save**, then close Min-Pin Intro.

You created a drop cap and a soft return, which moved text to the next line without creating a new paragraph.

Create and
APPLY STYLES

What You'll Do

In this lesson, you will use the Character Styles and Paragraph Styles panels to create and apply styles to text.

Working with Character and Paragraph Styles

Imagine that you are writing a book. Let's say it's a user's manual for how to care for houseplants. This book will contain seven chapters. In each chapter, different sections will be preceded by a headline that is the same font as the chapter title, but a smaller font size. Within those sections there will be subheads that, again, use the same font but in an even smaller size. Such a scenario is perfect for using styles.

A **style** is a group of formatting attributes, such as font, font size, color, and tracking, that is applied to text—whenever and wherever you want it to appear—throughout a document or multiple documents. Using styles saves you time and it keeps your work consistent. Styles are given descriptive names for the type of text to which they are applied. Figure 29 shows three styles on the Character Styles panel. You use the Character Styles panel to create styles for individual words or characters, such as a footnote, which you would want in a smaller, superscript font. You use the Paragraph Styles panel to apply a style to an entire paragraph. Paragraph styles include formatting options such as indents and drop caps. The Paragraph Styles panel is shown in Figure 30.

QUICK **TIP**

You can easily import character and paragraph styles from other InDesign documents. Click the Character Styles or Paragraph Styles panel list arrow, then click Load Character Styles or Load Paragraph Styles. You'll be prompted to navigate to the documents that have the styles you wish to import.

In the scenario of the houseplant book, if you weren't using styles, you would be required to format those chapter headlines one at a time, for all seven chapter heads. You'd need to remember the font size, the font style, and any tracking, kerning, scaling, or other formatting. Then you'd need to do the same for every section headline, and every sub-headline. For any body copy, you'd risk inconsistent spacing, indents, and other formatting options. Using styles, you define those formats one time and one time only. A much better solution, don't you think?

Another important feature about styles is that they are useful when you change your mind and want to modify text. Simply modify the style, and all the text that is assigned to that style will be automatically updated—throughout the document!

Choosing the Next Style

Once you have more than one paragraph style saved in the Paragraph Styles panel, you can program which style will come next when you are currently in one style and create a new paragraph. For example, imagine you are creating a catalog and you have two styles called Item and Description. Now let's say that each time you finish typing the name of an item, you want to type the description of that item using the Description paragraph style. Then when you finish typing the description and start a new paragraph, you want to type the next item using the Item paragraph style. You can choose which style should follow which, by double-clicking a style in the Paragraph Styles panel, then clicking the Next Style list arrow and choosing the name of the style that should come next.

Using Quick Apply

A quick way to apply a character or paragraph style is to use Quick Apply.

The Quick Apply button is available on the Control panel, Character Styles panel, and Paragraph Styles panel. In the Quick Apply dialog box, there is a pull-down menu showing checked items, such as Character Styles. When Character Styles is checked, you can apply a character style quickly by typing its name in the Quick Apply text box. Your style will appear in a list below. Click the name in the list and your style is applied.

Quick Apply is not limited to applying styles. You can use Quick Apply to access menu commands and run scripts. Just be sure to click the Quick Apply list arrow in the Quick Apply dialog box and select Include Scripts and Include Menu Commands.

Figure 29 *Character Styles panel*

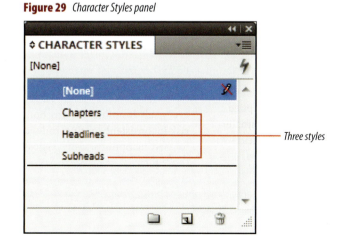

Three styles

Figure 30 *Paragraph Styles panel*

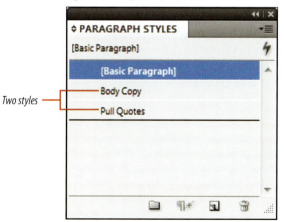

Two styles

Create character styles

1. Open ID 2-2.indd, then save it as **Jake's Diner**.

2. Display the Character Styles panel.

3. Click the **Character Styles panel options button** ▾≡, then click **New Character Style**.

4. Type **Dishes** in the Style Name text box of the New Character Style dialog box, then click **Basic Character Formats** in the left column, as shown in Figure 31.

5. Click the **Font Family list arrow**, click **Impact**, click the **Size list arrow**, click **14 pt**, click the **Leading text box**, type **16 pt**, then click **Advanced Character Formats** in the left column.

6. Type **85** in the Horizontal Scale text box, then click **OK**.

   The style "Dishes" now appears on the Character Styles panel.

7. Click the **Character Styles panel options button** ▾≡, click **New Character Style**, type **Descriptions** in the Style Name text box, then click **Basic Character Formats** in the left column.

8. Click the **Font Family list arrow**, click **Garamond** or a similar font, click the **Font Style list arrow**, click **Italic**, change the font size to **10 pt**, change the leading to **12 pt**, then click **OK**.

   The style "Descriptions" now appears on the Character Styles panel.

9. Click the **Character Styles panel options button** ▾≡, click **New Character Style**, type **Prices** in the Style Name text box, then click **Basic Character Formats** in the left column.

   (continued)

Figure 31 *New Character Style dialog box*

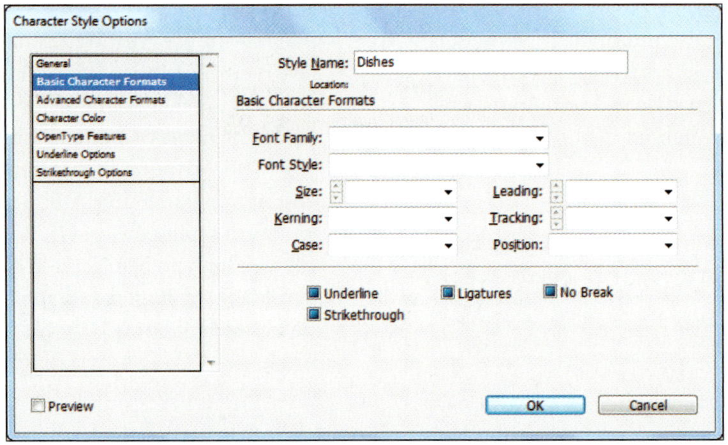

Using Data Merge

InDesign lets you create documents that are customized for each recipient, much like a mail merge in a word processing program, which you can use for such things as letters, name labels, and postcards. In a **data merge**, you use a data source (usually a text file) that contains **fields** (labels such as "First Name") and **records** (rows representing information for each recipient, such as "Bob Jones"). A **target document** is an InDesign file containing the text that will be seen by all recipients, such as a letter, as well as placeholders representing fields, such as <<First Name>>. In a data merge, InDesign places information from each record in the appropriate places in the target document, as many times as necessary. The result is a **merged document** containing the personalized letters.

To perform a data merge, click Window on the Application bar, point to Utilities, then click Data Merge. When the Data Merge panel opens, click the Data Merge panel options button, click Select Data Source, locate the data source file, then click Open. This displays the merge fields on the Data Merge panel. Click in a text frame and click field names to enter them in the frame. If you place placeholders on master pages, the merged document is connected to the data source, and you can automatically update the merged document with the most recent version of your data source.

To merge the document, click the Data Merge panel options button, then click Create Merged Document. Select the records to include, then click OK.

Figure 32 *Character Styles panel*

Figure 33 *Applying three different character styles*

Dishes style ——— **Eggs and Bacon**

Descriptions style ——— *Two eggs any style, two strips of lean bacon, one biscuit with our homestyle gravy, and home fries.*

Prices style ——— $5.95

Figure 34 *Viewing the document with all character styles applied*

Jake's Diner
Early Bird Breakfast Menu

Eggs and Bacon
Two eggs any style, two strips of lean bacon, one biscuit with our homestyle gravy, and home fries.
$5.95

Egg Sandwich
One egg over easy, served with American or Jack cheese on a soft French croissant.
$5.25

Belgian Waffle
A golden brown buttery waffle served with fresh-picked strawberries, raspberries and blueberries. Whipped fresh cream on request.
$4.95

Silver Dollar Pancakes
A stack of eight golden pancakes served with fresh creamery butter and warm maple syrup.
$4.95

French Toast
Four triangles of thick peasant bread dipped in a cinnamon-egg batter. Served with French Fries.
$6.95

Biscuits and Gravy
Light fluffy southern biscuits served with a hearty sausage gravy.
$3.95

Eggs Hollandaise
Three eggs lightly poached served on a bed of romaine lettuce and topped with a rich Hollandaise sauce.
$6.95

Steak and Eggs
A 6 oz. strip of peppered breakfast steak cooked to your liking, served with two eggs, any style.
$7.95

10. Change the font to **Garamond** or a similar font, change the font style to **Bold**, change the font size to **12 pt**, change the leading to **14 pt**, then click **OK**.

    Your Character Styles panel should resemble Figure 32.

You created three new character styles.

Apply character styles

1. Click the **Type tool** T, triple-click the word **Eggs** in the first title to select the entire title "Eggs and Bacon," then click **Dishes** in the Character Styles panel.

    The Dishes character style is applied to the title.

2. Select the entire next paragraph (beginning with the word Two), then click **Descriptions** in the Character Styles panel.

3. Select the first price (**$5.95**), click **Prices** on the Character Styles panel, click **Edit** on the Application bar, then click **Deselect All**.

    Your first menu item should resemble Figure 33. If you used a different font, your text lines may break differently.

4. Select all of the remaining text in the text frame, then apply the Descriptions style.

5. Apply the **Dishes style** to the remaining seven dish titles.

6. Apply the **Prices style** to the remaining seven prices, then deselect so that your document resembles Figure 34.

You applied character styles to format specific areas of a document.

Create paragraph styles

1. Close the Character Styles panel, then open the Paragraph Styles panel.

2. Click the **Paragraph Styles panel options button** ▼≣, then click **New Paragraph Style**.

3. Type **Prices** in the Style Name text box, then click **Indents and Spacing** in the left column.

TIP Note that the New Paragraph Style dialog box contains Basic Character Formats and Advanced Character Formats categories—the same that you find when working in the New Character Style dialog box.

4. Click the **Alignment list arrow**, then click **Center**.

5. Type **.25** in the Space After text box, then click **Paragraph Rules** in the left column, as shown in Figure 35.

TIP The term **rules** is layout jargon for lines. Rules can be positioned on a page as a design element, or text can be underlined with rules.

6. Click the **list arrow** directly beneath Paragraph Rules, click **Rule Below**, then click the **Rule On check box** to add a check mark.

7. Type **.125** in the Offset text box, type **.25** in the Left Indent text box, type **.25** in the Right Indent text box, press **[Tab]** so that your dialog box resembles Figure 35, then click **OK**.

   The paragraph style "Prices" now appears on the Paragraph Styles panel as shown on Figure 36.

You created a paragraph style, which included a center alignment, a space after value, and a paragraph rule.

Figure 35 *Paragraph Rules window in the New Paragraph Style dialog box*

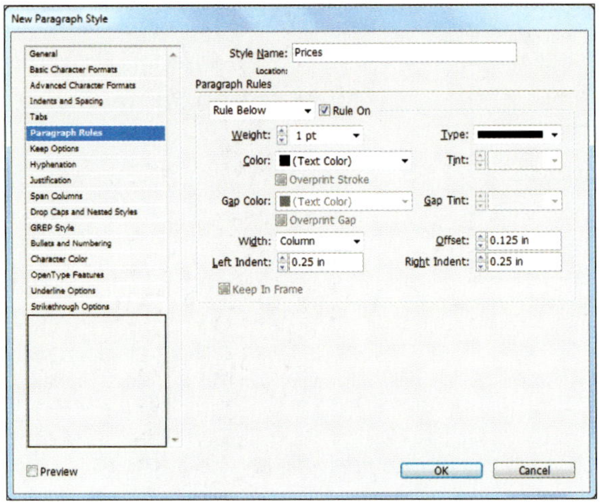

Figure 36 *Paragraph Styles panel*

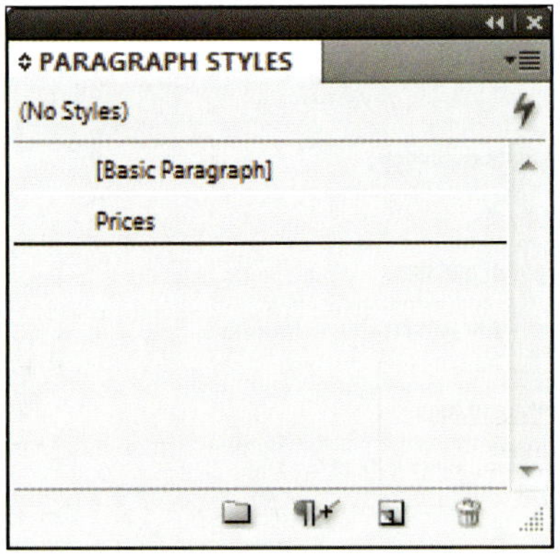

Figure 37 *Applying a paragraph style to two prices*

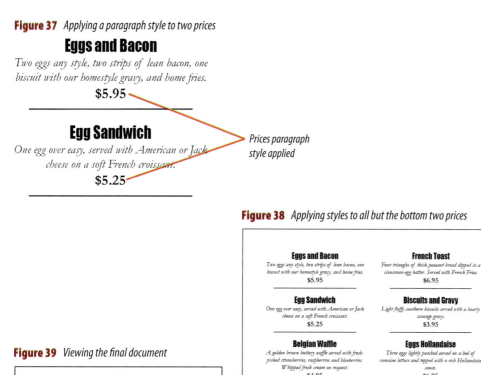

Eggs and Bacon

Two eggs any style, two strips of lean bacon, one biscuit with our homestyle gravy, and home fries.

$5.95

Egg Sandwich

One egg over easy, served with American or Jack cheese on a soft French croissant.

$5.25

Prices paragraph
style applied

Figure 38 *Applying styles to all but the bottom two prices*

Eggs and Bacon
Two eggs any style, two strips of lean bacon, one biscuit with our homestyle gravy, and home fries.
$5.95

French Toast
Four triangles of thick peasant bread dipped in a cinnamon-egg batter. Served with French Fries.
$6.95

Egg Sandwich
One egg over easy, served with American or Jack cheese on a soft French croissant.
$5.25

Biscuits and Gravy
Light fluffy southern biscuits served with a hearty sausage gravy.
$3.95

Belgian Waffle
A golden brown buttery waffle served with fresh-picked strawberries, raspberries and blueberries. Whipped fresh cream on request.
$4.95

Eggs Hollandaise
Three eggs lightly poached served on a bed of romaine lettuce and topped with a rich Hollandaise sauce.
$6.95

Silver Dollar Pancakes
A stack of eight golden pancakes served with fresh creamery butter and warm maple syrup.
$4.95

Steak and Eggs
A 6 oz. strip of peppered breakfast steak cooked to your liking, served with two eggs, any style.
$7.95

Figure 39 *Viewing the final document*

Jake's Diner
Early Bird Breakfast Menu

Eggs and Bacon
Two eggs any style, two strips of lean bacon, one biscuit with our homestyle gravy, and home fries.
$5.95

French Toast
Four triangles of thick peasant bread dipped in a cinnamon-egg batter. Served with French Fries.
$6.95

Egg Sandwich
One egg over easy, served with American or Jack cheese on a soft French croissant.
$5.25

Biscuits and Gravy
Light fluffy southern biscuits served with a hearty sausage gravy.
$3.95

Belgian Waffle
A golden brown buttery waffle served with fresh-picked strawberries, raspberries and blueberries. Whipped fresh cream on request.
$4.95

Eggs Hollandaise
Three eggs lightly poached served on a bed of romaine lettuce and topped with a rich Hollandaise sauce.
$6.95

Silver Dollar Pancakes
A stack of eight golden pancakes served with fresh creamery butter and warm maple syrup.
$4.95

Steak and Eggs
A 6 oz. strip of peppered breakfast steak cooked to your liking, served with two eggs, any style.
$7.95

You do not need
dividing rules at the
bottom of the menu

Hollandaise sauce
moves to a new line

Apply paragraph styles

1. Click the **Type tool** T, then select all the text in the document except for the two headlines at the top of the page.

2. Click the **Align center button** ≣ on the Paragraph panel.

   For this layout, all the menu items will be aligned center. It's not necessary to create a paragraph style for all items to align center, because you can simply use the Align center button on the Paragraph panel.

3. Click the first price (**$5.95**) once, click **Prices** on the Paragraph Styles panel, click the second price (**$5.25**), then click **Prices** on the Paragraph Styles panel again.

   Your first two menu items should resemble Figure 37.

   TIP When applying paragraph styles, just place the cursor in the paragraph you want to modify.

4. Apply the Prices paragraph style to the remaining prices in the document except the Silver Dollar Pancakes and Steak and Eggs prices, then compare your document to Figure 38.

5. Click **View** on the Application bar, point to **Grids & Guides**, then click **Hide Guides**.

6. Click before the word Hollandaise in the description text for Eggs Hollandaise, press and hold down **[Shift]**, while pressing **[Enter]** (Win) or **[return]** (Mac).

   Hollandaise sauce is moved to the next line. Using the same method, add soft returns to break any other lines that you think could look better, then compare your work to Figure 39.

7. Save your work, then close Jake's Diner.

You applied a paragraph style to specific areas of the menu.

Edit TEXT

What You'll Do

Find/Change

Query: [Custom]

Text | GREP | Glyph | Object

Find what:
Miniature Pincher

Change to:
Min-Pin

Search: Document

Find Format:

Change Format:

Done
Find
Change
Change All
Change/Find
Fewer Options

In this lesson, you will use the Find/Change and Check Spelling commands to edit the text of a document.

Using the Find/Change Command

One of the great things about creating documents using a computer is the ability to edit text quickly and efficiently. Imagine the days before the personal computer. When you finished typing a document, you needed to read through it carefully, looking for any errors. If you found any, you had three options: cover it up, cross it out, or type the whole document again.

The Find/Change dialog box, shown in Figure 40, is a powerful tool for editing a document. With this command, you can search for any word in the document, then change that word to another word or delete it altogether with a click of your mouse. For example, imagine that you have typed an entire document about Abraham Lincoln's early years growing up in Frankfurt, Kentucky. Then you find out that Lincoln actually grew up in Hardin County, Kentucky. You could use the Find/Change command to locate every instance of the word "Frankfurt" and change it to "Hardin County." One click would correct every instance of that error, throughout the entire document. Try that with a typewriter!

QUICK TIP

InDesign CS5 has a number of great features in the Find/Change dialog box. The Query menu lists pre-defined search options for finding (and changing) common formatting issues. For example, the Query menu has built-in searches for finding and changing dashes to en dashes and straight single or double quotes to typographer's quotes. There's a built-in search for trailing white space—useless extra spaces at the end of paragraphs or sentences—and there's even a search for telephone number formatting.

Checking Spelling

Since the earliest days of the personal computer, the ability to check and correct spelling errors automatically has been a much-promoted benefit of creating documents digitally. It has stood the test of time. The spell checker continues to be one of the most powerful features of word processing.

InDesign's Check Spelling dialog box, shown in Figure 41, is a comprehensive utility for locating and correcting typos and other misspellings in a document. If you've done word processing before, you will find yourself on familiar turf. The spell checker identifies words that it doesn't find in its dictionary, offers you a list of suggested corrections, and asks you what you want to do. If it is indeed a misspelling, type the correct spelling or choose the correct word from the suggested corrections list, then click Change to correct that instance or click Change All to correct all instances of the misspelling throughout the document.

Sometimes the spell checker identifies a word that is not actually a misspelling. For example, say you were typing a letter about your dog whose name is Gargantua. The spell checker is not going to find that word/name in its dictionary, and it is going to ask you what you want to do with it. You have two options. You could click Ignore, which tells the spell checker to make no changes and move on to the next questionable word. However, because in the future you will probably type the dog's name in other documents, you don't want the spell checker always asking you if this word/name is a misspelling. In this case, you'd be better off clicking the Add button. Doing so adds the name Gargantua to the spell checker's dictionary, and in the future, the spell checker will no longer identify Gargantua as a misspelling.

When you click the Add button, the word in question is added to the User Dictionary, which is InDesign's main dictionary. If you use the spell checker often, you will build up a list of words that you've chosen to ignore and a list of words that you've chosen to add to the dictionary. To see those lists and modify them, click the Dictionary button in the Check Spelling dialog box.

You can create your own user dictionary in the Dictionary section of the Preferences

dialog box. Click the Language list arrow to choose the language with which you want to associate your dictionary, then click the Add User Dictionary button, then select the user dictionary file. The user dictionary file is stored on the hard drive and includes a .udc or a .not extension. When you locate it, click Open. If you can't find the dictionary file, search your hard drive to locate the .udc files (try using *.udc or *.not in the search text box). The new user dictionary is added to the list under the Language menu. Then, when you are using the spell checker, click the Dictionary button, click the Target list arrow, then choose your new user dictionary from the list. You can add words to the new user dictionary using the Add button in the Check Spelling dialog box.

Using Dynamic Spell Checking

Another spell check feature is Dynamic Spelling. As you type, the program places a squiggly red line under words that its spell

Figure 40 *Find/Change dialog box*

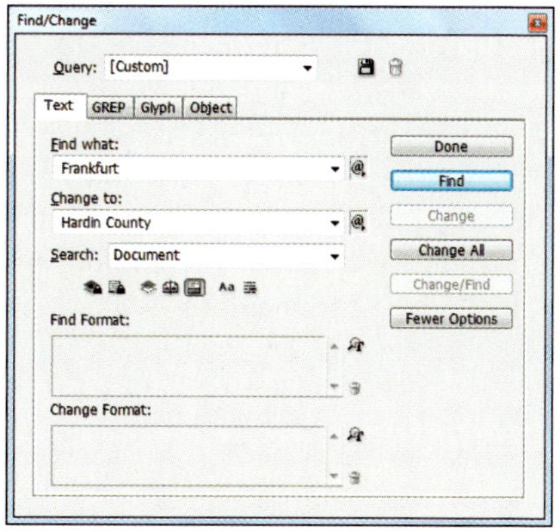

checker thinks are misspelled. To prevent the program from flagging a proper name, you can add that name to your customized dictionary. To enable dynamic spelling, click Edit on the Application bar, point to Spelling, then click Dynamic Spelling.

Correcting Text Automatically

Autocorrect takes dynamic spell checking one step farther. Instead of flagging a misspelled word, the Autocorrect feature actually corrects the misspelled word. So if you type the word "refered" and press [Spacebar], Autocorrect will change it to "referred."

Many commonly misspelled or easily mistyped words, such as "hte" for "the," are preprogrammed into the Autocorrect feature, and you can add words that might not already be listed. To turn on the Autocorrect feature, click Edit on the Application bar, point to Spelling, then click Autocorrect.

Figure 41 *Check Spelling dialog box*

Use the Find/Change command

1. Open ID 2-3.indd, then save it as **Final Edit**.

2. Click **Edit** on the Application bar, then click **Find/Change**.

3. Type **Miniature Pincher** in the Find what text box, then type **Min-Pin** in the Change to text box, as shown in Figure 42.

4. Click **Find**.

   The first use of "Miniature Pincher" in the document is highlighted. As this is the first use of the term, you don't want to change it to a nickname.

   TIP Drag the dialog box out of the way if you cannot see your document.

5. Click **Find Next**, then click **Change**.

   The second use of "Miniature Pincher" is changed to "Min-Pin."

6. Click **Find Next** again, then click **Change**.

7. Click **Find Next** three times.

   You don't want to change all instances of Miniature Pincher to Min-Pin.

8. Click **Change**, then click **Done**.

9. Click **Edit** on the Application bar, then click **Find/Change**.

10. Type **Pincher** in the Find what text box, type **Pinscher** in the Change to text box, then click **Change All**.

    A dialog box appears stating that the search is completed and 14 replacements were made.

11. Click **OK**, then click **Done**.

You used the Find/Change command to replace specific words in the document.

Figure 42 *Find/Change dialog box*

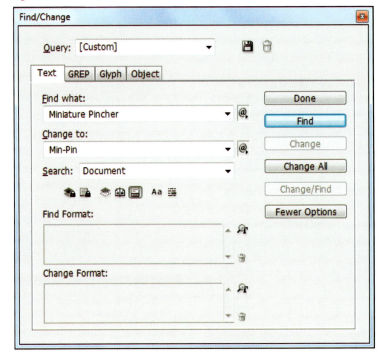

Editing Text Using Drag and Drop

InDesign has a Drag and Drop text editing feature that allows you to move text to locations within a document without having to cut and paste. This means that you can select text and simply drag it from one text frame into another text frame. You can drag and drop text between text frames on different pages. You can even drag and drop text between documents. Dragging and dropping text is usually a lot faster and easier than cutting and pasting. You can also drag and drop a copy of selected text by holding [Alt] (Win) or [option] (Mac) down when dragging. You can turn Drag and Drop text on or off in the Type window of the Preferences dialog box. In the Drag and Drop Text Editing section, check both the Enable in Layout View and the Enable in Story Editor check boxes so that the feature is activated for all of your editing methods. Give it a try!

Figure 43 *Check Spelling dialog box*

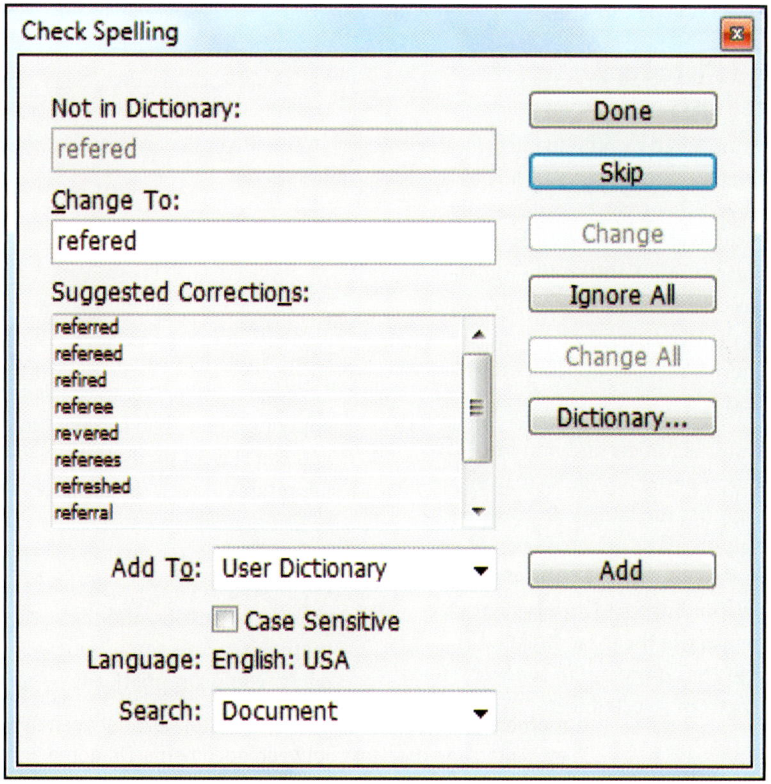

Check spelling

1. Click to the right of the drop cap T (between the T and the h) at the top of the page.

   Positioning your cursor at the top of a document forces the spell checker to begin checking for misspellings from the start of the document.

2. Click **Edit** on the Application bar, point to **Spelling**, then click **Check Spelling**.

   As shown in Figure 43, "refered" is listed as the first word the spell checker can't find in the dictionary. Suggested corrections are listed.

3. Click **referred** in the Suggested Corrections list, then click **Change**.

   The spell checker lists "racey" as the next word it can't find in the dictionary.

4. Click **racy** in the Suggested Corrections list, then click **Change**.

   The spell checker lists "Pinscher1" as not in the dictionary because of the number 1 footnote.

5. Click **Ignore All** for all remaining queries, click **OK**, then click **Done**.

6. Save your work, then close Final Edit.

TIP Never rely on the spell checker as the sole means for proofreading a document. It cannot determine if you have used the wrong word. For example, the spell checker did not flag the word "gate" in the first paragraph, which should be spelled "gait."

You used the Check Spelling dialog box to proof a document for spelling errors.

Create
BULLETED AND NUMBERED LISTS

 In this lesson, you will create bulleted and numbered lists, then change the typeface of the numbers.

Creating Bulleted and Numbered Lists

Creating numbered or bulleted lists is a common need in many types of layout, and InDesign allows you to do so easily. The best way to start is to type the list first, without formatting. Point to the Bulleted & Numbered Lists command in the Type menu and then choose whether you want to apply bullets or numbers to the selected text.

You can think of bullets and numbers like any other type of paragraph formatting. InDesign applies the bullets or numbers to each paragraph of the selected text. At any time, you can select the text and change the marks from bullets to numbers or vice versa. You also use the same Bulleted & Numbered Lists command to remove bullets or numbers from selected text.

Modifying Bulleted and Numbered Lists

You can think of bullets and numbers as being applied "virtually" to a paragraph. Let's use numbers as an example. When you apply numbers, you can see the numbers, but you can't select them. If you select the entire paragraph of text, the numbers won't appear to be selected. This is because the numbers are applied as a format to the paragraph. For example, let's say you had a list of nine numbered entries, and then you inserted a tenth entry between numbers 5 & 6. The new entry would automatically be numbered with a "6" and the numbers on all the following entries would be automatically updated.

Once you've finished a list, you might find that you want to modify the numbers by changing the type face, color, or size of the numbers. To do so, you must first convert the list to text so that the numbers can be selected and modified. Click the Bulleted & Numbered Lists command, then click the Convert Bullets and Numbering to Text command, shown in Figure 44. When you do this, the numbers (or bullets) will be converted to regular text. The list will still appear to be numbered, but it will have lost the functionality of the list formatting. If you insert or remove any component of the list, the numbers won't be updated. InDesign will see it only as a block of text.

Figure 44 *Convert Bullets to Text command*

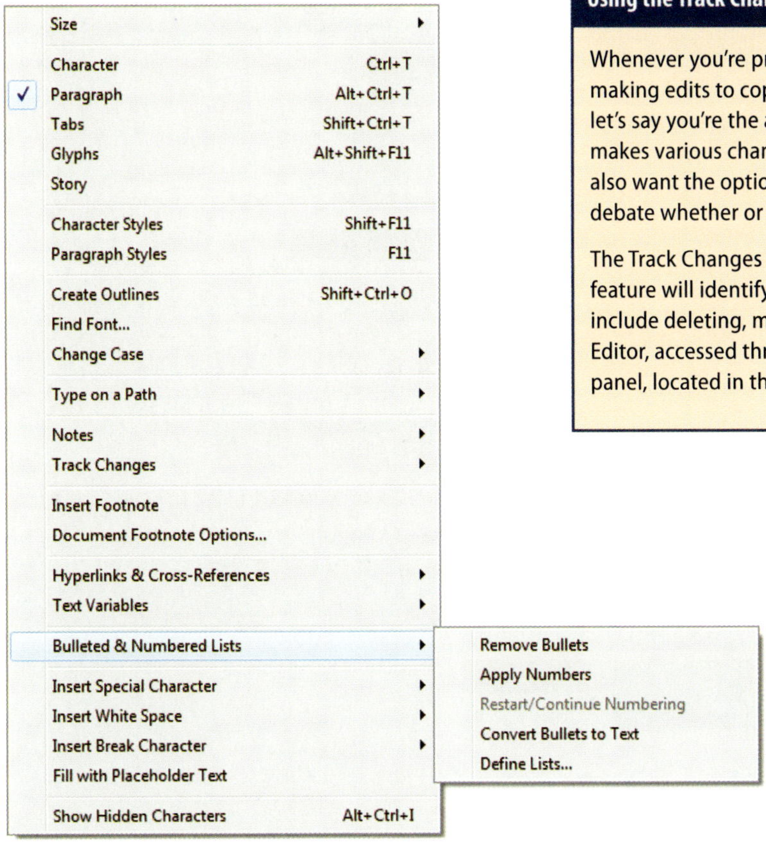

Using the Track Changes Feature

Whenever you're producing a document that involves a copy editor or more than one person making edits to copy, it becomes important that any edits made are recorded. For example, let's say you're the author of a story in a magazine. The copy editor goes through your text and makes various changes. You, as the author, will want to see what changes were made. You'll also want the option of approving or rejecting those changes, or at least the opportunity to debate whether or not the changes should be implemented.

The Track Changes feature allows for this important function within the editing process. The feature will identify each participant separately. Some of the changes that will be recorded include deleting, moving, and inserting new text. To view the changes, you use the Story Editor, accessed through the Edit menu. To accept or reject changes, use the Track Changes panel, located in the Window menu on the Editorial submenu.

Create a bulleted and a numbered list

1. Open ID 2-4.indd, then save it as **TOC**.

2. Click the **Type tool** T , then select all of the text below Chapter 1: Getting Started.

3. In the Paragraph panel, set the Space After value to **.125 in**.

4. Click **Type** on the Application bar, point to **Bulleted & Numbered Lists**, then click **Apply Bullets**.

   A shown in Figure 45, bullets are applied at each paragraph in the selected text. The text remains selected, though the bullets themselves do not appear selected.

5. Click **Type** on the Application bar, point to **Bulleted & Numbered Lists**, then click **Apply Numbers**.

   The bullets change to numbers that are the same type face, size, and color of the selected text.

6. Save your work.

You applied bullets to selected text, then changed the bullets to numbers.

Figure 45 *Bullets applied to text*

Photoshop CS5
Table of Contents

Chapter 1: Getting Started

- Defining Photo Editing Software
  understanding graphics programs

- Starting Photoshop
  getting help
  managing the workspace

- Using the Zoom Tool and the Hand Tool
  accessing the tools

- Saving a Document
  choosing the right file format

- Understanding Resolution
  the difference between Image Size and file size

- Changing Image Size
  what is "high-res" exactly

- Creating a New Document
  using the Revert command
  introducing color models

- Transforming the Canvas
  "rezzing up"

Figure 46 *Reformatting the numbers in the list*

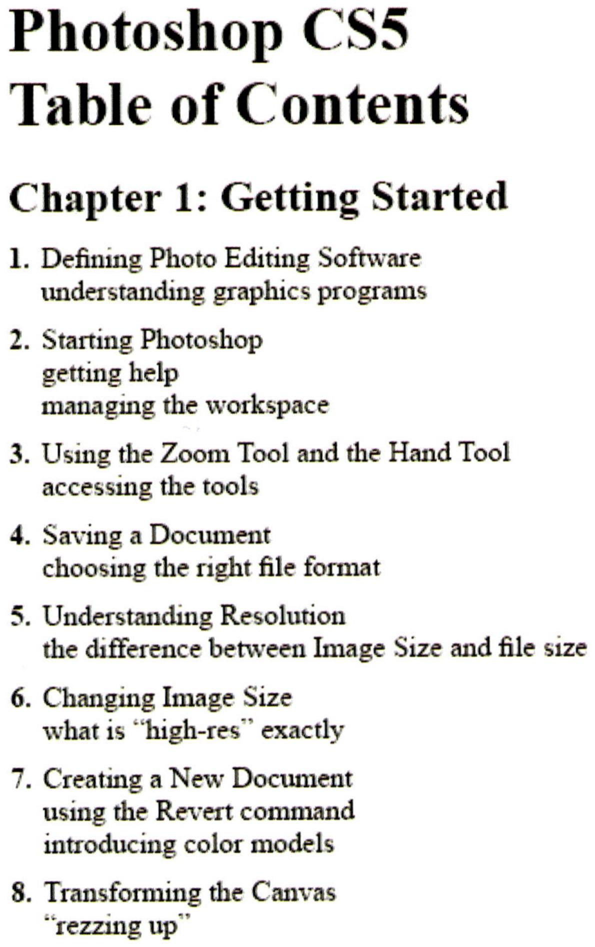

Photoshop CS5
Table of Contents

Chapter 1: Getting Started

1. Defining Photo Editing Software
   understanding graphics programs

2. Starting Photoshop
   getting help
   managing the workspace

3. Using the Zoom Tool and the Hand Tool
   accessing the tools

4. Saving a Document
   choosing the right file format

5. Understanding Resolution
   the difference between Image Size and file size

6. Changing Image Size
   what is "high-res" exactly

7. Creating a New Document
   using the Revert command
   introducing color models

8. Transforming the Canvas
   "rezzing up"

Convert numbers to text

1. Verify that all of the numbered text is still selected.

2. Click **Type** on the Application bar, point to **Bulleted & Numbered Lists**, then click **Convert Numbering to Text**.

3. Select the number 8 and the period that follows it.

4. In the Character panel, change the Type Style from Regular to Bold.

5. Change all the numbers and the periods that follow them to bold so that your list resembles Figure 46.

6. Save your work, then close TOC.indd.

You converted numbering to text so that you could format the numbers differently from the text in the list.

Format text.

1. Open ID 2-5.indd, then save it as **Independence**.
2. Click Window on the Application bar, point to Workspace, then click Reset Typography.
3. Click the Type tool, then triple-click the word Declaration at the top of the page.
4. On the Character panel, type **80** in the Horizontal Scale text box, then press [Enter] (Win) or [return] (Mac).
5. Click the Font Family list arrow, click Impact, click the Font Size list arrow, then click 36 pt.
6. Press and hold [Shift] [Ctrl] (Win) or [Shift] ⌘ (Mac), then press [<] two times.
7. Triple-click the word July on the next line, change the type face to Garamond, if necessary, change the type style to Italic, then click the Font Size up arrow until you change the font size to 18 pt.
8. Click Object on the Application bar, click Text Frame Options, change the Align setting to Center, then click OK.
9. Triple-click the word July, if necessary.
10. Type **100** in the Tracking text box, then press [Enter] (Win) or [return] (Mac).
11. Click between the letters r and a in the word Declaration, click the Kerning list arrow, then click 10.
12. Click View on the Application bar, click Fit Page in Window, if necessary, click the Zoom tool, then drag a selection box that encompasses all of the body copy on the page.
13. Click the Type tool, then select the number 1 at the end of the first paragraph.
14. Click the Character panel options button, then click Superscript.
15. Select the number 1 at the beginning of the last paragraph, then apply the Superscript command.

Format paragraphs.

1. Click View on the Application bar, click Fit Page in Window, then click the first word When in the body copy five times to select all the body copy.
2. Select (12 pt) in the Leading text box on the Character panel, type **13.25**, then press [Enter] (Win) or [return] (Mac).
3. Display the Paragraph panel, then click the Justify with last line aligned left button.
4. Click in the word Independence at the top of the document, then click the Align center button on the Paragraph panel.
5. Click the Type tool, if necessary, click anywhere in the body copy, click Edit on the Application bar, then click Select All.
6. On the Paragraph panel, click the Space After up arrow three times, so that the value reads .1875 in, click Edit on the Application bar, then click Deselect All.
7. Select the footnote (last paragraph of the document), double-click the Space Before text box on the Paragraph panel, type **.5**, then press [Enter] (Win) or [return] (Mac).
8. Apply the Deselect All command.
9. Click Type on the Application bar, then click Show Hidden Characters.
10. Select all the body copy on the page except for the last paragraph (the footnote), double-click the First Line Left Indent text box on the Paragraph panel, type **.25**, then press [Enter] (Win) or [return] (Mac).
11. Select July 4, 1776 beneath the headline, then click the Align right button on the Paragraph panel.
12. Double-click the Right Indent text box on the Paragraph panel, type **.6**, then press [Enter] (Win) or [return] (Mac).
13. Click anywhere in the first paragraph, then change the First Line Left Indent value to 0.
14. Click the Drop Cap Number of Lines up arrow three times, so that the text box displays a 3.

Working with Text

15. Click the Zoom tool, then drag a selection box that encompasses the entire second to last paragraph in the body copy.
16. Click the Type tool, position the pointer before the word these—the second to last word in the paragraph.
17. Press and hold [Shift], then press [Enter] (Win) or [return] (Mac).
18. Click Type on the Application bar, click Hide Hidden Characters, if necessary, click View on the Application bar, point to Grids & Guides, then click Hide Guides.
19. Click View on the Application bar, then click Fit Page in Window.
20. Compare your document to Figure 47, click File on the Application bar, click Save, then close Independence.

Figure 47 *Completed Skills Review, Part 1*

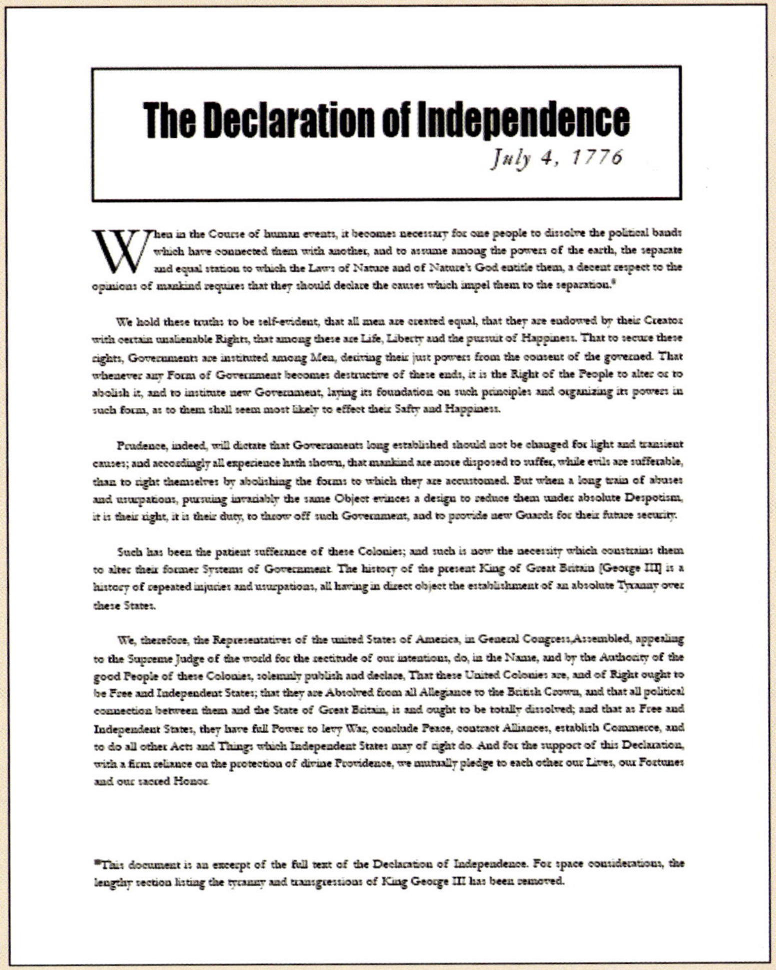

The Declaration of Independence

July 4, 1776

When in the Course of human events, it becomes necessary for one people to dissolve the political bands which have connected them with another, and to assume among the powers of the earth, the separate and equal station to which the Laws of Nature and of Nature's God entitle them, a decent respect to the opinions of mankind requires that they should declare the causes which impel them to the separation.*

We hold these truths to be self-evident, that all men are created equal, that they are endowed by their Creator with certain unalienable Rights, that among these are Life, Liberty and the pursuit of Happiness. That to secure these rights, Governments are instituted among Men, deriving their just powers from the consent of the governed. That whenever any Form of Government becomes destructive of these ends, it is the Right of the People to alter or to abolish it, and to institute new Government, laying its foundation on such principles and organizing its powers in such form, as to them shall seem most likely to effect their Safty and Happiness.

Prudence, indeed, will dictate that Governments long established should not be changed for light and transient causes; and accordingly all experience hath shown, that mankind are more disposed to suffer, while evils are sufferable, than to right themselves by abolishing the forms to which they are accustomed. But when a long train of abuses and usurpations, pursuing invariably the same Object evinces a design to reduce them under absolute Despotism, it is their right, it is their duty, to throw off such Government, and to provide new Guards for their future security.

Such has been the patient sufferance of these Colonies; and such is now the necessity which constrains them to alter their former Systems of Government. The history of the present King of Great Britain [George III] is a history of repeated injuries and usurpations, all having in direct object the establishment of an absolute Tyranny over these States.

We, therefore, the Representatives of the united States of America, in General Congress,Assembled, appealing to the Supreme Judge of the world for the rectitude of our intentions, do, in the Name, and by the Authority of the good People of these Colonies, solemnly publish and declare, That these United Colonies are, and of Right ought to be Free and Independent States; that they are Absolved from all Allegiance to the British Crown, and that all political connection between them and the State of Great Britain, is and ought to be totally dissolved; and that as Free and Independent States, they have full Power to levy War, conclude Peace, contract Alliances, establish Commerce, and to do all other Acts and Things which Independent States may of right do. And for the support of this Declaration, with a firm reliance on the protection of divine Providence, we mutually pledge to each other our Lives, our Fortunes and our sacred Honor.

*This document is an excerpt of the full text of the Declaration of Independence. For space consideration, the lengthy section listing the tyranny and transgressions of King George III has been removed.

Create and apply styles.

1. Open ID 2-6.indd, then save it as **Toy Breeds**.
2. Open the Character Styles panel.
3. Click the Character Styles panel options button, then click New Character Style.
4. Type **Breeds** in the Style Name text box, then click Basic Character Formats in the left column.
5. Change the font to Tahoma, change the size to 14 pt, change the leading to 16 pt, then click OK.
6. Click the Character Styles panel options button, click New Character Style, type **Info** in the Style Name text box, then click Basic Character Formats in the left column.
7. Change the font to Garamond, change the style to Italic, change the size to 10 pt, change the leading to 12 pt, then click OK.
8. Select all of the text except for the top two lines, then click Info on the Character Styles panel.
9. Double-click the Affenpinscher headline, then click Breeds on the Character Styles panel.
10. Apply the Breeds character style to the remaining seven breed headlines, then deselect all.
11. Open the Paragraph Styles panel.
12. Click the Paragraph Styles panel options button, then click New Paragraph Style.
13. Type **Info** in the Style Name text box, then click Indents and Spacing in the left column.
14. Click the Alignment list arrow, then click Center.
15. Type **.25** in the Space After text box, then click Paragraph Rules in the left column.
16. Click the list arrow directly below Paragraph Rules, click Rule Below, then click the Rule On check box.
17. Type **.1625** in the Offset text box, type **1** in the Left Indent text box, type **1** in the Right Indent text box, then click OK.
18. Select all of the text except for the top two lines, then click the Align center button on the Paragraph panel.
19. Click in the Affenpinscher description text, then click Info on the Paragraph Styles panel.
20. Apply the Info paragraph style to all the remaining descriptions except for the Pomeranian and the Pug.
21. Click View on the Application bar, point to Grids & Guides, then click Hide Guides.
22. Click before the word bred in the Manchester Terrier description, press and hold [Shift], then press [Enter] (Win) or [return] (Mac).
23. Click before the phrase even-tempered in the Pug description, press and hold [Shift], press [Enter] (Win) or [return] (Mac), click before the word and in the "Pug" description, press and hold [Shift], then press [Enter] (Win) or [return] (Mac). (*Hint:* Your text may break differently. Correct any other bad breaks you see.)
24. Save your work, compare your screen to Figure 48, then close Toy Breeds.

Figure 48 *Completed Skills Review, Part 2*

TOY BREEDS
A Guide to Small Dog Breeds

Affenpinscher
One of the oldest of the toy breeds, the Affenpinscher originated in Europe. The Affenpinscher is noted for its great loyalty and affection.

Chihuahua
A graceful, alert and swift dog, the Chihuahua is a clannish breed which tends to recognize and prefer its own breed for association.

Maltese
Known as the "ancient dog of Malta," the Maltese has been known as the aristocrat of the canine world for more than 28 centuries.

Manchester Terrier
Dubbed "the gentleman's terrier," this dog was bred in Manchester, England to kill vermin and to hunt small game.

Pekingese
Sacred in China, the Pekingese is a dignified dog who is happy in a rural or urban setting.

Poodle
The national dog of France, Poodles are known for their retrieving capabilities in cold water.

Pomeranian
A descendant of the sled dogs of Iceland and Lapland, the "Pom" is hearty and strong despite his fragile appearance.

Pug
One of the oldest breeds, the Pug is an even-tempered breed who is playful, outgoing and dignified.

Edit text.

1. Open ID 2-7.indd, then save it as **Declaration Edit.**
2. Select the Type tool, then click at the beginning of the first paragraph.
3. Click Edit on the Application bar, then click Find/Change.
4. Type **IV** in the Find what text box, then type **III** in the Change to text box. (*Hint*: Drag the dialog box out of the way if you cannot see your document.)
5. Click Find. (*Hint*: You want to change the IV to III in George IV, as in George III, however, the spell checker finds all instances of "IV," such as in the word "deriving."
6. Click the Case Sensitive button in the middle of the Find/Change dialog box (*Hint*: Look for an icon with Aa), then click Find.
7. Click Change All, click OK in the dialog box that tells you that two replacements were made, then click Done in the Find/Change dialog box. By specifying the search to be Case Sensitive, only uppercase IV instances were found and changed.
8. Click before the drop cap in the first paragraph, click Edit on the Application bar, point to Spelling, then click Check Spelling.
9. For the query on the word "Safty," click Safety at the top of the Suggested Corrections list, then click Change.
10. Click Ignore All to ignore the query on hath.
11. Click Ignore All to ignore all instances of III.
12. Click before the capital "S" in "States" in the Change To text box in the Check Spelling dialog box, press [Spacebar] once, then click Change.
13. Click Done.
14. Save your work, deselect, compare your screen to Figure 49, then close Declaration Edit.

Create bulleted and numbered lists.

1. Open ID 2-8.indd, then save it as **Chapter 2**.
2. Click the Type tool, then select all of the text beneath Chapter 2: Selecting Pixels.
3. In the Paragraph panel, set the Space After value to .125 in.
4. Click Type on the Application bar, point to Bulleted & Numbered Lists, then click Apply Bullets.
5. Click Type on the Application bar, point to Bulleted & Numbered Lists, then click Apply Numbers.
6. Click Type on the menu bar, point to Bulleted & Numbered Lists, then click Convert Numbering to Text.
7. Select the number 1 and the period that follows it.
8. In the Character panel, change the Type Style from Regular to Italic.
9. Change all the numbers and the periods that follow them to italic.
10. Save your work, then close Chapter 2.indd.

Figure 49 *Completed Skills Review, Part 3*

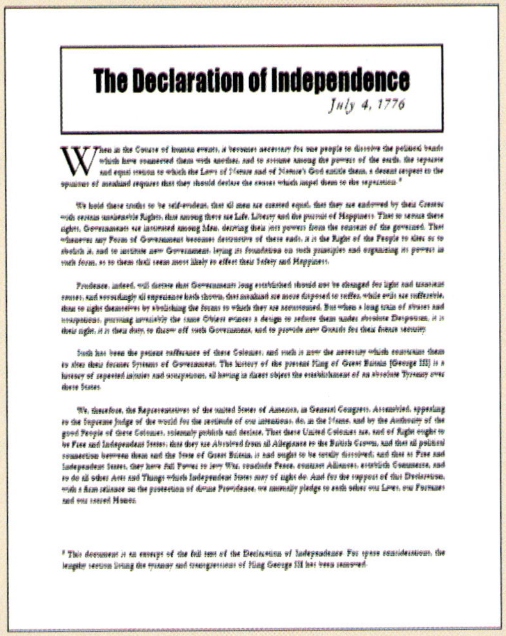

PROJECT BUILDER 1

You are a freelance designer. Your client returns a document to you, telling you that she wants you to make a change to a drop cap. She wants you to format not just the first letter but the entire first word as a drop cap, so that it is more prominent on the page.

1. Open ID 2-9.indd, then save it as **Drop Cap Modifications**.
2. Click the Zoom tool, then drag a selection box around the first paragraph.
3. Click the Type tool, click after the W drop cap, double-click the 1 in the Drop Cap One or More Characters text box on the Paragraph panel, type **4**, and then press Enter.
4. Click before the word in, in the top line, then type **100** in the Kerning text box on the Character panel.
5. Select the letters HEN, click the Character panel options button, click All Caps, click the Character panel options button again, then click Superscript.
6. With the letters still selected, type **–10** in the Baseline Shift text box on the Character panel.
7. Click between the W and H in the word WHEN, then type **-60** in the Kerning text box.
8. Save your work, compare your screen to Figure 50, then close Drop Cap Modifications.

Figure 50 *Completed Project Builder 1*

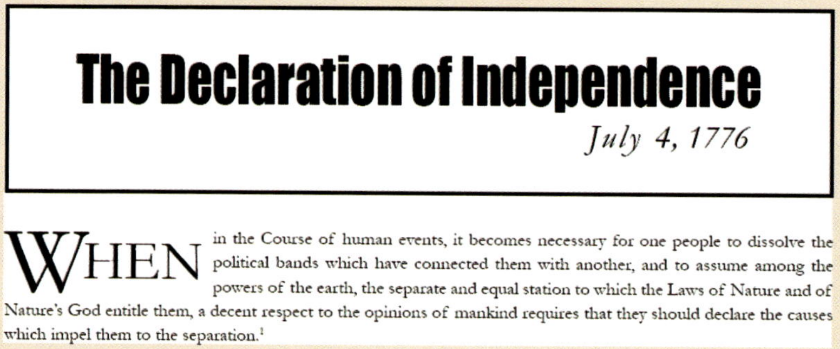
The Declaration of Independence

July 4, 1776

WHEN in the Course of human events, it becomes necessary for one people to dissolve the political bands which have connected them with another, and to assume among the powers of the earth, the separate and equal station to which the Laws of Nature and of Nature's God entitle them, a decent respect to the opinions of mankind requires that they should declare the causes which impel them to the separation.[1]

You have designed a document about miniature pinschers. Your client calls you with changes. He wants to show small pictures of miniature pinschers in the document, one beside each paragraph. He asks you to reformat the document to create space where the small pictures can be inserted.

1. Open ID 2-10.indd, then save it as **Hanging Indents**.
2. Select the four paragraphs of body copy, then change the first line left indent to 0.
3. Change the left indent to 2 in, then change the right indent to .5 in.
4. Create a half-inch space after each paragraph.
5. Type **–1.5** in the First Line Left Indent text box, then deselect all.
6. Save your work, compare your screen to Figure 51, then close Hanging Indents.

Figure 51 *Completed Project Builder 2*

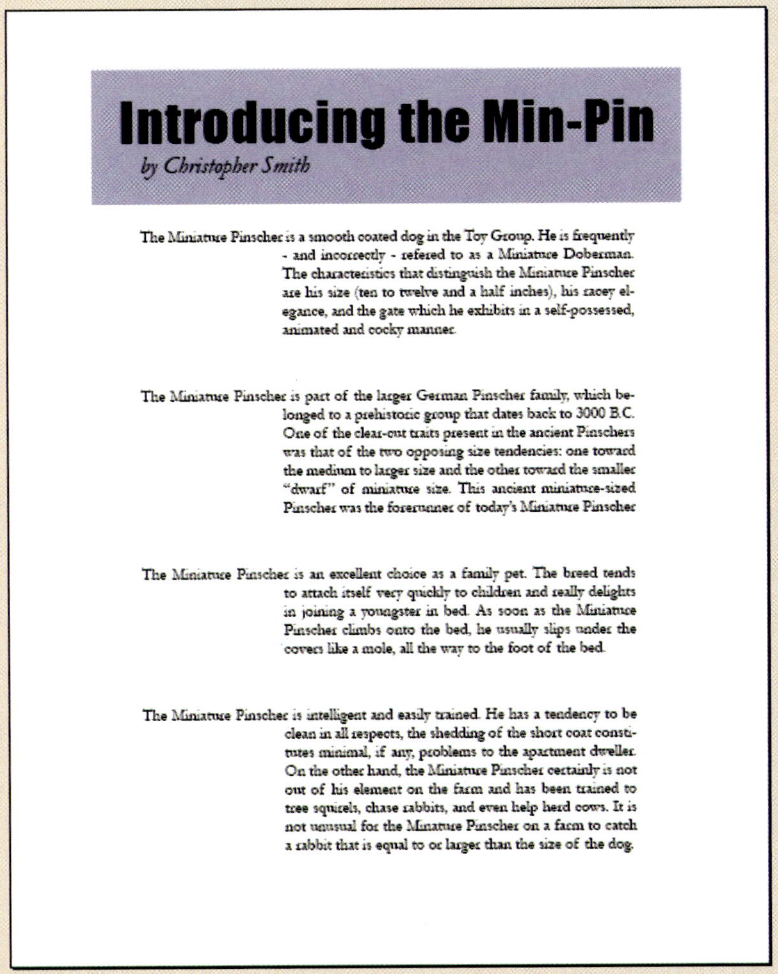

Introducing the Min-Pin
by Christopher Smith

The Miniature Pinscher is a smooth coated dog in the Toy Group. He is frequently - and incorrectly - refered to as a Miniature Doberman. The characteristics that distinguish the Miniature Pinscher are his size (ten to twelve and a half inches), his racey elegance, and the gate which he exhibits in a self-possessed, animated and cocky manner.

The Miniature Pinscher is part of the larger German Pinscher family, which belonged to a prehistoric group that dates back to 3000 B.C. One of the clear-cut traits present in the ancient Pinschers was that of the two opposing size tendencies: one toward the medium to larger size and the other toward the smaller "dwarf" of miniature size. This ancient miniature-sized Pinscher was the forerunner of today's Miniature Pinscher.

The Miniature Pinscher is an excellent choice as a family pet. The breed tends to attach itself very quickly to children and really delights in joining a youngster in bed. As soon as the Miniature Pinscher climbs onto the bed, he usually slips under the covers like a mole, all the way to the foot of the bed.

The Miniature Pinscher is intelligent and easily trained. He has a tendency to be clean in all respects, the shedding of the short coat constitutes minimal, if any, problems to the apartment dweller. On the other hand, the Miniature Pinscher certainly is not out of his element on the farm and has been trained to tree squirels, chase rabbits, and even help herd cows. It is not unusual for the Miniature Pinscher on a farm to catch a rabbit that is equal to or larger than the size of the dog.

You are designing a title treatment for a poster for the new music CD titled, "Latin Lingo." After typing the title, you realize immediately that the phrase poses obvious kerning challenges. You note that the central letters—TIN LIN—appear close together, but the outer letters are much further apart. You decide to kern the outer letters to bring them closer together.

1. Open ID 2-11.indd, then save it as **Latin Lingo**.
2. Using the Type tool, click between the A and T, then apply a kerning value of −105.
3. Apply a kerning value of −75 between the N and the G.
4. Apply a kerning value of −80 between the G and the O.
5. Position your cursor to the immediate left of the L in the word Lingo.
6. Apply a kerning value of −75.
7. Save your work, compare your screen to Figure 52, then close Latin Lingo.

Figure 52 *Completed Design Project*

LATIN LINGO

You have been assigned the task of designing a headline for a billboard for the movie "Crushing Impact." The client has asked for a finished design in black letters on a white background. Before you design the title, you consider the following questions.

Discussion.

1. Open ID 2-12.indd, then save it as **Crushing Impact**.
2. Look at the title for a full minute.
3. What font family might be best for the title?
4. Does the title demand a big, bold font, or could it work in a fine, delicate font?
5. Should the two words be positioned side-by-side or one on top of the other?
6. Does the title itself suggest that, visually, one word should be positioned on top of the other?

Exercise.

1. Position the word Impact on a second line, select all the text, change the font to Impact, then change the font size to 64 pt.
2. Select the word Impact, change the horizontal scale to 200, then change the vertical scale to 80.
3. Select the word Crushing, change the horizontal scale to 50, change the font size to 190, then change the leading to 190.
4. Select the word Impact, then change the leading to 44.
5. Save your work, compare your screen to Figure 53, then close Crushing Impact.

Figure 53 *Completed Portfolio Project*

CHAPTER 3 SETTING UP A DOCUMENT

1. Create a new document and set up a master page
2. Create text on master pages
3. Apply master pages to document pages
4. Modify master pages and document pages
5. Place and thread text
6. Create new sections and wrap text

CHAPTER 3

SETTING UP
A DOCUMENT

The setup of a document is a critical phase of any design project, because you make decisions that determine the fundamental properties of the layout. When you start a new document, you specify the size, number of pages, and the basic layout of the document. At this stage, you also position columns and guides to help you plan and work with the layout. Though all of these elements can be modified, it is best if you have already determined these basic properties beforehand, so that you will not need to go back and "retro-fit" the document and its design.

Chapter 3 explores all of the basic principles and features that Adobe InDesign offers for setting up a new document. You will create a complex layout using master pages, and you will create placeholders for text, graphics, and page numbers. You will also learn how to import or place text into a document and how to "thread" text from text frame to text frame.

Along the way, you'll learn some great techniques for designing a layout, simplifying your work, avoiding time-consuming repetition of your efforts, and ensuring a consistent layout from page to page.

New Document

Document Preset: [Custom]

Intent: Print

Number of Pages: 10   ☑ Facing Pages

Start Page #: 1   ☐ Master Text Frame

Page Size: [Custom]

Width: 6.25 in   Orientation:

Height: 4.75 in

Columns

Number: 2   Gutter: 0.1667 in

Margins

Top: 0.5 in   Inside: 0.5 in

Bottom: 0.5 in   Outside: 0.5 in

OK   Cancel   Save Preset...   More Options

New Section

☑ Start Section

○ Automatic Page Numbering

● Start Page Numbering at: 2

Page Numbering

Section Prefix:

Style: 1, 2, 3, 4...

Section Marker:

☐ Include Prefix when Numbering Pages

Document Chapter Numbering

Style: 1, 2, 3, 4...

● Automatic Chapter Numbering

○ Start Chapter Numbering at: 1

○ Same as Previous Document in the Book

Book Name: N/A

OK   Cancel

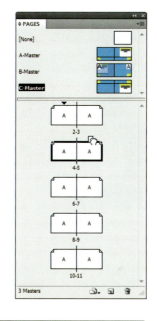

◇ PAGES

[None]

A-Master

B-Master

C-Master

2-3

4-5

6-7

8-9

10-11

3 Masters

◇ TEXT WRAP

☐ Invert

⊤ 0 in   ⊢▪ 0.08 in

⊥ 0 in   ▪⊣ 0.08 in

Wrap Options:

Wrap To: Both Right & Left Sides

Contour Options:

Type:

☐ Include Inside Edges

Create a New Document
AND SET UP A MASTER PAGE

What You'll Do

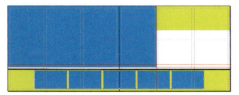

▶ *In this lesson, you will create a new document, position guides on a master page, and position placeholder frames for text, tints, and graphics.*

Creating a New Document

When you are ready to create a new document in InDesign, you begin in the New Document dialog box, shown in Figure 1. Here you specify the number of pages the document will contain. You also specify the **page size**, or, **trim size**—the width and height of the finished document. In addition, you specify whether or not the document will have **facing pages**. When you choose this option, the document is created with left and right pages that *face* each other in a spread, such as you would find in a magazine. If this option is not selected, each page stands alone, like a *stack* of pages.

The New Document dialog box also allows you to specify the width of margins on the outer edges of the page and the number of columns that will be positioned on the page. Margins and columns are very useful as layout guides, and they play an important role in flowing text. When working with

Figure 1 *New Document dialog box*

Enter number of pages that you want in your document here

Page size options

Document Preset list arrow

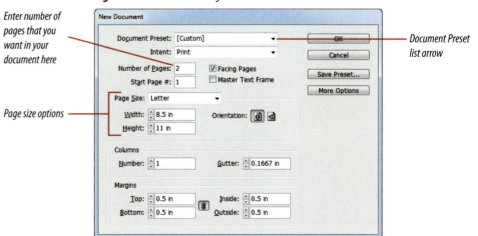

columns, the term **gutter** refers to the space between the columns. Figure 2 shows margins and columns on a typical page.

When creating a document with specific settings that you plan on using again and again, you can save the settings as a preset by clicking Save Preset in the New Document dialog box. Your named preset will then become available in the Document Preset list in the New Document dialog box.

Setting the Starting Page Number

Imagine that you are holding a closed book in your hands—perhaps this book—and you open the front cover. The first page of the book is a single right-hand page. If you turn the page, the next two pages are pages 2-3, which face each other in a spread. Now imagine closing the book and flipping it over so that you are looking at the back cover. If you open it, the last page is a single left-hand page.

With the above in mind, consider that, by default, whenever you create a multiple page document with facing pages, InDesign automatically creates the first page on a single right-hand page and the last page on a single left-hand page. Figure 3 shows how InDesign, by default, would create a four-page document: with a single right-hand page as the first page and a single left-hand page as the last page.

But what if you wanted to design those four pages as two spreads—what if you wanted the first page to be a left page?

Figure 2 *Identifying margins and columns*

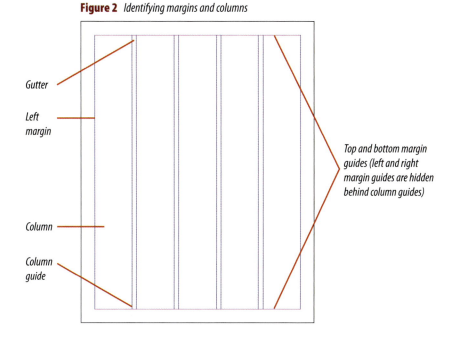

Gutter

Left margin

Column

Column guide

Top and bottom margin guides (left and right margin guides are hidden behind column guides)

Figure 3 *Four page document with default page layout*

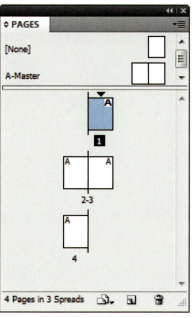

You accomplish this in the Start Page # text box in the New Document dialog box. The number that you enter in this text box determines the page number of the first page and whether it is a left-hand or a right-hand page. If you enter a 2 (or any other even number), the first page will be a left-hand page. Figure 4 shows the same four-page document set up as two spreads. Note that the first page is page 2. It is a left-hand page. There is no page 1 in the document.

Modifying Margins and Columns

The New Document dialog box offers you options for specifying measurements for margins and for the number of columns in the document. Once you click OK though,

you can't return to the New Document dialog box to modify those settings. The Document Setup dialog box allows you to change the page size and the number of pages, among other choices, but it doesn't offer the option to modify margins or the number of columns. Don't worry though; once you've created a document, you can modify margins and columns with the Margins and Columns command under the Layout menu.

Understanding Master Pages

Imagine that you are creating a layout for a book and that every chapter title page will have the same layout format. If that book had 20 chapters, you would need to create that chapter title page 20 times. And you'd need

to be careful to make the layout consistent every time you created the page. Now imagine that you've finished your layout, but your editor wants you to change the location of the title on the page. That would mean making the same change—20 times!

Not so with master pages. **Master pages** are templates that you create for a page layout. Once created, you apply the master page to the document pages you want to base on that layout. With master pages, you create a layout one time, then use it as many times as you like. Working with master pages saves you from time-consuming repetition of efforts, and it offers consistency between document pages that are meant to have the same layout.

Figure 4 *Four-page document set up as two spreads*

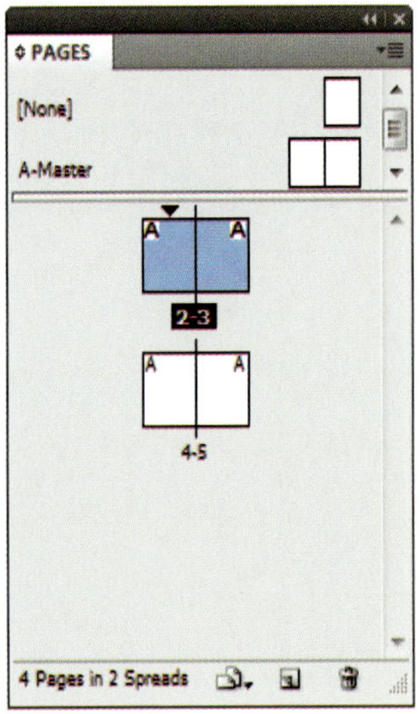

So what happens when your editor asks for that change in location of the title? Simply make the change to the master page, and the change will be reflected on all the document pages based on that master.

When you create a new document, one default master page is created and listed on the Pages panel, as shown in Figure 5. The Pages panel is command central for all things relating to pages and master pages. You use the Pages panel to add, delete, and apply master pages to document pages.

Creating Master Items on Master Pages

In InDesign, text is positioned in **text frames** and graphics are positioned in **graphics frames**. To create a text frame, you click the Type tool and then drag it in the document window. You can then type into the text frame. You use the Rectangle, Ellipse, or Polygon Frame tools in the same way to create graphics frames.

When you create a frame for text or graphics on a master page, it is referred to as a **master item**. All objects on a master page are called master items and function as a "placeholder" where objects on the document pages are to be positioned. For example, if you had a book broken down into chapters and you created a master page for the chapter title pages, you would create a text frame placeholder for the chapter title text. This text frame would appear on every document page that uses the chapter title master page. Working this way—with the text frame

placeholder on the master page—you can feel certain that the location of the chapter title will be consistent on every chapter title page in the book.

Creating Guides

Guides, as shown in Figure 6, are horizontal or vertical lines that you position on a page. As their name suggests, guides are used to help guide you in aligning objects on the page. You have a number of options for creating guides. You can create them manually by "pulling" them out from the horizontal and vertical

rulers. You can also use the Create Guides command on the Layout menu. Once created, guides can be selected, moved, and deleted, if necessary. You can also change the color of guides, which sometimes makes it easier to see them, depending on the colors used in your document.

> **QUICK TIP**
>
> Press and hold [Ctrl] (Win) or ⌘ (Mac), then drag a guide from the horizontal ruler to create a guide that covers a spread instead of an individual page in a spread.

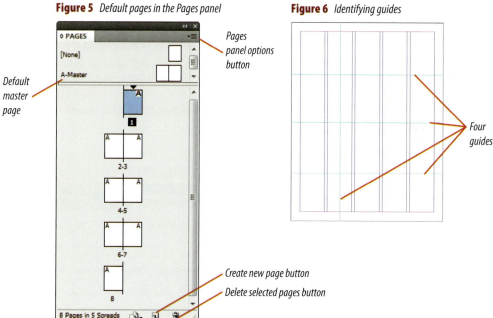

Figure 5 *Default pages in the Pages panel*

Pages panel options button

Default master page

Create new page button

Delete selected pages button

Figure 6 *Identifying guides*

Four guides

Changing the Color of Guides, Margins, and Columns

By default, guides are cyan, column guides are violet, and margin guides are magenta. Depending on your preferences and on the color of objects in the layout you are creating, you may want to change their colors.

In InDesign, you modify individual guide colors by selecting them, then clicking the Ruler Guides command on the Layout menu. Choosing a new color in the Ruler Guides dialog box affects only the selected guides. When you create more guides, they will be created in the default color.

You modify the default color of margins and columns in the Guides & Pasteboard section of the Preferences dialog box. Once you've modified the color of margins and columns, each new page you create in an existing document will appear with those colors. However, when you create a new document, the margins and columns will appear in their default colors.

Locking Column Guides

InDesign lets you lock Column Guides independently from any ruler guides you create. Click View on the Application bar, point to Grids & Guides, and then click Lock Column Guides to add or remove the check mark, which toggles the lock on or off. By default, column guides are locked.

Choosing Default Colors for Guides, Margins, and Columns

When you choose colors for guides, margins, and columns, you may want those choices to affect every document you create. You do so by making the color changes in the appropriate dialog boxes without any documents open. The new colors will be applied in all new documents created thereafter. Remember, if you change default colors when a document is open, the changes are only applied to that document.

Using the Transform Panel

The Transform panel identifies a selected object's width and height, and its horizontal and vertical locations on the page. As shown in Figure 7, the width and height of the selected object appears in the Width and Height text boxes of the Transform panel.

When you position an object on a page, you need some way to describe that object's position on the page. InDesign defines the position of an object using X and Y Location values on the Transform panel. To work with X and Y locations, you first need to understand that the **zero point** of the page is, by default, at the top-left corner of the page. X and Y locations are made in reference to that zero point.

There are nine reference points on the Transform panel that correspond to the nine points available on a selected item's bounding box. Clicking a reference point tells InDesign that you wish to see the horizontal and vertical locations of that point of the selected object.

Figure 7 *Transform panel shows coordinates and size of selected frame*

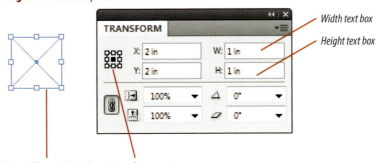

Width text box

Height text box

Selected frame is 1" × 1"   Nine reference points

When an object is selected, the X Location value is the horizontal location—how far it is across the page—and the Y Location value is the vertical location—how far it is down the page. The selected object in Figure 8 has an X Location of 1 inch and a Y Location of 1 inch. This means that its top-left point is 1 inch across the page and 1 inch down. Why the top-left point? Because that is the reference point chosen on the Transform panel, also shown in Figure 8.

QUICK TIP

X and Y Location values for circles are determined by the reference points of the bounding box that is placed around circles when they are selected.

Be sure to note that the text boxes on the Transform panel are interactive. For example, if you select an object and find that its X Location value is 2, you can enter 3 in the X Location text box, press [Enter] (Win) or [return] (Mac), and the object will

be relocated to the new location on the page. You can also change the width or height of a selected object by changing the value in the Width or Height text boxes.

QUICK TIP

You can perform calculations in the text boxes on the Transform panel. For example, you could select an object whose width is three inches. By typing 3 - .625 in the W text box, you can reduce the object's width to 2.375 inches. What a powerful feature!

Using the Control Panel

You can think of the Control panel, docked at the top of the document window by default, as InDesign's "super panel." The Control panel mimics all the other panels, housing a wide variety of options for working with text and objects. Rather than always moving from one panel to another, you can usually find the option you are looking for in the Control panel.

The options on the Control panel change based on the type of object selected. For example, if a block of text is selected, the Control panel changes to show all of the type-related options for modifying text, such as changing the font or font size. When any object is selected, the Control panel display is similar to the Transform panel. It offers X/Y coordinate reference points and text boxes and the same options for modifying a selected object. For example, you can change the width and height of a frame using the Control panel, just as you can with the Transform panel.

Unlike the Transform panel, the Control panel offers a multitude of additional options for working with frames, making the Control panel perhaps the most-used panel in InDesign.

In Figure 9, the Control panel shows options for a selected graphics frame.

QUICK TIP

The Info panel displays information about the current document and selected objects, such as text and graphics frames. For example, if you click inside a text frame with the Type tool, the Info panel displays the number of characters, words, lines, and paragraphs in the frame. If you click the same text frame with the Selection tool, you can find out the size and location of the text frame. The Info panel is available only for viewing information. You cannot make changes to a selected object using this panel.

Figure 8 *Identifying an object's X and Y locations*

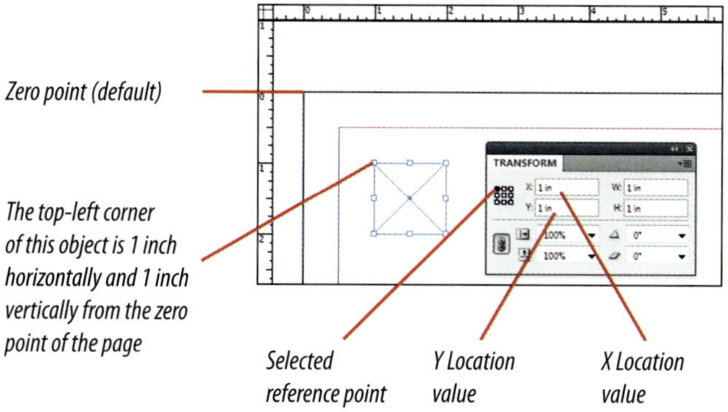

Zero point (default)

The top-left corner of this object is 1 inch horizontally and 1 inch vertically from the zero point of the page

Selected reference point

Y Location value

X Location value

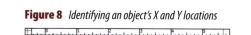

Figure 9 *Control panel*

Using the Line Tool

The Line tool makes lines—no surprise there. Use the Line tool to make horizontal, vertical and diagonal lines in your layouts. When you click the Line tool, the Fill/Stroke colors at the bottom of the Tools panel default to a fill of None and a stroke color of black. You can apply a fill color to a line, but generally speaking, you only want to stroke a line with color. You specify the weight of a line with the Stroke panel, and you can use the length text box in the Control and Transform panels to specify the length. You can use all nine reference points in the Control and Transform panels to position a line in your layout.

Transforming Objects

Transform is a term used to describe the act of moving an object, scaling it, skewing it, or rotating it. You can do all of the above in the Transform or Control panels. Figure 10 shows a rectangular frame that is 3" wide and 1.5" tall. Its center point is identified on the Transform panel, because the center reference point is selected on the

Figure 10 *A rectangle with its center point identified*

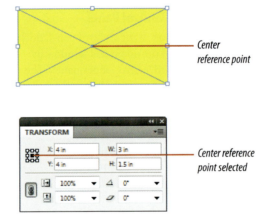

Center reference point

Center reference point selected

Transform panel. In Figure 11, the same frame has been rotated 90 degrees—note the 90∞ value in the Rotation Angle text box on the Transform panel. Note also that the object was rotated at its center point. This is because the center reference point was selected when the transformation was executed. The center point of the rectangle was the **point of origin** for the transformation. Think of the point of origin as the point from where the transformation happens. Whichever reference point is selected determines the point of origin for the transformation of the selected object.

In Figure 12, the object has not been moved. The top-left reference point on the Transform panel has been selected, so the X/Y text boxes now identify the location of the top-left corner of the rectangle.

Don't trouble yourself trying to guess ahead of time how the choice of a point of origin in conjunction with a transformation will affect an object. Sometimes it will be easy to foresee how the object will be transformed; sometimes you'll need to use trial and error. The important thing for you to remember is

that the point of origin determines the point where the transformation takes place.

Using the Transform Again Command

The Transform Again command is a very powerful command that repeats the last transformation executed. For example, let's say you rotate a text frame. If you select another text frame and apply the Transform Again command, the same rotation will be applied to the second object. The Transform Again command is useful for creating multiple objects at specified distances.

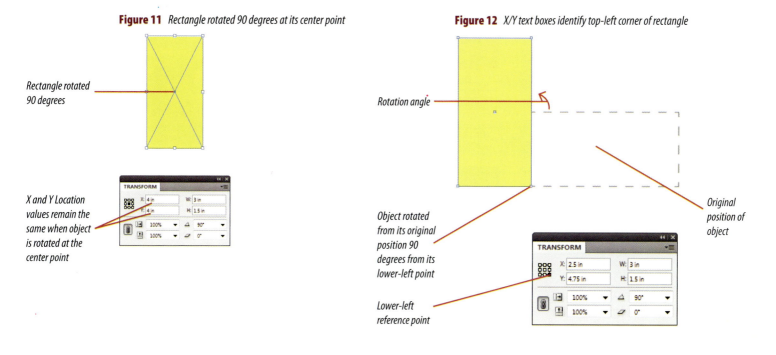

Figure 11 *Rectangle rotated 90 degrees at its center point*

Rectangle rotated 90 degrees

X and Y Location values remain the same when object is rotated at the center point

Figure 12 *X/Y text boxes identify top-left corner of rectangle*

Rotation angle

Object rotated from its original position 90 degrees from its lower-left point

Lower-left reference point

Original position of object

View a multi-page document

1. Open ID 3-1.indd.
2. Press **[Shift][W]** to enter Presentation mode.
3. Use the right and left arrow keys on your computer keypad to view all of the pages in the document.

   The document is composed of five two-page spreads for a total of ten pages. The document has been designed as a pamphlet for a travel company advertising destinations for a tour of Italy. Page numbers are visible at the bottom of every spread. The five spreads are based on three layout versions. The layout will be used for both a printed piece and for an interactive PDF that can be emailed.

4. Press **[Esc]** to leave Presentation mode.
5. Press **[Tab]** to show panels, then show the Pages panel.

   The first page of the document is page 2, and it is a left-hand page.

6. View spread 4-5.

   Spread 4-5, shown in Figure 13, is the basis for the document you will build using master pages in this chapter.

7. Close the file.

You viewed a finished document that will be the basis for the document you will build in this chapter.

Create a new document

1. Verify that no documents are open.
2. Click **Edit** (Win) or **InDesign** (Mac) on the Application bar, point to **Preferences**, then click **Units & Increments**.

(continued)

Figure 13 *Layout used as the basis for this chapter*

Figure 14 *Settings in the New Document dialog box*

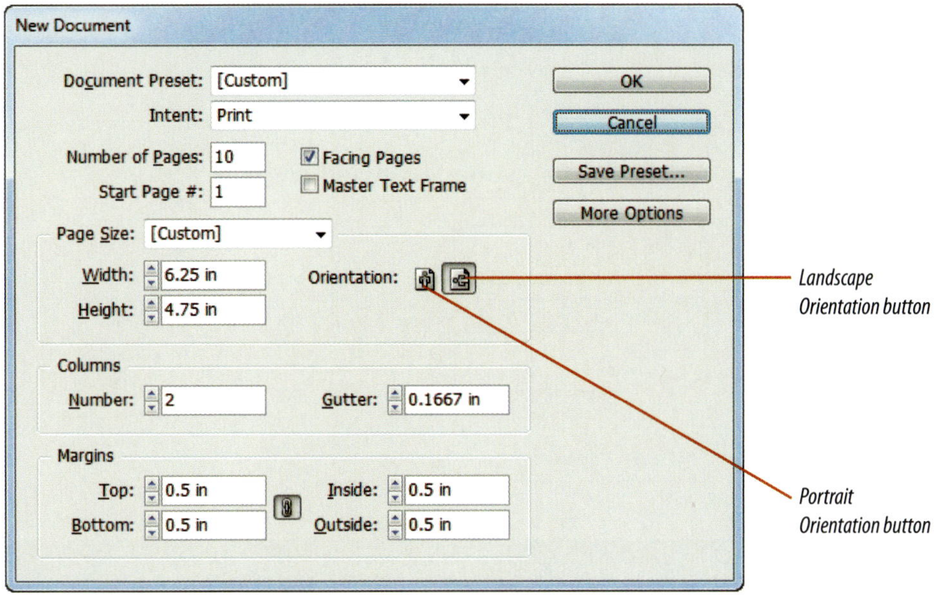

Landscape
Orientation button

Portrait
Orientation button

3. Click the **Horizontal list arrow**, click **Inches**, click the **Vertical list arrow**, click **Inches**, then click **OK**.

4. Click **File** on the Application bar, point to **New**, then click **Document**.

5. Type **10** in the Number of Pages text box, verify that the Facing Pages check box is checked, then verify that the Start Page # is set to 1.

6. Type **6.25** in the Width text box, press **[Tab]**, type **4.75** in the Height text box, then click the **Landscape Orientation button**.

TIP Press [Tab] to move your cursor forward from text box to text box. Press [Shift][Tab] to move backward from text box to text box.

7. Type **2** in the Number text box in the Columns section, then verify that the Gutter text box is set to .1667 in.

8. Type **.5** in the Top Margins text box, then verify that the Make all settings the same button 🔒 is activated.

9. Compare your dialog box to Figure 14, click **OK**, then look at the pages panel.

   Page 1 is a single right-hand page, and page 10 is a single left hand page.

10. Click **File** on the Application bar, then click **Document Setup**.

    Note that the Margins and Columns sections are not available in the Document Setup dialog box.

(continued)

11. Change the Start Page # to **2**, click **OK**, then compare your Pages panel to Figure 15.

The document is now composed of five two-page spreads, numbered 2-11.

12. Save the document as **Setup**.

You set the Units & Increments preferences to specify that you will be working with inches for horizontal and vertical measurements. You then created a new document using the New Document dialog box. You specified the number of pages in the document, the page size for each page, and the number of columns on each page. You then modified the start page number in the Document Setup dialog box to start the document on a left-hand page.

Modify margins and the number of columns

1. Click **Layout** on the Application bar, then click **Margins and Columns**.

The Margins and Columns dialog box opens.

2. Set the number of columns to 3.

3. Reduce the width of the margins on all four sides to .125 in, then click **OK**.

Note that the width and height of the columns change to fill the area within the margins.

4. Save the file.

You changed the number of columns and the width of margins in an open document.

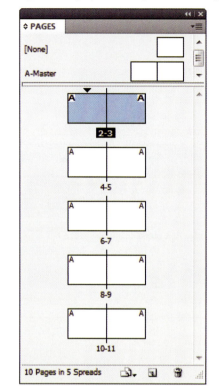

Figure 15 *Pages panel showing document starting on a left-hand page*

Using the Move Pages Command

As you have learned, if you have a multiple-page document, you can change the sequence of pages simply by moving them around on the Pages panel. Easy enough. But for documents with more pages—let's say 100 pages—dragging and dropping page icons on the Pages panel isn't so simple. Imagine, for example, trying to drag page 84 so that it follows page 14. Whew! With InDesign CS5's powerful Move Pages command, you can specify which pages you want to move and where you want to move them. Click the Pages panel options button click Move Pages, then choose options in the Move Pages dialog box. Be sure to check it out.

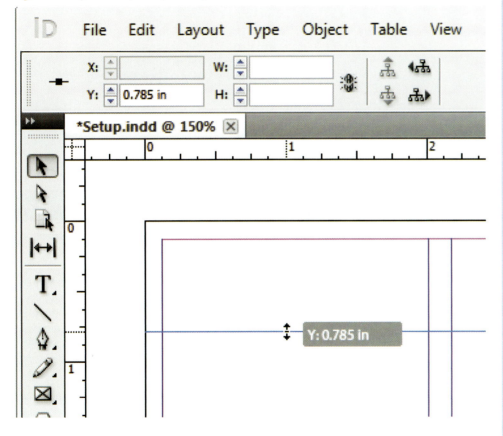

Figure 16 *Using the Control panel to position a guide*

Add guides to a master page

1. Set the workspace to Essentials.

2. Double-click the word **A-Master** on the Pages panel, note that both master pages in the Pages menu become blue, then note that the page menu at the lower-left corner of the document window lists A-Master.

   A-Master is now the active page.

3. If rulers are not visible at the top and left of the document window, click **View** on the Application bar, then click **Show Rulers**.

4. Click the **Selection tool** , position the pointer over the horizontal ruler, then click and slowly drag down a guide, releasing it anywhere on the page.

   A guide is positioned only on the left page of the spread.

TIP As you drag the new guide onto the page, the value in the Y Location text box on the Control panel continually changes to show the guide's current location. See Figure 16.

5. Click **Edit** on the Application bar, then click **Undo Add New Guide.**

6. Press and hold **[Ctrl]**(Win) or **[Command]**(Mac), then drag down a guide from the horizontal ruler, releasing it anywhere on the page.

   The guide extends across the entire spread.

7. Type **2.5** in the Y Location text box on the Control panel, then press **[Enter]** (Win) or **[return]** (Mac).

   The guide jumps to the specific vertical location you entered: 2.5" from the top of the page.

TIP For this entire chapter, you can use the Transform panel interchangeably with the Control panel.

(continued)

8. Drag a second spread guide from the horizontal ruler, drop the guide anywhere on the page, then set its Y Location to 3.5 in.

9. Click **Edit** (Win) or **InDesign** (Mac), point to **Preferences**, then click **Units & Increments**.

10. In the Ruler Units section, verify that Origin is set to Spread, then click **OK**.

    With the Origin value set to spread, the ruler and all X values are continuous across the entire spread. In other words, there's one ruler across both pages, as opposed to one ruler for the left page and another for the right page.

11. Drag a guide from the vertical ruler on the left side of the document window, then use the Control panel to position its X value at 8.35 in.

12. Using the Selection Tool, click the **first horizontal guide** you positioned at 2.5 inches to select it, double-click the **Y Location text box** on the Transform panel, type **3.4**, then press **[Enter]** (Win) or **[return]** (Mac).

    The guide is moved to the new location.

TIP   Selected guides appear darker blue.

13. Position a third horizontal guide at 3.25" from the top of the page.

14. Compare your spread and guides to Figure 17, then save your work.

You positioned guides on the master page by dragging them from the horizontal and vertical rulers. You used the Control panel to position them at precise locations.

Figure 17 *Master spread with guides in position*

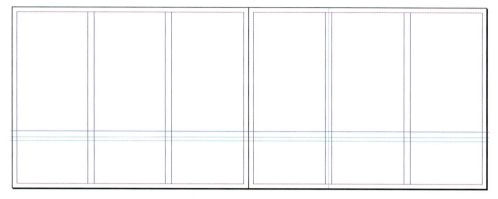

Working with Conditional Text

Using conditional text is a great way to create different versions of the same InDesign document. You create conditional text by first creating conditions and then applying them to text. Later, you hide or show the text that has the condition applied to it by hiding or showing conditions using the Conditional Text panel. Showing and hiding conditions works just like showing and hiding layers on the Layers panel. You assign a new condition to text, and then hide it by clicking the "Eye" (visibility) icon on the Conditional Text panel. When you have many conditions, you can create a **condition set**, which is a snapshot of the current visibility of the applied conditions. Click the Conditional Text panel options button then click Show Options. On the Conditional Text panel, click the Set list arrow, then click Create New Set. Name the set, then click OK. Instead of turning individual conditions on or off on the panel, you can choose a condition set to do the same job in one step.

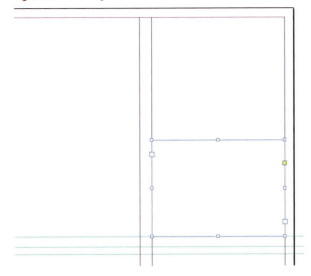

Figure 18 *Positioning the text frame*

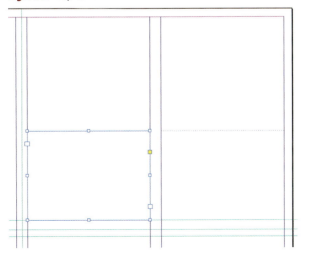

Figure 19 *Duplicated text frame*

Create placeholder text frames

1. Verify that the Fill and Stroke colors at the bottom of the Tools panel are both set to None.

2. Click the **Type tool** T , then drag to create a small text frame anywhere in the rightmost column above the horizontal guides.

3. Click the **Selection tool** , drag the **left and right handles of the text frame** so that it is the full width of the column.

4. Drag the **bottom handle** down until it snaps to the topmost horizontal guide.

5. Click the **bottom-center reference point** on the Control panel, type **1.375** in the Height text box on the Transform panel, then press **[Enter]** (Win) or **[return]** (Mac).

   Your right page should resemble Figure 18. The bottom of the text frame did not move with the change in height.

6. Press and hold **[Shift][Alt]**(Win) or **[Shift] [Option]**(Mac), then drag and drop a copy of the text frame into the column to the left so that your page resembles Figure 19.

   Note that the new text frames are difficult to distinguish from the ruler guides.

7. Save your work.

You created two text frames, which will be used as placeholders for body copy the document.

Change the color of guides, margins, and columns

1. Click **Edit** (Win) or **InDesign** (Mac) on the Application bar, point to **Preferences**, then click **Guides & Pasteboard**.

2. Verify that the Guides in Back check box is unchecked.

   When this option is deactivated, guides appear in front of all items on the document, rather than hidden behind them.

3. In the Color section, click the **Margins list arrow**, then click **Light Gray**.

4. Click the **Columns list arrow**, then click **Light Gray**.

5. Click **OK**.

6. Click the **Selection tool** , click the **vertical guide** to select it, press and hold **[Shift]**, then click the three **horizontal guides**, so all the guides you created are selected.

   All four guides appear dark blue.

7. Click **Layout** on the Application bar, then click **Ruler Guides**.

8. Click the **Color list arrow**, click **Red**, then click **OK**.

9. Click the **pasteboard** to deselect the guides, then compare your page to Figure 20.

You changed the color of margins, columns, and guides to improve your ability to distinguish text frames from page guides.

Figure 20 *Viewing changed guide colors*

Figure 21 *Viewing the copied frame*

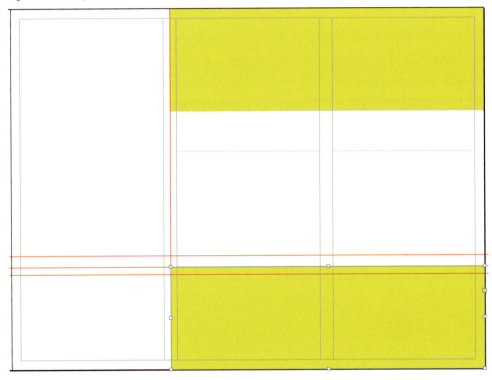

Create color tint frames on a master page

1. Verify that the Fill and Stroke colors at the bottom of the Tools panel are both set to None.

   TIP You will learn much more about fills and strokes in Chapters 4 and 5.

2. Click the **Rectangle tool** , then drag a small **rectangle** anywhere above the two text frames in the two rightmost columns.

3. Click the **Selection tool** , click **Window** on the Application bar, point to **Object & Layout**, then click **Transform**.

   The Transform panel appears.

4. Drag the **left handle of the frame** so that it snaps to the red vertical guide.

   TIP To verify that Snap to Guides is activated, click View on the Application bar, then point to Grids & Guides.

5. Drag the **right handle of the frame** so that it snaps to the right edge of the document.

   The Width text box in the Transform panel should read 4.15 in.

6. Drag the **top handle of the frame** so that it snaps to the top edge of the document.

7. Click the **top-center reference point** on the Transform panel, then verify that the Y text box on the Transform panel reads 0.

   If the top edge of the frame is aligned to the top edge of the page, its Y coordinate must be zero.

8. Change the height value on the Transform panel to **1.35** in.

   Because the Units & Increments preferences are set to Inches, you do not need to—nor should

   (continued)

you—type the abbreviation for inches in the text box. Just type the number.

TIP Don't deselect the frame.

9. At the bottom of the Tools panel, click the **Fill Color swatch** once so that it is in front of the Stroke Color swatch.

10. Open the Swatches panel, then click the **yellow swatch**.

   The frame fills with the yellow tint.

11. Drag and drop **a copy of the yellow frame** to the bottom of the page, as shown in Figure 21.

12. Drag the **top edge of the bottom frame** down so that it aligns with the bottommost of the three guides, then drag the left edge to align with the left edge of the document.

   The Width & Height text boxes on the Transform panel should read 12.5 in and 1.25 in, respectively.

13. Deselect all, then click the **light blue swatch** in the Swatches panel.

   The Fill Color swatch changes to the light blue color.

14. Create a small rectangle anywhere in the upper-left section of the document.

   The new rectangle is created with the light blue fill.

15. Click the **top-left reference point** on the Transform panel, enter **0** in the X text box, press **[Tab]**, enter **0** in the Y text box, press **[Tab]**, type **8.35** in the Width text box, press **[Tab]**, then enter **3.4** in the Height text box.

   Your spread should resemble Figure 22.

16. Save your work.

You created three color-filled frames on the page and used the Transform panel to position them and modify their sizes.

Figure 22 *Viewing tints on the spread*

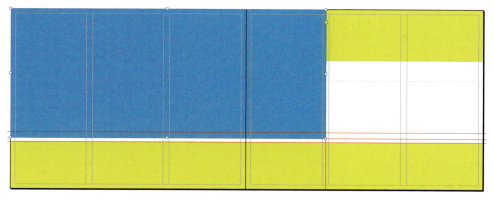

Use the Line tool

1. Close the Transform panel, click anywhere in the pasteboard to deselect all, then click the **Line tool**.

   Verify that the Fill color automatically changes to None, and the Stroke color changes to black.

2. Position the cursor at the left edge of the document, press and hold **[Shift]**, then click and drag to create a line of any length.

   Pressing and holding [Shift] constrains the line so that it is straight.

3. Expand the Stroke panel, then increase the weight of the stroke to 4 pt.

4. Click the **top-left reference point** on the Control panel, type **0** in the X text box, press **[Tab]**, type **3.5** in the Y text box, press **[Tab]**, then type **12.5** in the L (length) text box so that your spread resembles Figure 23.

5. Save your work.

You created a line with the line tool, specified its weight in the Stroke panel, then positioned it on the spread and specified its length with the Control panel.

Figure 23 *Viewing the line*

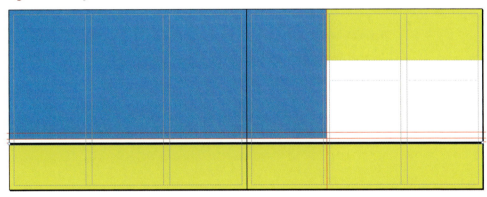

Use the Transform Again command

1. Click the **Rectangle tool** , then draw a small rectangle in the first column anywhere at the bottom of the page.

2. Click the **top-left reference point** on the Control panel, type **0** in the X text box, type **3.6** in the Y text box, type **1.8** in the Width text box, then type **1** in the Height text box.

3. Press **[I]** on your keypad to access the Eyedropper tool , then click the **large blue frame** at the top of the page.

   The Eyedropper tool samples the fill and stroke colors from the large frame; the small rectangle takes on the same fill and stroke color.

4. Press **[V]** to access the Selection Tool , press and hold **[Shift][Alt]**(Win) or **[Shift][Option]** (Mac), then drag a copy approximately 1/8" to the right of the original, as shown in Figure 24.

   (continued)

Figure 24 *Duplicating the frame*

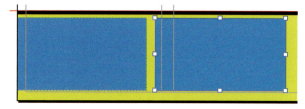

Setting Up a Document

5. Click **Object** on the Application bar, point to **Transform Again**, then click **Transform Again**.

   The last transformation you made—dragging and dropping the copy—is duplicated.

6. Apply the Transform Again command two more times.

7. Select all five of the small blue rectangles.

8. Click the **center reference point** in the Control panel.

   With the center reference point selected, the X/Y coordinates in the Control panel now identify the center point of all five boxes as a unit.

9. Change the X value in the Control panel to 6.25.

   6.25 is half of the full horizontal width of 12.5," thus the five boxes, as a unit, are centered horizontally on the page.

10. Compare your layout to Figure 25, then save your work.

You created a single rectangle, then changed its fill and stroke color with the Eyedropper tool. You duplicated it with the drag-and-drop method, then used the Transform Again command three times. You then used the Control panel to center all five rectangles as a unit.

Figure 25 *Viewing five frames centered horizontally on the spread*

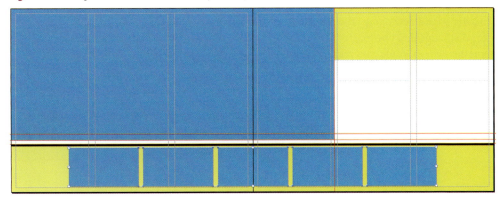

Create Text
ON MASTER PAGES

What You'll Do

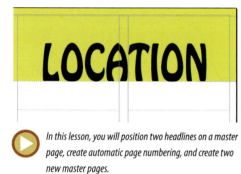

In this lesson, you will position two headlines on a master page, create automatic page numbering, and create two new master pages.

Creating a New Master Page

You create new master pages by clicking the New Master command on the Pages panel menu. When you create a new master page, you have the option of giving the master page a new name. This is useful for distinguishing one master page from another. For example, you might want to use the name "Body Copy" for master pages that will be used for body copy and then use the name "Chapter Start" for master pages that will be used as a layout for a chapter title page. Figure 26 shows three named master pages on the Pages panel.

When you create a new master page, you have the option of changing the values for the margins and for the number of columns on the new master page.

Figure 26 *Three master pages on the Pages panel*

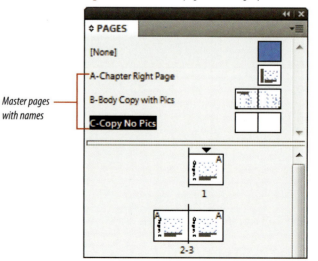

Master pages
with names

Loading Master Pages

You can load master pages from one InDesign document to another by simply clicking the Pages panel options button, then clicking Load Master Pages. You will be prompted to navigate to the file that has the master pages you wish to load. Select the InDesign document, then click Open. The master pages are added to the Pages panel. You will be prompted to rename master pages that have the same name or replace the existing master pages.

Creating Automatic Page Numbering

When you create a document with multiple pages, chances are you'll want to have page numbers on each page. You could create a text frame on every page, then manually type the page number on every page, but think of what a nightmare that could turn out to be! You would have to create a text frame of the same size and in the same location on every page. Imagine what would happen if you were to remove or add a page to the middle of the document: you'd need to go back and renumber your pages!

Fortunately, InDesign offers a solution for this. You can create placeholder text frames for page numbers on your master pages. Click inside the text frame, click Type on the Application bar, point to Insert Special Character, point to Markers, then click Current Page Number. A letter will appear in the text frame, as shown in Figure 27.

Figure 27 *A text frame on a master page containing an auto page number character*

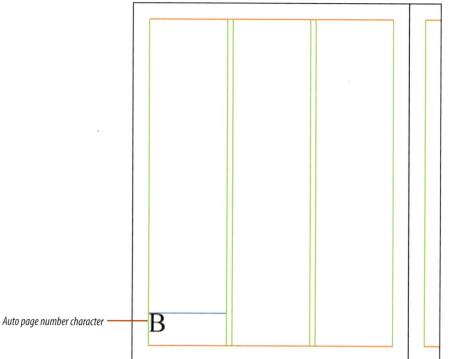

Auto page number character — B

That letter represents the page number. You can format it using any font, size, and alignment that you desire. On document pages based on that master, the letter in the text frame will appear as the number of the page. Page numbering is automatic. This means that the page number is automatically updated when pages are added or removed from the document.

When you work with multiple master pages, make sure that each page number placeholder is the same size, in the same location, and formatted in the same way on each master page. This will make the appearance of page numbers consistent throughout the document, regardless of the master upon which a particular document page is based.

Inserting White Space Between Text Characters

In Chapter 2, you learned that you should not press the spacebar more than once to create extra spacing between characters. However, sometimes a single space does not provide enough space between words or characters. You may want to insert additional space to achieve a certain look. You could tab the text or, as you'll learn in this lesson, you can insert white space.

The Type menu contains commands for inserting white space between words or characters. The two most-used white spaces are **em space** and **en space**. The width of an em space is equivalent to that of the lowercase letter m in the current typeface

at that type size. The width of an en space is narrower—that of the lowercase letter n in that typeface at that type size. Use these commands—not the spacebar—to insert white space. To insert an em space or an en space, click Type on the Application bar, point to Insert White Space, then click either Em Space or En Space. Figure 28 shows an em space between a page number placeholder and a word.

Inserting Em Dashes and En Dashes

Sometimes you'll want to put a dash between words or characters and you'll find that the dash created by pressing the hyphen key is not wide enough. That's because hyphens are shorter than dashes.

Rotating the Spread View

Sometimes, with certain layouts, not all of your content will be right-side-up on your page spread. For example, you might be designing a poster that will fold four ways, so when the poster is laid out flat in your InDesign document, some of the content will be rotated on its side—or maybe even upside down! Whatever the case, when you're working with these types of layouts, you don't need to lie on your side or do a headstand to see your work right-side-up. Instead, use the Rotate Spread View command in the Pages panel or the Rotate Spread command on the View menu. These commands rotate the view of the spread so that you can work right-side-up. They don't actually affect the content on the page—just the view.

Figure 28 *Identifying an em space*

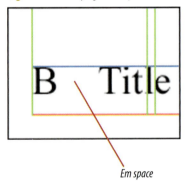

Em space

Setting Up a Document

InDesign offers two types of dashes to insert between words or characters—the em dash and the en dash. The width of an em dash is equivalent to that of the lowercase letter m in the current typeface at that type size. The width of an en dash is narrower—that of the lowercase letter n in that typeface at that type size. To insert an em dash or an en dash, click Type on the Application bar, point to Insert Special Character, point to Hyphens and Dashes, then click either Em Dash or En Dash. Figure 29 shows an example of an en dash.

Creating a New Master Page Based on Another Master Page

Imagine that you've created a master page for a magazine layout. The master contains master items for the headline, the body copy, and the page number. It also contains master items for pictures that will appear on the page. Now imagine that you need to create another master page that will be identical to this master page, with the one exception that this new master will not contain frames for graphics. You wouldn't want to duplicate all of the work you did to create the first master, would you?

To avoid repeating efforts and for consistency between masters, you can create a new master page based on another master page. The new master would appear identical to the first. You would then modify only the elements that you want to change on the new master, keeping all of the elements that you don't want to change perfectly consistent with the previous one.

Basing a new master on another master is not the same thing as duplicating a master.

When you base a new master on another, any changes you make to the first master will be updated on masters based on it. Think of how powerful this is. Let's say that your editor tells you to change the type size of the page numbers. Making a change in only one place offers you a substantial savings in time and effort and provides you with the certainty that the page numbers will be consistent from master to master.

Remember that all master items on new master pages will also be locked by default. To unlock a master item, you must press and hold [Shift][Ctrl] (Win) or [Shift] ⌘ (Mac) to select those objects on the new master. InDesign does this so that you don't accidentally move or delete objects from the new master or the original master.

Figure 29 *Identifying an en dash*

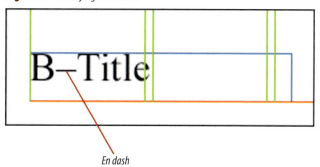

En dash

Add placeholders for headlines

1. Verify that the Fill and Stroke colors at the bottom of the Tools panel are both set to None.

2. Click the **Type tool** T, then drag a small **rectangle** anywhere in the two rightmost columns above the two text frames already there.

3. Click the **Selection tool** , then drag the **left handle of the frame** so that it snaps to the red vertical guide.

4. Drag the **right handle of the frame** so that it snaps to the right edge of the document.

   The Width text box in the Control panel should read 4.15 in.

5. Click the **bottom-center reference point** on the Control panel, then enter **1.35** in the Y text box.

   The text frame moves to align its bottom edge to the Y coordinate.

6. Change the height value on the Control panel to 1.2.

7. Click the **Type tool** T, click inside the new frame, then type **LOCATION** in all caps.

8. In the Control panel, center the text, set the typeface to Hobo Std Medium, set the type size to 60 pt, then set the Horizontal Scale to 75%.

9. Enter **[Ctrl][B]**(Win) or **[Command][B]**(Mac) to open the Text Frame Options dialog box, click the **Align list arrow**, click **Bottom**, then click **OK**.

10. Deselect, then compare your text to Figure 30.

11. Click the **Selection Tool** , press and hold **[Shift][Alt]**(Win) or **[Shift][Option]**(Mac), then drag and drop a **copy of the text frame** anywhere straight down below the original.

(continued)

Figure 30 *Formatted headline on a master page*

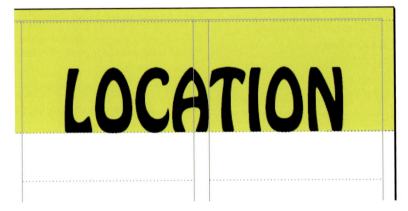

Figure 31 *Formatted sub-headline on a master page*

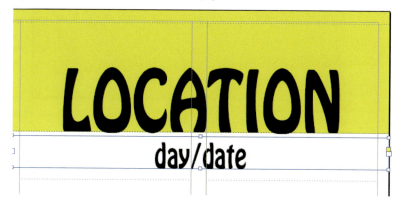

Figure 32 *The inserted page number*

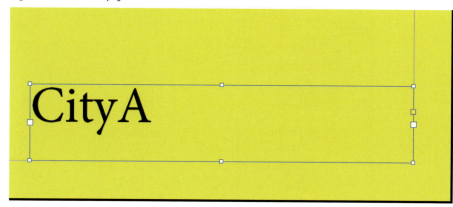

12. Click the **Type tool** T , select the duplicated text, reduce the type size to 24 pt, then type **day/date** in all lowercase letters.

13. Click the **Selection tool** , then verify that the bottom-center reference point in the Control panel is selected.

14. Type **1.75** in the Y text box, type **.35** in the Height text box, then compare your layout to Figure 31.

15. Save your work.

You created and positioned two text frames on the master page, then formatted text in each.

Create automatic page numbering and insert white space between characters

1. Click the **Type tool** T , draw a text frame anywhere in the lower-right corner of the spread, set its width to 1.25", then set its height to .25".

2. Position the textframe in the lower-right corner of the spread, inside the margin guide.

3. Type the word **City** in the textframe with no space after the word, choose any typeface and size you like, then verify that the text cursor is blinking to the right of the word.

4. Click **Type** on the Application bar, point to **Insert Special Character**, point to **Markers**, then click **Current Page Number**.

   As shown in Figure 32, the letter A appears in the text frame. This letter will change on document pages to reflect the current document page. For example, on page 4, the A will appear as the number 4.

(continued)

5. Click the cursor between the y and the A, click **Type** on the Application bar, point to **Insert White Space**, then click **Em Space**.

6. In the Control panel, set the text to Align Right, click **Object** on the Application bar, click **Text Frame Options**, then set the Vertical Justification to Bottom.

   Your text box should resemble Figure 33.

7. Copy the **selected text frame**, paste it in place, click the **bottom-left reference point** on the Control panel, then change the X value to .125.

   The text frame moves to the left page, inside the margin guide.

8. Reformat the text so that the copied text frame resembles Figure 34.

TIP You copy/paste the Em Space just like any other character.

9. Save your work.

You created automatic page numbering on the right and left pages of the master page and inserted em spaces.

Create a new master page spread based on another master page spread

1. Expand the Pages panel if necessary, click the **Pages panel options button**, then click **New Master**.

2. Click the **Based on Master list arrow**, click **A-Master**, then click **OK**.

   As shown in Figure 35, the B-Master page icons in the Pages panel display an A, because B-Master is based on A-Master.

(continued)

Figure 33 *Formatted text on the right-hand page*

Figure 34 *Reformatted text on the left-hand page*

Figure 35 *Viewing the new master in the Pages panel*

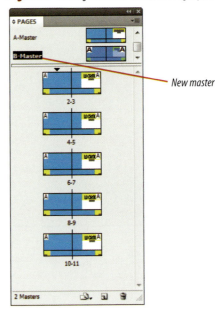

New master

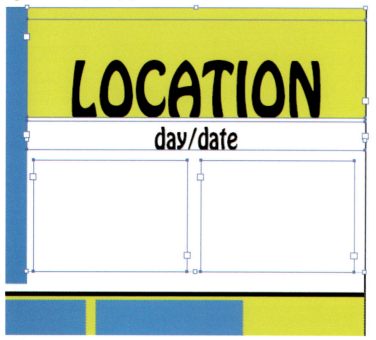

Figure 36 *Selecting specific page elements*

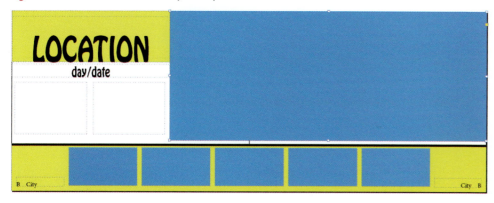

Figure 37 *Five frames centered horizontally on the spread*

3. Double-click the words **B-Master** in the Pages panel to view the B-Master master page.

   If necessary, fit spread in window. B-Master is identical to A-Master, except that the automatic page number reads B rather than A.

4. Hide guides.

5. Click the **Selection tool** , then try to select objects on the page.

   Objects on a master page based on another master cannot be selected in the standard way.

6. Press and hold **[Shift][Ctrl]**(Win) or **[Shift] [Command]**(Mac), then drag a marquee to select all the elements above the black horizontal line, except the large blue frame, as shown in Figure 36.

TIP Make sure you start dragging on the pasteboard and not on the document or you might accidentally select and move an object on the master.

7. Click the **middle-left reference point** on the Control panel, then set the X value to 0.

8. Select the **large blue frame**, click the **middle-right reference point** on the Control panel, then set the X value to 12.5.

   Your B-Master spread should resemble Figure 37.

9. Save your work.

You created a new master spread based on the A-Master spread. You modified the location of elements on the new master to differentiate it from the original.

Create a new blank master page spread

1. Click the **Pages panel options button**, then click **New Master**.

2. Click the **Based on Master list arrow**, then verify that None is selected so that your New Master dialog box resembles Figure 38.

3. Click **OK**.

   C-Master appears as two blank (white) page thumbnails in the Pages panel.

4. Double-click the words **A-Master** in the top part of the Pages panel to view the A-Master spread, select all, then copy.

5. Double-click **C-Master** to view the C-Master spread, click **Edit** on the Application bar, click **Paste in Place**, then deselect all.

   As shown in Figure 39, the A-Master layout is pasted into the C-Master spread. The only change is that the automatic page numbering reads C.

6. Click the **Selection tool** ➤, if necessary, then select the five blue frames at the bottom of the page as well as the yellow frame behind them.

   Because C-Master is not based on A-Master, the items are not locked.

7. Click the **top-center reference point** on the Control panel, then set the Y value to 0.

8. Click **Object** on the Application bar, then click **Hide**.

   (continued)

Figure 38 *New Master dialog box*

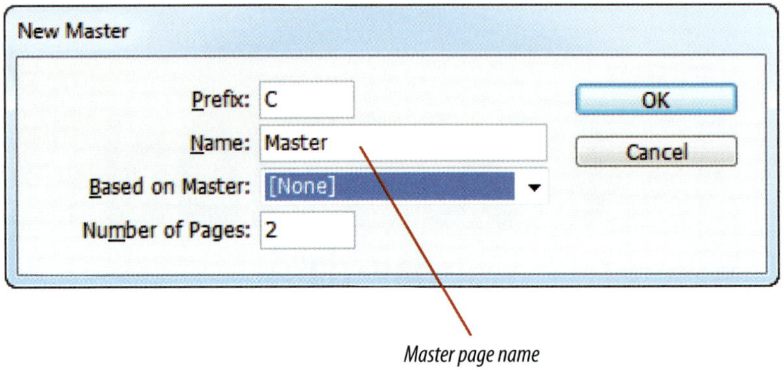

New Master

Prefix: C
Name: Master
Based on Master: [None]
Number of Pages: 2

OK
Cancel

Master page name

Figure 39 *A-Master pasted into C-Master*

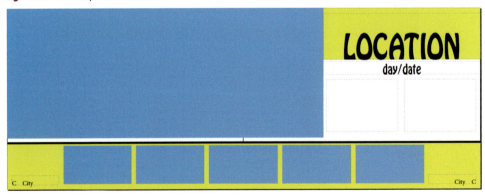

LOCATION
day/date

C City
City C

9. Select all the objects above the horizontal black line, click the **bottom-center reference point** on the Control panel, then set the Y value to 4.75.

10. Delete the **automatic numbering text frame** at the bottom of the right-hand page.

   Pages based on C-Master will have page numbers only on the left page of the spread.

11. Show the hidden frames, then deselect all.

12. Select the large yellow frame at the top of the page, click the **bottom-center reference point** on the Control panel, then note the Y value.

13. Select the horizontal black line, then set the Y value to be the same as that of the large yellow frame.

   Your C-Master spread should resemble Figure 40.

14. Save your work.

You created a new blank master spread not based on any other master. You modified the location of elements on the new master to differentiate it from the original.

Figure 40 *Modified layout in C-Master*

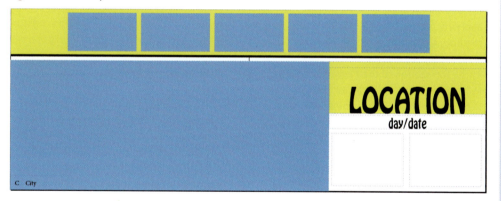

Apply Master Pages
TO DOCUMENT PAGES

What You'll Do

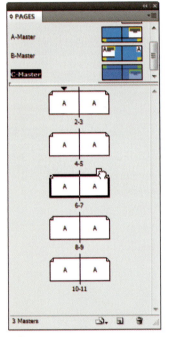

 In this lesson, you will apply master pages to document pages.

Applying Master Pages to Document Pages

Once you have created master pages, you then use the Pages panel to apply them to the document pages. One method for applying master pages is the "drag and drop" method. Using this method, you drag the master page icon or the master page name, in the top section of the Pages panel, down to the page icons in the lower section of the Pages panel. To apply the master to a single page, you drag the master onto the page icon, as shown in Figure 41. To apply the master to a spread, you drag the master onto one of the four corners of the left and right page icons until you see a dark border around both pages in the spread, as shown in Figure 42.

When you apply a master page to a document page, the document page inherits all of the layout characteristics of the master.

> **QUICK TIP**
>
> You can apply the default None master page to a document page when you want the document page not to be based on a master.

A second method for applying master pages to document pages is to use the Apply Master to Pages command on the Pages panel menu. The Apply Master dialog box, shown in Figure 43, allows you to specify which master you want to apply to which pages. This method is a good choice when you want to apply a master to a series of consecutive pages—it's faster than dragging and dropping.

Figure 41 *Applying C-Master to Page 2*

Figure 42 *Applying C-Master to Pages 2 & 3*

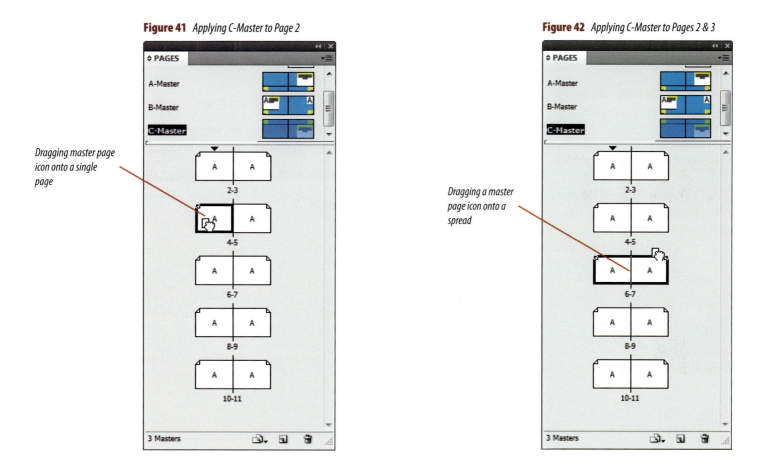

Dragging master page icon onto a single page

Dragging a master page icon onto a spread

Figure 43 *Using the Apply Master dialog box*

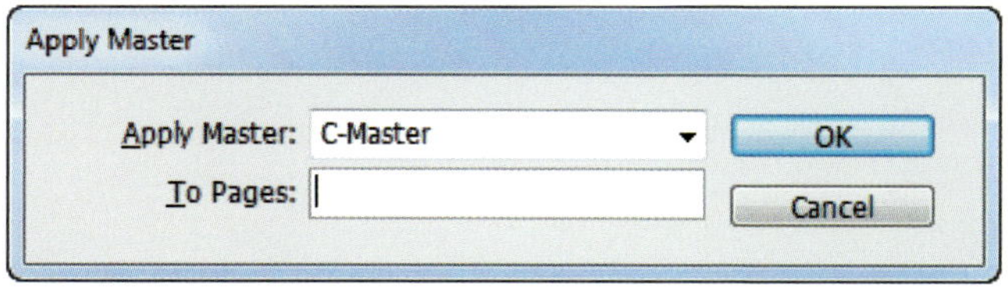

Apply master pages to document pages

1. Click the **Pages panel options button**, then click **Panel Options**.

2. Verify that your Pages section matches Figure 44, then click **OK**.

   Because the three master pages are similar in color, having thumbnails hidden and page icons showing will make it easier to see which masters have been applied to which spreads.

3. Scroll through the document and note that the A-Master has been automatically applied to all the pages in the document.

   (continued)

Figure 44 *Panel Options dialog box*

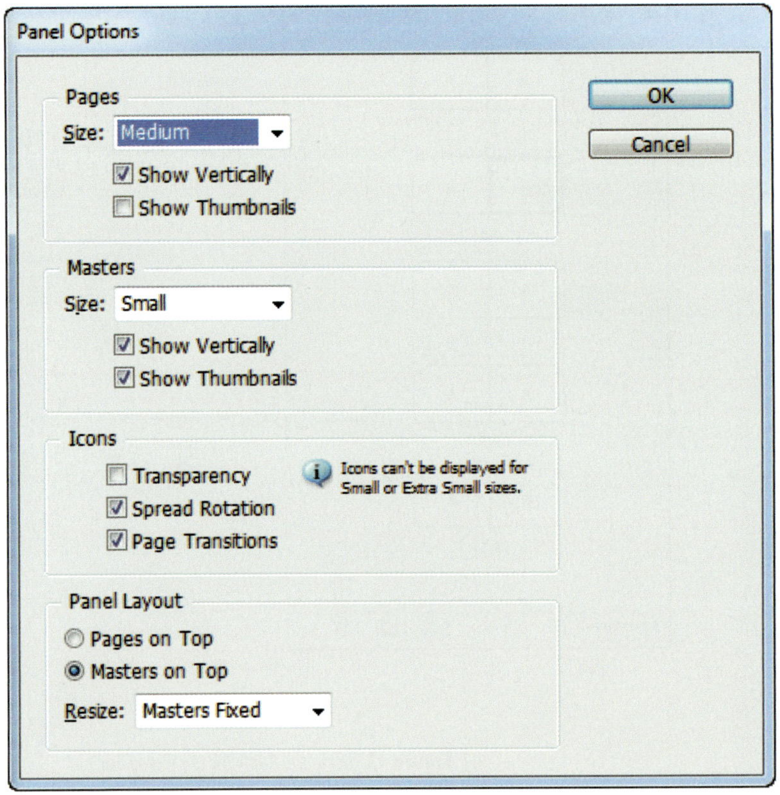

Setting Up a Document

Figure 45 *Applying the master to the document spread*

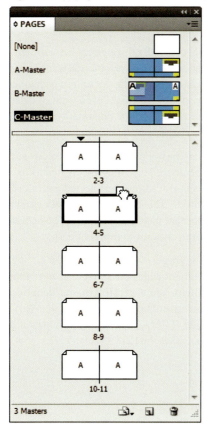

Figure 46 *Pages panel reflecting applied masters*

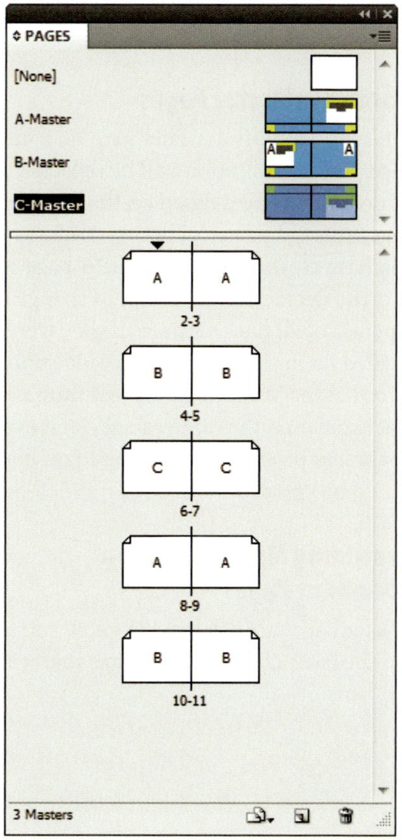

4. In the Pages panel, drag **B-Master** to the upper-right corner of spread 4-5 until a black frame appears around both thumbnails, as shown in Figure 45, then release your mouse.

5. Using the same method, apply the C-Master to spread 6-7.

6. Click the **Pages panel options button**, then click **Apply Master to Pages**.

7. Click the **Apply Master list arrow**, then click **B-Master**.

8. Type **10-11** in the pages text box, then click **OK**.

    The master is applied to the spread. Your Pages panel should resemble Figure 46.

9. Navigate to page 2, then switch to Presentation mode.

10. Navigate through the spreads to see the masters applied and the automatic page numbering.

11. Exit Presentation mode, then save your work.

You applied master spreads to document spreads using the drag-and-drop method and the Apply Master dialog box.

Modify Master Pages
AND DOCUMENT PAGES

What You'll Do

▶ *In this lesson, you will make modifications to both master pages and document pages and explore how each affects the other.*

Modifying Master Pages

When you modify a master item on a master page, that modification will be reflected on all document pages based on that master page. This is a powerful option. Let's say that you have created a layout for a 36-page book, and you decide that you want to change the typeface of all the headlines. If they were created on master pages, you could simply reformat the headline in the text frame placeholder on the master pages, and every document page in the book based on it would be updated.

Overriding Master Items on Document Pages

Master pages are designed to allow you to lay out the basic elements for a page that will be used repeatedly throughout a document. In most cases, however, you will want to make modifications to the document page once it is created—you might even want to delete some objects on the document page that were created on the master page.

When master page items are first created on a document page, they are created as fixed objects and cannot be selected with normal methods. This is to protect master items on document pages, but there will be occasions where you want to modify them.

Modifying a master page item on a document page is referred to as **overriding** the item. You override a master item by pressing and holding [Shift][Ctrl] (Win) or [Shift]⌘ (Mac), then clicking a master item. This makes the item selectable.

You very well might find that fixed master items on document pages are annoying! Long after the master page has served its purpose, you will find—especially with long documents—that the inability to just simply select master items with the Selection tool impedes your progress. You can quickly override all master items on a targeted document page on the Pages panel options menu, by clicking Override All Master Page Items.

Making changes to a document page is often referred to as making a local change. When you override a master item, that item nevertheless maintains its status as a master item and will still be updated with changes to the master page. For example, if you resize a master item on a document page, but you do not change its color, it will retain its new size, but if the color of the master item is changed on the master page, the master item's color will be updated on the document page.

Once a master item has been released from its fixed position, it remains selectable. You can return a master item on a document page back to its original state by selecting the item, clicking the Pages panel options button, then clicking Remove Selected Local Overrides.

Detaching Master Items

When you are sure you no longer want a master item to be affected by updates made to the associated master page, you can detach a master item. To detach a master item, you must first override it by pressing and holding [Shift][Ctrl] (Win) or [Shift] [⌘] (Mac) while selecting it. Next, click the Pages panel options button, then click Detach Selection From Master.

That's the official move. Note though, that when you modify text in a text frame on a document page, the relationship between the text on the document page and the text on the master page tends to detach automatically. Therefore, when it comes to text, it's a smart idea to use master pages for the placement of text frames on the page, but use character and paragraph styles for global formatting of the text itself.

Override master items on a document page

1. Verify that the document has been saved.

2. Double-click the **page 3 icon** on the Pages panel, click the **Selection tool** ➤ , then try to select any objects on the page.

   Because all objects on page 3 are master items, they're fixed and can't be selected with standard methods.

3. Press and hold **[Shift][Ctrl]** (Win) or **[Shift]** ⌘ (Mac), then click the word **LOCATION**.

4. Click the **Type tool** T , select the text, type **MANAROLA**, then click the **pasteboard** to deselect.

5. Save your work.

You overrode a master item on a document page.

Modify master items on a master page

1. View the right-hand page in the A-Master, select the word city, the Em Space, and the Automatic Page icon, then change the type size and typeface to 12 pt Garamond.

2. Select only the word City, then change its typeface to Garamond Italic.

   Your text should resemble Figure 47.

   (continued)

Figure 47 *Modifying text on a master page*

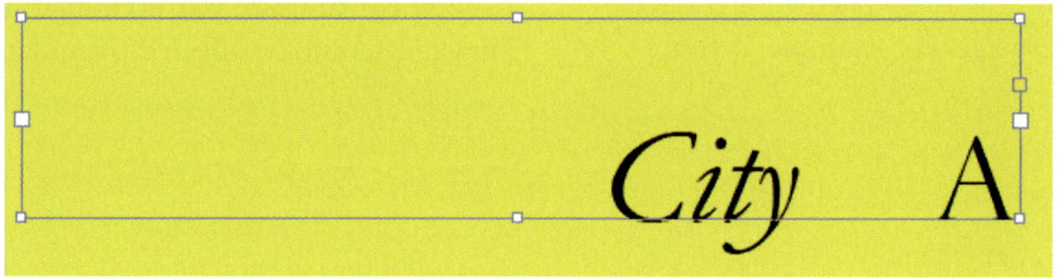

Figure 48 *Stroke button in the Swatches panel*

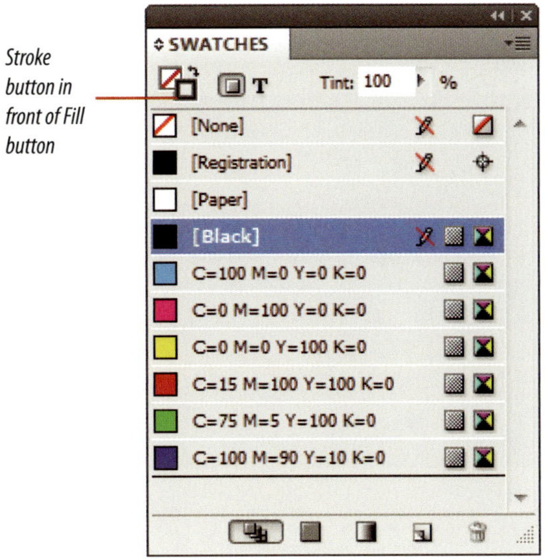

Stroke button in front of Fill button

3. Make the same changes to the text on the bottom of the left-hand page of the spread.

4. Double-click the word **LOCATION** to select it, click the **Swatches panel**, then click **Paper**.

   The Fill color of the text changes to white.

5. Click the **Selection tool** ▶ , then select the two yellow frames on the page.

6. Click the **Swatches panel**, then click the **green swatch**.

   The fill changes to green.

7. Select the black horizontal line, then click the **Stroke button** ☰ at the top of the Swatches panel so that it is in front of the Fill button, as shown in Figure 48.

   (continued)

8. Click the **red swatch**, then compare your layout to Figure 49.

9. Double-click **B-Master**.

   All of the changes you made to A-Master, except one, are reflected on B-Master because B-Master was created based on A-Master. Note though that the headline on B-Master is still black. Type tends to behave unpredictably on master pages. The fact that this frame has been relocated from its original position when it was created as a duplicate of A-Master might explain why it didn't update.

10. Double-click **C-Master** to view the spread.

    None of the changes from A-Master affect C-Master.

11. View spread 8-9.

    All of the changes you made on the master page, including the white headline, are reflected on the spread. No items on this page have been touched since the page was created.

12. View spread 2-3.

    All of the changes you made on the master page, except the white headline, are reflected on the spread.

You modified document pages by editing text within text frames created from master items.

Figure 49 *A-Master modifications*

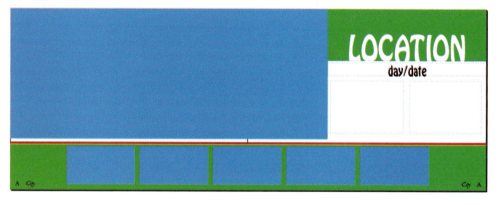

Remove local overrides and detach master items

1. View spread 10-11, then select the large blue frame.

2. Click the **Pages panel options button**, then click **Detach Selection from Master**.

3. Double-click **B-Master**, then change the fill color on the large blue frame to red.

4. Double-click **page 4** in the Pages panel, then scroll through the document to note the changes.

   The change is reflected on spread 4-5, but not on spread 10-11.

5. Navigate to page 3 in the document, then select the text frame of MANAROLA.

6. Click the **Pages panel options button**, then click **Remove Selected Local Overrides**.

   The modified headline changes to reflect that which is on the A-Master, as shown in Figure 50.

7. Save your work, then close Setup.indd.

You detached a frame from its master. You then modified the master, noting that the change did not affect the detached frame. You selected a modified master item on a document page, then used the Remove Selected Local Overrides command to restore the item's relationship to its master.

Figure 50   *Change reflected on spread 4-5*

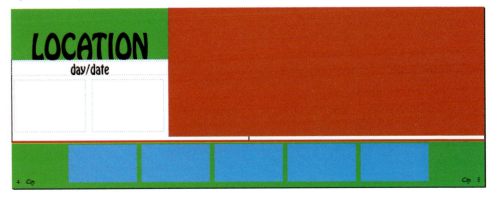

Place
AND THREAD TEXT

What You'll Do

tuesday august 9

Lorem ipsum dolor sit amet, consect
etuer adipiscing elit, sed diam no
nummy nibh euismod tincidunt ut
laoreet dolore magna aliquam
volutpat. Ut wisi enim ad
veniam, quis nostrud exerci
ullamcorper suscipit lobortis
aliquip ex ea commodo conseq
Duis autem vel eum iriure dolor
hendrerit in vulputate velit esse
molestie consequat, vel illum dolore

In this lesson, you will place text, thread text from frame to frame, then view text threads.

Placing Text

Once you have created a text frame—either on a master page or on a document page—you can type directly into the frame, or you can place text from another document into it. When creating headlines, you usually type them directly into the text frame. When creating body copy, however, you will often find yourself placing text from another document, usually a word processing document.

Placing text in InDesign is simple and straightforward. Click the Place command on the File menu, which opens the Place dialog box. Find the text document that you want to place, then click Open.

The pointer changes to the loaded text icon. With a loaded text icon, you can drag to create a text frame or click inside an existing text frame. Position the loaded text icon over an existing text frame, and the icon appears in parentheses, as shown in Figure 51. The parentheses indicate that you can click to place the text into the text frame. Do so, and the text flows into the text frame, as shown in Figure 52.

QUICK TIP

The loaded text icon displays a thumbnail image of the first few lines of text that is being placed. This helps to make sure you are placing the correct file.

Figure 51 *Loaded text icon positioned over a text frame*

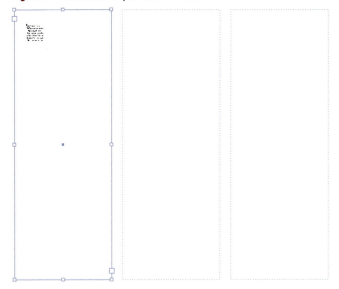

Figure 52 *Text placed into a text frame*

Text placed in text frame

Threading Text

InDesign provides many options for **threading text**—linking text from one text frame to another. Text frames have an **in port** and an **out port**. When threading text, you use the text frame ports to establish connections between the text frames.

In Figure 53, the center text frame is selected, and the in port and out port are identified. The in port represents where text would

flow into the text frame, and the out port represents from where text would flow out.

In the same figure, note that the out port on the first text frame is red and has a plus sign in its center. This indicates the presence of **overset text**—more text than can fit in the frame.

To thread text manually from the first to the second text frame, first click the Selection tool, then click the frame with the overset

text so that the frame is highlighted. Next, click the out port of the text frame. When you position your cursor over the next text frame, the cursor changes to the link icon, as shown in Figure 54. Click the link icon and the text flows into the frame, as shown in Figure 55. When the Show Text Threads command on the View menu is activated, a blue arrow appears between any two text frames that have been threaded, as shown in Figure 56.

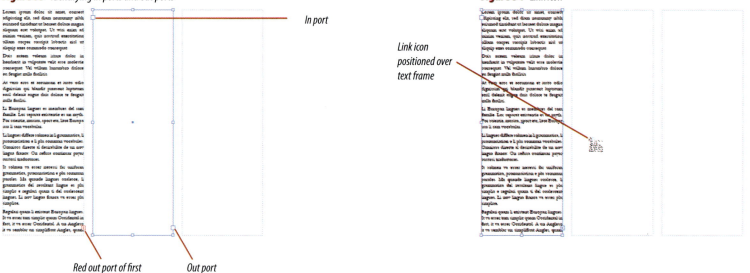

Figure 53 *Identifying in ports and out ports*

In port

Red out port of first text frame indicates overset text

Out port

Figure 54 *Link icon*

Link icon positioned over text frame

Figure 55 *Threading text between frames*

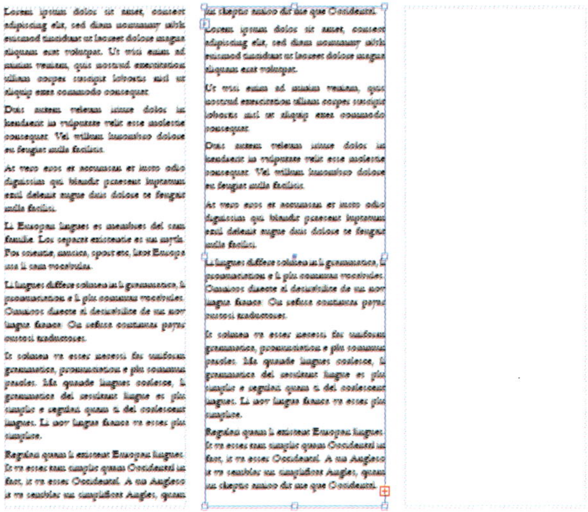

Figure 56 *Showing text threads*

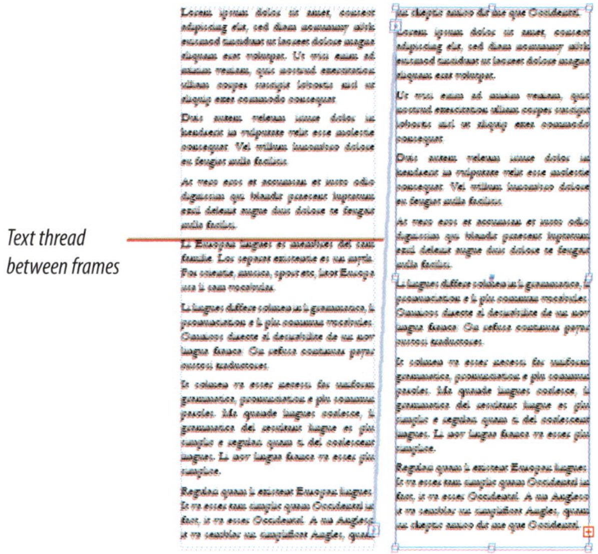

Text thread
between frames

Using Smart Text Reflow

Smart Text Reflow is a feature that adds pages automatically to an InDesign document when you edit text in InDesign. The only requirement for Smart Text Reflow to work is that the text frame you are editing must already have at least one text thread to another text frame. For example, you can add text to a text frame that is already threaded to another and if you add more text than will fit the frame, a new page will be automatically added to accommodate the reflowed text. The reverse is also true. If you delete text from a text frame, pages that are no longer necessary will automatically be deleted. To work with Smart Text Reflow, open the Type Preferences dialog box, then verify that the Smart Text Reflow check box is checked. Be sure to remove the check mark in the Limit to Master Text Frames check box if you are not using text frames on the master pages. Otherwise, this feature will only work if you create a text frame on the master page.

Place text on document pages

1. Open ID3-2.indd, then save it as **Wraps and Sections.indd**.

   This data file has the same parameters as the document you created at the start of this chapter. The only changes are that the local document pages have been colorized and the headlines and dates have been filled in. Also, small blue frames are positioned over the text frames on each spread.

2. Click the **Workspace switcher**, then click **Typography**.

3. Double-click the **page 3 icon** on the Pages panel to go to page 3.

4. Click **File** on the Application bar, click **Place**, navigate to the drive and folder where your Data Files are stored, then double-click **Greek text**.

5. Point to the interior of the **left text frame**.

   As shown in Figure 57, the loaded text icon appears in parentheses, signalling that you can insert the loaded text into the text frame.

6. Click the loaded text icon in the left text frame.

   As shown in Figure 58, text flows into the frame. The red out port with the plus sign indicates that there is overset text—more text than can fit in the text frame.

   (continued)

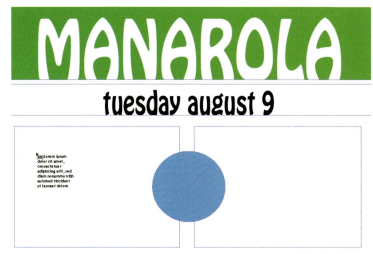

Figure 57 *Loaded text icon*

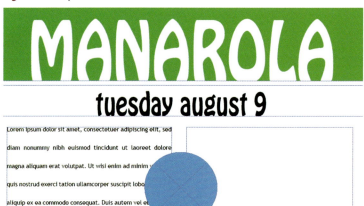

Figure 58 *Text placed into a frame*

Setting Up a Document

Figure 59 *Loaded text icon with a link icon*

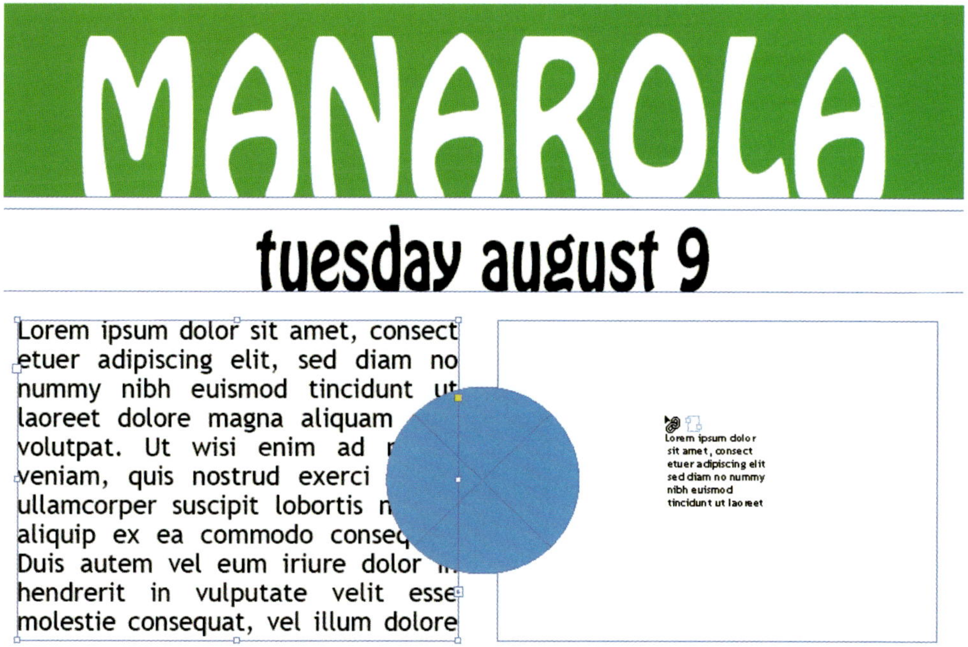

7. Click the **Type tool**, click **any word** five times to select all the text in the frame, set the typeface to Garamond, set the type size to 8 pt, set the leading to 9 pt, then set the alignment to Justify with last line aligned left.

TIP Clicking five times selects even the text that is not currently visible in the frame. If you only select the text that is visible, only that text will be affected by your format change.

8. Click the **Selection tool**, click the **red out port**, then position the loaded text icon over the right text frame.

   As shown in Figure 59, a link icon appears in the loaded text icon, indicating you are about to flow text from one frame to another. The red out port turns blue when you click it.

TIP To unlink text frames, double-click the blue out port.

(continued)

9. Click in the right text frame.

   As shown in Figure 60, the text flows into the right text frame, and a new red out port appears at the bottom-right of the right frame.

You used the Place command to load text into a text frame, then threaded text from that frame into another.

Thread text through multiple text frames

1. Click **View** on the Application bar, point to **Extras**, then click **Show Text Threads** if necessary.

   With the Show Text Threads command activated, blue arrows appear between threaded text frames when they are selected.

2. Reduce the view of the document to 75% so that you can see more than one spread in your monitor window.

3. Click the **Selection tool** , then click the **out port** of the right text frame.

   The loaded text icon appears.

4. Scroll so that you can see both page 3 & 4 in the monitor window.

   (continued)

Figure 60 *Text flowed from one frame to another*

Lorem ipsum dolor sit amet, consectetuer adipiscing elit, sed diam nonummy nibh euismod tincidunt ut laoreet dolore magna aliquam volutpat. Ut wisi enim ad veniam, quis nostrud exerci ullamcorper suscipit lobortis aliquip ex ea commodo conseq Duis autem vel eum iriure dolor hendrerit in vulputate velit esse molestie consequat, vel illum dolore

eu feugiat nulla facilisis at vero eros et accumsan et iusto odio dignissim qui blandit praesent luptatum zzril it augue duis dolore te feugait facilisi. Ut wisi enim ad minim , quis nostrud exerci tation orper suscipit lobortis nisl ut p ex ea commodo consequat. uis autem vel eum iriure dolor in hendrerit in vulputate velit esse molestie consequat, vel illum dolore

Mapping Style Names when Importing Word or RTF Files

When you place a Word document or RTF text in InDesign you have a number of options to choose from regarding how text is imported. After you click Place on the File menu and find the Word or RTF document that you want to place, click the Show Import Options check box, then click Open. The Import Options dialog box opens. In this dialog box you can choose to include or not include footnotes, endnotes, table of contents text, and index text. You can also choose to remove any previous styles applied to text, and any table formatting. Conversely you can opt to retain styles and table formatting applied to incoming text. You can import styles automatically by clicking the Import Styles Automatically option button and then tell InDesign how to deal with conflicts when incoming styles have the same names as existing styles in InDesign. Finally, you can map style names from the placed text file to specific styles in InDesign by clicking the Customize Style Import option button, then clicking the Style Mapping button. The Style Mapping dialog box opens and allows you to choose which InDesign style to map to each incoming text style. For example, you can specify that the Normal style in Word is mapped to the [Basic Paragraph] style in InDesign.

Figure 61 *Text threads showing text flowing from one spread to another*

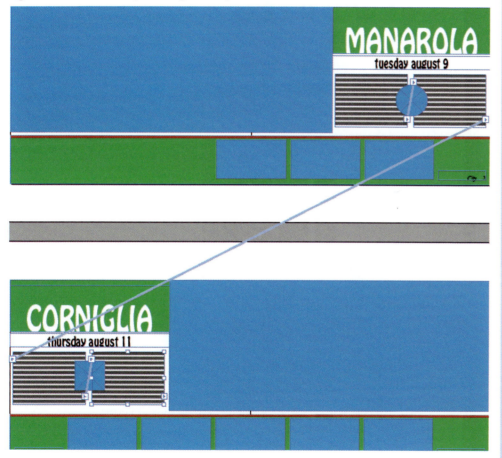

5. Press and hold **[Alt]**(Win) or **[Option]**(Mac), position the loaded text icon over the left text frame on page 4, click, and do not release the **[Alt]/[Option] key**.

   With the Alt/Option key pressed, the loaded text icon remains active. To continue threading, you don't need to click the out port of the left text frame.

6. Position the pointer over the right text frame, then click.

   As shown in Figure 61, the text is threaded through both frames on page 4.

7. Using the same process, thread text through the remaining pages of the document. When you're done threading. It's OK that you will still have loaded text.

8. Save your work.

You used a keyboard command to thread text more quickly and easily between multiple text frames.

Create New Sections
AND WRAP TEXT

What You'll Do

In this lesson, you will create two different numbering sections and create two text wraps around graphics frames.

Creating Sections in a Document

Sections are pages in a document where page numbering changes. For example, sometimes in the front pages of a book, in the introduction or the preface, the pages will be numbered with lowercase Roman numerals, then normal page numbering will begin with the first chapter.

You can create as many sections in a document as you wish. You determine the page on which the new section will start by clicking that page icon on the Pages panel. Choose the Numbering & Section Options command on the Pages panel menu, which opens the New Section dialog box, shown in Figure 62.

QUICK TIP

The first time you choose a type of page numbering for a document, the Numbering & Section Options dialog box opens instead of the New Section dialog box.

Figure 62 *New Section dialog box*

New section will begin with this number

Numbering in the new section will have this style

Setting Up a Document

Wrapping Text Around a Frame

When you position a text frame or a graphics frame near another frame that contains text, you can apply a text wrap to the overlapping frame in order to force the underlying text to wrap around it. InDesign offers many options for wrapping text around a frame. One quick method is to click the Wrap around bounding box button on the Text Wrap panel, shown in Figure 63.

Figure 64 shows a rectangular frame using the No text wrap option on the Text Wrap panel. Figure 65 shows that same frame using the Wrap around bounding box option on the Text Wrap panel.

QUICK TIP

To turn off text wrap in a text frame, select the text frame, click Object on the Application bar, click Text Frame Options, click the Ignore Text Wrap check box, and then click OK.

When you choose the Wrap around bounding box option, you can control the **offset**—the distance that text is repelled from the frame—by entering values in the Top, Bottom, Left, and Right Offset text boxes on the panel. Figure 66 shows the frame with a .125-inch offset applied to all four sides of the frame.

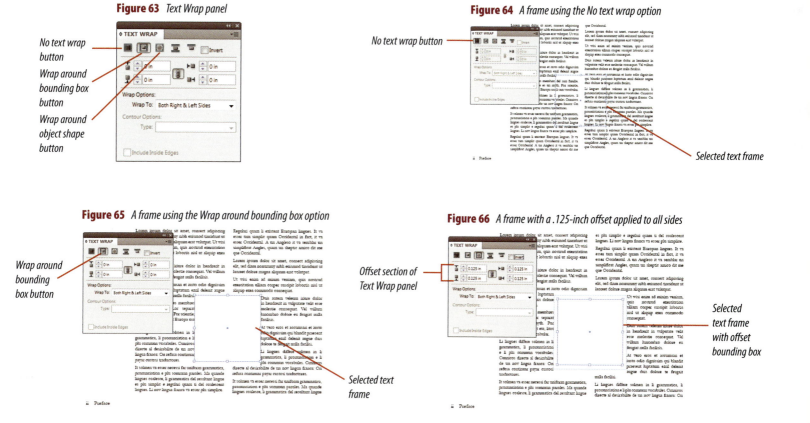

Figure 63 *Text Wrap panel*

No text wrap button

Wrap around bounding box button

Wrap around object shape button

Figure 64 *A frame using the No text wrap option*

No text wrap button

Selected text frame

Figure 65 *A frame using the Wrap around bounding box option*

Wrap around bounding box button

Selected text frame

Figure 66 *A frame with a .125-inch offset applied to all sides*

Offset section of Text Wrap panel

Selected text frame with offset bounding box

Create sections in a document

1. Double-click the **page 8 icon** on the Pages panel.

   The document has been designed so that page 8 represents a new section in the document. The color theme changes to red, and the city is Firenze.

2. Click the **Pages panel options button**, then click **Numbering and Section Options**.

   The dialog box opens as New Section.

3. Verify that Start Section is checked.

4. Click the **Start Page Numbering at option**, then type **2**.

   Your Dialog box should resemble Figure 67. With these choices, you are starting a new section at page 8, renumbered as page 2.

   (continued)

Figure 67 *New Section dialog box*

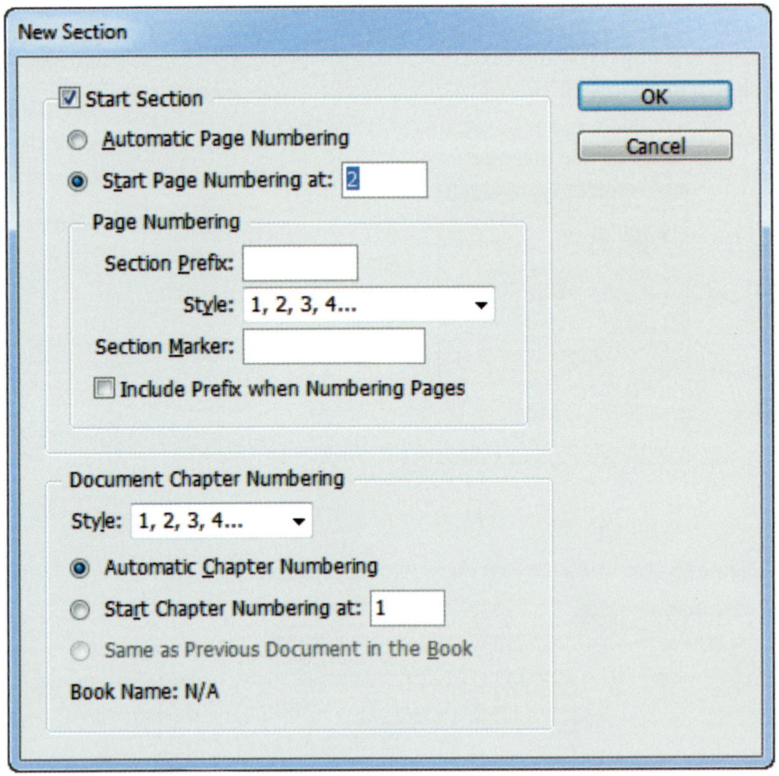

Setting Up a Document

Figure 68 *Viewing renumbered pages in the Pages panel*

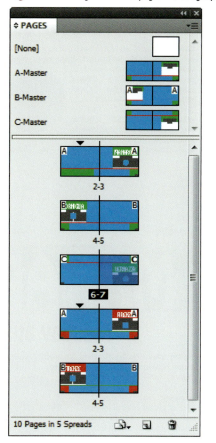

5. Click **OK**, then compare your Pages panel to Figure 68.

TIP If you get a Warning that a page number in this section already exists in another section, click OK.

The pages are renumbered. Spread 8-9 is now spread 2-3.

6. Note that the automatic page numbering has updated to reflect the new numbering in the new section.

7. Save the file.

You used the New Section dialog box to change the sequence of the automatic page numbering in the document.

Wrap text around a frame

1. Double-click the **original Page 3 icon** on the Pages panel, click the **Selection tool** , then select the small blue **ellipse frame**.

2. Show the Text Wrap panel.

3. Click the **Wrap around bounding box button** at the top of the panel.

   The text wraps around the rectangular bounding box, as shown in Figure 69.

4. Click the **Wrap around object shape button** , then type **.125** in the Top Offset text box on the Text Wrap panel.

   The text wraps around the ellipse, as shown in Figure 70.

5. Navigate to page 4, select the small blue rectangular frame, then click the **Wrap around bounding box button** on the Text Wrap panel.

6. Click the **Make all settings the same button** to deactivate it if necessary.

   The deactivated Make all settings the same button looks like this: .

(continued)

Figure 69 *Text wrapped around the ellipse's bounding box*

Figure 70 *Text wrapped around the object shape*

7. Set the Top Offset text box and the Bottom Offset text box to 0.

8. Set the Left Offset text box and the Right Offset text box to .08.

9. Compare your result to Figure 71.

10. Save your work, then close Wraps and Sections.

You used the Text Wrap panel to flow text around two graphics frames.

Figure 71 *Text wrapped at different offset values*

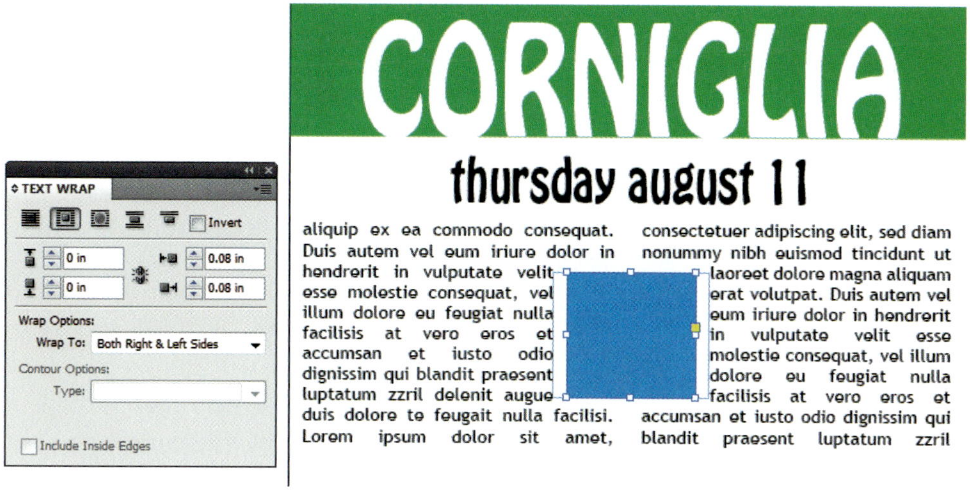

Create a new document and set up a master page.

1. Start Adobe InDesign.
2. Without creating a new document, click Edit (Win) or InDesign (Mac) on the Application bar, point to Preferences, then click Guides & Pasteboard.
3. In the Guide Options section, click the Guides in Back check box to select, if necessary, click Units & Increments in the Preferences list in left side of the dialog box, verify that the horizontal and vertical ruler units are set to inches then click OK.
4. Click File on the Application bar, point to New, then click Document.
5. Type **8** in the Number of Pages text box, press [Tab], then verify that the Facing Pages check box is checked.
6. Type **5** in the Width text box, press [Tab], then type **5** in the Height text box.
7. Using [Tab] to move from one text box to another, type **1** in the Number text box in the Columns section.
8. Type **.25** in the Top, Bottom, Inside, and Outside Margins text boxes.
9. Click OK, then save the document as **Skills Review**.
10. Click the Workspace Switcher on the Application bar, then click Advanced, if necessary.
11. Double-click the words A-Master on the Pages panel to center both pages of the master in your window.

12. Click Window on the Application bar, point to Object & Layout, then click Transform.
13. Click the Selection tool, press and hold [Ctrl] (Win) or ⌘ (Mac), create a guide across the spread using the horizontal ruler, releasing the mouse pointer when the Y Location text box on the Transform panel reads 2.5 in.
14. Create a guide on the left page using the vertical ruler, releasing the mouse pointer when the X Location text box on the Transform panel reads 2.5 in.
15. Click Edit (Win) or InDesign (Mac) on the Application bar, point to Preferences, click Units & Increments, click the Origin list arrow, click Page, then click OK.
16. Create a vertical guide on the right page, releasing the mouse pointer when the X Location text box on the Transform panel reads 2.5 in.
17. Verify that the Fill and Stroke icons in the Tools panel are set to None, click the Rectangle Frame tool, then draw a rectangle anywhere on the left page.
18. Click the top-left reference point on the Transform panel.
19. With the rectangle frame selected, type **0** in the X Location text box on the Transform panel, type **0** in the Y Location text box, type **5** in the Width text box, type **5** in the Height text box, then press [Enter] (Win) or [return] (Mac).

20. Using the same method, create an identical rectangle on the right page.
21. Type **0** in the X Location text box on the Transform panel, type **0** in the Y Location text box, then press [Enter] (Win) or [return] (Mac).
22. Click the Pages panel option button, then click New Master.
23. Type **Body** in the Name text box, click the Based on Master list arrow, click A-Master, then click OK.
24. Click the Selection tool, press and hold [Shift][Ctrl] (Win) or [Shift] ⌘ (Mac), select both rectangle frames, then delete them.
25. Double-click B-Body on the Pages panel to center both pages of the master in your window.
26. Click Layout on the Application bar, then click Margins and Columns.
27. Type **2** in the Number text box in the Columns section, then click OK.

Create text on Master Pages.

1. Click the Type tool, create a text frame of any size anywhere in the right column on the left page, then click the Selection tool.
2. Verify that the top-left reference point is selected on the Transform panel, type **2.6** in the X Location text box, type **.25** in the Y Location text box, type **2.15** in

the Width text box, type **4.5** in the Height text box, then press [Enter] (Win) or [return] (Mac).

3. Click Edit on the Application bar, click Copy, click Edit on the Application bar again, then click Paste in Place.

4. Press and hold [Shift], then drag the copy of the text frame onto the right page, releasing the mouse button when it "snaps" into the left column on the right page.

5. Click the Type tool, then draw a small text box anywhere on the left page of the B-Body master.

6. Select the text frame, and verify that the top-left reference point is selected on the Transform panel, type **.25** in the X Location text box, type **4.5** in the Y Location text box, type **1.65** in the Width text box, type **.25** in the Height text box, then press [Enter] (Win) or [return] (Mac).

7. Select the Type tool, click in the text frame, click Type on the Application bar, point to Insert Special Character, point to Markers, then click Current Page Number.

8. Click Type on the Application bar, point to Insert Special Character, point to Hyphens and Dashes, then click En Dash.

9. Type the word **Title**.

10. Click the Selection tool, select the text frame if necessary, click Edit on the Application bar, click Copy, click Edit on the Application bar again, then click Paste in Place.

11. Press and hold [Shift], then drag the copy of the text frame so that it is positioned in the lower-right corner of the right page of the master page.

12. Open the Paragraph panel, click the Align right button, then delete the B and the dash after the B.

TIP Switch your workspace to Typography to access the Paragraph panel if necessary.

13. Click after the word Title, click Type on the Application bar, point to Insert Special Character, point to Hyphens and Dashes, then click En Dash.

14. Click Type on the Application bar, point to Insert Special Character, point to Markers, then click Current Page Number.

Apply master pages to document pages.

1. Double-click the page 2 icon on the Pages panel.

2. Drag the B-Body master page title to the bottom-left corner of the page 2 icon until you see a black rectangle around the page 2 and 3 icons, then release the mouse button.

3. Drag the word B-Body from the top of the Pages panel to the bottom-left corner of the page 4 icon until you see a black rectangle around the page 4 icon, then release the mouse button.

4. Click the Pages panel option button, then click Apply Master to Pages.

5. Click the Apply Master list arrow, click B-Body if necessary, type **6-8** in the To Pages text box, then click OK.

6. Double-click the page 2 icon on the Pages panel.

7. Hide guides.

Place and thread text.

1. Click File on the Application bar, click Place, navigate to the drive and folder where your Data Files are stored, then double-click Skills Review Text.

2. Click anywhere in the text frame in the right column on page 2.

3. Click View on the Application bar, point to Extras, then click Show Text Threads.

4. Click the Selection tool, then click the out port of the text frame on page 2.

5. Click the loaded text icon anywhere in the text frame on page 3.

Modify master pages and document pages.

1. Double-click the page 6 icon on the Pages panel.

2. Click the bottom-middle reference point on the Transform panel.

3. Click the Selection tool, press and hold [Shift][Ctrl] (Win) or [Shift] ⌘ (Mac), then click the large text frame.

4. Type **.3** in the Height text box on the Transform panel, then press [Enter] (Win) or [return] (Mac).

5. Double-click A-Master in the top of the Pages panel, then select the graphics placeholder frame on the left page.
6. Click the center reference point on the Transform panel.
7. On the Transform panel, type **3** in the Width text box, type **3** in the Height text box, then press [Enter] (Win) or [return] (Mac).
8. Double-click the right page icon of the A-Master on the Pages panel, then select the graphics placeholder frame on the right page.
9. On the Transform panel, type **2** in the Width text box, type **4** in the Height text box, then press [Enter] (Win) or [return] (Mac).
10. View the two right-hand pages on the Pages panel that are based on the A-Master right-hand page to verify that the modifications were updated.
11. Double-click B-Body on the Pages panel, click the Rectangle Frame tool, then create a frame anywhere on the left page of the B-Body master page.

12. Click the center reference point on the Transform panel, then type **2** in the X Location text box, type **2.6** in the Y Location text box, type **2.25** in the Width text box, type **1.5** in the Height text box, then press [Enter] (Win) or [return] (Mac).

Create new sections and wrap text.

1. Double-click the page 1 icon on the Pages panel, click the Pages panel options button, then click Numbering & Section Options.
2. In the Page Numbering section, click the Style list arrow, click the lower-case style letters (a, b, c, d), click OK, then note the changes to the pages on the Pages panel and in the document.
3. Double-click the page e icon on the Pages panel, click the Pages panel option button, then click Numbering & Section Options.
4. In the Page Numbering section, click the Start Page Numbering at option button, type **5** in the text box, then verify that the Style text box in the Page Numbering

section shows ordinary numerals (1, 2, 3, 4). (If it does not, click the Style list arrow and select that style.)
5. Click OK, then view the pages in the document, noting the new style of the page numbering on the pages and on the Pages panel.
6. Double-click the page b icon on the Pages panel, click the Selection tool, press and hold [Shift][Ctrl] (Win) or [Shift] ⌘ (Mac), then select the rectangular graphics frame.
7. Click Window on the Application bar, then click Text Wrap.
8. Click the Wrap around bounding box button on the Text Wrap panel.
9. Type **.125** in the Right Offset text box on the Text Wrap panel, then press [Enter] (Win) or [return] (Mac).
10. Click View on the Application bar, click Fit Spread in Window, then click anywhere to deselect any selected items.
11. Compare your screen to Figure 72, save your work, then close Skills Review.

Figure 72 *Completed Skills Review*

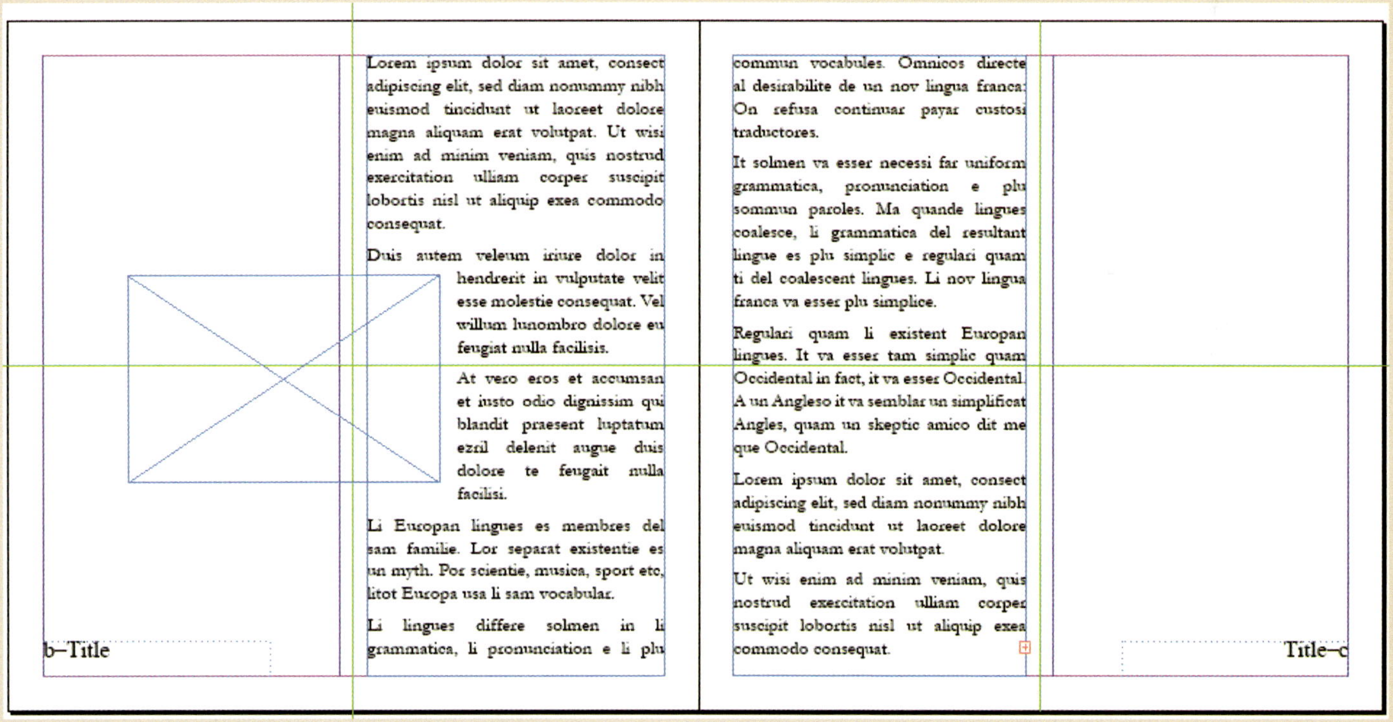

Lorem ipsum dolor sit amet, consect adipiscing elit, sed diam nonummy nibh euismod tincidunt ut laoreet dolore magna aliquam erat volutpat. Ut wisi enim ad minim veniam, quis nostrud exercitation ulliam corper suscipit lobortis nisl ut aliquip exea commodo consequat.

Duis autem veleum iriure dolor in hendrerit in vulputate velit esse molestie consequat. Vel willum lunombro dolore eu feugiat nulla facilisis.

At vero eros et accumsan et iusto odio dignissim qui blandit praesent luptatum ezril delenit augue duis dolore te feugait nulla facilisi.

Li Europan lingues es membres del sam familie. Lor separat existentie es un myth. Por scientie, musica, sport etc, litot Europa usa li sam vocabular.

Li lingues differe solmen in li grammatica, li pronunciation e li plu

commun vocabules. Omnicos directe al desirabilite de un nov lingua franca: On refusa continuar payar custosi traductores.

It solmen va esser necessi far uniform grammatica, pronunciation e plu sommun paroles. Ma quande lingues coalesce, li grammatica del resultant lingue es plu simplic e regulari quam ti del coalescent lingues. Li nov lingua franca va esser plu simplice.

Regulari quam li existent Europan lingues. It va esser tam simplic quam Occidental in fact, it va esser Occidental. A un Angleso it va semblar un simplificat Angles, quam un skeptic amico dit me que Occidental.

Lorem ipsum dolor sit amet, consect adipiscing elit, sed diam nonummy nibh euismod tincidunt ut laoreet dolore magna aliquam erat volutpat.

Ut wisi enim ad minim veniam, quis nostrud exercitation ulliam corper suscipit lobortis nisl ut aliquip exea commodo consequat.

b–Title

Title–c

You are a graphic designer working out of your home office. A local investment company has contracted you to design their monthly 16-page newsletter. You've sketched out a design and created a new document at the correct size, and now you need to add automatic page numbering to the document.

1. Open ID 3-3.indd, then save it as **Newsletter**.
2. Double-click A-Master on the Pages panel.
3. Click the Type tool, then draw a text frame about one inch tall and one column wide.
4. Position the text frame at the bottom of the center column, being sure that the bottom edge of the text frame snaps to the bottom margin of the page.
5. Set the Preference settings so that the guides are sent to the back of the layout—so that all four sides of the text frame are visible.
6. Click the Type tool, then click inside the text box.
7. Click Type on the Application bar, point to Insert Special Character, point to Hyphens and Dashes, then click Em Dash.
8. Click Type on the Application bar, point to Insert Special Character, point to Markers, then click Current Page Number.
9. Click Type on the Application bar, point to Insert Special Character, point to Hyphens and Dashes, then click Em Dash.
10. Select all three text elements and change their font size to 20 pt.
11. Click the Align center button on the Paragraph panel.
12. Click the dark blue swatch on the Swatches panel.

13. Click the Selection tool, click the bottom-center reference point on the Transform panel, double-click the Height text box on the Transform panel, type **.25**, then press [Enter] (Win) or [return] (Mac).

14. Double-click the page 5 icon on the Pages panel, compare your page 5 to Figure 73, save your work, then close Newsletter.

Figure 73 *Completed Project Builder 1*

You work in the design department for a bank, and you are responsible for creating a new weekly bulletin, which covers various events within the bank's network of branches. You have just finished creating three master pages for the bulletin, and now you are ready to apply the masters to the document pages.

1. Open ID 3-4.indd, then save it as **Bulletin Layout**.
2. Apply the B-Master to pages 2 and 3.
3. Click the Pages panel options button, then click Apply Master to Pages.
4. Apply the C-Master to pages 4 through 6, then click OK.
5. Place Bulletin text.doc in the text frame on page 1.
6. Select the text frame, click the out port on the text frame, double-click page 2 in the Pages panel, then click anywhere in the text frame on page 2.
7. Thread the remaining text through each page up to and including page 6 in the document.
8. Click the Preview button, deselect any selected items, then compare your page 6 to Figure 74.
9. Save your work, then close Bulletin Layout.

Figure 74 *Completed Project Builder 2*

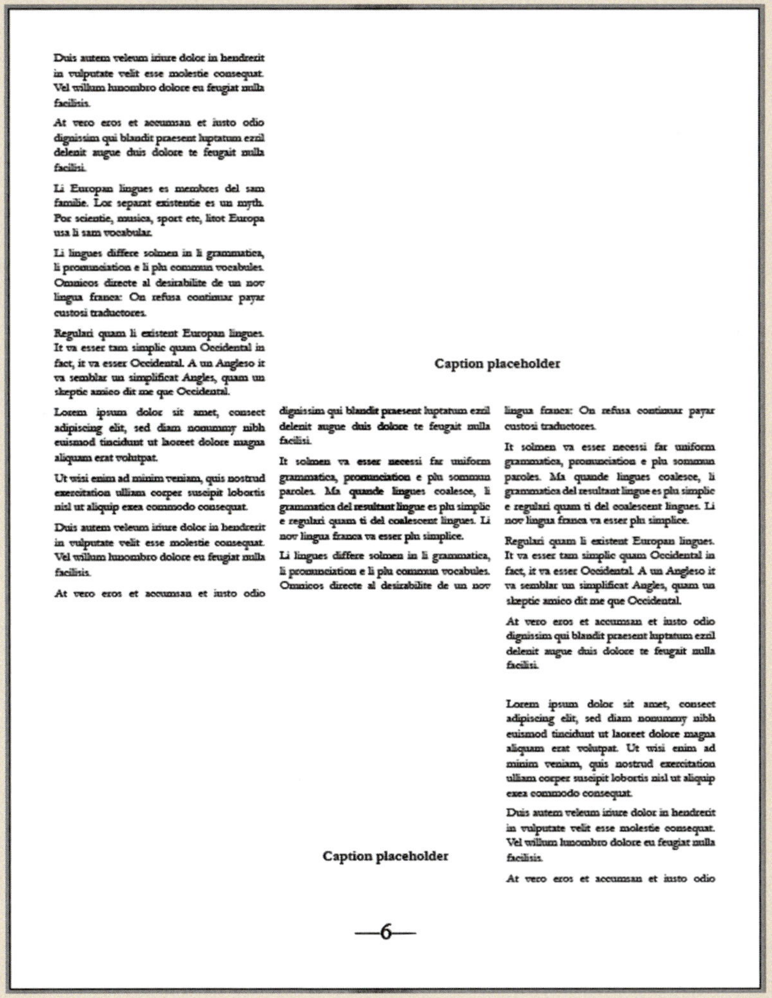

Your client has provided you with a page layout that she wants to use for the background of the design project for which she has hired you. Knowing that she'll want to use this background design for multiple pages, you decide to "tweak" her document to be sure that the background elements are the same size and are aligned evenly.

1. Open ID 3-5.indd, then save it as **Four Square**.
2. Click File on the Application bar, click Document Setup, note the width and height of the page, then close the Document Setup dialog box.
3. Hide the guides and the frame edges if necessary, then verify that only the Transform panel and the Tools panel are visible.
4. Click the Selection tool, then click the top-left reference point on the Transform panel.
5. Click the top-left square on the page, type **0** in the X Location text box, type **0** in the Y Location text box, type **7.75** in the Width text box, then press [Enter] (Win) or [return] (Mac).
6. Click to place the insertion point after the number 7.75 in the Width text box, type **/2**, then press [Tab].
7. Type **3.875** in the Height text box, then press [Enter] (Win) or [return] (Mac).
8. Click the top-right square, type **3.875** in the X Location text box, type **0** in the Y Location text box, type **3.875** in the Width and Height text boxes, then press [Enter] (Win) or [return] (Mac).
9. Click the lower-left square, type **0** in the X Location text box, type **3.875** in the Y Location text box, type **3.875** in the Width and Height text boxes, then press [Enter] (Win) or [return] (Mac).
10. Click the lower-right square, type **3.875** in the X Location text box, type **3.875** in the Y Location text box, type **3.875** in the Width and Height text boxes, press [Enter] (Win) or [return] (Mac), then deselect all.
11. Compare your screen to Figure 75, save your work, then close Four Square.

Figure 75 *Completed Design Project*

In this Portfolio Project, you're going to work on a fun puzzle that will test your problem-solving skills when using X and Y locations. You will open an InDesign document with two pages. On the first page are four 1-inch squares at each corner of the page. On the second page, the four 1-inch squares appear again—this time forming a large red square that is positioned at the exact center of the 7.75-inch × 7.75-inch document page. Just looking at the second page, your challenge will be to write down the X and Y coordinates of each of the four boxes at the center of the page. Then, you will test out your answers with the boxes on the first page.

Setup.

1. Open ID 3-6.indd, then save it as **Center Squares**.
2. On page 1, verify that each red square is 1" × 1", then deselect all.
3. Go to page 2, then press [Tab] to hide all panels.
4. Do not select any of the squares at the center.
5. Write down what you think is the X/Y coordinate of the top-left point of the top-left square.
6. Write down what you think is the X/Y coordinate of the top-right point of the top-right square.
7. Write down what you think is the X/Y coordinate of the bottom-right point of the bottom-right square.

8. Write down what you think is the X/Y coordinate of the center point of the bottom-left square.
9. Press [Tab] to show all hidden panels.
10. Go to page 1, select the top-left square, then click the top-left reference point on the Transform panel.
11. Enter the X/Y coordinates that you wrote down for this point, then press [Enter](Win) or [return](Mac).

12. Using the same method, test out the X/Y coordinates you wrote down for the other three boxes. (*Hint*: Be sure to click the appropriate reference point on the Transform panel for each of the three remaining boxes.)
13. When you are done, does your page 1 match page 2 exactly as shown in Figure 76?

Figure 76 *Completed Portfolio Project*

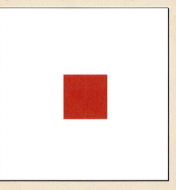

CHAPTER 4 WORKING WITH
FRAMES

1. Align and distribute objects on a page
2. Stack and layer objects
3. Work with graphics frames
4. Work with text frames

CHAPTER 4 WORKING WITH FRAMES

When you position objects on a page, they are positioned in text frames or graphics frames. Chapter 4 focuses on frames and various techniques for working with them.

The first lesson gives you the chance to pause and explore basic options for aligning and distributing frames on the page. In this lesson, you'll explore two features that are new to CS5: Live Distribute and the Gap tool.

In the second lesson, you'll learn how to manipulate the stacking order of frames, and you'll get a thorough tour of the Layers panel. After going through these lessons, you'll feel confident in your ability to position frames precisely on a page and get them to overlap the way you want them to.

The third lesson is an immersion into the world of placing graphics in graphics frames. Put on your thinking caps—there's a lot going on here, all of it interesting. You'll learn the specifics of placing graphics and the all-important difference between the graphics frame and the graphic itself. Finally, you'll finish by working with text frames and exploring the power of autoflowing text in a document. Watch InDesign create dozens of text frames with a click of a button!

Step and Repeat

Repeat

Count: 2

☐ Create as a grid

OK

Cancel

☑ Preview

Offset

Vertical: 2 in   Horizontal: 1 in

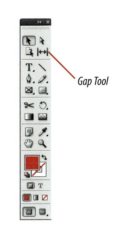

Gap Tool

ALIGN

Align Objects:

Distribute Objects:

☐ Use Spacing   0 in

Align to Selection ▼

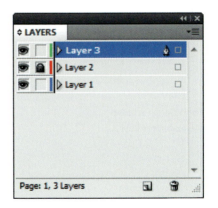

LAYERS

Layer 3

Layer 2

Layer 1

Page: 1, 3 Layers

LESSON 1

Align and Distribute
OBJECTS ON A PAGE

What You'll Do

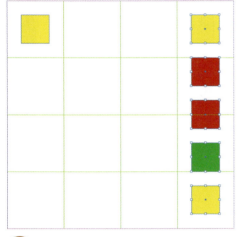

▶ In this lesson, you will explore various techniques for positioning objects in specific relationships to one another.

Applying Fills and Strokes

A **fill** is a color you apply to the inside of an object. A **stroke** is a color that you apply to the outline of an object. Figure 1 shows an object with a blue fill and a yellow stroke.

InDesign offers you a number of options for filling and stroking objects. The simplest and most direct method for doing so is to select an object and then pick a color from the Swatches panel, shown in Figure 2. The color

that you choose on the Swatches panel will be applied to the selected object as a fill or as a stroke, depending on whether the Fill or the Stroke button is activated on the Tools panel.

To activate either the Fill or the Stroke button, simply click it once on the Tools panel. The Fill button is activated when it is in front of the Stroke button, as shown in Figure 3. When the Fill button is activated, clicking a swatch on the

Figure 1 *An object with a fill and a stroke*

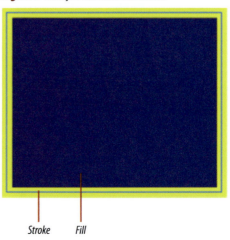

Stroke   Fill

Swatches panel applies that swatch color as a fill to the selected object(s). When the Stroke button is activated, as shown in Figure 4, the swatch color is applied as a stroke.

Once a stroke is applied, you can modify the **stroke weight**—how heavy the outline

appears—using the Stroke panel. The Stroke panel is command central for all the modifications you can apply to a stroke, including making dotted and dashed strokes and varying stroke styles.

The Align Stroke section of the Stroke panel is critical for determining *where* on the object

the stroke is applied. By default, a stroke is aligned to the center of the object's perimeter. This means that it's centered on the edge, halfway inside and halfway outside the object. For example, if you apply a 10 pt stroke to a rectangle, five points of the stroke will be inside the object, and five points will be outside.

Figure 2 *Swatches panel*

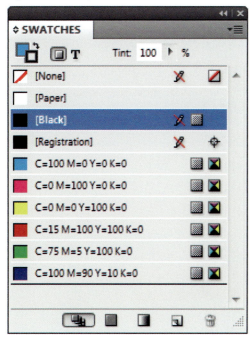

Figure 3 *Viewing the activated Fill button*

Fill button is in front of the Stroke button

Figure 4 *Viewing the activated Stroke button*

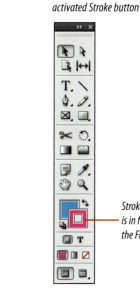

Stroke button is in front of the Fill button

The Stroke panel offers three Align Stroke options: Align Stroke to Center, Align Stroke to Inside, and Align Stroke to Outside. Figure 5 shows examples of all three. Note that in all three examples, the object itself is the same size, but the way the stroke is aligned to the object changes how much of the fill color is visible.

Using the Step and Repeat Command

Many times, when laying out a page, you will want to create multiple objects that are evenly spaced in lines or in grids. InDesign CS5 offers many great utilities for accomplishing this, one of which is the Step and Repeat dialog box, as shown in Figure 6.

Before you choose the Step and Repeat command, you need to decide which objects you want to copy and how many copies of it you want to create. After selecting the object, choose Step and Repeat on the Edit menu. In the Step and Repeat dialog box, you choose the number of copies. You also specify the **offset** value for each successive copy. The offset is the horizontal and vertical distance the copy will be from the original.

QUICK TIP

Click the Preview check box to see transformations before you execute them.

Figure 5 *A 10 pt stroke with three different alignments*

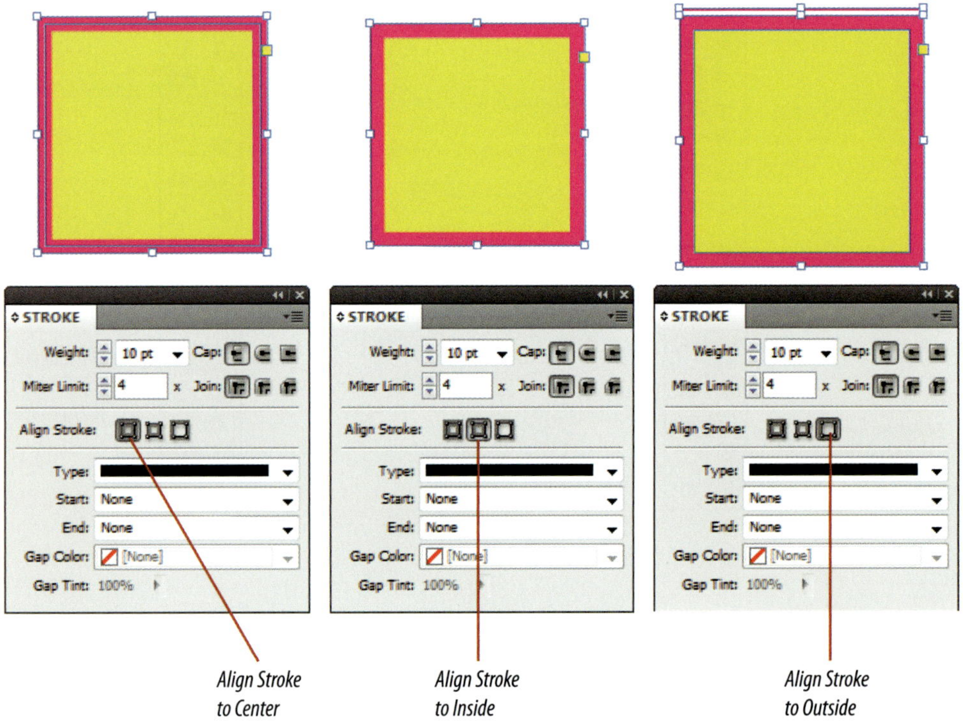

Align Stroke
to Center

Align Stroke
to Inside

Align Stroke
to Outside

Figure 6 *Step and Repeat dialog box*

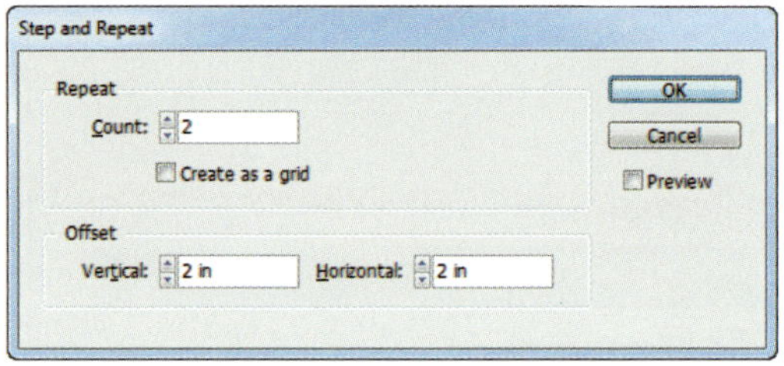

Figure 7 shows an original 1-inch square frame and three copies created using the Step and Repeat command. that the horizontal offset is two inches and the vertical offset is two inches. Thus, each copy is two inches to the right and two inches down from the previous copy.

Note that positive and negative offset values create copies in specific directions. On the horizontal axis, a positive value creates copies to the right of the original; a negative value creates copies to the left of the original.

On the vertical axis, a positive value creates copies *below* the original; a negative value creates copies above the original. Figure 8 is a handy guide for remembering the result of positive and negative offset values.

Use the vertical ruler on the left side of the document page to remember positive and negative values on the vertical axis. You are used to thinking of positive as up and negative as down, but remember that in InDesign, the default (0, 0) coordinate is in the top-left corner of the page. On the ruler,

positive numbers *increase* as you move *down* the ruler.

Aligning Objects

The Align panel offers quick and simple solutions for aligning and distributing multiple objects on a page. To **align** objects is to position them by their tops, bottoms, left sides, right sides or centers. To **distribute** objects is to space them equally on a page horizontally, vertically, or both. Using the top section of the Align panel, you can

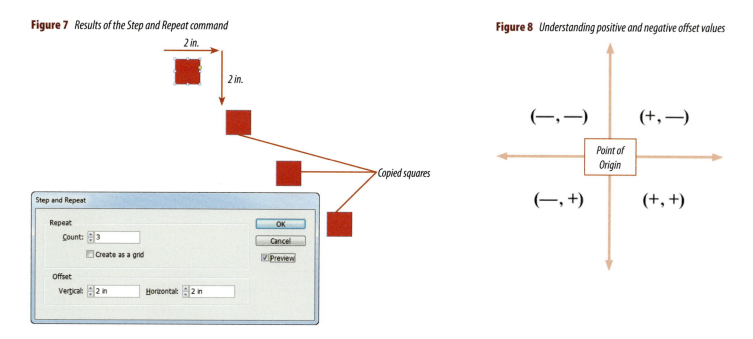

Figure 7 *Results of the Step and Repeat command*

Figure 8 *Understanding positive and negative offset values*

choose from six alignment buttons, shown in Figure 9. Each option includes an icon that represents the resulting layout of the selected objects, after the button has been clicked. Figure 10 shows three objects placed randomly on the page. Figure 11 shows the same three objects after clicking the Align left edges button.

Compare Figure 10 to Figure 11. Only the bottom two objects moved; they moved left to align with the left edge of the top object. This is because the top object was originally the leftmost object. Clicking the Align left edges button aligns all selected objects with the leftmost object.

Figure 12 shows the same three objects after clicking the Align top edges button. The red and yellow boxes move up so that their tops are aligned with the top of the blue box.

QUICK TIP

The Align panel has four choices for aligning objects. In addition to aligning objects using the boundaries of the selection, you can also align one or more objects to the page, margins, or spread.

Distributing Objects

You use the Distribute Objects section of the Align panel to distribute objects. As stated earlier, to distribute objects is to space them equally on a page, horizontally, vertically, or both.

Figure 9   *Align Objects section of the Align panel*

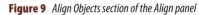
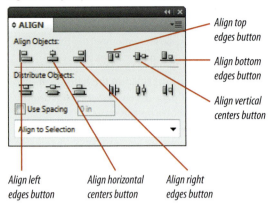

Align top edges button

Align bottom edges button

Align vertical centers button

Align left edges button

Align horizontal centers button

Align right edges button

Figure 10   *Three objects not aligned*

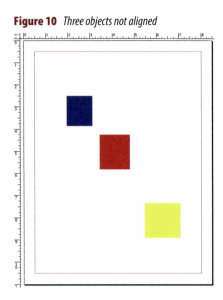

Figure 11   *Objects aligned with the Align left edges button*

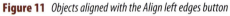
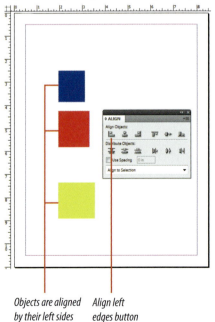

Objects are aligned by their left sides

Align left edges button

Figure 12   *Objects aligned with the Align top edges button*

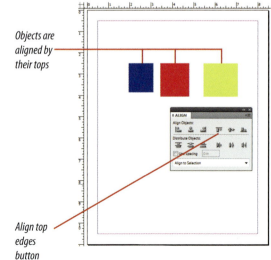

Objects are aligned by their tops

Align top edges button

Figure 13 shows three objects that are not distributed evenly on either the horizontal or vertical axis. Figure 14 shows the same three objects after clicking the Distribute horizontal centers button. Clicking this button means that—on the horizontal axis— the distance between the center point of the first object and the center point of the second

object is the same as the distance between the center point of the second object and the center point of the third object.

Figure 15 shows the same three objects after clicking the Distribute vertical centers button. Clicking this button means that—on the vertical axis—the distance between the

center points of the first two objects is the same as the distance between the center points of the second and third objects.

Why are the Align and Distribute buttons on the same panel? Because their power is how they work in conjunction with each other. Figure 16 shows three text frames without any

Figure 13 *Three objects, positioned randomly*

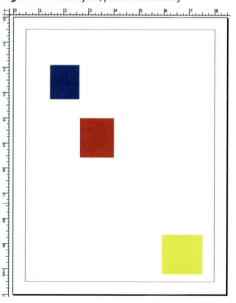

Figure 14 *Objects distributed by their horizontal centers*

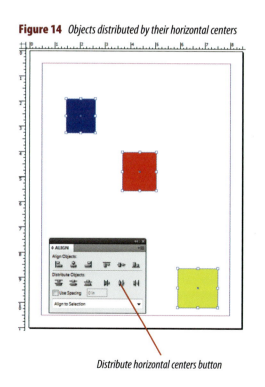

Distribute horizontal centers button

Figure 15 *Objects distributed by their vertical centers*

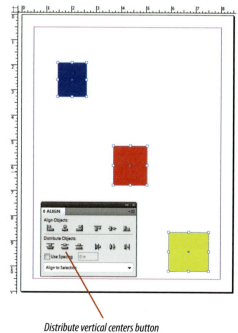

Distribute vertical centers button

alignment or distribution applied. Figure 17 shows the three frames after clicking the Align top edges button and the Distribute left edges button. Compare the two figures.

NEW Using the Live Distribute Technique

When you select multiple objects, a bounding box appears around the objects. As you already know, you can drag the handles of that bounding box to transform all the selected objects. The Live Distribute option offers a different behavior. Instead of resizing the objects, you can use the Live Distribute option to proportionally resize the *space between* the objects.

To access the Live Distribute option, select multiple objects, start dragging a bounding box handle and then hold down the Spacebar as you drag. The spaces between the objects will be resized, and the alignment of the objects will change depending on where and in what direction you drag.

Figure 18 shows 20 frames aligned in a grid. Figure 19 shows the same 20 frames modified with the Live Distribute option.

Figure 16 *Three text frames, positioned randomly*

Figure 17 *Objects aligned at their top edges and distributed from left edges*

Aligned at top edge ——

Even horizontal distribution from left edge to left edge

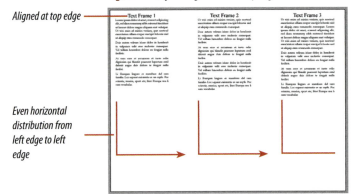

Figure 18 *20 frames*

Figure 19 *Space between frames increased proportionately with the Live Distribute option*

Working with Frames

Note that the frames haven't changed size—only the space between them has changed.

Using the Gap Tool

The Gap tool is a new tool in InDesign CS5. When you're working with multiple objects, the Gap tool offers a quick way to adjust the size of the gaps between them.

It also allows you to resize several items that have commonly aligned edges at once, while maintaining the size of the gaps between them. Think of it this way: the Gap tool moves the gap.

Figure 20 shows a grid of 12 frames with the Gap tool positioned over the center gap. The shaded area indicates the length of the gap that will be modified by the tool. Figure 21 shows the result of dragging the Gap tool to the left. Note that only the gap moved; the size of the gap didn't change. The width of the associated frames changed.

You can use the Gap tool while pressing and holding various keys to perform other tasks as well, as shown in Table 1.

Figure 20 *Gap tool positioned over a grid of frames*

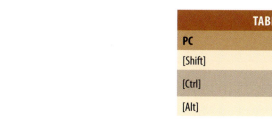

Gray area identifies frames that will be affected

Figure 21 *Result of dragging the Gap tool to the left*

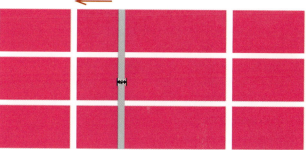

TABLE 1: GAP TOOL BEHAVIORS AND KEYBOARD COMBINATIONS		
PC	**Mac**	**Behavior**
[Shift]	[shift]	Affects the gap only between the two items nearest to the cursor
[Ctrl]	⌘	Increases the width and height of the gap
[Alt]	[option]	Moves the items with the gap instead of resizing the items

Apply fills and strokes

1. Open ID 4-1.indd, then save it as **Orientation**. Verify that guides are showing.

2. Click the **workspace switcher list arrow** on the Application bar, then click **[Advanced]**.

3. Click the **Rectangle tool** , then click anywhere on the page.

   TIP When a shape tool is selected on the Tools panel, clicking the document window opens the tool's dialog box, where you can enter values that determine the size of the resulting object.

4. Type **2** in the Width text box, type **2** in the Height text box, then click **OK**.

5. Click **Swatches** in the stack of collapsed panels to open the Swatches panel.

6. Verify that the Fill button is activated.

7. Click **Green** on the Swatches panel.
   The rectangle frame fills with green.

8. Click the **Stroke button** on the Tools panel.

9. Click **Brick Red** on the Swatches panel.

10. Open the Stroke panel, type **6** in the Weight text box, then press **[Enter]** (Win) or **[return]** (Mac).

11. Click the **Align Stroke to Outside button** .

12. Click the **Align Stroke to Center button** .

13. Click the **Align Stroke to Inside button** .

14. Click the **top-left reference point** in the Control panel, type **0** in the X and Y text boxes, then press **[Enter]**(Win) or **[Return]**(Mac). Your page should resemble Figure 22.

(continued)

Figure 22 *Positioning the rectangle frame*

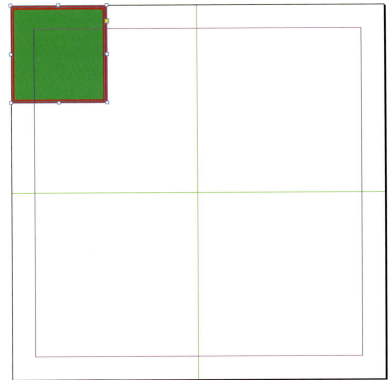

Figure 23 *The Apply None button*

Apply None button

Figure 24 *Viewing results of the Step and Repeat command*

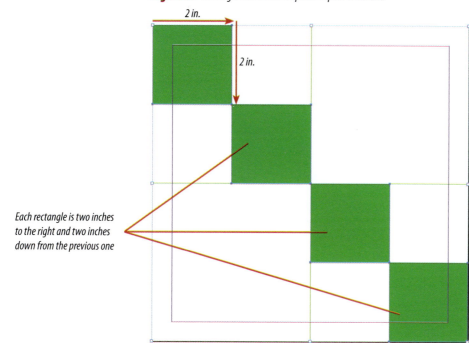

2 in.

2 in.

Each rectangle is two inches
to the right and two inches
down from the previous one

15. Click **File** on the Application bar, then click **Save**.

You created a rectangle using the Rectangle dialog box. You then used the Swatches panel to choose a fill color and a stroke color for the rectangle frame. You chose a weight for the stroke and tested three options for aligning the stroke. Finally, you used the Control panel to position the square at the top-left corner of the page.

Use the Step and Repeat command

1. Click the **green rectangle**, click the **Stroke button** on the Tools panel, then click the **Apply None button** ⬜, as shown in Figure 23.

   The stroke is removed from the green rectangle. With the loss of the stroke, the rectangle is no longer aligned with the top-left corner.

2. Press **[V]** to access the Selection tool, then drag **the frame** so that its top-left corner is aligned with the top-left corner of the page.

3. Click **Edit** on the Application bar, then click **Step and Repeat**.

4. Verify that the Horizontal and Vertical text boxes are set to 0 on the Control panel, type **3** in the Repeat Count text box, type **2** in the Horizontal Offset text box, type **2** in the Vertical Offset text box, then click **OK**.

   Three new rectangles are created, each one two inches to the right and two inches down from the previous one, as shown in Figure 24.

5. Click the pasteboard to deselect all, click the **top-left rectangle**, press and hold **[Shift]**, click the **second rectangle**, click **Edit** on the Application bar, then click **Step and Repeat**.

   (continued)

6. Type **1** in the Repeat Count text box, type **0** in the Vertical Offset text box, type **4** in the Horizontal Offset text box, then click **OK**.

7. Select the bottom two rectangles on the page, click **Edit** on the Application bar, then click **Step and Repeat**.

8. Type **1** in the Repeat Count text box, type **0** in the Vertical Offset text box, type **-4** in the Horizontal Offset text box, then click **OK**.

9. Press **[W]** to switch to Preview, click anywhere to deselect the new rectangles, then compare your page to Figure 25.

10. Save the file.

You used the Step and Repeat command to create a checkerboard pattern, duplicating a single rectangle multiple times.

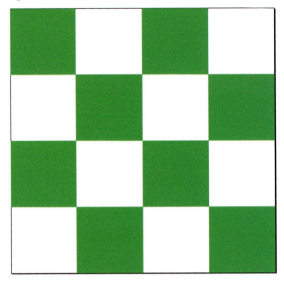 Use the Live Distribute technique

1. Hide guides, select all, copy, then paste in place.

2. Click the **Center Reference Point** on the Control panel, type **90** in the Rotation Angle text box in the Control panel, then press **[Enter]**(Win) or **[Return]**(Mac).

3. Verify that the Fill button is in front on the Tools panel, click **Dark Blue** in the Swatches panel, then compare your screen to Figure 26.

(continued)

Figure 25 *Checkerboard created using the Step and Repeat command*

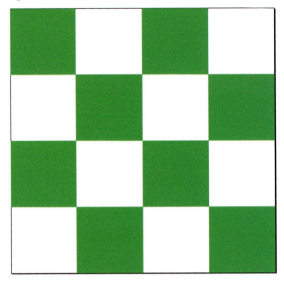

Figure 26 *Viewing the complete checkerboard*

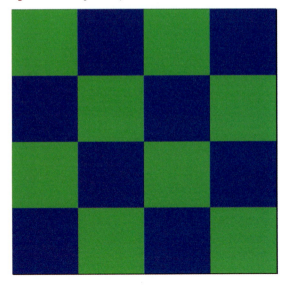

Working with Frames

Figure 27 *Scaling the checkerboard in a standard manner*

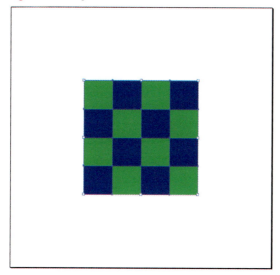

Figure 28 *Expanding the space between frames with Live Distribute*

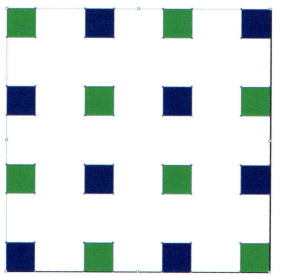

4. Select all, press and hold **[Shift][Alt]**(Win) or **[Shift][Option]**(Mac), then click and drag the **upper-right handle of the bounding box** toward the center of the page, releasing your mouse when your checkerboard resembles Figure 27.

   The objects are scaled from their center point.

5. Click and drag the **upper-right corner of the bounding box** toward the upper-right corner of the document, then, while you are still dragging, press and hold **[Spacebar]**.

   When you press [Spacebar] while dragging, the Live Distribute option is enabled. The space between the objects is modified—larger or smaller—depending on the direction in which you drag.

6. With the Spacebar still pressed, drag the **handle** in different directions on the document.

   Regardless of the direction you drag, the frames do not change size or shape—only the space between the frames changes.

7. With the Spacebar still pressed, press and hold **[Shift][Alt]**(Win) or **[Shift][Option]**(Mac), then drag the handle to the upper-right corner of the document and release your mouse button.

   Pressing and holding [Spacebar][Shift][Alt] when dragging enlarges the space between the frames in proportion from the center. Your page should resemble Figure 28.

8. Begin dragging the **upper-right handle of the bounding box** slowly toward the center of the document.

   (continued)

9. As you're dragging, press **[Spacebar]** to activate Live Distribute, then press **[Shift][Alt]**(Win) or **[Shift][Option]**(Mac) and continue dragging toward the center until your artwork resembles Figure 29.

10. Deselect all, then save your work.

You pasted and rotated a copy of the squares to create a complete checkerboard. You selected all the frames, then dragged a bounding box handle to reduce all the objects in a standard manner. You then used the Live Distribute technique to modify the space between the objects.

NEW Use the Gap tool

1. Click the **Gap tool** |↔| on the Tool bar.

2. Position the Gap tool over the **middle-vertical gap**, then click and drag left so that your grid resembles Figure 30.

3. Position the Gap tool over the **bottom-horizontal gap**, then click and drag up so that your grid resembles Figure 31.

4. Position the Gap tool over the **gap between the top two frames in the upper-right corner**, press and hold **[Shift]**, then click and drag to the left so that your grid resembles Figure 32.

5. Press and hold **[Ctrl]**(Win) or ⌘ (Mac), then click and drag the **left edge of the grid**.

   The width of the four frames on the left is increased.

6. Press and hold **[Alt]**(Win) or **[Option]**(Mac), position the Gap tool over the **bottom-horizontal gap**, then click and drag down.

(continued)

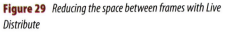

Figure 29 *Reducing the space between frames with Live Distribute*

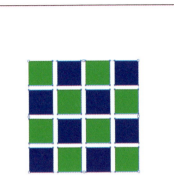

Figure 30 *Moving the vertical gap*

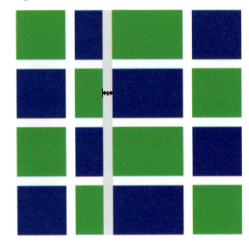

Figure 31 *Moving the horizontal gap*

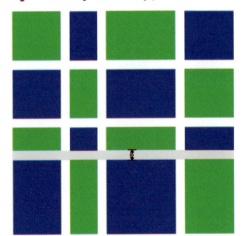

Figure 32 *Moving the gap only between two rectangles*

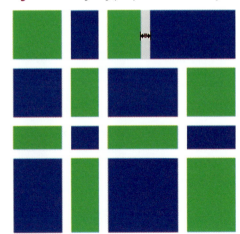

Figure 33 *Moving frames with the Gap tool*

Figure 34 *Aligning three objects by their top edges*

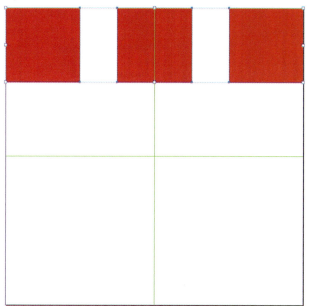

As shown in Figure 33, the frames on both sides of the gap move. Neither the frames nor the gap are resized—only relocated.

7. Save your work, then close Orientation.

You used the Gap tool with various key combinations to affect the gaps in a grid of frames.

Align objects

1. Open ID 4-2.indd, then save it as **Alignment**.

2. Click **Window** on the Application bar, point to **Object & Layout**, then click **Align**.

   The Align panel opens.

3. Press **[Ctrl][A]** (Win) or ⌘ **[A]** (Mac) to select all three objects on the page, then click the **Align left edges button** in the Align Objects section of the Align panel.

   The frames are aligned to the leftmost of the three.

4. Click **Edit** on the Application bar, then click **Undo Align**.

5. Click the **Align top edges button** on the Align panel.

   As shown in Figure 34, the top edges of the three frames are aligned to the topmost of the three.

6. Undo the previous step, then click the **Align horizontal centers button** .

7. Click the **Align vertical centers button** .

   The three frames are stacked, one on top of the other, their center points aligned both horizontally and vertically.

8. Save your work, then close Alignment.

You used the buttons in the Align Objects section of the Align panel to reposition frames with various alignments.

Distribute objects

1. Open ID 4-3.indd, then save it as **Distribution**. Verify that guides are showing.

2. Select the top two yellow squares and the two red squares, then click the **Align top edges button** 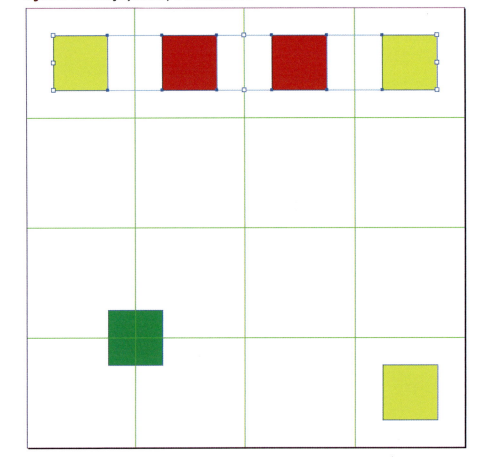 in the Align Objects section of the Align panel.

    The four objects are aligned by their top edges.

3. Click the **Distribute horizontal centers button** in the Distribute Objects section of the Align panel.

    The center points of the two red squares are distributed evenly on the horizontal axis between the center points of the two yellow squares, as shown in Figure 35.

4. Click **Edit** on the Application bar, click **Deselect All**, select the top-left yellow square, select the two red squares, then select the bottom-right yellow square.

    (continued)

Figure 35 *Distributing objects evenly on the horizontal axis*

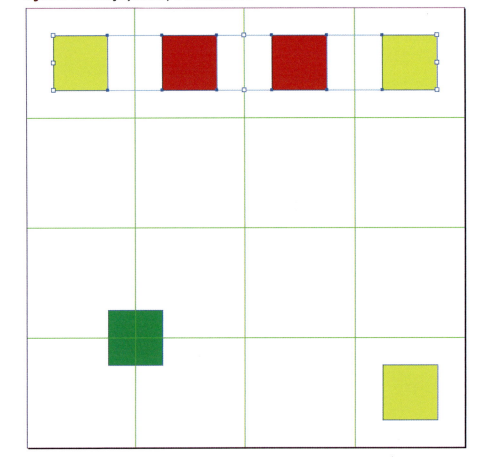

Figure 36 *Distributing 4 objects evenly on the vertical axis*

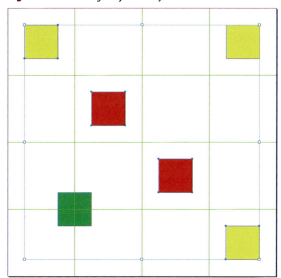

5. Click the **Distribute vertical centers button** ☰, then compare your screen to Figure 36.

6. Select the green square, the two red squares and the bottom yellow square, then click the **Align right edges button** ▤.

7. Press and hold **[Shift]**, then click the **top-right yellow square** to add it to the selection.

8. Click the **Distribute vertical centers button** ☰.

   The center points of the five squares are distributed evenly on the vertical axis, as shown in Figure 37.

9. Save your work, then close Distribution.

You spaced objects evenly on the horizontal and vertical axes.

Figure 37 *Distributing 5 objects evenly on the vertical axis*

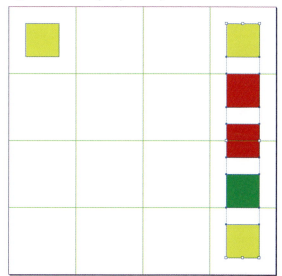

Stack
AND LAYER OBJECTS

What You'll Do

▽ Images		
<P8241453.psd>		
▽ <group>		
<P8251520.psd>		
<P8251555.jpg>		
<P8241476.psd>		
<P8241449.psd>		
<P8241483.psd>		
<P8251552.psd>		
▷ Text		
▷ Tints		

Pages: 2-3, 3 Layers

In this lesson, you will manipulate the stacking order of objects on the page, and you'll use the Layers panel to control how objects are layered.

Understanding the Stacking Order

The **stacking order** refers to how objects are arranged in hierarchical order. When you create multiple objects, it is important for you to remember that every object is on its own level. For example, if you draw a square frame, and then draw a circle frame, the circle frame is automatically created one level in front of the square, whether or not they overlap. If they did overlap, the circle would appear in front of the square.

QUICK TIP

Use the word "level" when discussing the hierarchy of the stacking order, not the word "layer," which has its own specific meaning in InDesign.

You control the stacking order with the four commands on the Arrange menu. The Bring to Front command moves a selected object to the front of the stacking order. The Send to Back command moves a selected object to the back of the stacking order. The Bring Forward command moves a selected object one level forward in the stacking order, and the Send Backward command moves a selected object one level backward in the stacking order.

Using these four commands, you can control and arrange how every object on the page overlaps other objects.

NEW Understanding Layers

The Layers panel, as shown in Figure 38, is a smart solution for organizing and managing elements of a layout. With InDesign CS5, Adobe has dramatically improved the Layers panel interface, making it similar to the Layers panel in Adobe Illustrator. Of the numerous improvements, the Layers panel now features the option for locking and hiding individual objects on a layer.

By default, every document is created with one layer. You can create new layers and give them descriptive names to help you identify a layer's content. For example, if you were working on a layout that contained both text and graphics, you might want to create a layer for all of the text frames called Text and create another layer for all of the graphics called Graphics.

Why would you do this? Well, for one reason, you have the ability to lock layers on the Layers panel. Locking a layer makes its contents non-editable until you unlock it.

In the example, you could lock the Text layer while you work on the graphic elements of the layout. By doing so, you can be certain that you won't make any inadvertent changes to the text elements. Another reason is that you have the ability to hide layers. You could temporarily hide the Text layer, thus providing yourself a working view of the graphics that is unobstructed by the text elements.

You can also duplicate layers. You do so by clicking the Duplicate Layer command on the Layers panel menu or by dragging a layer on top of the Create new layer icon on the Layers panel. When you duplicate a layer, all of the objects on the original layer are duplicated and will appear in their same locations on the new layer.

Layers are a smart, important solution for organizing your work and improving your workflow, especially for complex layouts. Invest some time in working with layers—it will pay off with lots of saved time and fewer headaches.

Working with Layers

You can create as many layers on the Layers panel as you need to organize your work.

Figure 39 shows the Layers panel with three layers. Notice the Lock icon on Layer 2. The Lock icon indicates that this layer cannot be edited. All objects on Layer 2 are locked. Clicking the Lock icon will unlock the layer, and the lock icon will disappear.

Think of layers on the Layers panel as being three-dimensional. The topmost layer is the front layer; the bottommost layer is the back layer. Therefore, it follows logically that objects on the topmost layer are *in front* of objects on any other layer. Layers themselves are transparent. If you

Figure 38 *Layers panel*

Figure 39 *Layers panel with three layers*

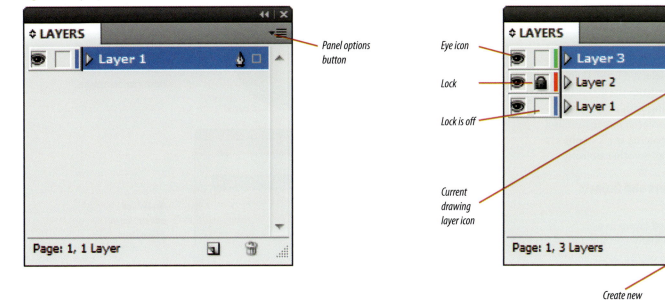

have a layer with no objects on it, you can see through the layer to the objects on the layers behind it.

Note that each layer contains its own stacking order. Let's say that you have three layers, each with five objects on it. Regardless of the stacking order of the top layer, all the objects on that layer are in front of any objects on the other layers. In other words, an object at the back of the stacking order of the top layer is still in front of any object on any layer beneath it.

One great organizational aspect of layers is that you can assign a selection color to a layer. When you select an object, its bounding box appears in the selection color of the layer on which it is placed, as shown in Figure 40.

You determine a layer's selection color by selecting the layer, clicking the Layers panel options button, clicking Layer Options for the name of the selected layer, then choosing a new color from the Color menu. When you are working with a layout that contains numerous objects, this feature is a great visual aid for keeping track of objects and their relationships to other objects.

Manipulating Layers and Objects on Layers

Once you have created layers in a document, you have many options for manipulating objects on the layers and the layers themselves. You can move objects between layers, and you can reorder the layers on the Layers panel.

Clicking a layer on the Layers panel to select it is called **targeting** a layer. The layer that you click is called the **target layer**. When you create a new object, the object will be added to whichever layer is targeted on the Layers panel. The pen tool icon next to a layer's name on the Layers panel is called the Current drawing layer icon. This icon will help remind you that anything placed or drawn will become part of that layer.

You can select any object on the page, regardless of which layer is targeted. When you select the object, the layer that the object is on is automatically targeted on the Layers panel.

Figure 40 *Assigning a selection color to a layer*

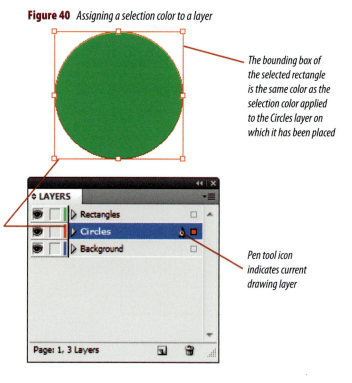

The bounding box of the selected rectangle is the same color as the selection color applied to the Circles layer on which it has been placed

Pen tool icon indicates current drawing layer

Working with Frames

When one or more objects are selected, a small, square icon on the far right of a layer in the Layers panel, fills with color to show that items on the layer are selected as shown in Figure 41. That small button, called the Selected items icon, represents the selected objects. When you click and drag the Selected items icon and move it to another layer, the selected objects move to that layer. Therefore, you should never feel constrained by the layers you have chosen for objects; it's easy to move them from one layer to another.

You can also change the order of layers on the Layers panel by dragging a layer up or down on the panel. As you drag, a heavy black line indicates the new position for the layer when you release the mouse button. In Figure 42, the Rectangles layer is being repositioned under the Circles layer.

Selecting Artwork on Layers

Let's say you have three layers in your document, each with six objects. That means your document has a total of 18 objects. If you apply the Select All command on the Edit menu, all 18 objects will be selected, regardless of which layer is targeted on the Layers panel.

In many situations, you'll want to select all the objects on one layer only. The easiest way to do this is with the Selected items icon. Even when nothing is selected, the icon is available on every layer—as a hollow square. Click that icon, and all objects on that layer will be selected. This is a powerful and useful option—make note of it.

Selecting Objects Behind Other Objects

When you have multiple overlapping objects on a page, objects behind other objects can sometimes be difficult to select. Pressing and holding [Ctrl] (Win) or ⌘ (Mac) allows you to "click through the stacking order" to select objects behind other objects. Simply click the top object, press and hold [Ctrl] (Win) or ⌘ (Mac), then click the top object again, which will select the object immediately behind it. Click the top object again and the next object down in the stacking order will be selected.

Figure 41 *Viewing the Selected items icon*

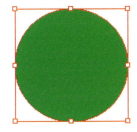

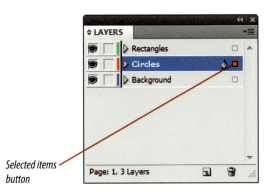

Selected items button

Figure 42 *Changing the order of two layers on the Layers panel*

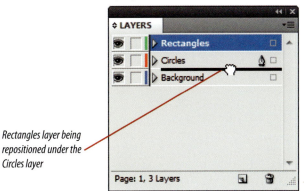

Rectangles layer being repositioned under the Circles layer

Use the Arrange commands to change the stacking order of objects

1. Open ID 4-4.indd, then save it as **Stack and Layer**.

2. Press **[V]** to access the Selection tool, then click the **yellow rectangle**.

3. Click **Object** on the Application bar, point to **Arrange**, then click **Bring Forward**.

   The yellow rectangle moves forward one level in the stacking order.

4. Click the **red square**, click **Object** on the Application bar, point to **Arrange**, then click **Bring to Front**.

5. Select both the yellow rectangle and the blue circle, click **Object** on the Application bar, point to **Arrange**, then click **Bring to Front.**

   Both objects move in front of the red square, as shown in Figure 43.

6. Click the **green circle**, click **Object** on the Application bar, point to **Arrange**, then click **Bring to Front**.

7. Select all, then click the **Align horizontal centers button** 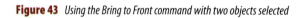 on the Align panel.

   The blue circle is completely behind the green circle.

(continued)

Figure 43 *Using the Bring to Front command with two objects selected*

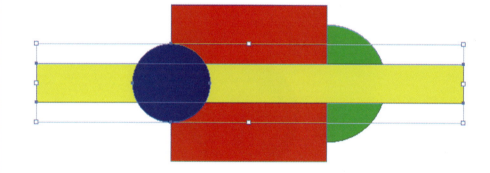

Figure 44 *Sending the green circle backward one level in the stacking order*

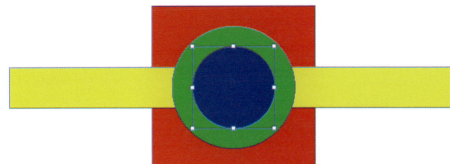

8. Deselect all, then click the **center of the green circle**.

9. Press and hold **[Ctrl]**(Win) or ⌘ (Mac), then click the **center of the green circle** again.

   The blue circle behind the green circle is selected.

10. Click **Object** on the Application bar, point to **Arrange**, then click **Bring Forward**.

    As shown in Figure 44, the blue circle moves forward one level in the stacking order, in front of the green circle.

11. Deselect all, select the blue circle, press and hold **[Ctrl]** (Win) or ⌘ (Mac), then click the **blue circle center** again to select the green circle behind it.

12. Still pressing and holding [Ctrl] (Win) or ⌘ (Mac), click the **blue circle center** again to select the yellow rectangle, then click the **blue circle center** once more to select the red square.

TIP Commit this selection technique to memory, as it is useful for selecting overlapping objects.

13. Save your work, then close Stack and Layer.

You used the Arrange commands to manipulate the stacking order of four objects.

Create new layers on the Layers panel

1. Open ID 4-5.indd, save it as **Layers Intro**, then click **Layers** in the stack of collapsed panels to open the Layers panel.

   As shown in Figure 45, the Layers panel has one default layer named Layer 1. All the objects on the spread are on Layer 1.

2. Double-click **Layer 1** on the Layers panel.

   The Layer Options dialog box opens. In this box you can change settings for Layer 1, such as its name and selection color.

3. Type **Tints** in the Name text box, then click **OK**.

4. Click the **Create new layer button** on the Layers panel, then double-click **Layer 2**.

5. Type **Images** in the Name text box, click the **Color list arrow**, click **Orange**, then click **OK**.

6. Click the **Layers panel options button**, then click **New Layer**.

7. Type **Text** in the Name text box, click the **Color list arrow**, click **Purple**, then click **OK**.

   Your Layers panel should resemble Figure 46.

You renamed Layer 1, then created two new layers on the Layers panel.

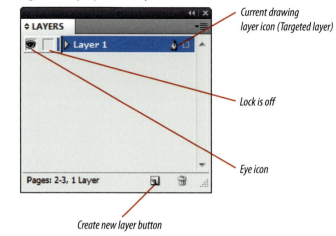

Figure 45 *Layers panel with Layer 1*

Current drawing layer icon (Targeted layer)

Lock is off

Eye icon

Create new layer button

Figure 46 *Layers panel with three layers*

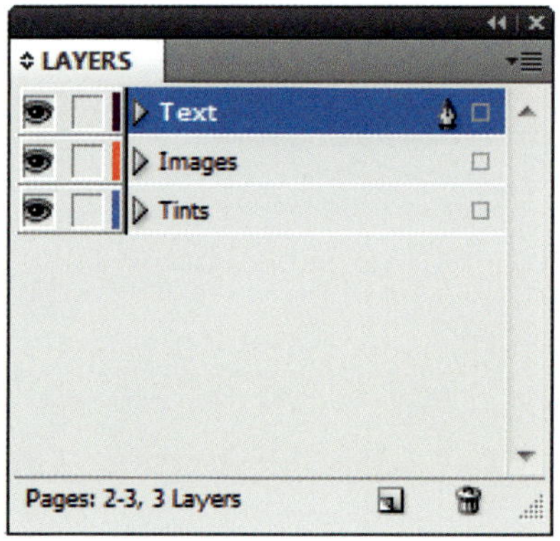

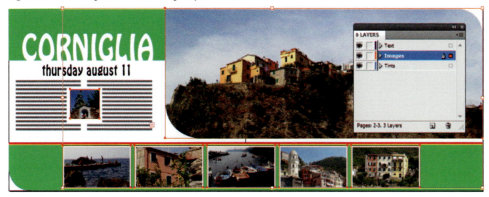

Figure 47 *Seven images moved to the Images layer*

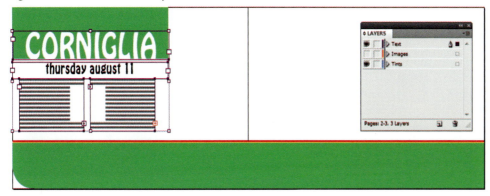

Figure 48 *Text frames moved to Text layer*

Position objects on layers

1. Press **[V]** to access the Selection tool, if it is not already active, then select the seven images on the spread.

   The Tints layer on the Layers panel is highlighted and the Selected items icon appears next to the layer name.

2. Click and drag the **Selected items button** from the Tints layer up to the Images layer.

   The seven images are moved to the Images layer. As shown in Figure 47, the selection edges around the frames are now orange, the color assigned to the Images layer.

3. Click the **Eye icon** on the **Images layer** to hide that layer.

4. Select the four text frames on the left page, then drag the **Selected items icon** up to the Text layer.

   As shown in Figure 48, the text frames are moved to the Text layer and the selection marks are now purple. Note that the text wrap is still affecting the text, even though the Images layer containing the images is hidden.

5. Show the Images layer, then click the **Selected items icon** on the Images layer.

   All objects on the Images layer are selected, and all the objects on the Text layer are deselected.

6. Click the **Text layer** in the Layers panel, click the **Rectangle tool**, then draw a small rectangle anywhere on the page.

   Because the Text layer was selected on the Layers panel, the new object is positioned on the Text layer.

(continued)

7. Verify that the Fill button is active on the Tools panel, click **Tan** on the Swatches panel, then remove any stroke if necessary.

8. Click the **top-left reference point** on the Control panel, enter **0** in the X text box, enter **0** in the Y text box, enter **12.5** in the W text box, then enter **4.75** in the H text box.

   The rectangle should cover the entire spread. Because the rectangle is the newest object created, it is at the top of the stacking order on the Text layer.

9. Click **Object** on the Application bar, point to **Arrange**, click **Send to Back**, then compare your spread to Figure 49.

   The rectangle is at the back of the stacking order of the Text layer. But because the Text layer is at the top of the Layers panel, the rectangle is in front of all images and all tints on the layers below.

10. Drag the **Selected items button** down to the Tints layer.

    The rectangle is moved to the tints layer. It is at the top of the stacking order on the Tints layer, so the green tints are not visible.

11. Click **Object** on the Application bar, point to **Arrange**, then click **Send to Back**.

    As shown in Figure 50, the tan rectangle is at the bottom of the stacking order on the Tints layer.

12. Save your work.

You used the Layers panel to move selected objects from one layer to another. You targeted a layer, then created a new object, which was added to that layer. You then pasted objects into a targeted layer.

Figure 49 *Rectangle moved to back of the stacking order on Text layer*

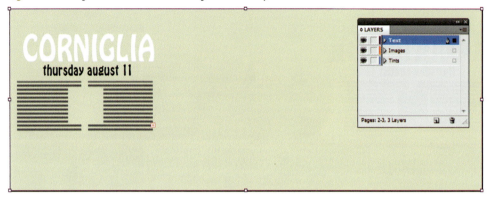

Figure 50 *Rectangle moved to back of the stacking order on Tints layer*

Figure 51 *Moving the Tints layer*

Figure 52 *Text layer, reordered and locked*

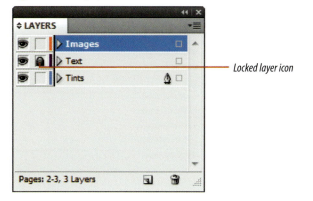

Locked layer icon

Change the order of layers on the Layers panel

1. Switch to the Selection tool ▶, deselect all, then click and drag the **Tints layer** to the top of the Layers panel.

   As shown in Figure 51, a heavy black line appears indicating where the layer will be positioned when dragged.

2. Drag the **Text layer** to the top of the Layers panel.

3. Drag the **Images layer** to the top of the Layers panel.

4. Click the empty square next to the Text layer name to lock the layer, then compare your Layers panel to Figure 52.

   The Lock icon appears when it is clicked, indicating the layer is now locked.

5. Save the file.

You changed the order of layers and locked the Text layer.

NEW Group items on layers

1. Click the **triangle** on the Images layer, then see Figure 53.

   Clicking the triangle expands the layer to show the objects on the layer. The seven frames are listed on the layer with the name of the images pasted into them.

2. Select the first four small frames at the bottom of the layout.

   The Selected items icon becomes activated for each individual object that is selected.

3. Click **Object** on the Application bar, then click **Group**.

   The four selected objects are moved into a folder named Group.

4. Click the **triangle** to expand the group folder, select the fifth thumbnail frame on the layout, then compare your screen to Figure 54.

   The Selected items icon is activated beside the fifth thumbnail layer in the Layers panel. Because this image is not part of the group, it is not within the group folder.

   (continued)

Figure 53 *Expanding a layer in the Layers panel*

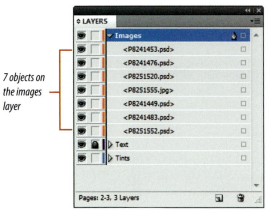

7 objects on the images layer

Figure 54 *Four objects in a group folder*

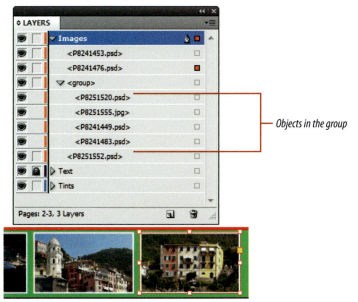

Objects in the group

Figure 55 *Dragging the ungrouped thumbnail into the group*

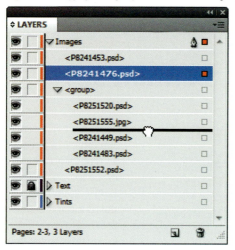

Figure 56 *Locking the group on the layer*

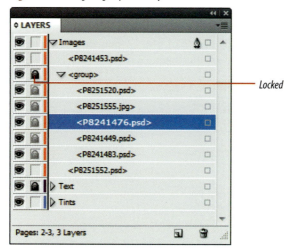

Locked

5. Click and drag the **fifth thumbnail layer** into the middle of the group folder, as shown in Figure 55.

6. Deselect all, then click the **leftmost of the five thumbnails** on the layout with the Selection tool.

   The fifth thumbnail is now part of the group.

7. Lock the group folder so that your Layers panel resembles Figure 56.

   When you expand a layer, you can lock and hide individual objects on a layer. In this example, the Images layer has seven images on it, but only five of them are locked.

8. Save your work, then close Layers Intro.

You modified a group using layers. You grouped four of five frames. You then added the fifth frame to the group by dragging the fifth frame into the group folder in the Layers panel.

Work with GRAPHICS FRAMES

What You'll Do

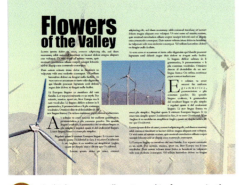

In this lesson, you will create graphics frames, resize them, and manipulate graphics that you import into them.

Placing Graphics in a Document

The term **graphic** is quite broad. In its most basic definition, a graphic is an element on the page that is not text. A simple square with a fill color could be called a graphic. However, when you are talking about placing graphics in an InDesign document, the term graphic usually is referring to bitmap images or vector graphics. **Bitmap images** are images that consist of pixels created in a program like Adobe Photoshop or downloaded from the internet or a digital camera. Anything that has been scanned is a bitmap image. **Vector graphics** are artwork comprised of geometrically defined paths and curves, usually illustrations created and imported from drawing programs like Adobe Illustrator.

There are two essential methods for placing a graphic in a document. The first is to create a graphics placeholder frame using any of the InDesign's shape tools—Rectangle, Ellipse or Polygon. Once you have created the frame and it is selected on the page, you use the Place command on the File menu to locate the graphic you want to import into the document. The graphic will appear in the graphics frame.

The second method is to place a graphic without first creating a graphics frame. If you click the Place command and then locate the graphic you want to import, you will see the loaded graphics icon when you position the pointer over the page. See Figure 57. Click the loaded graphics icon on the page to place

Figure 57 *Loaded graphics icon*

Loaded graphics icon

the graphic. The graphic will be placed on the page in a graphics frame whose top-left corner will be positioned at the location where you clicked the loaded graphics icon.

Which is the better method? It depends on what you want to do with the graphic. If the size and location of the graphics frame is important, it's probably better to create and position the frame first, then import the graphic and make it fit into the frame. If the size and location of the frame are negotiable, you might want to place the graphic anywhere in the layout and then modify its size and location.

Understanding the Difference Between the Graphics Frame and the Graphic

One of the essential concepts in InDesign is keeping in mind the distinction between the graphics frame and the graphic itself. Think of the graphics frame as a window through which you see the placed graphic. Sometimes, the graphic will be smaller than the frame and will fit entirely within the frame. At other times, the graphic will be larger than the frame that contains it. In that case, you see only the areas of the graphic that fit in the frame. The other areas of the graphic are still there, you just can't see them because they are outside of the frame.

Understanding the Difference Between the Selection Tool and the Direct Selection Tool

The difference between the graphics frame and the graphic itself is reflected on the Tools panel by the Selection tool and the Direct Selection tool. Specifically, the Selection tool addresses the graphics frame while the Direct Selection tool addresses the *contents* of the frame. Anything you want to do to the frame, you do with the Selection tool. Anything you want to do to the contents—to the graphic itself—you do with the Direct Selection tool. This concept is the key to manipulating graphics within a graphics frame.

Figure 58 shows a graphics frame selected with the Selection tool. The Transform panel shows the X and Y locations of the frame and the width and height of the frame. In this figure, the Transform panel shows no information about the placed image.

Figure 59 shows the same object, but this time it has been selected with the Direct Selection tool. The graphic itself is selected. The selection frame is brown, which is the default color for a selected graphic. The selected frame around the image is called the bounding box. The **bounding box**—always rectangular—is the frame that defines the horizontal and vertical dimensions of the graphic. Finally, note that even though you can see the entire bounding box, there are parts of the graphic that you can't see. That's because the graphic is being cropped by the graphics frame.

It's important to note that the notations on the Transform panel are different. The + signs beside the X and Y text boxes are a visual indication that the Transform panel is now referring to the graphic, not the frame. The X and Y values are *in*

relation to the top-left corner of the frame. Let's explore this: The upper-left reference point in the Transform panel is selected. The X/Y coordinates in the Transform panel refer to the location of the upper-left

Figure 58 *Selected frame*

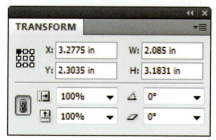

corner of the graphic. The upper-left corner of the graphic is .04" above and 1.07" to the left of the top-left corner *of the frame*. This is illustrated in Figure 60, which shows the graphic positioned at an X/Y value of 0/0.

Using the Content Indicator

When you're working with lots of graphics in lots of frames, you'll want a quicker solution for selecting graphics and frames. The quickest and easiest solution is to double-click the image. Double-clicking the image toggles between the frame being selected and the graphic being selected.

NEW InDesign CS5 debuts the content indicator, the donut-shaped circle shown in Figure 61. The content indicator is available whenever a graphic is placed in a frame. If you click the content indicator with the Selection tool, the graphic will be selected. Thus, the content indicator allows you to select the graphic with the Selection tool without having to switch to the Direct Selection tool.

You'll just need to make sure that when you intend to select a frame, you don't accidentally select the content indicator and, thus, the graphic. Then it's easy to make

modifications to the graphic, when you really mean to modify the frame.

Moving a Graphic Within a Graphics Frame

When you want to move the graphic within the frame, select the graphic by any method you prefer, then click and drag the graphic. You can also move the selected graphic using the arrow keys on the keypad. When you click and drag the graphic to move it, you see a ghosted image of the areas of the graphic that are outside the graphics frame, as shown

Figure 59 *Selected graphic*

Bounding box of graphic

Figure 60 *X/Y values of the selected graphic at 0/0*

X/Y of graphic is 0/0 aligned with top-left corner of frame

Figure 61 *The content indicator*

Content indicator

in Figure 62. The ghosted image is referred to as a **dynamic preview**.

Once you release the mouse button, the graphic will be repositioned within the frame. Remember, though, that regardless of where you move the graphic within the frame, the frame crops the graphic.

Copying and Pasting a Graphic

When designing layouts, you'll often find that you want to copy and paste a graphic from one frame to another. This is easy to do in InDesign. First, select the graphic (not the frame), then copy it. Select the frame where you want to paste the copy, then choose the Paste Into command on the Edit menu.

Resizing a Graphic

When you select a graphic with the Direct Selection tool, you can then resize the graphic within the frame. Changes that you make to the size of the graphic do not affect the size of the graphics frame.

You can drag the handles of the graphic to scale it. You can also use the Transform or Control panels. With the graphic selected, change the Scale X Percentage and the Scale Y Percentage values on the Transform or Control panels, as shown in Figure 63, to reduce or enlarge the graphic.

You can also use the Transform/Scale command on the Object menu to scale the graphic. Remember, when the graphic is selected with the Direct Selection tool, only the graphic will be scaled when you use this command.

Figure 62 *Dynamic preview of the entire graphic*

Figure 63 *Using the Control panel to scale the graphic*

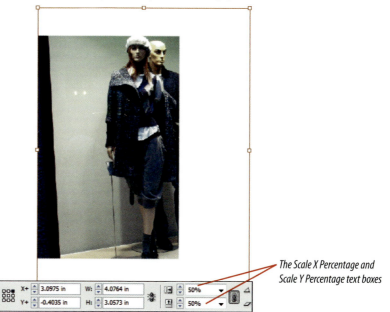

The Scale X Percentage and Scale Y Percentage text boxes

Using the Fitting Commands

While it's not difficult to select a graphic with the Direct Selection tool and then scale it using the Transform panel, there are a lot of steps in the process.

For a quick solution, you can use the Fitting commands, located on the Object menu. The Fitting commands offer different options for positioning the graphic in the frame. These commands are smart and useful but beware—they're easy to confuse with one another. It's important that you keep each command straight in your head, because one of the commands distorts the image to fit the frame. See Table 2.

Of all the fitting commands, the Fill Frame Proportionally command is the one you're likely to use most often, because it resizes the placed graphic to a size that is guaranteed to fit the frame, with no negative space in the frame. This means that some of the graphic may not be visible if it exceeds the size of the frame, but you can be confident that it will not be distorted to fit the frame.

Wrapping Text Around an Imported Photoshop Graphic Saved with a Named Clipping Path

In Chapter 3, you learned how to use the Text Wrap panel to wrap text around a bounding box using the Wrap around bounding box button. You can also wrap text around a graphic inside the frame, as shown in Figure 64.

The Text Wrap panel offers a number of methods for doing so. In this chapter, you will focus on wrapping text around an image that was saved with a named clipping path in Photoshop. Figure 65 shows

Figure 64 *Wrapping text around a graphic*

The text is able to enter the graphics frame to wrap around the picture

TABLE 2: FITTING COMMANDS		
Command	**Result**	**Proportion Issues**
Fill Frame Proportionally	The graphic is scaled proportionally to the minimum size required to fill the entire frame.	No proportion issues. The graphic is scaled in proportion.
Fit Content Proportionally	The graphic is scaled proportionally to the largest size it can be without exceeding the frame. Some areas of the frame may be empty.	No proportion issues. The graphic is scaled in proportion.
Fit Frame to Content	The frame is resized to the exact size of the graphic.	No proportion issues. The graphic is not scaled.
Fit Content to Frame	The content is resized to the exact size and shape of the frame.	The content will almost always be distorted with this fitting command.
Center Content	The center point of the graphic will be aligned with the center point of the frame.	No proportion issues. The graphic is not scaled.

Figure 65 *A Photoshop image with a clipping path*

Clipping path created in Photoshop

Working with Frames

a Photoshop image with a clipping path drawn around a man. A **clipping path** is a graphic that you draw in Photoshop that outlines the areas of the image you want to show when the file is placed in a layout program like InDesign. When you save the Photoshop file, you name the clipping path and save it with the file.

When you place a graphic that has a named clipping path saved with it into your layout, InDesign is able to recognize the clipping path. With the graphic selected, click the Wrap around object shape button on the Text Wrap panel, click the Type list arrow in the Contour Options section of the panel,

and then choose Photoshop Path, as shown in Figure 66. When you do so, the Path menu will list all the paths that were saved with the graphic file. (Usually, you will save only one path with a file.) Choose the path that you want to use for the text wrap.

QUICK TIP

To define the way text wraps around a graphic, click the Wrap To list arrow in the Wrap Options section, then choose one of the available presets.

Remember, in every case, you can always manually adjust the resulting text wrap boundary. Though the clipping path is

created in Photoshop, the text wrap itself is created in InDesign—and it is editable. As shown in Figure 67, you can relocate the path's anchor points using the Direct Selection tool. You can also use the Add Anchor Point and Delete Anchor Point tools to add or delete points to the path as you find necessary. Click the Add Anchor Point tool anywhere on the path to add a new point and increase your ability to manipulate the path. Click any anchor point with the Delete Anchor Point tool to remove it. Changing the shape of the path changes how text wraps around the path.

Figure 66 *Choosing the Wrap around object shape button*

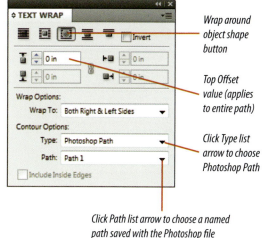

Wrap around object shape button

Top Offset value (applies to entire path)

Click Type list arrow to choose Photoshop Path

Click Path list arrow to choose a named path saved with the Photoshop file

Figure 67 *Manipulating the text wrap path*

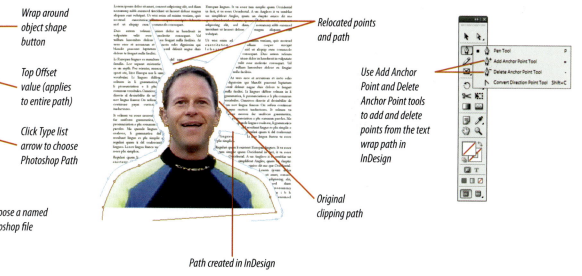

Relocated points and path

Use Add Anchor Point and Delete Anchor Point tools to add and delete points from the text wrap path in InDesign

Original clipping path

Path created in InDesign

Place graphics in a document

1. Open ID 4-6.indd, then save it as **Flowers**.

2. On the Layers panel, click the empty square next to the Text layer name to lock the Text layer, as shown in Figure 68.

   TIP When a layer is locked, the contents of the layer cannot be modified; this is a smart way to protect the contents of any layer from unwanted changes.

3. Click the **Background layer** to target it, click the **Rectangle Frame tool** ⊠, then draw a graphics frame in the center of the page that is approximately the size shown in Figure 69.

   The bounding box of the graphics frame is orange because orange is the selection color applied to the Background layer.

4. Click **File** on the Application bar, click **Place**, navigate to the drive and folder where your Data Files are stored, then double-click **Windmills Ghost.psd**.

   Because the frame was selected, the graphic is placed automatically into the frame, as shown in Figure 70.

5. Click the **Selection tool** ▶, click anywhere to deselect the frame, click the **Eye icon** 👁 on the Background layer to hide it, then click the **Images layer** to target it on the Layers panel.

6. Click **File** on the Application bar, click **Place**, navigate to the drive and folder where your Data Files are stored, click **Windmills Color.psd**, then click **Open**.

   (continued)

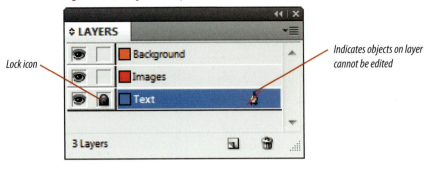

Figure 68 *Locking the Text layer*

Lock icon

Indicates objects on layer cannot be edited

Figure 69 *Drawing a graphics frame*

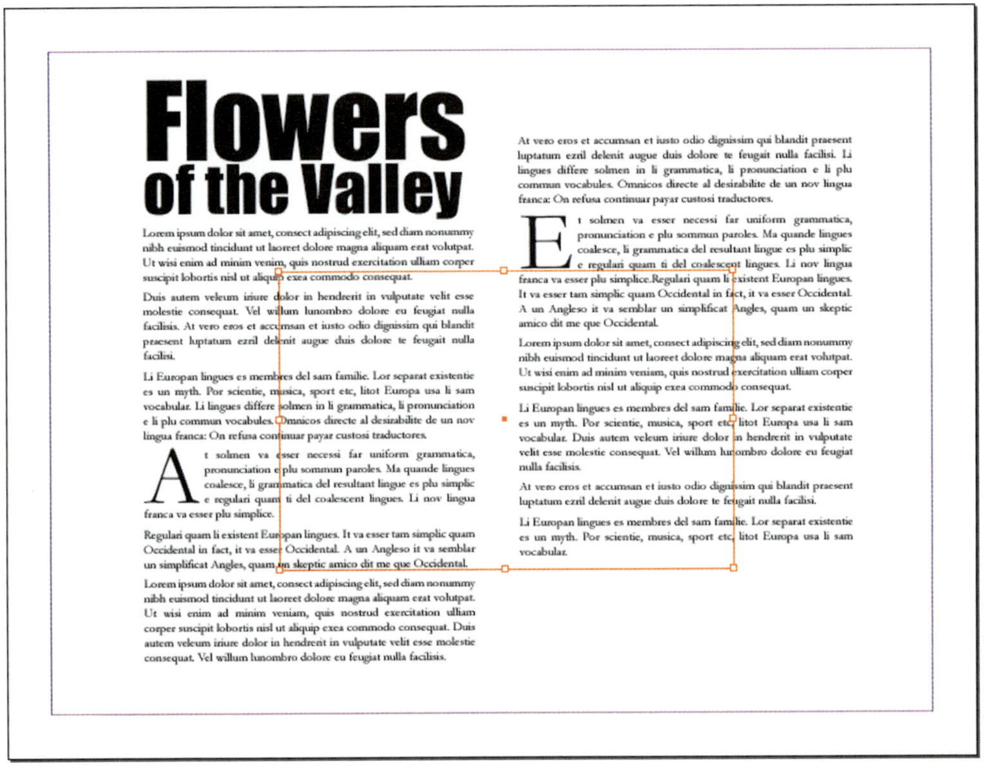

Figure 70 *Viewing the placed graphic*

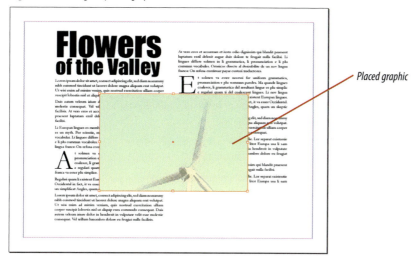

Placed graphic

Figure 71 *Viewing the graphic placed with the loaded graphics icon*

Top-left corner of placed graphic
located at same spot where loaded
graphics icon was clicked

TIP You can also access the Place command by pressing [Ctrl][D] (Win) or ⌘ [D] (Mac).

7. Position the pointer over the document.

    The pointer changes to the loaded graphics icon and shows a thumbnail of the graphic.

8. Click the loaded graphics icon on the **F** in the word Flowers.

    As shown in Figure 71, the graphic is placed in a new graphics frame whose top-left corner is located where the loaded graphics icon was clicked.

You imported two graphics using two subtly different methods. You created a graphics frame then used the Place command to place a graphic in that frame. You used the Place command to load a graphic file then clicked the loaded graphics icon to create a new frame for the new graphic.

Move a graphic in a graphics frame

1. Hide the Images layer, show and target the Background layer, click the **Selection tool** , then click the **Windmills Ghost graphic** in the layout.

2. Click the **top-left reference point** on the Transform panel.

3. Click the **Direct Selection tool** , position the tool over the graphic, then click the **graphic**.

TIP As soon as you position the Direct Selection tool over the graphic, the pointer becomes a hand pointer.

    The X and Y text boxes on the Transform panel change to X+ and Y+, indicating that the graphic—not the frame—is selected.

(continued)

4. Note the width and height of the graphic, as listed on the Transform panel.

The graphic is substantially larger than the frame that contains it, thus there are many areas of the graphic outside the frame that are not visible through the frame.

5. Press and hold the **hand icon** on the graphic until the hand icon changes to a black arrow, then drag inside the graphics frame, releasing your mouse when the windmill is centered in the frame, as shown in Figure 72.

The graphic moves within the frame, but the frame itself does not move. Note that the blue bounding box, now visible, is the bounding box for the graphic within the frame.

6. Click the **Selection tool** , then click the **graphic**.

The orange graphics frame appears and the blue bounding box of the graphic disappears. Note that the values on the Transform panel are again specific to the frame only.

7. Click and drag the **top-left selection handle** of the graphics frame so that it is aligned with the top-left corner of the document page.

As shown in Figure 73, the graphic within the frame does not change size or location.

8. Drag the **bottom-right corner** of the graphics frame so that it is aligned with the bottom-right corner of the document page.

As the frame is enlarged, more of the graphic within the frame is visible.

9. Click the **Direct Selection tool** , click the **graphic**, type **0** in the X+ text box on the

(continued)

Figure 72 *Viewing the graphic as it is moved in the frame*

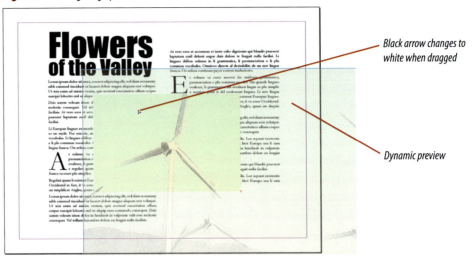

Black arrow changes to white when dragged

Dynamic preview

Figure 73 *Resizing the graphics frame*

Top-left corner of bounding box

Graphic does not change size

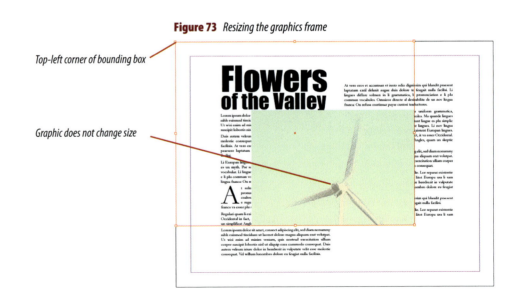

Figure 74 *Viewing the entire graphic in the enlarged frame*

Figure 75 *Scaling a graphic*

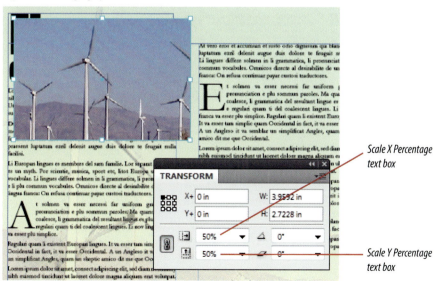

Scale X Percentage text box

Scale Y Percentage text box

Transform panel, type **0** in the Y+ text box, then press **[Enter]** (Win) or **[return]** (Mac).

As shown in Figure 74, the top-left corner of the graphic is aligned with the top-left corner of the frame.

You used the Direct Selection tool and X+ and Y+ values on the Transform panel to move a graphic within a graphics frame.

Resize graphics frames and graphics

1. Drag the **Background layer** below the Text layer on the Layers panel, then show and target the Images layer.

2. Press **[A]** to access the Direct Selection tool, then click the **Windmills Color graphic** in the layout.

3. Verify that the Constrain proportions for scaling option is activated on the Transform panel—represented by a link icon.

   The Constrain proportions for scaling option is activated by default. If you click it, you will deactivate this feature and see a broken link icon.

4. Type **50** in the Scale X Percentage text box on the Transform panel, as shown in Figure 75, then press **[Enter]** (Win) or **[return]** (Mac).

   Because the Constrain proportions for scaling option is activated, the graphic is scaled 50% horizontally and 50% vertically, as shown in Figure 75.

5. Press **[V]** to access the Selection tool, then click the **Windmills Color graphic** in the layout.

   The size of the graphics frame was not affected by scaling the graphic itself.

6. Click **Object** on the Application bar, point to **Fitting**, then click **Fit Frame to Content**.

(continued)

7. Click the **top-left reference point** on the Transform panel.

8. With the frame still selected, type **4.5** in the X Location text box, type **3** in the Y Location text box, type **3.32** in the Width text box, type **2.125** in the Height text box, then press **[Enter]** (Win) or **[return]** (Mac).

9. Press **[A]** to access the Direct Selection tool, click the **graphic**, then note the Scale X Percentage and Scale Y Percentage text boxes on the Transform panel, as shown in Figure 76.

   The graphic retains its 50% scale.

TIP When you resize a graphics frame using the Width and Height text boxes on the Transform panel, the graphic is not resized with the frame.

10. Click **Object** on the Application bar, point to **Fitting**, then click **Fit Content Proportionally**.

    The Transform panel shows that the graphic is scaled proportionately to fit the resized frame.

11. Deselect, press **[V]**, then click the **graphic**.

12. Click **Object** on the Application bar, point to **Fitting**, then click **Fit Frame to Content**.

    As shown in Figure 77, the right edge of the frame moves left to fit to the right edge of the graphic.

13. Deselect all.

You scaled a graphic using the Transform panel, noting that the graphics frame did not change with the scale. You then scaled the graphics frame with the Transform panel, noting that the graphic itself was not scaled. Lastly, you used the Fitting command to fit the graphic proportionally to the new frame size.

Figure 76   *Noting the Scale X and Scale Y Percentage values*

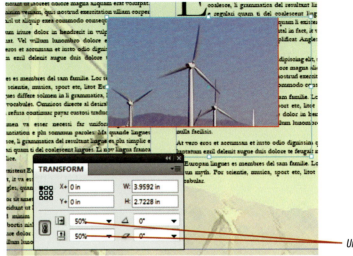

Unchanged

Figure 77   *Fitting the frame to the content*

Figure 78 *Wrapping text around a frame's bounding box*

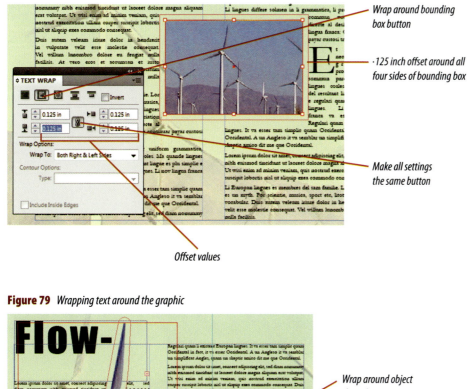

Wrap around bounding box button

·125 inch offset around all four sides of bounding box

Make all settings the same button

Offset values

Figure 79 *Wrapping text around the graphic*

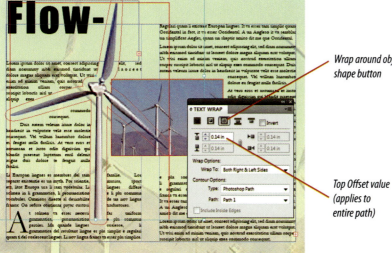

Wrap around object shape button

Top Offset value (applies to entire path)

Wrap text around a graphic

1. Verify that the Selection tool is selected, click the **graphic**, then click the **Wrap around bounding box button** ▤ on the Text Wrap panel.

2. Verify that the Make all settings the same button ▤ is active, type **.125** in the Top Offset text box, then press **[Enter]** (Win) or **[return]** (Mac).

   Your page and Text Wrap panel should resemble Figure 78.

3. Deselect all, press **[Ctrl][D]** (Win) or ⌘ **[D]** (Mac), navigate to the drive and folder where your Data Files are stored, then double-click **Windmills Silhouette.psd**.

4. Click the loaded graphics icon on the **F** in the word Flowers.

   Windmills Silhouette.psd was saved with a clipping path named "Path 1" in Photoshop.

5. Click the **Wrap around object shape button** ▣ on the Text Wrap panel, click the **Type list arrow**, click **Photoshop Path**, then note that Path 1 is automatically listed in the Path text box.

6. Type **.14** in the Top Offset text box, then press **[Enter]** (Win) or **[return]** (Mac).

   As shown in Figure 79, the text wraps around the graphic's shape, as defined by the path created in Photoshop. The Text Wrap panel specifies a default offset of .14 inches for the wrap.

(continued)

7. Deselect, click the **Selection tool** ▶ , then click the **graphic** to verify that the frame—not the graphic within the frame—is selected.

8. Type **-1.25** in the X Location text box on the Transform panel, type **3.8** in the Y Location text box, then press **[Enter]** (Win) or **[return]** (Mac).

   As shown in Figure 80, because of the shape of the path around the graphic, a couple of words appear in an odd position near the graphic.

9. In the Wrap Options section, click the **Wrap To list arrow**, click **Right Side**, then deselect the graphic.

   As shown in Figure 81, the words are moved to the right because the wrap option forces all items to wrap against the right edge of the graphic.

TIP Whenever you have a stray word or a stubborn area after applying a text wrap, you can fine tune the text wrap using the Delete Anchor Point tool ✑ to remove unwanted anchor points along the path. You can also move anchor points along the path using the Direct Selection tool.

(continued)

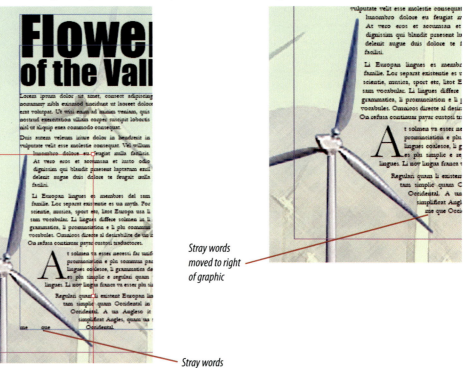

Figure 80 *Noting a minor problem with the wrap*

Figure 81 *Results of wrapping text to the right side*

Stray words moved to right of graphic

Stray words

Creating a Caption Based on Metadata

Metadata is text-based information about a graphics file. For example, you can save a Photoshop file with metadata that lists information such as the image's file name, file format, and resolution. When the file is placed in an InDesign layout, you can specify that InDesign automatically generates a caption listing the metadata. These types of captions would be useful if you were creating a contact sheet of photography, for example, that listed important information about a bunch of photos on a DVD or server.

InDesign offers several methods for generating captions of placed images. The most exciting one is Live Caption. Simply click to select a frame containing an image, click the Object menu, point to Captions, then click Generate Live Caption. InDesign creates a textbox immediately below the selected frame listing the metadata saved with the image, which is, at minimum, the file name. Here's the "Live" part: if you move that text frame to touch another frame containing a placed image, the text in the frame will update automatically to list the metadata information of the new image. To customize the data or formatting of the caption, click the Object menu, point to Captions, then click Caption Setup.

Figure 82 *Resizing the graphics frame*

Figure 83 *Viewing the completed document*

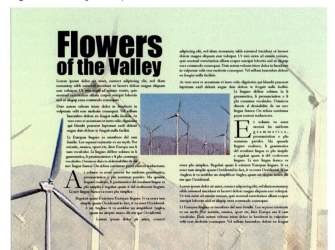

10. Click the **Selection tool** , click the **graphic**, drag the **left-middle handle** of the bounding box to the right so that it abuts the left edge of the page, then drag the **bottom-middle handle** of the bounding box up so that it abuts the bottom of the page, as shown in Figure 82.

TIP You may need to reduce the page view to see the bottom handles on the bounding box.

11. Click the **pasteboard** to deselect the frame, press **[W]** to change to Preview, then compare your work to Figure 83.

12. Save your work, then close Flowers.

You wrapped text around a graphic, specified an offset value, then specified Wrap Options.

Work with TEXT FRAMES

What You'll Do

▶ *In this lesson, you will explore options for autoflowing text through a document. You will also learn how to add column breaks to text.*

Semi-Autoflowing Text

In Chapter 3, you learned how to thread text manually—to make it flow from text frame to text frame. When you click the out port of one text frame with the Selection tool, the pointer changes to the loaded text icon. When you click the loaded text icon in another text frame, text flows from the first frame to the second frame—and the pointer automatically changes back to the Selection tool. That's great, but what if you wanted to keep threading text? Would you need to repeat the process over and over again?

This is where **semi-autoflowing** text comes in handy. When you are ready to click the loaded text icon in a text frame where you want text to flow, press and hold [Alt] (Win) or [option] (Mac) then click the text frame. Text will flow into the text frame, but the loaded text icon will remain active; it will not automatically revert back to the Selection tool. You can then thread text into another text frame. In a nutshell, semi-autoflowing text is a method for manually threading text through multiple frames.

Autoflowing Text

You can also **autoflow** text, which is a powerful option for quickly adding text to your document. Let's say that you create a six-page document and you specify that each page has three columns. When you create the document, the pages have no text frames on them—they're just blank, with columns and margin guides. To auto-flow text into the document, you click the Place command and choose the text document that you want to import. Once you choose the document, the pointer changes to the loaded text icon. If you press and hold [Shift], the loaded text icon becomes the autoflow loaded text icon. When you click the autoflow loaded text icon in a column, InDesign creates text frames within column guides on that page and all subsequent pages and flows the text into those frames. Because you specified that each page has three columns when you created the document, InDesign will create three text frames in the columns on every page into which the text will flow. Figure 84 shows a page with three text frames created by autoflowing text. Note that if you autoflow more text than the document size can handle, InDesign will add as many pages as necessary to autoflow all of the text. Note also that, if your document pages contain objects such as graphics, the text frames added by the autoflow will be positioned in front of the graphics already on the page.

As you may imagine, autoflowing text is a powerful option, but don't be intimidated by it. The text frames that are generated are all editable. You can resize them or delete them. Nevertheless, you should take some time to practice autoflowing text to get the hang of it. Like learning how to ride a bicycle, you can read about it all you want, but actually doing it is where the learning happens.

Inserting a Column Break

When you are working with text in columns, you will often want to move text from the bottom of one column to the top of the next. You do this by inserting a column break. A **column break** is a typographic command that forces text to the next column. The Column Break command is located within the Insert Break Character command on the Type menu.

In Figure 85, the headline near the bottom of the first column would be better positioned at the top of the next column. By inserting a column break, you do exactly that, as shown in Figure 86.

Inserting a "Continued on page..." Notation

When threading text manually or auto-flowing text, you will get to a point where text has filled all the text frames on the page and continues to another page. Usually, the text continues onto the very next page—but not always. In many cases, the next page will be reserved for pictures or other publication elements, such as tables or graphs. When the reader gets to the bottom of the page of text,

Figure 84 *Three text frames created in columns by autoflowing text*

Figure 85 *Viewing text that needs a column break*

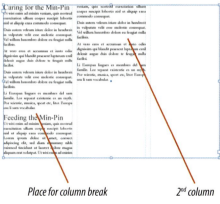

Place for column break   *2nd column*

Figure 86 *Viewing text after inserting a column break*

Text is forced to top of next column

they need to know on which page the text is continued. You can insert a "Continued on page..." notation to let the reader know where to go to continue reading.

If you've ever read a magazine or newspaper article, you are familiar with "Continued on page..." notations. In InDesign, a page continuation is formatted as a special character. Simply create a text frame, then type the words "Continued on page X." Select the X, then apply the Next Page Number command. The X changes to the page number of the page that contains the text frame into which the text flows. If for any reason you move pages within the Pages panel and page numbers change, the Next Page Number character will automatically update to show the page number where the text continues.

The Next Page Number command is located within the Insert Special Character command under Markers on the Type menu.

There's one important point you need to note when creating a "Continued on page..." notation. Below the text frame on the page of the text you are flowing, you will need to create another text frame to contain the "Continued on page..." notation. In order for the notation to work—for it to list the page where the text continues—the top edge of the text frame that contains the notation must be touching the frame that contains the body copy that is to be continued.

Using the Story Editor

InDesign has a feature called the Story Editor that makes it easier to edit text in complex documents. Imagine that you are doing a layout for a single magazine article. The text for the article is flowed through numerous text frames across 12 pages. Now imagine that you want to edit the text. May be you want to proofread it or spell check it. Editing the text within the layout might be difficult—you'd have to scroll from page to page. Instead, you could use the Edit in Story Editor command on the Edit menu. This opens a new window, which contains all the text in a single file, just like a word processing document. Any changes that you make in the Story Editor window will be immediately updated to the text in the layout. It's a great feature!

Paragraphs that Span or Split Columns

Imagine having one textbox that contains five paragraphs, with the fourth needing to be split into two columns within the textbox. Or imagine that you have a single text frame with three columns, but you want to run a headline across all three columns. With InDesign CS5, you can format text to span multiple columns or split into columns within a single text frame. Not only is this feature unprecedented, it's remarkably easy to use. Simply click your cursor in the paragraph you want to modify. Choose the Span Columns command from the Paragraph Panel menu, then select to split the paragraph or span the paragraph.

Figure 87 *Creating a text frame using the loaded text icon*

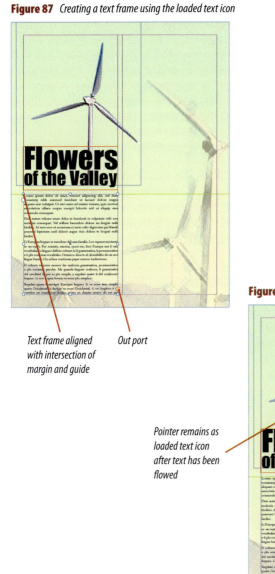

Text frame aligned
with intersection of
margin and guide

Out port

Figure 88 *Flowing text with the semi-autoflow loaded text icon*

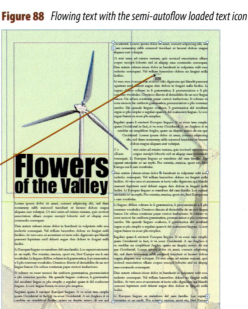

Pointer remains as
loaded text icon
after text has been
flowed

Autoflow text

1. Open ID 4-7.indd, save it as **Autoflow**, then look at each page in the document.

   Other than the text frame that holds the headline on page 1, there are no text frames in the document.

2. Click the **Selection tool** ▶, double-click the **page 1 icon** on the Pages panel, click **File** on the Application bar, click **Place**, navigate to the drive and folder where your Data Files are stored, then double-click **Windmill text.doc**.

   The pointer changes to the loaded text icon.

3. Drag a **text frame** in the position shown in Figure 87.

   Note that once you have drawn the frame, the loaded text icon automatically changes back to the Selection tool.

4. Click the **out port** of the text frame, then position the loaded text icon over the right column on the page.

5. Press and hold **[Alt]** (Win) or **[option]** (Mac) so that the pointer changes to the semi-autoflow loaded text icon.

6. Still pressing and holding [Alt] (Win) or [option] (Mac), click the **top-left corner** of the right column, so that a new text frame is created.

   Because you used the semi-autoflow loaded text icon, the pointer remains as a loaded text icon and does not revert back to the Selection tool, as shown in Figure 88.

7. Double-click the **page 2 icon**, then click the **top-left corner** of the left column on the page.

   (continued)

A new frame is created and text flows into the left column.

8. Click the **out port** of the new text frame on page 2, then position the pointer over the right column on page 2.

9. Press and hold **[Shift]**, note the change to the loaded text icon, then click the **top-left corner** of the second column.

   Because you were pressing [Shift], InDesign created text frames within column guides on all subsequent pages. InDesign has added new pages to the document to accommodate the autoflow.

You placed text by clicking and dragging the loaded text icon to create a new text frame. You flowed text using the semi-autoflow loaded text icon and the autoflow loaded text icon.

Reflow text

1. Double-click the **page 4 icon** on the Pages panel, then create a horizontal guide at 5.875 in.

2. Click the **left text frame** to select it, drag the **bottom-middle handle** of the text frame's bounding box up until it snaps to the guide, then do the same to the right text frame, so that your page resembles Figure 89.

   The text is reflowed in the document.

3. Double-click the numbers **2-3** on the Pages panel to center the spread in the document window, click **View** on the Application bar, point to **Extras**, click **Show Text Threads**, then click the **right text frame** on page 2.

   (continued)

Figure 89 *Resizing text frames*

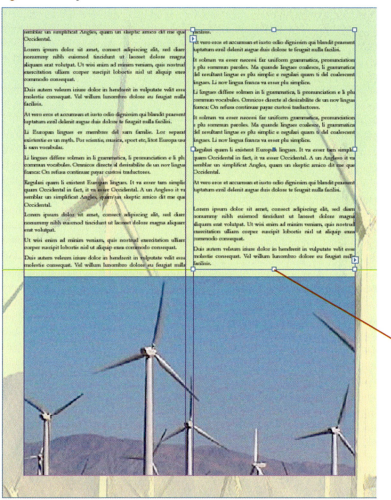

Drag middle handle up to guide

Figure 90 *Flowing text after deleting a text frame*

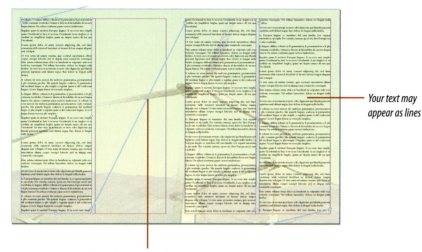

Your text may appear as lines

Text flow continues between remaining text frames

Figure 91 *Threading text to a new text frame*

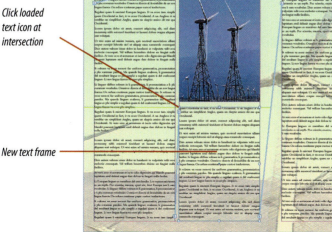

Click loaded text icon at intersection

New text frame

4. With the right frame on page 2 still selected, press **[Delete]** (Win) or **[delete]** (Mac), then click the **text frame** remaining on page 2.

   As shown in Figure 90, the text is reflowed from the first text frame on page 2 to the first text frame on page 3.

5. Press **[Ctrl][D]**(Win) or ⌘ **[D]** (Mac), navigate to the drive and folder where your Data Files are stored, then double-click **2 Windmills.psd**.

6. Click the **top-left corner** of the right column on page 2.

7. Create a horizontal guide at 5.375 in.

8. Click the **text frame** on page 2, then click the **out port**.

9. Click the **intersection** between the guide you created and the left edge of the right column, beneath the graphic.

   As shown in Figure 91, text is now threaded through the new text frame.

You resized two text frames, noting that text was reflowed through the document. You deleted a text frame, then created a text frame, noting that text continued to flow through the document.

Add a column break

1. Double-click the **page 5 icon** on the Pages panel, then delete the two text frames on page 5.

2. Click **Layout** on the Application bar, click **Margins and Columns**, change the number of columns to 3, then click **OK**.

3. Press **[Ctrl][D]**(Win) or ⌘ **[D]** (Mac), navigate to the drive and folder where your Data Files are stored, then double-click **Sidebar copy.doc**.

4. Drag the **loaded text icon** to create a text frame, as shown in Figure 92.

5. Click **Object** on the Application bar, click **Text Frame Options**, change the number of columns to 3, then click **OK**.

6. Click the **Type tool** T , then click to place the pointer before the W in the Windmill Speeds headline.

7. Click **Type** on the Application bar, point to **Insert Break Character**, then click **Column Break**.

   The Windmill Speeds text is forced into the second column.

8. Click before the W in the Windmill Productivity headline, click **Type** on the Application bar, point to **Insert Break Character**, then click **Column Break**.

   Your page should resemble Figure 93.

You deleted two text frames on a page, then changed the number of columns on that page. You then placed text, formatted the text frame to have three columns, and, finally, used the Column Break command to create two new column breaks.

Figure 92 *Creating a text frame with the loaded text icon*

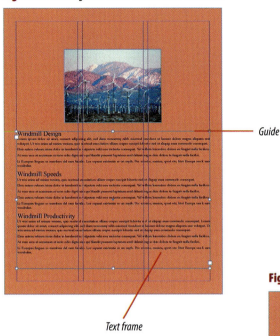

Guide

Text frame

Figure 93 *Viewing the text frame with column breaks*

Figure 94 *Creating a text frame for the page continuation notation*

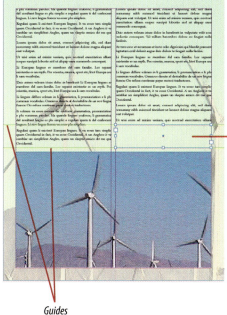

Text frame

Guides

Figure 95 *Viewing the page continuation notation*

Notation

(Continued on page 6)

Insert a page continuation notation

1. Double-click the **page 4 icon** on the Pages panel, then create a horizontal guide at 5 in.

2. Click the **Selection tool**, click the text frame in the right column, then drag the **bottom middle bounding box handle** up until it snaps to the guide at 5 in.

3. Click the **Type tool**, then create a text frame between the two guides, as shown in Figure 94.

   The edges of the two text frames should overlap slightly at the guide, which is critical in order for page continuation notation to work.

4. Click **Object** on the Application bar, click **Text Frame Options**, change the vertical justification to Center, then click **OK**.

5. Click the **Type tool** inside the new text box, type **(Continued on page X)**, click anywhere within the (Continued on Page X) text, show the Paragraph Styles panel, then click the style named **Continued**.

6. Select the letter **X**, click **Type** on the Application bar, point to **Insert Special Character**, point to **Markers**, then click **Next Page Number**.

   The text now reads (Continued on Page 6), as shown in Figure 95.

   TIP You can use the Previous Page Number command along with "Continued from page . . ." text to indicate that a story is continued from a previous page.

7. Click the **Selection tool**, click the **text frame** above the "Continued" text frame, then follow the text thread to verify that the text does indeed continue on page 6.

8. Save your work, then close Autoflow.

You inserted a page continuation notation in the document.

Align and distribute objects on a page.

1. Open ID 4-8.indd, then save it as **Dog Days**.
2. Click the workspace switcher list arrow on the Application bar, then click Advanced or Reset Advanced if Advanced is already checked.
3. Click the Type tool, then drag a text frame that fills the left column on the page.
4. Click the Selection tool, press and hold [Shift][Alt] (Win) or [Shift][option] (Mac), then drag a copy of the text frame and position it in line with the right column.
5. Click the Rectangle Frame tool, click anywhere on the page, type **1.5** in both the Width and Height text boxes, then click OK.
6. Click the top-left reference point on the Transform panel, type **0** in the X Location text box, type **0** in the Y Location text box, then press [Enter] (Win) or [return] (Mac).
7. Verify that the frame has no fill and no stroke.
8. Click Edit on the Application bar, click Step and Repeat, type **1** in the Repeat Count text box, type **9.5** in the Horizontal Offset text box, type **0** in the Vertical Offset text box, then click OK.
9. Select both graphics frames, click Edit on the Application bar, click Step and Repeat, type **1** in the Repeat Count text box, type **0** in the Horizontal Offset text box, type **7** in the Vertical Offset text box, then click OK.
10. Click the Rectangle Frame tool, click anywhere in the left column, type **3** in both the Width and Height text boxes, click OK, then verify that the frame has no fill or stroke.
11. Click the Selection tool, press and hold [Shift], click the top-left graphics frame, then click the top-right graphics frame so that three frames are selected.
12. Click Window on the Application bar, point to Object & Layout, click Align, then click the Distribute horizontal centers button on the Align panel.
13. Deselect all, select the top-left and bottom-left graphics frames and the 3"× 3" frame, click the Distribute vertical centers button on the Align panel, then compare your page to Figure 96.

Stack and layer objects.

1. Display the Layers panel.
2. Double-click Layer 1, type **Background Graphic** in the Name text box, then click OK.
3. Click the Create new layer button on the Layers panel, double-click the new layer, type **Dog Pics** in the Name text box, then click OK.
4. Click the Layers panel options button, click New Layer, type **Body** in the Name text box, then click OK.
5. Click the Selection tool, select the five graphics frames, then drag the Selected items icon from the Background Graphic layer up to the Dog Pics layer.
6. Select the two text frames, then drag the Selected items icon from the Background Graphic layer up to the Body layer.
7. Verify that the Body layer is selected, select only the left text frame, click File on the Application bar, click Place, navigate to the drive and folder where your Data Files are stored, then double-click Skills Text.doc.
8. Click any word five times to select all the text, then format the text as Garamond 12-point with 14-point leading.
9. Click the Selection tool, click the out port of the left text frame, then click the loaded text icon anywhere in the right text frame.
10. On the Layers panel, drag the Body layer down below the Dog Pics layer.
11. Save your work.

Figure 96 *Completed Skills Review, Part 1*

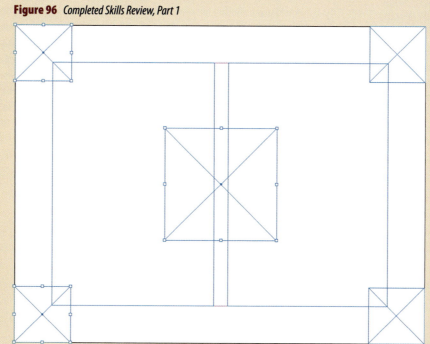

Work with graphics frames.

1. Click the Selection tool, select the top-left graphics frame, press [Ctrl][D] (Win) or ⌘ [D] (Mac), navigate to the drive and folder where your Data Files are stored, then double-click Red 1.psd.
2. Select the top-right graphics frame, press [Ctrl][D] (Win) or ⌘ [D] (Mac), navigate to the drive and folder where your Data Files are stored, then double-click Black 1.psd.
3. Select the bottom-left graphics frame, press [Ctrl] [D] (Win) or ⌘ [D] (Mac), navigate to the drive and folder where your Data Files are stored, then double-click Red 2.psd.
4. Select the bottom-right graphics frame, press [Ctrl] [D] (Win) or ⌘ [D] (Mac), navigate to the drive and folder where your Data Files are stored, then double-click Black 2.psd.
5. Select the top two graphics frames, click Object on the Application bar, point to Fitting, then click Fit Content to Frame.
6. Deselect all, click the Direct Selection tool, press and hold your pointer on the bottom-left graphic, then drag until the dog's nose is at the center of the frame.
7. Click the center reference point on the Transform panel, type **40** in both the Scale X Percentage and Scale Y Percentage text boxes, then click and drag to center the dog's head in the frame.
8. Deselect all, click the Selection tool, select the four corner graphics frames, click the Wrap around bounding box button on the Text Wrap panel, then type **.125** in all four of the Offset text boxes.
9. Select the center graphics frame, press [Ctrl][D] (Win) or ⌘ [D] (Mac), navigate to the drive and folder where your Data Files are stored, then double-click Dog Silo.psd.
10. Click the Direct Selection tool, click the new graphic, then click the Wrap around object shape button on the Text Wrap panel.
11. Click the Type list arrow in the Contour Options section, choose Same as Clipping, type **.15** in the Top Offset text box, then press [Enter] (Win) or [return] (Mac).
12. Press [W] to switch to Preview, deselect all, compare your page to Figure 97, save your work, then close Dog Days.

Figure 97 *Completed Skills Review, Part 2*

Lorem ipsum dolor sit amet, consect adipiscing elit, sed diam nonummy nibh euismod tincidunt ut laoreet dolore magna aliquam erat volutpat. Ut wisi enim ad minim venim, quis nostrud exercitation ulliam corper suscipit lobortis nisl ut aliquip exea commodo consequat.

Duis autem veleum iriure dolor in hendrerit in vulputate velit esse molestie consequat. Vel willum lunombro dolore eu feugiat nulla facilisis. At vero eros et accumsan et iusto odio dignissim qui blandit praesent luptatum ezril delenit augue duis dolore te feugait nulla facilisi.

Li Europan lingues es membres del sam familie. Lor separat existentie es un myth. Por scientie, musica, sport etc, litot Europa usa li sam vocabular. Li lingues differe solmen in li grammatica, li pronunciation e li plu commun vocabules. Omnicos directe al desirabilite de un nov lingua franca: On refusa continuar payar custosi traductores.

At solmen va esser necessi far uniform grammatica, pronunciation e plu sommun paroles. Ma quande lingues coalesce, li grammatica del

resultant lingue es plu simplic e regulari quam ti del coalescent lingues. Li nov lingua franca va esser plu simplice.

Regulari quam li existent Europan lingues. It va esser tam simplic quam Occidental in fact, it va esser Occidental. A un Angleso it va semblar un simplificat Angles, quam un skeptic amico dit me que Occidental.

Lorem ipsum dolor sit amet, consect adipiscing elit, sed diam nonummy nibh euismod tincidunt ut laoreet dolore magna aliquam erat volutpat. Ut wisi enim ad minim veniam, quis nostrud exercitation ulliam corper suscipit lobortis nisl ut aliquip exea commodo consequat. Duis autem veleum iriure dolor in hendrerit in vulputate velit esse molestie consequat. Vel willum lunombro dolore eu feugiat nulla facilisis.

At vero eros et accumsan et iusto odio dignissim qui blandit praesent luptatum ezril delenit augue duis dolore te feugait nulla facilisi. Li lingues differe solmen in li grammatica, li pronunciation e li plu commun vocabules. Omnicos directe al desirabilite de un nov lingua franca: On refusa continuar payar custosi traductores.

Solmen va esser necessi far uniform grammatica,

Work with text frames.

1. Open ID 4-9.indd, click Update Links, then save it as **Dog Days Part 2**.
2. Click the Selection tool, click the right text frame on page 1, then click the out port of the text frame.
3. Double-click page 2 on the Pages panel, position the loaded text icon over the left column, press and hold [Shift], then click the top-left corner of the left column.
4. Click View on the Application bar, point to Extras, click Show Text Threads, double-click page 3 on the Pages panel, then click the Eye icon in the Dog Pics layer on the Layers panel to hide it temporarily. (*Hint*: Autoflowing the text created two text frames on page 3, but they weren't visible because the Body Copy layer is behind the Dog Pics layer.)
5. Verify that the Body Copy layer is selected, select and delete the left text frame on page 3, select and delete the right text frame on Page 3, then click the Eye icon in the Dog Pics layer so that the layer is visible again.
6. Double-click page 2 on the Pages panel, select the right text frame, then drag the bottom-middle handle of the right text frame up so that it slightly overlaps the top edge of the small text frame at the bottom of the column.
7. Click the Type tool, click in the small text frame at the bottom of the right column, then type **Turn to page X**.
8. Click the Continued style on the Paragraph Styles panel, select the letter X, click Type on the Application bar, point to Insert Special Character, point to Markers, then click Next Page Number.
9. Deselect all, compare your screen to Figure 98, save your work, then close Dog Days Part 2.

Figure 98 *Completed Skills Review, Part 3*

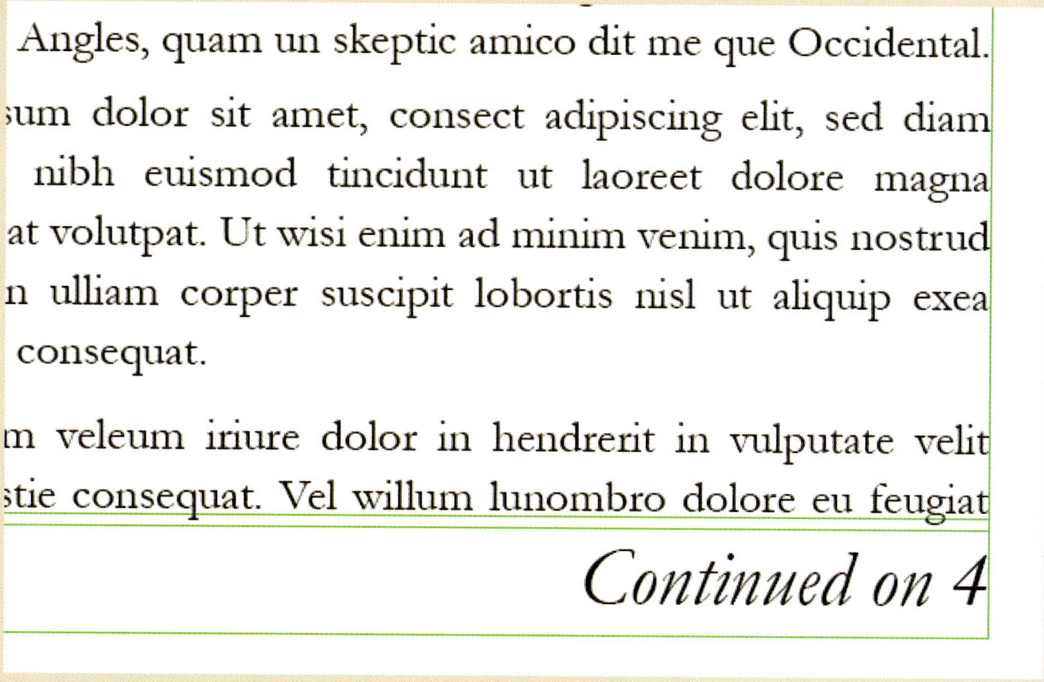

Angles, quam un skeptic amico dit me que Occidental.

sum dolor sit amet, consect adipiscing elit, sed diam
nibh euismod tincidunt ut laoreet dolore magna
at volutpat. Ut wisi enim ad minim venim, quis nostrud
n ulliam corper suscipit lobortis nisl ut aliquip exea
consequat.

m veleum iriure dolor in hendrerit in vulputate velit
stie consequat. Vel willum lunombro dolore eu feugiat

Continued on 4

You work for a design firm, and you are creating a logo for a local shop that sells vintage board games. You decide to create an 8" × 8" checkerboard, which you will later incorporate into your logo.

1. Open ID 4-10.indd, then save it as **Checkerboard**.
2. Click the Rectangle Frame tool, create a 1" square frame anywhere on the board, fill it with black and no stroke, then position it so that its top-left corner has a (0, 0) coordinate.
3. Use the Step and Repeat command to make one copy, one inch to the right of the original square
4. Select the new square, if necessary, change its fill color to Brick Red, then select both squares.
5. Use the Step and Repeat command again, type **3** in the Repeat Count text box, type **0** in the Vertical Offset text box, type **2** in the Horizontal Offset text box, then click OK.
6. Verify that all squares are still selected, use the Step and Repeat command again, type **1** in the Repeat Count text box, type **1** in the Vertical Offset text box, type **0** in the Horizontal Offset text box, then click OK.
7. Deselect all, select the eight squares in the second row, click the center reference point on the Transform panel, then change the Rotation Angle text box to 180°.

8. Select all, use the Step and Repeat command again, type **3** in the Repeat Count text box, type **2** in the Vertical Offset text box, type **0** in the Horizontal Offset text box, then click OK.

9. Press [W] to switch to Preview, deselect all, then compare your work to Figure 99.
10. Save your work, then close Checkerboard.

Figure 99 *Completed Project Builder 1*

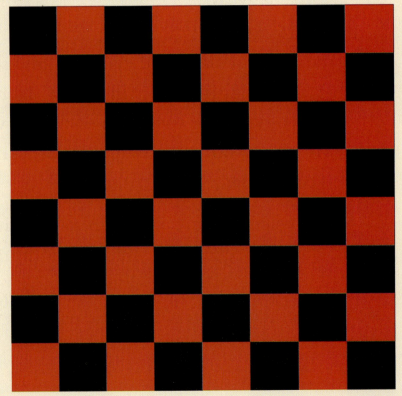

You are a designer at a design firm that specializes in travel. A client comes in with a disk that contains a layout she created in InDesign. She wants you to use it as a template for future layouts. You open the file and decide that it's best to move the basic elements onto layers.

1. Open ID 4-11.indd, then save it as **Brochure Layers**.
2. On the Layers panel, rename Layer 1 as **Background Colors**.
3. Create a new layer, then name it **Pictures**.
4. Create a new layer, then name it **Text**.
5. Select the four graphics frames, then move them onto the Pictures layer.
6. Select the two text frames, then move them onto the Text layer.
7. Use the Layers panel to select all the frames on the Pictures layer, then compare your work to Figure 100.
8. Save your work, then close Brochure Layers.

Figure 100 *Completed Project Builder 2*

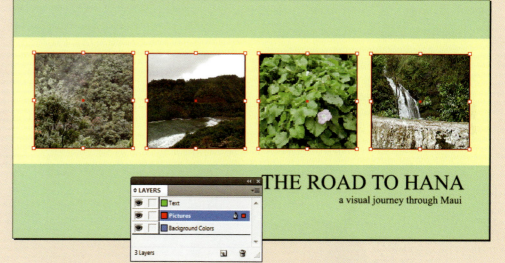

You head up the layout team for a design firm. Your client has delivered you a Photoshop file with a clipping path. He wants you to use it in the layout he has supplied. He tells you he wants the graphic placed in the middle of the page with text wrapping around it on all four sides. You import the graphic and realize that you will need to modify the path in InDesign that controls the wrap.

1. Open ID 4-12.indd, then save it as **Four Leg Wrap**.
2. Click File on the Application bar, then click Place, navigate to the drive and folder where your Data Files are stored, then double-click Red Silo.psd.
3. Click the loaded graphics icon anywhere on the page, click the Selection tool, then center the graphic on the page.

4. Verify that you can see the Transform panel, press and hold [Ctrl][Shift] (Win) or [Command] [Shift] (Mac), then drag the top-left corner of the frame toward the center of the frame, reducing the frame until the Width text box on the Transform panel reads approximately 5 in.
5. Click the center reference point on the Transform panel, type **4.25** in the X Location text box, type **4.2** in the Y Location text box, then press [Enter] (Win) or [return] (Mac).
6. Click the Direct Selection tool, click the graphic, click the Wrap around object shape button on the Text Wrap panel, then adjust the offset so it is visually pleasing.

7. Draw a graphics frame in the position shown in Figure 101, being sure the bottom edges of the two graphics frames are aligned.
8. With only the lower graphics frame selected, click the Wrap around bounding box button on the Text Wrap panel. (*Hint*: Adjust the new frame as necessary to move any stray text.)
9. Deselect all, press [W] to switch to Preview, then compare your work to Figure 102.
10. Save your work, then close Four Leg Wrap.

Figure 101 *Positioning the graphics frame*

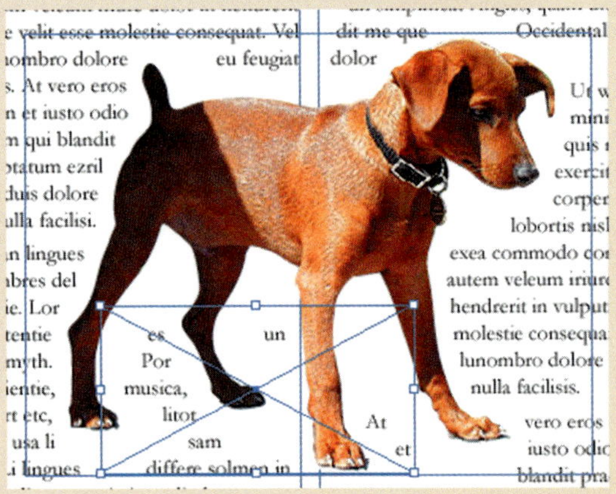

Figure 102 *Completed Design Project*

This project will test your problem-solving skills when using the Step and Repeat command and the Align panel. Your challenge is to recreate the graphic shown in Figure 103. First read the rules, then proceed with the exercise steps below.

Rules.

1. You will start by opening an 8" × 8" InDesign document that contains a single red 1.45" square.
2. To recreate the graphic in the figure, you may use only the Step and Repeat command and the Align panel. (*Hint*: You may also drag single objects.) You can't scale any objects.
3. In the final graphic, the top-left square must be aligned with the top-left corner of the page. The bottom-right square must be aligned with the bottom-right corner of the page, and the eight squares in between must all be equidistant, forming a perfect staircase.
4. Devise the simplest solution for recreating the graphic.
5. If you can't recreate the figure on your own, refer to the steps below.

Exercise.

1. Open ID 4-13.indd, then save it as **Test Your Alignment**.
2. Select the top-left square, click Step and Repeat, type **.5** in the Vertical Offset text box, type **.5** in the Horizontal Offset text box, type **9** in the Repeat Count text box, then click OK.
3. Deselect all.
4. Drag the bottommost square down and align its bottom-right corner with the bottom-right corner of the page.
5. Select all, click the Distribute vertical centers button on the Align panel, then click the Distribute horizontal centers button.
6. Press [W] to switch to Preview.
7. Deselect all, compare your screen to Figure 103, save your work, then close Test Your Alignment.

Figure 103 *Completed Portfolio Project*

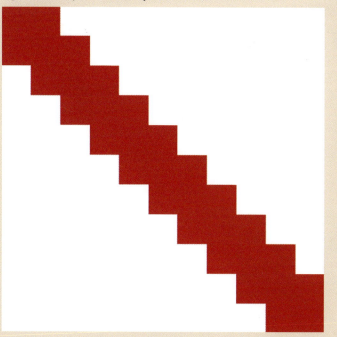

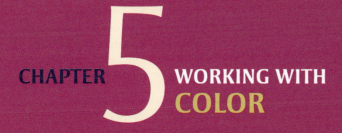

CHAPTER 5 WORKING WITH
COLOR

1. Work with process colors
2. Apply color
3. Work with spot colors
4. Work with gradients

CHAPTER 5 WORKING WITH COLOR

In Chapter 5, you will explore InDesign's many methods for creating and applying color. You'll use the Swatches panel to create new colors, and you'll learn a number of tips and tricks for applying color quickly. You'll also use the Color panel to quickly mix colors and modify the color of selected objects.

As a fully functional layout application, InDesign is equipped with a user-friendly interface for creating process tints and spot colors. You'll use the Swatches panel again to create spot colors, and you'll explore the built-in spot color libraries.

Finally, you'll work with gradients. Be prepared to be impressed by InDesign's sophisticated interface for creating, applying, and manipulating gradients.

New Color Swatch

Swatch Name: Gold

☐ Name with Color Value

Color Type: Process

Color Mode: CMYK

Cyan 0 %
Magenta 10 %
Yellow 90 %
Black 0 %

OK
Cancel
Add

◇ SWATCHES

Tint: 100 ▶ %

☐ [None]
☐ [Paper]
■ [Black]
■ [Registration]
■ C=100 M=0 Y=0 K=0
■ C=0 M=100 Y=0 K=0
■ C=0 M=0 Y=100 K=0
■ Gold
■ Blue
■ Pink

◇ COLOR

C 10 %
M 0 %
Y 100 %
K 0 %

New Color Swatch

Swatch Name: New Color Swatch

☐ Name with Color Value

Color Type: Spot

Color Mode: PANTONE solid coated

PANTONE _____ C

■ PANTONE Yellow C
■ PANTONE Yellow 012 C
■ PANTONE Orange 021 C
■ PANTONE Warm Red C
■ PANTONE Red 032 C
■ PANTONE Rubine Red C

OK
Cancel
Add

New Gradient Swatch

Swatch Name: Blue/Gold/Red Linear

Type: Linear

Stop Color: Swatches

☐ [Paper]
■ [Black]
■ C=100 M=0 Y=0 K=0
■ C=0 M=100 Y=0 K=0
■ C=0 M=0 Y=100 K=0

Gradient Ramp

Location: 0 %

OK
Cancel
Add

Work with PROCESS COLORS

What You'll Do

New Color Swatch

Swatch Name: Gold
☐ Name with Color Value

Color Type: Process

Color Mode: CMYK

OK
Cancel
Add

Cyan 0 %
Magenta 10 %
Yellow 90 %
Black 0 %

In this lesson, you will create new process colors and a tint swatch.

Understanding Process Colors

Process colors are colors that you create (and eventually print) by mixing varying percentages of cyan, magenta, yellow, and black (CMYK) inks. CMYK inks are called **process inks**. Lighter colors are produced with smaller percentages of ink, and darker colors with higher percentages. By mixing CMYK inks, you can produce a large variety of colors, and you can even reproduce color photographs. Think about that for a second—when you look at any magazine, most if not all the color photographs you see are created using only four colors!

In Adobe InDesign, you create process colors by creating a new swatch on the Swatches panel or in the New Color Swatch dialog box. You then mix percentages of CMYK to create the color. Figure 1 shows the New Color Swatch dialog box, where you name and define a color. You can choose Process or Spot as your type of color using the Color Type list arrow in the New Color Swatch dialog box. Choosing Process defines the swatch as a process swatch, meaning that it is created with percentages of CMYK ink. Any color that you create in this manner

is called a **named color** and is added to the Swatches panel, as shown in Figure 2. You can choose to have the color's name defined by CMYK percentages, as shown in the figure, or you can give it another name that you prefer.

One major benefit of working with named colors is that you can update them. For example, let's say you create a color that is 50% cyan and 50% yellow and you name it Warm Green. Let's say that you fill 10 objects on 10 different pages with Warm Green, but your client tells you that she'd prefer the objects to be filled with a darker green. You could simply modify the Warm Green color—change the cyan value to 70% for example—and every object filled with Warm Green would automatically update to show the darker green.

Understanding Tints

In the print world, the term "tint" is used to refer to many things. For example, some print professionals refer to all process colors as tints. In Adobe InDesign, however, the term **tint** refers specifically to a lighter version of a color.

Working with Color

Figure 3 shows four objects, all of them filled with the color cyan. The first is filled with 100% cyan, the second is filled with a 50% tint of cyan, the third—25%, and the fourth—10%. Note the variation in color.

Here's the tricky thing to understand about tints—the four swatches are all filled with the *same* cyan ink. The only difference is that, in the lighter objects, there's more white space that's not covered with cyan, thus creating

the illusion that the object is filled with a lighter blue.

The best way to keep the concept of tints clear in your head is to think of a checkerboard. In a checkerboard, 50% of the squares are black and the other 50% are red. Now imagine that the red squares are filled with solid cyan. Imagine that the other 50% are filled with white. That's exactly what's happening in the 50% cyan swatch in the figure. It's just that the

checkerboard is so small and contains so many squares that your eye perceives the illusion that the object is filled with a light blue.

Tints can also be created from more complex process colors. Figure 4 shows a process color that is C16 M100 Y100. It follows logically that the 50% tint of the color is C8 M50 Y50. A tint of any process color is created by multiplying each of the original colors' CMYK values by the desired tint percentage.

Figure 1 *New Color Swatch dialog box*

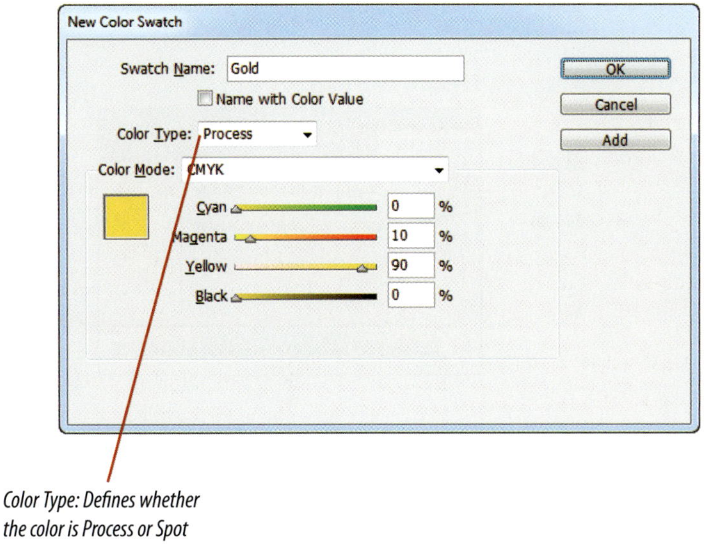

Figure 2 *Swatches panel*

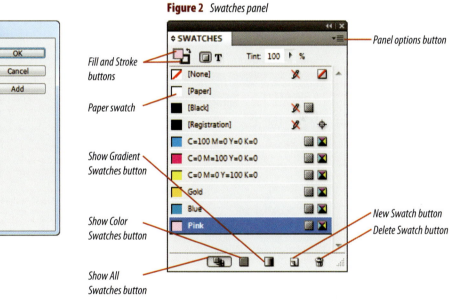

Panel options button

Fill and Stroke buttons

Paper swatch

Show Gradient Swatches button

Show Color Swatches button

Show All Swatches button

New Swatch button

Delete Swatch button

Color Type: Defines whether the color is Process or Spot

Figure 3 *Four objects filled with cyan*

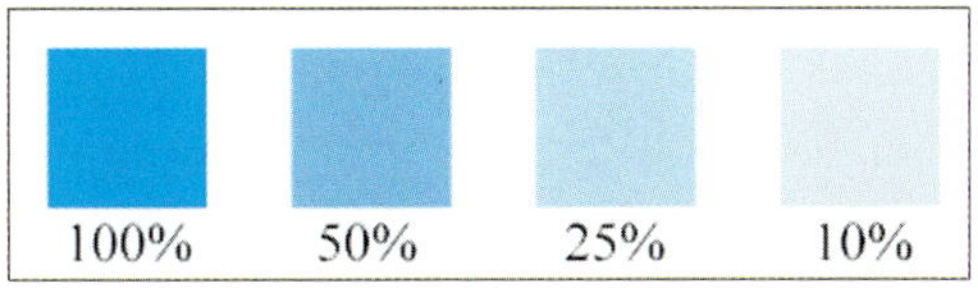

100%   50%   25%   10%

Figure 4 *A red process color and a 50% tint of that color*

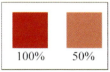

100%   50%

Creating Tint Swatches

Like process colors, you use the Swatches panel to create tint swatches. You can select a swatch on the Swatches panel, and then create a tint based on that original swatch by clicking the Swatches panel option button, clicking New Tint Swatch, and then dragging the Tint slider to the desired percentage. The resulting tint swatch is given the same name of the color on which it was based, plus the tint percentage next to it, as shown in Figure 5.

If you modify the original swatch, any tint swatch that is based on the original will automatically update to reflect that modification. For example, if your client says she wants that Warm Green color to be darker, then any modifications you make to Warm Green will affect all objects filled with Warm Green and all objects filled with tints of Warm Green.

Working with Unnamed Colors

It is not a requirement that you create named swatches for every color that you

want to use in your layout. Many designers prefer to use the Color panel, shown in Figure 6, to mix colors and apply them to objects. Using the Color panel, you can apply a color to an object by selecting it, then dragging the sliders on the Color panel until you are happy with the new color. As you drag the sliders, the color is continually updated in the selected object. In this way, you can experiment with different colors and allow the document's color scheme to evolve.

Figure 5 *Tint swatch on the Swatches panel*

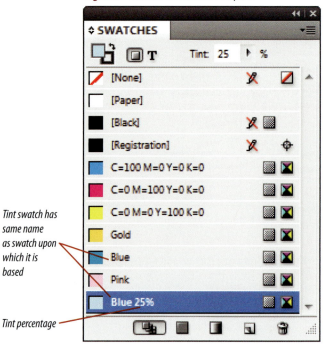

Tint swatch has same name as swatch upon which it is based

Tint percentage

Figure 6 *Color panel*

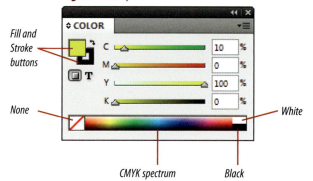

Fill and Stroke buttons

None

CMYK spectrum

Black

White

When you create colors using the Color panel, those colors are not saved anywhere. Any colors that you create that aren't saved to the Swatches panel are called **unnamed colors**.

There's nothing wrong, per se, with working with unnamed colors. You can mix a color on the Color panel, then apply it to an object. No problem. But it's important that you understand that the color is not saved anywhere. This can result in problems. For example, let's say that you mix a royal blue color and apply it to a document, then you

show the document to your client, who says that he'd prefer it to be green. So you mix a new green color. Then the client says he prefers the royal blue after all. If you didn't write down the CMYK values of that royal blue, you are out of luck because InDesign does not retain a record of it for you.

Other problems can develop too. Let's say you used that royal blue to fill multiple objects throughout the document. If you want to modify the color, you would need to modify each individual usage of the color. This could get very time consuming.

Does this mean that you'd be smart not to use the Color panel to mix colors? Not at all. Once you've decided on a color, simply save it on the Swatches panel. It couldn't be easier. Just drag the Fill (or Stroke) button from the Tools panel or the Color panel into the Swatches panel. You can even drag the Fill (or Stroke) button from the top of the Swatches panel down into the Swatches panel. The swatch will instantly be added to the Swatches panel as a process color and its CMYK values will be used as its name, as shown in Figure 7.

Figure 7 *Viewing a formerly unnamed color dragged into the Swatches panel*

Color dragged into Swatches panel

Create process color swatches

1. Open ID 5-1.indd, click **Update Links** if necessary, then save it as **Oahu Magazine Cover**.

2. Display the Swatches panel.

3. Click the **Swatches panel options button** , then click **New Color Swatch**.

4. Verify that the Color Type text box displays Process and that the Color Mode text box displays CMYK.

5. Remove the check mark in the Name with Color Value check box, then type **Gold** in the Swatch Name text box.

6. Type **0**, **10**, **90**, and **0** in the Cyan, Magenta, Yellow, and Black text boxes, as shown in Figure 8.

7. Click **OK**, click the **Swatches panel options button** , then click **New Color Swatch**.

8. Remove the check mark in the Name with Color Value check box, then type **Blue** in the Swatch Name text box.

9. Type **85**, **10**, **10**, and **0** in the CMYK text boxes, then click **OK**.

10. Create a new process color named **Pink**, type **20** in the Magenta text box, type **0** in the Cyan, Yellow, and Black text boxes, then click **OK**.

    Your Swatches panel should resemble Figure 9.

You created three new process colors.

Figure 8 *Creating a process color*

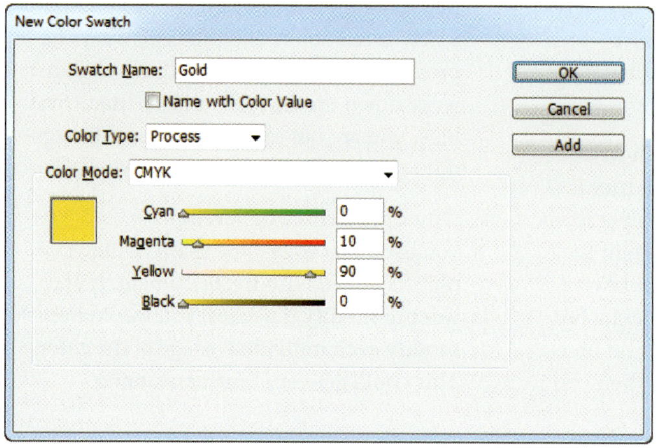

Figure 9 *Swatches panel*

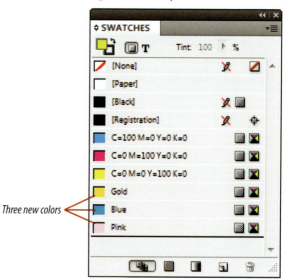

Three new colors

Figure 10 *Viewing the new tint swatch*

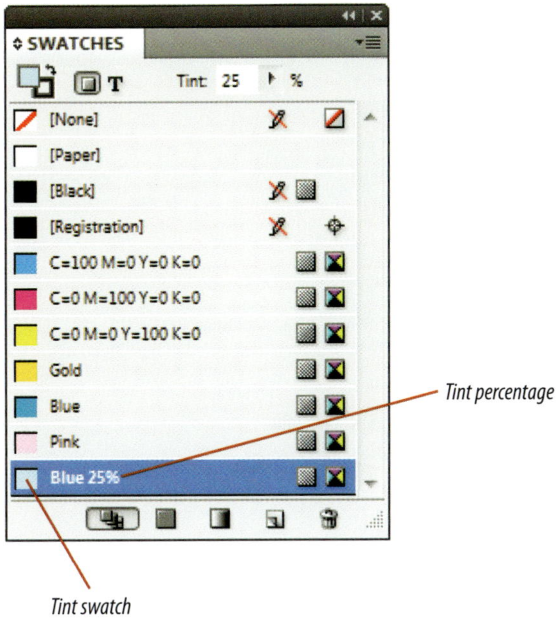

Tint percentage

Tint swatch

Figure 11 *Viewing changes to the tint swatch*

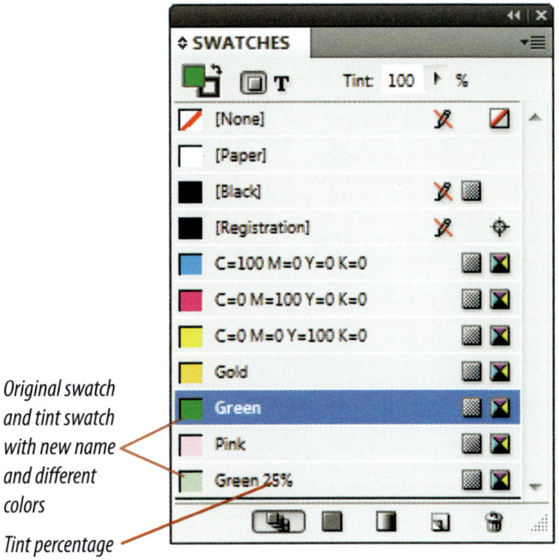

Original swatch and tint swatch with new name and different colors

Tint percentage

Create a tint swatch and modify the original color swatch

1. Click **Blue** on the Swatches panel, click the **Swatches panel options button** [icon], then click **New Tint Swatch**.

2. Drag the **Tint slider** to 25%, then click **OK**.

   As shown in Figure 10, a new 25% tint swatch named Blue 25% appears on the Swatches panel.

3. Double-click the original **Blue swatch** that you created on the Swatches panel.

4. Rename it by typing **Green** in the Swatch Name text box, drag the **Yellow slider** to 100%, then click **OK**.

   As shown in Figure 11, the blue swatch is renamed Green and the 25% tint swatch is renamed Green 25%.

5. Drag the **Green 25% tint swatch** up and relocate it immediately below the Green swatch you just created on the Swatches panel.

6. Drag the **Gold swatch** to the bottom of the panel so that it won't be confused with the Yellow swatch.

7. Click **File** on the Application bar, then click **Save**.

   Be sure to save your work at this step, as you will later revert to this point in the project.

You created a new tint swatch. You then modified the original swatch on which the tint swatch was based, noting that the tint swatch was automatically updated. You also rearranged swatches on the Swatches panel.

Use the Color panel

1. Verify that the Fill button on the Tools panel is activated.

2. Click the **Selection tool** 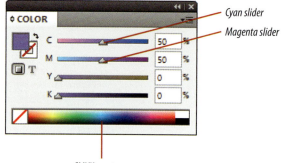, if necessary, click the **cyan-filled frame** that surrounds the image on the page, then display the **Color panel**.

3. Click the **Color panel options button** , then click **CMYK**.

4. Drag the **Magenta slider** on the Color panel to 50%, then drag the **Cyan slider** to 50%, as shown in Figure 12.

   The fill color of the selected frame changes to purple.

   TIP When you create a new color on the Color panel, it becomes the active fill or stroke color on the Tools panel, depending on which button is active.

5. Drag the **Yellow slider** to 100%, then drag the **Cyan slider** to 0%.

   The purple color that previously filled the frame is gone—there's no swatch for that color on the Swatches panel.

   TIP Colors that you mix on the Colors panel are not automatically saved on the Swatches panel.

6. Click the **green area** of the CMYK spectrum on the Color panel.

7. Drag the **Cyan slider** to 70%, drag the **Magenta slider** to 20%, then drag the **Yellow** and **Black sliders** to 0%.

You selected an object, then used the Color panel to change its fill to a variety of process colors, none of which were saved on the Swatches panel.

Figure 12 *Color panel*

Cyan slider
Magenta slider
CMYK spectrum

Figure 13 *An unnamed color is added to the Swatches panel*

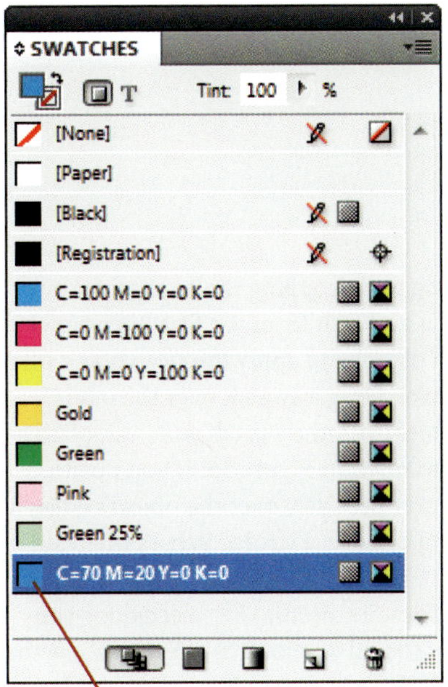

Color dragged into
Swatches panel

Figure 14 *A tint swatch is added to the Swatches panel*

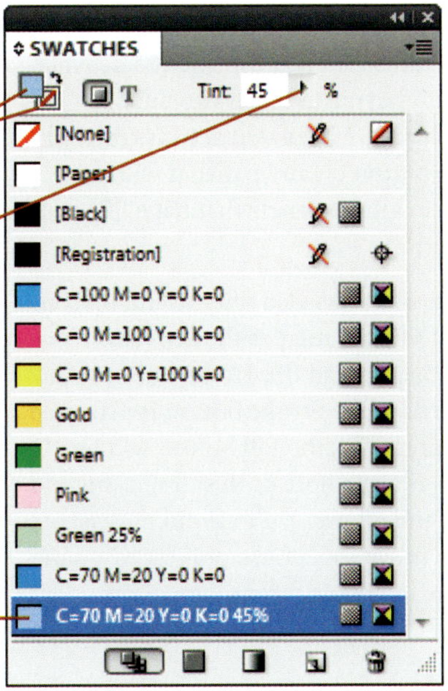

Fill and
Stroke
buttons

Tint slider

Tint swatch

Save an unnamed color on the Swatches panel

1. Drag the **Fill color** from the Tools panel into the Swatches panel.

   Your Swatches panel should resemble Figure 13.

2. Drag the **Tint slider** on the Color panel to 45%.

3. Save the new color as a swatch by dragging the **Fill button** from the top of the Swatches panel to the bottom of the list of swatches on the Swatches panel.

   Your Swatches panel should resemble Figure 14.

4. Double-click the **darker blue swatch** on the Swatches panel, remove the check mark in the Name with Color Value check box, type **Purple** in the Name text box, drag the **Magenta slider** to 100%, then click **OK**.

   The darker blue swatch becomes purple, and the tint swatch based on the darker blue swatch is also updated.

5. Click **File** on the Application bar, click **Revert**, then click **Yes** (Win) or **Revert** (Mac) in the dialog box that follows.

   The document is reverted back to its status when you last saved. The new color swatches you created are no longer on the Swatches panel.

You saved an unnamed color on the Swatches panel, created a tint swatch based on that swatch, then reverted the document.

Apply COLOR

What You'll Do

FALL 2012 · $4.95

A·MAZE·ING
get lost in a
pineapple maze

TWIST & SHOUT
boogie-boarding
daredevils stare down
the north coast waves

MAVERICK
a sizzling interview
with Chef Mavre

 In this lesson, you will explore various techniques for applying and modifying color swatches.

Applying Color to Objects

InDesign offers a number of options for applying fills and strokes to objects. The most basic method is to select an object, activate either the Fill or the Stroke button on the Tools panel, then click a color on the Swatches panel or mix a color on the Color panel.

As shown in Figure 15, both the Color panel and the Swatches panel have Fill and Stroke buttons that you can click to activate rather than having to always go back to the Tools panel. When you activate the Fill or Stroke button on any panel, it will be activated in all the panels that have Fill and Stroke buttons.

Keyboard shortcuts also offer useful options. Pressing [X] once toggles the activation between the Fill and the Stroke buttons. In other words, if the Stroke button is activated and you press [X], the Fill button will be activated. Make a note of this. It's useful and practical and allows you to avoid always having to move the mouse pointer to a panel to activate the fill or the stroke.

Dragging and dropping is also useful. You can drag a swatch from the Swatches panel onto an object and apply the swatch as a fill or a stroke. Drag a swatch over the interior of an object and the swatch will be applied as a fill, as shown in Figure 16. If you position the pointer precisely over the object's edge, it will be applied as a stroke. What's interesting about the drag and drop method is that the object does not need to be selected for you to apply the fill or the stroke. You can use the drag and drop method with any panel that has Fill and Stroke buttons.

The Tools panel offers useful buttons for working with color, as shown in Figure 17. The Default Fill and Stroke button reverts the Fill and Stroke buttons to their default colors—no fill and a black stroke. Clicking this button will apply a black stroke and no fill to a selected object. The Swap Fill and Stroke button swaps the fill color with the stroke color.

Finally, the three "Apply" buttons on the Tools panel are useful for speeding up your work. The Apply Color and Apply Gradient buttons display the last color and gradient that you've used. This makes for quick and easy access when you are using the same color or gradient repeatedly. The Apply None button is available for removing the fill or stroke from a selected object, depending on which button (Fill or Stroke) is active on the Tools panel.

QUICK **TIP**

If you are viewing your Tools panel as a single column, you will not see all three of these buttons. Press and hold the current button on the Tools panel, then click the desired button.

Figure 15 *Fill and Stroke buttons on the Color and Swatches panels*

Fill and Stroke buttons

Fill and Stroke buttons

Figure 16 *Dragging and dropping a swatch to fill an object*

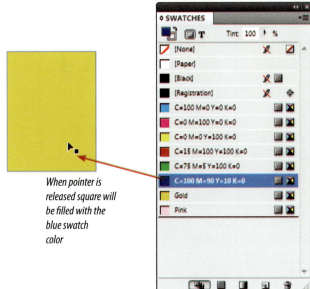

When pointer is released square will be filled with the blue swatch color

Figure 17 *Useful color buttons on the Tools panel*

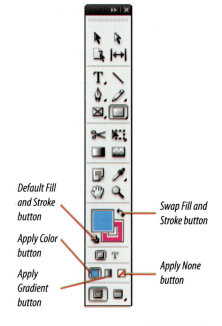

Default Fill and Stroke button

Apply Color button

Apply Gradient button

Swap Fill and Stroke button

Apply None button

Understanding the Paper Swatch

If I gave you a white piece of paper and a box of crayons and asked you to draw a white star against a blue background, you would probably color all of the page blue except for the star shape, which you would leave blank. The star would appear as white because the paper is white. The Paper swatch, shown in Figure 18, is based on this very concept. Use the Paper swatch whenever you want an object to have a white fill or stroke.

Don't confuse a Paper fill with a None fill. When you fill a frame with Paper, it is filled with white. When you fill it with None, it has no fill—its fill is transparent. Figure 19 illustrates this distinction. In the figure, two text frames are positioned in front of a frame with a yellow fill. The text frame on the left has None as its fill; therefore the yellow frame is visible behind the text. The text frame on the right has Paper as its fill.

Figure 18 *Paper swatch*

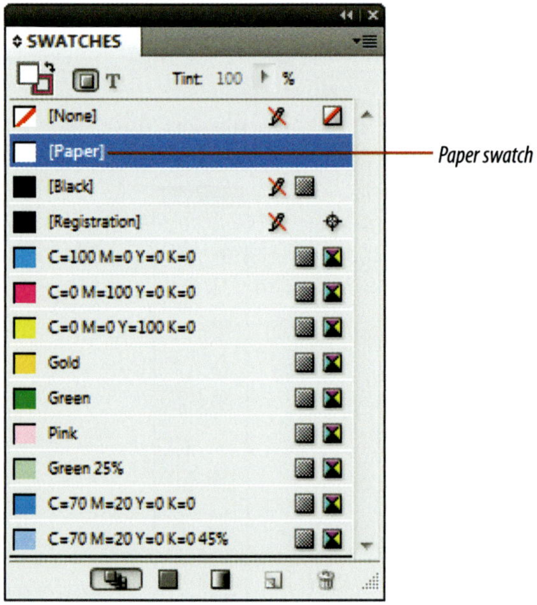

Figure 19 *Understanding a Paper fill*

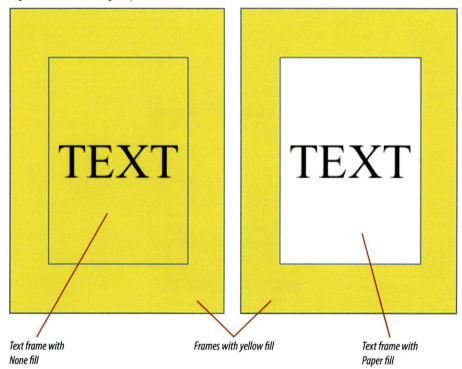

Paper swatch

Text frame with None fill

Frames with yellow fill

Text frame with Paper fill

Applying Color to Text

Applying color to text is easy. There are two different methods for applying color to text, depending on which tool you are using to select the text.

When you select text with the Type tool, the Fill and Stroke buttons on the Tools panel display the letter T, as shown in Figure 20. This is a visual indication that you are filling or stroking text. Click a swatch on the Swatches panel or mix a color on the Color panel and the text will be filled or stroked with that color.

QUICK TIP

The color of the T on the Fill and Stroke buttons is always the same color as the selected text.

When you select a text frame with a selection tool, you need to tell InDesign what you want to do—apply a fill or stroke to the frame itself or apply a fill or stroke to the text in the frame. If you want to apply color to the text, click the Formatting affects text button on the Tools panel, as shown in Figure 21. If you want to apply color to the frame, click the Formatting affects container button. It's that simple. Note that the two buttons can also be found in the Swatches and Color panels.

Figure 20
Fill and Stroke buttons applied to text

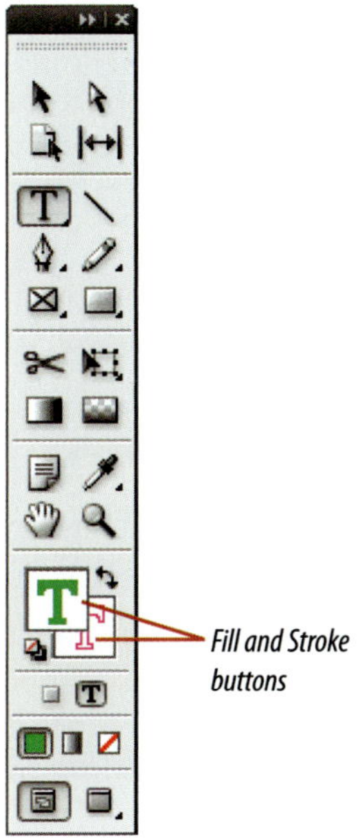

Fill and Stroke buttons

Figure 21
Formatting buttons

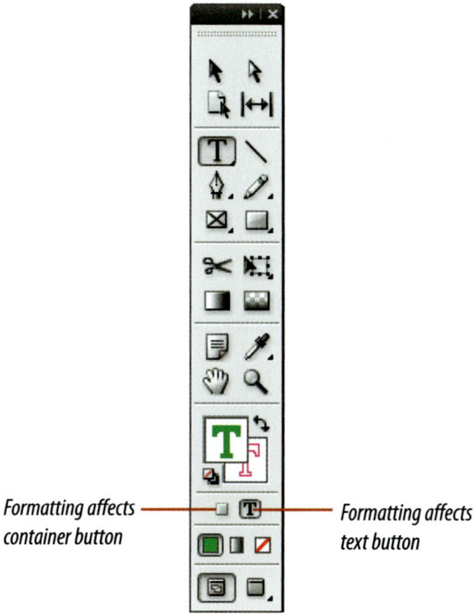

Formatting affects container button

Formatting affects text button

Creating Black Shadow Text

When you position text against a background color or against a photographic image, sometimes it's not easy to see the text, as shown in Figure 22. To remedy this, many designers use the classic technique of placing a black copy of the text behind the original text, as shown in Figure 23. This trick adds much-needed contrast between the text and the image behind it.

QUICK TIP

Placing a black copy of text behind original text produces a different effect than using InDesign's Drop Shadow command.

Modifying and Deleting Swatches

Once you've created a swatch or added a swatch to the Swatches panel, it is a named color and will be saved with the document. Any swatch can be modified simply by double-clicking it, which opens the Swatch Options dialog box, as shown in Figure 24. Any modifications you make to the swatch will be updated automatically in any frame that uses the color as a fill or a stroke.

You can also delete a swatch from the Swatches panel by selecting the swatch, then clicking the Delete Swatch button on the Swatches panel or clicking the Delete Swatch command on the Swatches panel menu.

Figure 22 *Text positioned against an image*

Figure 23 *Text with a black copy behind it*

Black text placed behind purple text

If you are deleting a swatch that is used in your document, the Delete Swatch dialog box opens, as shown in Figure 25.

You use the Delete Swatch dialog box to choose a color to replace the deleted swatch. For example, if you've filled (or stroked) a number of objects with the color Warm Green and then you delete the Warm Green swatch, the Delete Swatch dialog box wants to know to what color those objects should be changed. You choose another named color that is already on the Swatches panel by clicking the Defined Swatch list arrow, clicking a color, and then clicking OK. When you do so, all the objects with a Warm Green fill or stroke will change to the named color you chose. Note that this can be a very quick and effective method for changing the fill (or stroke) color of multiple objects simultaneously.

If you click the Unnamed Swatch option button in the Delete Swatch dialog box, all the objects filled or stroked with the deleted color will retain their color. However, since that color is no longer on the Swatches panel, those objects are now filled with an unnamed color.

Figure 24 *Swatch Options dialog box*

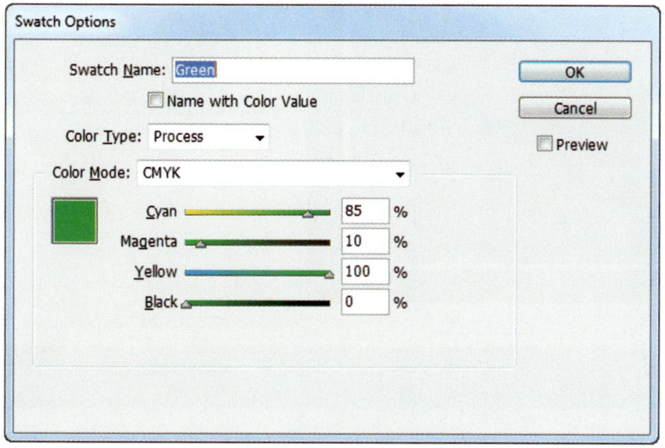

Figure 25 *Delete Swatch dialog box*

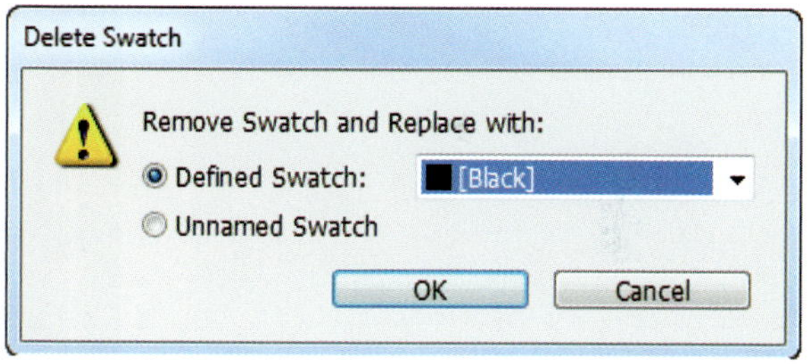

Drag and drop colors onto objects

1. Click **View** on the Application bar, point to **Extras**, then click **Hide Frame Edges**.

2. Drag and drop the **Green swatch** on top of the blue frame, as shown in Figure 26, then release the mouse button.

   The frame is filled with green.

3. Click the **Toggles visibility button**  on the Photo layer on the Layers panel to hide the background image.

4. Drag the **Pink swatch** to the inside of the white text frame.

   The fill changes to pink.

You dragged and dropped colors from the Swatches panel to objects in the document window.

Figure 26 *Dragging and dropping a color swatch*

Using the Color Picker

In addition to using the Tools panel and the Swatches panel to apply colors, you can use the Color Picker to choose and mix colors. Select the object you want to fill, then double-click the Fill or Stroke button on the Tools panel to open the Color Picker. In the color spectrum, click or drag to select a color, drag the color slider triangles, or type values in the text boxes. To save the color as a swatch, click Add CMYK Swatch, Add RGB Swatch, or Add Lab Swatch. The color appears on the Swatches panel, displaying its color values as a name.

Figure 27 *Applying the Default Fill and Stroke to the frame*

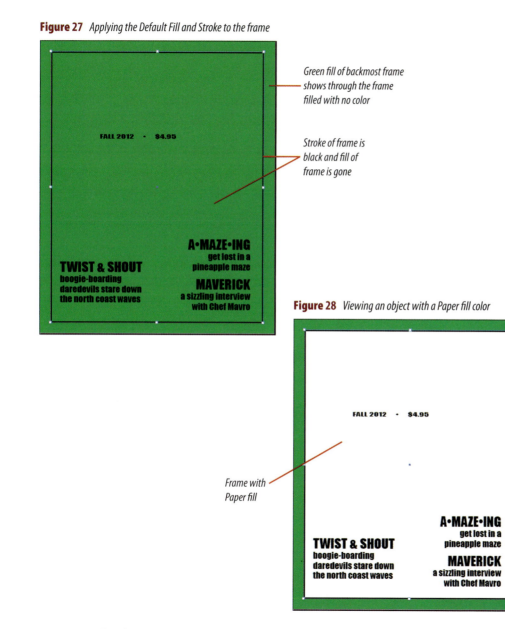

Green fill of backmost frame
shows through the frame
filled with no color

Stroke of frame is
black and fill of
frame is gone

Figure 28 *Viewing an object with a Paper fill color*

Frame with
Paper fill

Use the Swap Fill and Stroke and Default Fill and Stroke buttons

1. Click the **Selection tool** ➤ if necessary, click the center of the pink frame, then note the Fill and Stroke buttons on the Tools panel.

   The Fill button is activated—it is in front of the Stroke button.

2. Press **[X]** to activate the Stroke button on the Tools panel, then click **Gold** on the Swatches panel.

3. Click the **Swap Fill and Stroke button** ↰.

   In the selected frame, the fill and stroke colors are swapped.

4. Click the **Default Fill and Stroke button** ▣.

   The fill color of the selected frame is removed and replaced with no fill, and the stroke changes to black as shown in Figure 27.

5. Press **[X]** to activate the Fill button, click the **Paper swatch** on the Swatches panel, then compare your work to Figure 28.

You used the Swap Fill and Stroke and Default Fill and Stroke buttons to explore ways to modify your document, and then applied the Paper swatch to the center frame.

Apply color to text

1. Click the **Selection tool** 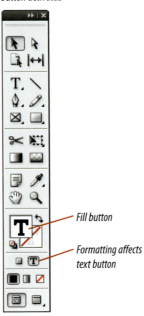, click the **TWIST & SHOUT text frame**, then click the **Formatting affects text button** T on the Tools panel.

   As shown in Figure 29, the Fill and Stroke buttons display the letter T, indicating that any color changes will affect the text in the selected frame, not the frame itself.

2. Click **Gold** on the Swatches panel.

3. Click the **A•MAZE•ING text frame**, then note that the Formatting affects container button is active on the Tools panel because you have selected a frame.

4. Click the **Type tool** T, then select all of the text in the A•MAZE•ING text frame.

TIP When you select text with the Type tool, the Formatting affects text button on the Tools panel is automatically activated.

5. Click **Pink** on the Swatches panel.

6. Click the **Selection tool**, click the **MAVERICK text frame**, then click the **Formatting affects text button** T on the Swatches panel.

7. Click the **Green 25% swatch** on the Swatches panel so that your document resembles Figure 30.

You explored two methods for applying color to text. In the first, you selected text with the Selection tool, clicked the Formatting affects text button, then chose a new color. In the second, you selected text with the Type tool, then chose a new color.

Figure 29 *Tools panel with the Formatting affects text button activated*

Fill button

Formatting affects text button

Figure 30 *Viewing the colors applied to text*

FALL 2012 - $4.95

A•MAZE•ING
get lost in a
pineapple maze

TWIST & SHOUT
boogie-boarding
daredevils stare down
the north coast waves

MAVERICK
a sizzling interview
with Chef Mavre

Figure 31 *Layer Options dialog box*

Layer Options		
Name: Color Headlines		OK
Color: ■ Orange ▼		Cancel
☑ Show Layer	☑ Show Guides	
☐ Lock Layer	☐ Lock Guides	
☑ Print Layer		
☐ Suppress Text Wrap When Layer is Hidden		

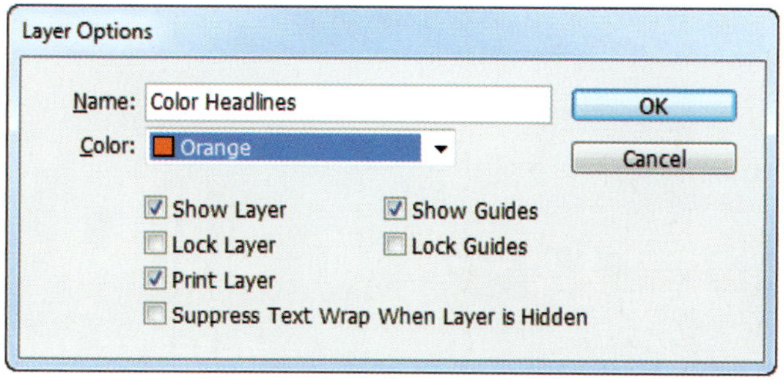

Create black shadow text

1. Click the **Toggles visibility button**  (in its off state) on the Photo layer on the Layers panel, then assess the legibility of the text in the three text frames against the background graphic.

   The text is legible, but some letters like the M in Maverick are more difficult to distinguish from the background.

2. Click the **Original Black Text layer** on the Layers panel, click the **Layers panel options button** , then click **Duplicate Layer "Original Black Text."**

3. Double-click the name of the new layer on the Layers panel to open the Layer Options dialog box.

4. Type **Color Headlines** in the Name text box, click the **Color list arrow**, then click **Orange**, so that your Layer Options dialog box resembles Figure 31.

5. Click **OK**, then hide the Original Black Text layer.

6. With the Color Headlines layer still selected, delete the Fall 2012 text frame on the Color Headlines layer since you will not need a duplicate of this text.

7. Hide the Color Headlines layer, then show the Original Black Text layer.

(continued)

8. Click the **Click to select items button** ☐ on the Original Black Text layer to select all the objects on the layer.

9. Click the **Formatting affects text button** **T** on the Swatches panel, apply a 100% black fill to all the text, then deselect all.

10. Show the Color Headlines layer, then click the **Click to select items button** ☐ to select all objects on the layer.

11. Click **Object** on the Application bar, point to **Transform**, then click **Move**.

12. Activate the Preview option if necessary, type **-.04** in the Horizontal text box, type **-.04** in the Vertical text box, click **OK**, deselect all, then compare your work to Figure 32.

You duplicated a layer containing text. You changed the fill color of the text on the lower layer to black, then repositioned the colored text on the upper layer so that the black text acts as a shadow. By doing so, you added contrast to the colored text, making it more legible against the picture on the Photo layer.

Figure 32 *Viewing the colored text with a black shadow*

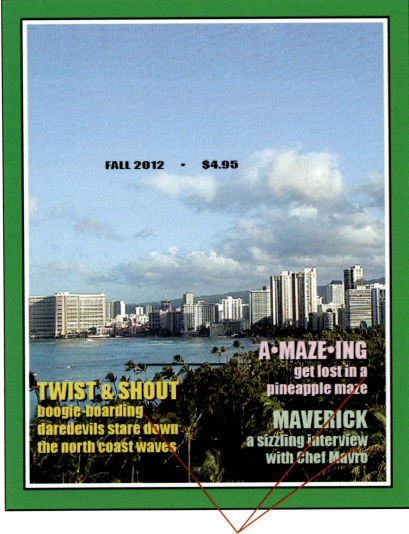

Black text placed behind
colored text adds contrast

Figure 33 *Viewing modifications to the Gold swatch*

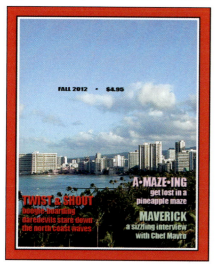

Figure 34 *Delete Swatch dialog box*

Gold swatch will be
replaced with Pink

Modify and delete swatches

1. Deselect all, then drag the **Gold swatch** onto the Green frame to change its fill color to Gold.

2. Double-click the **Gold swatch** on the Swatches panel.

3. Activate the Preview option if necessary, then drag the **Black slider** to 20%.

   You may need to move the Swatch Options dialog box to see the effect on the document page.

4. Drag the **Black slider** to 5%, then drag the **Magenta slider** to 100%.

5. Click **OK**, then compare your work to Figure 33.

   All usages of the Gold swatch—the frame and the "Twist & Shout" text—are updated with the modification.

6. Drag the **Gold swatch** to the Delete Swatch button 🗑 on the Swatches panel.

7. Click the **Defined Swatch list arrow**, click **Pink**, as shown in Figure 34, then click **OK**.

   As shown in Figure 35, all usages of the Gold swatch in the document are replaced by the Pink swatch.

You modified a swatch and noted that it updated throughout the document. You then deleted the swatch, replacing all of its usages with a different swatch.

Figure 35 *Gold swatch replaced with pink swatch*

Work with
SPOT COLORS

What You'll Do

In this lesson, you will create and apply spot colors, and import graphics that contain spot colors.

Understanding Spot Colors

Spot colors are non-process inks that are manufactured by companies. Though printing is based on the four process colors, CMYK, it is not limited to them. It is important to understand that though combinations of CMYK inks can produce a wide variety of colors—enough to reproduce any color photograph quite well—they can't produce every color. For this reason, and others, designers often turn to spot colors.

Imagine that you are an art director designing the masthead for the cover of a new magazine. You have decided that the masthead will be electric blue—vivid and eye-catching. If you were working with process tints only, you would have a problem. First, you would find that the almost-neon blue that you want to achieve is not within the CMYK range; it can't be printed. Even if it could, you would have a bigger problem with consistency issues. You would want that blue to be the same blue on every issue of the magazine, month after month. But offset printing is never perfect; variations in dot size are factored in. As the cover is printed, the blue color

in the masthead will certainly vary, sometimes sharply.

Designers and printers use spot colors to solve this problem. **Spot colors** are special pre-mixed inks that are printed separately from process inks. The color range of spot colors far exceeds that of CMYK. Spot colors also offer consistent color throughout a print run.

The design and print worlds refer to spot colors by a number of names:

- Non-process inks: Refers to the fact that spot colors are not created using the process inks—CMYK.
- Fifth color: Refers to the fact that the spot color is often printed in addition to the four process inks. Note, however, that a spot color is not necessarily the "fifth" color. For example, many "two-color" projects call for black plus one spot color.
- PANTONE color: PANTONE is a manufacturer of non-process inks. PANTONE is simply a brand name.
- PMS color: An acronym for PANTONE Matching System.

A good way to think of spot colors is as ink in a bucket. With process inks, if you want red, you must mix some amount of magenta ink with some amount of yellow ink. With spot colors, if you want red, you pick a number from a chart, open the bucket, and there's the red ink—pre-mixed and ready to print.

Creating Spot Color Swatches

You create spot color swatches in Adobe InDesign using the New Color Swatch dialog box. Instead of choosing CMYK values, as you would when you create a process color,

you choose Spot from the Color Type list, then choose a spot color system from one of 30 systems in the Color Mode list. After you choose a system, the related library of spot colors loads into the New Swatch dialog box, allowing you to choose the spot color you want. Figure 36 shows the PANTONE solid coated color system.

Importing Graphics with Spot Colors

When you create graphics in Adobe Illustrator or Adobe Photoshop, you can create and apply spot colors in those

applications as well. For example, you can create a logo in Adobe Illustrator and fill it with a spot color.

Because InDesign, Illustrator, and Photoshop are all made by Adobe, InDesign recognizes the spot colors applied to graphics created in those applications. In the above example, when you place the graphic from Illustrator, InDesign identifies the spot color that was used and adds it to the InDesign Swatches panel. If you double-click the swatch on the Swatches panel, you will see that the swatch is automatically formatted as a spot color.

Figure 36 *Creating a spot color swatch*

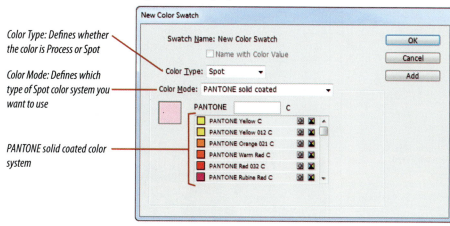

Color Type: Defines whether the color is Process or Spot

Color Mode: Defines which type of Spot color system you want to use

PANTONE solid coated color system

Create a spot color swatch

1. Click the **Swatches panel options button**, then click **New Color Swatch**.

2. Click the **Color Type list arrow**, then click **Spot**.

3. Click the **Color Mode list arrow**, then click **PANTONE solid coated**.

4. Type **663** in the PANTONE text box, so that your New Color Swatch dialog box resembles Figure 37.

5. Click **OK**, then compare your Swatches panel with Figure 38.

6. Change the fill of the pink frame to PANTONE 663.

7. Change the fill of the TWIST & SHOUT text to PANTONE 663, deselect the TWIST & SHOUT text frame, then compare your document to Figure 39.

You created a spot color swatch and then applied it to elements in the layout.

Figure 37 *Creating a spot color*

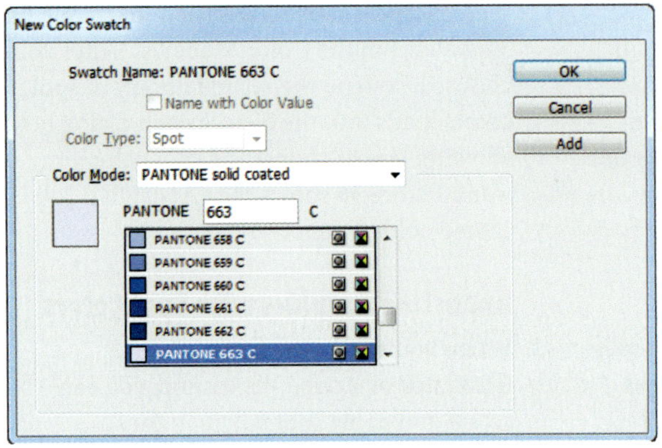

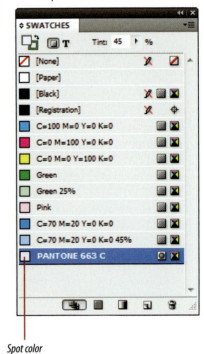

Figure 38 *Identifying a spot color on the Swatches panel*

Figure 39 *Viewing the document with the spot color applied*

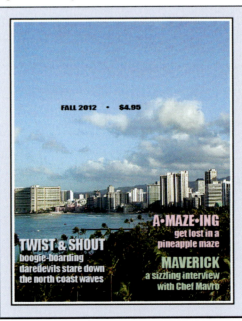

Spot color

Figure 40 *Selecting a frame for a graphic*

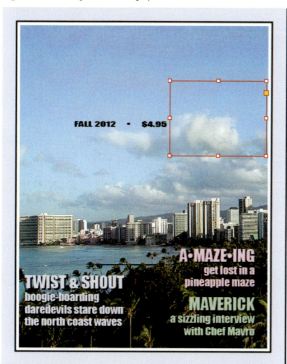

FALL 2012 · $4.95

A·MAZE·ING
get lost in a
pineapple maze

TWIST & SHOUT
boogie-boarding
daredevils stare down
the north coast waves

MAVERICK
a sizzling interview
with Chef Mavro

Figure 41 *Identifying a new spot color on the Swatches panel*

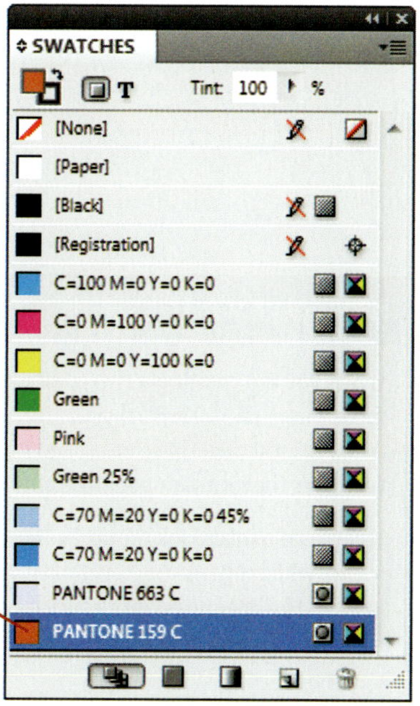

PANTONE swatch added to the Swatches panel when the Illustrator graphic was imported

SWATCHES

Tint: 100 ▸ %

[None]
[Paper]
[Black]
[Registration]
C=100 M=0 Y=0 K=0
C=0 M=100 Y=0 K=0
C=0 M=0 Y=100 K=0
Green
Pink
Green 25%
C=70 M=20 Y=0 K=0 45%
C=70 M=20 Y=0 K=0
PANTONE 663 C
PANTONE 159 C

Import graphics with spot colors

1. Click the **Imported Graphics layer** on the Layers panel to target it, click the **Selection tool** ⭢, then select the frame shown in Figure 40.

    TIP Clicking in the general area of the selected frame shown in Figure 40 will select the frame.

2. Click **File** on the Application bar, click **Place**, navigate to the drive and folder where your Data Files are stored, click **Living Graphic.ai**, then click **Open**.

3. Click **Object** on the Application bar, point to **Fitting**, then click **Center Content**.

    The graphic that is placed in the frame was created in Adobe Illustrator.

4. Click **View** on the Application bar, point to **Display Performance**, then click **High Quality Display**.

5. Compare your Swatches panel to Figure 41.

    The PANTONE 159 C swatch was automatically added to the Swatches panel when the graphic was placed, since it was a color used to create the graphic.

6. Deselect the graphics frame, double-click **PANTONE 159 C** on the Swatches panel, note that PANTONE 159 C was imported as a spot color as indicated in the Color Type text box, then click **Cancel**.

    (continued)

7. Select the **frame** shown in Figure 42.

8. Click **File** on the Application bar, click **Place**, navigate to the drive and folder where your Data Files are stored, then double-click **OAHU graphic.ai**.

OAHU graphic.ai is an Adobe Illustrator file. The fill color of O, A, H, and U is PANTONE 663—the same PANTONE 663 fill that was created in InDesign and applied to the border and the TWIST & SHOUT text. For this reason, PANTONE 663 does not need to be added to the Swatches panel.

TIP If, when you import the graphic, a dialog box appears warning you that the PANTONE color in the graphic is defined differently and asking if you want to replace it, click No.

(continued)

Figure 42 *Selecting a frame for a graphic*

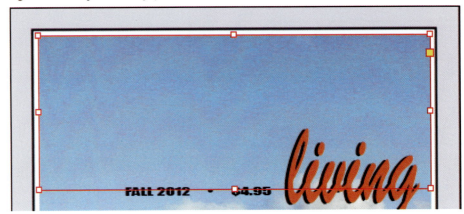

Working with Mixed Ink Swatches

When you are creating a two color job—let's say Black and PMS 100—you will want to work with more than just 100% Black and 100% PMS 100. You'll want to work with tints, such as a 70% Black and 20% PMS100 mix. These are called mixed swatches. A mixed ink group is a group of many mixed ink swatches that you can generate automatically based on the two or more inks in your color job.

You create a mixed ink group by clicking the New Mixed Ink Group command on the Swatches panel menu, which opens the New Mixed Ink Group dialog box. Use this dialog box to specify the inks involved for the mixed ink group, the initial mixture, and the increments (percentages) at which new tint swatches will be generated. All of the swatches will appear in the Swatches panel.

Figure 43 *Viewing the document page*

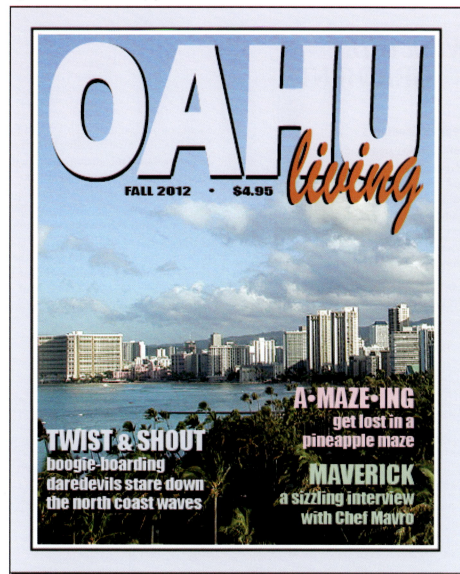

9. Click **Object** on the Application bar, point to **Fitting**, then click **Center Content**.
10. Deselect all, then compare your document with Figure 43.
11. Save your work, then close OAHU Magazine Cover.

You imported a graphic that was created with a spot color in another application, then noted that the spot color was automatically added to the Swatches panel. Next, you imported a graphic that was filled with the same spot color that you had already created in InDesign.

Work with
GRADIENTS

What You'll Do

In this lesson, you will create gradients and explore options for applying them to frames.

Creating Gradients

A **gradient** is a graduated blend of two or more colors. By definition, every gradient must have at least two colors, which are commonly referred to as the **starting** and **ending colors** of the gradient. You can add more colors to a gradient—colors that come between the starting and ending colors. The colors that you add are called **color stops**.

In InDesign, you create gradients by clicking New Gradient Swatch in the Swatches panel options. This opens the New Gradient Swatch dialog box, as shown in Figure 44. In this dialog box, you define all the elements of the gradient. Like new colors, you can give your gradient a descriptive name. You use the Gradient Ramp to define the starting and ending colors, as well as any intermediary colors for your gradient. You choose whether your gradient will be radial or linear using the Type list arrow. You can think of a **radial gradient** as a series of concentric

Figure 44 *New Gradient Swatch dialog box*

New Gradient Swatch

Swatch Name: Blue/Gold/Red Linear

Type: Linear

Stop Color: Swatches

☐ [Paper]
■ [Black]
■ C=100 M=0 Y=0 K=0
■ C=0 M=100 Y=0 K=0
■ C=0 M=0 Y=100 K=0

OK
Cancel
Add

Type: Defines a gradient as Linear or Radial

Gradient Ramp

Location: 0 %

circles. With a radial gradient, the starting color appears at the center of the gradient, then radiates out to the ending color.

You can think of a **linear gradient** as a series of straight lines that gradate from one color to another (or through multiple colors). Figure 45 shows a linear and a radial gradient, each composed of three colors.

Figure 46 shows the dialog box used to create the linear gradient. The Gradient Ramp represents the gradient, and the blue color stop is selected. The sliders show the CMYK values that make the blue tint. Note that the Stop Color text box reads CMYK.

You can create gradients using swatches already on the Swatches panel as color stops.

In Figure 47, the selected color stop is a spot color named PANTONE Red 032 C. Note that the Stop Color text box reads Swatches. When you choose Swatches from the Stop Color menu, all the named colors on the Swatches panel are listed and available to be used in the gradient.

When you close the New Gradient Swatch dialog box, the new gradient swatch appears on the Swatches panel when you click the Show All Swatches button or when you click the Show Gradient Swatches button on the Swatches panel.

Figure 45 *A linear and a radial gradient*

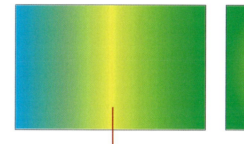
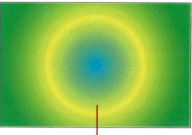

Linear gradient

Radial gradient

Figure 46 *Viewing a linear gradient*

Figure 47 *Viewing the formatting of a gradient with a named color*

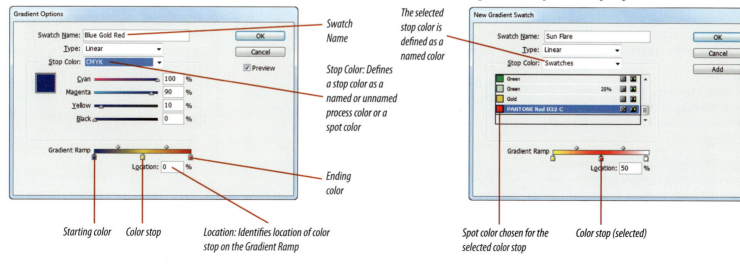

Swatch Name

Stop Color: Defines a stop color as a named or unnamed process color or a spot color

Ending color

The selected stop color is defined as a named color

Starting color   Color stop   Location: Identifies location of color stop on the Gradient Ramp

Spot color chosen for the selected color stop   Color stop (selected)

Applying Gradients

You apply a gradient to an object the same way you apply a color to an object. Simply select the object, then click the gradient on the Swatches panel. A gradient swatch can be applied as a fill or as a stroke.

If you use a gradient to fill an object, you can further control how the gradient fills the object using the Gradient Swatch tool or the Gradient Feather tool. The Gradient Swatch tool allows you to change the length and/or direction of a linear or radial gradient. You can also use it to change the angle of a linear gradient and the center point of a radial gradient. To use the Gradient Swatch tool, you first select an object with a gradient fill, then drag the Gradient Swatch tool over the object. For both linear and radial gradients, where you begin dragging and where you stop dragging determines the length of the gradient, from starting color to ending color. The Gradient Feather tool works exactly like the Gradient Swatch tool, except that it produces a softer progression of the colors in the gradient.

For linear gradients, the direction in which you drag the Gradient Swatch tool determines the angle of the blend that fills the object.

Figure 48 shows six rows of six square frames filled with rainbow gradients. The Gradient Swatch tool was dragged in varying lengths and directions across each row—represented by the black lines you see in the examples—to create different effects.

Modifying a Gradient Fill Using the Gradient Panel

Like color swatches, gradients can be modified. When you modify a gradient, all instances of the gradient used in the document will be automatically updated. Let's say you create a gradient and use it to fill 10 objects. Then you decide that, in only one of those 10 objects, you want to modify the gradient by removing one color. What do you do? If you modify the gradient swatch, by removing a color stop, it's going to affect all usages of the gradient. You could, of course, duplicate the gradient swatch, remove the unwanted color stop, then apply the new gradient to the single object. But there's a better way. You can use the Gradient panel, shown in Figure 49.

When you select an object with a gradient fill, the Gradient panel shows the Gradient Ramp that you used to create the gradient in the New Gradient Swatch dialog box. You can manipulate the Gradient Ramp on the Gradient panel. You can add, move, and delete color stops. You can also select color stops and modify their color using the Color panel. And here's the great part: the modifications you make on the Gradient panel only affect the gradient fill of the selected object(s).

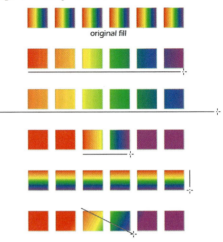

Figure 48 *Using the Gradient Swatch tool*

original fill

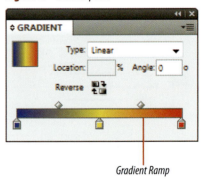

Figure 49 *Gradient panel*

Gradient Ramp

Figure 50 *New Gradient Swatch dialog box*

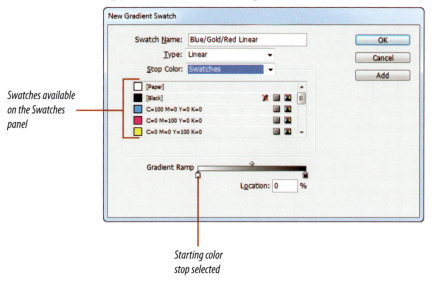

Swatches available on the Swatches panel

Starting color stop selected

Figure 51 *Creating a linear gradient swatch*

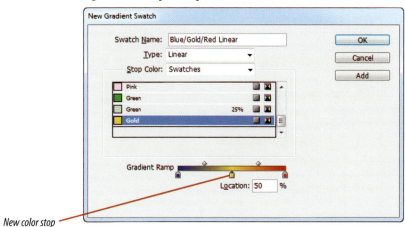

New color stop

Create a linear gradient swatch

1. Open ID 5-2.indd, then save it as **Making the Gradient**.

2. Click the **Swatches panel options button**, then click **New Gradient Swatch**.

3. In the Swatch Name text box, type **Blue/Gold/ Red Linear**.

4. Click the **left color stop** on the Gradient Ramp, click the **Stop Color list arrow**, then click **Swatches** so that your dialog box resembles Figure 50.

   When you choose Swatches, the colors on the Swatches panel are listed below.

5. Click the swatch named **Blue**.

   The left color stop on the Gradient Ramp changes to blue.

6. Click the **right color stop** on the Gradient Ramp, click the **Stop Color list arrow**, click **Swatches**, then click the swatch named **Red**.

7. Click directly below the Gradient Ramp to add a new color stop.

TIP Click anywhere to add the new color stop. You can adjust the location using the Location text box.

8. Type **50** in the Location text box, then press **[Tab]**.

   The new color stop is located at the exact middle of the Gradient Ramp.

9. Click the **Stop Color list arrow**, click **Swatches**, then click the swatch named **Gold** so that your New Gradient Swatch dialog box resembles Figure 51.

(continued)

10. Click **OK**.

The new gradient swatch is added to the Swatches panel.

You created a three-color linear gradient swatch using three named colors.

Create a radial gradient swatch

1. Click the **Swatches panel options button** ▼≣, then click **New Gradient Swatch**.

The New Gradient Swatch dialog box opens with the settings from the last created gradient.

2. In the Swatch Name text box, type **Cyan Radial**.

3. Click the **Type list arrow**, then click **Radial**.

4. Click the **center color stop**, then drag it straight down to remove it from the Gradient Ramp.

5. Click the **left color stop** on the Gradient Ramp, click the **Stop Color list arrow**, then click **CMYK**.

6. Drag each slider to **0%** so that your dialog box resembles Figure 52.

7. Click the **right color stop** on the Gradient Ramp, click the **Stop Color list arrow**, then click **CMYK**.

8. Drag the **Cyan slider** to 100%, then drag the **Magenta**, **Yellow**, and **Black sliders** to 0% so that your dialog box resembles Figure 53.

9. Click **OK**.

The new gradient swatch is added to the Swatches panel.

You created a two-color radial gradient swatch using CMYK values.

Figure 52 *Formatting the left color stop*

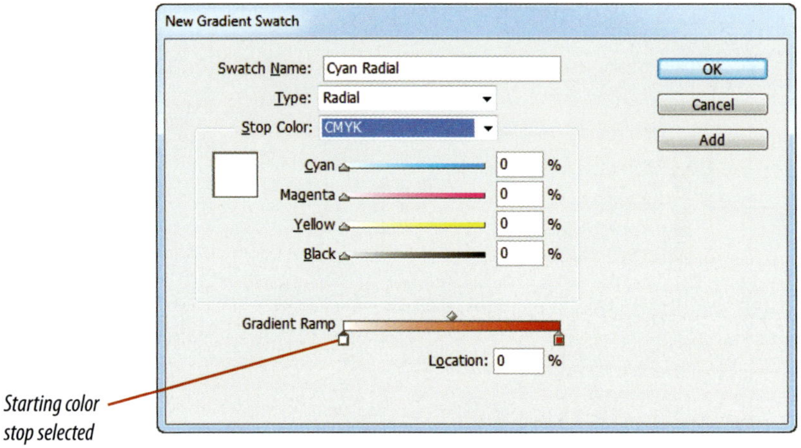

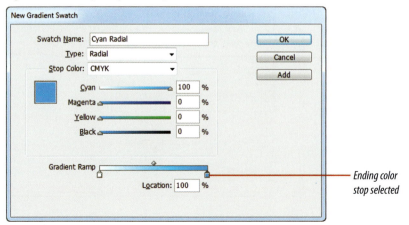

Starting color stop selected

Figure 53 *Formatting the right color stop*

Ending color stop selected

Figure 54 *Dragging the Gradient Swatch tool straight down*

*Drag Gradient Swatch tool
cursor straight down*

Figure 55 *Linear gradient applied vertically to the frame*

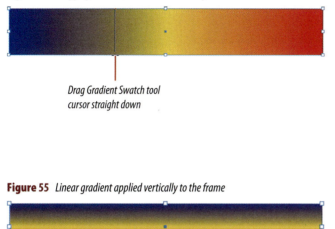

Figure 56 *Dragging the Gradient Swatch tool from left to right*

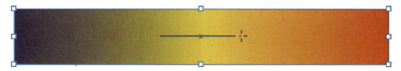

Apply gradient swatches and use the Gradient Swatch tool

1. Click the **Show Gradient Swatches button** on the Swatches panel.

2. Click the **Selection tool**, click the **border** of the top rectangular frame, verify that the Fill button is activated on the Tools panel, then click **Blue/Gold/Red Linear** on the Swatches panel.

TIP Make sure you are in Normal view and that you are viewing frame edges.

3. Click the **Gradient Swatch tool**, then, using Figure 54 as a guide, place the mouse pointer anywhere on the top edge of the rectangular frame, click and drag down, and release the mouse button at the bottom edge of the frame.

    Your frame should resemble Figure 55.

TIP Pressing and holding down [Shift] while dragging the Gradient Swatch tool constrains the movement on a horizontal or vertical axis.

4. Drag the **Gradient Swatch tool** from the bottom-middle handle of the frame to the top-right handle.

5. Drag the **Gradient Swatch tool** from the left edge of the document window to the right edge of the document window.

6. Drag the **Gradient Swatch tool** a short distance from left to right in the center of the frame, as shown in Figure 56.

7. Click the **Selection tool**, click the edge of the circular frame, then click **Cyan Radial** on the Swatches panel.

(continued)

8. Click the **Gradient Swatch tool** [icon], press and hold down **[Shift]**, then drag the **Gradient Swatch tool** from the center point of the circle up to the bottom edge of the center rectangle above the circle so that your document resembles Figure 57.

You filled two objects with two different gradients, and you used the Gradient Swatch tool to manipulate how the gradients filled the objects.

Use the Gradient Swatch tool to extend a gradient across multiple objects and modify a gradient

1. Click **Window** on the Application bar, point to **Color**, then click **Gradient** to open the Gradient panel.

2. Deselect all, click the **Selection tool** [icon], then select the three rectangular frames above the circle.

3. Click **Blue/Gold/Red Linear** on the Swatches panel.

   As shown in Figure 58, the gradient fills each frame individually.

(continued)

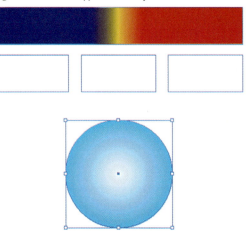

Figure 57 *Gradients applied to two objects*

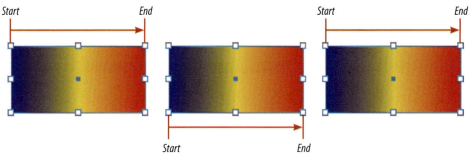

Figure 58 *A gradient fill applied individually to three objects*

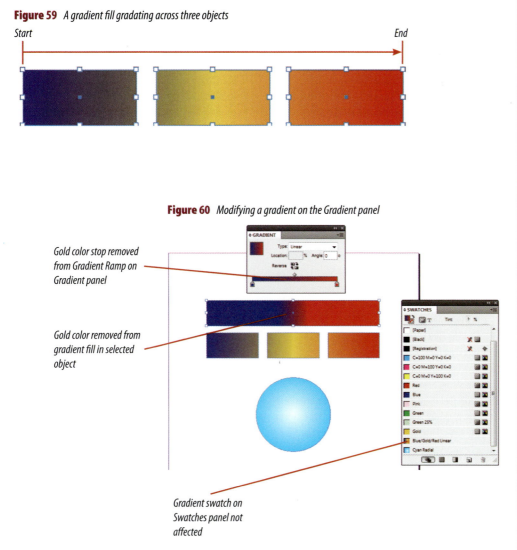

Figure 59 *A gradient fill gradating across three objects*

Start   End

Figure 60 *Modifying a gradient on the Gradient panel*

Gold color stop removed
from Gradient Ramp on
Gradient panel

Gold color removed from
gradient fill in selected
object

Gradient swatch on
Swatches panel not
affected

4. With the three objects still selected, click the **Gradient Swatch tool** ⬛, then drag it from the left edge of the leftmost frame to the right edge of the rightmost frame.

   As shown in Figure 59, the gradient gradates across all three selected objects.

5. Click the **Selection tool** ▶, then click the **rectangular frame** at the top of the document window.

6. Remove the center gold color stop from the Gradient Ramp on the Gradient panel, then click the **Show All Swatches button** ⬛ on the Swatches panel.

   As shown in Figure 60, the gold color is removed only from the gradient fill in the *selected* frame. The original gradient on the Swatches panel (Blue/Gold/Red Linear) is not affected.

7. Save your work, then close Making the Gradient.

You selected three objects, applied a gradient to each of them, then used the Gradient Swatch tool to extend the gradient across all three selected objects. You then modified the gradient fill of a selected object by removing a color stop from the Gradient panel.

Work with process colors.

1. Open ID 5-3.indd, then save it as **LAB cover**.
2. Verify that the Swatches panel is open, click the Swatches panel option button, then click New Color Swatch.
3. Verify that Process is chosen in the Color Type text box and that CMYK is chosen in the Color Mode text box.
4. Remove the check mark in the Name with Color Value check box, then type **Pink i**n the Swatch Name text box.
5. Type **15** in the Cyan text box, press [Tab], type **70** in the Magenta text box, press [Tab], type **10** in the Yellow text box, press [Tab], type **0** in the Black text box, press [Tab], then click OK.
6. Display the Color panel if necessary.
7. Click the Color panel options button, click CMYK, then verify that the Fill button is activated.
8. Drag the Cyan slider on the Color panel to 50%, drag the Magenta slider to 10%, then drag the Yellow and Black sliders to 0%.
9. Drag the color from the Fill button on the Color panel to the Swatches panel.
10. Verify that the C=50 M=10 Y=0 K=0 swatch is still selected on the Swatches panel, click the Swatches panel options button, then click New Tint Swatch.
11. Drag the Tint slider to 35%, then click OK.

Apply color.

1. Duplicate the Text layer, then rename it **Colored Text**.
2. Click View on the Application bar, point to Extras, then click Hide Frame Edges.

3. Drag and drop C=50 M=10 Y=0 K=0 from the Swatches panel to the outermost black-filled frame.
4. Click the Selection tool, click the BRUSH UP text frame, then click the Formatting affects text button on the Tools panel.
5. Click the C=50 M=10 Y=0 K=0 swatch on the Swatches panel.
6. Click the Holiday Issue text frame in the lower left corner of the cover, click the Formatting affects text button on the Swatches panel, then click the Paper swatch on the Swatches panel.
7. Click the Type tool, select all of the text in the PUPPY LOVE text frame, then click Pink on the Swatches panel.
8. Select all of the text in the FETCH text frame, then click the C=50 M=10 Y=0 K=0 35% tint swatch on the Swatches panel.
9. Click the Click to select items button on the Colored Text layer to select all the items on the layer.
10. Click Object on the Application bar, point to Transform, then click Move.
11. Verify that there is a check mark in the Preview check box, type **-.03** in the Horizontal text box, type **-.03** in the Vertical text box, click OK, then deselect all.

Work with spot colors.

1. Click the Swatches panel options button, then click New Color Swatch.
2. Click the Color Type list arrow, then click Spot.
3. Click the Color Mode list arrow, then click PANTONE solid coated.
4. Type **117** in the PANTONE text box, then click OK.

5. Change the fill on the C=50 M=10 border to PANTONE 117 C.
6. Click the Imported Graphics layer on the Layers panel to target it, click the Selection tool, then click between the dog's eyes to select the frame for placing a new image.
7. Click File on the Application bar, click Place, navigate to the drive and folder where your Chapter 5 Data Files are stored, click LAB.ai, then click Open. (*Hint*: LAB.ai is an Adobe Illustrator graphic filled with PANTONE 117 C.)
8. Click the Photo layer on the Layers panel, click the dog graphic in the document window, click Edit on the Application bar, click Copy, click Edit on the Application bar, then click Paste in Place.
9. On the Layers panel, drag the Indicates selected items button from the Photo layer up to the Imported Graphics layer.
10. Click File on the Application bar, click Place, navigate to the drive and folder where your Chapter 5 Data Files are stored, then double-click Wally Head Silo. psd. (*Hint*: Wally Head Silo.psd is identical to the dog photo, with the exception that it was saved with a clipping path around the dog's head in order to remove the red background.)
11. Deselect all, compare your work to Figure 61, save your work, then close the document.

Work with gradients.

1. Open ID 5-4.indd, then save it as **Gradient Skills Review**.
2. Click the Swatches panel options button, then click New Gradient Swatch.

Working with Color

3. In the Swatch Name text box, type **Red/Golden/Green Linear**.
4. Click the left color stop on the Gradient Ramp, click the Stop Color list arrow, then click Swatches.
5. Click the swatch named Red.
6. Click the right color stop on the Gradient Ramp, click the Stop Color list arrow, click Swatches, then click the swatch named Green.
7. Position your pointer anywhere immediately below the Gradient Ramp, then click to add a third color stop.
8. Type **50** in the Location text box, then press [Tab].

9. Click the Stop Color list arrow, choose Swatches, click the swatch named Gold, then click OK.
10. Click the Show Gradient Swatches button on the Swatches panel.
11. Click the Selection tool, select the border of the top rectangular frame, verify that the Fill button is activated on the Tools panel, then click Red/Golden/Green Linear on the Swatches panel.
12. Click the Gradient Swatch tool, then drag from the top-middle handle of the rectangular frame down to the bottom-right handle.

13. Display the Gradient panel if necessary.
14. Click the Selection tool, deselect the top rectangular frame, then select the three lower rectangular frames.
15. Click Red/Golden/Green Linear on the Swatches panel.
16. Click the Gradient Swatch tool, and with all three objects still selected, drag the Gradient Swatch tool from the left edge of the leftmost frame to the right edge of the rightmost frame.
17. Deselect all, then compare your work to Figure 62.
18. Save your work, then close Gradient Skills Review.

Figure 61 *Completed Skills Review, Part 1*

Figure 62 *Completed Skills Review, Part 2*

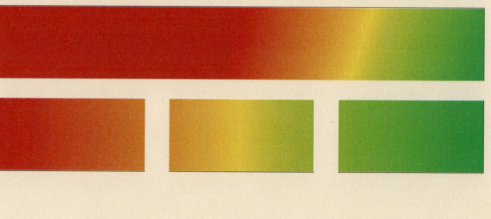

You are a freelance graphic designer. You have recently been contracted to create a newsletter for a local financial investment company. The newsletter will be 8.5" × 11" and will be printed using the CMYK process inks. You decide on the colors you want to use, open InDesign, create a new document, then, before you start designing, create a process color and a 40% tint of that color.

1. Open ID 5-5.indd, then save it as **Process Colors**.
2. Click the Swatches panel options button, then click New Color Swatch.
3. Create a CMYK color named **Tan** using the following values: Cyan 0%, Magenta 30%, Yellow 55%, and Black 20%.
4. Create a new tint swatch based on Tan, then change the tint amount to 40%.
5. Compare your Swatches panel to Figure 63, save your work, then close Process Colors. (Don't be concerned if your swatch order differs.)

Figure 63 *Completed Project Builder 1*

Working with Color

You are a freelance graphic designer. You have recently been contracted to create a cover for LAB magazine. The magazine is usually published only with one color—in black and white—but the publishers have some extra money for this issue. They want you to create a design for this cover so that it will print as a two-color job. It will be printed with black and one spot color. They provide you with the black and white version of the cover. You are free to choose the spot color and apply it in whatever way you think is best.

1. Open ID 5-6.indd, then save it as **2 Color Cover**.
2. Click the Swatches panel options button, then click New Color Swatch.
3. Click the Color Type list arrow, then choose Spot.
4. Click the Color Mode list arrow, then choose PANTONE solid coated.
5. Choose PANTONE 195 C, then click OK.
6. Click the Swatches panel option button, then click New Tint Swatch.
7. Drag the Tint slider to 25%, then click OK.
8. Change the fill of the outermost frame that is filled with black to PANTONE 195 C.
9. Click the inner white border that is filled with Paper and stroked with Black, then change its fill color to PANTONE 195 C 25%.
10. Change the fill color on the three white headlines to PANTONE 195 C 25%.
11. Compare your cover to Figure 64, save your work, then close 2 Color Cover.

Figure 64 *Completed Project Builder 2*

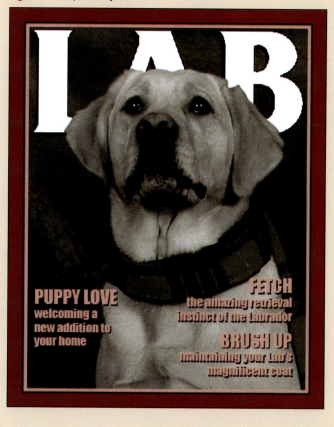

You have recently been contracted to create a logo for the Hypnotists Foundation. Their representative tells you that he wants the logo to be a circle filled with a radial gradient. Starting from the inside of the circle, the colors should go from white to black to white to black to white to black. He tells you that he wants each color to be very distinct—in other words, he doesn't want the white and black colors to blend into each other, creating a lot of gray areas in the logo.

1. Open ID 5-7.indd, then save it as **Concentric Circle Gradient**.
2. Click the Swatches panel options button, then click New Gradient Swatch.
3. Create a radial gradient named **Six Ring Radial**.
4. Add four new color stops to the Gradient Ramp, then position them so that they are equally spaced across the ramp.
5. Format the first, third, and fifth color stops as 0% CMYK (White).
6. Format the second, fourth and sixth color stops as 100% Black.
7. Close the New Gradient Swatch dialog box, then apply the new gradient to the circle.
8. Hide the frame edges, then compare your work to Figure 65.
9. Save your work, then close Concentric Circle Gradient.

Figure 65 *Completed Design Project*

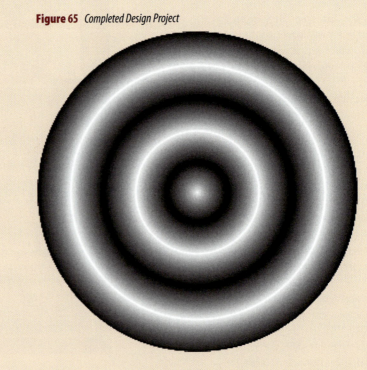

This project will test your familiarity with process colors. You will open an InDesign document that shows nine process colors. Each process color is numbered from 1 to 9. All nine colors are very basic mixes. None of the nine is composed of more than two process inks. The inks used to create the nine colors are used at either 100% or 50%. Your challenge is to guess the CMYK components of each color.

1. Open ID 5-8.indd, then save it as **Guessing Game**. The color squares are shown in Figure 66.
2. Use the Type tool to enter your guesses for each process color. You can type directly on top of each of the nine squares or directly below each, for example, **Magenta=100**.
3. When finished, double-click each color on the Swatches panel to identify the actual CMYK mix.
4. Enter the total number of your correct answers on your document window, save your work, then close Guessing Game.

Figure 66 *Portfolio Project Quiz*

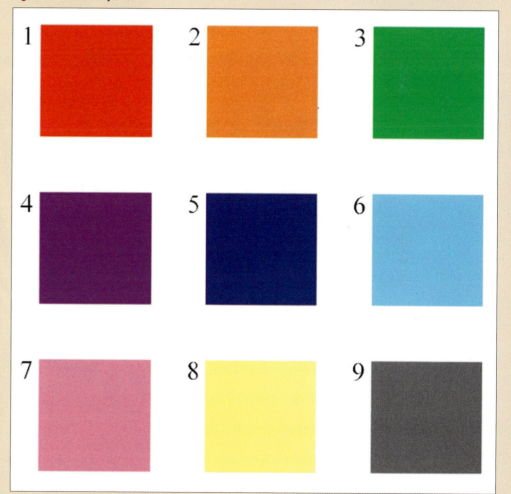

CHAPTER 6 WORKING WITH
PLACED IMAGES

1. Place multiple graphics
2. Use the Links panel
3. Explore image resolution issues
4. Place vector graphics
5. Interface InDesign with Photoshop
6. Use Libraries

CHAPTER **6** WORKING WITH
PLACED IMAGES

As a layout program, InDesign offers you a number of options for importing graphics from other applications and placing them into your design. Chapter 6 focuses on working with placed images from Adobe Photoshop and Adobe Illustrator. First, you will learn how to place multiple images quickly and easily, using the standard Place command in InDesign, then using InDesign CS5's new Mini Bridge feature. Once your images are placed, you will explore the Links panel, a great resource for managing the relationship between your InDesign document and the imported files. The Links panel allows you to find imported graphics in the document. It tells you the status of the link to a graphic, and it alerts you if the graphic has been modified or is missing.

Chapter 2 also focuses on vector and bitmap graphics. You'll learn the difference between the two and what rules apply when working with each. You'll do an extensive exploration of the resolution issues involved in placing Photoshop imagery and discover InDesign's powerful relationship with Photoshop through the manipulation of Photoshop graphics right in InDesign. You'll remove a white background from an image and load alpha channels and clipping paths— all without having to open Photoshop!

Finally, you'll learn about libraries—another great feature for managing your work with imported graphics.

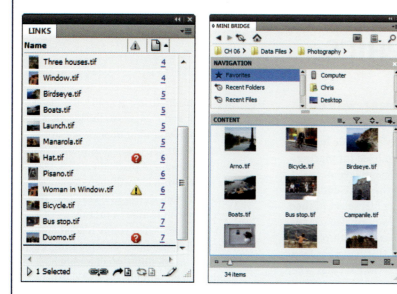

Place Multiple GRAPHICS

What You'll Do

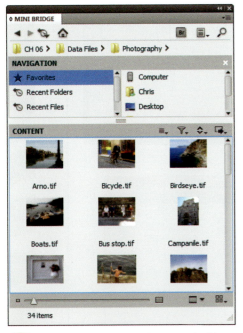

 In this lesson, you will use the Place command and the Mini Bridge panel to place multiple images into a layout.

Placing Multiple Images with the Place Command

The Place command on the File menu is the basic command used for placing graphics into an InDesign layout. In Chapter 4, you used the Place command to navigate to a single file, select it, then place it in a layout. You can also use the Place command to import multiple image files simultaneously. This is a great feature that offers substantial time savings when working with multiple images.

Figure 1 *Place gun icon*

Number indicates the number of images loaded in the place gun

To place multiple images, click the Place command and navigate to the location where the graphics you want to place are stored. Use the [Ctrl] key to select as many graphic files as you want to place, then click Place. The place command will then display the place gun icon, shown in Figure 6-1. The place gun icon features a thumbnail of a loaded image. When you've loaded multiple images, the thumbnail showing is the current "loaded" image, and a small number against a white background indicates how many total images are loaded. You can use the right-arrow and left-arrow keys to scroll through all the loaded images. Simply click the place gun on the page or in a frame and the current "loaded" image will be placed.

When you place an image, you always have two options for how it's placed. If you click the place gun in an already existing frame, the image will be placed into the frame. If you click the place gun on the page, InDesign will create a frame for the placed image. By default, the frame will be sized to display the entire image at 100%. In other words, the frame will be the same size as the image itself.

When placing graphics into frames, be aware at what size the graphic is being placed. When you create a new frame and then place a graphic into that frame, by default the graphic will be placed at 100%—even if the graphic is larger than the frame itself. However, if you place a graphic into a "used" frame, the rules can change. For example, let's say you have a frame that contains an image, and that image has been resized to 74%. If you click the Place command and place a different image into the frame, the new image will be placed at 74%. In other words, when placing a graphic into a used frame, the new graphic is placed at the same size as the previous graphic.

Setting Frame Fitting Options

As discussed in Chapter 4, the Fitting menu lists a number of commands that affect how a graphic fits into its frame. Generally speaking, you'll find that the Fill Frame Proportionally

and Fit Content Proportionally commands are the one you'll use most often.

When they're designing a layout, most designers position frames at a specific size and location that works for the layout. Therefore, it makes sense that when they import graphics into those frames, they'll want the graphic to fill the frame. The Fill Frame Proportionally fitting command does just that: it scales the graphic so that it fills the entire frame—without distorting the graphic.

On the other hand, some designers like to see the entire graphic when it's placed into a frame—even if it doesn't fill the entire frame. Then, they scale the graphic to fill the frame. The Fit Content Proportionally fitting command scales a placed graphic so that the entire graphic is visible when placed into any size frame.

When you're placing many graphics into a layout, you will find it tiring to be choosing the same fitting command over and over again. To alleviate this, you can set up options in the Frame Fitting Options dialog box, shown in Figure 6-2. This dialog box allows you a specific fitting option for all placed graphics. If you want the options applied to all frames you create in all future documents, set the frame fitting options with no documents open. By doing so, the frame fitting options you choose will be applied to all frames you create when you open a document.

If you apply settings in the Frame Fitting Options dialog box with a document open and no frames selected, the options will apply to all frames you create in that document only. If you apply frame fitting options to a selected frame, the options affect only that frame.

Figure 2 *Frame Fitting Options dialog box*

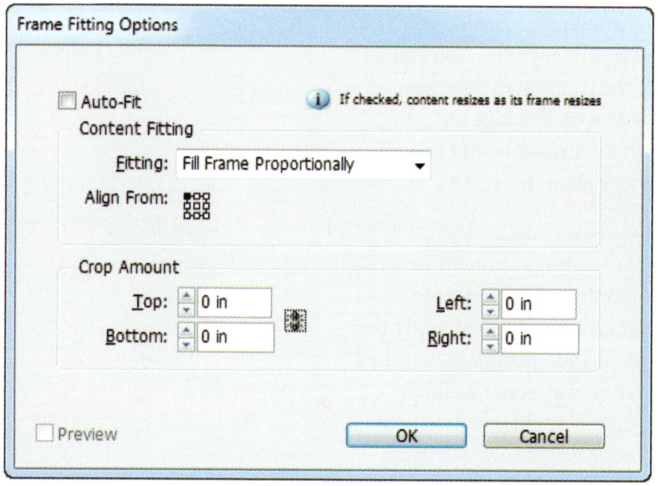

You can also use the Frame Fitting Options dialog box to specify the reference point for the alignment of the image in the frame.

Adobe Bridge

Adobe Bridge is a free-standing **content management application**.

What is content management? Imagine that you are designing a 200-page catalog, like the quarterly catalog for L.L. Bean or IKEA. Think about the hundreds of images that you'll need to import to complete your layout. Now consider that those images—the ones that you actually use in the catalogue—are only a subset of the thousands of product shots that the photographers deliver after the photo shoot.

Adobe Bridge is designed to help you manage this content. Let's say you have a folder with 500 image files. If you view that folder using Adobe Bridge as the interface, Bridge will show you a thumbnail of each file. You can choose the size of the thumbnail, allowing you to sample and preview each image quickly. Compare that with the time it would take to open each image to look at it.

Adobe Bridge also allows you to apply color labels and text data to images to help you categorize them. Continuing the example above, the photography team could apply the text tag SHOES to all shoe products that they shoot, and SWEATERS to every sweater. Then you, the designer, could use Bridge to sort through the images to show only the shoe or sweater photographs.

Placing Multiple Images with Mini Bridge

InDesign CS5 marks the debut of Mini Bridge. Mini Bridge allows you to access the power of Adobe Bridge without leaving InDesign by incorporating Adobe Bridge into InDesign as a panel. You access it in the Windows menu, just like any other panel. You then navigate to the folder where your images are stored. As shown in Figure 3, the Mini Bridge panel provides you with a thumbnail preview and other useful information about the files in the target folder. Use the slider at the bottom of the panel to enlarge or decrease the size of the preview thumbnails.

Mini Bridge is great for previewing and a great resource for placing graphics. Simply select one or more images, then drag and drop into the InDesign document. The place gun will appear, allowing you to place the image(s) in the location of your choice.

Figure 3 *Mini Bridge panel*

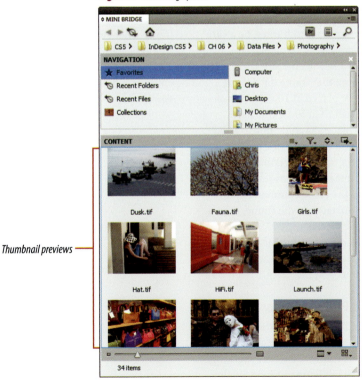

Thumbnail previews

Figure 4 *Setting Frame Fitting Options*

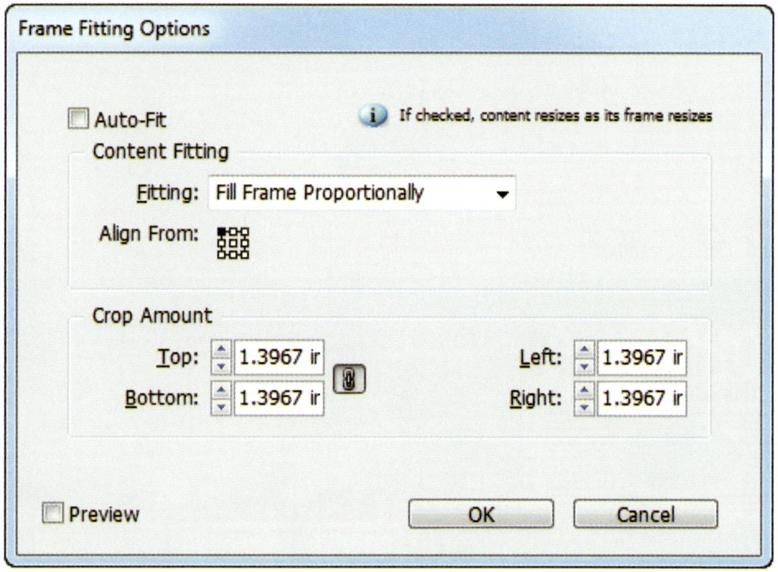

Frame Fitting Options

☐ Auto-Fit   ⓘ If checked, content resizes as its frame resizes

Content Fitting

Fitting: Fill Frame Proportionally ▼

Align From: ▦

Crop Amount

Top: 1.3967 ir   Left: 1.3967 ir

Bottom: 1.3967 ir   🔗   Right: 1.3967 ir

☐ Preview   [OK]   [Cancel]

Place multiple images with the Place command

1. Verify that no documents are open in InDesign, click **Object** on the Application bar, point to **Fitting**, then click **Clear Frame Fitting Options**.

   Before specifying a frame fitting option, it's a good idea to first clear any existing options.

2. Open ID 6-1.indd, then save it as **Multiple Placements**.

3. Click **Object** on the Application bar, point to **Fitting**, then click **Frame Fitting Options**.

4. Click the **Fitting list arrow**, then click **Fill Frame Proportionally**.

5. Verify in the Align From section that the top-left reference point is checked, then compare your dialog box to Figure 4.

   With these settings, the graphics you place *should* all be fit proportionally when you place them. However, depending on various factors, such as other work you've done on your computer, other fitting settings that might have been loaded, or if the data file has been used by someone else, your placed files might not be placed as specified. Don't worry: the last part of this lesson will correct any inconsistencies.

6. Click **OK**, click the **Selection tool** ▶, then select the large blue frame on pages 2-3.

7. Click **File**, click **Place**, navigate to the folder where your Chapter 6 data files are stored, open the Photography folder, then click the file **Corniglia** once to select it.

(continued)

8. Press and hold **[Ctrl]**(Win) or ⌘ (Mac), then click the following files in this order: **David**, **Divers**, **Sheets**, **Fauna**, **Dusk**

   You will need to scroll in the Place dialog box to select all the files.

9. Click **Open**.

   As shown in Figure 5, the place gun is loaded, showing the Corniglia graphic and the number 6, indicating that six files are loaded.

10. Press the **right arrow key** [→] on your keypad repeatedly to see all the files loaded in the place gun.

    Despite the order in which you selected them when you chose them, the files are loaded alphabetically: Corniglia, David, Divers, Dusk, Fauna, Sheets

11. Press the **right arrow key** [→] repeatedly until the **Corniglia image** is the visible loaded file.

12. Click the **place gun** on the large **blue frame**.

    As shown in Figure 6, the Corniglia image fills the frame and the place gun now shows the next file in line.

13. Place the remaining five loaded images into the five frames at the bottom of the page in any order that you wish.

14. Select all six frames, click **Object**, point to **Fitting**, then click **Fill Frame Proportionally**.

    Theoretically, with Fill Frame Proportionally set as the Frame Fitting Option, this step should be unnecessary. However, for this lesson, it's necessary to verify that your layout is consistent with that of the book.

    (continued)

Figure 5 *Place gun icon*

Six images loaded

Figure 6 *Placing the Corniglia image*

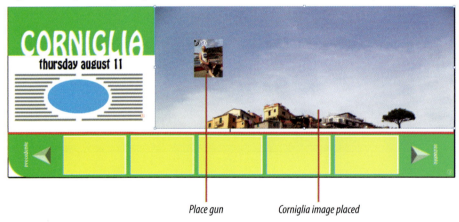

Place gun   Corniglia image placed

15. Select the Corniglia image only, click **Object**, point to **Fitting**, then click **Center Content**. Your layout should resemble Figure 7.

16. Save your work.

With no documents open, you chose the Clear Frame Fitting Options. You opened a document and chose a frame fitting option. You used the Place command to select six files to be placed, then used the arrow key to view those six files in the Place gun. You then placed the files and applied a fitting command to all the frames to verify that they were consistent.

Figure 7 *Six images loaded and fitted*

NEW Place multiple images with Mini Bridge

1. Navigate to spread 4-5, then compress all of your open panels except the Tools panel.

   The Mini Bridge panel can get pretty large, so you want to maximize the available space on your screen.

2. Click **Window**, then click **Mini Bridge**.

   The Mini Bridge panel, shown in Figure 8, opens.

(continued)

Figure 8 *Mini Bridge panel*

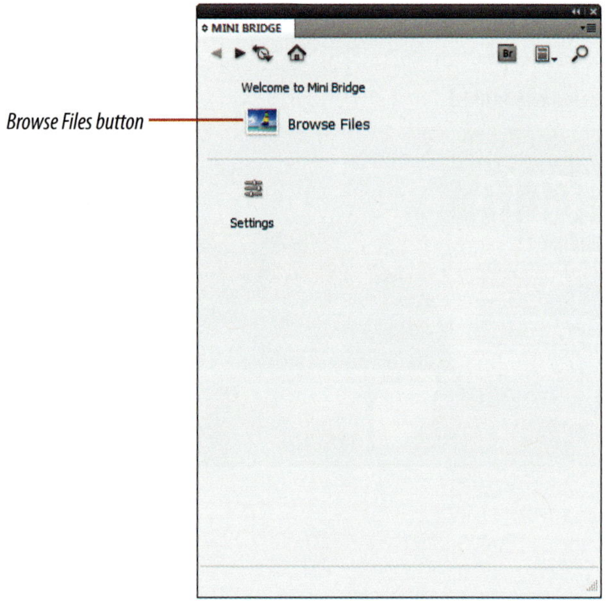
Browse Files button
MINI BRIDGE
Welcome to Mini Bridge
Browse Files
Settings

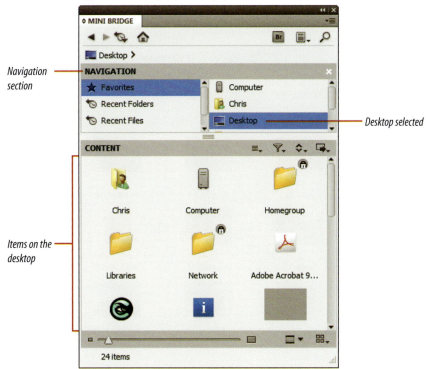

Figure 9 *Mini Bridge panel displaying contents of desktop*

Navigation section

Desktop selected

Items on the desktop

3. Click the **Browse Files button** then, when the Navigation section appears at the top of the Mini Bridge panel, click **Desktop**.

As shown in Figure 9, when you click Desktop, the Content section lists the files currently on your desktop. Figure 9 shows our desktop, so your panel will show different files.

(continued)

4. Navigate to the chapter where you store your Chapter 6 data files, open the Photography folder, then compare your Mini Bridge panel to Figure 10.

   Mini Bridge displays thumbnail previews of the contents of the Photography folder.

5. Drag the **scale slider** at the bottom of the panel left and right to enlarge and reduce the thumbnails.

6. Drag the **scale slider** so that nine thumbnails are visible in the panel.

7. Use the scrollbar on the right of the panel to scroll through all the thumbnails.

8. Click the file named **Manarola**, then note what the image looks like so you'll remember it.

9. Press and hold **[Ctrl]**(Win) or ⌘ (Mac), then click the following five files: **Birdseye**, **Boats**, **Launch**, **Three Houses**, **Window**.

(continued)

Figure 10 *Mini Bridge panel displaying contents of Photography folder*

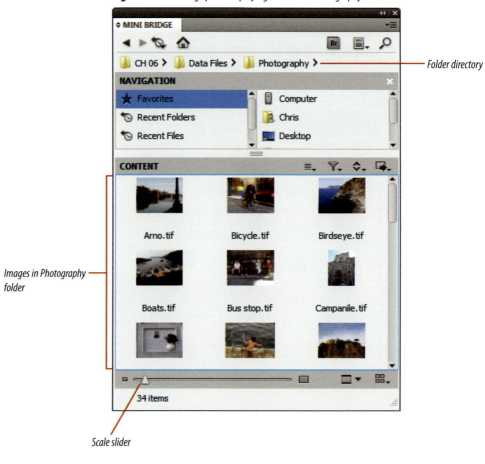

Folder directory

Images in Photography folder

Scale slider

Figure 11 *Place gun loaded with images from Mini Bridge*

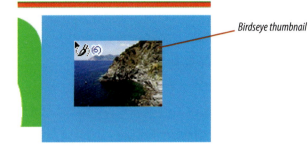

Birdseye thumbnail

Figure 12 *Placing the Manarola image*

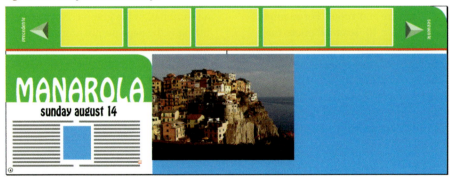

10. Position your mouse over **any of the selected thumbnails**, then click and drag the **files** from the Mini Bridge panel into the document.

    As shown in Figure 11, the place gun appears, showing the Birdseye thumbnail and the number 6—indicating that six files are loaded.

11. Minimize the Mini Bridge panel.

12. Press → to scroll through the loaded thumbnails, then scroll to the Manarola thumbnail.

13. Click in the **large blue frame** with the place gun.

    As shown in Figure 12, the Manarola image fills the frame.

14. Place the remaining five loaded images into the five frames at the top of the page in any order that you wish.

15. Select all six frames, click **Object**, point to **Fitting**, then click **Fill Frame Proportionally**.

16. Save your work, then close the file.

You previewed files on your computer using the Mini Bridge. You selected multiple files in Mini Bridge then placed them in an InDesign layout.

Use the
LINKS PANEL

What You'll Do

 In this lesson, you will use the Links panel to manage links to imported graphics.

Understanding Preview Files

When you use the Place command to place a graphic file, the image that you see in the graphics frame in InDesign is a **preview file**; it is *not* the graphic itself. Why does InDesign work this way? Because of file size considerations.

Remember that many graphics files—especially those of scanned photos or other digital images—have very large file sizes. Some of them are enormous. For example, if you had an 8" × 10" scanned photo that you wanted to use in a layout for a magazine, that graphic would be approximately 21 megabytes—at minimum. If you placed that graphic in your InDesign layout, your InDesign file size would increase dramatically. Now imagine placing 10 of those graphics!

The preview is a low-resolution version of the placed graphic file. As such, its file size is substantially smaller than the average graphics file. The role of the preview file in the layout is ingenious. As a proxy for the actual graphic, it allows you to see a representation of the graphic in your layout without having to carry the burden of the graphic's full file size.

Using the Links Panel

You can think of the Links panel, shown in Figure 13, as command central for managing the links to placed graphics. The Links panel lists all of the graphics files that you place into an InDesign document. By default, text that you place in InDesign is not linked to the original text file and therefore not listed in the Links panel.

By default, graphics files are listed with a thumbnail of the graphic. Next to each listing is the page number on which the file is located. The Links panel menu offers options for sorting this list. For example, you can sort the list alphabetically or by page number.

You can use the Links panel to locate a placed file in your document quickly. If you select a file on the Links panel and then click the Go to Link button on the panel, InDesign will go to the page where the placed file is located and will automatically select its frame. Conversely, when you select a placed file on the document, the file's listing is automatically highlighted on the Links panel.

Viewing the Link Info Section of the Links Panel

Double-clicking a filename on the Links panel displays the Link Info section of the Links panel. Shown in Figure 14, the Link Info section displays important information about the placed file, including its file size, resolution, the date it was last modified, the application that created it, and its file format. The file format identifies what type of file it is, such as a Photoshop or an Illustrator file.

QUICK TIP

You can also click the Show/Hide Link Information triangle to expose this section of the panel.

It's always good to know the file format of a graphic and the application that created it in case you wish to edit the original. The Links panel is a big help in this regard, as well. Simply click the Edit Original button on the panel and the selected graphic will open in its original application (that is, if

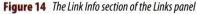
Figure 14 *The Link Info section of the Links panel*

Figure 13 *The Links Panel*

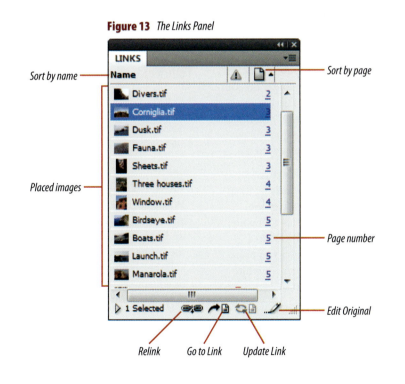

Sort by name

Sort by page

Placed images

Page number

Edit Original

Relink   Go to Link   Update Link

Show/Hide Link Info

you have that application installed on your computer).

Generally speaking, you will find the default information listed in the Link Info section of the panel to be more than satisfactory for your work. It might even be too much information. You can specify the categories of information you want to see listed in the Link Info section, by clicking the Links panel options button, clicking Panel Options, then selecting only the check boxes of the categories you want to view.

Placing Text Files

When you place text in InDesign, the text is usually from a Word processing program like Microsoft Word or Word Perfect. By default, when you place text in InDesign, the text is not linked to the original text file and the placed text does not appear in the Links panel. The formatting changes you apply in InDesign don't affect the original text file and, more importantly, any changes that you might make to the original text file don't affect the formatting of the text in InDesign. You can override the default and link text you place in InDesign to the original text document. If you select the Create Links When Placing Text And Spreadsheet Files option in File Handling preferences before you place a file, the name of the text file appears in the Links panel.

When text is linked to its original file in this manner, you can use the Links panel to update and manage the file. But beware: when you update a linked text file, any

editing or formatting changes that you applied in InDesign are lost. That's why placed text in InDesign isn't linked by default: it's too risky. Even when you override the default and link text to its original file, text files in the InDesign document are not automatically updated when the original file is edited and saved. You must manually update the linked file using the Links panel.

Managing Links to Placed Graphics

When you place a graphics file, InDesign establishes a link between the graphics frame and the placed file. That link is based on the location of the file. When you first place the graphic, you must navigate through the folder structure on your computer to locate the file. You may navigate to a folder on your computer's hard drive, external drive or network. In either case, InDesign remembers that navigation path as the method for establishing the location of the placed file.

The Links panel uses icons to alert you to the status of a placed file. The Missing icon appears beside the file's name when the established link no longer points to the file. In other words, if you move the file to a different folder (or trash it), *after* you place it in InDesign. The Missing icon is a white question mark inside a red circle.

The Modified icon is a black exclamation point in a yellow triangle. A placed file's status is noted as Modified when the original file has been edited and saved *after* being placed in InDesign. For example, if you place a Photoshop graphic in InDesign, then open

the graphic in Photoshop, edit it and save changes, the graphic you placed in InDesign is no longer the most up-to-date version of the graphic. If you have the InDesign document open when you save the Photoshop file, InDesign automatically updates the graphic in the layout. Otherwise, the Links panel displays the Modified icon beside the file. Figure 15 shows files in the Links panel with the Missing and Modified icons.

The OK status does not have an icon. The OK status means that the established link still points to the location of the placed graphic, and the graphic itself has not been modified since being placed.

QUICK TIP

If a linked or embedded file contains metadata, you can view the metadata using the Links panel. Select a file on the Links panel, click the Links panel options button, click Utilities, then click XMP File Info.

Updating Missing and Modified Files

When the Links panel displays modified and missing icons, those links need to be updated, meaning you need to reestablish the connection between the preview file and the graphic file that has been moved or edited.

It is very easy to update modified files on the Links panel. To do so, you click the filename on the Links panel, then click the Update Link button on the panel. The link will update to the newest saved version of the file, and the status of the file will change to OK.

Files that have the Missing status need to be relinked to the graphic. To do so, you click the filename on the Links panel, click the Relink button, then navigate to the new location of the graphic file. Once the link is reestablished, the status of the file changes to OK.

When you reestablish a link, none of the formatting that you did to the graphic when you placed it the first time is lost. If, for example, you scaled a placed graphic to 35% and centered it proportionally in the graphics frame, those modifications will still be in place when you reestablish the link.

Embedding Files

InDesign CS5 allows you to embed a placed file into the InDesign document. When you embed a placed file, the file literally becomes part of the InDesign document; it no longer links to a source file. In fact, if you edit the source file, you cannot update the embedded file; the link is literally broken.

You would do this for one reason: to have a self-contained InDesign document without the need for supporting files. Rather than having to package an InDesign document with all its supporting files, an InDesign document with embedded graphics offers you the simplicity of having to work with only a single document.

Figure 15 *Placed graphics with Missing and Modified status*

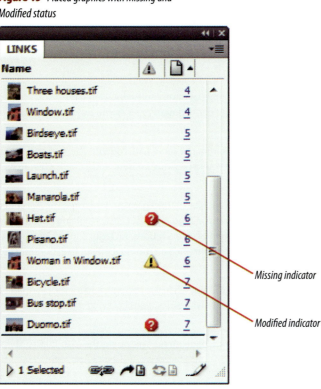

Missing indicator

Modified indicator

Figure 16 *Embedding a placed file*

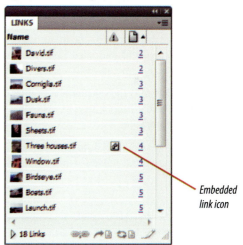

Embedded link icon

To embed a placed graphic file, simply select it on the Links panel, click the Links options button, then click Embed File. The file will continue to be listed on the Links panel, but it will appear with the Embedded icon beside its name, as shown in Figure 16.

To relink an embedded file, click the file on the Links panel, click the Links panel options button, then click Relink. You'll be prompted to navigate to the location of the source file to reestablish the link. The file will then be linked, not embedded.

Because an embedded file is part of the InDesign document, embedded files increase the file size of the InDesign document substantially. For this reason, you may want to avoid embedding files in InDesign and work with the standard methodology of linking to graphics.

Exporting XML

XML is a versatile language that describes content, such as text, graphics, and design elements, in a way that allows that content to be output in a variety of ways. Like HTML, XML uses coded information, called "tags," to identify and organize content. Unlike HTML, XML does not describe how the information will appear or how it will be laid out on a page. Instead, XML creates an identity for the content.

XML can distinguish and identify such elements as chapter titles, headlines, body copy, an author's name, or numbered steps. Here's the hook: XML information is not specific to any one kind of output, so you can use that same information to create different types of documents, just as you can use the English alphabet to speak and write other languages.

For example, many designers work in XML to generate catalogs, books, magazines, or newspapers, all from the same XML content. The Tags panel and the Structure pane, which are two XML utilities in InDesign, interface smoothly with XML code and allow you to organize content and list it in a hierarchical order, which is essential to XML.

Before items can be exported to an XML file, they must be tagged, using the Tags panel. You can also apply an "autotag" to an item using the Autotag command on the Tags panel menu. When you do so, InDesign applies the default tag for that item type defined in the Tagging Preset Options dialog box. You can change the default tag settings in this dialog box by clicking the Tags panel options button, then clicking Tagging Preset Options. All tagged items appear in the Structure pane. You can opt to show or hide tagged frames as well as tag markers using the Structure commands on the View menu. To export an XML file, click Export, then choose XML from the Format list menu.

Because XML tags are data descriptions and carry no formatting instructions, you will need to format XML content when you import it into a layout. A smart solution for doing that quickly and with consistency is to "map" XML tags to paragraph, character, table, or cell styles. As with all solutions involving styles, mapping tags to pre-defined styles makes formatting imported XML content easier and less time-consuming.

To map XML tags to various styles, choose Map Tags to Styles from the Tags panel menu or the Structure pane menu. This opens the Map Tags to Styles dialog box, where you can choose an XML tag and apply a style to it.

Figure 17 *Links warning dialog box*

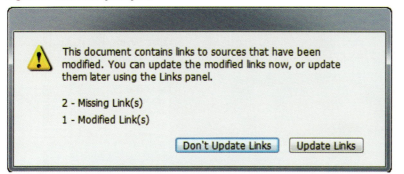

Creating and Using Snippets

In the same way that libraries let you store page elements for reuse, snippets let you export any elements from a document for reuse in other documents or in an object library. A **snippet** is an XML file with an .inds file extension that contains complete representation of document elements, including all formatting tags and document structure. To create a snippet, use the Selection tool to select the frames you want to reuse, click File on the Application bar, click Export, then choose InDesign Snippet from the Save as type list arrow. Remember that you can create a single snippet from multiple objects. For example, you can select all the objects on a page and create one snippet from everything on the page. (It's a good idea to group the elements before exporting the snippet.) An even easier method is to drag selected items onto the desktop, into Adobe Bridge, a Library panel, or an e-mail message, each of which automatically creates a snippet file. To use a snippet in another file, you can use the Place command or just drag the snippet from the desktop into an InDesign document.

Use the Links panel to update modified and missing graphics

1. Open ID 6-2.indd, then compare the warning dialog box you see to Figure 17. Your dialog box might differ from the figure.

2. Click **Don't Update Links**, then save the file as **Update Links**.

   Normally you would click Update Links and the modified links would be updated. The missing links wouldn't be updated because they are missing. For this lesson, you were instructed to not update links so that you can do so manually in the Links panel.

3. Open the Links panel.

4. Scroll through the Links panel to view the list of the placed graphics.

   All of the placed files in this document—except two—are located in the Photography folder in the Data Files folder for Chapter 6. Two files have been moved out of the Photography folder and into the Moved Files folder. If your Links panel shows all the files as modified (an exclamation point in a yellow triangle), that is only because they have been relocated to your computer; they're not really modified.

(continued)

5. Click the **Woman in Window.tif link** in the Links panel, then click the **Go to Link** button.

   As shown in Figure 18, the window refreshes to show the Woman in Window graphic, which is automatically selected. Note that the graphic—not the frame—is selected.

6. Click the **Update Link button** 🗘.

   As shown in Figure 19, the graphic was listed as modified because its color had been modified in Photoshop and the file resaved since it had been placed in InDesign.

7. If necessary, select any other graphic files that show the Modified icon, then click the **Update Link button** 🗘.

8. Note that the Hat and Duomo graphics are listed as missing.

9. Click the **Hat** graphic in the Links panel, then click **Go to Link**.

10. Press and hold **[Alt]**(Win) or **[Option]**(Mac) then click the **Relink button** 🔗 in the Links panel.

(continued)

Figure 18   *Viewing modified graphic on the page and in the Links panel*

Modified indicator

Modified graphic selected

Go to Link   Update Link

Figure 19   *Viewing updated graphic on the page and in the Links panel*

Modified Indicator disappears

Graphic updated

Figure 20 *InDesign finds and relinks another missing graphic*

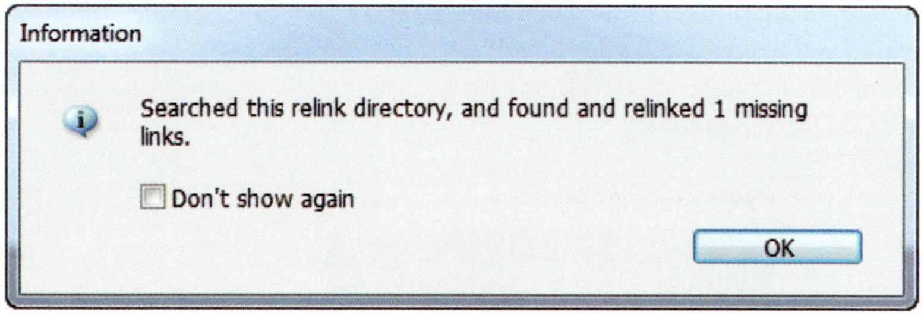

Information

Searched this relink directory, and found and relinked 1 missing links.

☐ Don't show again

OK

Because you know that both missing files are in the same location—the Moved files folder—you can relink them simultaneously.

11. Navigate to the Moved Files folder where you store your Chapter 6 data files, click **Hat**, then click **Open**.

As shown in Figure 20, an Information dialog box appears indicating that one file has been found and relinked. This refers to the other missing file, Duomo.tif.

12. Click **OK**, then note in the Links panel that both missing files have been relinked.

13. Save your work.

You used the Links panel to update one modified link, then you updated two missing links simultaneously.

Explore Image
RESOLUTION ISSUES

What You'll Do

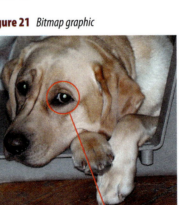

In this lesson, you will learn about effective image resolution in an InDesign layout and how to modify image resolution in Adobe Photoshop.

Understanding Bitmap Graphics

Photographic images are created on computers using a rectangular grid of colored squares called **pixels**. Because pixels (a contraction of "picture elements") can render subtle gradations of tone, they are the most common medium for continuous tone images—what you perceive as a photograph on your computer. Graphics created from pixels are called **bitmap graphics**.

All scanned images are composed of pixels. All "digital images" are composed of pixels. Adobe Photoshop is the leading graphics application for working with digital "photos." Figure 21 shows an example of a bitmap image. The enlarged section shows you the pixels that compose the image.

Figure 21 *Bitmap graphic*

Enlarged view of eye shows pixels

Understanding Image Resolution

The number of pixels in a given inch is referred to as the image's **resolution**. To be effective, pixels must be small enough to create an image with the illusion of continuous tone. The standard resolution for images for the web is 72 pixels per inch (ppi). For images that will be professionally printed, the standard resolution is 300 pixels per inch (ppi).

The term **effective resolution** refers to the resolution of a placed image based on its size in the layout. The important thing to remember about bitmap images in relation to InDesign is that the size of the image placed in the InDesign layout has a direct effect on the image's resolution. Think about it—if you enlarge a placed image in InDesign, the pixels that make up the image are spread out over a larger area. Thus, the effective resolution of the image goes down, because there are now fewer pixels per inch. This decrease in resolution will have a negative impact on the quality of an image when it is printed.

This is why enlarging an image in InDesign usually creates a problem with effective resolution: the greater the enlargement, the lower the effective resolution of the image.

QUICK TIP

The Links panel, in the Link Info section, lists the effective resolution for all placed graphics.

Let's use a clear example to illustrate this. Let's say you have a Photoshop image that is 1" × 1" at 300 ppi. 300 ppi is the resolution of the image. The image contains a total of 90,000 pixels (300 × 300 = 90,000).

Now, let's say you place the image into a 2" × 2" frame and enlarge the image 200% to fill the frame. Those same 90,000 pixels are spread out to fill a 2" × 2" frame. Thus, the effective resolution is 150 (ppi)—too low for professional printing. Figure 22 illustrates this example.

QUICK TIP

Vector graphics, like those you create in Adobe Illustrator, have no pixels, thus they have no resolution. Graphics professionals refer to vector graphics as **resolution independent**.

Figure 22 *Illustration of effective resolution*

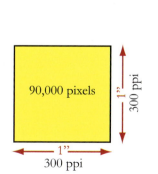

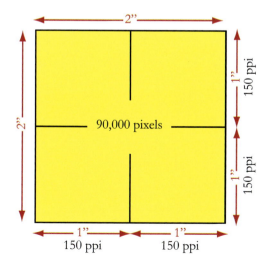

Enlarging a Graphic in Adobe Photoshop

Photoshop is the best-selling pixel-based image manipulation software application by Adobe Systems, the same company that produces InDesign. In fact, InDesign and Photoshop are sold as a unit with Illustrator. It's important that you understand that scaling a graphic in Photoshop is different from scaling a graphic in InDesign. When you scale a graphic in InDesign, it either spreads the existing pixels over a larger area (enlargement) or squeezes them into a smaller area (reduction). Photoshop, because it specializes in image manipulation, allows you to actually change the number of pixels when you scale a graphic.

Let's continue with the same example from above. If you have a 1" × 1" graphic at 300 ppi, it has a total of 90,000 pixels. If you enlarge it in Photoshop to a 2" × 2" graphic, Photoshop offers you the ability to maintain the image resolution. Thus, after the scale, the image will still be 300 ppi, meaning the 2" square image will be 600 pixels wide and 600 tall, for a total of 360,000 pixels. But from where do those extra 270,000 pixels come?

When enlarging a graphic in Photoshop, Photoshop creates the new pixels necessary to maintain an image's resolution by a process called **interpolation**. The color of the new pixels is based on the color information of the original pixels in the image. Thus, in the example above, the colors of the 270,000 new pixels are created based on the 90,000 original pixels.

QUICK TIP

To be an effective designer in InDesign, you need to understand effective resolution issues and be able to work in Photoshop to modify an image's resolution.

Enlarging a bitmap graphic always results in a loss of quality—even if you do it in Photoshop. That's because interpolated data is only duplicated data—inferior to the original data that you get from a scan or a digital image that you download from your digital camera.

In a nutshell, you should try your best to create all bitmap graphics in Adobe Photoshop at both the size and resolution that they will be used at the final output stage. You then import the graphic into InDesign and leave its size alone.

If you find that you need to enlarge the graphic substantially (more than 10%), remember that all resizing of bitmap graphics should be done in Photoshop, not in InDesign. Use InDesign simply to place the graphics in a layout, create text wraps, and perform other layout related tasks.

Is there any leeway here? Yes. If you need to reduce the size of a placed bitmap graphic in InDesign, you can do so without worrying about it too much. Reducing a bitmap graphic in InDesign is not a problem, because you *increase* the effective resolution of the bitmap graphic (the same number of pixels in a smaller area means more pixels per inch). If you need to enlarge a graphic slightly in InDesign, you can feel comfortable enlarging it up to 110%. For anything larger, enlarge it in Photoshop.

QUICK TIP

Remember, nothing in this discussion applies to vector graphics. Vector graphics are resolution independent. You can feel free to enlarge and reduce placed vector graphics in InDesign to your heart's content.

Figure 23 *Viewing resolution info for Dusk*

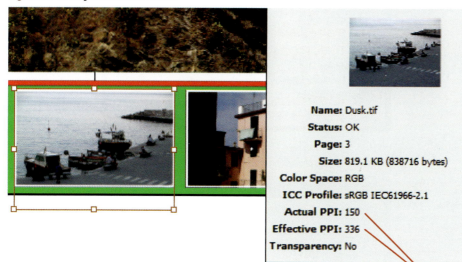

Resolution information

Change the resolution of a placed graphic

1. Go to spread 2-3, double-click **Dusk**, then compare your screen to Figure 23.

   The Link Info panel shows that the Actual PPI of the image is 150, but the Effective PPI of the placed image is 336, making it high enough to print with quality. Because the image was placed at 44%, the effective resolution is more than double the actual.

2. Double-click the **Corniglia** image at the top of the page.

   The actual resolution of the image is 150 ppi, and the effective ppi is 144, which is too low for quality printing.

3. Click the **Edit Original button** at the bottom of the Links panel.

   The image opens in Adobe Photoshop. You will need to have Adobe Photoshop installed on your computer to complete this lesson.

   (continued)

4. In Photoshop, click **Image** on the Application bar, then click **Image Size**.

   As shown in Figure 24, the resolution of the image is 150.

5. Note the Resample Image option at the bottom of the dialog box is checked.

   The Resample Image option is a key option in the dialog box. When it is checked, Photoshop will add pixels to the image when enlarging, and it will remove pixels from the image when reducing. If you uncheck the option, changing the image size would be no different than doing so in InDesign—no pixels would be added or removed.

6. Verify that the Resample Image option is checked.

7. Type **300** in the Resolution text box, then compare your Image Size dialog box to Figure 25.

   Note that the physical dimensions of the image do not change, but the number of pixels and the file size increase dramatically.

8. Click **OK**, click **File**, then click **Save**.

9. Return to the InDesign layout.

   Because the InDesign document was open when you saved the change in Photoshop, the graphic in InDesign was automatically updated and deselected.

   (continued)

Figure 24 *Image size information for the original image*

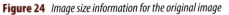

Actual PPI—same as listed in InDesign Links panel

Figure 25 *Results of doubling resolution*

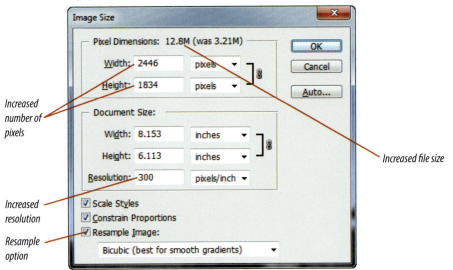

Increased number of pixels

Increased file size

Increased resolution

Resample option

10. Double-click the **Corniglia image**, then compare your screen to Figure 26.

    The Actual PPI in the Link Info panel now reads 300 and the Effective PPI is 293—close enough to 300 to be acceptable.

11. Save your work, then close the file.

You noted the actual and effective PPI for a placed graphic, opened the graphic in Photoshop, then increased its resolution.

Figure 26 *Viewing updated resolution information*

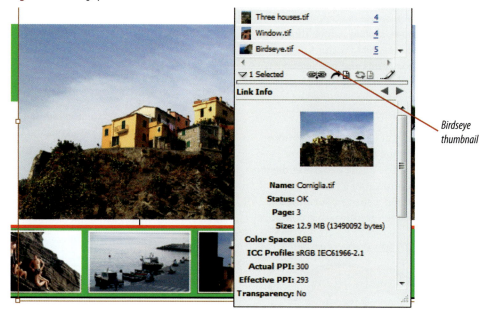

Birdseye thumbnail

Place Vector
GRAPHICS

What You'll Do

In this lesson, you will place vector graphics in InDesign, resize them, then choose display performance settings.

Understanding Vector Graphics

Graphics that you create in computer drawing programs, such as Adobe Illustrator, are called **vector graphics**. Vector graphics consist of anchor points and line segments, together referred to as **paths**. Paths can be curved or straight; they are defined by geometrical characteristics called **vectors**.

For example, if you use Adobe Illustrator to render a person's face, the software will identify the iris of the eye using the geometrical definition of a circle with a specific radius and a specific location in respect to the other graphics that compose the face. It will then fill that circle with a color you have specified. Figure 27 shows an example of vector graphics used to draw a cartoon boy. The graphic on the left is filled with colors, and the graphic on the right shows the vector shapes used to create the graphic.

As geometric objects, vector graphics can be scaled to any size with no loss in quality. This means that a graphic that you create in an application like Adobe Illustrator can be output to fit on a postage stamp … or on a billboard!

Computer graphics rely on vectors to render bold graphics that must retain clean,

Figure 27 *Example of vector graphics*

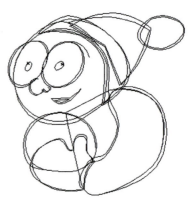

crisp lines when scaled to various sizes. Vectors are often used to create logos or "line art," and they are often the best choice for typographical illustrations.

Placing Vector Graphics in InDesign

When you place vector graphics in InDesign, you can enlarge or reduce them to any size; scaling a vector graphic does not have any impact on its visual quality.

When you place a vector graphic from Illustrator, only the objects that compose the graphic are placed. If you draw a 2" square on an 8" artboard in Illustrator, then place the file in InDesign, the 2" square will be placed, not the entire 8" artboard.

When you create a graphic in Illustrator, Illustrator draws an imaginary bounding box that defines the perimeter of the graphic. This will have an impact when the graphic is placed in InDesign. Let's say you create a 1" circle in Illustrator. When you place it in InDesign and you apply a text wrap, the text will wrap around the imaginary 1" bounding box—not the circle. You must click Detect Edges in the Contour section of the Text Wrap panel to make the InDesign text wrap around the graphic. Remember this technique, because, as shown in Figure 28, you can create interesting text wraps around a complex Illustrator graphic.

Choosing the Default Display Performance

When you place a graphic file in InDesign, a low-resolution preview file appears in the graphics frame. The appearance of the preview file—the quality at which it is displayed—is determined by default in the **Display Performance section** of the Preferences dialog box.

You can choose between Fast, Typical, or High Quality views of placed graphics.

- The Fast Display view shows no preview file. Instead, it shows a gray box within the graphics frame. Most up-to-date computers have enough memory that you won't need to resort to this option.
- The Typical Display view displays a low resolution preview. This is an adequate display for identifying and positioning an image within the layout.
- The High Quality Display view displays the preview file at high resolution. This option provides the highest quality, but requires the most memory. However, given the power and speed of today's computers, this is unlikely to be a factor. You may want to use High Quality Display to get a "final view" of a completed layout or to present the layout onscreen to a client.

The setting that you choose in the Display Performance section of the Preferences dialog box will determine the default display

Figure 28 *Placed Illustrator graphic with a text wrap*

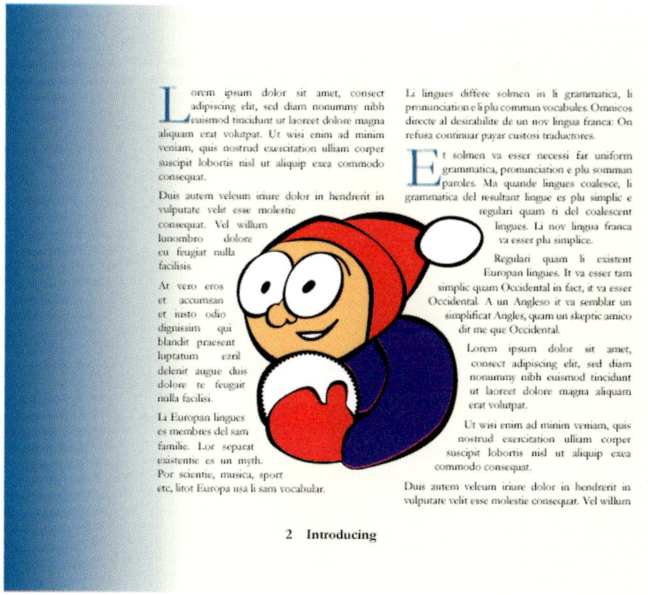

Lorem ipsum dolor sit amet, consect adipiscing elit, sed diam nonummy nibh euismod tincidunt ut laoreet dolore magna aliquam erat volutpat. Ut wisi enim ad minim veniam, quis nostrud exercitation ulliam corper suscipit lobortis nisl ut aliquip exea commodo consequat.

Duis autem veleum iriure dolor in hendrerit in vulputate velit esse molestie consequat. Vel willum lunombro dolore eu feugiat nulla facilisis.

At vero eros et accumsan et iusto odio dignissim qui blandit praesent luptatum ezril delenit augue duis dolore te feugait nulla facilisi.

Li Europan lingues es membres del sam familie. Lor separat existentie es un myth. Por scientie, musica, sport etc, litot Europa usa li sam vocabular.

Li lingues differe solmen in li grammatica, li pronunciation e li plu commun vocabules. Omnicos directe al desirabilite de un nov lingua franca: On refusa continuar payar custosi traductores.

Et solmen va esser necessi far uniform grammatica, pronunciation e plu sommun paroles. Ma quande lingues coalesce, li grammatica del resultant lingue es plu simplic e regulari quam ti del coalescent lingues. Li nov lingua franca va esser plu simplice.

Regulari quam li existent Europan lingues. It va esser tam simplic quam Occidental in fact, it va esser Occidental. A un Angleso it va semblar un simplificat Angles, quam un skeptic amico dit me que Occidental.

Lorem ipsum dolor sit amet, consect adipiscing elit, sed diam nonummy nibh euismod tincidunt ut laoreet dolore magna aliquam erat volutpat.

Ut wisi enim ad minim veniam, quis nostrud exercitation ulliam corper suscipit lobortis nisl ut aliquip exea commodo consequat.

Duis autem veleum iriure dolor in hendrerit in vulputate velit esse molestie consequat. Vel willum

2 Introducing

for every graphic that you place in InDesign. In addition, there are two sets of Display Performance commands on the Application bar. There is one set on the Object menu and another set on the View menu. Use the View menu commands when you want to change the display performance of all of the placed graphics in an open document. Use the Object menu commands when you want to change the display performance for graphics on an individual basis.

Options for Placing Illustrator Graphics

There are two different ways you can put your Illustrator graphics into an InDesign document. If you know you won't need to modify the graphic at all in InDesign, just place it using the Place command on the File menu. However, if you want to retain the option of editing the file from within InDesign, copy and paste the Illustrator graphic. When you copy and paste the Illustrator graphic into your InDesign document, it becomes an InDesign object—not a placed graphic—and will be fully editable in InDesign because InDesign is also an Adobe vector-based program. Figure 29 shows an Illustrator graphic placed in InDesign and selected with the Direct Selection tool.

Pasting an Illustrator graphic into InDesign is not a common practice, but it does have its uses. Once the graphic is pasted in InDesign, you can apply the layout's colors and gradients to the graphic, rather than having to recreate those colors and gradients in Illustrator. You also have a bit more control for modifying the graphic to produce very specific text wraps. These are all minor considerations, however. In general, the best method for incorporating Illustrator graphics into your layouts is to place them.

Figure 29

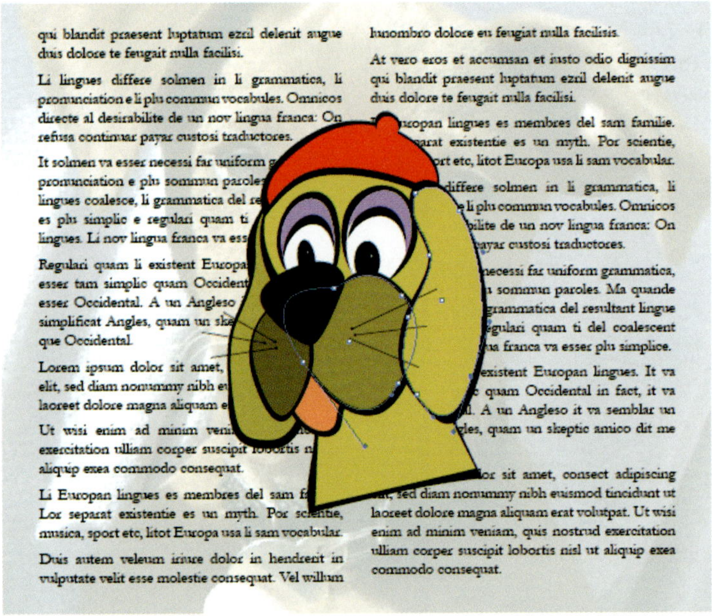

Figure 30 *Illustrator graphic placed in InDesign and selected with Direct Selection tool*

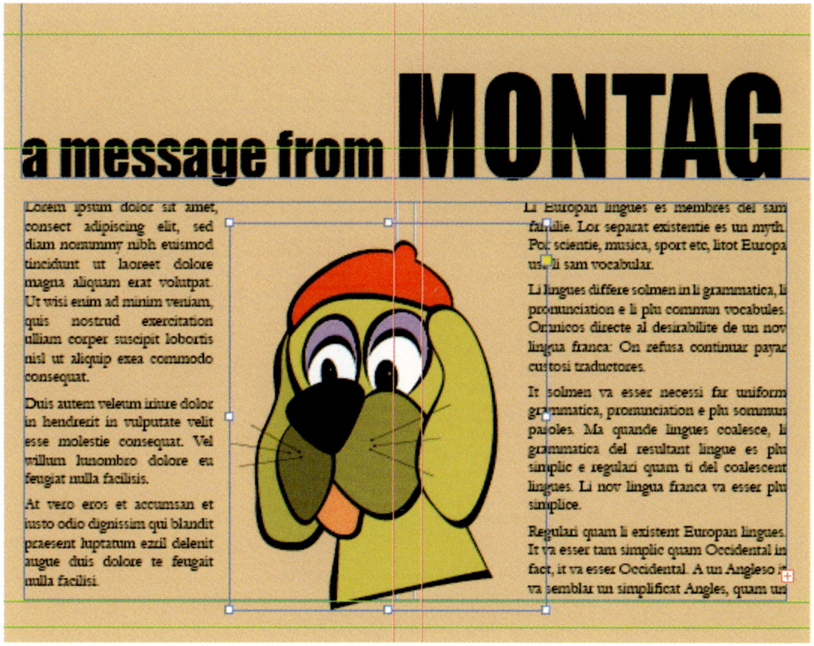

Place vector graphics in InDesign

1. Open ID 6-3.indd, then save it as **Min-Pin Graphics**.
2. Go to page 6, then verify that frame edges are showing.
3. Click the **Selection tool**, then click the **large graphics frame** at the center of the page.
4. Click **File** on the Application bar, click **Place**, navigate to the drive and folder where your Data Files are stored, click **Montag.ai**, then click **Open**.
5. Click **Object** on the Application bar, point to **Fitting**, then click **Fit Content Proportionally**.

   Your screen should resemble Figure 30.
6. Go to page 5, fit the spread in the document window, then click between the text frames to select the large graphics frame.

   The graphics frame is behind the text frames in the stacking order.
7. Click **File** on the Application bar, click **Place**, navigate to the drive and folder where your Data Files are stored, click **Orange Dogs.ai**, then click **Open**.
8. Click **Object** on the Application bar, point to **Fitting**, then click **Fit Content Proportionally**.

   The graphic is enlarged to fit the frame. Note that the dramatic enlargement does not have an effect on the quality of the lines and curves of the graphic.

TIP If your dogs look bitmapped, go to Display Performance on the View menu and select High Quality Display.

(continued)

9. Click the **No text wrap button** 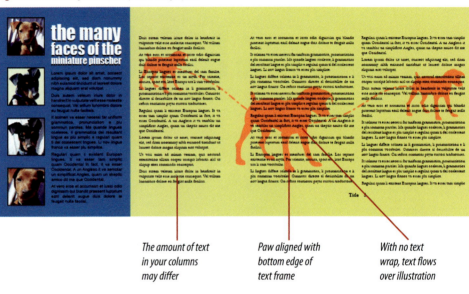 on the Text Wrap panel.

10. Deselect, switch to Preview mode, then compare your page to Figure 31.

11. Switch back to Normal mode, then save the file.

You placed two vector graphics in InDesign. You enlarged the second graphic dramatically, noting no effect on its quality.

Figure 31 *Removing the text wrap from the graphic*

The amount of text
in your columns
may differ

Paw aligned with
bottom edge of
text frame

With no text
wrap, text flows
over illustration

Figure 32 *Wrapping text around the graphic*

1. Go to page 6, then select the frame with the cartoon dog illustration.

2. Click the **Wrap around object shape button** on the Text Wrap panel.

3. In the Wrap Options section of the Text Wrap panel, click the **Wrap To list arrow**, then click **Both Right & Left Sides**.

4. In the Contour Options section, click the **Type list arrow**, then click **Detect Edges**.

5. In the upper section of the panel, set the Top Offset value to .1875.

6. Compare your page to Figure 32.

7. Save your work.

You wrapped InDesign text around a placed Illustrator graphic.

Interface InDesign
WITH PHOTOSHOP

What You'll Do

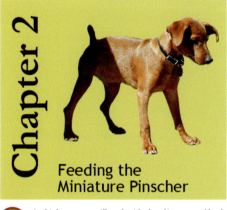

Chapter 2

Feeding the
Miniature Pinscher

In this lesson, you will work with placed images and load clipping paths and alpha channels.

Understanding the Relationship of InDesign with Other Adobe Products

Adobe makes a number of software products. InDesign is a layout application. Illustrator is a drawing application. Photoshop is a photo manipulation application. Because they are all Adobe products, they have been engineered to work together, in most cases, seamlessly. This is a good thing. Also, because they are all Adobe products, many of their functions overlap. For example, you can draw complex graphics and manipulate bitmap images in InDesign. This overlapping of functions is a good thing. It allows you to do things to placed graphics in InDesign, for example, without having to go back to either Illustrator or Photoshop. However, this overlapping can also blur the distinctions between the applications. So it's important that you keep clear in your head what those distinctions are—what you can and cannot and should and should not do to a placed graphic in InDesign. For example, though it is possible to enlarge a placed bitmap graphic 800% in InDesign, you must educate yourself to understand the ramifications of doing so, and why it

might not be something you *should* do, even though it's something that you *can* do.

Removing a White Background from a Placed Graphic

In many cases, bitmap graphics that you place in InDesign will have a white background. One useful overlap between InDesign and Photoshop is the ability to remove a white background from a placed graphic in InDesign. Using the Detect Edges function in the Clipping Path dialog box, as shown in Figure 33, InDesign identifies pixels in the graphic based on their values—from light to dark—and makes specific pixels transparent.

The Threshold value determines the pixel values that will be made transparent. For example, if the Threshold value is set to 10, the 10 lightest pixel values (out of a total of 256 values from light to dark) would be made transparent. Your best method for using this feature is to start with a Threshold value of 0—no pixels will be transparent. To make only the white pixels transparent, use a Threshold value of 1 and use the Preview function to see how that setting affects the image. If some unwanted almost-white pixels remain, increase the Threshold value until you are happy with the preview.

The Tolerance value determines how smooth the edge of the image will be once pixels are made transparent. A Tolerance value of 1 or 2 is usually acceptable.

Figure 34 shows a placed graphic, first with a white background, then with the white background removed using the Detect Edges section of the Clipping Path dialog box.

The Detect Edges feature works most effectively with darker foreground images against a white background. One drawback to using the Detect Edges feature is that it affects all white pixels, whether they are in the background or foreground. In other words, if you have an image of a man with a white beard against a white background, there's no way to make the white background transparent without making the white beard transparent as well.

Loading Alpha Channels in InDesign

Many times, when working with bitmap graphics, you'll find that you want to select only a specific area of the graphic. For example, you may want to isolate an image of a person from its background. Using selection tools in Photoshop, you can do just that. The selection, known as a **silhouette**, can be saved with the Photoshop file for use in another Photoshop document or in another program, such as InDesign. **Alpha channels** are selections created and saved in Photoshop. InDesign has the ability to load alpha channels that have been saved with a Photoshop file. This is another useful overlap between InDesign and Photoshop.

Figure 33 *Detect Edges function in the Clipping Path dialog box*

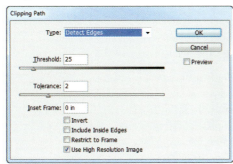

Figure 34 *A placed graphic with a white background and with the white background made transparent*

White background

White background made transparent

Alpha channels are rendered in terms of black and white, with the white areas representing the selected pixels and the black areas representing the non-selected areas. Figure 35 shows a graphic in Photoshop and an alpha channel that was saved with the graphic.

When you place the Photoshop graphic in InDesign, the alpha channel saved with it is not automatically loaded. The graphic will be placed by default as a **square-up**—the entire image, including the background. You can then use the Clipping Path command to load the alpha channel, thereby creating a silhouette in your layout.

QUICK TIP

If you have saved multiple alpha channels with a Photoshop file, you can choose them from the Clipping Path dialog box by clicking the Alpha list arrow after clicking Alpha Channel from the Type list.

Loading Clipping Paths in InDesign

Like alpha channels, clipping paths are another type of selection you can create in Photoshop. Paths are created with the Pen tool, which is a sophisticated selection tool in Photoshop that allows you to make very specific selections. Once created, one or more paths can be saved or exported with a Photoshop file.

What's the difference between saving and exporting a path with a Photoshop file? It's a difference of intended usage. If a path is exported with the Photoshop file, the path will be loaded automatically when you place the graphic in InDesign. If you create a path for a Photoshop graphic and you know you want to use it to silhouette the graphic in your InDesign layout, you might as well export the path with the Photoshop file so you won't have to load it in InDesign.

Figure 35 *A Photoshop file and an alpha channel*

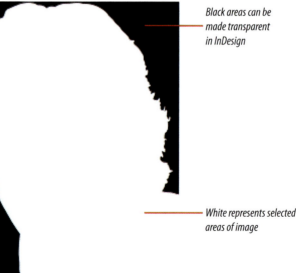

Black areas can be made transparent in InDesign

White represents selected areas of image

If you save, rather than export, a path with a Photoshop file, it won't automatically load when you bring it into InDesign, though you can use the Clipping Path command in InDesign to load it. Sometimes, you'll only want to save a path with a Photoshop document rather than export it, so you have the option to use the entire graphic or a silhouette in InDesign.

Placing a Graphic with a Transparent Background in InDesign

When placing a bitmap graphic with a feathered edge against a colored background in InDesign, the best solution is to save the graphic against a transparent background in Photoshop. You do this by making the selection with a feathered edge, then copying the selection to a new layer. You then make the original layer invisible. This solution is shown in Figure 36. Note that the graphic now appears against a transparent background (identified in Photoshop as a checkerboard). If you save the graphic in Photoshop with this configuration in the Photoshop Layers panel, when you place the graphic in InDesign, only the visible layer—the graphic with the feathered edge—appears.

Remember this solution and remember the nature of the challenge: How do you place a Photoshop graphic with a feathered edge against a colored background in InDesign?

Someday, in some situation, you will encounter this scenario at work in a design department or production facility, and you can be the hero who has the answer!

Figure 36 *Layers panel in Photoshop and a graphic against a transparent background*

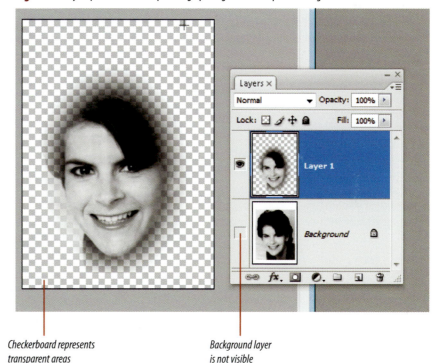

Checkerboard represents transparent areas

Background layer is not visible

Remove a background from a placed graphic

1. Go to page 1, click the **Selection tool** 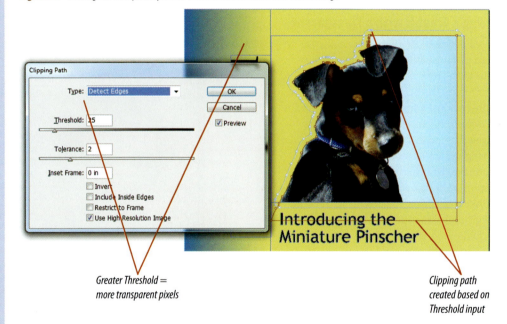, click the **center of the page** to select the graphics frame, then place the graphic named **Blake.psd**.

TIP Fit the page in the window if you cannot see it all.

2. Click **Object** on the Application bar, point to **Clipping Path**, then click **Options**.

3. Click the **Type list arrow**, then click **Detect Edges**.

4. Click the **Preview check box** to add a check mark if it is not checked.

   The Detect Edges option instructs InDesign to create a clipping path around the object. InDesign uses the Threshold and Tolerance sliders in conjunction with the given image to define where that path will be positioned in relation to the image. As shown in Figure 37, at the default threshold and tolerance settings, the white part of the background is made transparent, but the blue areas of the background are still visible.

   (continued)

Figure 37 *Viewing the transparency at the default Threshold and Tolerance settings*

Greater Threshold = more transparent pixels

Clipping path created based on Threshold input

Figure 38 *Setting the Threshold slider set to remove the background*

Background totally
transparent

5. Drag the **Threshold** and **Tolerance sliders** to 0.

   The Threshold slider finds light areas of the image
   and makes them transparent—starting with
   white. At 0, no pixels are made invisible. The
   farther you move the slider to the right, the more
   the darker tones are included in the areas that
   are made invisible. That's why it's a smart idea to
   start with the Threshold set to 0. You want to use
   as small a Threshold value as possible.

6. Drag the **Threshold slider** slowly right until the
   entire background disappears.

   As shown in Figure 38, the Threshold slider
   needs to be set as high as 53 to make the entire
   background invisible. Note how many anchor
   points are on the brown clipping path.

   (continued)

7. Slowly drag the **Tolerance slider** all the way to the right, stopping along the way to view the effect on the path.

The Tolerance slider defines how many points are used to draw the path and, therefore, how accurately the path is drawn. As shown in Figure 39, at a very high tolerance, the path is no longer articulate enough to differentiate the dog from the background.

8. Drag the **Tolerance slider** to 0, click **OK**, deselect, then compare your result to Figure 40.

9. Save the file.

Using the Detect Edges feature in the Clipping Path dialog box, you were successful in making a white background from a placed graphic transparent.

Figure 39 *Tolerance set too high*

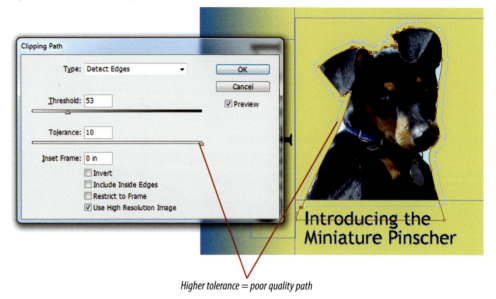

Higher tolerance = poor quality path

Figure 40 *Viewing the final result*

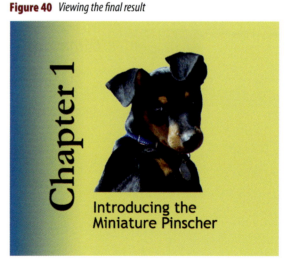

Figure 41 *Photoshop file saved with two alpha channels*

Alpha channels

Figure 42 *Whole Body alpha channel*

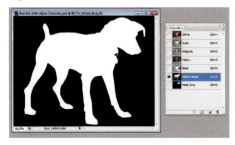

Figure 43 *Head Only alpha channel*

Figure 44 *Placed graphic with Head Only alpha channel loaded*

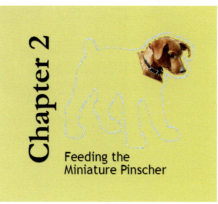

Chapter 2

Feeding the
Miniature Pinscher

Figure 45 *Placed graphic with Whole Body alpha channel loaded*

Chapter 2

Feeding the
Miniature Pinscher

Load alpha channels in InDesign

1. Go to page 7, click the **Selection tool**, click the **center of the page** to select the graphics frame, then fit the page in the window if necessary.

2. Looking at Figures 41, 42, and 43, observe that Figure 41 shows a Photoshop file that has been saved with two alpha channels. Figures 42 and 43 show the two alpha channels in detail.

3. Click **File** on the Application bar, click **Place**, navigate to the drive and folder where your Data Files are stored, then place **Red Silo with Alpha Channels.psd**.

4. Click **Object** on the Application bar, point to **Fitting**, then click **Fit Content Proportionally**.

5. Click **Object** on the Application bar, point to **Clipping Path**, click **Options**, then verify that the Preview check box is checked in the Clipping Path dialog box.

6. Click the **Type list arrow**, click **Alpha Channel**, click the **Alpha list arrow**, click **Head Only**, click **OK**, then compare your page to Figure 44.

7. Click **Object** on the Application bar, point to **Clipping Path**, click **Options**, click the **Alpha list arrow**, click **Whole Body**, then click **OK**.

8. Deselect, press **[W]** to switch to Preview, then compare your page to Figure 45.

You placed a file with two alpha channels. You loaded each of the alpha channels, then previewed the results in the graphics frame.

Load clipping paths in InDesign

1. Go to page 1, click the **Direct Selection tool** , select the graphic, then delete it.

2. Click the **Selection tool** , select the empty graphics frame, then place **Puppies.psd**.

   Puppies.psd is a Photoshop file saved with three paths.

3. Click **Object** on the Application bar, point to **Fitting**, then click **Fill Frame Proportionally**.

4. Click **Object** on the Application bar, point to **Clipping Path**, click **Options**, then verify that the Preview check box is checked.

   TIP You may need to move the Clipping Path dialog box out of the way to see the results of your choices made in the dialog box.

5. Click the **Type list arrow**, click **Photoshop Path**, click the **Path list arrow**, click **Blake Alone**, then click **OK**.

   Your page should resemble Figure 46.

6. Click **Object** on the Application bar, point to **Clipping Path**, click **Options**, click the **Path list arrow**, then click **Rex Alone**.

7. Click the **Path list arrow**, click **Blake and Rex**, then click **OK**.

8. Deselect all, then compare your page to Figure 47.

You imported a file that was saved with three clipping paths. In the Clipping Path dialog box, you loaded each of the paths, and previewed the results in the graphics frame.

Figure 46 *Placed graphic with the Blake Alone path loaded*

Figure 47 *Placed graphic with the Blake and Rex path loaded*

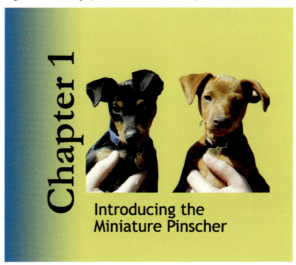

Working with Placed Images

Figure 48 *Photoshop file with graphic on a transparent layer*

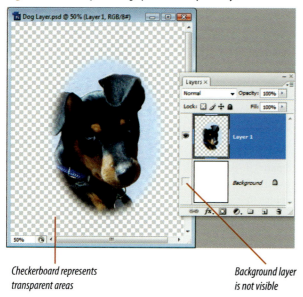

Checkerboard represents transparent areas

Background layer is not visible

Figure 49 *Viewing the result of importing the graphic*

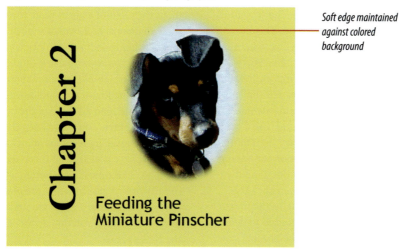

Soft edge maintained against colored background

Place a graphic saved with a transparent background in InDesign

1. Go to page 7, click the **Direct Selection tool** , click the **image of the dog** to select it, then press **[Delete]** (Win) or **[delete]** (Mac).

2. Click the **Selection tool** , then click the **middle of the page** to select the graphics frame.

3. Drag the **top-middle handle** of the graphics frame straight up to the top edge of the page.

4. Place Dog Layer.psd from the drive and folder where your Data Files are stored.

   As shown in Figure 48, Dog Layer.psd is a Photoshop file containing two layers. Layer 1 contains a selection of the dog with a feathered edge against a transparent background, and the Background layer, which is hidden, is white.

5. Click **Object** on the Application bar, point to **Fitting**, then click **Fill Frame Proportionally**.

6. Click **Object** on the Application bar, point to **Fitting**, then click **Center Content**.

7. Deselect all, then compare your document to Figure 49.

   The bitmap graphic is placed in InDesign exactly the way it was saved in Photoshop, with a transparent background.

8. Save your work.

You placed a graphic in InDesign that was saved in Photoshop with a transparent background.

Use LIBRARIES

What You'll Do

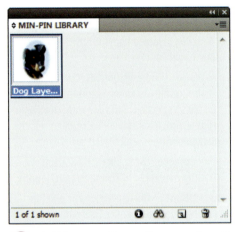

In this lesson, you will create a library to store the graphics you've placed in the document, then use them in another document.

Working with Libraries

Libraries (also called Object Libraries) are files you create that appear as a panel in your InDesign document. You can use this library panel to organize and store graphics that you use most often. You can also store other page elements, such as text, ruler guides, and grids. Figure 50 shows a library containing two graphics. Notice the four buttons on the Library panel. The first button, called Library Item Information, opens the Item Information dialog box for a selected library item. This dialog box displays the item's name, type, and creation date. The second is the Show Library Subset button. This button opens the Show Subset dialog box, where you define a subset of library items you want to view in the library while temporarily hiding all others. For example, you can choose to show only those library items containing "dog" in the filename. The third button is called the New Library Item button. This button offers another option for adding an item to a library instead of dragging the item. Simply select an item, then click the New Library Item button. Finally, the fourth button, Delete Library Item, is used to delete a selected library item from the library.

Library files exist as named files on your computer's hard drive, just like any other files. When you create a library file, you specify where it will be stored. You can open and close a library file just as you would any other file. Libraries exist independently of whatever InDesign document is open and you can open multiple libraries, as needed.

For an example of the usefulness of libraries, imagine that you are an art director for an advertising agency. A major banking chain is your client. You design hundreds of ads for them throughout a given year. The bank has three divisions, each with a slightly different logo. Rather than having to place a logo every time you want to use it (and having to remember which filename refers to which version of the logo), you could simply create a library and load all three of the bank's logos into that library. You could keep that library open whenever InDesign is launched. That way, you have access to all three versions of the logo at all times. Even better, when you modify linked graphics that are placed in a library, those library items are updated in the library as soon as you update the images on the Links panel.

When you use a file from a library in a document, you can edit the file any way you like. The edits that you make to the file in the document do not affect the original file in the library in any way. For example, if you scale a graphic file that you used from the library in the document, the file in the library is not scaled. You can delete the graphic file from the document, but it won't be deleted from the library. Nothing you do to a graphic in the document affects any object in a library. It is only when you modify the original source file that library items are affected.

Adding All Page Objects to a Library

InDesign has two great commands that allow you to add all the objects on a page to a library as one single object or as separate objects.

Both commands are found on the Library panel menu, as shown in Figure 51.

You don't need to select any objects on the page before choosing either of these two commands. Figure 52 shows the results of adding all objects on the page as separate objects.

QUICK **TIP**

Snippets can be added to a library. Simply drag a snippet from the InDesign page into the Library panel to add it as a library element.

Figure 50 *Sample library*

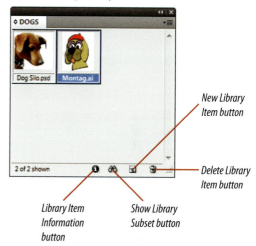

New Library
Item button

Delete Library
Item button

Library Item
Information
button

Show Library
Subset button

Figure 51 *Library panel menu*

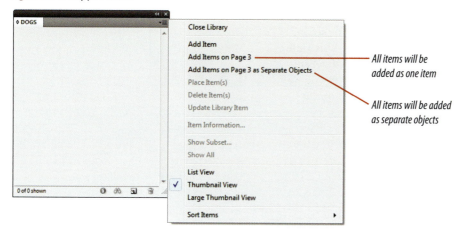

All items will be
added as one item

All items will be added
as separate objects

Figure 52 *All items on page added to library as separate objects*

Create a library and add items to it

1. Click **File** on the Application bar, point to **New**, then click **Library**.

2. Name the library **Min-Pin Library**, then click **Save**.

   A library panel named Min-Pin Library appears.

3. Click the **Selection tool** , then drag the **Dog Layer graphic** from page 7 into the Min-Pin Library.

   As shown in Figure 53, a thumbnail of the image appears on the panel.

4. Go to page 1, click the **Min-Pin Library panel options button**, then click **Add Items on Page 1 as Separate Objects**.

5. Save, then close Min-Pin Graphics.

   The Min-Pin Library does not close with the document.

You created a new library, then added graphics from the document into the library.

Figure 53 *Graphic added to library*

Figure 54 *Placing an image from the Min-Pin Library*

Lorem ipsum dolor sit amet, consect adipiscing elit, sed diam nonummy nibh euismod tincidunt ut laoreet dolore magna aliquam erat volutpat. Ut wisi enim ad minim venim, quis nostrud exercitation ulliam corper suscipit lobortis nisl ut aliquip exea commodo consequat.

Duis autem veleum iriure dolor in hendrerit in vulputate velit esse molestie consequat. Vel wilhm hunombro dolore eu feugiat nulla facilisis. At vero eros et accumsan et iusto odio dignissim qui blandit praesent luptatum ezril delenit augue duis dolore te feugait nulla facilisi.

Li Europan lingues es membres del sam familie. Lor separat existentie es un myth. Por scientie, musica, sport etc, litot Europa usa li sam vocabular. Li lingues differe solmen in li grammatica, li pronunciation e li plu commun vocabules. Omnicos directe al desirabilite de un nov lingua franca: On refusa continuar payar custosi traductores.

At solmen va esser necessi far uniform grammatica, pronunciation e plu sommun paroles. Ma quande lingues coalesce, li grammatica del resultant

lingue es plu simplic e regulari quam ti del coalescent lingues. Li nov lingua franca va esser plu simplice.

Regulari quam li existent Europan lingues. It va esser tam simplic quam Occidental in fact, it va esser Occidental. A un Angleso it va semblar un simplificat Angles, quam un skeptic amico dit me que Occidental.

Lorem ipsum dolor sit amet, consect adipiscing elit, sed diam nonummy nibh euismod tincidunt ut laoreet dolore magna aliquam erat volutpat. Ut wisi enim ad minim veniam, quis nostrud exercitation ulliam corper suscipit lobortis nisl ut aliquip exea commodo consequat. Duis autem veleum iriure dolor in hendrerit in vulputate velit esse molestie consequat. Vel willum hunombro dolore eu feugiat nulla facilisis.

At vero eros et accumsan et iusto odio dignissim qui blandit praesent luptatum ezril delenit augue duis dolore te feugait nulla facilisi. Li lingues differe solmen in li grammatica, li pronunciation

Add a library object to a document

1. Open ID 6-4.indd, click **Update Links**, navigate to the Missing Graphic folder to locate Red 1.psd, open Red 1.psd, click **No** in the Warning dialog box regarding text edits, then save the file as **Library Test**.

TIP Do not be concerned if some of the files show the Modified icon on the Links panel.

2. Drag **Dog Layer.psd** from the Min-Pin Library onto the document page.

3. Display the Links panel.

   Dog Layer.psd is listed on the Links panel.

4. Center the graphic on the page, display the Text Wrap panel, then click the **Wrap around object shape button** if it is not already selected.

5. Type **.5** in the Top Offset text box on the Text Wrap panel.

6. Click the **Type list arrow** in the Contour Options section of the Text Wrap panel, then click **Alpha Channel**.

7. Deselect all, switch to Preview mode, if you are not already in it, then compare your document to Figure 54.

8. Save your work, then close Library Test.

You dragged a graphic from the Min-Pin Library to the Library Test document.

Use the Links panel.

1. Open ID 6-5.indd, click Don't Update Links, then save the document as **Program Cover**.
2. If necessary, select each graphic file that shows the Modified icon, then click the Update Link button.
3. Click the Selection tool, click the spotlight graphic on page 1, then note that the graphic's name is highlighted on the Links panel.
4. Click Final Logo.ai on the Links panel, then click the Go to Link button.
5. Click susan.psd on the Links panel, then click the Go to Link button.
6. Click the Relink button, navigate to the EOU Moved folder, click susan.psd, then click Open.
7. Go to page 1, fit the page in the window, then click the center of the spotlight oval to select the empty graphics frame.

Place vector graphics.

1. Click File on the Application bar, click Place, navigate to your Data Files folder, click Logo with Shadow.ai, then click Open.
2. Press [W] to switch to Preview.
3. Go to page 2, click the Selection tool, then click the graphic named susan.psd.
4. Click Object on the Application bar, point to Clipping Path, then click Options.
5. Click the Type list arrow, then click Detect Edges.
6. Verify that there is a check mark in the Preview check box.
7. Drag the Threshold slider to 40, then click OK.

8. With susan.psd still selected, click Object on the Application bar, point to Clipping Path, then click Options.
9. Click the Type list arrow, then click Alpha Channel.
10. Click the Alpha list arrow, then click Head Silhouette Only.
11. Drag the Threshold slider to 1, verify that the Tolerance slider is set to 2, then click OK.
12. With susan.psd still selected, click Object on the Application bar, point to Clipping Path, then click Options.
13. Click the Type list arrow, click Photoshop Path, then click OK.
14. Deselect all, then fit the page in the window.

Use libraries.

1. Click File on the Application bar, point to New, then click Library.
2. Name the library **Susan's Library**, then click Save.
3. Click the Selection tool, then drag the susan.psd graphic from page 2 into Susan's Library.
4. Drag Final Logo.ai from page 2 into Susan's Library.
5. Double-click page 1 in the Pages panel.
6. Click the Susan's Library panel options button, then click Add Items on Page 1 as Separate Objects.
7. Resize the Susan's Library panel so that you can see all four graphics, then compare your page to Figure 55.
8. Save your work, then close Program Cover and Susan's Library.

Place multiple graphics.

1. Open ID 6-6.indd, then save it as Dog's Best Friend.
2. Collapse all of your open panels except the Tools panel.
3. Click Window on the Application bar, then click Mini Bridge.
4. Click the Browse Files button then, when the Navigation section appears at the top of the Mini Bridge panel, click Desktop.
5. Navigate to the chapter where you store your Chapter 6 data files.
6. Drag the scale slider at the bottom of the panel left and right to enlarge and reduce the thumbnails.
7. Use the scrollbar on the right of the panel to scroll through all the thumbnails.
8. Click the file named Black 1.psd.
9. Press and hold [Ctrl](Win) or ⌘ (Mac), then click the following three files: Black 2, Red 1, Red 2.
10. Position the pointer over any of the selected thumbnails, then click and drag the files from the Mini Bridge panel into the document.
11. Minimize the Mini Bridge panel.
12. Press the right-arrow key to scroll through the loaded thumbnails, then scroll to the Black 1 thumbnail.
13. Click the place gun in the top frame at the left of the page.
14. Place the remaining three loaded images into the remaining three frames in any order that you wish.
15. Select all four frames, click Object, point to Fitting, then click Fill Frame Proportionally.
16. Save your work.

Interface InDesign with Photoshop.

1. Click the Selection tool, then click the graphic on the right-hand page.
2. Click Wrap around object shape button on the Text Wrap panel.
3. Click Object on the Application bar, point to Clipping Path, then click Options.
4. Click the Type list arrow, then click Detect Edges.
5. Click the Preview check box to add a check mark, if necessary.
6. Drag the Threshold and Tolerance sliders to 0.
7. Drag the Threshold slider to 10, click OK.
8. Save the file.
9. Verify that the large dog image on the right hand page is selected.
10. Click Object on the Application bar, point to Clipping Path, click Options, then verify that the Preview check box is checked in the Clipping Path dialog box.
11. Click the Type list arrow, click Alpha Channel, click the Alpha list arrow, then click Petey.
12. Drag the Threshold slider to 1 and the Tolerance slider to 0.
13. Click OK.
14. Verify that the large dog image on the right hand page is selected.

Figure 55 *Completed Skills Review Part 1*

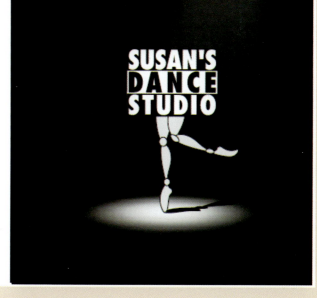

15. Click Object on the Application bar, point to Clipping Path, click Options, then verify that the Preview check box is checked.
16. Click the Type list arrow, click Photoshop Path, click the Path list arrow, click Path 1, then click OK.
17. Deselect all, then switch to Preview mode.
18. Compare your page to Figure 56.

Explore image resolution issues.

1. Verify that the large dog image is selected, double-click the thumbnail in the Links panel, then note the information in the Link Info section.

2. Click the Edit Original button at the bottom of the Links panel.
   The image opens in Adobe Photoshop. You will need to have Adobe Photoshop installed on your computer to complete this lesson.
3. In Photoshop, click Image on the Application bar, then click Image Size.
4. Verify that the Resample Image option is checked.
5. Enter 600 in the Resolution text box, then click OK.
6. Click File, then click Save.
7. Return to the InDesign layout.

Because the InDesign document was open while you saved the change in Photoshop, the graphic in InDesign was automatically updated and deselected.

8. Verify that the dog graphic is selected, then note the change to the Effective PPI.
   The Actual PPI in the Link Info panel now reads 600 and the Effective PPI is 319.
9. Save your work, then close the file.

Figure 56 *Skills Review Part 2*

You are a designer at a local studio. A client has delivered an Adobe Illustrator graphic for you to place in an InDesign document. She says she wants you to place it with a text wrap, then show her the results on your monitor.

1. Open ID 6-7.indd, click Don't Update Links in the alert dialog box, then save it as **Snowball**.

2. Switch to Normal mode if you are not already in it.
3. Select the graphics frame in the center of the page, then place the file Snowball.ai.
4. Fit the content proportionally in the graphics frame.
5. Click the Wrap around object shape button on the Text Wrap panel.
6. Click the Wrap To list arrow on the Text Wrap panel, then click Both Right & Left Sides.

7. Click the Type list arrow on the Text Wrap panel, then click Detect Edges.
8. Deselect all, then switch to Preview.
9. Save your work, compare your page to Figure 57, then close Snowball.

Figure 57 *Completed Project Builder 1*

You work for a print production service bureau. You have just been given a job to print 10 color copies of a supplied file. You open the file and decide that you need to update the links before printing the copies.

1. Open ID 6-8.indd, click Don't Update Links, then save the file as **Hawaii Links**.
2. Switch to Preview mode if you are not already in it.
3. Click the link for Tree coverage.psd that is on page 1, then click the Go to Link button. (*Hint*: You will need to expand the Tree coverage.psd (2) link to see the two instances of the graphic, one on page 1, and one on page 2. See Figure 58.)
4. Click the Relink button, navigate to the Hidden Tree folder in your Data Files folder, click Tree coverage. psd, then click Open.
5. Relink Tree coverage.psd that is on page 2.
6. Update the remaining files on the Links panel if they are not updated.
7. Compare your Links panel to Figure 58.
8. Save your work, then close Hawaii Links.

Figure 58 *Completed Project Builder 2*

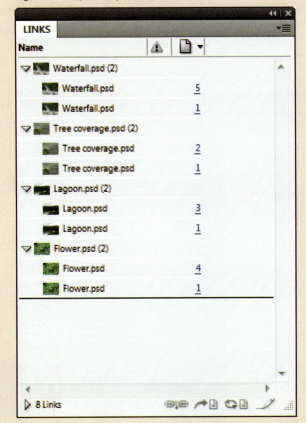

You are designing a cover for LAB magazine and run into a problem. The way the cover photograph has been shot, the dog's face is hidden behind the magazine's title. You open the photograph in Photoshop, then create a path around the dog's head. You are now ready to use the image in InDesign.

1. Open ID 6-9.indd, click Update Links, then save it as **Lab Cover**.
2. Switch to Normal view you are not already in it.
3. Verify that guides are showing.
4. Click the Selection tool, click the dog photograph, copy it, click Edit on the Application bar, then click Paste in Place.
5. Place the file Wally Head Silo.psd from your data files. (*Hint*: When the new graphic is placed, it will look exactly the same as the previous graphic.)
6. Click Object on the Application bar, point to Clipping Path, then click Options.
7. Click the Type list arrow, click Photoshop Path, then click OK. (*Hint*: The Direct Selection tool becomes automatically selected.)
8. Click the Selection tool, then click the dog's face.
9. Click Object on the Application bar, point to Arrange, then click Send Backward.
10. Deselect all, click View on the Application bar, point to Display Performance, then click High Quality Display.
11. Hide guides, hide frame edges, then compare your page to Figure 59.
12. Save your work, then close Lab Cover.

Figure 59 *Completed Design Project*

In this portfolio project, you will explore how to save a graphic in Photoshop with a transparent background and then place it against a colored background in InDesign.

Note: This project requires that both Photoshop and InDesign are available on the computer being used for the exercise.

1. Start Photoshop, open ID 6-10.psd, then save it as **Soft Circle**.
2. Expand the Layers panel if it is collapsed.
3. Click the Elliptical Marquee tool, press and hold [Shift], then create a circle that is approximately the diameter of a compact disc on top of the flower. (*Hint*: The Elliptical Marquee tool may be hidden beneath the Rectangular Marquee tool.)
4. Click Select on the Application bar, point to Modify, click Feather, type **18**, then click OK.
5. Click Edit on the Application bar, click Copy, click Edit on the Application bar, then click Paste.
6. On the Layers panel, click the Eye icon on the Background layer to make the Background layer invisible. (*Hint*: Your Photoshop window canvas should resemble Figure 60.)
7. Save your work, click OK in the Photoshop Format Options dialog box if necessary, close Soft Circle, then close Photoshop.

Figure 60 *Soft Circle.psd*

Soft Circle.psd @ 66.7% (Layer 1, RGB/8)

66.67%   Doc: 1.60M/4.19M

8. Start InDesign, open ID 6-11.indd, then save it as **Soft Circle Layout**.

9. Switch to Normal view if you are not already in it.

10. Place Soft Circle.psd in the graphics frame at the center of the page.

11. Click Object on the Application bar, point to Fitting, then click Fit Content to Frame.

12. Click Object on the Application bar, point to Display Performance, then click High Quality Display.

13. Deselect all, press [W], save your changes, compare your page to Figure 61, then close Soft Circle Layout.

Figure 61 *Completed Portfolio Project*

Working with Placed Images

CHAPTER  CREATING
GRAPHICS

1. Use the Pen tool

2. Reshape frames and apply stroke effects

3. Work with polygons and compound paths

4. Work with advanced text features

CHAPTER 7 CREATING GRAPHICS

By now, you are aware that InDesign is a sophisticated layout program, but you may be surprised to find out that it is a cool little graphics program as well. You can use the Pen tool to create any shape, which is why it's often called "the drawing tool." More precisely, the Pen tool is a tool for drawing straight lines, curved lines, polygons, and irregularly shaped objects. The Pen tool can be challenging, but only when you first experiment with it. After a while, it becomes easier, and soon it becomes second-nature. Like most everything else in graphic design (and in life!), mastery comes with practice. So make it a point to learn Pen tool techniques. Use the Pen tool often, even if it's just to play around making odd shapes.

In addition to the Pen tool, you can create simple shapes with the Rectangle, Ellipse, and Polygon tools, and then reshape them using the Direct Selection tool. You can also apply drop shadows, stroke effects, and corner effects, such as rounded corners. If you're into typography, you can use the Type on a Path tool to position type on any path. You can even wrap it around a circle.

So sit down and get ready to have fun with Chapter 7. In InDesign, there are so many ways to create shapes, from simple to complex. Chapter 7 is designed to teach you all of the moves you'll need to know. It's back to the drawing board!

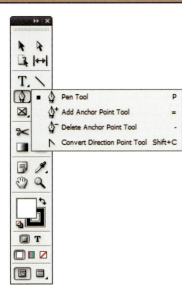

Pen Tool P
Add Anchor Point Tool =
Delete Anchor Point Tool -
Convert Direction Point Tool Shift+C

Polygon Settings

Options

Number of Sides: 5

Star Inset: 60%

OK

Cancel

STROKE

Weight: 1 pt   Cap:

Miter Limit: 4   x   Join:

Align Stroke:

Type:

Start: None

End: None

Gap Color: [None]

Gap Tint: 100%

Corners: Adjust dashes and gaps

12 pt

dash   gap   dash   gap   dash   gap

Effects

Settings for: Object

Transparency

☑ Drop Shadow
☐ Inner Shadow
☐ Outer Glow
☐ Inner Glow
☐ Bevel and Emboss
☐ Satin
☐ Basic Feather
☐ Directional Feather
☐ Gradient Feather

OBJECT: Normal 100%; Drop Shadow
STROKE: Normal 100%; (no effects)
FILL: Normal 100%; (no effects)

☐ Preview

Drop Shadow

Blending

Mode: Multiply   Opacity: 75%

Position

Distance: 0.1375 in   X Offset: 0.0972 in

Angle: 135°   Y Offset: 0.0972 in

☐ Use Global Light

Options

Size: 0.0694 in   ☑ Object Knocks Out Shadow

Spread: 0%   ☐ Shadow Honors Other Effects

Noise: 0%

OK   Cancel

Use the
PEN TOOL

In this lesson, you will use the Pen tool to create a complex vector graphic.

Understanding the Pen Tool

You use the Pen tool to create **paths**, which are straight or curved lines that consist of anchor points and line segments. You create paths by clicking the Pen tool pointer on the page. Each time you click the Pen tool pointer on the document, you create an anchor point. Line segments automatically fall into place between every two anchor points. You start off by creating one anchor point, then creating another at a different location. Once the second anchor point is created, a line segment is automatically placed between the two anchor points, as shown in Figure 1. The number of anchor points and line segments you'll need depends on the type of object you are creating.

QUICK **TIP**

The Pen tool can also be found in both Adobe Illustrator and Adobe Photoshop. In Illustrator, as in InDesign, the Pen tool is used to draw create shapes. In Photoshop, the Pen tool is most often used to create clipping paths to silhouette images.

You can create open paths or closed paths with the Pen tool. The letter U or a simple straight line are both good examples of open paths. An **open path** is a path whose end points are not connected. You can think of a circular object, such as a melon or the letter O, as examples of closed paths. **Closed paths** are continuous lines that do not contain end points. In fact, when you create a closed path, you end your drawing at the same point where you started it by clicking the Pen tool on the first anchor point. Figure 2 shows examples of open and closed paths.

Notice that in this example, some paths are filled with color. You can apply fills and strokes to paths. In general, you will seldom want to fill an open path. Usually, when a path is open, you will want only to apply a stroke to it.

Drawing Straight Segments with the Pen Tool

Drawing straight segments with the Pen tool is easy. Simply click with the Pen tool, then click again in a new location and your first straight segment appears. Straight segments are connected by **corner points**—anchor

points that create a corner between the two segments. Figure 3 shows a simple path drawn with five anchor points and four segments.

Reconnecting to a Path

There will be times when you are working with the Pen tool that you will become disconnected from a path. This often

happens when you stop drawing, change tools to do something else, and then go back to the Pen tool. When you create a new anchor point, you will be surprised that it stands alone. No path segment connects it to the path you made previously.

Whenever you need to reconnect to a path, simply position the Pen tool over the path's end point until a diagonal line appears beside the Pen tool. Then, click the end point. You have successfully reconnected to the path and can continue drawing.

Figure 1 *Creating paths with the Pen tool*

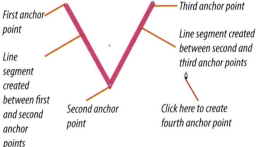

First anchor point

Line segment created between first and second anchor points

Second anchor point

Third anchor point

Line segment created between second and third anchor points

Click here to create fourth anchor point

Figure 2 *Examples of open and closed paths*

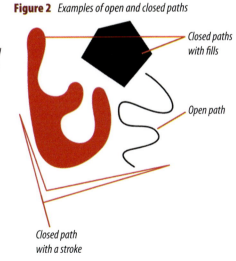

Closed paths with fills

Open path

Closed path with a stroke

Figure 3 *Elements of a path composed of straight segments*

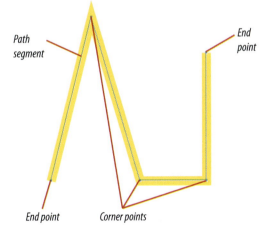

Path segment

End point

End point

Corner points

Adding Anchor Points and Using the Direct Selection Tool

Perfection is an unnecessary goal when you are using the Pen tool. Anchor points and line segments can be moved and repositioned. New points can be added and deleted. Use the Pen tool to create the general shape that you have in mind. Once the object is complete, you can use the Direct Selection tool to perfect, or, tweak, the points and paths. "Tweaking" a finished object is making small, specific improvements to it, and is always part of the drawing process.

To use the Direct Selection tool, make sure your path is deselected, then click the path with the Direct Selection tool. The anchor points, which normally contain a solid fill color, appear hollow or empty. This means that you can use the Direct Selection tool to move each anchor point independently. Simply click an anchor point, then drag it to a new location. You can also use the Direct Selection tool to move a line segment independently.

When the Pen tool is positioned over a line segment, it automatically changes to the Add Anchor Point tool. Click the path and an anchor point will be added, which you can use to manipulate the path further.

Deleting Anchor Points

When the Pen tool is positioned over an existing anchor point, it automatically changes to the Delete Anchor Point tool. Click the anchor point to delete it from the path. When you delete an anchor point, the two segments on both sides of it are joined as one new segment. The Delete Anchor Point tool will delete a point from the path without breaking the path into two paths. This is very different from selecting an anchor point and using the Cut command or the Delete key to delete it. Using either of these methods would delete the anchor point but also the line segments on both sides of it, thus creating a break in your path.

Drawing Curved Segments with the Pen Tool

So far you have learned about creating straight paths. You can also draw curved paths with the Pen tool. To draw a curved path, click an anchor point, then click and drag the Pen tool when creating the next point. A curved segment will appear between the new point and the previous point.

Anchor points that connect curved segments are called **smooth points**. A smooth point has two **direction lines** attached to it. Direction lines determine the arc of the curved path, depending on their direction and length. Figure 4 shows a curved path made from three smooth points. Since the center point

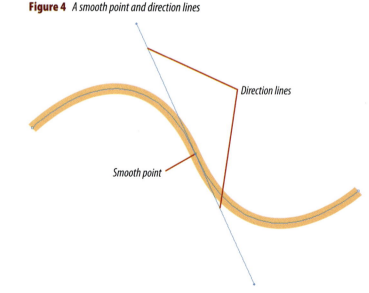

Figure 4 *A smooth point and direction lines*

Direction lines

Smooth point

is selected, you can see the two direction lines attached to it.

Changing the Shape of a Path Using Direction Lines

Using the Direct Selection tool, you can manipulate the direction lines of a smooth point. When you do this, you alter the arc of both segments attached to the point, always maintaining a smooth transition through the anchor point. Simply click the point that you want to modify, then drag the **direction handle**—the round blue circle at the top of the direction line—in a new direction or to shorten or elongate it.

When two segments are joined at a corner point, the two segments can be manipulated independently. A corner point can join two straight segments, one straight segment and one curved segment, or two curved segments, having zero, one, and two direction lines, respectively.

Figure 5 compares smooth points and corner points and shows how direction lines define the shape of a path.

Converting Anchor Points

Direction lines work in tandem. When you move one, the other one also moves. This is often very useful when making curved paths. However, in some cases, you will want to move one direction line independently of the other, especially when creating or tracing a path that abruptly changes direction.

The Convert Direction Point tool "breaks" a smooth point's direction lines and allows you to move one independently of the other. When you do so, the smooth point is converted to a corner point that now joins two unrelated curved paths. Once the direction lines are broken, they remain broken. You can manipulate them independently with the Direct Selection tool;

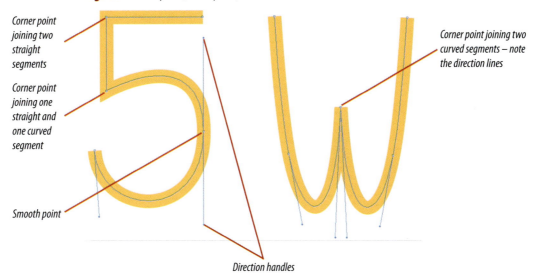

Figure 5 *Smooth points, corner points, and direction lines*

Corner point joining two straight segments

Corner point joining one straight and one curved segment

Smooth point

Corner point joining two curved segments – note the direction lines

Direction handles

you no longer need the Convert Direction Point tool to do so.

The Convert Direction Point tool can also be used to change corner points to smooth points and smooth points to corner points. To convert a corner point to a smooth point, click the Convert Direction Point tool on the anchor point, then drag the pointer. As you drag, new direction lines appear, as shown in Figure 6.

To convert a smooth point to a corner point, simply click the Convert Direction Point tool on the smooth point. The direction lines disappear and the two attached paths become straight paths, as shown in the center object in Figure 7.

Note the rightmost object in Figure 7. If you drag a direction line with the Convert Direction Point tool, the point is automatically converted from a smooth point to a corner point. Therefore, the direction line you are dragging moves independently from the other direction line.

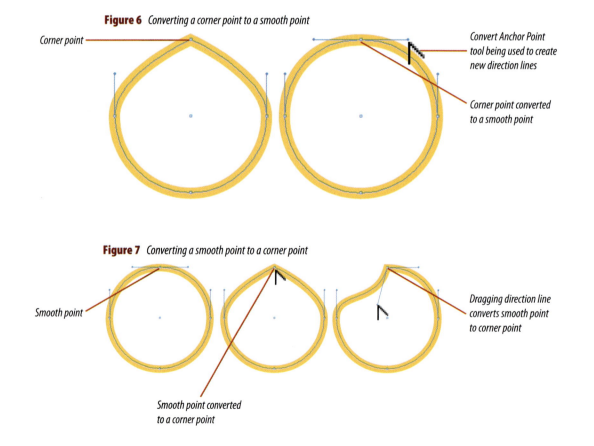

Figure 6 *Converting a corner point to a smooth point*

Corner point

Convert Anchor Point tool being used to create new direction lines

Corner point converted to a smooth point

Figure 7 *Converting a smooth point to a corner point*

Smooth point

Dragging direction line converts smooth point to corner point

Smooth point converted to a corner point

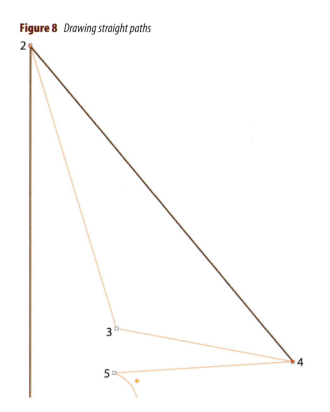

Figure 8 *Drawing straight paths*

2

3

5

4

Create straight segments

1. Open ID 7-1.indd, then save it as **Halloween Witch**.

2. Click **View** on the Application bar, point to **Display Performance**, then click **High Quality Display** if necessary.

3. Click **View** on the Application bar, point to **Grids & Guides**, then verify that both Snap to Guides and Smart Guides are not checked.

   When drawing with the Pen tool, you'll find that Snap to Guides inhibits your ability to draw freely and Smart Guides can be distracting if you aren't using them.

4. Click the **Default Fill and Stroke button** on the Tools panel.

5. Click the **Zoom tool**, then draw a selection box around the bottom half of the witch template.

6. Verify that Layer 2 is targeted on the Layers panel, click the **Pen tool**, then click the **center of the purple star** at the bottom-right corner of the witch template.

TIP The Pen tool may be hidden behind the Add Anchor Point tool, the Delete Anchor Point tool, or the Convert Direction Point tool.

7. Press and hold **[Shift]**, then click **point 1** by clicking the small white square next to it.

TIP As you proceed, click the small white square next to each consecutive number.

Pressing and holding [Shift] constrains the Pen tool to create either straight lines or diagonal lines at 45 degrees.

(continued)

8. Press and hold **[Spacebar]** to access the Hand tool, then click and drag the document window using the Hand tool to scroll to the top of the witch's hat.

9. Press and hold **[Shift],** then click **point 2**.

10. Release [Shift], bypass point 3, then click **point 4**, so that your screen resembles Figure 8 on the previous page.

You created straight segments with the Pen tool.

Add an anchor point to a path

1. Position the Pen tool pointer over the path between point 2 and point 4.

TIP When the Pen tool pointer is positioned directly over a path, it changes to the Add Anchor Point tool pointer (the Pen tool with a plus sign).

2. Click anywhere on the path between the two points.

   An anchor point is added where you clicked.

3. Click the **Direct Selection tool** 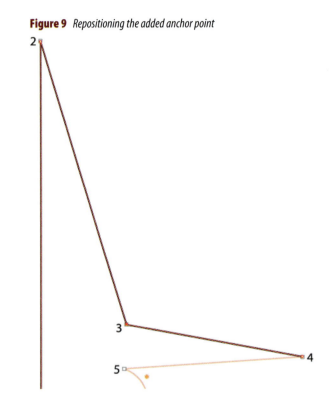, click the **new anchor point**, then drag it to point 3, so that your path resembles Figure 9.

TIP Only the Direct Selection tool allows you to select a single point on a path.

4. Click the **Pen tool** , then click **point 5**.

   An anchor point is created, but it is not joined to the existing path; the software doesn't recognize that you want to continue the path—it thinks you want to start a new path.

5. Click **Edit** on the Application bar, then click **Undo Add New Item**.

   The stray anchor point is removed.

(continued)

Figure 9 *Repositioning the added anchor point*

Figure 10 *Creating a new direction line from an anchor point*

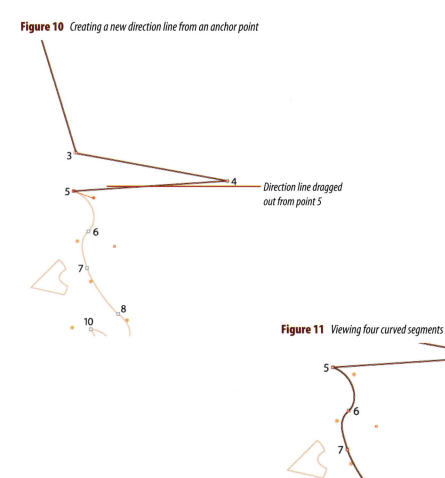

Direction line dragged
out from point 5

Figure 11 *Viewing four curved segments*

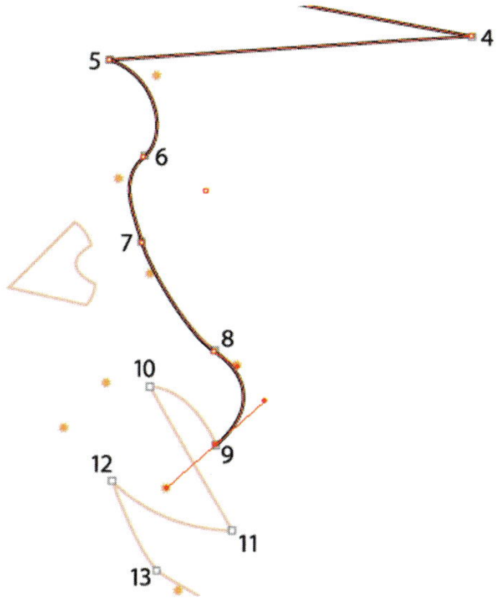

6. Click **point 4** with the Pen tool pointer to reconnect with the path, then click **point 5**.

TIP To reconnect to an open path, simply click the end point with the Pen tool pointer.

7. Click **point 5**.

8. Click and drag a **direction line** from point 5 to the center of the yellow star, so that your screen resembles Figure 10.

    The direction line you just created from point 5 indicates the direction that the path will go—towards point 6. The path has now made an abrupt change in direction. Note that the yellow stars on the witch template are there to give you a sense of how to position direction lines when drawing curved paths.

You added an anchor point to the path, then repositioned it. You then reconnected to the path, which allowed you to continue drawing.

Create curved segments

1. Position the Pen tool pointer over point 6, then click and drag a **direction line** to the next yellow star.

2. Position the Pen tool pointer over point 7, then click and drag a **direction line** to the next yellow star.

3. Position the Pen tool pointer over point 8, then click and drag a **direction line** to the next yellow star.

4. Position the Pen tool pointer over point 9, then click and drag a **direction line** to the yellow star between points 12 and 11, so that your screen resembles Figure 11.

You created four curved segments.

Use the Convert Direction Point tool to change directions while drawing

1. Click the **Pen tool pointer** on point 10.

   As shown in Figure 12, the path does not follow the template because the direction line on point 9 points in a different direction.

2. Click the **Direct Selection tool** ▶, then drag the **direction line** from point 9 to position the path properly between points 9 and 10.

   As shown in Figure 13, because the direction lines are joined by the same anchor point, manipulating the path between points 9 and 10 also repositions the path between points 8 and 9.

3. Click **Edit** on the Application bar, then click **Undo Modify Path**.

4. Click the **Convert Direction Point tool** ↖., then drag the **direction line** from point 9 to position the path properly between points 9 and 10.

   As shown in Figure 14, the Convert Direction Point tool allows you to alter the path between points 9 and 10 without affecting the path between points 8 and 9.

5. Click the **Pen tool** ✎., click **point 10** to reconnect to the path, then click **point 11**.

6. Position the Pen tool pointer over point 12, then click and drag a **direction line** to the yellow star above and to the left of it.

   The direction line does not point toward the next point—point 13, so the direction line must be either repositioned or removed.

   (continued)

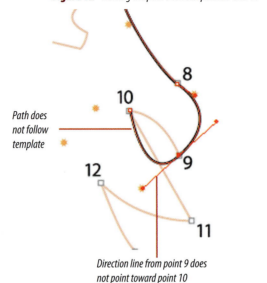

Figure 12 *Viewing the path between points 9 and 10*

Path does not follow template

Direction line from point 9 does not point toward point 10

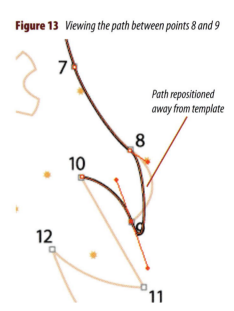

Figure 13 *Viewing the path between points 8 and 9*

Path repositioned away from template

Figure 14 *Viewing the path altered with the Convert Direction Point tool*

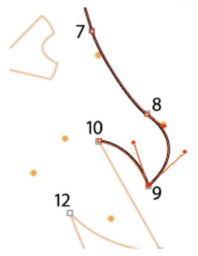

Figure 15 *Viewing the finished drawing*

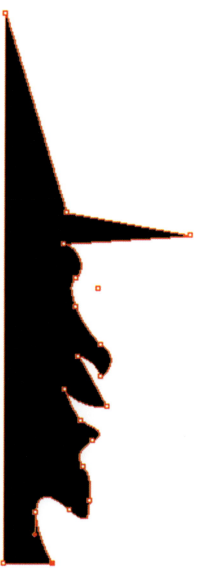

7. Click **point 12** with the Pen tool pointer.

   Clicking a point with the Pen tool pointer removes the direction line that pointed away from point 13.

8. Position the Pen tool pointer over point 13, then click and drag a **direction line** to the nearest yellow star.

9. Position the Pen tool pointer over point 14, then click and drag a **direction line** to the next yellow star.

10. Using the same skills used in Steps 6 through 9, create points 15 through 18.

11. Click the **starting anchor point** (on the purple star) to close the path.

    A small circle appears next to the Pen tool pointer when the Pen tool pointer is directly over the starting anchor point.

12. Click the **Swap Fill and Stroke button** ⤵ on the Tools panel, fit the page in the window, then hide Layer 1 on the Layers panel.

13. Save your work, compare your page to Figure 15, then close Halloween Witch.

You finished drawing a closed path. You used the Convert Direction Point tool to change direction while drawing.

Reshape Frames and
APPLY STROKE EFFECTS

What You'll Do

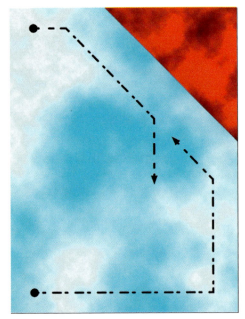

▶ In this lesson, you will use the Pen tool to reshape frames and create stroke effects, including dashed line patterns.

Reshaping Frames

The Tools panel offers a number of tools for creating basic shapes. The graphics frame tools include the Rectangle, Polygon, and Ellipse; you can also use the regular Rectangle, Polygon, and Ellipse tools. The objects that you create with any of these tools can be modified using the Direct Selection tool or the Pen tool.

When you select an object, the appearance of the object will differ depending on which of the two selection tools is selected on the Tools panel. Figure 16 shows the appearance of the same object when the Selection tool and the Direct Selection tool are active on the Tools panel.

When the Selection tool is selected, you'll see the object's bounding box. The bounding box includes eight handles, which you can manipulate to change the object's size.

When you click the Direct Selection tool, the object's bounding box disappears and is replaced by its path. You can select and move anchor points or path segments along the path. Figure 17 shows a rectangle reshaped, using the Direct

Using the Rectangle Tools

The Tools panel contains two tools for creating rectangles: the Rectangle Frame tool and the Rectangle tool. What is the difference, you may ask? The surprising answer is that there really is no difference. Both create rectangular shaped objects. Both can be filled and stroked with color. Both can contain a placed graphic. About the only distinction between the two is that the Rectangle Frame tool is considered one of the frame tools in which graphics are placed, whereas the Rectangle tool creates rectangles that are meant to be used as simple illustrations. However, as stated above, both can be filled and stroked, and both can contain placed graphics.

Creating Graphics

Selection tool. Figure 18 shows that, when the Selection tool is activated, the reshaped object is once again positioned within its bounding box.

When an object is selected, clicking the Pen tool has the same effect as clicking the Direct Selection tool—the eight handles disappear and are replaced by anchor points. Just as with any other path, you can use the Pen tool to add or delete anchor points to give you further control for reshaping an object. Figure 19 shows the same object reshaped with three added anchor points.

Remember, when the Direct Selection tool or the Pen tool is active on the Tools panel, any selected object is essentially a path, composed of anchor points and path segments, which you can manipulate like any other path. This means that, using the Direct Selection tool or the Pen tool, you can reshape any of the basic objects you create with the shape tools—rectangles, ellipses, and polygons—into anything that your imagination can dream up!

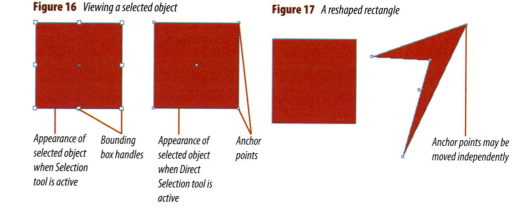

Figure 16 *Viewing a selected object*

Appearance of selected object when Selection tool is active *Bounding box handles* *Appearance of selected object when Direct Selection tool is active* *Anchor points*

Figure 17 *A reshaped rectangle*

Anchor points may be moved independently

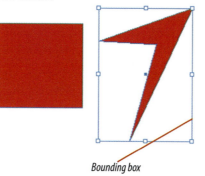

Figure 18 *A reshaped rectangle with the Selection tool activated*

Bounding box

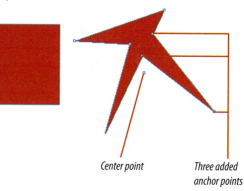

Figure 19 *A rectangle reshaped with three added anchor points*

Center point *Three added anchor points*

Using the Convert Shape Command

Once you create a frame, you are always free to change its basic shape using the Convert Shape command. For example, if you create a circular frame and want to change it to a rectangular frame, there's no need to delete the circular frame and redraw a rectangle. Instead, simply select the circular frame, go to the Object menu, then use the Convert Shape menu item to select the Rectangle command. The new rectangle will appear in the same position on the page that the circle occupied.

Defining Strokes

Color that you apply to a path is called a stroke. Once you've applied a stroke to a path, you can manipulate characteristics of the stroke using the Stroke panel, such as the weight or thickness of the stroke. You have options for changing the design of the stroke, such as making it a dotted line instead of a solid line. You can format the stroke as a dashed stroke, and you can apply end shapes to the stroke, such as arrowheads and tail feathers.

Defining Joins and Caps

Once you've applied a stroke to a path, you should decide upon joins and caps for the path. Make a note of this because your choice for joins and caps can have a subtle but effective impact on your illustration.

These are attributes that many designers forget about or just plain ignore to the detriment of their work.

Joins define the appearance of a corner point when a path has a stroke applied to it. There are three types of joins: miter, round, and bevel. The miter join, which produces pointed corners, is the default. The round join produces rounded corners, and the bevel join produces squared corners. Figure 20 shows examples of all three joins.

Sometimes, it is hard to see which type of join is being used. The greater the weight of the stroke, the more apparent the join will be.

Caps define the appearance of end points when a stroke is added to a path. The Stroke panel offers three types of caps: butt, round, and projecting. Butt caps produce squared

ends and round caps produce rounded ends. Generally, round caps are more appealing to the eye. The projecting cap applies a squared edge that extends the anchor point at a distance one-half the weight of the stroke. With a projecting cap, the weight of the stroke is equal in all directions around the line. The projecting cap is useful when you align two anchor points at a right angle, as shown in Figure 21.

Joins and caps are subtle features, but they are effective. Note the different appearances of the three heads in Figure 22. Note the round caps vs. the bluntness of the butt caps, especially visible on the character's nose. Note, too, the corners of the character's mouth, which are sharp with miter joins, rounded with round joins, and blunt with bevel joins.

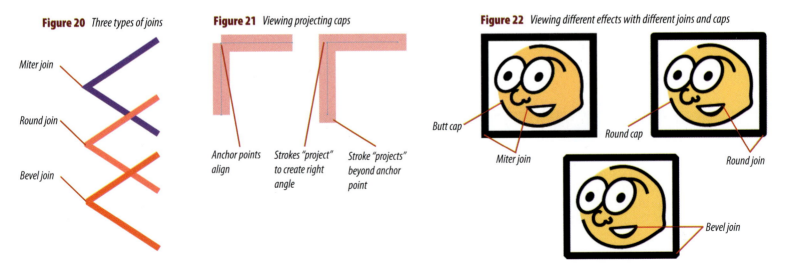

Figure 20 *Three types of joins*

Miter join

Round join

Bevel join

Figure 21 *Viewing projecting caps*

Anchor points align

Strokes "project" to create right angle

Stroke "projects" beyond anchor point

Figure 22 *Viewing different effects with different joins and caps*

Butt cap

Miter join

Round cap

Round join

Bevel join

Defining the Miter Limit

The miter limit determines when a miter join will be squared off to a beveled edge. The miter is the length of the point, from the inside to the outside, as shown in Figure 23. The length of the miter is not the same as the stroke weight. When two stroked paths are at an acute angle, the length of the miter will greatly exceed the weight of the stroke, which results in an extreme point that can be very distracting.

The default miter limit is 4, which means that when the length of the miter reaches 4 times the stroke weight, it will automatically be squared off to a beveled edge. Generally, you will find the default miter limit satisfactory, but be conscious of it when you draw objects with acute angles, such as stars or triangles.

Creating a Dashed Stroke

Dashed strokes, which are created and formatted using the Stroke panel, are strokes that consist of a series of dashes and gaps. You define the dash sequence for a dashed stroke by entering the lengths of the dashes and the gaps between them in the dash and gap text boxes on the Stroke panel. You can create a maximum of three different sized dashes separated by three different sized gaps. The pattern you establish will be repeated across the length of the stroke. Figure 24 shows a dashed stroke and its formatting on the Stroke panel.

Figure 23 *Understanding miters and miter limits*

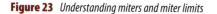

Figure 24 *Formatting a dashed stroke*

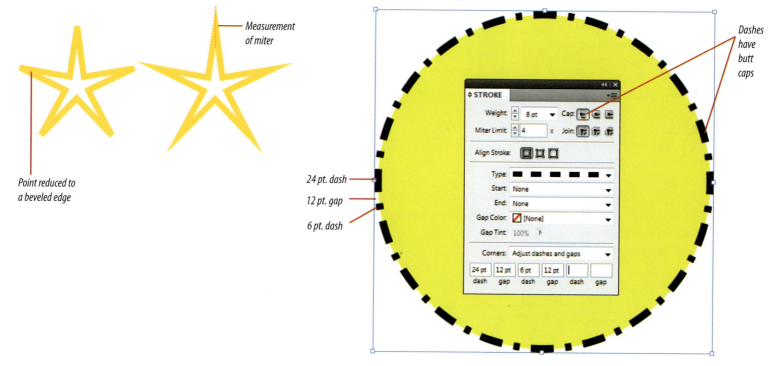

Reshape a frame using the Direct Selection tool and Pen tool

1. Open ID 7-2.indd, then save it as **Halloween Invitation**.

2. Click the **Selection tool** , click the **Orange Clouds graphic** in the document, copy it, click **Edit** on the Application bar, then click **Paste in Place**.

   A duplicate frame and graphic is placed directly in front of the original.

3. Place Blue clouds.tif, from the location where your Chapter 7 Data Files are stored, in this new frame.

4. Click the **Direct Selection tool** then click anywhere in the pasteboard to deselect all.

5. Drag the **top-right corner point** toward the center so that it is in the approximate location shown in Figure 25.

6. Click **Edit** on the Application bar, then click **Undo Move**.

7. Click the **Pen tool** , then add an anchor point on the top path of the frame, where it intersects with the vertical burgundy guide.

8. Add an anchor point on the right path of the frame, where it intersects with the horizontal burgundy guide.

   Your page should resemble Figure 26.

9. Position the Pen tool pointer over the top-right corner point.

   The Pen tool pointer becomes the Delete Anchor Point tool .

10. Click **the top-right corner point** to delete it.

    Your screen should resemble Figure 27.

You used the Pen tool to reshape a graphics frame.

Figure 25 *Moving the top-right corner point independently*

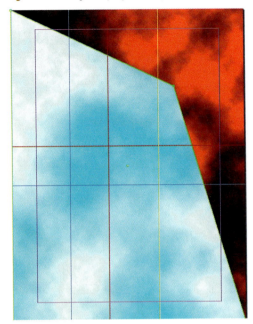

Figure 26 *Viewing two added anchor points*

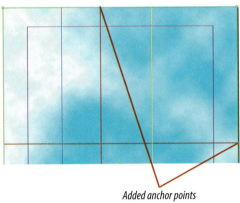

Added anchor points

Figure 27 *Viewing the results of deleting an anchor point*

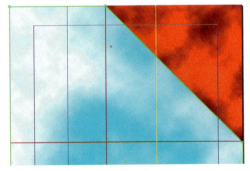

Figure 28 *Creating a rectangle*

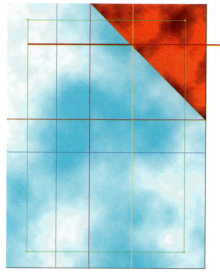

Path positioned on
margin guides

Figure 30 *Viewing the path*

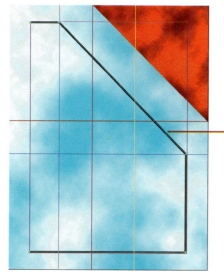

Clicking the Default Fill and
Stroke button changes the
stroke color to black

Figure 29 *Segments deleted when anchor
point is cut*

End point

Segments are
deleted

End point

1. Verify that None is selected for both the fill
   and stroke colors on the Tools panel, click the
   Rectangle tool 🔲, then create a rectangle
   that snaps to the inside of the four margin
   guides, as shown in Figure 28.

TIP If you prefer, turn on the Snap to Guides function.

2. Click the **Pen tool** ✒️, then add an anchor
   point anywhere on the left segment of the frame.

3. With the new anchor point still selected, click
   Edit on the Application bar, then click **Cut**.

   As shown in Figure 29, when the anchor point
   is cut, the two segments connected to it are
   also deleted.

4. Click the **Default Fill and Stroke button** 🔲
   on the Tools panel.

5. Click the **Stroke panel name tab** to display the
   Stroke panel.

6. Click the **Weight list arrow** on the Stroke panel,
   then click **4 pt**.

7. Place the Pen tool pointer on the top path of the
   frame, where it intersects with the blue guide;
   then, when it changes to the Add Anchor Point
   tool pointer, click to add an anchor point.

8. Add an anchor point on the right path of the
   frame, where it intersects with the blue guide.

9. Click the **Delete Anchor Point tool** ✒️, then
   click the **top-right anchor point**.

   Your screen should resemble Figure 30.

You created a simple rectangle, then reshaped it into an
open path.

Use the Stroke panel to add end shapes to a path

1. Press **[W]** to switch to Preview, click the **Selection tool** , then click the **black-stroked path**.

   TIP All objects, even open paths, are selected within a rectangular bounding box.

2. Click the **Start list arrow** on the Stroke panel, then click **CircleSolid**.

   TIP Click the Stroke panel menu icon, then click Show Options if necessary.

3. Click the **End list arrow**, click **Circle Solid**, then compare your page to Figure 31.

4. Press **[W]** to return to Normal view, click the **Pen tool** , then position it over the location where the diagonal section of the black path intersects with the yellow guide.

5. When the Pen tool pointer changes to the Add Anchor Point tool pointer , click.

6. Add another anchor point where the black path intersects with the horizontal burgundy guide.

7. Add a third new anchor point approximately halfway between the two new anchor points.

8. Click the **Direct Selection tool** , select only the third anchor point you added in Step 7, click **Edit** on the Application bar, then click **Cut**.

   Your page should resemble Figure 32.

9. Click the **Selection tool** , deselect all, click the **top black path**, click the **Pen tool** , point to the anchor point where the top black path intersects with the yellow guide, then stop when a diagonal line appears beside the Pen tool pointer.

   (continued)

Figure 31 *Viewing end shapes*

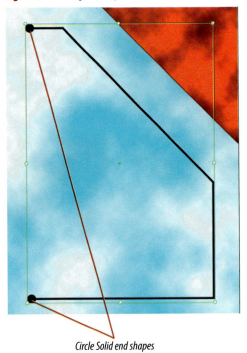

Circle Solid end shapes

Figure 32 *Viewing end shapes on two paths*

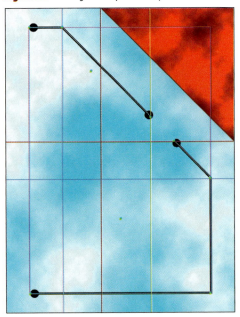

Creating Graphics

Figure 33 *Adding a triangle end shape to an extended path*

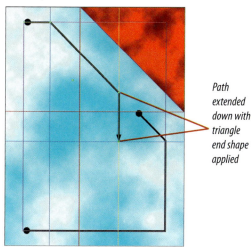

Path
extended
down with
triangle
end shape
applied

Figure 34 *Formatting a dashed line*

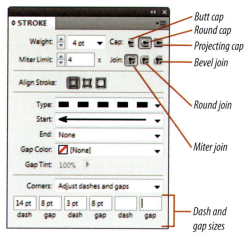

Butt cap
Round cap
Projecting cap
Bevel join

Round join

Miter join

Dash and
gap sizes

Figure 35 *Viewing dashed strokes*

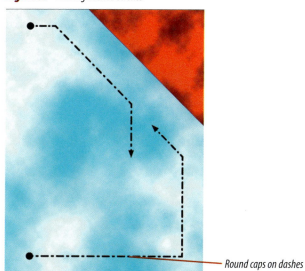

Round caps on dashes

The diagonal line indicates that the Pen tool is being used to reconnect to the path.

10. Click the **Pen tool pointer** on the anchor point, press and hold **[Shift]**, then click where the yellow guide intersects with the blue guide.

11. On the Stroke panel, click the **Start list arrow**, then click **Triangle**.

    Your page should resemble Figure 33.

12. Click the **Selection tool** , select the bottom black path, on the Stroke panel, click the **End list arrow**, then click **Triangle**.

You added end shapes to a path, split the path, then noted that the end shapes were applied to the two new paths.

Create a dashed stroke

1. Click **View** on the Application bar, point to **Grids & Guides**, then click **Hide Guides**.

2. Click the **Selection tool** if necessary, then select both black paths.

3. Click the **Type list arrow** on the Stroke panel, then click **Dashed**.

4. Type **14**, **8**, **3**, and **8** in the dash and gap text boxes on the Stroke panel, as shown in Figure 34.

5. Click the **Round Cap button** on the Stroke panel, deselect all, then compare your page to Figure 35.

6. Save your work.

You used the Stroke panel to format a path with a dashed stroke using round caps.

Work with Polygons
AND COMPOUND PATHS

What You'll Do

In this lesson, you will work with polygons and use them to create compound paths and anchored objects.

Creating Polygons

The Tools panel offers the Polygon tool and the Polygon Frame tool for creating multi-sided objects, such as triangles, pentagons, and hexagons. You can place graphics into objects you create with either tool.

To determine how many sides you want your polygon to be, double-click the tool to open the Polygon Settings dialog box, as shown in Figure 36. If, for example, you enter 5 in the Number of Sides text box and then click OK, when you click and drag with the Polygon tool selected, you will create a pentagon. Press and hold [Shift] when dragging to create a perfect pentagon with all 5 sides of equal length.

Figure 36 *Polygon Settings dialog box*

Creating Compound Paths

The Star Inset setting allows you to use the Polygon tool or the Polygon Frame tool to create star shapes. The greater the star inset percentage, the more acute and longer the points of the star will be, as shown in Figure 37. The number entered in the Number of Sides text box determines the number of points on the star.

Creating Compound Paths

Imagine you were going to use the Pen tool to trace the outline of a doughnut. You would draw an outer circle for the doughnut itself, then an inner circle to define the doughnut hole. Then, you would want to format the two paths so that the inner circle "cuts a hole" in the outer circle.

Figure 37 *Comparing different star inset percentages*

70% star inset

40% star inset

You create **compound paths** when you want to use one object to cut a hole in another object. In the above example, you would select both circles and then apply the Make Compound Path command. Figure 38 shows an example of the result. Note that you can see the blue square through the hole in the gold circle.

Once compounded, the two paths create one object.

Compound paths are not only used for the practical purpose of creating a hole. When you work with odd or overlapping shapes, the Make Compound Path command can produce results that are visually interesting and can be used as design elements, as shown in Figure 39.

Creating Anchored Objects

Anchored objects are objects that you create and use as text characters within a block of text. Figure 40 shows a red star used as an anchored object to make a block of text appear more eye-catching.

Anchored objects are placed or pasted into text blocks at the insertion point. Any modifications you make to the text after they are placed, such as rotating the text box, will also affect the anchored objects. The default position for anchored objects is Inline. In the Inline position, the anchored object is aligned with the baseline. You can adjust the Y Offset value of the anchored object to raise or lower it. The other possible positions are referred to as Above Line and Custom. You can choose one of these three positions and

many other options in the Insert Anchored Object dialog box.

If you want to reserve a space for an anchored object that is not yet available, click the Type tool where you would like to insert the anchored object, click Object on the Application bar, point to Anchored Object, then click Insert (Defaults). To change an anchored object's current settings, select the anchored object, click Object on the Application bar, point to Anchored Object, then click Options (Defaults).

Anchored objects can be used for practical purposes. For example, if you were designing a form that required check boxes, you could create a simple rectangle and then use it as an anchored object wherever you needed a check box to appear.

Figure 38 *Identifying two paths compounded as a single path*

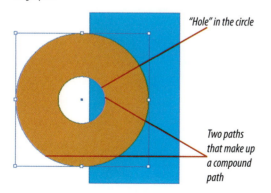

"Hole" in the circle

Two paths that make up a compound path

Figure 39 *Using compound paths to design interesting graphics*

A "hole" is created where the letter overlaps the circle

Figure 40 *Viewing anchored objects*

Our annual Summer Sale ★ begins on Tuesday ★ Get huge discounts from many of your favorite departments.

Anchored object

Create polygons, circles, and lines

1. On the Tools panel, set the fill color to black and the stroke color to None, then double-click the **Polygon tool** ⬡, on the Tools panel.

TIP The Polygon tool may be hidden beneath the Rectangle tool or the Ellipse tool.

2. Type **8** in the Number of Sides text box, type **70** in the Star Inset text box, then click **OK**.

3. Drag anywhere on the page to create a polygon of any size.

4. Click **Window** on the Application bar, point to **Object & Layout**, then click **Transform** to show the Transform panel if necessary.

5. On the Transform panel, verify that the center reference point on the proxy is selected, type **1.25** in both the Width and Height text boxes, press **[Enter]** (Win) or **[return]** (Mac), then position the polygon in the top-right corner of the page, as shown in Figure 41.

6. Deselect the polygon, change the fill color on the Tools panel to yellow, click the **Ellipse tool** ⬭, then position the pointer at the center of the black star.

7. Press and hold **[Shift][Alt]** (Win) or **[Shift] [option]** (Mac), then drag a **circle** approximately the size shown in Figure 42.

TIP Pressing and holding [Alt] (Win) or [option] (Mac) allows you to draw a circle from its center. Pressing and holding [Shift] constrains the shape to a perfect circle.

8. Click the **Selection tool** ▸ , click the **pasteboard** to deselect all, click the

(continued)

Figure 41 *Positioning the polygon*

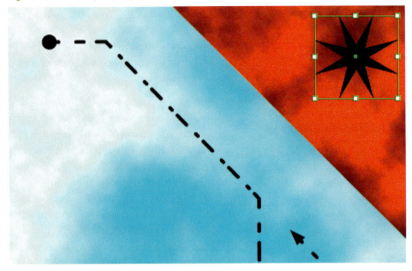

Figure 42 *Drawing the circle*

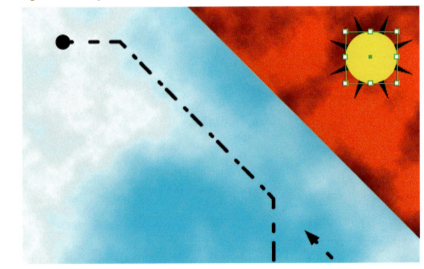

Figure 43 *Drawing the line*

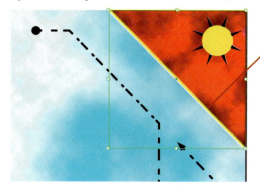

Diagonal line

Figure 44 *Positioning the witch polygon*

Figure 45 *Viewing the witch polygon with the placed graphic and black stroke*

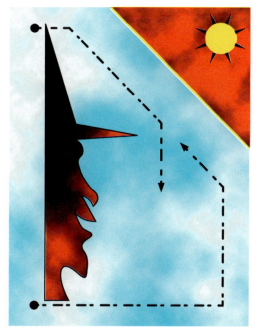

Swap Fill & Stroke button ↰ on the Tools panel, click the **Stroke button** ▤ to activate it, then change the weight on the Stroke panel to 4 pt and the type to Solid.

9. Click the **Line tool** ╲ , position the pointer on the top edge of the page where the orange clouds graphic meets the blue clouds graphic, then drag a **diagonal line** along the base of the orange clouds triangle, as shown in Figure 43.

You created an eight-pointed polygon, a circle, and a line.

Place graphics in polygons

1. Open the Halloween Witch file that you created, select the witch graphic, copy it, click **Window** on the Application bar, click **Halloween Invitation.indd**, click **Edit** on the Application bar, then click **Paste**.

2. Position the witch polygon in the location shown in Figure 44.

3. Verify that the witch is still selected, click **File** on the Application bar, click **Place**, navigate to the drive and folder where your Chapter 7 Data Files are stored, then double-click **Orange Clouds.tif**.

4. Click the **Swap Fill & Stroke button** ↰ on the Tools panel, change the stroke weight to 2 pt, then deselect.

   Your page should resemble Figure 45.

5. Select the star polygon, then place the Blue clouds.tif graphic in it.

TIP When you place a graphic into a polygon that has a fill, the fill remains, even though it may not be visible because of the placed graphic.

(continued)

6. Click **Object** on the Application bar, point to **Fitting**, then click **Fit Content to Frame**.

7. Change the fill color of the star polygon to None, deselect, then compare your page to Figure 46.

8. Select the small ten-pointed polygon in the pasteboard, then place Orange Clouds.tif into it.

9. Click **Object** on the Application bar, point to **Fitting**, then click **Fit Content to Frame**.

You placed three graphics into three polygons.

Create compound paths

1. Click the **Selection tool** , select the yellow "eye" polygon on the pasteboard, click **Object** on the Application bar, point to **Arrange**, then click **Bring to Front**.

2. Position the eye on top of the witch polygon as shown in Figure 47.

3. Verify that the eye polygon is still selected, press **[Shift]**, then click the **witch polygon** so that both polygons are selected.

4. Click **Object** on the Application bar, point to **Paths**, then click **Make Compound Path**.

   As shown in Figure 48, the eye polygon becomes a "hole" in the witch polygon through which you can see the Blue clouds graphic.

5. Select both the yellow circle and the star polygons in the top-right corner of the page.

6. Click **Object** on the Application bar, point to **Paths**, click **Make Compound Path**, then deselect all.

   Your page should resemble Figure 49.

You created two compound paths.

Figure 46 *Viewing two graphics placed in polygons*

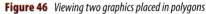

Blue clouds.tif placed into the star polygon

Orange Clouds.tif placed into "witch" polygon

Figure 47 *Positioning the "eye" polygon*

"Eye" polygon

Figure 48 *Creating a compound path*

Figure 49 *Viewing two compound paths*

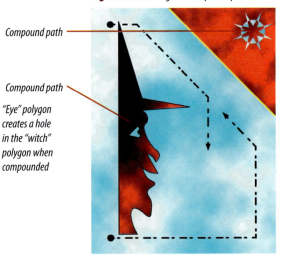

Compound path

Compound path

"Eye" polygon creates a hole in the "witch" polygon when compounded

Creating Graphics

Figure 50 *Placing the anchored object*

Anchored
object

Figure 51 *Selecting the anchored object*

The anchored
object and
spaces before
and after it
are selected

Figure 52 *Viewing three anchored objects*

Use a polygon as an anchored object

1. Drag the **Text layer** to the top of the Layers panel.

2. Click the **ten-pointed polygon** in the pasteboard, click **Edit** on the Application bar, then click **Cut**.

3. Click the **Type tool** T, click between the words Kids and We're, then paste.

   As shown in Figure 50, the polygon is pasted into the block of text.

4. Press **[Spacebar]** to create a space after the anchored object, position your cursor before the graphic, then press **[Spacebar]** to create a space before the graphic.

5. Select the space, the graphic, and the space after the graphic, as shown in Figure 51.

6. On the Character panel, type **-3** in the Baseline Shift text box, then press **[Enter]** (Win) or **[return]** (Mac).

   The anchored object is positioned more inline with the text.

7. With the space-graphic-space still selected, click **Edit** on the Application bar, then click **Copy**.

8. Click between the words school and Door, then paste.

9. Click between the words costume and Bring, then paste.

10. Select the words "We're having," type **It's**, then save your work.

    As shown in Figure 52, when the text is edited, the anchored objects reflow with the text.

You used a polygon as an anchored object within a block of text.

Work with
ADVANCED TEXT FEATURES

What You'll Do

In this lesson, you will position type on a line, convert type to outlines, and apply drop shadows and corner effects to graphics.

Positioning Type on a Line

Once you've created an object—a line or a polygon—the Type on a Path tool allows you to position text on the outline of the object. Simply float the Type on a Path tool pointer over the path until a plus sign appears beside the pointer, and then click the path. A blinking cursor appears, allowing you to begin typing.

Figure 53 shows text positioned on a path. Whenever you position text on a path, a default start, end, and center bracket are created, as well as an in port and an out port used for threading text. Drag the start bracket with either of the selection tools to move the text along the path.

If you drag the center bracket across the path, the text will flow in the opposite direction, as shown in Figure 54.

> **QUICK TIP**
>
> The center bracket is small and often difficult to see amid the letters.

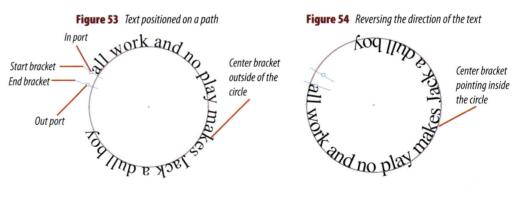

Figure 53 *Text positioned on a path*

In port

Start bracket

End bracket

Out port

Center bracket outside of the circle

Figure 54 *Reversing the direction of the text*

Center bracket pointing inside the circle

Once the text is entered, you can edit the text just as you would in a text frame. You can also modify the path. For example, if you modify the curve of the ellipse, the text will flow with the new shape.

One key design technique that many designers use in conjunction with text on a line is a baseline shift. You can use the Baseline Shift text box on the Character panel to make the text float above or below the path. Figure 55 shows text floating above the path of the ellipse.

Converting Text to Outlines

After you create text in InDesign, you can convert the text to outlines. When text is converted to outlines, each character is converted to a closed path and shares the same characteristics of all paths. As shown in Figure 56, the individual characters—which were once text—are now individual paths.

Why would you do this? One good reason is that when you convert text to outlines, you can place graphics into the outlines, as shown in Figure 57. You do this using the Place command or the Paste Into command.

The ability to convert text to paths is a powerful feature. Beyond allowing you to use text as a frame for graphics, it makes it possible to create a document with text and *without* fonts. This can save you time in document management when sending files to your printer, and it can circumvent

potential problems with missing fonts. Remember, though, that once text is converted to outlines, the outlines are no longer editable as text. So, be sure to save a copy of your file with text before converting an entire document to outlines for output.

Does this mean that you should always convert all of your text in all of your documents to outlines? No. For quality purposes, it is best for text—especially small text such as body copy—to remain formatted as text as opposed to outlines. However, converting to outlines can be a good choice when you've used a typeface that you suspect your client or printer doesn't have. Rather than send them the font, you could choose simply to convert the text to outlines. Remember though, this is an option for larger text, like headlines, and is not recommended for body copy.

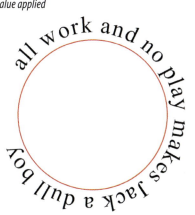

Figure 55 *Viewing text with a positive baseline shift value applied*

all work and no play makes Jack a dull boy

Figure 56 *Text converted to outlines*

Text shapes drawn with anchor points and line segments

Figure 57 *Placing a graphic in outlined text*

Blue stroke applied to paths

Position type on a line

1. Click the **Selection tool** ![arrow], then click the **yellow diagonal line**.

2. Click the **Type on a Path tool** ![tool], then position the pointer over the yellow line until a plus sign appears beside it.

3. Click the **yellow line**.

   A blinking type cursor appears at the top of the yellow line.

4. Type the word **happy** in lower-case letters, as shown in Figure 58.

5. Double-click **happy**, change the font to Impact, change the font size to 60 pt, then change the fill color to Paper on the Swatches panel.

6. Click the **Selection tool** ![arrow], then click the **text**.

   The Fill button on the Tools panel changes to None, and the Stroke button changes to yellow, because these are the attributes of the line that the type is positioned on, not the type itself.

7. Change the stroke color to None.

8. Position the word happy as shown in Figure 59.

9. Press and hold **[Shift][Alt]** (Win) or **[Shift] [option]** (Mac), then drag a **copy of the word happy** into the blue area beneath the orange triangle.

10. Click the **Type on a Path tool** ![tool], double-click **happy**, then type **halloween**.

11. Click the **Selection tool** ![arrow], then position the word halloween as shown in Figure 60.

You used the Type on a Path tool to position text on a diagonal line. You then created a copy of the text to create another word on the identical angle.

Figure 58 *Typing the word happy*

Figure 59 *Positioning the word happy*

Figure 60 *Positioning the word halloween*

Figure 61 *Viewing text converted to paths*

Figure 62 *Viewing graphics pasted into text outlines*

Convert text to outlines

1. Click the **Selection tool** ⬆ then select the "happy" text.
2. Click **Type** on the Application bar, then click **Create Outlines**.
3. Select the "halloween" text.
4. Click **Type** on the Application bar, then click **Create Outlines**.
5. Click the **Direct Selection tool** ⬆.

   Figure 61 shows that the halloween text has been converted to nine paths.

You converted text to outlines.

Place graphics into outlines

1. Deselect all, click the **Selection tool** ⬆, then click the word **happy**.
2. Click **File** on the Application bar, click **Place**, navigate to the drive and folder where your Data Files are stored, then place Blue clouds.tif.
3. Click **Object** on the Application bar, point to **Fitting**, then click **Fit Content to Frame**.
4. Deselect all, verify that the Selection tool ⬆ is selected, click the **Orange Clouds graphic** visible as a triangle in the top-right corner of the document, click **Edit** on the Application bar, then click **Copy**.
5. Click the word **halloween**, click **Edit** on the Application bar, then click **Paste Into**.
6. Compare your page to Figure 62.
7. Save your work, then close Halloween Invitation.indd.

You used two methods for using a graphic to fill text outlines. You placed a graphic into text outlines, then pasted a graphic into text outlines.

Reshape frames.

1. Open ID 7-3.indd, save it as **Garden Party**, then verify that all guides are locked.
2. Click the top edge of the frame containing the ghosted image with the Direct Selection tool, then drag the top middle anchor point down to the first horizontal (cyan) guide.
3. Click the Pen tool, position the pointer over the bottom edge of the frame so that a plus sign appears beside the tool, then click to add an anchor point at the 3" mark on the horizontal ruler.
4. Deselect all, click the Direct Selection tool, click one edge of the frame to select the frame, then select the new anchor point.
5. Click Edit on the Application bar, then click Cut.

Use the Pen tool.

1. Click the Pen tool, position the pointer over the bottom-left anchor point of the frame until a diagonal line appears beside the Pen tool, then click the anchor point.
2. Moving up and to the right, click the intersection of the pink vertical guide and the orange horizontal guide. (*Hint*: The intersection of the pink vertical guide and the orange horizontal guide is at the 1" mark on the horizontal ruler.)
3. Moving down and to the right, click where the next vertical guide intersects with the bottom of the page.
4. Repeat Steps 2 and 3 until your image matches Figure 63, then click the anchor point in the bottom-right corner to close the path.

Work with polygons and compound paths.

1. Deselect all, then click the Default Fill and Stroke button on the Tools panel.
2. Click the Ellipse tool, then position the pointer at the intersection of the cyan guide and the center pink guide.
3. Press and hold [Alt] (Win) or [option] (Mac), then click.
4. Type **1.65** in the Width text box, type **1.65** in the Height text box, then click OK.
5. Click the Selection tool, press and hold [Shift], then select the frame that contains the ghosted image. (*Hint*: Both the circle and the frame should be selected.)
6. Click Object on the Application bar, point to Paths, then click Make Compound Path.
7. Using the Selection tool, select the text in the pasteboard, click Object on the Application bar, point to Arrange, click Bring to Front, then position it as shown in Figure 64. (*Hint*: If both lines of text don't appear in the frame, enlarge it slightly.)
8. Click the Selection tool, click the compound path, then add a 1 pt black stroke to the path.

Figure 63 *Skills Review, Part 1*

Apply stroke effects.

1. Click the Ellipse tool, then position the pointer at the intersection of the cyan guide and the center pink guide.
2. Press and hold [Shift][Alt] (Win) or [Shift][option] (Mac), then drag a circle that is the width of two columns.
3. Change the stroke color to magenta by clicking C=0 M=100 Y=0 K=0 on the Swatches panel, then change the stroke weight to 3.5 pt.
4. Click the Pen tool, then click to add an anchor point in the two locations where the circle intersects with the black diagonal lines.
5. Click the Direct Selection tool, deselect all, select the magenta circle, select only the top anchor point of the larger circle, click Edit on the Application bar, then click Cut. (*Hint*: Your screen should resemble Figure 65.)

Figure 64 *Skills Review, Part 2*

Creating Graphics

6. Click the Start list arrow on the Stroke panel, then click Barbed.
7. Click the End list arrow, then click Barbed.
8. Click the Type list arrow, then click Dashed.
9. Type **12** in the first dash text box, type **8** in the first gap text box, type **4** in the second dash text box, then type **8** in the second gap text box.
10. Click the Round Cap button on the Stroke panel.

Work with advanced text features, corner effects, and drop shadows.

1. Click the Ellipse tool, position the pointer at the intersection of the cyan guide and the center pink guide, press and hold [Alt] (Win) or [option] (Mac), then click.

2. Type **3.25** in the Width text box, type **3.25** in the Height text box, then click OK.
3. Click the Pen tool, then click to add an anchor point in the two locations where the new circle intersects with the black diagonal lines.
4. Click the Direct Selection tool, deselect all, click the edge of the new circle, select its top anchor point, click Edit on the Application bar, then click Cut.
5. Click the Selection tool.
6. Click the Type on a Path tool, position it over the circle so that a plus sign appears beside the pointer, then click the path at approximately 9 o'clock.

7. Type **We're having a garden party! You're invited!**.
8. Select all of the text, change the font to Trajan or a similar font, then change the horizontal scale to 58%.
9. Change the font to 28 pt bold, then change the baseline shift to -5 pt.
10. Increase the Tracking value to 25.
11. Click the Direct Selection tool, then move the start bracket on the left until the text is evenly distributed.
12. Click the Selection tool, then change the stroke color to None.
13. Compare your results to Figure 66.
14. Save your work, then close Garden Party.

Figure 65 *Skills Review, Part 3*

Figure 66 *Completed Skills Review*

You are a freelance designer, and you have just created an invitation for a Halloween party that features a black cat. Your client tells you that she loves the blue clouds and the orange clouds in the background, but she thinks the cat and its yellow eyes are "too flat." She says that she'd prefer that the cat and the eyes had texture.

1. Open ID 7-4.indd, then save it as **Black Cat**.
2. Click the Selection tool, select the cat, then change the fill color to None. The cat image will disappear but its frame will remain selected.
3. Place the file named Gray Clouds.tif.
4. Press and hold [Shift], then select the left eye, so that both the cat and the left eye are selected.
5. Create a compound path from the cat and the left eye objects, then deselect all.
6. Select both the cat and the right eye are selected.
7. Create a compound path from the cat and the right eye objects, then deselect all.
8. Drag the circle from the pasteboard and position it so that it covers both of the cat's eyes.
9. Click Object on the Application bar, point to Arrange, then click Send Backward.
10. With the frame still selected, use the arrow keys to position the circle behind the cat's head in a way that you think is best, save your work, then compare your screen to Figure 67.
11. Close Black Cat.

Figure 67 *Completed Project Builder 1*

Creating Graphics

You are designing an advertisement for a travel magazine. The ad will promote tourism for a small island in the Caribbean named Lagoon Key. Unfortunately, the company you are working with doesn't have a huge budget. They've sent you only one photo. You decide to combine the photo with type to create a more complex design.

1. Open ID 7-5.indd, then save it as **Lagoon**.
2. Click the Selection tool, click the text, click Type on the Application bar, then click Create Outlines.
3. Copy the selection, click Edit on the Application bar, then click Paste In Place.
4. Click File on the Application bar, click Place, then place the Color Lagoon.psd file.
5. Click Object on the Application bar, point to Fitting, then click Fit Content to Frame.
6. Click View on the Application bar, point to Extras, then click Hide Frame Edges if necessary.
7. Press the up arrow four times, then press the right arrow four times.
8. Apply a 1 pt black stroke to the text outlines, then deselect all.
9. Save your work, compare your screen to Figure 68, then close Lagoon.

Figure 68 *Completed Project Builder 2*

You have been contracted to design an ad for Bull's Eye Barbecue. They supply you with their logo. You decide to position their name on a circle that surrounds the logo.

1. Open ID 7-6.indd, then save it as **Bull's Eye**.
2. Click the Selection tool, then click the black stroked circle that surrounds the logo.
3. Click the Type on a Path tool, position the pointer over the selection until a plus sign appears beside the pointer.
4. Click the path at approximately the 10 o'clock point.
5. Type **BULL'S EYE BARBECUE**, select the text, change the font to Garamond or a similar font, then change the type size to 62 pt. (*Hint*: Depending on the font you chose, you may need to resize the text so it fits.)
6. Click the Selection tool, change the stroke color to None, then save your work.
7. Deselect all, compare your screen to Figure 69, then close Bull's Eye.

Figure 69 *Completed Design Project*

Creating Graphics

This Portfolio Project is designed to give you some practice time working with type on a path. You will create type on a path, format it, then reposition it on the path. The design and the position of the type is completely up to you.

Figure 70 *Sample Portfolio Project*

1. Open ID 7-7.indd, then save it as **Atlas**.
2. Click the Selection tool, then select the black-stroked circle on the artwork.
3. Click the Type on a Path tool, then click the black-stroked circle anywhere above the letter "T" in ATLAS.
4. Type EVENT TV in all capital letters.
5. Format the text to any size, fill, and stroke color that you like.
6. Click the Selection tool, then click and drag the Start bracket to position the text anywhere above the word ATLAS that you like.
7. Remove the black stroke from the circle.
8. Click Edit on the Application bar, then click Copy.
9. Click Edit on the Application bar, then click Paste In Place.
10. Rotate the pasted copy from its center point 180-degrees.
11. Compare your results to Figure 70. Your results will vary based on the formatting options you chose in this exercise.
12. Save your work, then close Atlas.

CHAPTER 8 EXPLORING EFFECTS AND
ADVANCED TECHNIQUES

1. Use the Pathfinder panel
2. Create new stroke styles
3. Incorporate gridify behavior
4. Work with multiple page sizes
5. Work with nested styles
6. Apply Live Corner Effects
7. Work with effects and object styles

CHAPTER 8

EXPLORING EFFECTS AND
ADVANCED TECHNIQUES

Now that you've experienced a broad array of InDesign's basic features and functions, it's time for you to try out some of the more complex and exotic options that InDesign offers. Think of Chapter 8 as something of a buffet. For an appetizer, you'll use the Pathfinder panel. For side dishes, you'll create new stroke styles, incorporate gridify behavior, and work with multiple page sizes and nested styles. Your entrée will be applying Live Corner Effects, and your dessert will be working with effects and object styles. With seven lessons, covering so many different features, Chapter 8 will satisfy you with some really useful—and in some cases, surprising—tips, tools, and techniques.

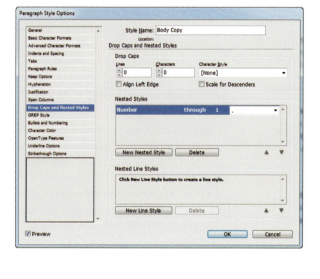

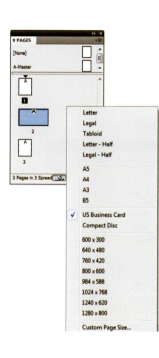

Use the
PATHFINDER PANEL

What You'll Do

Using the Pathfinder Panel

The Pathfinder panel is essentially a drawing tool. As shown in Figure 1, it is divided into three sections: Paths, Pathfinder, Convert Shape, and Convert Point. The Paths section is useful when creating paths with the Pen tool. You can join, open, close, or reverse a path using the four buttons in this section. The Convert Point section also applies to paths and points, allowing you to manipulate points to create different corners and arcs with a path. Chapter 7 covers paths and points extensively.

The Pathfinder section in the Pathfinder panel helps you easily create new complex shapes by overlapping simple objects. The panel does this by offering five buttons that work as follows:

Add: Combines two or more overlapping objects into one object, as shown in Figure 2. The resulting object assumes the color properties of the frontmost object.

Subtract: The frontmost object(s) "punch a hole" in the backmost object, as shown in Figure 3. The resulting object retains the color properties of the backmost object.

Intersect: The resulting shape is the intersection of the overlapping object(s) and assumes the color properties of the frontmost object, as shown in Figure 4.

Exclude Overlap: A hole is created where the two objects overlap, as shown in Figure 5. The resulting object assumes the color properties of the frontmost object.

Minus Back: The backmost object "punches a hole" in the object(s) in front, as shown in Figure 6. You can think of the Minus Back pathfinder as the opposite of the Subtract pathfinder. The resulting object assumes the color properties of the frontmost object.

Using the Convert Shape Section of the Pathfinder Panel

The Convert Shape section of the Pathfinder panel offers practical solutions and is easy to use. Create a frame of any shape and size, then click any of the buttons in the Convert Shape section of the panel, such as the ellipse, triangle, polygon, or line. The selected frame will then change to that shape.

Figure 1 *Pathfinder panel*

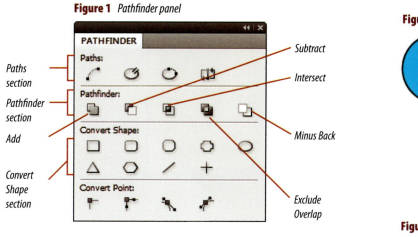

Subtract

Intersect

Paths section

Pathfinder section

Add

Convert Shape section

Minus Back

Exclude Overlap

Figure 2 *Add pathfinder*

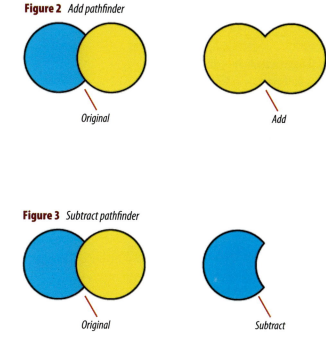

Original

Add

Figure 3 *Subtract pathfinder*

Original

Subtract

Figure 4 *Intersect pathfinder*

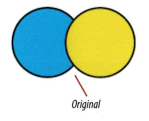

Original

Intersect

Figure 5 *Exclude Overlap pathfinder*

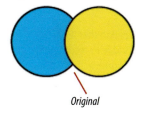

Original

Exclude Overlap

Negative space

Figure 6 *Minus Back pathfinder*

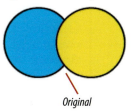

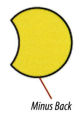

Original

Minus Back

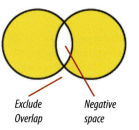

Use the Add pathfinder

1. Open ID 8-1.indd, then save it as **Add and Subtract**.

2. Click the **Selection tool** 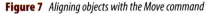, click the **green circle**, click **Object** on the Application bar, point to **Transform**, then click **Move**.

3. Type **2** in the Horizontal text box, then click **OK**.

4. Click the **yellow circle**, click **Object** on the Application bar, point to **Transform**, then click **Move**.

5. Type **-2** in the Horizontal text box, then click **OK** so that the objects are positioned as shown in Figure 7.

6. Select all three objects—the green and yellow circles and the red diamond.

7. Click **Window** on the Application bar, point to **Object & Layout**, then click **Pathfinder**.

(continued)

Figure 7 *Aligning objects with the Move command*

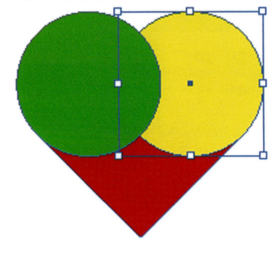

Understanding Color Management in InDesign

In the modern world of digital printing, printing shops have a wide variety of output devices. In one shop alone, a printer might have a number of different output devices from different manufacturers; some of them might even be based on different types of printing technologies. In this type of environment, color management becomes critical. When you send a job to a printer, the printer will need to color manage your job to print on a specific device.

Adobe has endowed InDesign CS5 with the same color management sophistication that it has invested in Photoshop. With these advanced color capabilities, InDesign CS5 is able to incorporate all types of color presets and configurations to interface with almost any digital printer that a print professional might employ. The end result is that you, the designer, can feel confident that the final printed product will match the color proof that you signed off on.

Exploring Effects and Advanced Techniques

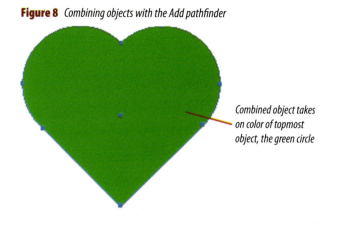

Figure 8 *Combining objects with the Add pathfinder*

Combined object takes
on color of topmost
object, the green circle

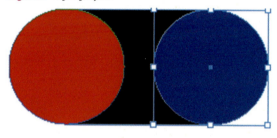

Figure 9 *Aligning objects*

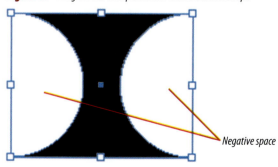

Figure 10 *Using the Subtract pathfinder to create a new shape*

Negative space

8. Click the **Add button** 🔲 on the Pathfinder panel.

   The three objects are combined into a single object, as shown in Figure 8.

   TIP When objects are added, the resulting object assumes the color of the topmost of the original objects.

You used the Move command to align three objects, selected them, then combined them into one object using the Add pathfinder.

Use the Subtract pathfinder

1. Click the **red circle**, click **Object** on the Application bar, point to **Transform**, then click **Move**.

2. Type **1.5** in the Horizontal text box, then click **OK**.

3. Click the **blue circle**, click **Object** on the Application bar, point to **Transform**, then click **Move**.

4. Type **-1.5** in the Horizontal text box, then click **OK** so that the objects are positioned as shown in Figure 9.

5. Select all three objects—the red and blue circles and the black rectangle.

6. Click the **Subtract button** 🔲 on the Pathfinder panel.

   The two front objects—the circles—"punch holes" in the backmost object, leaving negative space in place of the circles, as shown in Figure 10.

   TIP When the Subtract pathfinder is used on multiple objects, the backmost object retains its original fill color.

(continued)

7. Click the **green heart shape**, click **Object** on the Application bar, point to **Transform**, then click **Rotate**.

8. Type **180** in the Angle text box, then click **OK**.

9. Reposition the green heart shape in relation to the black shape, as shown in Figure 11.

10. Select both objects, click the **Add button** 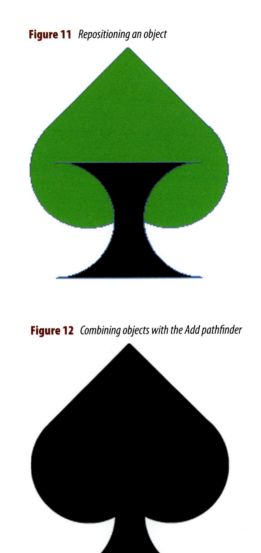 on the Pathfinder panel, deselect, then compare your work with Figure 12.

11. Save your work, then close Add and Subtract.

You aligned three objects, selected them, then used the Subtract pathfinder to transform the backmost object into an entirely new shape. You combined that object with another using the Add pathfinder to create a spade shape.

Figure 11 *Repositioning an object*

Figure 12 *Combining objects with the Add pathfinder*

Exploring Effects and Advanced Techniques

Figure 13 *Overlapping objects*

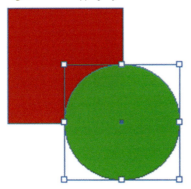

Figure 15 *Viewing two shapes created from pathfinders*

Figure 14 *Overlapping objects*

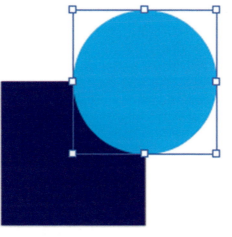

Use the Intersect and Minus Back pathfinders

1. Open ID 8-2.indd, then save it as **Intersect and Minus Back**.

2. Click the **Selection tool** , then move the green circle so that it overlaps the red square, as shown in Figure 13.

3. Select both objects, then click the **Intersect button** on the Pathfinder panel.

   The resulting single object is the intersection of the two overlapping objects.

4. Move the light blue circle so that it overlaps the blue square, as shown in Figure 14.

5. Select both objects, click the **Minus Back button** on the Pathfinder panel, deselect, then compare the shapes in your document to Figure 15.

   Where the two objects overlap, the backmost object "punches a hole" in the frontmost object.

6. Save your work, then close Intersect and Minus Back.

You used the Intersect and Minus Back pathfinders to create new shapes from two overlapping objects.

Create New
STROKE STYLES

In this lesson, you will create new stroke styles using the New Stroke Style dialog box.

Creating Stroke Styles

The Stroke panel offers a number of stroke styles that you can apply to objects. You can also create and customize your own stroke styles and make them available for use on the Stroke panel.

InDesign allows you to create and customize three types of stroke styles: Dash, Dotted, and Stripe. To create one of these stroke styles, you simply access the Stroke Styles dialog box by clicking the Stroke panel options button.

Creating a Dash Stroke Style

To create a new dash stroke style, open the New Stroke Style dialog box by clicking New in the Stroke Styles dialog box, then choosing Dash from the Type list, as shown in Figure 16. First, enter a descriptive name in the Name text box. Next, enter a measurement in the Length text box to specify the length of the dash, then enter another measurement in the Pattern Length text box to specify the intervals at which the dashes will occur.

You can add additional dashes to the pattern. Simply click the white space below

the ruler, as shown in Figure 17. You can change the length of the new dash by dragging the two white triangles (Win) or black triangles (Mac) above the dash. As you modify the new dash stroke style, you can see what it looks like in the preview window at the bottom of the dialog box. Using this dialog box, you can create dash stroke styles that are complex and visually interesting.

Creating a Dotted Stroke Style

To create a dotted stroke style, open the New Stroke Style dialog box and choose Dotted from the Type list. As with dash strokes, you can add additional dots to the stroke pattern. Enter a value in the Center text box to specify where the additional dot will be positioned horizontally in relation to the original dot. Enter a value in the Pattern Length text box to specify the intervals at which the dot pattern will occur. See Figure 18.

Creating a Stripe Stroke Style

To create a stripe stroke style, open the New Stroke Style dialog box and choose Stripe from the Type list, as shown in Figure 19.

By default, a stripe stroke style begins with two stripes, as shown in Figure 19. Enter a value in the Start text box to specify where the stripe will be positioned on the vertical axis. Enter a value in the Width text box to determine the width—from top to bottom—of the stripe.

Click anywhere in the white space to add additional stripes. As shown in Figure 20, you can specify additional stripes as having different widths, thus creating a style that is unique and visually interesting.

Figure 16 *New Stroke Style dialog box*

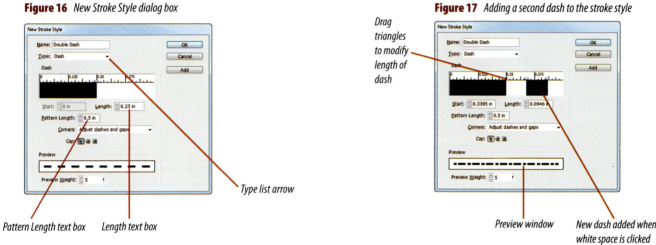

Type list arrow

Pattern Length text box   Length text box

Figure 17 *Adding a second dash to the stroke style*

Drag triangles to modify length of dash

Preview window   New dash added when white space is clicked

Figure 18 *Creating a dotted stroke style*

Drag triangle to change center location

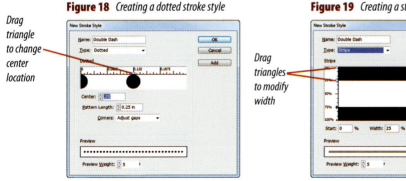

Figure 19 *Creating a stripe stroke style*

Drag triangles to modify width

Figure 20 *Adding two new stripes to a stroke style*

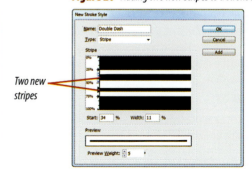

Two new stripes

Create a new dash stroke style

1. Open ID 8-3.indd, then save it as **Custom Strokes**.

2. Open the Stroke panel.

3. Click the **Stroke panel options button** 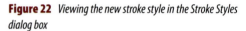, click **Stroke Styles**, then click **New**.

4. Type **Custom Dash Style** in the Name text box, then verify that Dash is listed in the Type text box.

5. Select the value in the Pattern Length text box, type **.5**, then press **[Tab]**.

   When you press [Tab] the value in the Length text box might automatically change to .25". If it does, you can skip step 6.

TIP If your measurement reverts to 0p3 after you press [Tab], verify that you typed the inch abbreviation after .5. (You can also type the letter "i" instead of "in".) Then all future measurements will be in inches. To change back to picas, type the measurement using "p" to indicate picas, such as 0p3.

6. Select the value in the Length text box, type **.25**, then compare your dialog box to Figure 21.

7. Click **anywhere in the white space in the ruler** to the right of the black dash to add a new dash.

8. Type **.35** in the Start text box, press **[Tab]**, type **.1** in the Length text box, press **[Tab]**, then note the change in the Preview window in the dialog box.

9. Click **OK**.

   The new stroke style is listed in the Stroke Styles dialog box, shown in Figure 22.

You created a new dash stroke style using the New Stroke Style dialog box.

Figure 21 *Defining a new dash stroke style*

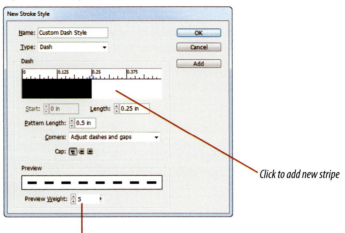

Click to add new stripe

The preview weight only affects the preview size of the new stroke style, not the actual weight of the stroke

Figure 22 *Viewing the new stroke style in the Stroke Styles dialog box*

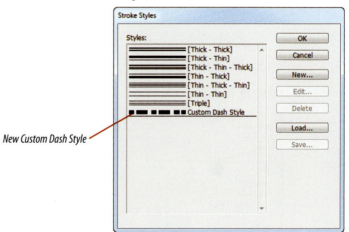

New Custom Dash Style

Figure 23 *Defining the width of the top stripe*

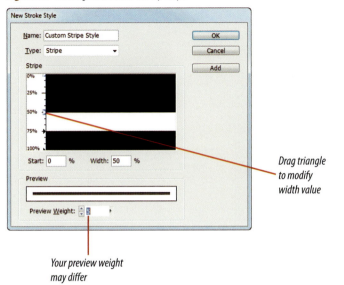

Drag triangle
to modify
width value

Your preview weight
may differ

Figure 24 *Defining the location and width of the new stripe*

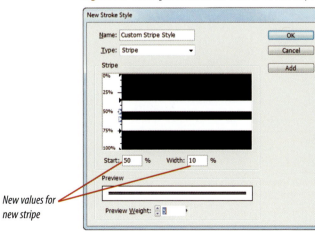

New values for
new stripe

Create a new stripe stroke style

1. Click **New** in the Stroke Styles dialog box.

2. Type **Custom Stripe Style** in the Name text box, click the **Type list arrow**, then click **Stripe**.

3. Select the value in the Width text box, type **50**, then press **[Tab]**.

   As shown in Figure 23, the top stripe doubles in width and remains selected, as noted by the highlighted triangles.

4. Drag the **triangle** at the 50% mark up until the value in the Width text box reads 35%.

5. Click **anywhere in the white space between the two stripes** to add a third stripe.

6. Select the contents of the Start text box, type **50**, then press **[Tab]**.

7. Type **10** in the Width text box, then press **[Tab]**.

   Your dialog box should resemble Figure 24.

8. Click **OK**, then note that the new stroke style has been added to the Styles list.

You created a new stripe stroke style using the New Stroke Style dialog box.

Create a new dotted stroke style

1. Click **New** in the Stroke Styles dialog box.

2. Type **Custom Dot Style** in the Name text box, click the **Type list arrow**, then click **Dotted**.

3. In the Pattern Length text box, type **1**, press **[Tab]**, then note the change to the preview.

   The default dotted stroke is a pattern of dots that are evenly spaced, regardless of the pattern length.

4. Click **anywhere in the white space beneath the ruler** to add another dot to the pattern.

5. Type **.25** in the Center text box, then press **[Tab]**.

   Your dialog box should resemble Figure 25.

TIP The Preview window is useful when you are designing a stroke style. Feel free to increase the Preview Weight value. The greater the value, the bigger the preview.

6. Click **anywhere in the white space to the right of the new dot** to add another dot.

7. Noting the change to the preview, drag the **triangle** above the new dot until the value in the Center text box reads .5.

   Your dialog box should resemble Figure 26.

8. Click **OK**, then note that the new stroke style has been added to the list.

You created a new dotted stroke style using the New Stroke Style dialog box.

Figure 25 *Positioning a new dot at the .25 mark*

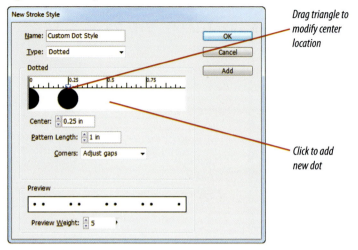

Drag triangle to modify center location

Click to add new dot

Figure 26 *Positioning a new dot at the .5 mark*

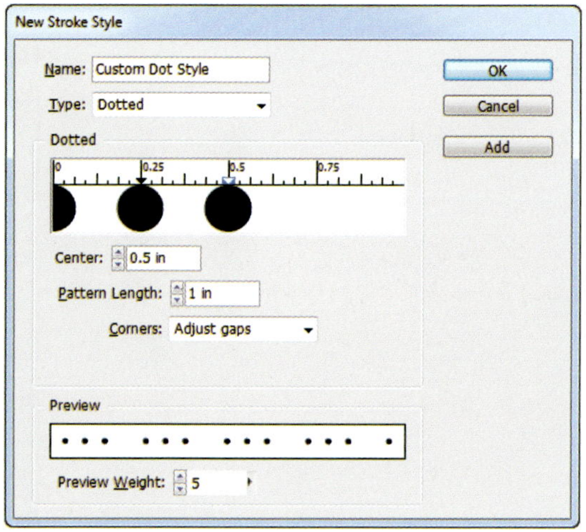

Figure 27 *Viewing three lines with stroke styles applied*

Apply stroke styles

1. Click **OK** in the Stroke Styles dialog box.
2. Click the **Selection tool** if it is not already selected, then click the **top line** on the page.
3. Click the **Type list arrow** on the Stroke panel, then click **Custom Dash Style**.
4. Click the **second line**, then apply the Custom Stripe Style.
5. Click the **third line**, then apply the Custom Dot Style.
6. Select all three lines on the page, then change the weight on the Stroke panel to 12 pt.
7. Deselect all, select the second line on the page, click the **Gap Color list arrow** on the Stroke panel, then click **Gold** if it is not already selected.
8. Deselect, then compare your page to Figure 27.
9. Save your work, then close Custom Strokes.

You applied three different stroke styles to three lines. You also applied a color to the gaps in the stripe stroke style.

Incorporate GRIDIFY BEHAVIOR

What You'll Do

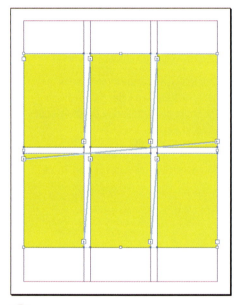

In this lesson, you will use keypad inputs to create multiple frames in grid formats in one move.

NEW Working with Gridify Behaviors

Grids are a common layout design. Whether you're doing a layout for a magazine, designing a high-school yearbook, or putting together a family photo album, you'll often find the need to place frames in a grid pattern.

With InDesign CS5, Adobe introduces both a new feature and a new word—**gridify**. Gridify means positioning frames into a grid pattern in just one move. You can make a variety of these moves using a combination of tools and keypad inputs. Adobe refers to these various moves as **gridify behaviors**.

You can use any of the frame creation tools, such as Rectangle, Polygon, and Type, to create a grid of frames in one move. Select the Rectangle tool, for example, then start dragging. While you're dragging, press the Right Arrow key three times, and InDesign will create three rectangle frames side by side. While you're still dragging, press the Up or Down arrows three times, and you'll get three more rows of frames. Figure 28 shows an example of this. Note that the frames are all equally spaced in the grid.

If you set up your document with column guides, InDesign will automatically use the gutter width specified for the column guides as the width for the columns of the grid you create. Having the grid align to the columns is especially useful when creating text frames. As an added bonus, the text frames you create with gridify behavior will automatically be threaded.

Gridify behaviors are powerful in conjunction with the place gun. When you've loaded multiple images into the place gun, you can use the same keyboard inputs to place all the loaded images in a grid layout. If you're into photography, this is a great way to make a quick contact sheet!

 **Executing a "Super" Step and Repeat**

Earlier in this book, you learned that you can "drag and drop" a copy of a frame.

You also learned to use the Step and Repeat command. Gridify behavior merges the two.

If you press and hold the [Alt](Win) or [option](Mac) key while dragging an object with the Selection tool, you can let go of the [Alt]/[option] key, then start using arrow keys to create a single row, a single column, or a grid of duplicates of the object. Voila! A "super" Step and Repeat.

Figure 28 *Frames in a grid*

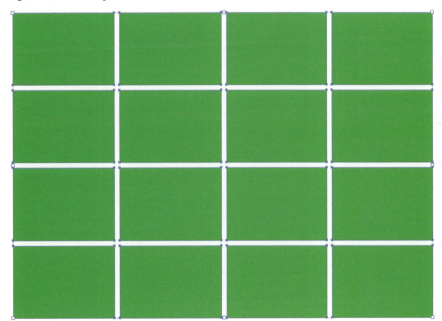

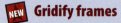 **Gridify frames**

1. Open ID 8-4.indd, then save it as **Gridify**.

2. Set the Fill color to Red.

3. Click the **Rectangle tool** 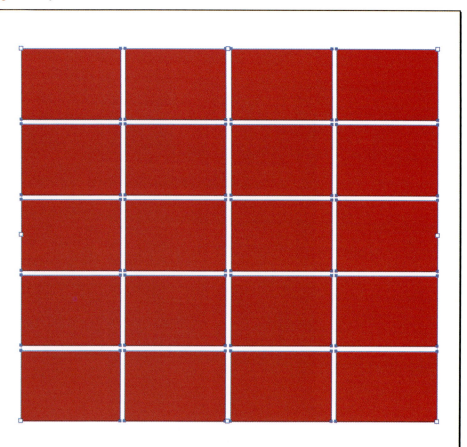, position the **crosshair pointer** near the upper-left corner of the page, then begin dragging.

4. While still dragging, press [→] three times.

5. While still dragging, press [↑] four times.

6. Continue dragging until the grid is the full width of the page, then release your mouse.

   Your grid should resemble Figure 29.

7. Save your work, then close the file.

You used gridify behavior to create a grid of rectangular frames.

Figure 29 *A grid of frames*

Exploring Effects and Advanced Techniques

Figure 30 *Placed images in a grid*

1. Open ID 8-5.indd, then save it as **Place Gun Gridified**.

2. Click **File**, click **Place**, navigate to your Chapter 8 Data Files, open the folder named Florence, select all, then click **Open**.

   The Place Gun indicates that 16 images are loaded.

3. Position the Place Gun near the upper-left corner of the document, then begin dragging.

4. While still dragging, press [→] three times, then press [↑] three times.

5. Continue dragging until the grid is the full width of the page, then release.

6. Set the fill on the selected frames to Black.

7. Deselect, then compare your screen to Figure 30.

8. Save your work, then close the file.

You used gridify behavior to place 16 images into a grid quickly.

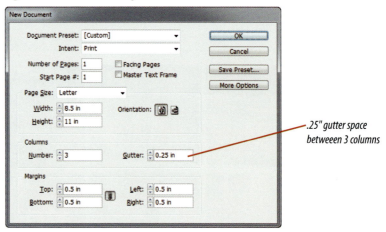 Gridify text frames

1. Click **File**, click **New**, then click **Document**.

2. Enter the settings shown in Figure 31, then click **OK**.

   Note that the number of columns is set to 3 and that .25" is set for the gutter width.

3. Click the **Type tool** T, , then position the cursor on the **left margin guide** near the upper-left corner of the page.

   A white arrow will appear beside the cursor when it is positioned on the left margin guide.

4. Start dragging right and down.

5. While still dragging, press [→] two times, then press [↑] one time.

6. Continue dragging to the right margin column, then release your mouse.

7. Fill the six frames with yellow.

8. Click **View**, point to **Extras**, then click **Show Text Threads**.

   As shown in Figure 32, the three text frames are aligned to the columns and they have been automatically threaded.

9. Save the file as **Gridify Text Frames**.

10. Close the file.

You used gridify behavior to create three threaded text frames aligned automatically to column guides.

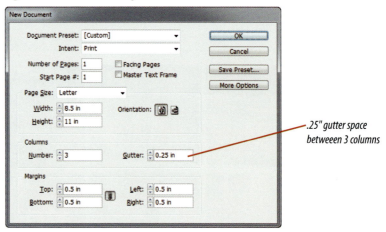

Figure 31 *New Document dialog box*

.25" gutter space betweeen 3 columns

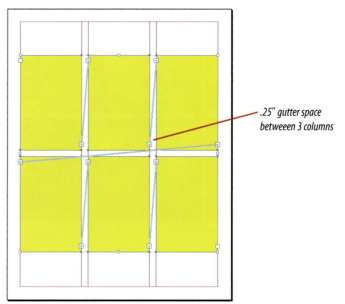

Figure 32 *Six frames threaded*

.25" gutter space betweeen 3 columns

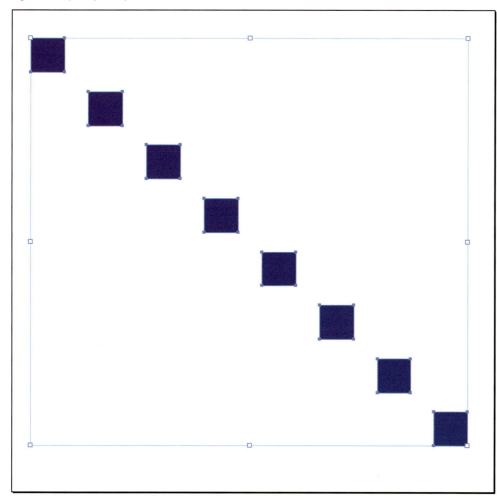

Figure 33 *Super step and repeat*

1. Open ID 8-6.indd, then save it as **Super Step and Repeat**.

2. Click the **Selection tool** , then select the blue square.

3. Press and hold **[Alt]**(Win) or **[option]**(Mac), then begin dragging to the right.

4. While still dragging right, release the **[Alt]/[option]** key, then press the [→] six times.

   With each press of the right arrowkey, a copy is added between the original and the dragged copy.

5. Drag down to the lower right corner, release your mouse, then compare your result to Figure 33.

6. Save your work, then close the file.

You used gridify behavior to do a "super" step and repeat.

Work with MULTIPLE PAGE SIZES

What You'll Do

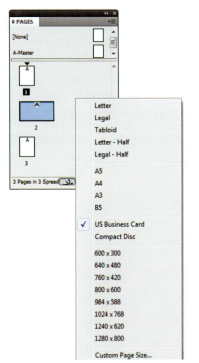

In this lesson, you will specify three different page sizes in a single document.

Working with Multiple Page Sizes

Imagine that you're a designer, and your boss tells you that you need to create layouts for a new client, including letterhead, a business card, and a 4" × 6" postcard. Each piece will contain the same elements: the client's logo, contact information, and a background pattern placed from Photoshop. What do you do? In earlier versions of InDesign, you would create three separate documents. You'd need to copy and paste the elements from one document to another. Then, if you needed to make any changes, you'd have to do so in all three documents.

Some designers thought up a work-around solution. In the above case, they'd create one really big document—say 18" × 18"—then they'd position all three elements in that large space. The problem with that is that the document size has no relationship to the artwork. You'd need to manually create and position crop marks for each of these three elements.

Why are we telling you how this *used to be* done? So that you can appreciate the brilliant upgrade to InDesign CS5 that allows you to work with multiple page sizes in a single document. Sticking with the same scenario, in InDesign CS5, you could start by creating a letter-sized document for the letterhead. Create the document with three pages. Then, for the business card, select one of the page thumbnails in the Pages panel and click the Edit page size button at the bottom of the panel, identified in Figure 34. When you do so, a sub-menu appears listing numerous standard-size choices which you can apply to the selected page. See Figure 35. If none of those is what you want, you can simply click Custom Page Size and enter specific page dimensions.

Working in this manner, you can change the size of any and every page in the Pages panel. Then, let's say you print the document—in this case, all three pages—with crop marks. InDesign will print unique crop sizes for each page to match the dimensions of that page. How cool is that? Figure 36 shows a PDF file of three different page sizes from one document, each with its own set of crops.

Working with Multiple Size Master Pages

The new multiple page size feature also works with master pages.

Exploring Effects and Advanced Techniques

Imagine that you customize all the stationery for the employees at your company. Each employee gets his or her own stationery, business cards, and business envelopes customized with their name. You could create a single document with three master pages—one for the letterhead, one for the business cards, and one for the envelopes. You could then apply the master to any page in the document. For example, a document page might be letter size, but if you drag your business card master to that page, it will be resized to 2" × 3.5". Think about it—in this scenario, you could keep customized stationery, business cards, and envelopes for every employee in a single document!

Figure 34 *Edit page size button*

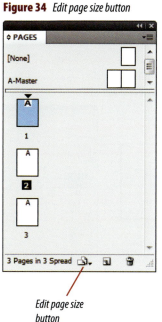

Edit page size button

Figure 35 *Edit page size menu*

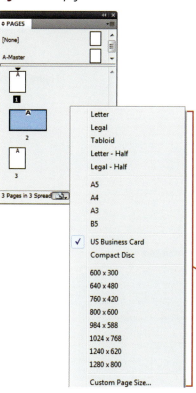

Pre-set page sizes

Figure 36 *Three page sizes output to PDF*

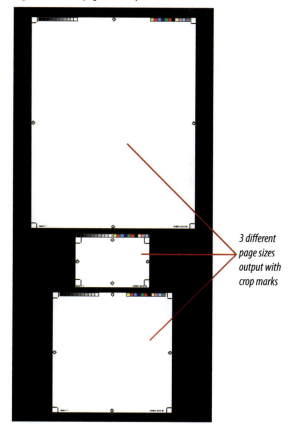

3 different page sizes output with crop marks

Create multiple page sizes in a single document

1. Click **File**, click **New**, then click **Document**.

2. Enter the values shown in Figure 37, then click **OK**.

   The document is a three-page letter-size document with a .5" margin.

3. Open the Pages panel, then double-click the **page 2 thumbnail**.

4. Click the **Edit page size button** at the bottom of the Pages panel, then click **US Business Card**.

   As shown in Figure 38, the page size changes to 2" × 3.5"—the standard size of a US business card. Note that the .5" margin, which worked for the letter size page, is impractically large for a business card layout.

5. With page 2 still targeted in the Pages panel, click **Layout** on the Application bar, click **Margins and Columns**, set the four Margins to .125, then click **OK**.

   The margin width is reduced.

6. Double-click **page 3** in the Pages panel.

   The change to the margins affected only page 2. Pages 1 and 3 retain the .5" margins.

7. Click the **Edit page size button** at the bottom of the Pages panel, then click **Custom Page Size**.

   The Custom Page Size dialog box opens.

8. Type **4 × 6 Postcard** in the Name text box, set the Width to 4, then set the Height to 6.

9. Click **Add**, then compare your dialog box to Figure 39.

   (continued)

Figure 37 *New dialog box*

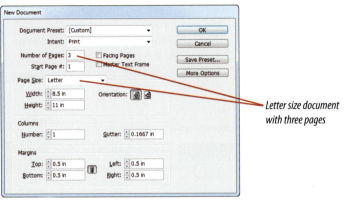

Letter size document with three pages

Figure 38 *US Business Card page size*

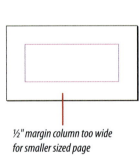
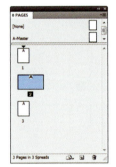

½" margin column too wide for smaller sized page

Figure 39 *Custom Page Size dialog box*

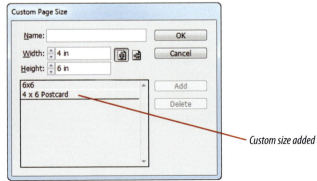

Custom size added

Exploring Effects and Advanced Techniques

Figure 40 *Tabloid master applied*

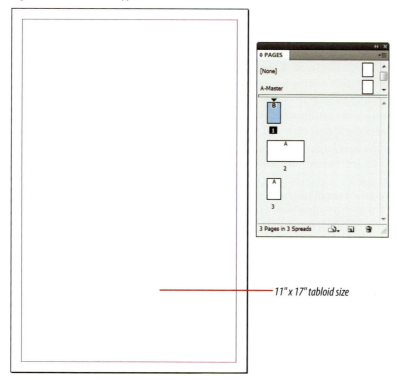

11" x 17" tabloid size

4 × 6 Postcard is added to the list. 4 × 6 Postcard will now be available in the Edit Page Size menu if you want to use it again.

10. Click **OK**, then save the file as **Multiple Page Sizes**.

You specified two different page sizes in a single document.

NEW Create a master page of a different size in a document

1. Click the **Pages panel options button** , click **New Master**, then click **OK** in the New Master dialog box.

   A new master page is created and targeted in the Pages panel. The new master is created at 8.5" × 11"—the document size specified when the document was created.

2. Click the **Edit Page Size button** at the bottom of the Pages panel, then click **Tabloid**.

   Only the B-Master changes to the Tabloid size of 11" × 17".

3. Drag the **B-Master icon** to the page 1 thumbnail in the Pages panel.

4. Double-click the **page 1 thumbnail**, then compare your screen to Figure 40.

   Page 1, originally letter-size, is now tabloid size.

5. Save your work, then close the document.

You created a new master page, then changed its page size. You then applied that master page to a document page, noting the change in size of the document page when the master was applied.

Work with Nested STYLES

What You'll Do

Great American Novels

1. **The Grapes of Wrath:** Regulari quam li existent Europan lingues. It va esser tam simplic quam Occidental in fact, it va esser Occidental. A un Angleso it va semblar un simplificat Angles, quam un skeptic amico dit me que Occidental.

2. **The Adventures of Huckleberry Finn:** Li Europan lingues es membres del sam familie. Lor separat existentie es un myth. Por scientie, musica, sport etc, litot Europa usa li sam vocabular. Li lingues differe solmen in li grammatica, li pronunciation e li plu commun vocabules.

3. **Tender is the Night:** It solmen va esser necessi far uniform grammatica, pronunciation e plu sommun paroles. Ma quande lingues coalesce, li grammatica del resultant lingue es plu simplic e regulari quam ti del coalescent lingues.

4. **To Kill a Mockingbird:** Ut wisi enim ad minim veniam, quis nostrud exercitation ulliam corper suscipit lobortis nisl ut aliquip exea commodo consequat. Duis autem veleum iriure dolor in hendrerit consequat.

▶ *In this lesson, you will use nested styles to format a block of text.*

Understanding Nested Styles

The term **nested styles** is based on real-world objects. If you like to cook, you've probably seen "nested" mixing bowls. These are mixing bowls—usually six—of different sizes. For storage, you set the smallest one inside the next largest one, then you set those two in the next largest one, until the five small bowls are "nested" in the largest bowl. This metaphor is also used for end tables, in which one small table slides underneath a taller table and both of those slide underneath an even taller table. These are called "nested" tables.

In InDesign, nested styles are paragraph styles that contain two or more character styles. In other words, two or more character styles are "nested" within the paragraph style.

In Figure 41, each paragraph contains elements that were formatted with character styles. The numbers were formatted with a character style named Red Number, and the blue names were formatted with a character style named Artist Name.

Without nested styles, you would need to apply the character styles one at a time. For example, in the first paragraph, you'd need to select the number 1 and the period that follows it, then apply the Red Number character style. Then, you'd select "Pablo Picasso:" and apply the Artist Name

Exploring Effects and Advanced Techniques

character style. Then you'd need to do the same for the next paragraphs. Imagine if your document profiled 100 artists!

With nested styles, you would format the entire block of text with a single paragraph style. That paragraph style would contain both the Red Number and the Artist Name character styles. They would be "nested" within the paragraph style and formatted in such a way that the first would format the number and the period and the second would format the artist's name. Then, because it's a paragraph style, the formatting would be reapplied after every paragraph break.

Applying Nested Styles

Nested styles are useful in specific situations, especially for blocks of text that contain repeating formatting at the beginning of each paragraph. Figure 42 shows how nested styles were applied to the text in Figure 41.

In the Nested Styles section, two character styles were loaded—Red Number and Artist Name. The values entered for Red Number translate as follows: the Red Number character style will be applied to each paragraph through the first (1) period and the Artist Name character style will be applied to each paragraph through the first em space.

If you regard the text in Figure 41 with this in mind, you see that the Red Number character is indeed applied up to and including the first period. An em space has been inserted after each artist's name, and the Artist Name character style has indeed been applied up to that em space. If you wanted, you could also have, instead, specified that the character style be applied up to and including the colon after each artist's name. They are just two different ways of indicating where you want the formatting to stop.

Figure 41 *Viewing a document with multiple character styles*

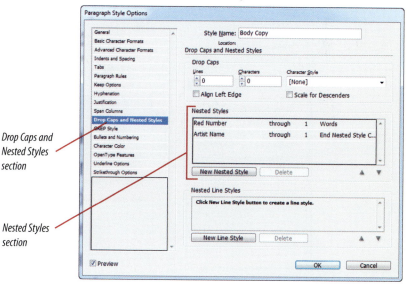

Red Number character style

Artist Name character style

Figure 42 *Paragraph Style Options dialog box*

Drop Caps and Nested Styles section

Nested Styles section

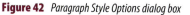

Using the End Nested Style Here Command

Clearly, implementing nested styles requires a bit of forethought when formatting paragraphs. You must have characters that you can use to identify where a nested style ends. Periods, colons, and em or en spaces can be entered in the paragraph style to mark where a nested style should end.

But what if your layout doesn't call for periods, colons, or em spaces? No problem. Simply insert a special character using the End Nested Style Here command. This command is located within the Insert Special Character command on the Type menu—the same list that you use to insert automatic page numbers on master pages or em dashes in body copy.

When you format the nested style in the Paragraph Style dialog box, you can specify that the nested style ends at the End Nested Style Here insertion. You do this by choosing End Nested Style Character in the Nested Styles section of the Paragraph Style Options dialog box, as shown in Figure 43.

Figure 43 *Formatting a nested style using the End Nested Style Character command*

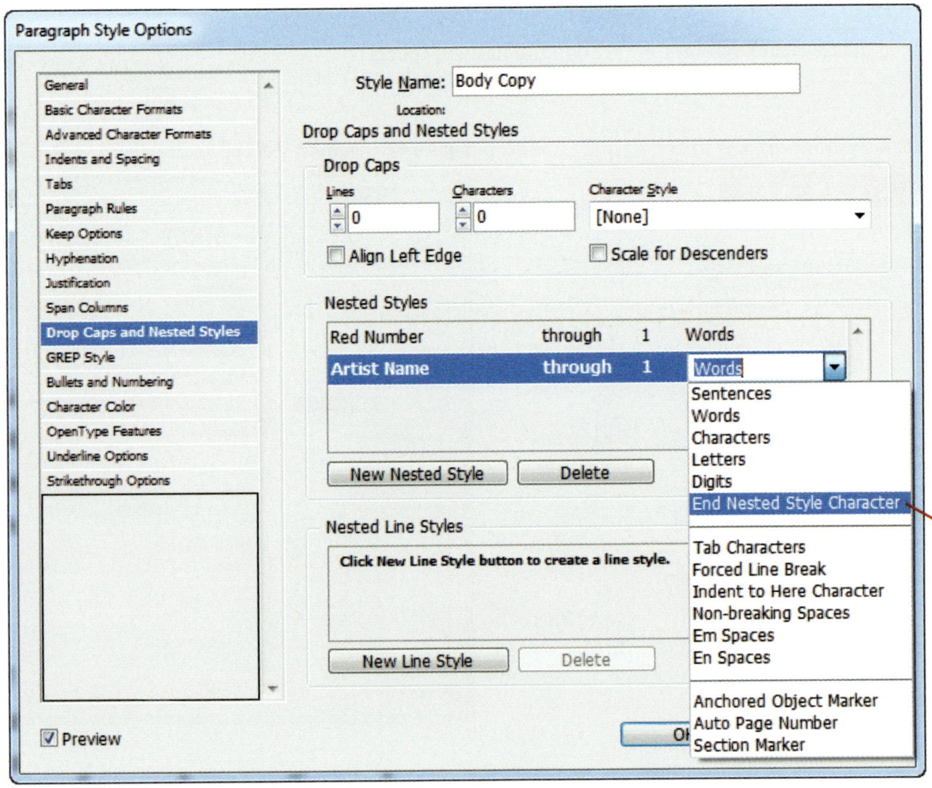

Specifies where Artist Name style will end

Figure 44 *Viewing two character styles applied to text*

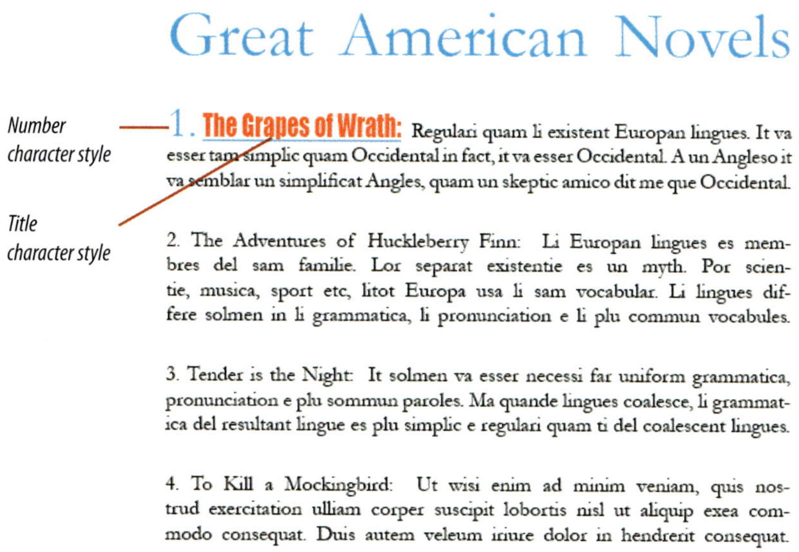

Great American Novels

Number
character style

1. **The Grapes of Wrath:** Regulari quam li existent Europan lingues. It va esser tam simplic quam Occidental in fact, it va esser Occidental. A un Angleso it va semblar un simplificat Angles, quam un skeptic amico dit me que Occidental.

Title
character style

2. The Adventures of Huckleberry Finn: Li Europan lingues es membres del sam familie. Lor separat existentie es un myth. Por scientie, musica, sport etc, litot Europa usa li sam vocabular. Li lingues differe solmen in li grammatica, li pronunciation e li plu commun vocabules.

3. Tender is the Night: It solmen va esser necessi far uniform grammatica, pronunciation e plu sommun paroles. Ma quande lingues coalesce, li grammatica del resultant lingue es plu simplic e regulari quam ti del coalescent lingues.

4. To Kill a Mockingbird: Ut wisi enim ad minim veniam, quis nostrud exercitation ulliam corper suscipit lobortis nisl ut aliquip exea commodo consequat. Duis autem veleum iriure dolor in hendrerit consequat.

Using GREP Styles

A **GREP style** is a style that is applied to patterns inside text based on code. The pattern can be as simple as a two-digit number or an e-mail address or it can be complex. You define a GREP style in the GREP Style section of the New Paragraph Style dialog box or the Paragraph Style Options dialog box when you create or modify a paragraph style. For example, if you want InDesign to search your document for all text inside quotation marks, and then change it to italics, you would first need to define the GREP expression. Click GREP Style in the New Paragraph Style dialog box, then click the New GREP Style button. Click the "To Text" box, then click the Special characters for search list arrow. Next, choose Quotation Marks, then the type of quotation mark, such as Double Left Quotation Mark. Continue to define the GREP expression using the available menu commands, then click OK. All text inside quotation marks will be italicized when you apply the paragraph style to the text. You can also search and change GREP expressions using the Find/Change dialog box. There is a GREP tab in the Find/Change dialog box with all of the same options on the Special characters for search menu in the New Paragraph Style dialog box.

Apply character styles using the Character Styles panel

1. Open ID 8-7.indd, then save it as **Nested Styles**.

2. Open the Paragraph Styles panel, click the **Type tool** T, , select all the black text, then note the paragraph style highlighted on the Paragraph Styles panel.

   All of the black text has the Body Copy paragraph style applied to it.

3. Deselect all, select the number 1 and the period that follows it, then click **Number** on the Character Styles panel.

4. Select The Grapes of Wrath and the colon that follows it, then click **Title** on the Character Styles panel.

5. Deselect, then compare your page to Figure 44.

   In order to format the remainder of the list, you would need to select each number and apply the Number character style, then select each title and apply the Title character style.

6. Click **File** on the Application bar, click **Revert**, then click **Yes** (Win) or **Revert** (Mac) in the dialog box that follows.

You used the Character Styles panel for applying character styles to text in a document.

Apply nested styles

1. Click the **Type tool** ⊤ , click to the immediate right of the colon after the word Wrath, click **Type** on the Application bar, point to **Insert Special Character**, point to **Other**, then click **End Nested Style Here**.

TIP Enlarge your document view to see it better if needed.

The special character is invisible, so you won't see any change to the text.

2. Using the same method, insert the End Nested Style Here special character after the colons in items 2–4.

3. Double-click **Body Copy** on the Paragraph Styles panel, then click the **Preview check box** in the bottom-left corner.

4. Click **Drop Caps and Nested Styles** on the left, then click the **New Nested Style button**.

5. Click **[None]** in the Nested Styles section to highlight it, click the **[None] list arrow**, then click **Number**.

6. Click **Words**, then type a **period (.)** to replace Words, so that your dialog box resembles Figure 45.

The Number character style will be applied through the first period in each entry.

TIP If necessary, move the dialog box to the side so that you can see the format changes as they are applied to the text.

(continued)

Figure 45 *Formatting a nested style*

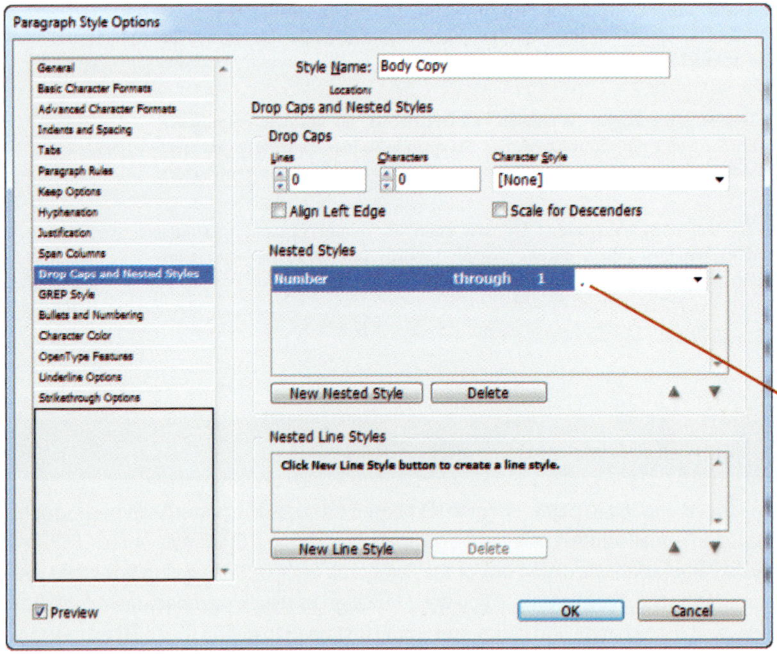

Number character style will be applied through the first period

Exploring Effects and Advanced Techniques

Figure 46 *Formatting a nested style through to the first colon*

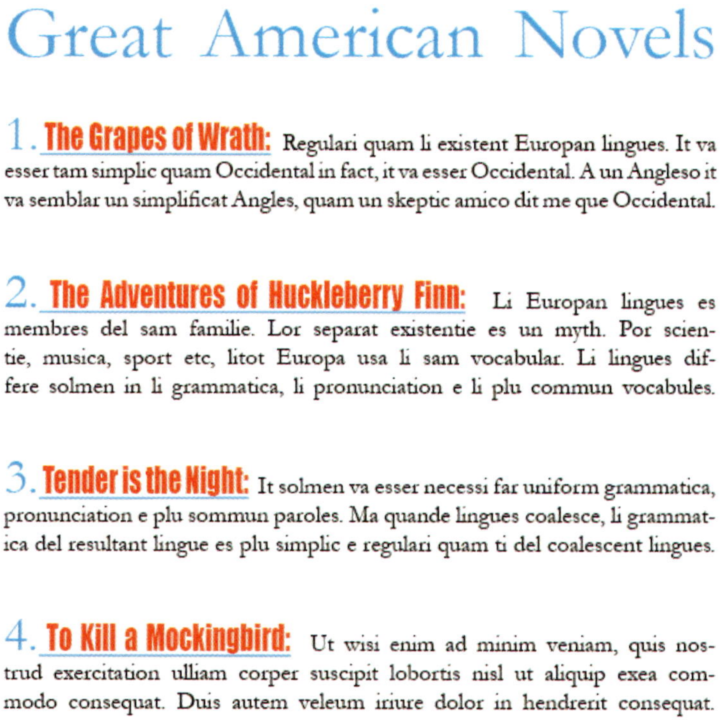

Great American Novels

1. The Grapes of Wrath: Regulari quam li existent Europan lingues. It va
esser tam simplic quam Occidental in fact, it va esser Occidental. A un Angleso it
va semblar un simplificat Angles, quam un skeptic amico dit me que Occidental.

2. The Adventures of Huckleberry Finn: Li Europan lingues es
membres del sam familie. Lor separat existentie es un myth. Por scientie, musica, sport etc, litot Europa usa li sam vocabular. Li lingues differe solmen in li grammatica, li pronunciation e li plu commun vocabules.

3. Tender is the Night: It solmen va esser necessi far uniform grammatica,
pronunciation e plu sommun paroles. Ma quande lingues coalesce, li grammatica del resultant lingue es plu simplic e regulari quam ti del coalescent lingues.

4. To Kill a Mockingbird: Ut wisi enim ad minim veniam, quis nos-
trud exercitation ulliam corper suscipit lobortis nisl ut aliquip exea commodo consequat. Duis autem veleum iriure dolor in hendrerit consequat.

7. Click **New Nested Style**, click the **[None] list arrow**, then click **Title**.

8. Click the word **Words** once, then note the format changes to the text on the page.

TIP The Title character style is applied to the first word only because the nested style specifies to do so.

9. Click the **Words list arrow**, click **End Nested Style Character**, press **[Enter]** (Win) or **[return]** (Mac) to execute the change, then click **OK**.

   As shown in Figure 46, the Title character style is applied to all the words up to the End Nested Style Character insertion.

10. Save your work, then close Nested Styles.

You applied two character styles to four paragraphs simultaneously by using nested styles.

Apply Live
CORNER EFFECTS

What You'll Do

CORNIGLIA
thursday august 11

In this lesson, you'll use Live Corner Effects to change the appearance of corners on frames.

Applying Live Corner Effects

As noted earlier, InDesign is a frame-based application. Everything goes in a frame—images, text, and even rules. From a design perspective, all of those rectangular frames everywhere can make your layouts look "boxy."

Live Corner Effects alleviate this issue by offering an interactive interface to apply different corner styles to a frame. Figure 47 shows the five styles available with Live Corner Effects.

What's great about the Live Corner Effects utility is that it allows you to click and drag to specify the extent of an effect. For example, with Round Corners, you click and drag to increase the radius of the corner. You can also apply an effect to a single corner, and you can apply multiple effects to a single frame.

To use the Live Corner Effects utility, select a frame with the Selection Tool. A yellow square appears on the frame, as shown in Figure 48. Click the yellow square to activate Live Corner Effects. Four yellow diamonds appear at each corner. If you click and drag any one of

the diamonds, round corners will be applied to all four corners, as shown in Figure 49. If you press [Shift] and click and drag a corner, only that corner will be affected. The ability to apply different effects to different corners offers the opportunity to create interesting frame shapes, as shown in Figure 50.

Round Corners is the default effect that is applied when you first drag the yellow diamond. To access the other effects shown in Figure 47, press and hold [Alt](Win) or [option](Mac), then click one of the diamonds repeatedly to cycle through the effects. When you do so, all the corners with

Figure 47 *Viewing corner effects*

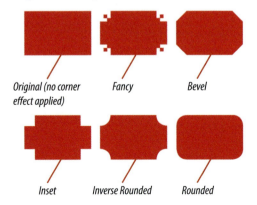

Original (no corner effect applied)   Fancy   Bevel

Inset   Inverse Rounded   Rounded

Exploring Effects and Advanced Techniques

effects applied will take on the current style. To cycle through effects on only one corner of the frame, press and hold [Shift][Alt] (Win) or [Shift][option](Mac), then click the diamond repeatedly. Figure 51 shows the Inset effect applied to the left side of the frame, the Fancy effect applied to the right and an image placed into the frame.

QUICK TIP

As an alternative to using Live Corner Effects, you can use the Corner Options dialog box in the Object menu.

Figure 48 *Click the yellow square to activate Live Corner Effects*

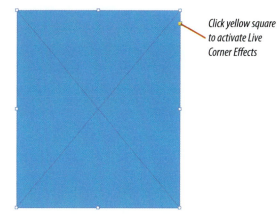

Click yellow square to activate Live Corner Effects

Figure 49 *Applying the same effect to four corners*

Figure 50 *Applying one effect to different degrees to two corners*

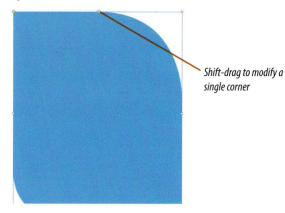

Shift-drag to modify a single corner

Figure 51 *Two effects applied and an image placed into the frame*

Fancy corner effect

Inset corner effect

Apply Round Corners with Live Corner Effects

1. Open ID 8-8.indd, then save it as **Advanced Techniques**.

2. On page 1, click the **Selection tool** , select the green frame behind the title CORNIGLIA, then click the **yellow square** on the frame.

   As shown in Figure 52, four yellow diamonds appear at the corners of the frame.

3. Click and drag the **top-left diamond** straight down until the frame resembles Figure 53.

   When you click and drag a diamond, all four corners are transformed simultaneously.

   (continued)

Figure 52 *Four Live Corner Effects diamonds*

Figure 53 *Four rounded corners*

Dragging one diamond affects all four corners

Figure 54 *Modifying only two corners*

Press [Shift] and drag

Figure 55 *Round corners on page 1*

4. Press and hold [Shift], then drag the **lower-left corner diamond** straight down.

   Pressing and holding shift when dragging a diamond affects only that corner.

5. Press and hold [Shift], then drag the **upper-right corner diamond** straight up.

   Your frame should resemble Figure 54.

6. Using the same methodology, apply Live Corner Effects so that the bottom of your page 1 resembles Figure 55.

(continued)

7. Using the same methodology, apply Live Corner Effects so that your page 2 resembles Figure 56.

8. Apply Live Corner Effects so that your page 3 resembles Figure 57.

9. Save your work.

You created round corners on frames using Live Corner Effects.

 **Cycle through Live Corner Effects**

1. Verify that you are on page 3, select the large image with the Selection tool, then click the **yellow square**.

2. Click and drag the **top-right diamond** to the left until the pop-up measurement box reads 1" as shown in Figure 58.

(continued)

Figure 56 *Round corners on page 2*

Figure 57 *Round corners on page 3*

Figure 58 *Modifying the Live Corner Effect*

Pop-up measurement box

Exploring Effects and Advanced Techniques

Figure 59 *Fancy corner effects on all four corners*

3. Press and hold **[Alt]**(Win) or **[Option]**(Mac), then click **any of the yellow diamonds** one time.

   As shown in Figure 59, all four corners of the frame change to the Fancy corner effect.

4. Press and hold **[Alt]**(Win) or **[Option]**(Mac), then click **any of the yellow diamonds** two times slowly.

5. Press and hold **[Shift]**[Alt](Win) or **[Shift]** [option](Mac), click the **top-left yellow diamond** one time, the click the **bottom-left diamond** one time.

   Your screen should resemble Figure 60.

6. Press and hold **[Alt]**(Win) or **[option]**(Mac), then click **any of the yellow diamonds**.

   All four corners are restored to right angles because you have cycled through all of the corner effects.

7. Save the file.

You cycled through corner effects, applying them to all four corners and to individual corners.

Figure 60 *Two different Live Corner Effects*

Work with Effects
AND OBJECT STYLES

What You'll Do

In this lesson, you'll apply various effects to type and objects, and you'll use the Object Styles panel and the New Object Style dialog box to format and apply object styles to type and frames.

Understanding Effects

The Effects dialog box, shown in Figure 61, offers a number of effects that you can apply to objects to make your layouts more visually interesting. All of the available effects are listed on the left side of the dialog box, and settings for each effect become available on the right side of the dialog box when you click the name of the effect on the left. You can apply multiple effects to a single object. Figure 62 shows text with a bevel and emboss effect, a pink drop shadow and a pink outer glow.

InDesign effects, such as glows, shadows, bevels, embosses, and feathers, are all **non-destructive**, which means that they are not necessarily permanent. At any time, you can apply, remove, or modify them. In other words, they don't permanently alter or "destroy" the object to which they're applied.

Figure 61 *Effects dialog box*

List of effects

Exploring Effects and Advanced Techniques

When you select a frame, the Effects panel lists information about any effects applied to the frame or to contents of the frame. When you have applied effects, the *fx* icon appears beside the word Object in the panel, as shown in Figure 63. The *fx* icon also appears at the bottom of the panel. If you click the *fx* icon at the bottom a menu will appear

showing the effects that have been applied. See Figure 64.

You apply an effect to an object or text by first selecting the frame or text frame with the Selection tool, then clicking the Effects command in the Object menu. This opens the Effects dialog box, where all effects are

applied and modified. Once you have applied effects, you can double-click the *fx* icon in the Effects panel to reopen the Effects dialog box if you want to modify or remove effects. This is an alternative to using the menu command. To remove an effect, simply uncheck the effect on the left side of the dialog box.

Figure 62 *Text with three effects applied*

effects

Figure 63 *Effects panel*

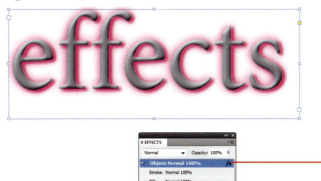

Indicates effects are applied

Figure 64 *Applied effects listed in Effects menu*

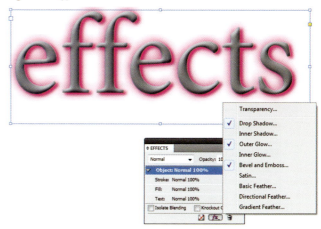

Copying Effects Between Objects

Use the *fx* icon in the Effects panel to copy effects between objects. Select any object that has an effect applied to it, then drag the *fx* icon to another object in the document. The effects applied to the first object will be applied to the second. See Figures 65 and 66.

Note that when you copy effects from one object to another, no relationship is created between the objects. If you modify the effects on one object, the other object won't be affected by the change.

Working with Object Styles

A lot of the work you do in InDesign is essentially formatting. As you learned in Chapter 2, you can save all of the formatting that you do to text as a Character Style or a Paragraph Style, then use those styles to format other text.

Object styles follow the same logic. They're styles saved for formatting. Let's say that you want to put a 1.5" black stroke and a white drop shadow effect on every picture frame in a document. It would be highly illogical to apply that formatting repeatedly to every picture frame. Not only would it be repetitive, but think about what would happen if tomorrow you wanted to make a change. Instead, save the formatting as an object style, then apply it to other objects. Any modification you make to the object style will update automatically to any object that uses the object style.

The New Object Style dialog box, shown in Figure 67, allows you to specify a variety of formatting choices for graphics frames and text frames. At first glance—wow—there's a lot of information there. But you'll find that the New Object Style dialog box is

straightforward, intuitive, and easy to incorporate into your day-to-day work with InDesign.

You can create a new object style from scratch in the New Object Style dialog box. First, you create and name a new style. Then, you specify formats for that style using the categories listed on the left.

You're likely to find that a more practical way to make new object styles is to first format an object on the page then save that formatting as an object style. This method allows you to incorporate some trial and error while you're formatting the object on the page. Once you've got it where you want it, click the Object Style panel options button, then click New Object Style. When the dialog box opens, all of the formatting you applied to the object will be activated in the dialog box,

Figure 65 *Dragging the fx icon*

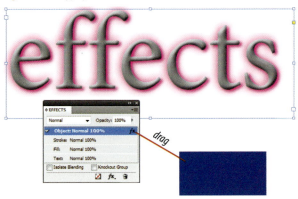

Figure 66 *Effects copied to the blue-filled frame*

ready to be saved as a style and applied to other objects.

Applying and Editing Object Styles

Once you've created an object style, the named style is listed on the Object Styles panel, as shown in Figure 68. Select an object on the page, such as a text frame, graphics frame, or shape that you created with the Pen tool, then click the object style on the panel that you want to use. As shown in Figure 69, all of the formatting that is specified as the style will be applied to the selected object.

The power of object styles is not limited simply to applying them to objects. In many ways, they are even more powerful when you want to edit effects. Editing object styles couldn't be easier. Simply double-click the style that you want to edit on the Object Styles panel. This will open the New Object Style dialog box, where you can make as many changes to the style as you like. It's when you click that OK button that the magic happens. With that one click, every object in your document that uses that style will update to reflect the changes you made.

Figure 67 *New Object Style dialog box*

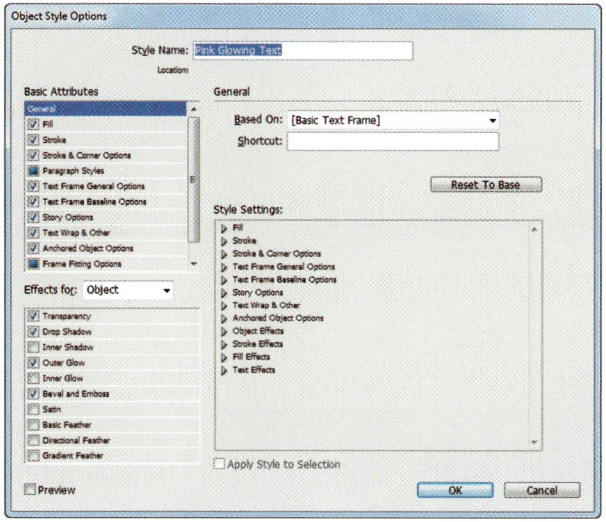

Figure 68 *Object Styles panel*

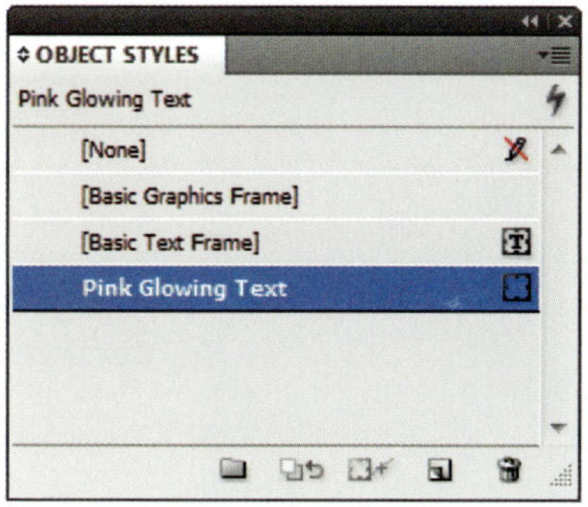

Figure 69 *Object style applied to different text*

Pink Glowing Text
style applied

Apply and copy an Inner Shadow effect

1. Navigate to page 1, click the **Selection tool** , then select the large image.

2. Click **Object** on the Application bar, point to **Effects**, then click **Inner Shadow**.

   The Effects dialog box opens with Inner Shadow checked in the box on the left and Inner Shadow settings on the right.

   TIP Move the dialog box to see as much of the selected image as possible.

3. Enter the settings shown in Figure 70, then click **OK**.

   Your result should resemble Figure 71.

   (continued)

Figure 70 *Effects dialog box with settings for an Inner Shadow*

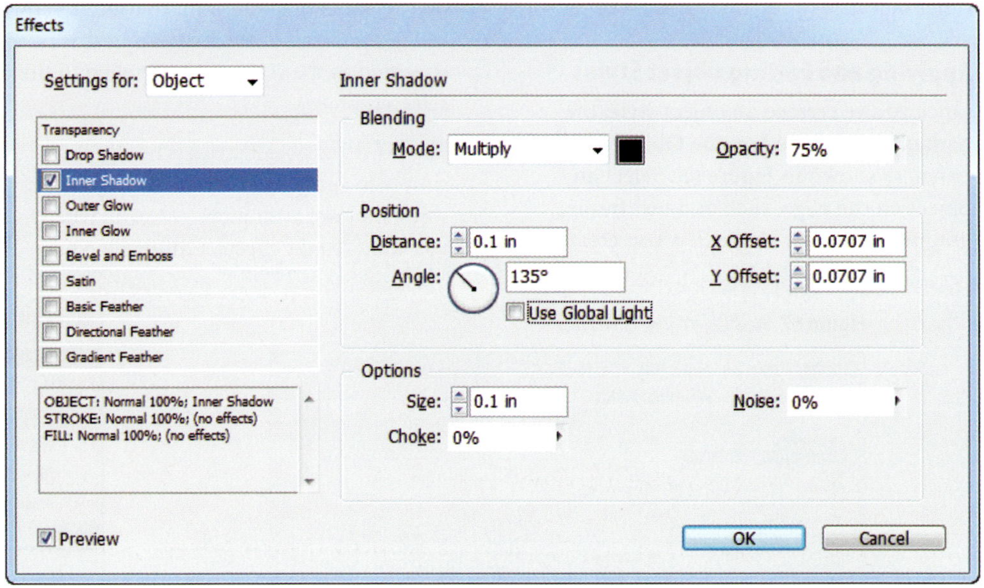

Figure 71 *Inner Shadow effect applied*

Inner shadow effect

Exploring Effects and Advanced Techniques

Figure 72 *Effects panel with Inner Shadow listed as applied*

Figure 73 *Copying the effect to the smaller image*

Figure 74 *Six frames with inner shadow effects*

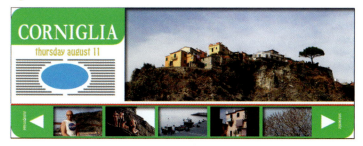

4. With the large image still selected, open the Effects panel, then click the *fx* **button** *fx.* at the bottom of the panel.

   As shown in Figure 72, the menu lists the Inner Shadow effect as having been applied to the image.

5. Select the five small frames at the bottom of the layout, then set the stroke color to none.

6. Select the large image, then drag the *fx* **icon** *fx.* from the Effects panel to the leftmost small frame, as illustrated in Figure 73.

   The Inner Shadow effect is applied to the small frame. The large frame remains selected.

7. Drag the *fx* **icon** *fx.* to the other four small frames, deselect all, then compare your result to Figure 74.

8. Save your work.

You applied an Inner Shadow effect to a frame with a placed graphic, then copied the effect to five other frames.

Apply a Bevel and Emboss and a Drop Shadow effect

1. Use the Selection Tool ▶ to select the CORNIGLIA text frame.

2. Click **Object** on the Application bar, point to **Effects**, then click **Bevel and Emboss**.

3. Enter the settings shown in Figure 75, but don't click OK when you're done.

(Steps are continued on page 46)

Figure 75 *Settings for a Bevel and Emboss effect*

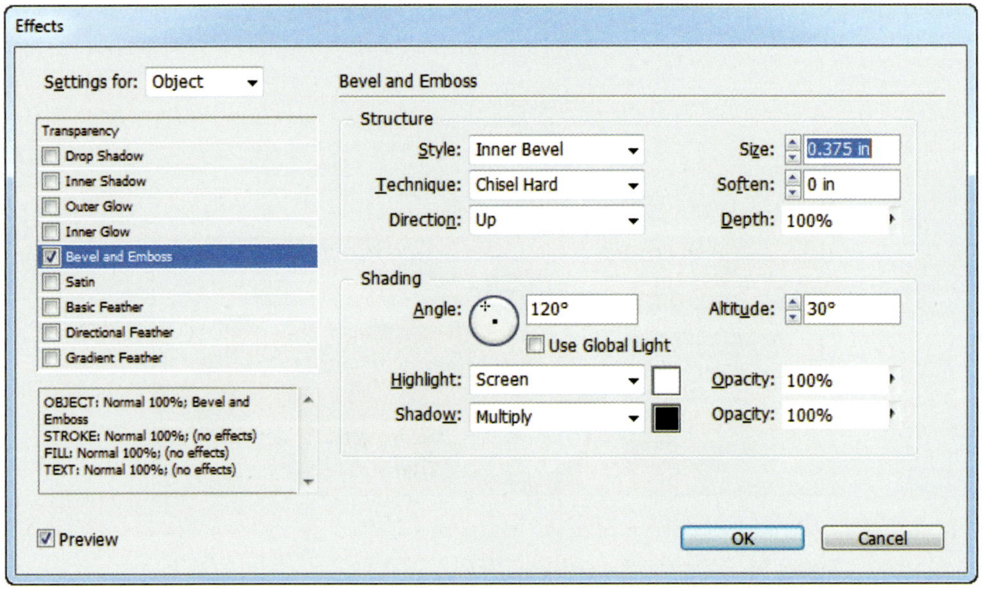

Understanding Blending Modes

By default, if you overlap one object with another, the bottom object will be hidden behind the top object where they overlap. One option that you have to manipulate this relationship is to apply a blending mode to the top object. **Blending modes** allow you to create different transparency and color effects where two or more objects overlap.

The Effects panel lists 15 blending modes. Some blending modes, such as Screen, are very practical and can be used to produce common effects. Others, such as Difference, produce more extreme effects and are therefore not used as often.

Blending modes work by comparing the colors in the overlapping graphics and then running those colors through a mathematical algorithm to produce an effect. They are almost always used on an experimental basis. Just try out different effects until you find one that works well with the objects you are blending.

Of the 15 blending modes, one in particular deserves special attention. **Multiply** is a practical and useful blending mode, so be sure to familiarize yourself with it. When Multiply is applied to an object, the object becomes transparent but retains its color. You can think of the effect as that of overlapping colors drawn by magic markers. Two important features to memorize about the Multiply blending mode are that any white areas of a graphic become transparent and any black areas remain black.

4. Click the words Drop Shadow on the left side of the dialog box, then enter the settings shown in Figure 76.

5. Click **OK**, then compare your text to Figure 77.

6. Save your work.

You applied two effects to text: a Bevel and Emboss and a Drop Shadow.

Figure 76 *Settings for a Drop Shadow*

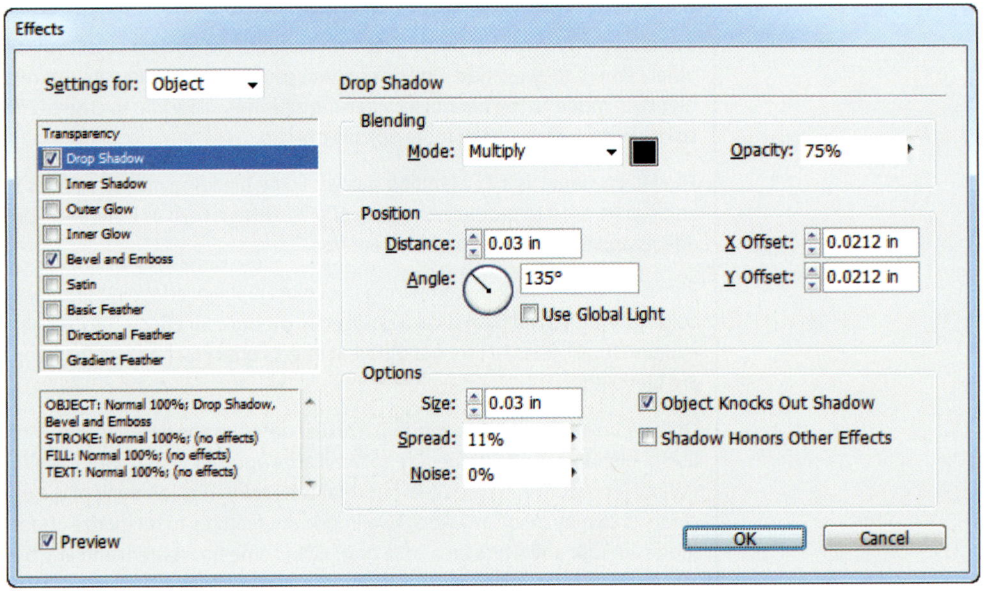

Effects

Settings for: Object ▼

Drop Shadow

Transparency
- ☑ Drop Shadow
- ☐ Inner Shadow
- ☐ Outer Glow
- ☐ Inner Glow
- ☑ Bevel and Emboss
- ☐ Satin
- ☐ Basic Feather
- ☐ Directional Feather
- ☐ Gradient Feather

OBJECT: Normal 100%; Drop Shadow, Bevel and Emboss
STROKE: Normal 100%; (no effects)
FILL: Normal 100%; (no effects)
TEXT: Normal 100%; (no effects)

Blending
Mode: Multiply ▼ ■ Opacity: 75% ▸

Position
Distance: 0.03 in   X Offset: 0.0212 in
Angle: 135°   Y Offset: 0.0212 in
☐ Use Global Light

Options
Size: 0.03 in   ☑ Object Knocks Out Shadow
Spread: 11% ▸   ☐ Shadow Honors Other Effects
Noise: 0% ▸

☑ Preview   OK   Cancel

Figure 77 *Text with two effects applied*

Understanding Global Light

Global Light is a setting that applies a uniform lighting angle to three of InDesign's effects that deal with shadows and transparency. They include Drop Shadow, Inner Shadow, and Bevel and Emboss. When you apply one of these effects to an InDesign object, you will see the Use Global Light check box in the corresponding dialog box. When checked, InDesign applies the global light settings defined in the Global Light dialog box. To set global lighting, click the Effects panel options button, then click Global Light. You can experiment with different values in the Angle and Altitude check boxes and preview them before you close the dialog box.

Create and apply an object style

1. Verify that the CORNIGLIA text frame is selected.

2. Click **Window**, point to **Styles**, then click **Object Styles**.

3. Click the **Object Styles panel options button** ▾≡ , then click **New Object Style**.

   The New Object Style dialog box opens.

4. Type **Bevel and Shadow** in the Style Name text box, then note in the lower-left section that the Bevel and Emboss and Drop Shadow effects are checked.

5. Uncheck all of the attributes in the General section.

   Your dialog box should resemble Figure 78. You will use this object style to apply the bevel and emboss and the drop shadow to other objects. The attributes in the General section include basic attributes of the CORNIGLIA text, such as the fill color, stroke color, and text wrap. You did not want to save these attributes with this object style, so you unchecked them.

   (continued)

Figure 78 *Object Styles dialog box*

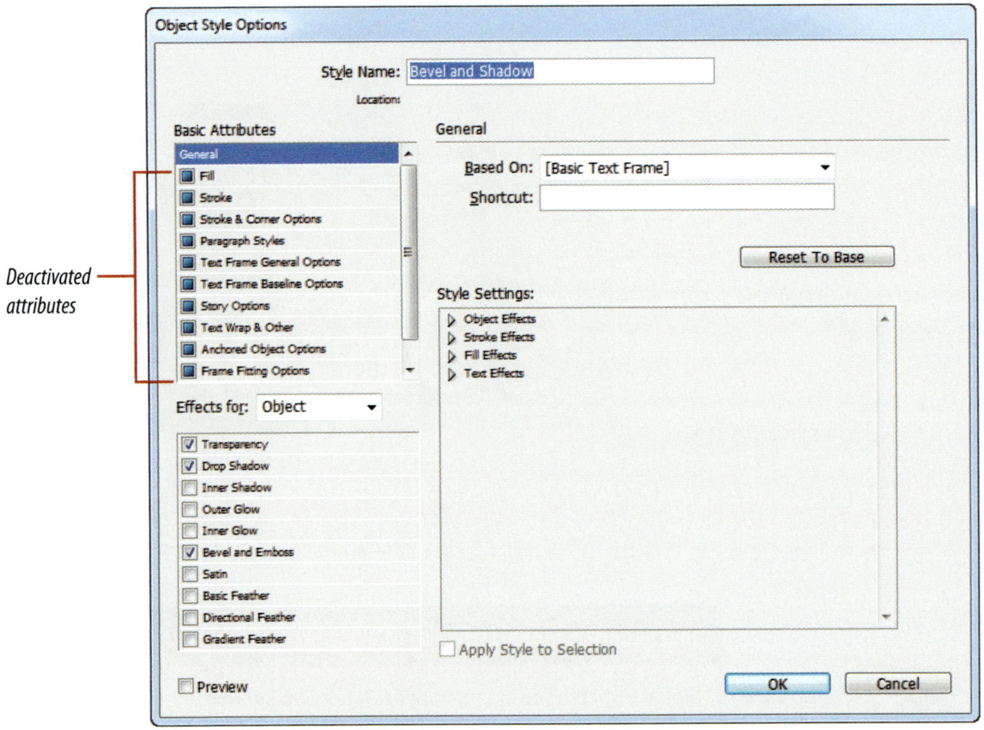

Deactivated attributes

Applying Transparency to Objects

When you manipulate an object's transparency, you are not limited to changing the opacity of the entire object. In fact, you can change the opacity of just the fill, just the stroke, or just the text. When you select the object that you want to modify, click the expand arrow next to Object on the Effects panel, then click Fill, Stroke or Text. For example, if you click Stroke, then change the opacity to 50%, only the stroke of the selected object will be 50% transparent. The object's fill will remain unchanged. You can also achieve the same results by selecting an object, clicking the Apply Effect to Object button on the Control panel, then clicking Fill, Stroke or Text. When Object is selected, both the fill and the stroke of the selected object will change.

Exploring Effects and Advanced Techniques

Figure 79 *New style in the panel*

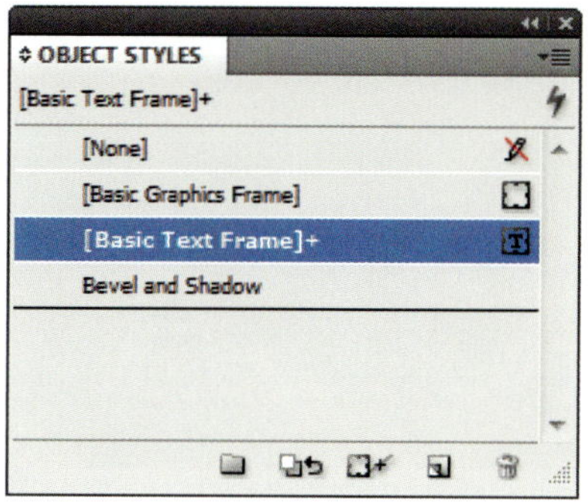

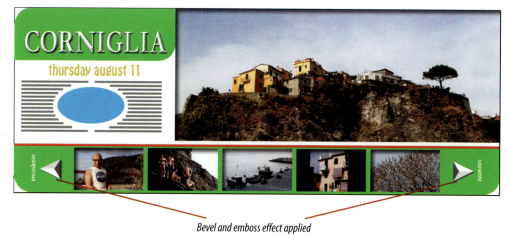

Figure 80 *Two arrows with effects*

Bevel and emboss effect applied

6. Click **OK**.

   As shown in Figure 79, the Bevel and Shadow object style is listed in the Object Styles panel.

7. Use the Selection Tool ▶ to select the white triangle to the left of the small images, then click Bevel and Shadow in the Object Styles panel.

   The Bevel and Shadow object style is applied to the triangle.

8. Apply the Bevel and Shadow object style to the other triangle, then compare your layout to Figure 80.

9. Apply the Bevel and Shadow object style to the two other headlines and four other triangles in the layout.

10. Save the file.

You selected text with two effects applied, then created a new object style. You then applied the object style to other objects in the layout.

Remove an object style from an object

1. Navigate to page 3, then select the MANAROLA headline with the bevel and shadow object style.

2. Note the *fx* icon *fx.* beside the highlighted Object line in the Effects panel.

3. Drag the *fx* icon *fx.* to the trash can icon at the bottom of the Effects panel.

   Both effects are removed, as shown in Figure 81.

4. Save the file.

You removed effects from text.

Apply feathering effects

1. Select the blue oval on page 1.

2. Click **Object** on the Application bar, point to **Effects**, then click **Basic Feather**.

3. Enter the settings shown in Figure 82, then click **OK**.

4. Click **File**, click **Place**, navigate to the Photography folder where you save your Chapter 8 Data Files, then choose the file named **Girls**.

(continued)

Figure 81 *Text with effects removed*

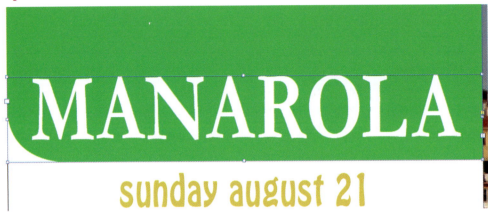

Figure 82 *Settings for a Basic Feather effect*

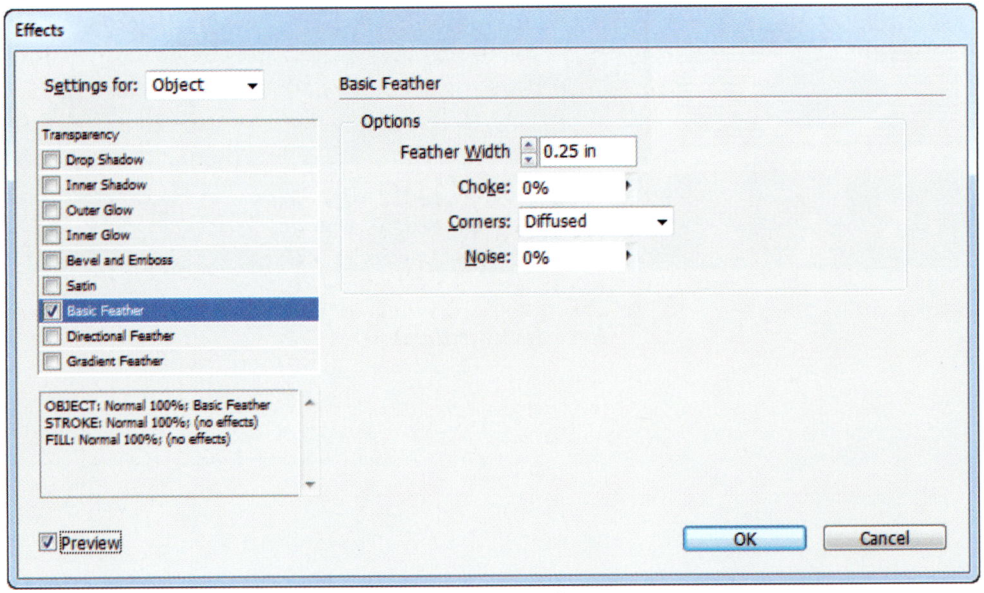

Figure 83 *Image placed in a feathered frame*

5. Fit the image so that your frame resembles Figure 83.

    When you place an image into a frame with a feather effect, the image takes on the effect.

6. Navigate to page 2, select the large image on the page, then click the **Gradient Feather tool** on the Tools panel.

    The Gradient Feather tool is a freehand effect tool. The feather is applied as an effect and can be modified or removed like any other effect.

    (continued)

Managing Color with Effects and Transparent Objects

When you overlap objects, InDesign allows you to create transparency effects, as though you are seeing one object through another. For example, if you overlap a blue circle with a yellow circle with a transparency effect, the overlapped area will appear green. Transparency also comes into play when you apply effects to objects. For example, when you apply a drop shadow or a glow to an object, those effects are transparent by definition.

When you are viewing transparency effects on your monitor, everything looks great. It's when you print a document that unexpected colors can result from transparency effects.

From the output perspective, it helps to think of overlapping areas as separate shapes with their own fills. To use the above example, think of the green overlapped area not as a section of the blue object overlapped by the yellow object but as a separate object with a green fill. That's how InDesign, on the code level, manages overlapped areas with transparency effects.

For example, when you flatten, or remove the layers of, a document for output, InDesign creates multiple objects from overlapping objects and assigns them their own colors to mimic transparency effects.

To avoid unexpected shifts in color, when you're outputting your document, you should assign a "color space" for InDesign to use when assigning colors to overlapped areas. If you are outputting for the web or for an on-screen presentation, choose the RGB color space. If you are outputting for print, choose the CMYK color space.

To assign a color space for transparency, click the Edit menu, point to Transparency Blend Space, then click Document RGB or Document CMYK. The blending space you choose is applied only to those spreads that contain transparency.

7. Position the tool over the left green shutter in the image, then click and drag to the left edge of the image, release your mouse, then deselect.

   As shown in Figure 84, the image gradually fades to white. The length of the fade is the length that you dragged the Gradient Feather tool.

8. Navigate to page 1, then select the large image.

9. Click **Object**, click **Effects**, then click the words **Directional Feather** in the box on the left.

10. Set the Bottom text box to 1" so that your dialog box resembles Figure 85.

11. Click **OK**, deselect, then compare your page to Figure 86.

12. Save your work, then close the file.

You applied three feather effects, including a basic feather, gradient feather, and directional feather.

Figure 84 *Gradient feather effect*

Fade to white

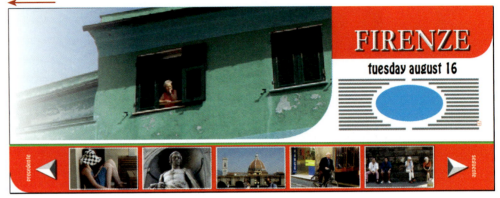

Figure 85 *Directional Feather settings*

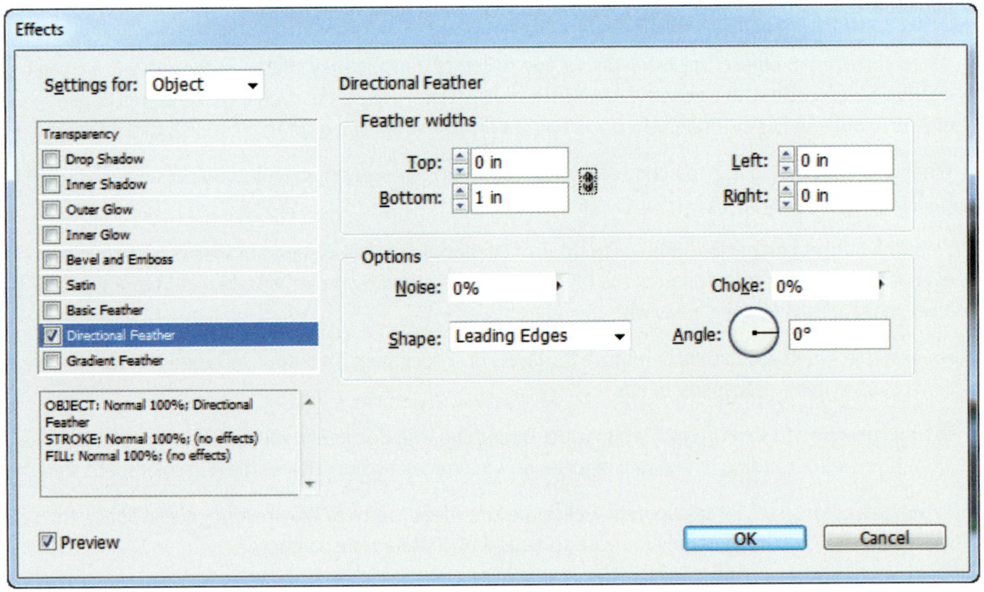

Exploring Effects and Advanced Techniques

Figure 86 *Final layout with the directional feather*

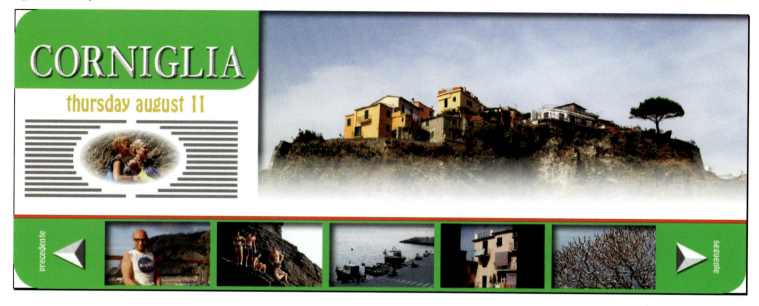

Using Creative Suite Color Settings

If you use other programs in the Adobe Creative Suite, such as Flash, Illustrator and Photoshop, you'll be glad to know that there is a way to ensure that color settings can be synchronized across each CS5 program. Before you start your work on a new document or even an old one, you should synchronize your color settings. Adobe Bridge is the tool for this job. Simply open Bridge from your current application by clicking File on the Application bar, then clicking Browse in Bridge. Once in Bridge, click Edit on the Application bar, then click Creative Suite Color Settings.

To see all of the color settings, click the Show Expanded List of Color Setting Files check box. Once you choose a color setting, click Apply. You can also install a custom settings file, such as a file you received from a printer or service bureau. To choose a custom settings file, click the Show Saved Color Settings Files button, then navigate to its location on your hard drive.

Use the Pathfinder panel.

1. Open ID 8-9.indd, then save it as **Pathfinder and Strokes Review**.
2. Click the Selection tool, then move the objects on the page so you can see how the graphic is built.
3. Revert the file to return the layout to its original state.
4. Display the Layers panel, then verify that only Layer 1 is visible and targeted.
5. Select all, then click the Subtract button on the Pathfinder panel.
6. Click Edit on the Application bar, click Copy, click Edit on the Application bar, click Paste in Place, then change the fill color to PANTONE 1797 C.
7. Make Layer 2 visible and active, press and hold [Shift], then click the yellow star to add it to the selection.
8. Click the Exclude Overlap button on the Pathfinder panel.
9. Click PANTONE Reflex Blue C on the Swatches panel.

Create new stroke styles.

1. Deselect all.
2. Click the Stroke panel options button, then click Stroke Styles.
3. Click New, then type **New Dash** in the Name text box.
4. Verify that Dash is listed in the Type text box.
5. Select the value in the Length text box, then type **.125 in**.
6. Click the white space to the right of the dash to add a new dash.
7. Select the value in the Start text box, type **.19 in**, press [Tab], type **.01 in** in the Length text box, then press [Tab].
8. Click OK.

9. Note the New Dash stroke in the Stroke Styles dialog box, then click OK.
10. Select the circle, click the Type list arrow on the Stroke panel, then click New Dash.
11. Change the stroke color to PANTONE Reflex Blue C, then compare your work to Figure 87.
12. Save your work, then close Pathfinder and Strokes Review.indd.

Work with nested styles.

1. Open ID 8-10.indd, then save it as **Nested Styles Skills**.
2. Click the Type tool, click to the immediate right of the colon after the word Picasso, click Type on the Application bar, point to Insert Special Character, point to Other, then click End Nested Style Here.
3. Using the same method, insert the End Nested Style Here special character after the colons in items 2–4.

4. Double-click Body Copy on the Paragraph Styles panel, then click the Preview check box in the bottom-left corner to select it if it is not already.
5. Click Drop Caps and Nested Styles in the box on the left, then click New Nested Style.
6. Click the [None] list arrow, click Red Number, then press [Enter] (Win) or [return] (Mac) to execute the change.
7. Click New Nested Style, click [None] to highlight it if it is not already, click the [None] list arrow, then click Artist Name.
8. Click Words once, click the Words list arrow, click End Nested Style Character, then press [Enter] (Win) or [return] (Mac) to execute the change.
9. Click OK, compare your work to Figure 88, save your work, then close Nested Styles Skills. (Your screen may look different if your computer substituted fonts.)

Figure 87 *Skills Review, Parts 1 and 2 completed*

Figure 88 *Skills Review, Part 3 completed*

Exploring Effects and Advanced Techniques

Incorporate gridify behavior.

1. Open ID 8-11.indd, then save it as **Gridify Skills**.
2. Set the Fill color to Red.
3. Click the Ellipse tool, position the crosshair near the upper-left corner of the page, then begin dragging.
4. While still dragging, press the Right Arrow key three times.
5. While still dragging, press the Up Arrow key four times.
6. Continue dragging until the grid is the full width of the page, then release your mouse. Your grid should resemble Figure 89.
7. Save your work, then close the file.

Execute a Super Step and Repeat.

1. Open ID 8-12.indd, then save it as **Super Step and Repeat Skills**.
2. Click the Selection tool, then select the blue circle.
3. Press and old [Alt](Win) or [option](Mac), then begin dragging to the right.
4. While still dragging right, release the Alt/option key, then press the Right Arrow key six times, but do not release the mouse button.
5. Drag down to the lower right corner, release your mouse button, then compare your result to Figure 90.
6. Save your work, then close the file.

Work with multiple page sizes.

1. Click File, point to New, then click Document.
2. Enter the values shown in Figure 91, then click OK.
3. Open the Pages panel, then double-click the page 2 thumbnail.

4. Click the Edit page size button at the bottom of the Pages panel, then click Compact Disc.
5. With page 2 still targeted in the Pages panel, click Layout on the Application bar, click Margins and Columns, set the four Margins text boxes to .125, then click OK.
6. Double-click page 3 in the Pages panel.
7. Click the Edit page size button at the bottom of the Pages panel, then click Custom Page Size. The Custom Page Size dialog box opens.
8. Type 3×5 Envelope in the Name text box, set the Width to 5, then set the Height to 3.
9. Click Add.
10. Click OK, then save the file as Multiple Page Size Skills.
11. Close the file.

Figure 89 *Skills Review, Part 4 completed*

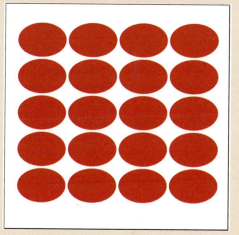

Figure 90 *Skills Review, Part 5 completed*

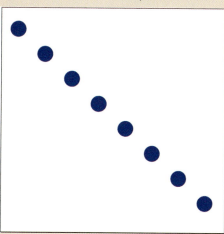

Figure 91 *New dialog box*

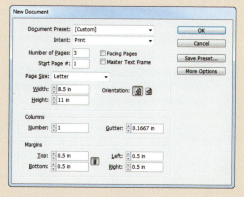

Apply Live Corner Effects.

1. Open ID 8-13.indd, then save it as Effects Skills.
2. Navigate to page 2, select the image, then click the small yellow square.
3. Drag the top-right diamond left inward approximately .25" to round all four corners.
4. Do the same to the images on pages 3, 4, and 5.
5. Select the image on page 2, click the yellow square, press and hold [Alt](Win) or [option](Mac), then click any of the yellow diamonds one time to change all four corners of the frame to the Fancy corner effect.
6. Select the image on page 3, click the yellow square, press and hold [Alt](Win) or [option](Mac), then click any of the yellow diamonds two times. All four corners of the frame change to the Bevel corner effect.
7. Select the image on page 4, click the yellow square, press and hold [Alt](Win) or [option](Mac), then click any of the yellow diamonds three times to change all four corners of the frame to the Inset corner effect.
8. Select the image on page 5, click the yellow square, press and hold [Alt](Win) or [option](Mac), then click any of the yellow diamonds four times so that all four corners of the frame change to the Inverse Rounded corner effect. Compare your spread to Figure 92.
9. Navigate to Page 1, then select all four frames on the page.
10. Click Object on the Application bar, then click Corner Options.
11. Verify that the Make All Settings The Same (link icon) is activated.
12. Enter **.1** in any of the four text boxes, then press [Tab].
13. Click any of the four shape list arrows, then click Rounded.
14. Click OK, then save the file.

Figure 92 *Live Corner Effects reviewed*

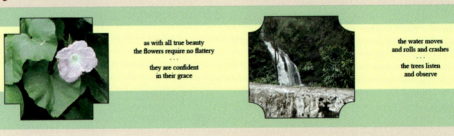

Exploring Effects and Advanced Techniques

Work with effects and object styles.

1. On page 1, select the second image from the left.
2. Click Object on the Application bar, point to Effects, then click the words Inner Shadow in the box on the left.
3. Enter the settings shown in Figure 93, but do not click OK.

Figure 93 *Inner Shadow settings*

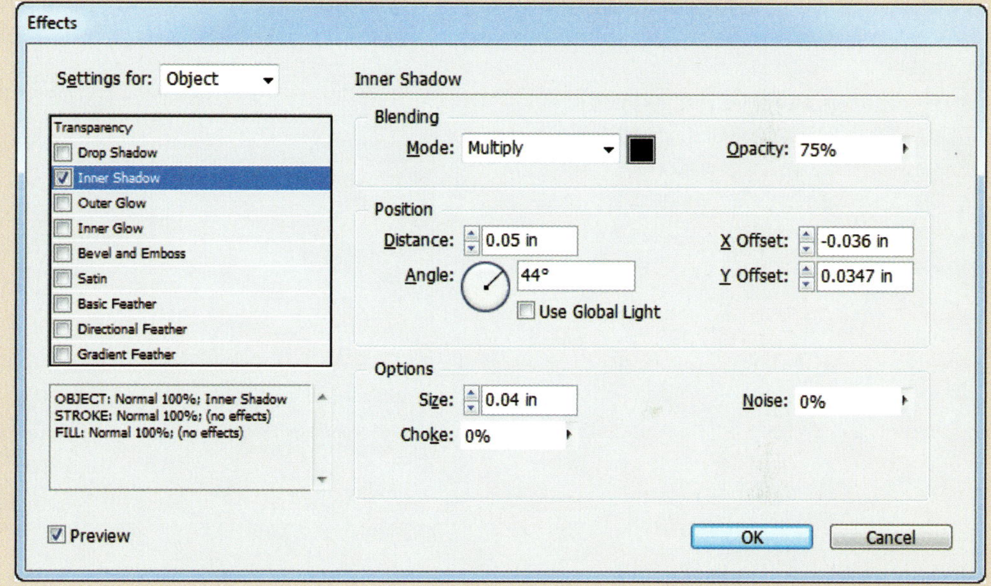

Effects

Settings for: Object ▾

Inner Shadow

Transparency
- ☐ Drop Shadow
- ☑ Inner Shadow
- ☐ Outer Glow
- ☐ Inner Glow
- ☐ Bevel and Emboss
- ☐ Satin
- ☐ Basic Feather
- ☐ Directional Feather
- ☐ Gradient Feather

OBJECT: Normal 100%; Inner Shadow
STROKE: Normal 100%; (no effects)
FILL: Normal 100%; (no effects)

Blending

Mode: Multiply ▾ ■   Opacity: 75% ▸

Position

Distance: 0.05 in   X Offset: -0.036 in
Angle: 44°   Y Offset: 0.0347 in
☐ Use Global Light

Options

Size: 0.04 in   Noise: 0% ▸
Choke: 0% ▸

☑ Preview   OK   Cancel

4. Click the words Drop Shadow in the box on the left side of the dialog box, then enter the settings shown in Figure 94.

5. Click OK.

6. With the image still selected, open the Effects panel, then click the *fx* button at the bottom of the panel to see which effects are applied to the image.

7. Drag the *fx* icon from the Effects panel beside Object: Normal 100% to the image of the flower to the right.

8. Save your work.

Figure 94 *Drop Shadow settings*

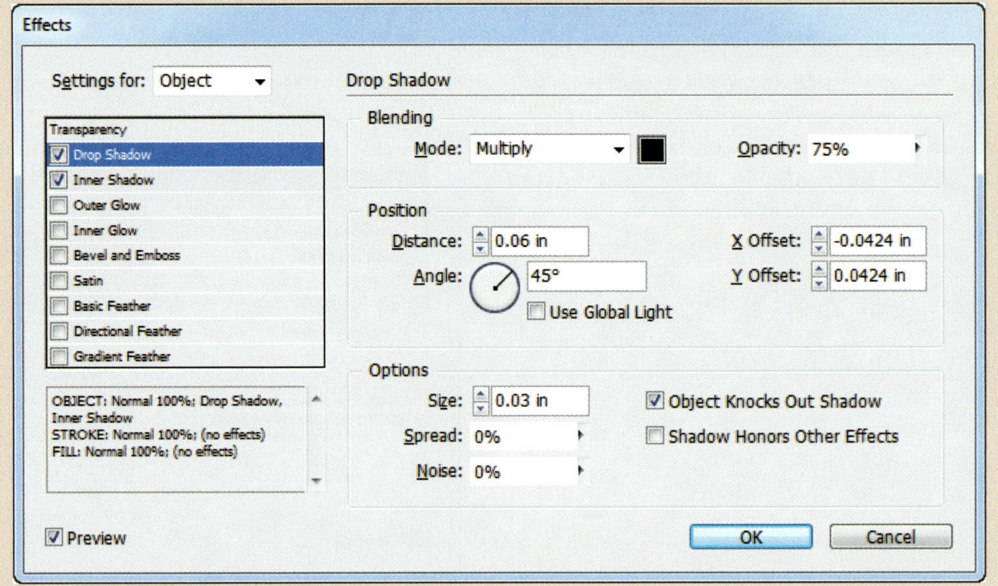

Effects

Settings for: Object ▾

Drop Shadow

Transparency
- ☑ Drop Shadow
- ☑ Inner Shadow
- ☐ Outer Glow
- ☐ Inner Glow
- ☐ Bevel and Emboss
- ☐ Satin
- ☐ Basic Feather
- ☐ Directional Feather
- ☐ Gradient Feather

OBJECT: Normal 100%: Drop Shadow, Inner Shadow
STROKE: Normal 100%: (no effects)
FILL: Normal 100%: (no effects)

Blending

Mode: Multiply   Opacity: 75% ▸

Position

Distance: 0.06 in   X Offset: -0.0424 in

Angle: 45°   Y Offset: 0.0424 in

☐ Use Global Light

Options

Size: 0.03 in   ☑ Object Knocks Out Shadow

Spread: 0% ▸   ☐ Shadow Honors Other Effects

Noise: 0% ▸

☑ Preview

OK   Cancel

Exploring Effects and Advanced Techniques

Work with effects and object styles.

1. With the second frame still selected, click Window, point to Styles, then click Object Styles.
2. Click the Object Styles panel options button, then click New Object Style.
3. Type Inner and Drop Shadow in the Style Name text box, then make sure in the lower left section that the Inner Shadow and Drop Shadow effects are checked.
4. Uncheck all of the attributes in the General section.
5. Click OK.
6. Use the Selection tool to select the leftmost image, then click Inner and Drop Shadow in the Object Styles panel.
7. Apply the Inner and Drop Shadow object style to all the other frames in the document, then compare your page 1 layout to Figure 95.
8. Save your work, then close the file.

Figure 95 *Object styles reviewed*

The Road to Hana
a visual journey through Maui

A new magazine named WEIRD is courting you with the idea of hiring you in their art department. They have asked you to submit a sample of a cover design. You are an avid fan of the magazine, and you know that every month they do something interesting with the title artwork. You decide to use a customized stroke style to create a 70s look.

1. Open ID 8-14.indd, then save it as **Weird**.
2. Open the Stroke Styles dialog box, click New, type **Vibe** in the Name text box, click the Type list arrow, then click Stripe.

3. Click the bottom stripe, then drag the top triangle down until the Start value reads 85.
4. Click the top stripe, then drag the bottom triangle up until the Width value reads 15.
5. Add a new stripe between the two stripes, change the Start value to 30, change the Width value to 42, then click OK twice.

6. Click the Direct Selection tool, click the W, then click the Swap Fill and Stroke button on the Tools panel to activate the Stroke tool.
7. Change the stroke type to Vibe, then change the stroke weight to 6 pt.
8. Change the fill color to white.
9. Deselect, compare your work to Figure 96, save your work, then close WEIRD.

Figure 96 *Completed Project Builder 1*

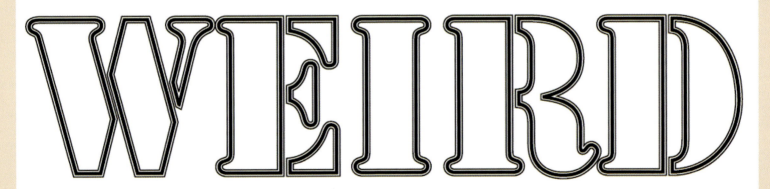

You run a small graphics business out of your home. A friend comes to you with an old photo of her grandmother. She wants to put it in a 3.5" × 5" frame, and asks you to create a soft oval effect for the photo.

1. Open ID 8-15.indd, then save it as **Vignette**.
2. Click the Selection tool if it is not active, select the frame, then fill it with the Tan swatch.
3. With the frame still selected, click the Ellipse tool, position the pointer over the center point of the selected frame, press and hold [Alt] (Win) or [option] (Mac), then click.
4. Type 3 in the Width text box, type 4.5 in the Height text box, then click OK.
5. Verify that the ellipse you just created has no fill or stroke.
6. Click the fx icon on the Effects panel, then click Basic Feather.
7. Click the Basic Feather check box, type .75 in the Feather Width text box, then click OK.
8. Place the file named Portrait.psd from the drive and folder where your Data Files are stored.
9. Click the Direct Selection tool, then center the woman's face in the oval.
10. Click View on the Application bar, point to Extras, click Hide Frame Edges if it is not already, deselect all, then compare your work to Figure 97.
11. Save your work, then close Vignette.

Figure 97 *Completed Project Builder 2*

Your client has opened a coffee shop near your home office. She doesn't have a big budget for purchasing artwork, so she's asked you to create some digital art to hang on her walls. She gives you an old photo and tells you she wants you to use it to create "something old and modern at the same time."

1. Open ID 8-16.indd, then save it as **Granny Warhol**.
2. Make the Photos layer visible, then select the top-left graphics frame using the Selection tool.
3. Click the Blending mode list arrow on the Effects panel and select Multiply.
4. Select the top-right graphics frame, then change the blending mode to Screen.
5. Select the bottom-left graphics frame, then change the blending mode to Hard Light.
6. Select the bottom-right graphics frame, drag the Opacity slider to 30%, then deselect all.
7. Press and hold [Alt] (Win) or [option] (Mac), then click the Background layer on the Layers panel to select the four colored squares behind the photos.
8. Verify that the center reference point on the Transform panel is selected.
9. Double-click the Rotate tool, type 90 in the Angle text box, then click OK.
10. Save your work, deselect all, compare your work to Figure 98, then close Granny Warhol.

Figure 98 *Completed Design Project*

Exploring Effects and Advanced Techniques

This project is designed to challenge your ability to recognize and distinguish pathfinders visually.

1. Open ID 8-17.indd or refer to Figure 99.
2. Number a piece of paper from 1 to 5 for recording answers to this project.
3. Identify the pathfinder used in each of the numbered examples shown in the file and Figure 99, and write your answers on your numbered piece of paper.

Figure 99 *Portfolio Project Challenge*

CHAPTER **9** WORKING WITH TABS
AND TABLES

1. Work with tabs

2. Create and format a table

3. Format text in a table

4. Place graphics in a table

CHAPTER 9 WORKING WITH TABS AND TABLES

InDesign offers many great options for creating charts and tables. You use tabs to position text at specific horizontal locations within a text frame, and you use the Tabs dialog box to determine the placement of those tabs. The Tabs dialog box is an excellent resource that features a sophisticated interface.

In addition to tabs, an important component to any layout application is the ability to create tables. By setting up data in the rows and columns of a table, you can often communicate large amounts of information more effectively. InDesign provides excellent options for creating tables quickly and easily—in fact, it provides both a Table panel and an entire Table menu!

Insert Table

Table Dimensions

Body Rows: 4
Columns: 4
Header Rows: 0
Footer Rows: 0

Table Style: [No Table Style]

OK
Cancel

Paragraph Rules

Rule Below   ☑ Rule On

Weight: 1 pt   Type: ▬▬▬▬
Color: ☑ (Text Color)   Tint:
☐ Overprint Stroke
Gap Color: ☑ (Text Color)   Gap Tint:
☐ Overprint Gap
Width: Column   Offset: 0 in
Left Indent: 0 in   Right Indent: 0 in
☐ Keep In Frame

☐ Preview   OK   Cancel

TABLE

Exactly

Tabs

X: Leader: Align On:

0   1   2   3

Work with
TABS

What You'll Do

Dancewear Sales				
Product	**# Purchased**	**# Sold**	**Best Color**	**Profit**
T-Shirts	50	45	White	$950.00
Sweatshirts	100	100	Navy	$1500.00
Leotards	200	150	White	$725.00
Tap Shoes	20	2	n/a	$60.50

In this lesson, you will use the Tabs dialog box to position text at specific horizontal positions within a frame.

Using Tabs

You use **tabs** to position text at specific horizontal locations within a text frame. Figure 1 shows a simple layout created using tabs. The heading "Column 2" and the five items beneath it are all aligned with the left-justified tab shown in the tab ruler of the Tabs dialog box.

Note that the left edge of the white ruler in the Tabs dialog box is aligned with the left edge of the text frame. This alignment occurs by default when you select a text frame and open the Tabs dialog box. The alignment of the text frame with the Tabs dialog box makes it easier to note the horizontal position of text within a frame. For example, in the same figure, you can see at a glance that Column 2 is positioned two inches in from the left edge of the text frame.

If you scroll up or down, or resize the page or the text frame, the text frame will no longer be aligned with the Tabs dialog box. To realign the two, simply click the Position

Panel above Text Frame button on the Tabs dialog box. The Tabs dialog box will move to realign itself with the text frame.

Once text has been aligned on a tab, moving the tab moves the text as well. In Figure 2, the tab has been moved right to 2.5" and the left edge of the text is also aligned at that position. The text does not need to be selected to be moved. Simply moving the tab moves the text.

To delete a tab from the tab ruler, simply drag it off the tab ruler, and then release the mouse button.

Using Different Tab Alignments

The Tabs dialog box offers four types of tab buttons for aligning text—Left-Justified Tab, Center-Justified Tab, Right-Justified Tab, and Align to Decimal Tab. To create a tab in the tab ruler, you can click a tab button, then click a location in the tab ruler or click a tab button, then enter a location in the X text box in the Tabs dialog box.

In Figure 3, the second column of text is aligned with a left-justified tab. Note that the tab is selected in the tab ruler—it is highlighted with blue. When a tab is selected, its horizontal location is indicated in the X text box. This tab is positioned at the 2.25" mark.

In Figure 4, the tab of the second column has been changed to a center-justified tab. Its horizontal location remains unchanged; however, now the center points of the text are aligned at the 2.25" mark.

QUICK TIP

You change a tab from one type to another by clicking the tab in the tab ruler, then clicking a different tab button in the Tabs dialog box.

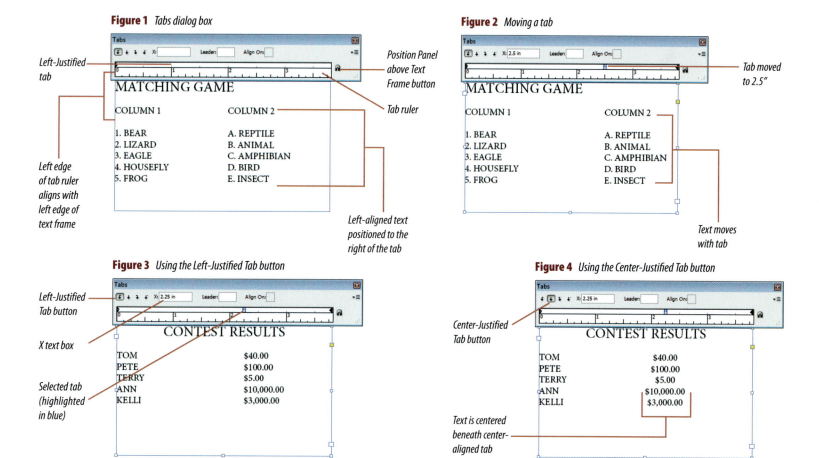

Figure 1 *Tabs dialog box*

Left-Justified tab

Position Panel above Text Frame button

Tab ruler

Left edge of tab ruler aligns with left edge of text frame

Left-aligned text positioned to the right of the tab

Figure 2 *Moving a tab*

Tab moved to 2.5"

Text moves with tab

Figure 3 *Using the Left-Justified Tab button*

Left-Justified Tab button

X text box

Selected tab (highlighted in blue)

Figure 4 *Using the Center-Justified Tab button*

Center-Justified Tab button

Text is centered beneath center-aligned tab

In Figure 5, the position of the right-column tab has not changed, but its alignment has changed to a right-justified tab. Notice that the lines of text are all aligned on the right.

In Figure 6, the tab alignment has been changed to an align-to-decimal tab.

The decimal points of each number in the column are aligned at the 2.25" mark. Clearly, this tab is a good choice when working with numbers.

When you use the align-to-decimal tab, you can align text with characters other than a

decimal point, such as an asterisk or a dollar sign. As shown in Figure 7, by clicking the Align to Decimal Tab button, then typing a $ in the Align On text box, the column is aligned on the dollar sign.

Figure 5 *Using the Right-Justified Tab button*

Figure 6 *Using the Align to Decimal Tab button*

Figure 7 *Using the Align On text box in the Tabs dialog box*

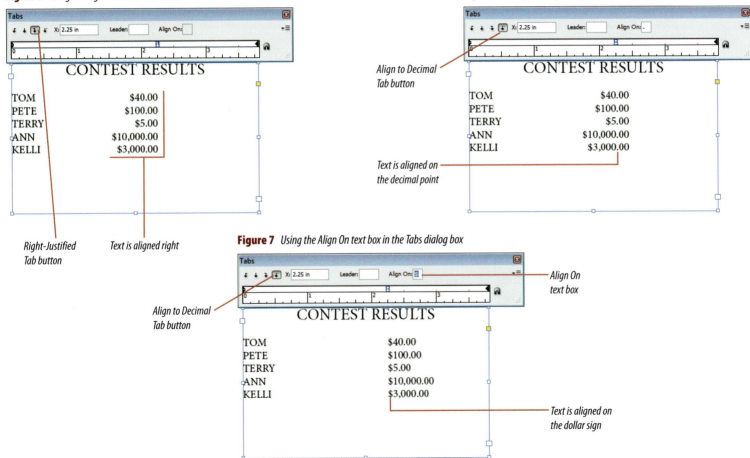

Using Text Insets

When you enter text in a text frame, **text insets** determine how far from the edge of the frame the text is positioned, or, how far it is *inset* into the frame. Text insets can be entered for all four sides of a text frame—top and bottom, left and right. For example, a .5" text inset means that text will be inset one-half inch on all four sides of a frame.

In Figure 8, a heavy black stroke has been added to the text frame. The addition of the stroke makes the position of the text visually unpleasing—the text is too close to the top and the left edges of the frame.

Text inset values are entered in the Text Frame Options dialog box. In Figure 9, a .25" text inset has been added to the top and left sides of the frame. Note the light blue line that indicates the top and left margins of the text within the text frame.

QUICK TIP

When you use tabs in a text frame that has a text inset, the tab ruler aligns itself with the light blue text inset line, not the left edge of the text frame.

Figure 8 *Applying a rule creates the need for a text inset*

Figure 9 *Applying a text inset to the top and left sides of the text frame*

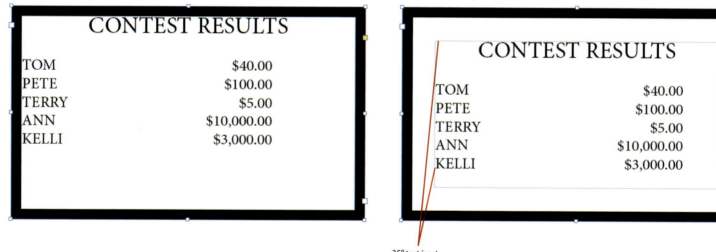

.25" text inset
top and left

Adding Rules above or below Paragraphs

Many times, you will want to add a horizontal rule above or below a line (or lines) of text. InDesign regards rules above and below text as paragraph attributes—in other words, they are part of the text formatting. If you resize the text—let's say you make it larger—the rule increases however much is necessary to continue underlining the text. If you move the text, the rule moves with it.

Rules for text are defined in the Paragraph Rules dialog box, shown in Figure 10. This dialog box allows you to specify a number of attributes for the rule, including its color and its weight. This is where you also specify whether the rule is positioned above or below the text.

When you apply a rule below text, the rule is positioned by default at the baseline of the text. Often, you will find this to be visually unpleasing. Figure 11 shows text with a rule positioned at its baseline.

Generally speaking, a rule below looks best when it is slightly below the baseline. Use the Offset text box in the Paragraph Rules dialog box to accomplish this. When the rule is defined as a Rule Below, a positive offset value moves the rule *down* from the baseline.

Rule offsets are best specified in points. A **point** is 1/72 of an inch. This small increment allows you to be very specific when positioning a rule. For a rule below, a two- or three-point offset value is usually best. Figure 12 shows the same rule with a three-point offset.

QUICK TIP

If your ruler units are set to inches, you can still enter values as points. Simply type p before a value to specify it as points. For example, if you want to specify a six-point offset value, type p6 in the Offset text box.

Figure 10 *Paragraph Rules dialog box*

Click to activate a rule

Figure 12 *Rule below, with a 3 point offset*

CONTEST RESULTS

TOM	$40.00
PETE	$100.00
TERRY	$5.00
ANN	$10,000.00
KELLI	$3,000.00

Figure 11 *Rule below, at the baseline*

Rule positioned with a zero offset value

CONTEST RESULTS

TOM	$40.00
PETE	$100.00
TERRY	$5.00
ANN	$10,000.00
KELLI	$3,000.00

Figure 13 *Insetting text*

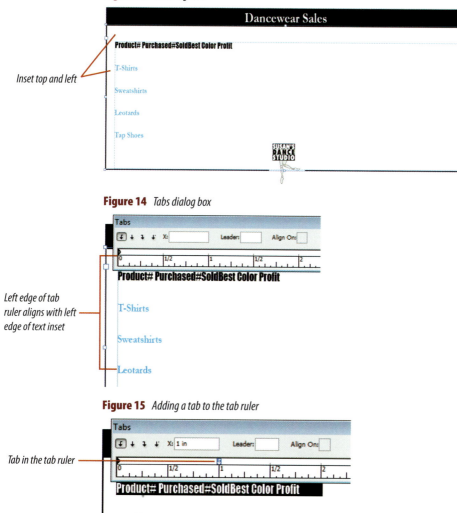

Inset top and left

Figure 14 *Tabs dialog box*

Left edge of tab
ruler aligns with left
edge of text inset

Figure 15 *Adding a tab to the tab ruler*

Tab in the tab ruler

Set a text inset and insert tabs

1. Open ID 9-1.indd, then save it as **Tabs**.

2. Click the **Selection tool** , click the **blue text**, click **Object** on the Application bar, then click **Text Frame Options**.

3. In the Inset Spacing section, type **.25** in the Top text box, type **.125** in the Left text box, click **OK**, then compare your work to Figure 13.

TIP You may need to disable the Make all settings the same feature (lock/unlock) button ⬚.

4. Click **Type** on the Application bar, then click **Tabs**.

   As shown in Figure 14, the left edge of the tab ruler (not the left edge of the Tabs dialog box) is automatically aligned with the left edge of the text inset so that the measurements in the ruler exactly match the text.

5. Click the **Type tool** T, select all of the text in the frame, then click the **Left-Justified Tab button** ↓ at the top left of the Tabs dialog box, if necessary.

6. Position the pointer in the white space in the top third of the tab ruler—just above the numbers—then click and drag until the X text box reads 1 in, as shown in Figure 15.

7. Repeat Step 6 to create a new tab at 2".

TIP To delete a tab from the tab ruler, simply drag it straight up.

8. Click anywhere in the tab ruler to the right of the second tab to add a third tab.

(continued)

The third tab remains selected, and its horizontal location is displayed in the X text box.

9. Double-click the **value** in the X text box, type **3**, then press **[Enter]** (Win) or **[return]** (Mac).

   The third tab is moved to the 3" mark.

10. Using either of the two methods from the above steps, add a new tab at 4", then compare your work to Figure 16.

You inset text from the top and left margins in the Text Frame Options dialog box. You then selected all the text in the frame and set four left-justified tabs at 1" intervals.

Enter text using tabs

1. Click the **Type tool** T , click to the left of the first # sign in the first line of text, then press **[Tab]**.

2. Tab the remaining text in the first line so that your page resembles Figure 17.

3. Click to the right of the word T-Shirts, press **[Tab]**, then type **50**.

4. Press **[Tab]**, type **45**, press **[Tab]**, type **White**, press **[Tab]**, then type **$950**.

   Your page should resemble Figure 18.

5. Using the same method, enter the information shown in Figure 19 so that your page matches the figure.

   Note that, now that the text is entered, the text is not centered in the frame—there is a large gap to the right of the last column.

6. Select all of the text, click **Object** on the Application bar, click **Text Frame Options**, change the Left inset value to **.5**, then click **OK**.

   (continued)

Figure 16 *Adding the fourth tab*

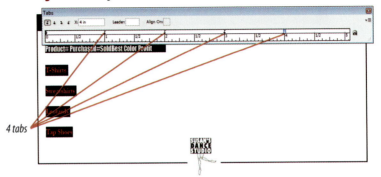

4 tabs

Figure 17 *Tabbing the first line of text*

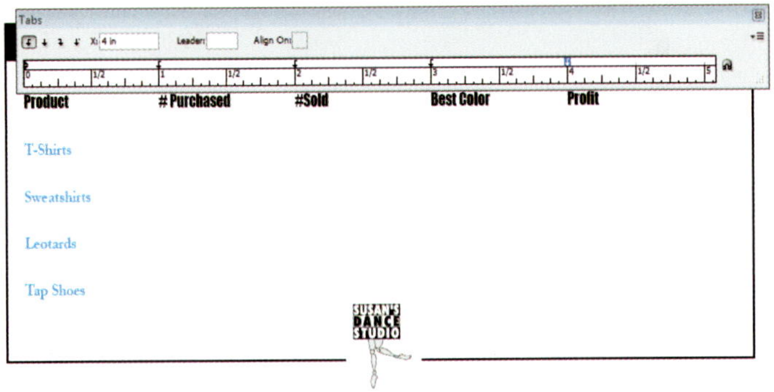

Figure 18 *Entering tabbed values for the first product line*

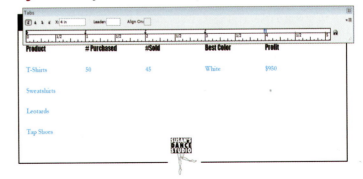

Figure 19 *Entering tabbed values for the remaining products*

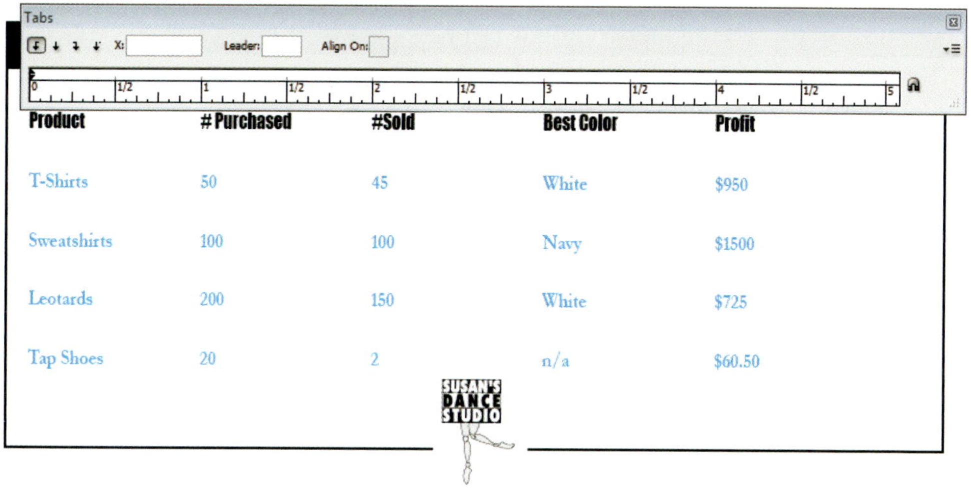

Product	# Purchased	#Sold	Best Color	Profit
T-Shirts	50	45	White	$950
Sweatshirts	100	100	Navy	$1500
Leotards	200	150	White	$725
Tap Shoes	20	2	n/a	$60.50

Figure 20 *Increasing the left inset*

Figure 21 *Changing a left-aligned tab to a center-aligned tab*

Center-aligned tab

Everything shifts to the right and the tabs remain spaced at 1" intervals. As shown in Figure 20, the left edge of the tab ruler is no longer aligned with the left edge of the text inset.

7. Click in the text to deselect it, then click the **Position Panel above Text Frame button** 🔒.

   The left edge of the tab ruler realigns itself with the left edge of the text inset.

8. Save your work.

You used tabs to enter text at specific horizontal locations. You modified the left text inset value, noting that the 1" tab intervals were not affected.

Change type of tabs and location of tabs

1. Select all of the blue text.

2. Click the **first tab** at the 1" location in the tab ruler to select it.

3. Click the **Center-Justified Tab button** ↓.

   The tab changes to a center-justified tab and the first column of text is now centered at the 1" mark.

4. With the first tab in the tab ruler still highlighted, select the **value** in the X text box, type **1.3**, then press **[Enter]** (Win) or **[return]** (Mac).

   As shown in Figure 21, the first column is now centered in relation to the # Purchased column headline.

5. Click the **second tab** to highlight it, click the **Center-Justified Tab button** ↓, then relocate the tab to 2.3".

6. Click the **third tab** to highlight it, click the **Center-Justified Tab button** ↓, then relocate the tab to 3.25".

(continued)

7. Click the **fourth tab** to highlight it, click the **Align to Decimal Tab button** ↓, then relocate the tab to 4.15.

8. Select only the **"# Sold"** text in the top row, then relocate its tab to **2.15"**.

9. Type **.00** after $950, $1500, and $725.

10. Click **Edit** on the Application bar, click **Deselect All**, save your work, then compare your page with Figure 22.

TIP The Tabs panel is hidden in the figure.

11. Save your work because you will revert to this point after the next set of steps.

You selected tabs, changed them to different types of tabs, then moved tabs in the tab ruler.

Apply tab leaders and rules

1. Select all of the blue text, then click the **first tab** in the tab ruler to highlight it.

2. Type a **period (.)** in the Leader text box in the Tabs dialog box, press **[Enter]** (Win) or **[return]** (Mac), then deselect all.

    As shown in Figure 23, the period is used as a character that connects the product listings to the first tab.

3. Select all of the blue text, click the **second tab** in the tab ruler, type a **period (.)** in the Leader text box, press **[Spacebar]**, then press **[Enter]** (Win) or **[return]** (Mac).

    Using the space creates a dot pattern that is more open.

(continued)

Figure 22 *Viewing reformatted tabs*

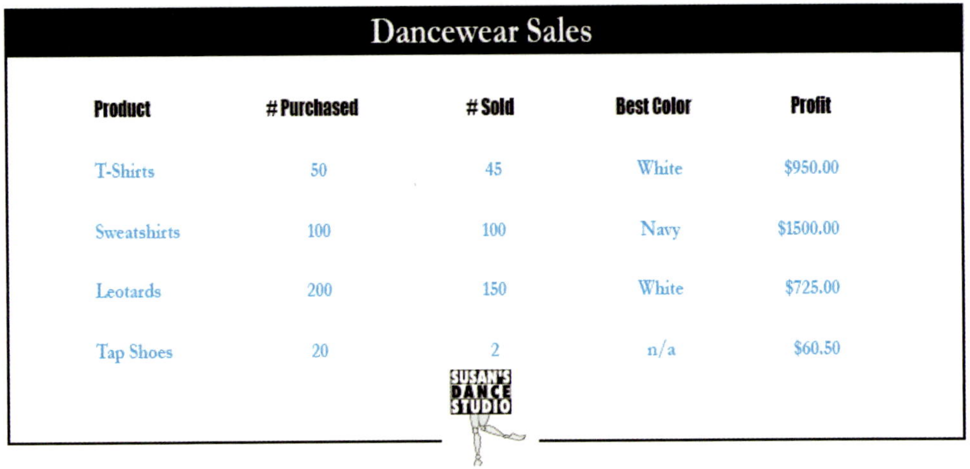

Dancewear Sales				
Product	# Purchased	# Sold	Best Color	Profit
T-Shirts	50	45	White	$950.00
Sweatshirts	100	100	Navy	$1500.00
Leotards	200	150	White	$725.00
Tap Shoes	20	2	n/a	$60.50

Figure 23 *Using a period as a tab leader*

Dancewear Sales				
Product	# Purchased	# Sold	Best Color	Profit
T-Shirts 50		45	White	$950.00
Sweatshirts 100		100	Navy	$1500.00
Leotards 200		150	White	$725.00
Tap Shoes...............20		2	n/a	$60.50

Working with Tabs and Tables

Figure 24 *Viewing various characters as tab leaders*

Figure 25 *Choosing attributes for the rule below*

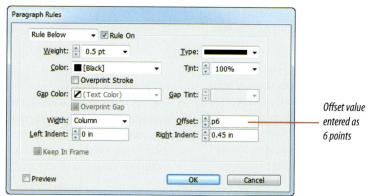

Offset value entered as 6 points

Figure 26 *Viewing the finished chart*

4. Click the **third tab** in the tab ruler, type an **asterisk (*)** in the Leader text box, then press **[Enter]** (Win) or **[return]** (Mac).

5. Click the **fourth tab** in the tab ruler, type a **hyphen (-)** in the Leader text box, press **[Enter]** (Win) or **[return]** (Mac), deselect, then compare your work to Figure 24.

6. Click **File** on the Application bar, click **Revert**, then click **Yes** (Win) or **Revert** (Mac).

7. Select all of the text, click the **Paragraph panel options button** , then click **Paragraph Rules**.

8. Click the **list arrow** at the top of the dialog box, click **Rule Below**, then click the **Rule On check box**.

9. Choose the settings for Weight, Color, Offset, and Right Indent as shown in Figure 25, click **OK**, then deselect all.

   Note that in the Offset text box, the intended six-point offset is specified as p6. When you tab from the Offset text box to the Right Indent text box, the p6 value is automatically converted to its equivalent in inches.

10. Select only the top line of text in the table, click the **Paragraph panel options button** , click **Paragraph Rules**, click the **Weight list arrow**, then click **2 pt**.

11. Click the **Type list arrow**, click **Dotted**, click the **Gap Color list arrow**, click **Paper**, then click **OK**.

12. Deselect all, save your work, compare your page to Figure 26, then close the Tabs document.

You used the Leader text box in the Tabs dialog box to set various characters as tab leaders. You used the Paragraph Rules dialog box to apply a rule below the rows of text in the text frame.

Create and Format
A TABLE

What You'll Do

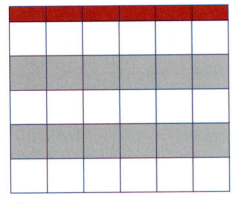

In this lesson, you will create a table and apply fills and strokes.

Working with Tables

As with tabs, **tables** are an efficient method for communicating information and an important component to any layout application, Tables consist of rectangles in horizontal **rows** and vertical **columns**. Each rectangle is called a **cell**. Figure 27 shows an example of a table.

The first important thing to note about tables is that InDesign regards them as text. Tables can only be created within a text frame. When you edit a table, you do so with the Type tool. If you select a table with the Selection tool, you can only modify the text frame, not the text or formatting of the table cells in the text frame.

Creating Tables

The first step in creating a table is to create a text frame. Once you've created the text frame, you can specify the number of rows and columns for the table in the Insert Table dialog box, shown in Figure 28. When you create the table, it always appears in a default layout, as shown in Figure 29. Note that the default width of the cells is determined by the number of columns and the width of the

text frame. In other words, the default width of the cells is the width of the text frame divided by the number of columns.

QUICK TIP

You can import a table from a Microsoft Word or Excel document using the Place command. The imported data appears in an InDesign table.

Formatting Tables

The Table panel, shown in Figure 30, is command central for manipulating a table. Even after you create the table, you can modify the number of rows and columns using the Table panel.

After you create the table, you determine the width of the columns and the height of the rows. Individual columns and rows in a table can have varying widths and heights. Column widths and row heights determine the size of any given cell in the table.

You can set the size of all the cells in a table simultaneously by selecting them all and entering values on the Table panel. You can also select a single column or row and specify a width just for that particular column or row.

Figure 31 shows the default table with a modified row height. The top row is .5" high, and the rest are all 1.625" high.

QUICK TIP

Long tables may continue over many pages in your document. To repeat information from the top or bottom row each time the table is divided, you can use headers or footers.

Headers and footers can be specified in the Insert Table dialog box at the time that you create the table, or you can convert existing rows to header or footer rows using the Convert Rows To Header or Footer commands on the Table menu.

Using Table Styles and Cell Styles

If you use tables a lot, you'll be glad to know that you can save any special formatting applied to tables or individual cells for future use by creating table styles or cell styles. This feature is especially useful if you need to create tables with identical formatting. Simply format your table with fills and strokes of your choice, select the table, click the Table Styles panel options button, then click New Table Style. In the New Table Style dialog box, assign a descriptive name for your new style and check out all of the options in the dialog box that allow you to further define the style, such as Row Strokes, Column Strokes, and Fills. Click OK, and you'll see your new style on the Table Styles panel. Create a new table, select it, then click the style on the Table Styles panel. The same process is used to create and apply cell styles. The difference is that you only select a cell with the formatting that you wish to save as a style, instead of an entire table. You can also import table and cell styles from other InDesign documents by clicking the Table Styles panel options button or the Cell Styles panel options button, then clicking Load Table and Cell Styles. Open the InDesign document with the table and/or cell styles you want and they will appear in your Table Styles and Cell Styles panels.

Figure 27 *An example of an InDesign table*

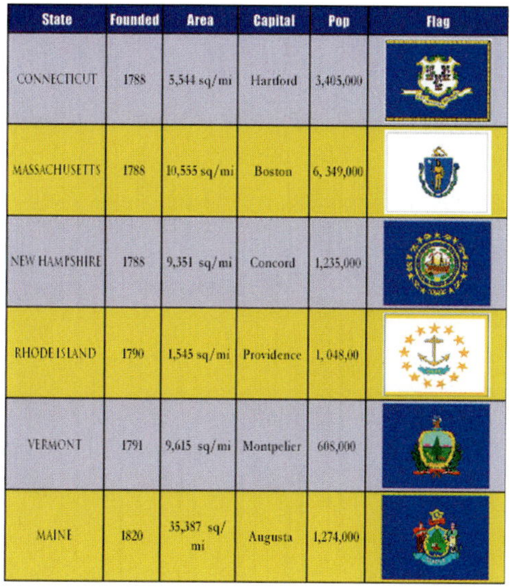

State	Founded	Area	Capital	Pop	Flag
CONNECTICUT	1788	5,544 sq/mi	Hartford	3,405,000	
MASSACHUSETTS	1788	10,555 sq/mi	Boston	6, 349,000	
NEW HAMPSHIRE	1788	9,351 sq/mi	Concord	1,235,000	
RHODE ISLAND	1790	1,545 sq/mi	Providence	1, 048,00	
VERMONT	1791	9,615 sq/mi	Montpelier	608,000	
MAINE	1820	35,387 sq/ mi	Augusta	1,274,000	

Figure 28 *Insert Table dialog box*

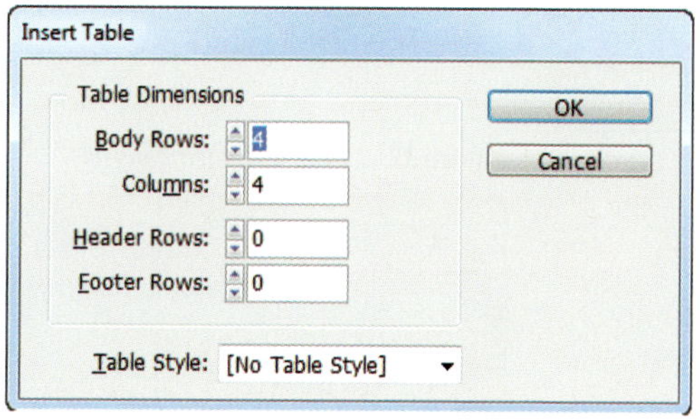

Figure 29 *Default table layout*

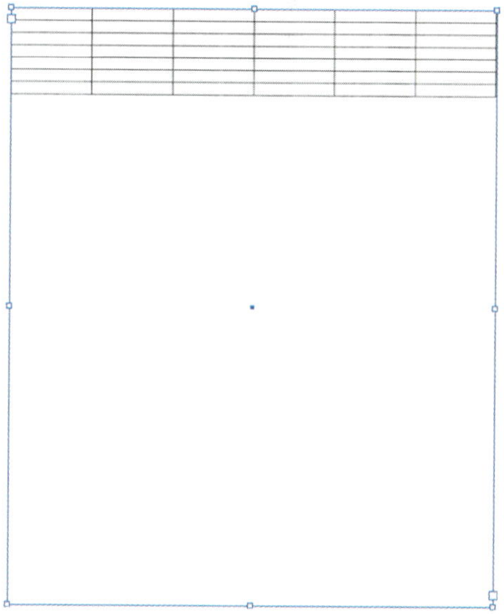

Applying Strokes and Fills to a Table

Adding color to a table can do wonders for its visual interest and improve the impact of the information it contains. You can apply strokes to the cells of the table to modify the color and the weight of the lines that make up the table grid.

You apply strokes and fills to a table just as you would to other InDesign objects. You can select a single cell, multiple cells, or an entire row or column. Remember, you use the Type tool to select elements of a table. You can then use the Swatches panel to add a fill color or to apply a stroke color, and the Stroke panel to modify the weight of the strokes.

You can also use the Table menu to apply fills and strokes. In addition, the Table menu provides options for alternating fills and strokes by row or column. Alternating fills is a technique that is often used to improve readability and enhance the look of a table. Figure 32 shows a table filled with two alternating colors.

Figure 30 *Table panel*

Figure 31 *Modified table*

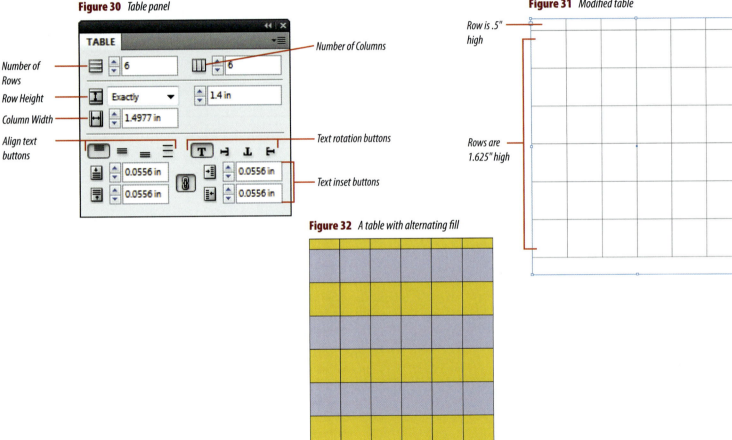

Figure 32 *A table with alternating fill*

Figure 33 *Insert Table dialog box*

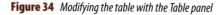

Figure 34 *Modifying the table with the Table panel*

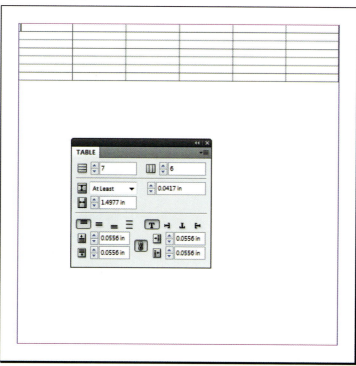

Create a table and change the number of rows

1. Open ID 9-2.indd, then save it as **Table**.

   The document is empty.

2. Close all open panels except for the Tools panel, click the **Type tool**, then create a text frame that snaps to all four margin guides.

3. Click **Table** on the Application bar, then click **Insert Table**.

4. Type **4** in the Body Rows text box, then type **6** in the Columns text box, as shown in Figure 33, then click **OK**.

5. Click **Window** on the Application bar, point to **Type & Tables**, then click **Table** to show the Table panel.

6. Click the **up arrow** next to the Number of Rows text box three times, so that there are seven rows in the table, as shown in Figure 34.

You created a table, then used the Table panel to increase the number of rows in the table.

Set a table's size

1. Position the pointer over the second cell in the first column, then click and drag to select all of the rows except the top row, as shown in Figure 35.

2. Click the **Row Height list arrow** on the Table panel, then click **Exactly**.

3. Type **1.4** in the text box to the right of the Row Height text box, press **[Enter]** (Win) or **[return]** (Mac), then compare your work to Figure 36.

4. Position the pointer over the left edge of the top cell in the first row so that a heavy black arrow appears pointing to the right.

(continued)

Figure 35 *Selecting multiple rows*

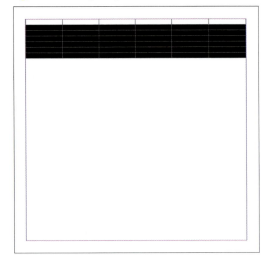

Figure 36 *Formatting the height of selected rows*

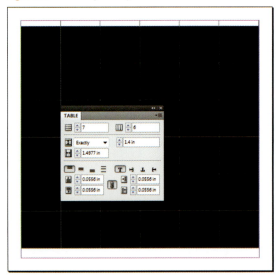

Figure 37 *Selecting a single row*

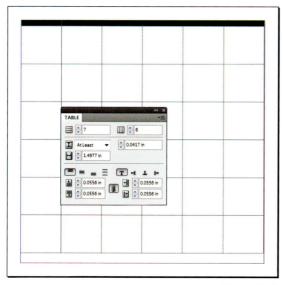

Figure 38 *Formatting the height of the top row*

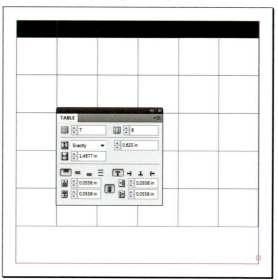

5. Click once to select the entire top row, as shown in Figure 37.

6. Click the **Row Height list arrow** on the Table panel, then click **Exactly**.

7. Type **.625** in the text box next to the Row Height text box, press **[Enter]** (Win) or **[return]** (Mac), then compare your work to Figure 38.

   The bottom row disappears and an overset text icon appears in the bottom-right corner of the text frame, indicating that there is no longer enough room in the text frame to hold all the rows in the table.

8. Position the pointer over the left edge of the second row so that a heavy black arrow appears pointing to the right.

9. Click to select the second row, click the **Table panel options button**, point to **Delete**, then click **Row**.

   The entire second row is deleted, and the overset text icon disappears because all six rows now fit in the text frame.

You selected six rows and entered a value for their height on the Table panel. You selected only the top row, then entered a different value for its height. You then deleted a row so that all rows could fit in the text frame.

Apply strokes to a table

1. Position the pointer over the top-left corner of the table so that a black diagonal arrow appears, as shown in Figure 39, then click to select the entire table.

2. Click **Table** on the Application bar, point to **Cell Options**, then click **Strokes and Fills**.

3. Click the **Weight list arrow** in the Cell Options dialog box, then click **2 pt**.

4. Click the **Color list arrow**, then click **Navy**.

5. Click **OK**, then click the pasteboard to deselect all.

6. Click **View** on the Application bar, point to **Grids & Guides**, click **Hide Guides**, click **View** on the Application bar again, point to **Extras**, click **Hide Frame Edges** if necessary, then compare your work to Figure 40.

You selected all the cells of the table, then applied strokes.

Figure 39 *Preparing to select the entire table*

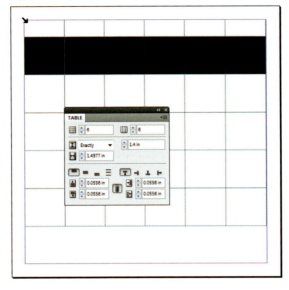

Figure 40 *Viewing strokes applied to cells*

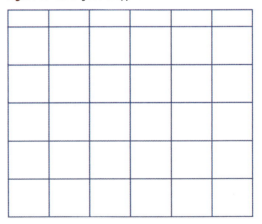

Figure 41 *Applying alternating fills*

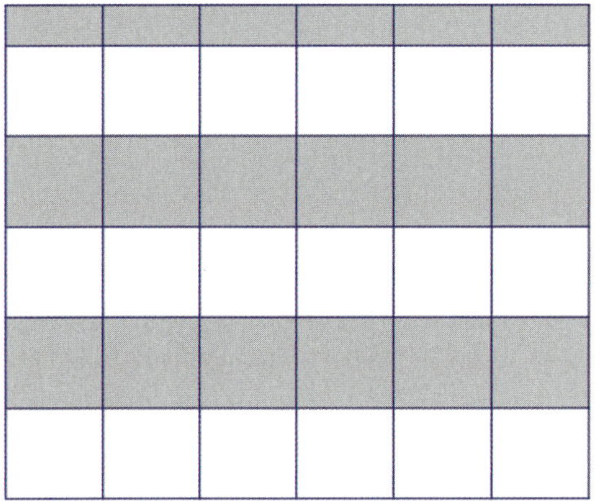

Figure 42 *Changing the fill color of the first row*

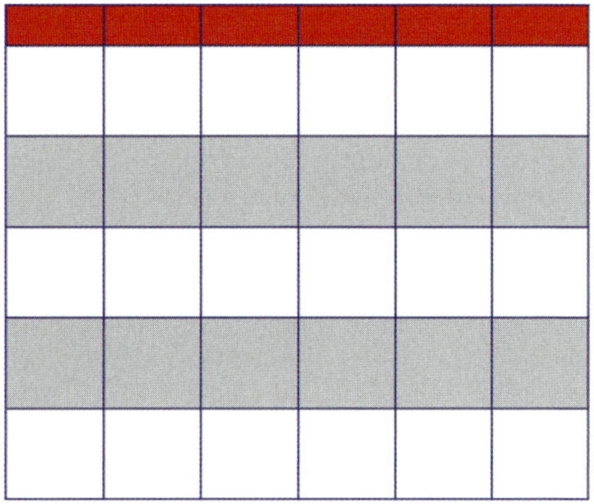

Apply fills to a table

1. Position the pointer over the top-left corner of the table so that a black diagonal arrow appears, then click once to select the entire table.

2. Click **Table** on the Application bar, point to **Table Options**, then click **Alternating Fills**.

3. Click the **Alternating Pattern list arrow**, then click **Every Other Row**.

4. Click the **first Color list arrow** on the left side of the dialog box, click **Black**, type **20** in the Tint text box, then click **OK**.

5. Click the **pasteboard** to deselect all, then compare your table to Figure 41.

6. Select the entire top row, click **Table** on the Application bar, point to **Cell Options**, then click **Strokes and Fills**.

7. Click the **Color list arrow** in the Cell Fill section of the dialog box, click **Red**, type **100** in the Tint text box, then click **OK**.

8. Click the **pasteboard** to deselect all, then compare your table to Figure 42.

You applied a fill to three rows simultaneously by using the Alternating Fills command. You then changed the fill color of the first row.

Format Text
IN A TABLE

What You'll Do

restaurant	signature	chef	review	hours	info
SHAME ON THE MOON		Bill Cohen	"The fish selection is imaginative and varied. Be sure to sample from the chef's seafood tasting menu on Thursday nights."	5-10	
BLAME IT ON MIDNIGHT		Ann Mahoney	"The pasta menu is Mahoney's secret weapon. The fettucine en brodo is rivaled only by the tortellini, which was simply a marvel."	3-11	
THE BLACK SWAN		Kelli Jacob	"With all of the incredible seafood specialty dishes, you might overlook the succulent beef and veal selections. That would be a tragedy."	4-11	
CHEZ BLAKE		Tim Brodt	"The juxtaposition of textures is stunning. My favorite was a crunchy crab salad served on a smooth lime gelée."	4-10	
THE GROOVE POD		Peter Panik	"Peter Panik is a culinary master of the unexpected."	5-11	

▶ In this lesson, you will explore options for formatting and positioning text within tables.

Entering Text in a Table

Because tables are always in text frames and, as such, are regarding as text, entering text in them is simple and straightforward. With the Type tool selected, simply click in a cell and begin typing. Press [Tab] to move from column to column. You can also use the arrow keys to move from cell to cell in any direction.

To select text in a cell and modify it, use the features on the Character panel, just as you would in a regular text frame.

When you enter text in a cell, by default, it is aligned to the left edge of the cell. You can select the text and change its alignment just as you would for any other text, using buttons, such as Align Right or Align Center, in the Paragraph panel.

By default, text that you enter in a cell is also aligned vertically to the top of the cell. To modify this, use the vertical alignment buttons on the Table panel, shown in Figure 43. Figure 44 shows text in a table that is centered both horizontally and vertically.

Modifying a Table to Fit Text

Once you have entered text into a table, you will often find that you need to modify the table to better fit the text. Sometimes the rows will not be tall enough to contain all the text, and sometimes the columns won't be wide enough. In Figure 45, for example, the left column is too narrow for the state names; note that four of them are broken by hyphens. However, the second column is more than wide enough to contain the four-digit dates. Wouldn't it be great if you could quickly reduce the size of the second column and increase the size of the first?

Fortunately, InDesign makes it very easy to modify the height of a row or the width of a column. One way to do this is to select the row or column and change the height or width value on the Table panel. Another option is simply to drag a cell border left or right to decrease or increase the width. Similarly, you can drag a cell border up or down to modify the height of a row.

In Figure 46, the width of the first column has been increased by dragging the cell border to the right. Note the double arrow that appears when you position the pointer over a cell border. Note too that increasing the width of the first column increased the width of the entire table. If you wanted to

return the table to its original width, you could decrease the width of another column. In Figure 47, the width of the second column has been reduced.

The ability to change the size of cells in this manner is a powerful option. It allows you

to experiment until the table looks the way you want it to look. Without this option, you would need to enter values repeatedly into the Table panel for each column and row, using trial-and-error guesswork, until you achieved a satisfactory result.

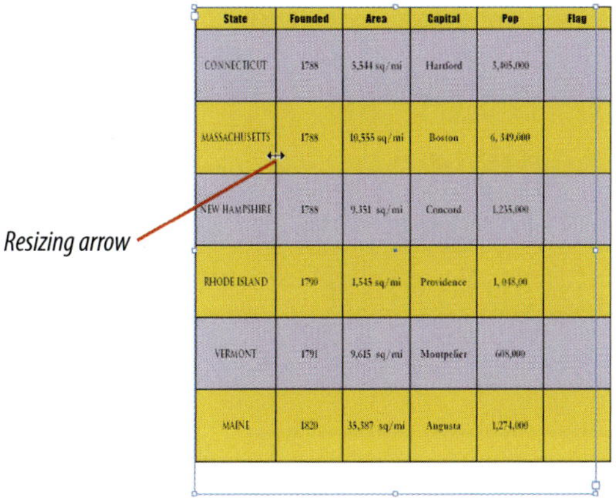

Figure 43 *Vertical alignment buttons*

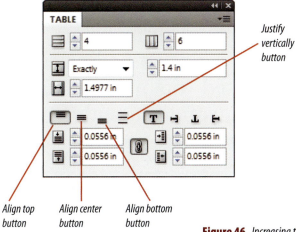

Justify
vertically
button

Align top
button

Align center
button

Align bottom
button

Figure 44 *Text centered horizontally and vertically*

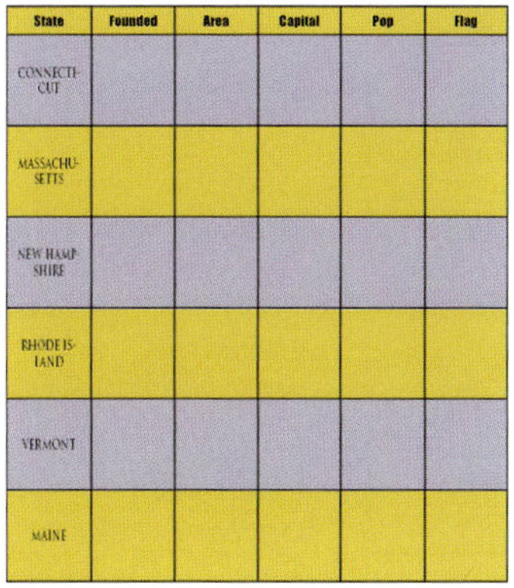

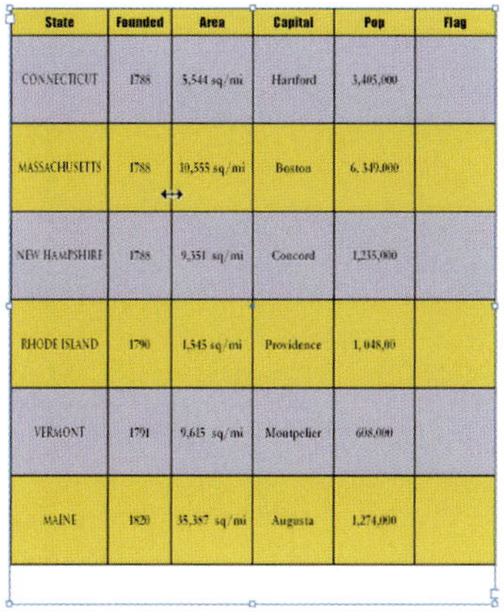

Figure 45 *A column that is too narrow*

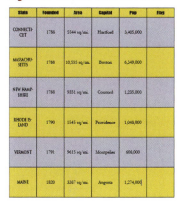

Figure 46 *Increasing the width of a column*

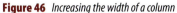

Resizing arrow

Figure 47 *Decreasing the width of a column*

Insetting Text Within a Cell

The cell inset text boxes on the Table panel, shown in Figure 48, allow you to control the text inset for all four sides of the cell. With the default inset of .0556 in, a block of text would appear as shown in Figure 49.

Note how on the left and right, the text is very close to the vertical borders of the cell, whereas there is a lot of "air" above and below. The reason the top and bottom margins are larger is because there is not enough text to take up more vertical space.

The result is that the text appears to "fight" the cell, as though it doesn't fit properly.

Figure 50 shows the same block of text with the left and right inset values increased to .1875 in. Note the improvement in appearance.

Figure 48 *Cell inset text boxes*

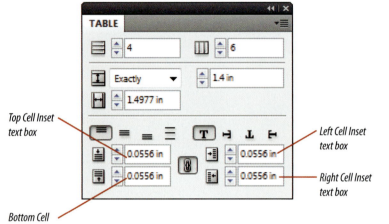

Top Cell Inset text box

Bottom Cell Inset text box

Left Cell Inset text box

Right Cell Inset text box

Figure 49 *Text with a default cell inset*

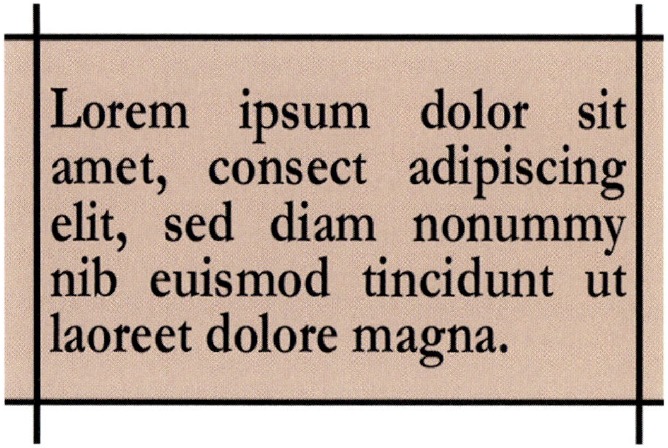

Lorem ipsum dolor sit amet, consect adipiscing elit, sed diam nonummy nib euismod tincidunt ut laoreet dolore magna.

Figure 50 *Text with increased right and left cell inset values*

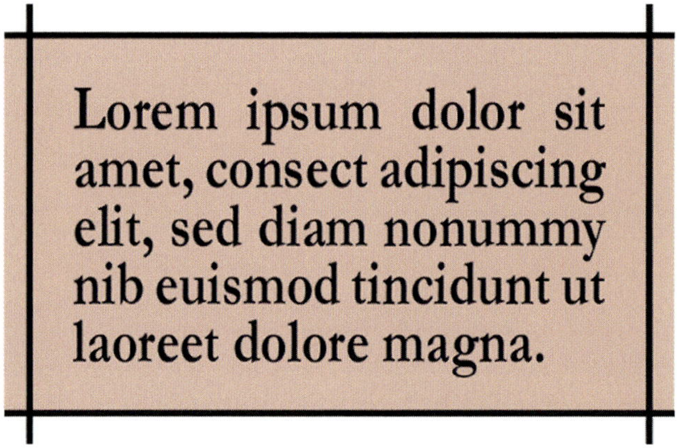

Lorem ipsum dolor sit amet, consect adipiscing elit, sed diam nonummy nib euismod tincidunt ut laoreet dolore magna.

Figure 51 *Entering text into a table*

restaurant	signature	chef	review	hours	info
SHAME ON THE MOON					
BLAME IT ON MIDNIGHT					
THE BLACK SWAN					
CHEZ BLAKE					
THE GROOVE POD					

Enter text in a table

1. Click the **Type tool** T, if necessary, click in the top-left cell, then type **restaurant**.

2. Press **[Tab]**, then type **signature**.

3. In the remaining four cells of the top row, type **chef**, **review**, **hours**, and **info**.

4. Click in the first cell of the second row, then type **SHAME ON THE MOON** in all caps.

5. Press ↓, then type **BLAME IT ON MIDNIGHT** in all caps.

6. Press ↓, then type **THE BLACK SWAN** in all caps.

7. Press ↓, then type **CHEZ BLAKE** in all caps.

8. Press ↓, type **THE GROOVE POD** in all caps, then compare your table to Figure 51.

You entered text into the cells of a table.

Format text in a table

1. Position the pointer over the left edge of the first cell in the top row so that a black arrow appears pointing right, then click once to select the entire row.

TIP The Type tool must be selected in order for the black arrow to appear.

2. Show the Swatches panel, click the **Formatting affects text button** **T**, click **Paper**, then verify that the stroke is set to **None**.

   The text changes to a white fill.

3. Show the Character panel, change the font to **Impact**, then change the font size to **18** pt.

4. Click anywhere in the first cell of the second row, then drag down to select all of the cells in the first column (except the top cell).

5. Show the Character Styles panel, then click **Restaurant name**.

TIP If you need to substitute fonts for this exercise, your restaurant name style may differ from that shown in the figures.

6. Position the pointer over the top-left corner of the table so that a black diagonal arrow appears, then click to select the entire table.

7. Click the **Align center button** ≡ on the Paragraph panel.

8. Click the pasteboard to deselect all, then compare your table to Figure 52.

   Your text may break differently. Use soft returns to adjust line breaks on the restaurant names if necessary.

9. Save your work, then close Table.

You modified the font, the font size, and the alignment of text in a table. You also applied a character style to selected text in a table.

INDESIGN 9-26

Figure 52 *Formatting text in a table*

restaurant	signature	chef	review	hours	info
SHAME ON THE MOON					
BLAME IT ON MIDNIGHT					
THE BLACK SWAN					
CHEZ BLAKE					
THE GROOVE POD					

Editing Tables in Story Editor

Just as you can edit InDesign text in Story Editor, you can edit tables in Story Editor. Simply select the table, click Edit on the Application bar, then click Edit in Story Editor. The text in each cell is identified by a column or row number and is easily editable. After making all necessary changes, close the Story Editor window to return to the updated table in InDesign. If you have added notes to table cells, they will also appear in Story Editor.

Working with Tabs and Tables

Figure 53   *Table with all text centered vertically and horizontally*

restaurant	signature	chef	review	hours	info
SHAME ON THE MOON		Bill Cohen	"The fish selection is imaginitive and varied. Be sure to sample from the chef's seafood tasting menu on	5-10	dress to impress late night menu entertainment
BLAME IT ON MIDNIGHT		Ann Mahoney	"The pasta menu is Mahoney's secret weapon. The fettucine en brodo is rivaled only by the tortellini.	3-11	children's menu take out
THE BLACK SWAN		Kelli Jacob	"With all of the incredible seafood specialty dishes, you might overlook the succulent beef and	4-11	dress to impress entertainment pre-theater menu
CHEZ BLAKE		Tim Brodt	"The juxtaposition of textures is stunning. My favorite was a crunchy crab salad served on a smooth	4-10	children's menu
THE GROOVE POD		Peter Panik	"Peter Panik is a culinary master of the unexpected."	5-11	late night menu children's menu

Setting up a Document Grid or a Baseline Grid

Grid lines are guides to which you can snap InDesign elements. Document grids are used for snapping objects, and baseline grids are used for aligning columns of text. Baseline grids look like ruled notebook paper and cover entire spreads. Document grids look more like grid paper and cover the entire pasteboard. You can view both grids by clicking View on the Application bar, pointing to Grids & Guides, then choosing Show Document Grid or Show Baseline Grid. You can change grid settings by opening the Grids Preferences dialog box. For example, you can change the color of grid lines, the vertical and horizontal space between document gridlines, and the number of subdivisions. Baseline grid preferences are for the gridlines for an entire document. It is possible, however, to create a baseline grid for an individual text frame. To do so, select the frame, click Object on the Application bar, then click Text Frame Options. Click the Baseline Options tab in the Text Frame Options dialog box, then choose an option for the First Baseline Offset. For example, you can choose Ascent, Cap Height, Leading, x Height, or Fixed. Click the Preview check box to see how each option affects your text. In the Baseline Grid section of the dialog box, you can customize the baseline grid for the text box.

Position text vertically within a cell

1. Open ID 9-3.indd, verify that you are in Normal view, then save it as **Table Complete**.

   This table has the exact formatting of the table you created but has additional text, a "key" graphic placed below the table, and icons on the pasteboard.

   TIP   If your computer substituted fonts when you opened ID 9-3.indd, your restaurant name style may differ from that shown in the figures.

2. Select the top row of cells, then click the **Align bottom button** ⊒ on the Table panel.

3. Click anywhere in the "BLAME IT ON MIDNIGHT" cell, then click the **Justify vertically button** ☰.

4. Position the pointer over the top-left corner of the table until a black diagonal arrow appears, then click to select the entire table.

5. Click the **Align center button** ☰ on the Table panel.

6. Deselect all, then compare your work to Figure 53.

You used the align buttons on the Table panel to format how text is positioned vertically within a cell.

Adjust column widths and cell insets

1. Click **View** on the Application bar, point to **Grids & Guides**, then click **Show Guides**.

2. Note the "review" text in the fourth column.

TIP Red circles in cells indicate that the cell content is too big to fit in the cell.

3. Position the pointer over the navy blue vertical cell border that separates the "hours" column from the "info" column so that a double arrow appears, as shown in Figure 54.

4. Click and drag the **arrow** left, so that the vertical cell border is aligned with the green vertical guide, as shown in Figure 55.

   The width of the "hours" column is reduced. The width of the "info" column is not reduced; it merely moves with the "hours" column.

5. Position the pointer over the navy blue vertical cell border to the right of the "review" column so that a double arrow appears.

(continued)

Figure 54 *Positioning the cursor over a column rule*

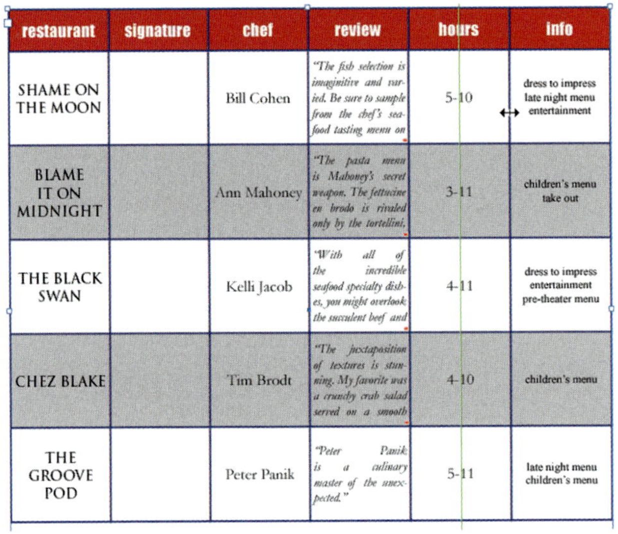

restaurant	signature	chef	review	hours	info
SHAME ON THE MOON		Bill Cohen	"The fish selection is imaginitive and varied. Be sure to sample from the chef's seafood tasting menu on	5-10	dress to impress late night menu entertainment
BLAME IT ON MIDNIGHT		Ann Mahoney	"The pasta menu is Mahoney's secret weapon. The fettucine en brodo is rivaled only by the tortellini,	3-11	children's menu take out
THE BLACK SWAN		Kelli Jacob	"With all of the incredible seafood specialty dishes, you might overlook the succulent beef and	4-11	dress to impress entertainment pre-theater menu
CHEZ BLAKE		Tim Brodt	"The juxtaposition of textures is stunning. My favorite was a crunchy crab salad served on a smooth	4-10	children's menu
THE GROOVE POD		Peter Panik	"Peter Panik is a culinary master of the unexpected."	5-11	late night menu children's menu

Figure 55 *Reducing the width of a column*

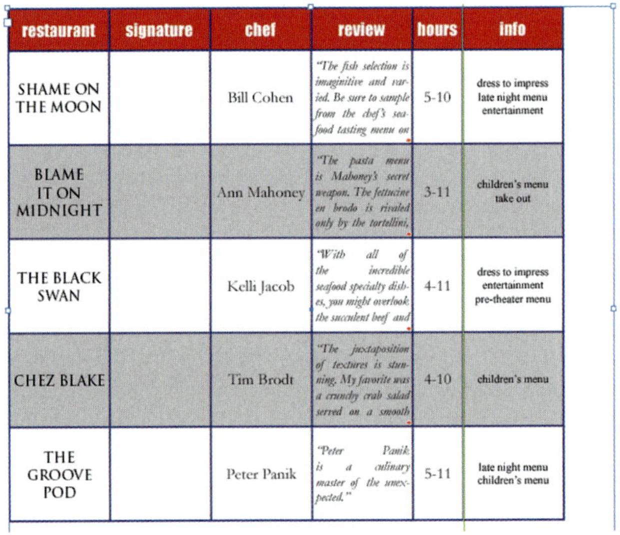

restaurant	signature	chef	review	hours	info
SHAME ON THE MOON		Bill Cohen	"The fish selection is imaginitive and varied. Be sure to sample from the chef's seafood tasting menu on	5-10	dress to impress late night menu entertainment
BLAME IT ON MIDNIGHT		Ann Mahoney	"The pasta menu is Mahoney's secret weapon. The fettucine en brodo is rivaled only by the tortellini,	3-11	children's menu take out
THE BLACK SWAN		Kelli Jacob	"With all of the incredible seafood specialty dishes, you might overlook the succulent beef and	4-11	dress to impress entertainment pre-theater menu
CHEZ BLAKE		Tim Brodt	"The juxtaposition of textures is stunning. My favorite was a crunchy crab salad served on a smooth	4-10	children's menu
THE GROOVE POD		Peter Panik	"Peter Panik is a culinary master of the unexpected."	5-11	late night menu children's menu

Working with Tabs and Tables

Figure 56 *Increasing the width of a column*

restaurant	signature	chef	review	hours	info
SHAME ON THE MOON		Bill Cohen	*"The fish selection is imaginitive and varied. Be sure to sample from the chef's seafood tasting menu on Thursday nights."*	5-10	dress to impress late night menu entertainment
BLAME IT ON MIDNIGHT		Ann Mahoney	*"The pasta menu is Mahoney's secret weapon. The fettucine en brodo is rivaled only by the tortel-lini, which was simply a marvel."*	3-11	children's menu take out
THE BLACK SWAN		Kelli Jacob	*"With all of the incredible seafood specialty dishes, you might overlook the succulent beef and veal selections. That would be a tragedy."*	4-11	dress to impress entertainment pre-theater menu
CHEZ BLAKE		Tim Brodt	*"The juxtaposition of textures is stunning. My favorite was a crunchy crab salad served on a smooth lime gelee."*	4-10	children's menu
THE GROOVE POD		Peter Panik	*"Peter Panik is a culinary master of the unexpected."*	5-11	late night menu children's menu

Figure 57 *Viewing the edited table*

restaurant	signature	chef	review	hours	info
SHAME ON THE MOON		Bill Cohen	*"The fish selection is imaginitive and varied. Be sure to sample from the chef's seafood tasting menu on Thursday nights."*	5-10	dress to impress late night menu entertainment
BLAME IT ON MIDNIGHT		Ann Mahoney	*"The pasta menu is Mahoney's secret weapon. The fettucine en brodo is rivaled only by the tortellini, which was simply a marvel."*	3-11	children's menu take out
THE BLACK SWAN		Kelli Jacob	*"With all of the incredible seafood specialty dishes, you might overlook the succulent beef and veal selections. That would be a tragedy."*	4-11	dress to impress entertainment pre-theater menu
CHEZ BLAKE		Tim Brodt	*"The juxtaposition of textures is stunning. My favorite was a crunchy crab salad served on a smooth lime gelee."*	4-10	children's menu
THE GROOVE POD		Peter Panik	*"Peter Panik is a culinary master of the unexpected."*	5-11	late night menu children's menu

6. Click and drag the **arrow** right until the right edge of the "review" column is aligned with the green guide, as shown in Figure 56.

7. Select only the five cells containing reviews.

8. On the Table panel, increase the Left Cell Inset value to .125, then increase the Right Cell Inset value to .125.

9. Deselect all, click **View** on the Application bar, point to **Grids & Guides**, click **Hide Guides**, then compare your table to Figure 57.

10. Save your work.

You decreased the width of one column and increased the width of another in order to fit text. You also increased the left and right cell insets so that the text was not too close to the vertical rules.

Place Graphics
IN A TABLE

What You'll Do

restaurant	signature	chef	review	hours	into
SHAME ON THE MOON		Bill Cohen	*"The fish selection is imaginitive and varied. Be sure to sample from the chef's seafood tasting menu on Thursday nights."*	5-10	
BLAME IT ON MIDNIGHT		Ann Mahoney	*"The pasta menu is Mahoney's secret weapon. The fettucine en brodo is rivaled only by the tortellini, which was simply a marvel."*	3-11	
THE BLACK SWAN		Kelli Jacob	*"With all of the incredible seafood specialty dishes, you might overlook the succulent beef and veal selections. That would be a tragedy."*	4-11	
CHEZ BLAKE		Tim Brodt	*"The juxtaposition of textures is stunning. My favorite was a crunchy crab salad served on a smooth lime gelee."*	4-10	
THE GROOVE POD		Peter Panik	*"Peter Panik is a culinary master of the unexpected."*	5-11	

 In this lesson, you will insert graphics into table cells using the Place command and the Copy and Paste commands.

Placing Graphics in a Table

InDesign makes it easy to place a graphic into a cell in a table. One simple method is to simply click in the cell and then use the Place command to choose and place the graphic.

Graphics that are placed in cells are treated like any other placed graphics. They appear in the Links panel and can be updated or edited, if necessary.

If the graphic you place is too large to fit in the cell, a red circle will appear in the bottom-right corner of the cell. Your only options are to increase the size of the cell or decrease the size of the graphic. Figure 58 shows a table with six graphics placed in the rightmost column.

If you've entered text into a table, you have the option of replacing text with graphics. Remember, InDesign regards tables as text. Thus, graphics in tables function as anchored objects, just like any other text element. Many designers, when they are building tables, will simply type a graphic's name in a cell as a placeholder and place the graphics in the pasteboard for later use. Then, when they're finished editing the table, they replace the text with the graphics.

You replace text in a cell with a graphic the same way you add anchored objects to a block of text. Select the graphic in the pasteboard with the Selection tool, copy it, select the text in the cell with the Type tool, then paste the graphic. The graphic will flow with any other text that is in the cell. This is a powerful option; it allows you to place both text and graphics in a single cell!

QUICK TIP

If a graphic you want to insert is in a separate file, you can use the Place command to put it at the insertion point location.

Merging and Splitting Table Cells

There may be times when you would like to convert one or more table cells into one large cell, a process known as merging. Merging cells allows you to accommodate more text or larger graphics in one cell.

For example, you may want to create a merged cell and place a heading in it, such as "Weekly Camp Activities," above a row of cells that includes the five weekdays. To merge a group of cells, select the cells, click Table on the Application bar, then click Merge Cells. Conversely, you can select one or more cells and split them horizontally or vertically. Just click Table on the Application bar and choose Split Cells Vertically or Split Cells Horizontally.

Figure 58 *Placing graphics in a table*

State	Founded	Area	Capital	Pop	Flag
CONNECTICUT	1788	5,544 sq/mi	Hartford	3,405,000	
MASSACHUSETTS	1788	10,555 sq/mi	Boston	6, 349,000	
NEW HAMPSHIRE	1788	9,351 sq/mi	Concord	1,235,000	
RHODE ISLAND	1790	1,545 sq/mi	Providence	1, 048,00	
VERMONT	1791	9,615 sq/mi	Montpelier	608,000	
MAINE	1820	35,387 sq/mi	Augusta	1,274,000	

Place graphics in a table

1. Click in the second cell of the second row.

2. Place the file named Sole.tif from the location where your Data Files are stored.

3. Click in the second cell of the third row.

4. Place the file named Crab salad.tif, then compare your work to Figure 59.

5. Click the **Selection tool** ⬈ if necessary, select the Crab Salad.tif graphic, click **Object** on the Application bar, point to **Clipping Path**, then click **Options**.

6. Click the **Type list arrow**, click **Alpha Channel**, then click **OK**.

7. Moving downward in the second column, place the following graphics: Striped bass.tif, Gnocchi.tif, and Tuna.tif.

8. Select the Gnocchi.tif graphic, click **Object** on the Application bar, point to **Clipping Path**, then click **Options**.

9. Click the **Type list arrow**, click **Alpha Channel**, click **OK**, then compare your table to Figure 60.

You used the Place command to place graphics in cells.

Replace text with graphics

1. Click the **Selection tool** ⬈, click the **moon graphic** in the pasteboard, then copy it.

TIP The "moon" graphic is the top-left graphic on the pasteboard.

2. Click the **Type tool** T, then select the "late night menu" text in the top cell of the info column.

(continued)

Figure 59 *Placing two graphics*

Figure 60 *Placing three additional graphics*

Figure 61 *Replacing two lines of text with graphics*

restaurant	signature	chef	review	hours	info
SHAME ON THE MOON		Bill Cohen	"The fish selection is imaginitive and varied. Be sure to sample from the chef's seafood tasting menu on Thursday nights."	5-10	dress to impress entertainment
BLAME IT ON MIDNIGHT		Ann Mahoney	"The pasta menu is Mahoney's secret weapon. The fettucine en brodo is rivaled only by the tortellini, which was simply a marvel."	3-11	children's menu take out
THE BLACK SWAN		Kelli Jacob	"With all of the incredible seafood specialty dishes, you might overlook the succulent beef and veal selections. That would be a tragedy."	4-11	dress to impress entertainment pre-theater menu
CHEZ BLAKE		Tim Brodt	"The juxtaposition of textures is stunning. My favorite was a crunchy crab salad served on a smooth lime gelee."	4-10	children's menu
THE GROOVE POD		Peter Panik	"Peter Panik is a culinary master of the unexpected."	5-11	children's menu

Figure 63 *Completing the table*

restaurant	signature	chef	review	hours	info
SHAME ON THE MOON		Bill Cohen	"The fish selection is imaginitive and varied. Be sure to sample from the chef's seafood tasting menu on Thursday nights."	5-10	
BLAME IT ON MIDNIGHT		Ann Mahoney	"The pasta menu is Mahoney's secret weapon. The fettucine en brodo is rivaled only by the tortellini, which was simply a marvel."	3-11	
THE BLACK SWAN		Kelli Jacob	"With all of the incredible seafood specialty dishes, you might overlook the succulent beef and veal selections. That would be a tragedy."	4-11	
CHEZ BLAKE		Tim Brodt	"The juxtaposition of textures is stunning. My favorite was a crunchy crab salad served on a smooth lime gelee."	4-10	
THE GROOVE POD		Peter Panik	"Peter Panik is a culinary master of the unexpected."	5-11	

Figure 62 *Placing three graphics in a cell*

3. Click **Edit** on the Application bar, then click **Paste**.

4. Select the "late night menu" text in the bottom cell of the info column, click **Edit** on the Application bar, then click **Paste**.

    Your table should resemble Figure 61.

TIP Press [Enter] (Win) or [return] (Mac) if "children's menu" is not on a separate line

5. Click the **Selection tool**, click the **tie graphic** in the pasteboard, copy it, then click the **Type tool**.

6. Triple-click **dress to impress** in the top cell of the info column to select the line of text, then paste.

    The tie graphic replaces the text; the moon graphic and tie graphic are on the same line.

7. Click the **Selection tool**, click the **music graphic** in the pasteboard, copy it, click the **Type tool**, select the "entertainment" text in the top cell of the info column, then paste.

    The top cell in your info column should resemble Figure 62.

8. Using the same method, replace all the text in the info column with corresponding icons so that your table resembles Figure 63.

TIP Use the key below the table to identify the icon that corresponds with the text.

TIP Each icon file has a clipping path that you can use to remove the background.

9. Save your work, then close Table Complete.

You replaced selected text elements with graphics.

Work with tabs.

1. Open ID 9-4.indd, then save it as **Tab Review**.
2. Click the Selection tool, click the text frame that contains the data, click Object on the Application bar, then click Text Frame Options.
3. In the Inset Spacing section, type **.3** in the Top text box, type **.3** in the Left text box, then click OK.
4. Click the Type tool, then select all of the text.
5. Click Type on the Application bar, then click Tabs.
6. Click the Left-Justified Tab button in the Tabs dialog box.
7. Position the pointer in the white space in the top third of the ruler—just above the numbers—then click and drag until the X text box reads 1 in.
8. Using the same method, create a new tab at 2.25", making sure the tab is left-justified.
9. Click anywhere to the right of the second tab to add a third tab.
10. Select the measurement in the X text box, type **3**, then press [Enter] (Win) or [return] (Mac), then make sure the tab is left-justified.
11. Click the Type tool pointer to the left of the first # sign in the first line of text, then press [Tab].
12. Click the Type tool pointer to the left of the second # sign, then press [Tab].
13. Click the Type tool pointer to the left of the word Profit, then press [Tab].
14. Using the same tabs, tab the numbers on the next four lines. (*Hint*: Be sure to click to the immediate left of each number before pressing [Tab]).
15. Select all of the text, click Object on the Application bar, click Text Frame Options, change the Left inset to .5, then click OK.
16. Click the Position Panel above Text Frame button in the Tabs dialog box.
17. Select only the bottom four rows of text.
18. Click the first left-justified tab at 1" in the tab ruler to select it.
19. Type **1.4** in the X text box, then press [Enter] (Win) or [return] (Mac).
20. Click the second left-justified tab at 2.25" in the tab ruler to select it.
21. Type **2.5** in the X text box, then press [Enter] (Win) or [return] (Mac).
22. Click the Align to Decimal tab button in the Tabs dialog box.
23. Click the third left-justified tab at 3" in the tab ruler to select it.
24. Click the Align to Decimal Tab button in the Tabs dialog box.
25. Type **3.2** in the X text box, then press [Enter] (Win) or [return] (Mac).
26. With the four rows of text still selected, click the first tab in the tab ruler to highlight it.

27. In the Leader text box, type **a period followed by a space**, then press [Enter] (Win) or [return] (Mac).
28. Click the second tab in the tab ruler to highlight it.
29. In the Leader text box, type **a period followed by a space**, then press [Enter] (Win) or [return] (Mac).
30. Click the third tab in the tab ruler to highlight it.
31. In the Leader text box, type **a period followed by a space**, then press [Enter] (Win) or [return] (Mac).
32. Click the Paragraph panel options button, then click Paragraph Rules.
33. Click the list arrow at the top of the dialog box, click Rule Below, then click the Rule On check box.
34. Choose the same settings shown in Figure 64 to define the rule, then click OK.
35. Deselect all, close the Tabs dialog box, then compare your page to Figure 65.
36. Save your work, then close Tab Review.

Figure 64 *Paragraph Rules dialog box*

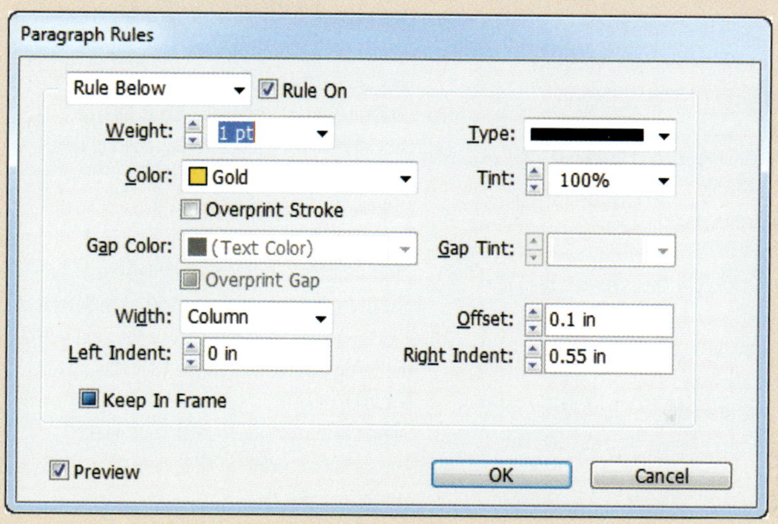

Figure 65 *Completed Skills Review, Part 1*

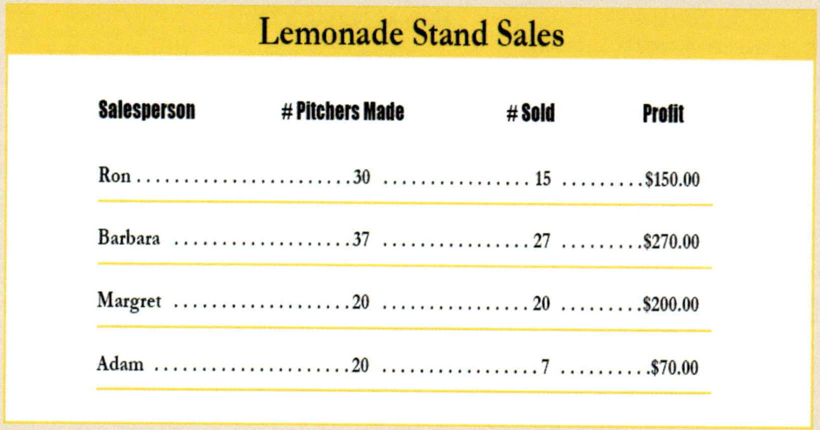

Lemonade Stand Sales			
Salesperson	# Pitchers Made	# Sold	Profit
Ron	30	15	$150.00
Barbara	37	27	$270.00
Margret	20	20	$200.00
Adam	20	7	$70.00

Create and format a table.

1. Open ID 9-5.indd, then save it as **Table Review**.
2. Close all open panels except for the Tools panel, click the Type tool, then create a text frame that snaps to all four margin guides.
3. Click View on the Application bar, point to Grids & Guides, then click Hide Guides.
4. Click Table on the Application bar, then click Insert Table.
5. Type **7** in the Body Rows text box, then type **6** in the Columns text box.
6. Click OK, click Window on the Application bar, point to Type & Tables, then click Table.
7. Position the pointer over the second cell in the first column, then click and drag to select all of the rows except the top row.
8. Click the Row Height list arrow on the Table panel, then click Exactly.
9. Type **1.625** in the text box next to the Row Height text box, then press [Enter] (Win) or [return] (Mac).
10. Position the pointer over the left edge of the top cell in the first row so that a heavy black arrow appears pointing to the right.
11. Click once to select the top row.
12. Click the Row Height list arrow on the Table panel, then click Exactly.
13. Type **.5** in the text box next to the Row Height text box, then press [Enter] (Win) or [return] (Mac).
14. Position the pointer over the top-left corner of the table so that a black diagonal arrow appears.

15. Click once to select the entire table.
16. Click Table on the Application bar, point to Cell Options, then click Strokes and Fills.
17. Click the Weight list arrow, then click 2 pt.
18. Click the Color list arrow, click Black, then click OK.
19. Click Table on the Application bar, point to Table Options, then click Alternating Fills.
20. Click the Alternating Pattern list arrow, then click Every Other Row.
21. Click the first Color list arrow on the left side of the dialog box, click Gold, then type **100** in the Tint text box.
22. Click the second Color list arrow on the right side of the dialog box, click Navy, type **18** in the Tint text box, then click OK.
23. Select the top row of cells, click Table on the Application bar, point to Cell Options, then click Strokes and Fills.
24. In the Cell Fill area, click the Color list arrow, click Navy, type **100** in the Tint text box, then click OK.

Format text in a table.

1. Click the Type tool in the top-left text box, then type **State**.
2. Press [Tab], then type **Founded**.
3. In the remaining four cells of the top row, type **Area**, **Capital**, **Pop**, and **Flag**.
4. Click in the first cell of the second row, then type **CONNECTICUT** in all caps.

Note: type all the state names in all caps.

5. Press ↓, then type **MASSACHUSETTS**.

6. Press ↓, then type **NEW HAMPSHIRE**.
7. Press ↓, then type **RHODE ISLAND**.
8. Press ↓, then type **VERMONT**.
9. Press ↓, then type **MAINE**.
10. Position the pointer over the left edge of the first cell in the top row so that a black arrow appears pointing right, then click to select the entire row.
11. Show the Swatches panel, click the Formatting affects text button, then click Paper.
12. Show the Character panel, change the font to Impact, then change the font size to 18 pt.
13. Click anywhere in the first cell of the second row, then drag down to select all of the cells in the first column (except the top row).
14. Show the Character Styles panel, then click Names. (*Hint*: If your computer substituted a different font and your state names are not all capital letters, select the state names and apply another all-capital font.)
15. Position the pointer over the top-left corner of the table so that a black diagonal arrow appears, then click to select the entire table.
16. Click the Align center button on the Paragraph panel, then deselect all.
17. Save your work, then close Table Review.
18. Open ID 9-6.indd, then save it as **Table Review Completed**.
19. Select the top row of cells, then click the Align bottom button on the Table panel.
20. Click anywhere in the "CONNECTICUT" cell, then click and drag to select the bottom six rows.

21. Click the Align center button on the Table panel.
22. Click View on the Application bar, point to Grids & Guides, then click Show Guides if necessary.
23. Position the pointer over the vertical cell border that separates the first two columns so that a double arrow appears.
24. Click and drag the arrow right, so that the vertical cell border is aligned with the green vertical guide.
25. Position the pointer over the vertical cell border that separates the second and third columns so that a double arrow appears.
26. Click and drag the arrow left, so that the vertical cell border is aligned with the red vertical guide.
27. Position the pointer over the vertical cell border that separates the fifth and sixth columns so that a double arrow appears.
28. Click and drag the arrow left, so that the vertical cell border is aligned with the blue vertical guide.
29. Position the pointer over the right edge of the table, then drag right until the right edge of the table is aligned with the margin guide.

Place graphics in a table.

1. Click in the sixth cell of the second row.
2. Place the file named CT State Flag.tif from the location where your Chapter 9 Data Files are stored.
3. Click in the next cell down.
4. Place the file named MA State Flag.tif.
5. Using the same method and moving downward in the column, place the following graphics: NH State Flag.tif, RI State Flag.tif, VT State Flag.tif, ME State Flag.tif.
6. Deselect all, hide guides, then compare your table with Figure 66. (Your screen may appear different if your computer substituted fonts.)
7. Save your work, then close Table Review Completed.

Figure 66 *Completed Skills Review, Part 2*

State	Founded	Area	Capital	Pop	Flag
CONNECTICUT	1788	5,544 sq/mi	Hartford	3,405,000	
MASSACHUSETTS	1788	10,555 sq/mi	Boston	6, 349,000	
NEW HAMPSHIRE	1788	9,351 sq/mi	Concord	1,235,000	
RHODE ISLAND	1790	1,545 sq/mi	Providence	1, 048,00	
VERMONT	1791	9,615 sq/mi	Montpelier	608,000	
MAINE	1820	35,387 sq/mi	Augusta	1,274,000	

You are a designer at a manufacturer of games. A junior designer has e-mailed you a chart that she created, showing the winners of a recent promotion. You note immediately that the chart is not well designed. You decide to make improvements before showing it to your boss.

1. Open ID 9-7.indd, then save it as **Contest Redesign**.
2. Select the headline only, then click the Align center button on the Paragraph panel.
3. Select all of the text in the frame, click Object on the Application bar, then click Text Frame Options.
4. In the Inset Spacing section, type **.4** in the Top text box only, verify that the other three textboxes are set to 0, then click OK.
5. Select only the five rows of data (not the headline).
6. Click Type on the Application bar, then click Tabs.
7. Click the left-justified tab already in the tab ruler to select it, then click the Align to Decimal Tab button.
8. Select the contents of the X text box on the Tabs panel, type **2.75**, then press [Enter] (Win) or [return] (Mac).
9. Click the Tab ruler approximately at the 2" mark to add a new tab.
10. Change the tab to a left-justified tab.
11. Select the contents of the X text box, type **.75**, then press [Enter] (Win) or [return] (Mac).
12. Click to the left of the first name, then press [Tab].
13. Tab the remaining four names, close the Tabs dialog box, then compare your work to Figure 67.
14. Save your work, then close Contest Redesign.

Figure 67 *Completed Project Builder 1*

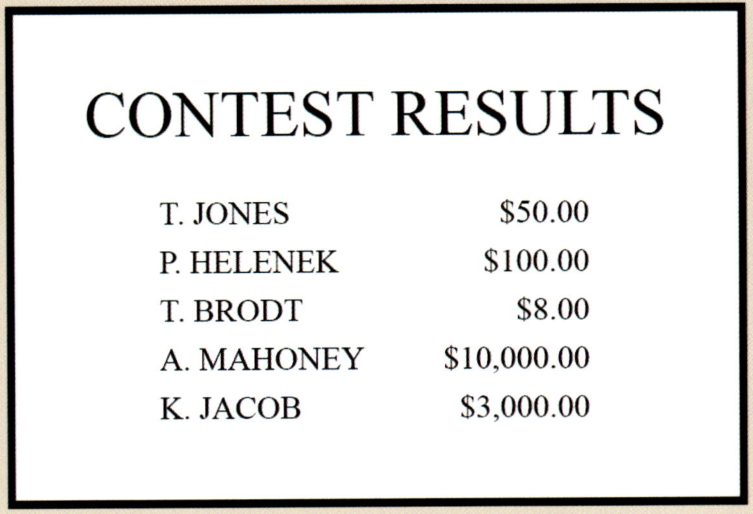

CONTEST RESULTS

T. JONES	$50.00
P. HELENEK	$100.00
T. BRODT	$8.00
A. MAHONEY	$10,000.00
K. JACOB	$3,000.00

Your company has recently held a sales contest. You are in charge of showing the contest results. One of your staff designers has e-mailed you a chart showing the results and says it's "ready to go." You feel that the chart looks a bit stark, so you decide to add rules to it.

1. Open ID 9-8.indd, then save it as **Contest Rules**.
2. Select the five lines of data, then increase the leading to 20 pts.
3. Click the Paragraph panel options button, then click Paragraph Rules.
4. Click the Rule On check box, type **.25** in the Left Indent text box, type **.25** in the Right Indent text box, type **p5** in the Offset text box, then click OK.
5. Select only the first row of text (T. Jones), click the Paragraph panel options button, then click Paragraph Rules.
6. Click the Rule Below list arrow, choose Rule Above, then click the Rule On check box.
7. Type **.25** in the Left Indent text box, type **.25** in the Right Indent text box, type **p15** in the Offset text box, then click OK.
8. Deselect all, save your work, compare your chart to Figure 68, then close Contest Rules.

Figure 68 *Completed Project Builder 2*

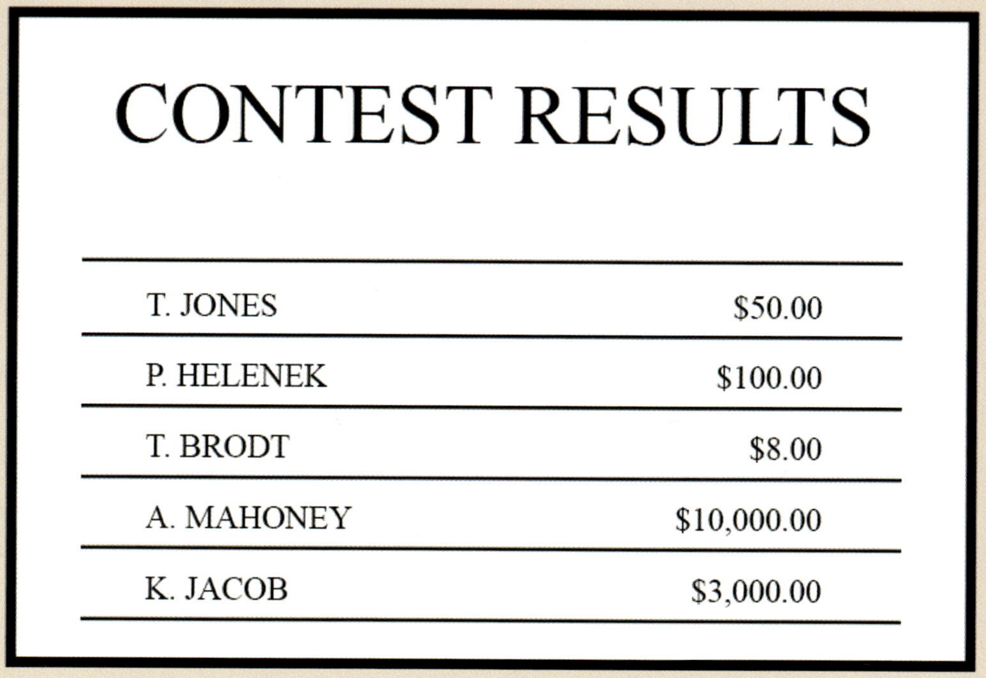

CONTEST RESULTS

T. JONES	$50.00
P. HELENEK	$100.00
T. BRODT	$8.00
A. MAHONEY	$10,000.00
K. JACOB	$3,000.00

You are a freelance designer. Your client has given you a table she created in InDesign and has asked you to "give it some life." You open the file and decide that it needs color and some reformatting.

1. Open ID 9-9.indd, then save it as **Mountain Table**.
2. Select all of the cells in the table, change their height to exactly .75 in, then change their width to exactly 2 in.
3. Center all the text horizontally and vertically.
4. Change the cell strokes to 2 pt Navy.
5. Apply alternating fills of 18% Navy and 18% Green.
6. Change the fill on the top row to 100% Navy.
7. Change the top row of text to 22 pt Impact.
8. Change the fill color of the text on the top row of text to Paper.
9. Select all of the text in rows 2 through 6, then change the type size to 22 pt.
10. Deselect all, then compare your work to Figure 69.
11. Save your work, then close Mountain Table.

Figure 69 *Completed Design Project*

Mountain	State	Elevation	First Scaled
Mount Jefferson	Utah	6288 ft.	1937
Mount Rustic	Colorado	7789 ft.	1933
Mount Green	Massachusetts	4953 ft.	1877
Bear Mountain	California	5784 ft.	1899
Goat Mountain	New Hampshire	6235 ft.	1910

In this project, you will build a chart from scratch, using tabs based on supplied information. You are free to choose the size of the chart and any colors, rules, tab leaders, or text formatting that might make the chart more visually pleasing. The chart will be based on the following information:

1. Create a new InDesign document, then save it as **Holiday Chart**.

   The title of the chart is: Annual Holiday Fund Raiser. Five students sold five different products during the holiday raffle. The sales information is as follows:

   - Karen sold 100 lollipops at a retail cost of 35 cents per unit, for a total net revenue of $35.00.
   - Jimmy sold 45 lapel pins at a retail cost of $2 per unit, for a total net revenue of $90.00.
   - Billy sold 30 candles at a retail cost of $2.50 per unit, for a total net revenue of $75.00.
   - Susan sold 10 rolls of mints at a retail cost of 50 cents per unit, for a total net revenue of $5.00.
   - Michael sold 20 calendars at a retail cost of $10 per unit, for a total net revenue of $200.00.

2. When you finish your chart, compare your work with Figure 70.
3. Save your work, then close Holiday Chart.

Figure 70 *Sample Portfolio Project*

Annual Holiday Fund Raiser

Sales Person	Product	Number Sold	Retail Cost	Net Revenue
Karen	Lollipops	100	$.35	$35.00
Jimmy	Lapel Pins	45	$2.00	$90.00
Billy	Candles	30	$2.50	$75.00
Susan	Mints	10	$.50	$5.00
Michael	Calendars	20	$10.00	$200.00

CHAPTER 10 MAKING BOOKS, TABLES OF CONTENTS, AND INDEXES

1. Create a book file
2. Organize a book file
3. Create a table of contents
4. Create an index

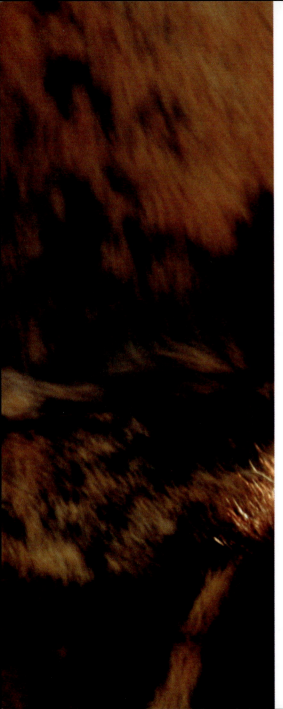

CHAPTER 10 MAKING BOOKS, TABLES OF CONTENTS, AND INDEXES

Imagine that you've created a number of InDesign documents, each of which is meant to be a chapter in a book. InDesign's Book feature allows you to combine and collate all of those separate documents into one book with continuous pagination. Want to switch the order of chapters? Feel free! The Book panel allows you to reorganize at will, and it will automatically repaginate your book every time you make a change.

This is a very cool feature. But InDesign's automatic table of contents and index features will really wow you! With a click of a button, InDesign examines all the documents on the Book panel, identifies text items that you've saved with specific paragraph styles, then sorts those text items into a table of contents or an index, complete with page numbers.

In the early days of desktop publishing, the ability to cut and paste text within an electronic document was revolutionary. Play around with InDesign's automatic table of contents and index features and you'll be amazed at how far we've come!

‡ DOG BREEDS

Table of Contents

TOC Style: [Default]

Title: Contents

Style: [No Paragraph Style]

OK

Cancel

Save Style...

More Options

Styles in Table of Contents

Include Paragraph Styles:

Other Styles:
- [No Paragraph Style]
- Breed Name
- [Basic Paragraph]
- Section Name

<< Add

Remove >>

Style:

Entry Style:

Options

☑ Create PDF Bookmarks

☐ Replace Existing Table of Contents

☐ Include Book Documents

Numbered Paragraphs: Exclude Numbers

Book Page Numbering Options

Options

Page Order: ○ Continue from previous document

● Continue on next odd page

○ Continue on next even page

☐ Insert Blank Page

☑ Automatically Update Page & Section Numbers

OK

Cancel

Generate Index

Title:

Title Style: Index Title

☑ Replace Existing Index

☐ Include Book Documents

☐ Include Entries on Hidden Layers

Book Name: Dog Breeds.indb

OK

Cancel

More Options

Create a
BOOK FILE

What You'll Do

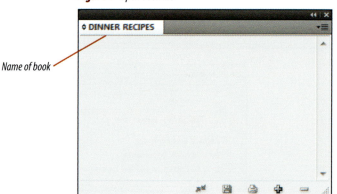

In this lesson, you will create a book file and add documents to create a book.

Creating a Book File

In Adobe InDesign, a book is a collection of two or more InDesign documents, which are paginated as a single book. For example, you can collect three 10-page documents as a single 30-page book.

Creating a book is similar to creating a document—you use the New command on the File menu; however, you choose Book instead of Document. A book is an individual InDesign file, like a library file, and when opened, it appears as a panel. Figure 1 shows an open book file.

QUICK TIP

Unlike InDesign documents, which have a filename extension of .indd (InDesign document), book files have a filename extension of .indb (InDesign book).

Adding Documents to a Book Panel

To create a book, you add InDesign documents to the Book panel. When you do so, the documents are paginated as though they were one book. For example, adding five 20-page documents would create a book that is paginated from 1–100. Figure 2 shows a Book panel after four documents have

Figure 1 *Open book file*

Name of book

Making Books, Tables of Contents, and Indexes

been added. Note the page ranges next to each document name.

When you add documents to a Book panel, the page numbering of those documents is also changed on the Pages panel, when the document is opened from the Book panel. For example, if you add two 20-page documents to the Book panel, the second document on the panel will be paginated from page 21–40. It is important to remember that page numbering changes that occur in your book file affect the original documents, as well, so always save backup copies of your original documents before adding them to a Book panel. You never know when you might need to go back to the original document.

Double-clicking a document on the Book panel opens the document. When a document is open, the Book panel shows the Document is open icon, as shown in Figure 3.

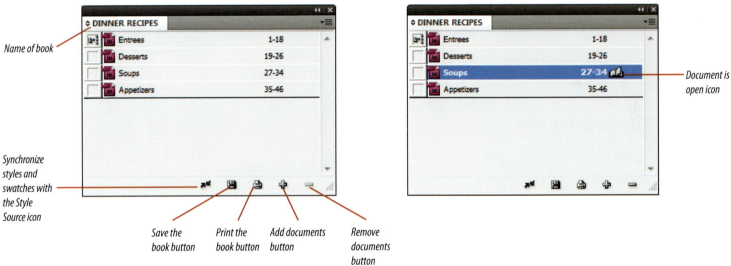

Figure 2 *Viewing documents on the book file*

Name of book

Synchronize styles and swatches with the Style Source icon

Save the book button

Print the book button

Add documents button

Remove documents button

Figure 3 *Book panel showing an open document*

Document is open icon

Create a book file

1. Open ID 10-1.indd, note the number of pages in the Pages panel, then save it as **Toy Breeds**.

   The document has 18 pages, numbered 1-18.

2. Open ID 10-2.indd, note the number of pages in the Pages panel, then save it as **Herding Breeds**.

   The document has 18 pages, numbered 1-18.

3. Open ID 10-3.indd, note the number of pages in the Pages panel, then save it as **Terrier Breeds**.

   The document has 26 pages, numbered 1-26.

4. Open ID 10-4.indd, note the number of pages in the Pages panel, then save it as **Hound Breeds**.

   The document has 20 pages, numbered 1-20.

5. Open ID 10-5.indd, note the number of pages in the Pages panel, then save it as **Sport Breeds**.

   The document has 24 pages, numbered 1-24.

6. Close all open documents.

7. Click **File** on the Application bar, point to **New**, then click **Book**.

8. Name the new file **Dog Breeds**, then click **Save**.

   As shown in Figure 4, a Book panel appears with a single tab named Dog Breeds. This panel is the book file.

You viewed each document that will be used in the book, then created a new book file.

Figure 4 *Dog Breeds book*

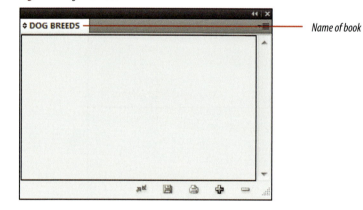

Name of book

Figure 5 *Adding a document to the Book panel*

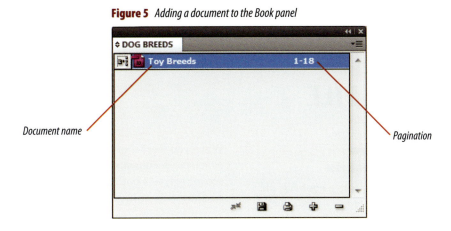

Document name

Pagination

Figure 6 *Dog Breeds book with five documents added*

Continuous
pagination

Add documents to a book file

1. Click the **Book panel options button** , then click **Add Document**.

2. Navigate to the drive and folder where you saved your files, click **Toy Breeds.indd**, then click **Open**.

   As shown in Figure 5, the document is listed on the Book panel along with its page range.

3. Click the **Add documents button** on the Book panel, then add the document named Herding Breeds.indd.

   The document, which was numbered 1-18 in its original file, is added to the Book panel as pages 19-36.

4. Using either of the two methods outlined above, add the following documents in the following order: Terrier Breeds.indd, Hound Breeds.indd, Sport Breeds.indd.

   As shown in Figure 6, the Book panel contains five documents and the pagination is continuous for a total of 106 pages in the book.

5. Click the **Save the book button** on the Book panel.

You added five documents to the Book panel to create a book with 106 pages.

Organize a BOOK FILE

What You'll Do

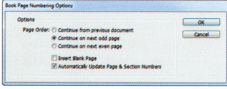

In this lesson, you will modify both the order and the page range of documents on the Book panel.

Manipulating the Order of Documents in a Book File

When you add documents to a book file, the documents are repaginated as you add them. However, you can reorder the documents at any time simply by dragging them up or down on the Book panel. Figure 7 shows four documents in the Dinner Recipes book reordered into the sequence of a meal, with appetizers first and desserts last.

When you reorder documents on the Book panel, the documents are repaginated accordingly—in both the panel and the documents themselves.

Modifying the Page Range of Documents

Typically, the documents that you add to a Book panel will start on page 1 in their original incarnation. In other words, if

Figure 7 *Reordering documents*

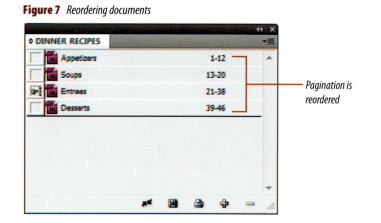

Pagination is reordered

Making Books, Tables of Contents, and Indexes

you add five documents, each would have originally been numbered starting with page 1. By default, page 1 is always a right-hand page.

As discussed previously, documents are repaginated when added to a book file. This can create left-hand page/right-hand page issues. For example, let's say you add two documents. Originally, the first is paginated with pages 1–11. The second is paginated with pages 1–12. Therefore, each begins on a right page. However, once both are added to a book file, the second document will be paginated with pages 12–23. This means that the first page of the second document is now a left-hand page.

This may or may not be a problem for your intended book layout. If it is a problem, you will want to repaginate the document so that it once again begins on a right-hand page. To do so, access the Book Page Numbering Options dialog box, shown in Figure 8, from the Book panel menu. This dialog box allows you to manipulate how documents are paginated as they are added to the book file.

In the above example, you would select the second document and then click the Continue on next odd page option button. This forces the next document to begin on the next odd page in the book. Thus, the second document once again begins on a right-hand page.

This method works on all documents on the Book panel except the first document, because the first document is not "continued" from any other document. In a book file, the first document starts on a right-hand page 1 by default. If you want it to start on an even left-hand page, you need to use a different method. Double-clicking the page numbers of a document on the Book panel opens both the document and the Document Numbering Options dialog box. You can use this dialog box to define the document start page as page 2, for example, as shown in Figure 9. Now the first document begins on an even left-hand page.

Figure 8 *Book Page Numbering Options dialog box*

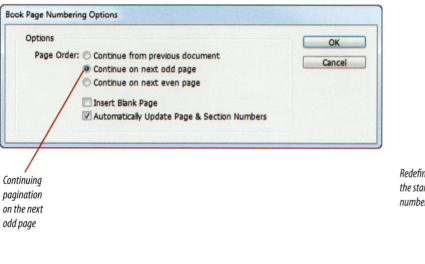

Continuing pagination on the next odd page

Figure 9 *Document Numbering Options dialog box*

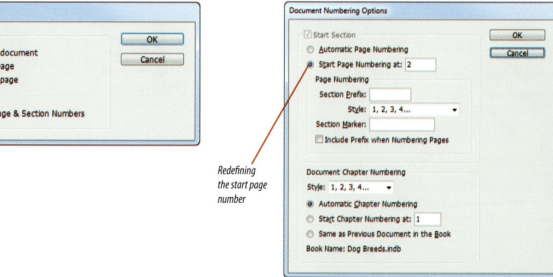

Redefining the start page number

Manipulate the order of documents

1. Note the order of documents on the Book panel.

   For this project, each document will be a chapter in the book. You want the chapters to flow in alphabetical order.

2. Drag **Toy Breeds** down to the bottom of the list.

TIP When you move a document in the list, a black horizontal line appears to denote its new location.

   As shown in Figure 10, when Toy Breeds is moved to the bottom of the list, the page range is renumbered—Toy Breeds now appears on pages 89–106.

3. Rearrange the list so that it is in alphabetical order, as shown in Figure 11.

4. Double-click **Toy Breeds** on the Book panel.

TIP Double-clicking the name of a document on the Book panel opens the InDesign document. Note the Document is open icon next to the page numbers for Toy Breeds in the Book panel.

5. Open the Pages panel.

   Manipulating a document on the Book panel affects the actual document. The Pages panel in Toy Breeds.indd lists the document pages as 89–106.

6. Close Toy Breeds.

You modified the order of documents on the Book panel, noting the changes in page range. You opened one of the documents and noted that the changes made on the Book panel directly affected the document.

Figure 10 *Moving Toy Breeds to the bottom of the list*

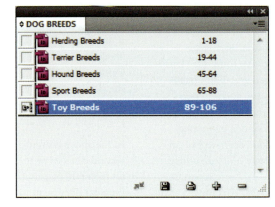

Figure 11 *Reordering the list into alphabetical order*

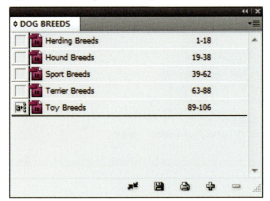

Figure 12 *Changing the pagination of 5 chapters*

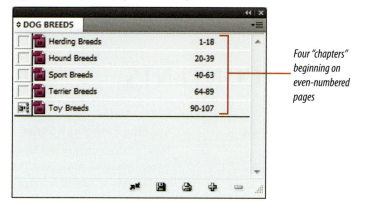

Four "chapters" beginning on even-numbered pages

Figure 13 *Changing the start page of the first chapter*

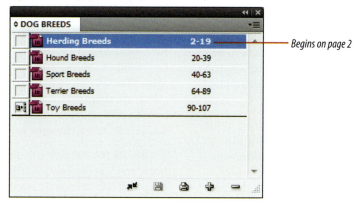

Begins on page 2

Modify the page range of documents

1. Click the **Book panel options button** ▾☰, then click **Book Page Numbering Options**.

   You will designate the first page of every chapter to appear on a left page—an even page number.

2. Click the **Continue on next even page option button**, then click **OK**.

   As shown in Figure 12, all chapters, except for chapter 1, begin on an even-numbered page.

3. On the Book panel, double-click the **page numbers** for Herding Breeds.

TIP Double-clicking the page numbers on the Book panel opens both the document and the Document Numbering Options dialog box.

4. Click the **Start Page Numbering at option button**, type **2** in the text box, then click **OK**.

   The first page of the document is now an even-numbered left-hand page, which is part of a two-page spread.

5. Save the change, close Herding Breeds, then note the page range on the Book panel.

   As shown in Figure 13, the book now begins on page 2 and ends on page 107, with all chapters beginning on an even-numbered left-hand page.

6. Click the **Save the book button** 🖫 on the Book panel.

You modified the page range of the book so that every chapter begins on a left-hand even-numbered page.

Create a TABLE OF CONTENTS

What You'll Do

▶ *In this lesson, you will create a table of contents based on the documents in the book file.*

Using Paragraph Styles to Create a Table of Contents

When you create a table of contents (TOC) for a book, it is generated from information contained within the documents that make up the book. Specifically, the entries in the TOC are text items from the documents that are formatted with specific paragraph styles.

Here's how it works: Let's say that you've created four documents that you want to collate into a recipe book. You want the title of every recipe from every document to be listed in the TOC. To make this happen, you must format the title of each recipe with the same paragraph style.

When you collate the four documents in the book file and then generate a TOC, InDesign searches through all four of the documents and locates all the text elements that were formatted with the paragraph style that you specified. In this example, that would be all the recipe titles. InDesign then copies all of those text elements into a TOC format. It lists all of the text elements and the pages on which they appear in the book. Isn't that an ingenious solution?

Loading Paragraph Styles

Now that you understand how InDesign uses paragraph styles to create a TOC, you need to understand how to manage paragraph styles properly. Remember, paragraph styles must be consistent for every document that has been added to the book.

The best method for assuring consistent paragraph styles is to load them between documents. This couldn't be easier. Once you've created the first document to be used in the book, create the second document, then use the Load Paragraph Styles command on the Paragraph Styles panel menu. You use this command to import the paragraph styles from the first document into the second document. Now, both documents access the same paragraph styles.

Do this for the remaining documents for the book, and you can be confident that all of the paragraph styles are consistent for all of the documents that make up the book.

Maintaining Consistent Styles Between Documents in a Book

In Figure 14, note the Indicates the Style Source icon to the left of Entrees.

Making Books, Tables of Contents, and Indexes

This means that InDesign regards the paragraph styles in the Entrees document as the master paragraph styles. In other words, the paragraph styles in the three other documents should be consistent with those in the Entrees document.

You can select two or more documents on the Book panel and then use the Synchronize Selected Documents command on the panel menu to synchronize styles. When you do so, InDesign automatically searches all the paragraph styles in the selected files and compares them to those in the style source document. If InDesign finds paragraph styles in any of the selected documents that are not consistent with the style source document, it will modify those styles so that they do match, thus insuring consistency throughout the book.

This is a great feature. However, you should note that in most cases, you should not need to use it. Creating a TOC requires foresight and planning. By the time that you add documents into a book file, if you've done your work properly, all your paragraph styles should be consistent. You should not need to rely on the Synchronize Selected Documents command.

Generating a Table of Contents

A table of contents is an individual InDesign document that you add to the Book panel to become part of the book.

When creating the TOC document, it is critical that you carefully choose the same document-setup specifications that were used to create the other documents in the book, such as page size and orientation. After creating the TOC document, add it to the Book panel. Figure 15 shows a TOC document added as page 1 on the Dinner Recipes Book panel.

Once you've added the TOC document to the Book panel, you must then load the paragraph styles used in the other documents in the book. The only way that the TOC document can access the paragraph styles necessary to create the TOC is to have those paragraph styles loaded into the TOC document itself. Simply use the Load Paragraph Styles command on the Paragraph Styles panel.

Figure 14 *Identifying the master paragraph style*

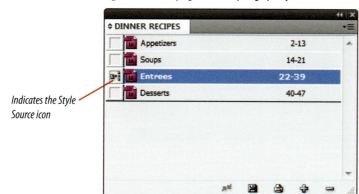

Indicates the Style Source icon

Figure 15 *TOC document on the Book panel*

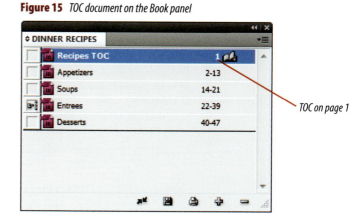

TOC on page 1

The Table of Contents dialog box, shown in Figure 16, is command central for creating a TOC. Once you have loaded the paragraph styles, they will be available in the Other Styles box. Choose which styles you want the TOC to use by adding them to the Include Paragraph Styles box.

One last thing: Be sure to check the Include Book Document check box in the dialog box. This tells InDesign to use the documents on the Book panel as the basis for the TOC.

When you click OK, the TOC is generated. The pointer will appear as the loaded text icon. Simply click it in the TOC document and it will flow the TOC data.

Figure 16 *Table of Contents dialog box*

Available paragraph styles

Check to include documents in open book file

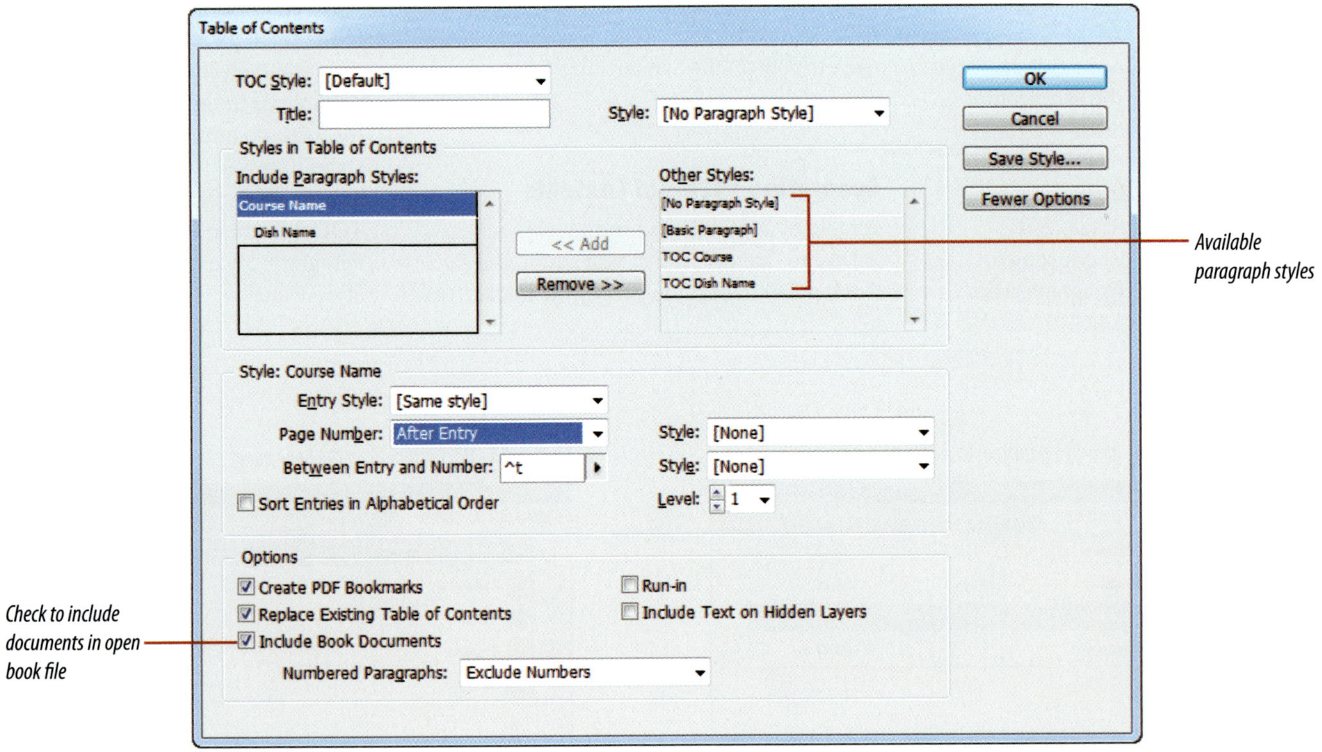

Reformatting Paragraph Styles

In most cases, the paragraph styles from which you generate your TOC will not be appropriate for the TOC layout. In the case of the recipe example, the recipe headlines were formatted as 24-pt headlines. As shown in Figure 17, this size is too large for TOC entries.

You have a number of options for formatting TOC entries. Once you generate the TOC, you can reformat the text any way you see fit or you can modify the paragraph styles in the TOC document only.

For a third solution, you can also create new paragraph styles in the TOC document that are more appropriate for the layout. Any new paragraph styles that you create will be listed in the Table of Contents dialog box.

In the Style section of the Table of Contents dialog box, you can use the new paragraph styles to modify the appearance of the loaded paragraph styles. In Figure 18, the loaded Course Name paragraph style is being modified by the TOC Course paragraph style (note the Entry Style text box).

Here's the concept in a nutshell. A TOC is created based on text that is formatted with specific paragraph styles in the documents that make up a book. Sometimes, those paragraph styles are not appropriate for the TOC layout—they're too big or too small, for example. To correct this, you can create new paragraph styles in the TOC document only. Those new paragraph styles will be listed in the Table of Contents dialog box, where you can use them to modify the loaded paragraph styles.

Figure 19 shows the same data reformatted with two new paragraph styles.

Figure 17 *TOC formatted with loaded paragraph styles*

Figure 18 *Modifying a loaded paragraph style*

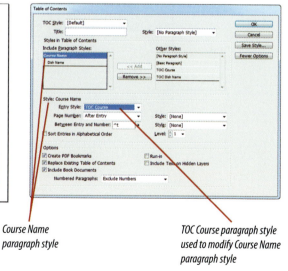

Course Name paragraph style

TOC Course paragraph style used to modify Course Name paragraph style

Figure 19 *TOC with reformatted paragraph styles*

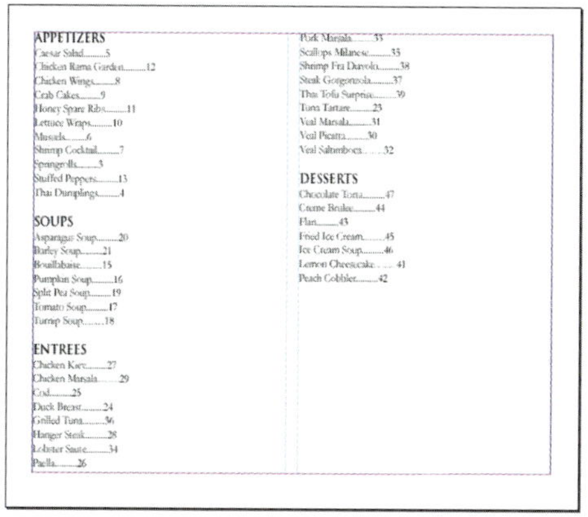

Identify and load paragraph styles for a TOC

1. Double-click **Toy Breeds** on the Book panel to open the document.

2. Open the Paragraph Styles panel.

3. Click the **Type tool** T, then click to place the pointer anywhere in the TOY BREEDS headline on the first page.

   The Paragraph Styles panel identifies the style applied to TOY BREEDS as Section Name.

4. Click to place the pointer in the Silky Terrier headline at the top of the next page.

   The Paragraph Styles panel identifies this style as Breed Name.

5. Close Toy Breeds.

6. Open ID 10-6.indd, then save it as **TOC**.

7. Click the **Paragraph Styles panel options button** ▾≡ , then click **Load Paragraph Styles**.

8. Navigate to the location where you store your files, click **Toy Breeds**, then click **Open**.

   The Load Styles dialog box appears, showing the two paragraph styles that are in the Toy Breeds file.

9. Click **OK**.

   As shown in Figure 20, the Breed Name and Section Name styles from the Toy Breeds file are added to the Paragraph Styles panel in the TOC file.

10. Click **File** on the Application bar, then click **Save**.

You opened a document and examined which text elements were formatted with paragraph styles. You then opened a document that will be used as the TOC and loaded the paragraph styles from the first document.

Figure 20 *Loading paragraph styles*

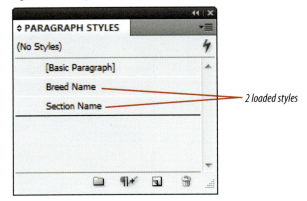

2 loaded styles

Figure 21 *Moving TOC to the top of the panel*

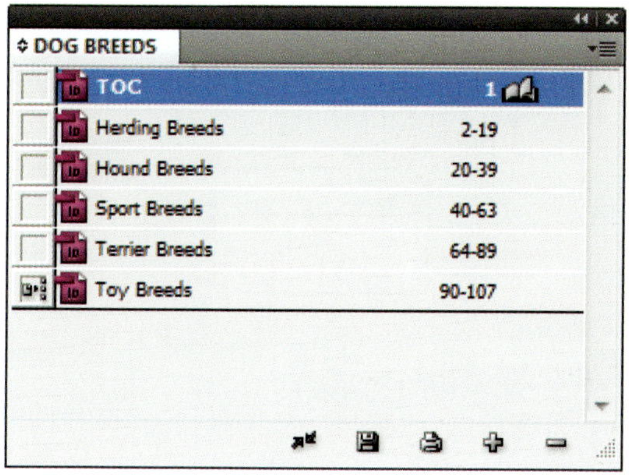

Figure 22 *Table of Contents dialog box*

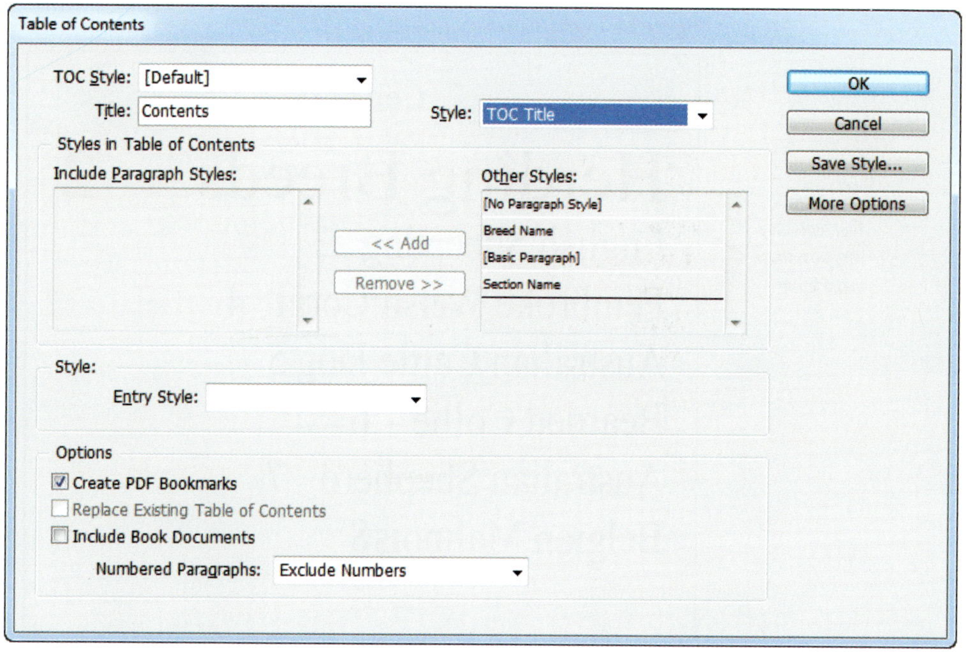

Create a table of contents

1. With TOC still open, click the **Add documents button** on the Book panel, then add TOC to the book.

   TOC is added to the bottom of the list.

2. Drag **TOC** to the top of the list so that your Book panel resembles Figure 21.

3. Click **Layout** on the Application bar, then click **Table of Contents**.

4. Verify that the Title text box reads Contents, then click the **Style list arrow**.

   The Breed Name and Section Name paragraph styles are in the list and available to be used.

5. Choose TOC Title so that your dialog box resembles Figure 22.

TIP TOC Title is a blank paragraph style available by default.

6. Note that the two paragraph styles that you loaded from Toy Breeds.indd are listed in the Other Styles section.

7. Click **Section Name**, then click **Add**.

   Section Name is now listed under Include Paragraph Styles.

(continued)

8. Double-click **Breed Name**.

   Breed Name is now listed beneath Section Name, as shown in Figure 23.

   TIP Double-clicking a style is an alternative to using the Add button.

9. In the Options section, click the **Include Book Documents check box**.

   This check box tells InDesign to create the TOC from the Dog Breeds book.

   TIP This step is easy to forget; make a mental note of it.

10. Click **OK**.

11. Position the pointer over the top-left corner of the margin guides, click, then click **Yes** in the warning box about overflow text, if necessary.

   Your page should resemble Figure 24. The paragraph styles loaded correctly, but those paragraph styles that were used in the source document, Toy Breeds, were formatted for that document's layout, not for a TOC layout. You will need to modify the paragraph styles in the TOC document so the fonts are smaller.

You specified the two paragraph styles that will be used in the TOC, then loaded the TOC into a text frame.

Create paragraph styles for a TOC

1. In the Paragraph Styles panel, click the **Paragraph Styles panel option button** ▼≡, then click **New Paragraph Style**.

2. Name the new style **TOC Section**, click **Basic Character Formats**, click the **Font Family list arrow**, click **Times New Roman** or a similar font, click the **Font Style list arrow**, click **Bold**, click the **Size list arrow**, click **14 pt**, click the **Leading List arrow**, then click **24 pt**.

   (continued)

Figure 23 *Adding two styles to be used in the TOC*

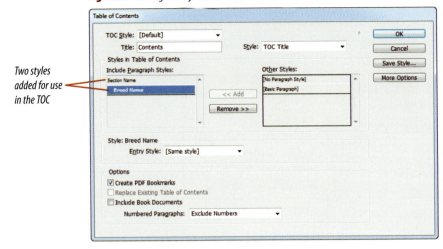

Two styles added for use in the TOC

Figure 24 *Loading the table of contents*

Your fonts may vary from those in the figure

Contents

Herding Breeds 2
English Sheepdog 3
Pembroke Welsh Corgi 4
Australian Cattle Dog 5
Bearded Collie 6
Australian Shepherd 7
Belgian Malinois 8

Figure 25 *Two new paragraph styles*

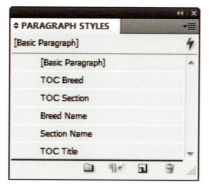

Figure 26 *Reformatting the Section Name paragraph style with the TOC Section paragraph style*

Section Name paragraph style

TOC Section paragraph style

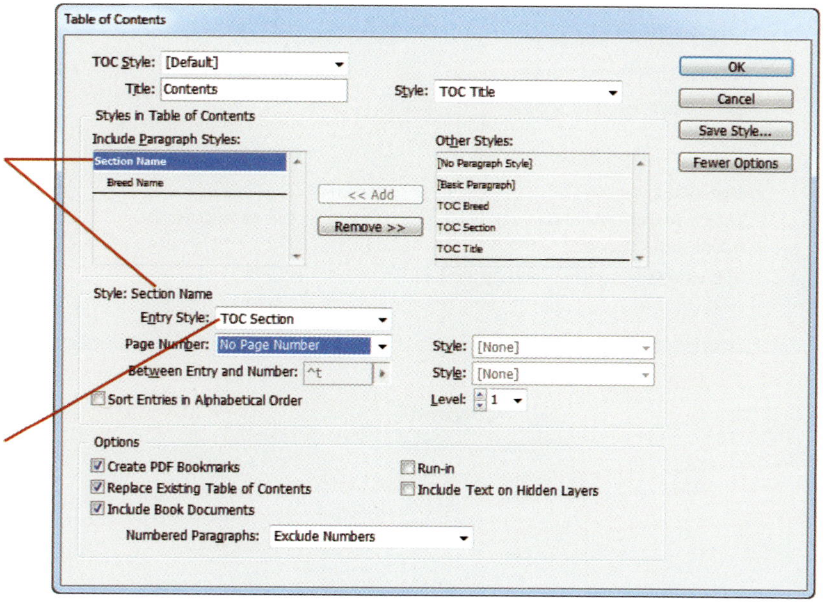

3. Click **OK**.

   A new paragraph style, TOC Section, appears on the Paragraph Styles panel.

4. Click the **Paragraph Styles panel options button** ▾☰, then click **New Paragraph Style**.

5. Name the new style **TOC Breed**, click **Basic Character Formats**, click the **Font Family list arrow**, click **Times New Roman** or a similar font, click the **Font Style list arrow**, click **Regular**, click the **Size list arrow**, click **10 pt**, then click **OK**.

   Your Paragraph Styles panel should resemble Figure 25.

You created two new paragraph styles for the TOC.

Reformat a table of contents

1. Click **Layout** on the Application bar, then click **Table of Contents**.

2. In the Include Paragraph Styles section, click **Section Name**.

   The Style section of the dialog box, directly beneath the Include Paragraph Styles box, now reads Style: Section Name.

3. Click the **Entry Style list arrow**, then click **TOC Section**.

   The Section Name paragraph style will be reformatted with the TOC Section paragraph style.

4. Click the **More Options button** if necessary, to expand the dialog box.

5. In the Style section of the dialog box, click the **Page Number list arrow**, then click **No Page Number**.

   Your dialog box should resemble Figure 26.

(continued)

6. In the Include Paragraph Styles section, click **Breed Name**.

   The Style section of the dialog box now reads Style: Breed Name.

7. Click the **Entry Style list arrow**, click **TOC Breed**, click the **Page Number list arrow**, then click **After Entry**.

8. Select all of the text in the **Between Entry and Number text box**, then type **. . . .** (four periods).

9. Click the **Sort Entries in Alphabetical Order check box**, then verify that the Replace Existing Table of Contents check box is checked.

   Your dialog box should resemble Figure 27.

10. Click **OK**. (Click **Yes** if you see a warning box about overset text.)

TIP You may see an Information dialog box stating that the table of contents has been updated successfully. If so, click **OK**.

(continued)

Figure 27 *Reformatting the Breed Name paragraph style with the TOC Breed paragraph style*

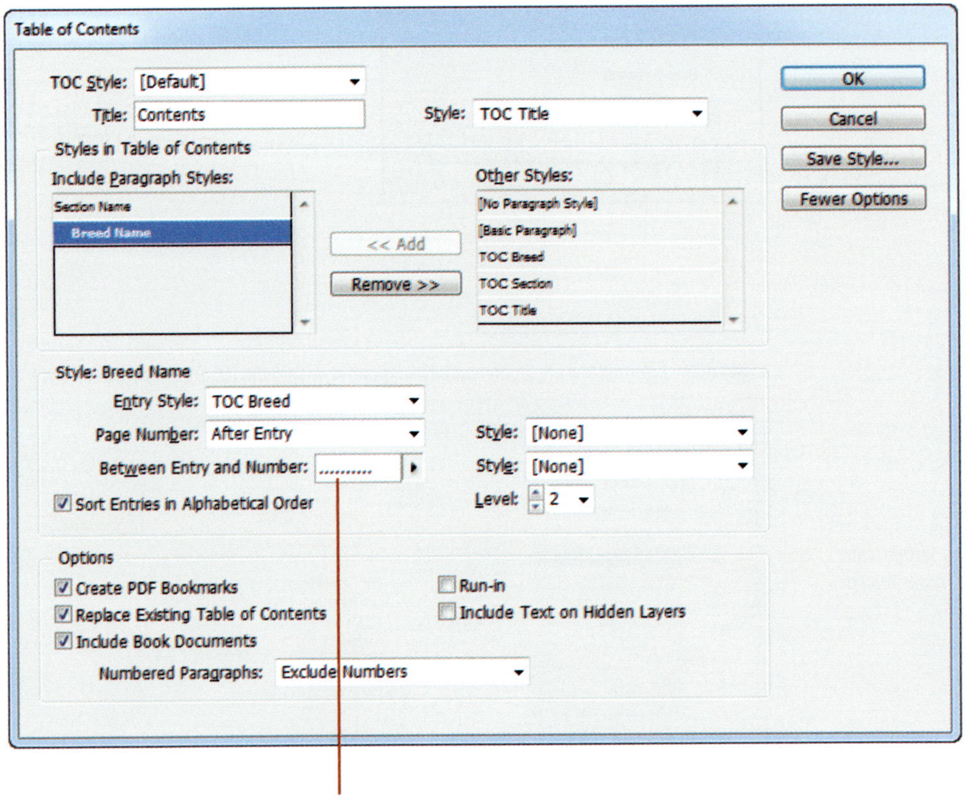

Characters between TOC entry and page number

Figure 28 *Viewing the reformatted TOC*

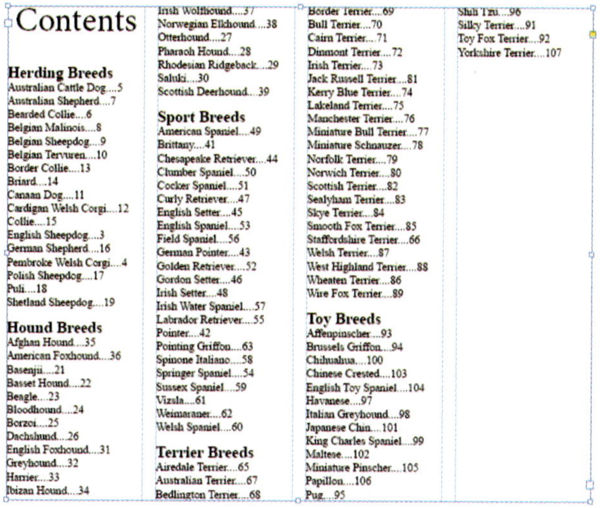

Contents

Herding Breeds
Australian Cattle Dog....5
Australian Shepherd....7
Bearded Collie....6
Belgian Malinois....8
Belgian Sheepdog....9
Belgian Tervuren....10
Border Collie....13
Briard....14
Canaan Dog....11
Cardigan Welsh Corgi....12
Collie....15
English Sheepdog....3
German Shepherd....16
Pembroke Welsh Corgi....4
Polish Sheepdog....17
Puli....18
Shetland Sheepdog....19

Hound Breeds
Afghan Hound....35
American Foxhound....36
Basenji....21
Basset Hound....22
Beagle....23
Bloodhound....24
Borzoi....25
Dachshund....26
English Foxhound....31
Greyhound....32
Harrier....33
Ibizan Hound....34

Irish Wolfhound....37
Norwegian Elkhound....38
Otterhound....27
Pharaoh Hound....28
Rhodesian Ridgeback....29
Saluki....30
Scottish Deerhound....39

Sport Breeds
American Spaniel....49
Brittany....41
Chesapeake Retriever....44
Clumber Spaniel....50
Cocker Spaniel....51
Curly Retriever....47
English Setter....45
English Spaniel....53
Field Spaniel....56
German Pointer....43
Golden Retriever....52
Gordon Setter....46
Irish Setter....48
Irish Water Spaniel....57
Labrador Retriever....55
Pointer....42
Pointing Griffon....63
Spinone Italiano....58
Springer Spaniel....54
Sussex Spaniel....59
Vizsla....61
Weimaraner....62
Welsh Spaniel....60

Terrier Breeds
Airedale Terrier....65
Australian Terrier....67
Bedlington Terrier....68

Border Terrier....69
Bull Terrier....70
Cairn Terrier....71
Dinmont Terrier....72
Irish Terrier....73
Jack Russell Terrier....81
Kerry Blue Terrier....74
Lakeland Terrier....75
Manchester Terrier....76
Miniature Bull Terrier....77
Miniature Schnauzer....78
Norfolk Terrier....79
Norwich Terrier....80
Scottish Terrier....82
Sealyham Terrier....83
Skye Terrier....84
Smooth Fox Terrier....85
Staffordshire Terrier....66
Welsh Terrier....87
West Highland Terrier....88
Wheaten Terrier....86
Wire Fox Terrier....89

Toy Breeds
Affenpinscher....93
Brussels Griffon....94
Chihuahua....100
Chinese Crested....103
English Toy Spaniel....104
Havanese....97
Italian Greyhound....98
Japanese Chin....101
King Charles Spaniel....99
Maltese....102
Miniature Pinscher....105
Papillon....106
Pug....95

Shih Tzu....96
Silky Terrier....91
Toy Fox Terrier....92
Yorkshire Terrier....107

11. Click the **Selection tool** , click the **text frame** on the page, click **Object** on the Application bar, click **Text Frame Options**, change the number of columns to 4, then click **OK**.

    Your page should resemble Figure 28.

12. Using the Type tool, position the cursor before Terrier Breeds, click **Type** on the Application bar, point to **Insert Break Character**, then click **Column Break**.

13. Deselect all, press **[W]** to hide guides, then compare your screen to Figure 29.

14. Save your work and close TOC.indd.

You reformatted the imported paragraph styles with other styles you created that were appropriate for the TOC layout.

Figure 29 *Viewing the final TOC*

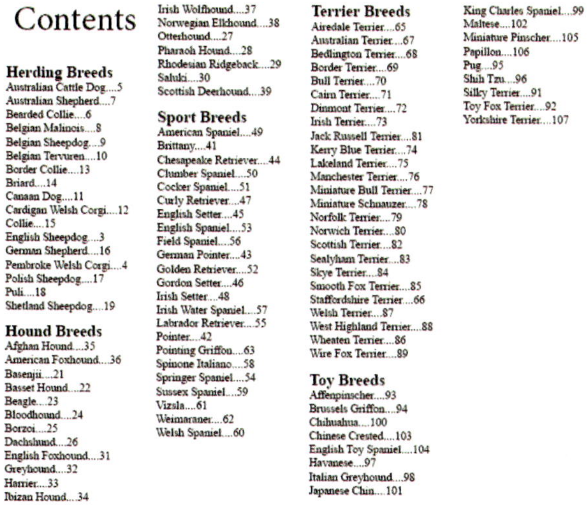

Contents

Herding Breeds
Australian Cattle Dog....5
Australian Shepherd....7
Bearded Collie....6
Belgian Malinois....8
Belgian Sheepdog....9
Belgian Tervuren....10
Border Collie....13
Briard....14
Canaan Dog....11
Cardigan Welsh Corgi....12
Collie....15
English Sheepdog....3
German Shepherd....16
Pembroke Welsh Corgi....4
Polish Sheepdog....17
Puli....18
Shetland Sheepdog....19

Hound Breeds
Afghan Hound....35
American Foxhound....36
Basenji....21
Basset Hound....22
Beagle....23
Bloodhound....24
Borzoi....25
Dachshund....26
English Foxhound....31
Greyhound....32
Harrier....33
Ibizan Hound....34

Irish Wolfhound....37
Norwegian Elkhound....38
Otterhound....27
Pharaoh Hound....28
Rhodesian Ridgeback....29
Saluki....30
Scottish Deerhound....39

Sport Breeds
American Spaniel....49
Brittany....41
Chesapeake Retriever....44
Clumber Spaniel....50
Cocker Spaniel....51
Curly Retriever....47
English Setter....45
English Spaniel....53
Field Spaniel....56
German Pointer....43
Golden Retriever....52
Gordon Setter....46
Irish Setter....48
Irish Water Spaniel....57
Labrador Retriever....55
Pointer....42
Pointing Griffon....63
Spinone Italiano....58
Springer Spaniel....54
Sussex Spaniel....59
Vizsla....61
Weimaraner....62
Welsh Spaniel....60

Terrier Breeds
Airedale Terrier....65
Australian Terrier....67
Bedlington Terrier....68
Border Terrier....69
Bull Terrier....70
Cairn Terrier....71
Dinmont Terrier....72
Irish Terrier....73
Jack Russell Terrier....81
Kerry Blue Terrier....74
Lakeland Terrier....75
Manchester Terrier....76
Miniature Bull Terrier....77
Miniature Schnauzer....78
Norfolk Terrier....79
Norwich Terrier....80
Scottish Terrier....82
Sealyham Terrier....83
Skye Terrier....84
Smooth Fox Terrier....85
Staffordshire Terrier....66
Welsh Terrier....87
West Highland Terrier....88
Wheaten Terrier....86
Wire Fox Terrier....89

Toy Breeds
Affenpinscher....93
Brussels Griffon....94
Chihuahua....100
Chinese Crested....103
English Toy Spaniel....104
Havanese....97
Italian Greyhound....98
Japanese Chin....101

King Charles Spaniel....99
Maltese....102
Miniature Pinscher....105
Papillon....106
Pug....95
Shih Tzu....96
Silky Terrier....91
Toy Fox Terrier....92
Yorkshire Terrier....107

Create an
INDEX

What You'll Do

Index

In this lesson, you will create an index based on the documents in the book file.

Creating Index Entries

Index entries are specified within the documents that make up the book and are saved with the documents. Specifying index entries is easy to do. Simply select the text that you want to be used as an index entry, click the Create a new index entry button on the Index panel, then click OK in the New Page Reference dialog box. The selected text will be added to the Index panel, as shown in Figure 30.

Generating an Index

An index is an individual InDesign document that you add to the Book panel to become part of the book. This will usually be a one- or two-page document. As with the TOC document, it is critical that you carefully choose the same document setup specifications that were used to create the other documents in the book. Once you have created the index document, add it to the Book panel.

After you've added the index document to the Book panel, click the Generate index button on the Index panel, shown in Figure 31. This opens the Generate Index dialog box, shown in Figure 32. As its name implies, this dialog box generates the index based on the index entries saved with the documents that compose the book. Be sure to check the Include Book Documents check box before clicking OK.

Figure 30 *Creating an index entry*

Selected text —

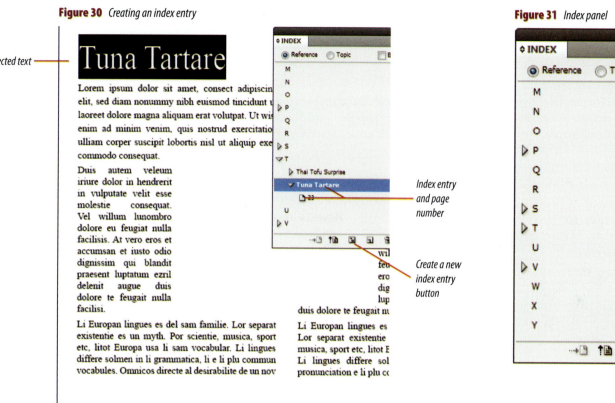

Index entry and page number

Create a new index entry button

Figure 31 *Index panel*

Generate index button

Figure 32 *Generate Index dialog box*

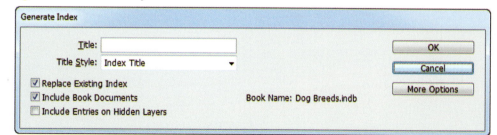

Generating a Cross-reference Index Entry

Creating an index is a linguistic challenge. One of your greatest challenges will be to anticipate the way a reader will search the index for specific topics. For example, if you have written a book on recipes, you might have an index entry for Bouillabaisse. That seems pretty straightforward, but you would also need to anticipate that some of your readers would go to the F section of your index looking for Bouillabaisse. *F*, you ask? Yes, F, for Fish Stew.

In this example, you could simply create an index entry for Fish Stew with the page number for Bouillabaisse. However, for consistency reasons, it would be better to create a cross-reference. You do this in the New Cross-reference dialog box, shown in Figure 33. You create this cross-reference entry in the document itself, when you create the other index entries. When you click OK, a new entry will be created, as shown in Figure 34.

Figure 33 *New Cross-reference dialog box*

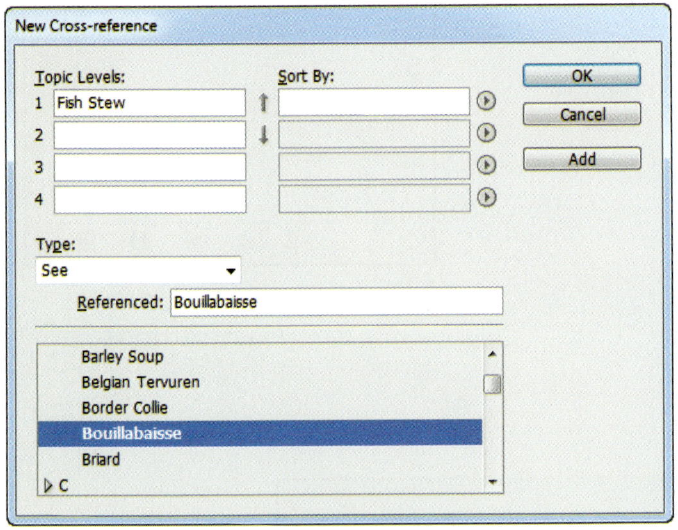

Figure 34 *Cross-referenced index entry*

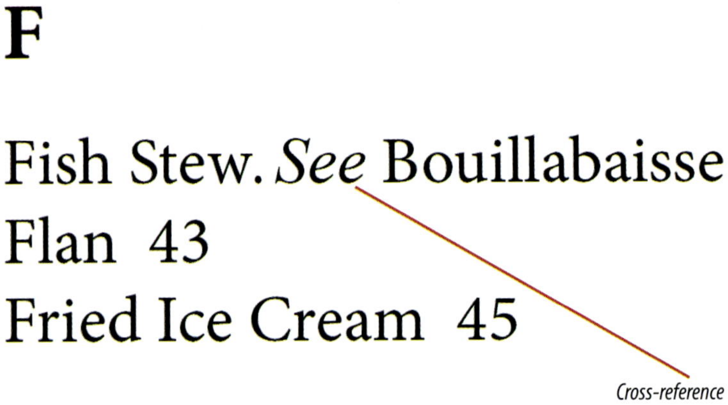

F

Fish Stew. *See* Bouillabaisse

Flan 43

Fried Ice Cream 45

Cross-reference

Making Books, Tables of Contents, and Indexes

Sorting Index Entries

Once you've created individual index entries for specific topics in your document, you may want to sort specific entries together under a new topic. For example, you might have three separate index entries for Veal Marsala, Chicken Marsala, and Pork Marsala. However, your reader might go to the "M" section of your index looking for the word "Marsala." For that reason, you would want an index entry that reads "Marsala Dishes" and lists the three Marsala dishes and their page numbers.

To do this, you must create a new index entry for Marsala Dishes. Go to the page for the first Marsala dish—in this example, that's Chicken Marsala—then click to place the pointer in the headline. Click the Create a new index entry button on the Index panel, which opens the New Page Reference dialog box. As shown in Figure 35, Marsala Dishes is entered in the number 1 text box and Chicken Marsala is entered in the number 2 text box. When you click OK, a new entry appears in the "M" section for Marsala Dishes with Chicken Marsala listed beneath it, as shown in Figure 36. Repeat this process for Veal Marsala and Pork Marsala, and your Index panel will resemble Figure 37.

When you save changes to the document and generate the index, the listing will appear as shown in Figure 38.

Figure 35 *New Page Reference dialog box*

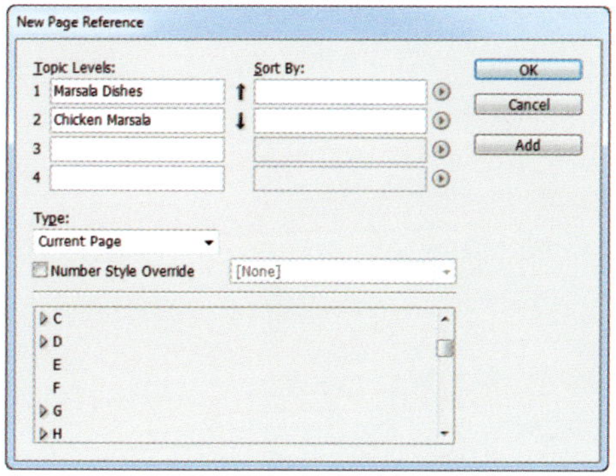

Figure 36 *An original index entry duplicated as a sub-entry*

Figure 37 *Three sorted sub-entries on the Index panel*

Figure 38 *Sorted entries in an index*

M

Marsala Dishes
Chicken Marsala 29
Pork Marsala 33
Veal Marsala 31
Mussels 6

New index entry

Three sorted entries

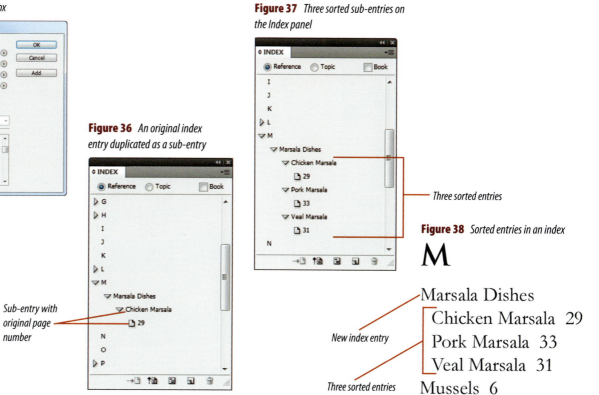

Create an index entry

1. On the Book panel, double-click **Toy Breeds**.

2. Click **Window** on the Application bar, point to **Type & Tables**, then click **Index**.

3. Click all the **triangles** on the Index panel to explore the index entries that have already been created.

   An index entry has been created for every breed in the document except the breed on page 91, Silky Terrier.

4. On the Pages panel, double-click **page 91** to center it in the window, click the **Type tool** T, then select the Silky Terrier headline.

   TIP Be sure that the Index panel is visible, and that you can see the "S" section.

5. Click the **Create a new index entry button** on the Index panel.

   When text is selected, clicking this button opens the New Page Reference dialog box. When nothing is selected, clicking this button will open the New Cross-reference dialog box.

6. Note that the Type list box contains Current Page, then click **OK**.

7. Expand the Silky Terrier entry on the Index panel, then compare your Index panel to Figure 39. An entry for Silky Terrier on page 91 is added to the Index panel.

8. Click **File** on the Application bar, click **Save**, then close Toy Breeds.indd.

You created an index entry.

Figure 39 *New entry on the Index panel*

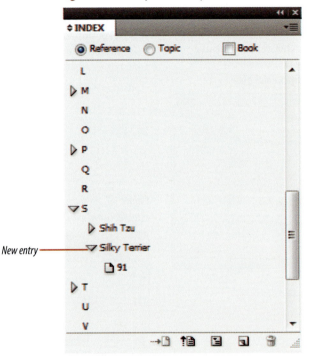

New entry

Figure 40 *Generate Index dialog box*

Generate Index

Title: [   ]

Title Style: [Index Title ▾]

☐ Replace Existing Index
☑ Include Book Documents   Book Name: Dog Breeds.indb
☐ Include Entries on Hidden Layers

[OK]
[Cancel]
[More Options]

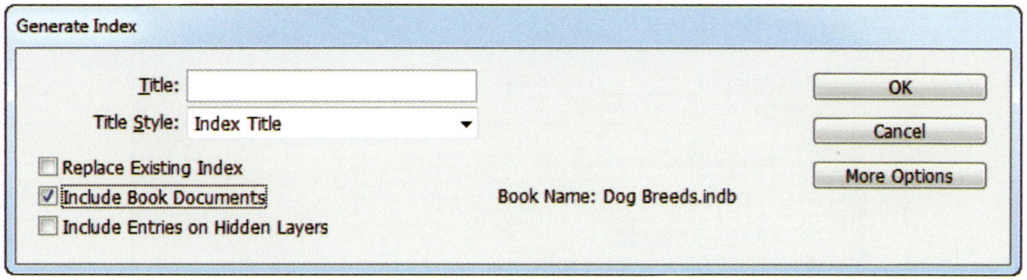

Figure 41 *Generating an index*

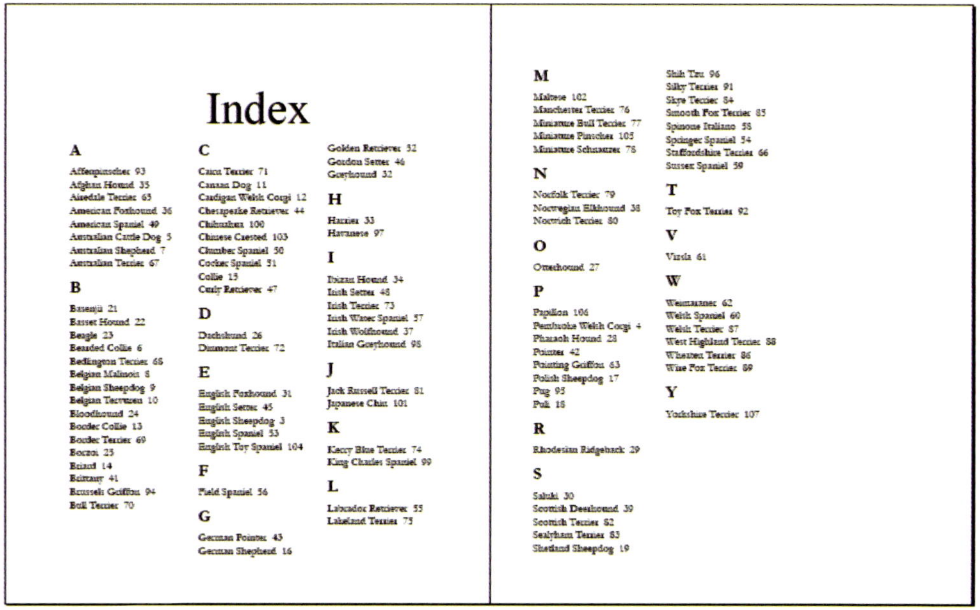

Index

A
Affenpinscher 93
Afghan Hound 35
Airedale Terrier 63
American Foxhound 36
American Spaniel 49
Australian Cattle Dog 5
Australian Shepherd 7
Australian Terrier 67

B
Basenji 21
Basset Hound 22
Beagle 23
Bearded Collie 6
Bedlington Terrier 66
Belgian Malinois 8
Belgian Sheepdog 9
Belgian Tervuren 10
Bloodhound 24
Border Collie 13
Border Terrier 69
Borzoi 25
Boxer 14
Brittany 41
Brussels Griffon 94
Bull Terrier 70

C
Cairn Terrier 71
Canaan Dog 11
Cardigan Welsh Corgi 12
Chesapeake Retriever 44
Chihuahua 100
Chinese Crested 103
Clumber Spaniel 50
Cocker Spaniel 51
Collie 15
Curly Retriever 47

D
Dachshund 26
Dumont Terrier 72

E
English Foxhound 31
English Setter 45
English Sheepdog 3
English Spaniel 53
English Toy Spaniel 104

F
Field Spaniel 56

G
German Pointer 43
German Shepherd 16

Golden Retriever 52
Gordon Setter 46
Greyhound 32

H
Harrier 33
Havanese 97

I
Ibizan Hound 34
Irish Setter 48
Irish Terrier 73
Irish Water Spaniel 57
Irish Wolfhound 37
Italian Greyhound 98

J
Jack Russell Terrier 81
Japanese Chin 101

K
Kerry Blue Terrier 74
King Charles Spaniel 99

L
Labrador Retriever 55
Lakeland Terrier 75

M
Maltese 102
Manchester Terrier 76
Miniature Bull Terrier 77
Miniature Pinscher 105
Miniature Schnauzer 78

N
Norfolk Terrier 79
Norwegian Elkhound 38
Norwich Terrier 80

O
Otterhound 27

P
Papillon 106
Pembroke Welsh Corgi 4
Pharaoh Hound 28
Pointer 42
Pointing Griffon 63
Polish Sheepdog 17
Pug 95
Puli 18

R
Rhodesian Ridgeback 29

S
Saluki 30
Scottish Deerhound 39
Scottish Terrier 82
Sealyham Terrier 83
Shetland Sheepdog 19

Shih Tzu 96
Silky Terrier 91
Skye Terrier 84
Smooth Fox Terrier 85
Spinone Italiano 58
Springer Spaniel 54
Staffordshire Terrier 66
Sussex Spaniel 59

T
Toy Fox Terrier 92

V
Vizsla 61

W
Weimaraner 62
Welsh Spaniel 60
Welsh Terrier 87
West Highland Terrier 88
Wheaten Terrier 86
Wire Fox Terrier 89

Y
Yorkshire Terrier 107

Generate an index

1. Open ID 10-7.indd, then save it as **Index**.
2. Click the **Add documents button** on the Dog Breeds Book panel, then add Index.

TIP Index should be added at the bottom of the list. If it appears elsewhere, drag it to the bottom of the list.

3. Click the **Generate index button** on the Index panel.
4. Delete the text in the Title text box.

   The title "Index" already exists in a text frame in the Index document.

5. Remove the check mark in the Replace Existing Index check box, then click the **Include Book Documents check box** so that your Generate Index dialog box resembles Figure 40.
6. Click **OK**, position the loaded text pointer over the **top-left corner of the text frame** on page 108, then click.
7. Adjust any bad column breaks.
8. Deselect all, hide all guides, then compare your index to Figure 41.

TIP If you are asked to save any of the "Breeds" documents, click Yes.

   The index is generated based on all the index entries created in each of the five documents. Note that Silky Terrier—the entry you created— is listed on page 91 in the "S" section.

9. Click **File** on the Application bar, then click **Save**.
10. Click the **Save the book button** on the Book panel.

You generated an index based on all the index entries in the five documents.

Create index cross-references

1. Double-click **Toy Breeds** on the Book panel.
2. Click the **Index panel options button** ▾▤, then click **New Cross-reference**.
3. In the Topic Levels section, type **Min-Pin** in the number 1 text box.
4. Click the **Type list arrow**, then click **See**.
5. In the large white box at the bottom, scroll to the "M" section, then click the **triangle** to expose the "M" index entries.
6. Drag **Miniature Pinscher** into the Referenced text box, as shown in Figure 42.

   The words Miniature Pinscher should appear in the Referenced text box, as shown in Figure 43.
7. Click **OK**, then scroll to the M section on the Index panel.

   A new entry for Min-Pin has been added, with the reference See Miniature Pinscher.
8. Save Toy Breeds, then close it.
9. Verify that Index.indd is the only open document, then click the **Generate index button** ▤ on the Index panel.
10. In the Generate Index dialog box, check the **Replace Existing Index check box** to replace the previous index, verify that the Include Book Documents check box is selected, then click **OK**. (If you receive a message telling you the index has been replaced successfully, click **OK**.)

    The replacement index now shows the cross-reference after the Min-Pin entry.

You created a new index entry that is cross-referenced to an already existing entry.

Figure 42 *Dragging an entry into the Referenced text box*

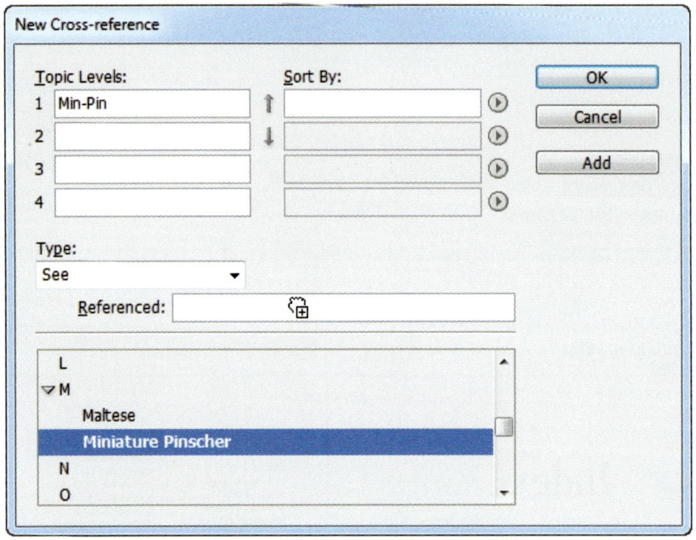

Figure 43 *Creating a cross-reference*

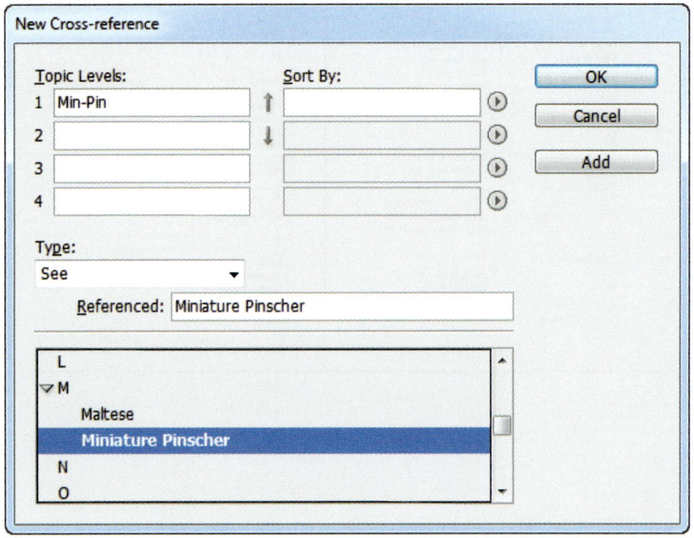

Figure 44 *New index entry with a sub-entry*

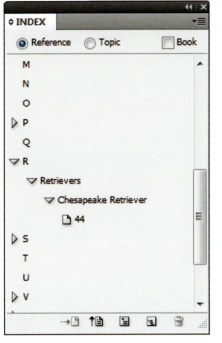

Figure 45 *Four sorted sub-entries*

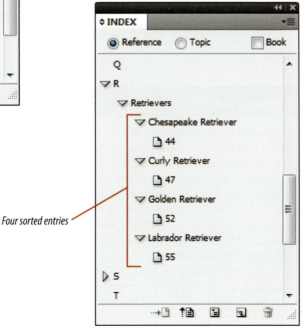

Four sorted entries

1. Open **Sport Breeds**.

   Sport Breeds contains four pages that profile retriever breeds of dogs.

2. Click the **Type tool** T, double-click **page 44** on the Pages panel, then click anywhere in the headline Chesapeake Retriever.

3. Click the **Index panel options button** , then click **New Page Reference**.

4. In the Topic Levels section, type **Retrievers** in the number 1 text box, type **Chesapeake Retriever** in the number 2 text box, click **OK**, then compare your Index panel to Figure 44.

5. Double-click **page 47** on the Pages panel, click anywhere in the Curly Retriever headline, click the **Index panel options button** , then click **New Page Reference** on the Index Panel Options menu.

6. Type **Retrievers** in the number 1 text box, type **Curly Retriever** in the number 2 text box, then click **OK**.

7. Using Pages 52 and 55, create new page references for the Golden Retriever and Labrador Retriever.

   Your Index panel should resemble Figure 45.

   (continued)

8. Save Sport Breeds, close the document, verify that Index is the only document open, then generate a replacement index.

   As shown in Figure 46, the new index has an entry for Retrievers with the four retriever breeds sorted beneath as sub-entries.

9. Read the sidebar on this page titled, "Exporting a Book File."

10. Save Index, close it, then close the Book panel. If you are prompted to save changes to Dog Breeds.indb before closing, click **Yes** (Win) **Save** (Mac).

You created a new index entry, then sorted four other entries.

Figure 46 *Updated index with four sorted entries*

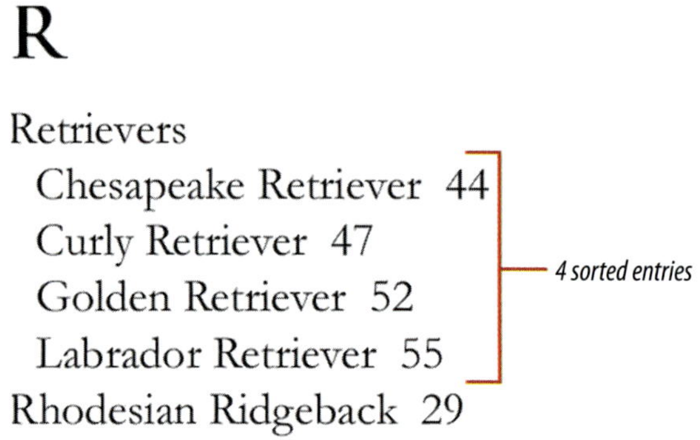

R

Retrievers
   Chesapeake Retriever 44
   Curly Retriever 47
   Golden Retriever 52   *4 sorted entries*
   Labrador Retriever 55
Rhodesian Ridgeback 29

Exporting a Book File

It is important you understand that the book file itself is the book. For example, as a result of doing the exercises in this chapter, you have created a book file named Dog Breeds. You have determined how the sections will flow, you have determined that each section will open on a left-hand, even-numbered page, and you have added a table of contents and an index. Remember that all of the work you've done in the Book panel has affected the original data files with which you started. They've been renumbered and, in some cases, pages have been moved to correspond to the moves you made in the Book panel. At this point, if you were ready to produce the book, you would have a number of options. You could click the Print the Book button at the bottom of the Book panel and the entire book would print. If this were a job that was being professionally printed, you could package and send the individual InDesign data files to the printer just like you would any other project. You could also export a single PDF that houses the entire book. In Chapter 12, you will do just that: export Dog Breeds as a single PDF.

Create a book file.

1. Open ID 10-8.indd, then save it as **Appetizers**.
2. Open ID 10-9.indd, then save it as **Soups**.
3. Open ID 10-10.indd, then save it as **Entrees**.
4. Open ID 10-11.indd, then save it as **Desserts**.
5. Close all open documents.
6. Click File on the Application bar, point to New, then click Book.
7. Name the new file **Dinner Recipes**, then click Save.
8. Click the Book panel options button, then click Add Document.
9. Add Entrees.indd.
10. Click the Add documents button on the Book panel, then add Desserts.indd.
11. Add the following two documents: Soups.indd and Appetizers.indd.
12. Click the Save the book button on the Book panel.

Organize a book file.

1. Click and drag Soups to the top of the list.
2. Click and drag Appetizers to the top of the list.
3. Note that all the documents on the Book panel begin on odd page numbers. (*Hint*: For this project, you want each chapter to begin on an even left-hand page.)
4. Click the Book panel options button, then click Book Page Numbering Options.
5. Click the Continue on next even page option button, then click OK.
6. On the Book panel, double-click the page numbers for Appetizers.
7. Click the Start Page Numbering at option button, type **2** in the text box, then click OK.
8. Save the change, close Appetizers, then note the page range on the Book panel.
9. Click the Save the book button on the Book panel.

Create a table of contents.

1. Open ID 10-12.indd, then save it as **Recipes TOC**.
2. Click the Paragraph Styles panel options button, then click Load Paragraph Styles.
3. Open Appetizers.indd.
4. Click OK in the Load Styles dialog box.
5. Click File on the Application bar, then click Save.
6. With Recipes TOC.indd still open, click the Add documents button on the Book panel.
7. Add Recipes TOC.indd.
8. Drag Recipes TOC to the top of the list.
9. Click Layout on the Application bar, then click Table of Contents.
10. Delete the text in the Title text box.
11. In the Other Styles list, click Course Name, then click Add.
12. Double-click Dish Name.
13. In the Options section at the bottom of the dialog box, click the Include Book Documents check box to select it.
14. Click OK.
15. Position the pointer over the top-left corner of the margin guides on the page, then click once.
16. Click Layout on the Application bar, then click Table of Contents.
17. In the Include Paragraph Styles section, click Course Name to select it.
18. Click the Entry Style list arrow, then click TOC Course.
19. Click the Page Number list arrow, then click No Page Number. (If necessary, click More Options to display the Page Number option.)
20. In the Include Paragraph Styles section, click Dish Name to select it.
21. Click the Entry Style list arrow, then click TOC Dish Name, click the Page Number list arrow, then click After Entry.
22. Select the contents of the Between Entry and Number text box, then type **.....** (five periods).
23. Click the Sort Entries in Alphabetical Order check box to select it, then verify that the Replace Existing Table of Contents check box is checked.

24. Click OK. (*Hint*: If you see a dialog box saying that the TOC was updated successfully, click OK.)
25. Click the Selection tool, select the text frame on the page, click Object on the Application bar, click Text Frame Options, change the number of columns to 2, click OK, then deselect all.
    Your page should resemble Figure 47.
26. Save the changes to Recipes TOC.indd, then close the document.

Create an index.

1. On the Book panel, double-click Entrees to open the document.
2. Click Window on the Application bar, point to Type & Tables, then click Index.
3. On the Pages panel, double-click page 23 to center it in the window, click the Type tool, then select the Tuna Tartare headline.
4. Click the Create a new index entry button on the Index panel.
5. Click OK.
6. Click File on the Application bar, click Save, then close Entrees.
7. Open ID 10-13.indd, then save it as **Recipes Index**.
8. Click the Add documents button on the Dinner Recipes Book panel, add Recipes Index.indd, then drag it to the bottom of the Book panel.
9. Click the Generate index button on the Index panel.
10. Delete the text in the Title text box.
11. Remove the check mark in the Replace Existing Index check box, then click to select the Include Book Documents check box.
12. Click OK.
13. Position the loaded text pointer over the top-left corner of the text frame in Recipes Index.indd, then click.
14. Click File on the Application bar, then click Save.
15. Click the Save the book button on the Book panel.
16. Double-click Soups on the Book panel to open the document.
17. Click the Index panel options button, then click New Cross-reference.

Figure 47 *Completed Skills Review, Part 1*

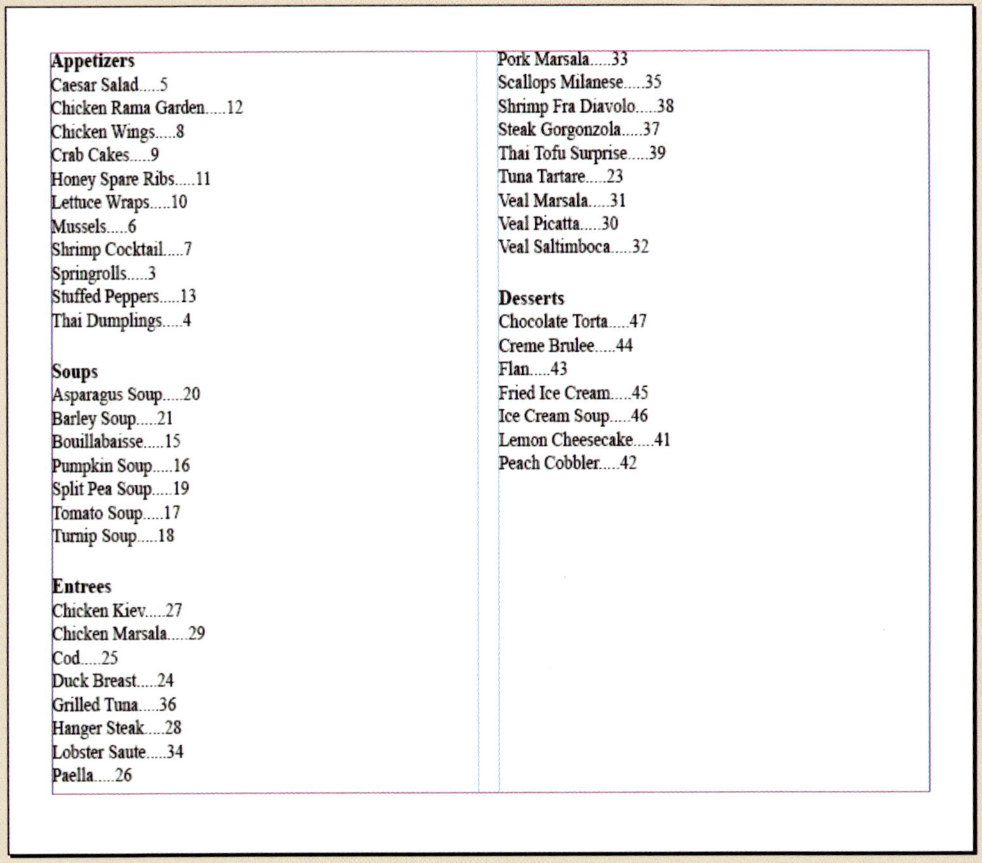

Appetizers
Caesar Salad.....5
Chicken Rama Garden.....12
Chicken Wings.....8
Crab Cakes.....9
Honey Spare Ribs.....11
Lettuce Wraps.....10
Mussels.....6
Shrimp Cocktail.....7
Springrolls.....3
Stuffed Peppers.....13
Thai Dumplings.....4

Soups
Asparagus Soup.....20
Barley Soup.....21
Bouillabaisse.....15
Pumpkin Soup.....16
Split Pea Soup.....19
Tomato Soup.....17
Turnip Soup.....18

Entrees
Chicken Kiev.....27
Chicken Marsala.....29
Cod.....25
Duck Breast.....24
Grilled Tuna.....36
Hanger Steak.....28
Lobster Saute.....34
Paella.....26

Pork Marsala.....33
Scallops Milanese.....35
Shrimp Fra Diavolo.....38
Steak Gorgonzola.....37
Thai Tofu Surprise.....39
Tuna Tartare.....23
Veal Marsala.....31
Veal Picatta.....30
Veal Saltimboca.....32

Desserts
Chocolate Torta.....47
Creme Brulee.....44
Flan.....43
Fried Ice Cream.....45
Ice Cream Soup.....46
Lemon Cheesecake.....41
Peach Cobbler.....42

18. In the Topic Levels section, type **Fish Stew** in the number 1 text box.
19. Click the Type list arrow, then click See.
20. In the large box at the bottom, scroll to the "B" section, then click the triangle to expose the "B" index entries.
21. Drag Bouillabaisse into the Referenced text box, then release the mouse button when the plus sign appears in the pointer.
22. Click OK.
23. Save Soups, then close the document.
24. Verify that Recipes Index.indd is the only open document, then click the Generate index button on the Index panel.
25. In the Generate Index dialog box, check the Replace Existing Index check box, then click OK.
26. Double-click Entrees on the Book panel to open the document. (*Hint*: Entrees contains three Marsala dishes—Pork, Veal, and Chicken.)
27. Click the Type tool, double-click page 29 on the Pages panel, then click anywhere in the headline.
28. Click the Index panel options button, then click New Page Reference.
29. In the Topic Levels section, type **Marsala Dishes** in the number 1 text box, type **Chicken Marsala** in the number 2 text box, then click OK.
30. Double-click page 31 on the Pages panel, click anywhere in the headline, click the Index panel options button, then click New Page Reference.
31. Type **Marsala Dishes** in the number 1 text box, type **Veal Marsala** in the number 2 text box, then click OK.
32. Double-click page 33 on the Pages panel, click anywhere in the headline, click the Index panel options button then click New Page Reference.

33. Type **Marsala Dishes** in the number 1 text box, type **Pork Marsala** in the number 2 text box, then click OK.
34. Save Entrees, close the document, verify that Recipes Index.indd is the only document open, then generate a replacement index.

35. Adjust column breaks to improve the layout, deselect all, press [W] to hide guides, then compare your index to Figure 48.
36. Save Recipes Index.indd, close it, then close the Dinner Recipes book.

Figure 48 *Completed Skills Review, Part 2*

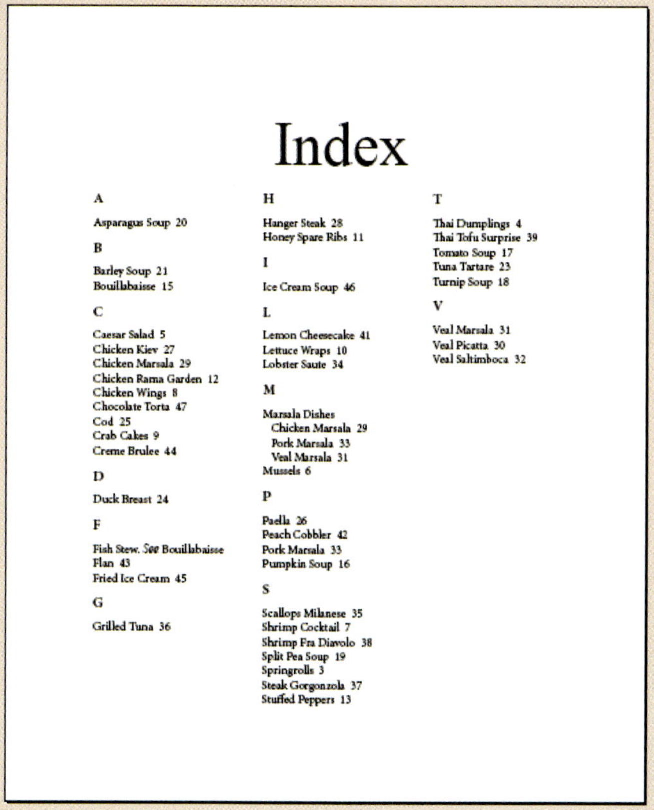

Index

A
Asparagus Soup 20

B
Barley Soup 21
Bouillabaisse 15

C
Caesar Salad 5
Chicken Kiev 27
Chicken Marsala 29
Chicken Rama Garden 12
Chicken Wings 8
Chocolate Torta 47
Cod 25
Crab Cakes 9
Creme Brulee 44

D
Duck Breast 24

F
Fish Stew. *See* Bouillabaisse
Flan 43
Fried Ice Cream 45

G
Grilled Tuna 36

H
Hanger Steak 28
Honey Spare Ribs 11

I
Ice Cream Soup 46

L
Lemon Cheesecake 41
Lettuce Wraps 10
Lobster Saute 34

M
Marsala Dishes
   Chicken Marsala 29
   Pork Marsala 33
   Veal Marsala 31
Mussels 6

P
Paella 26
Peach Cobbler 42
Pork Marsala 33
Pumpkin Soup 16

S
Scallops Milanese 35
Shrimp Cocktail 7
Shrimp Fra Diavolo 38
Split Pea Soup 19
Springrolls 3
Steak Gorgonzola 37
Stuffed Peppers 13

T
Thai Dumplings 4
Thai Tofu Surprise 39
Tomato Soup 17
Tuna Tartare 23
Turnip Soup 18

V
Veal Marsala 31
Veal Picatta 30
Veal Saltimboca 32

You work for a publishing company, and you have created an index for a book on dog breeds. Your boss comes to you and tells you that the index is not complete as is; he wants you to sort three breeds under a new index entry.

1. Open ID 10-14.indd, then save it as **Sort Setters**.
2. Click the Type tool, double-click page 6 on the Pages panel, then click in the headline.
3. Click the Index panel options button, then click New Page Reference.
4. In the Topic Levels section, type **Setters** in the number 1 text box, type **English Setter** in the number 2 text box, then click OK.
5. Double-click page 7 on the Pages panel, click in the headline, click the Index panel option button, then click New Page Reference.
6. Type **Setters** in the number 1 text box, type **Gordon Setter** in the number 2 text box, then click OK.
7. Double-click page 9 on the Pages panel, click in the headline, click the Index panel options button, then click New Page Reference.
8. Type **Setters** in the number 1 text box, type **Irish Setter** in the number 2 text box, then click OK.
9. Scroll to the S section, then compare your index to Figure 49.
10. Save your work, then close Sort Setters.

Figure 49 *Completed Project Builder 1*

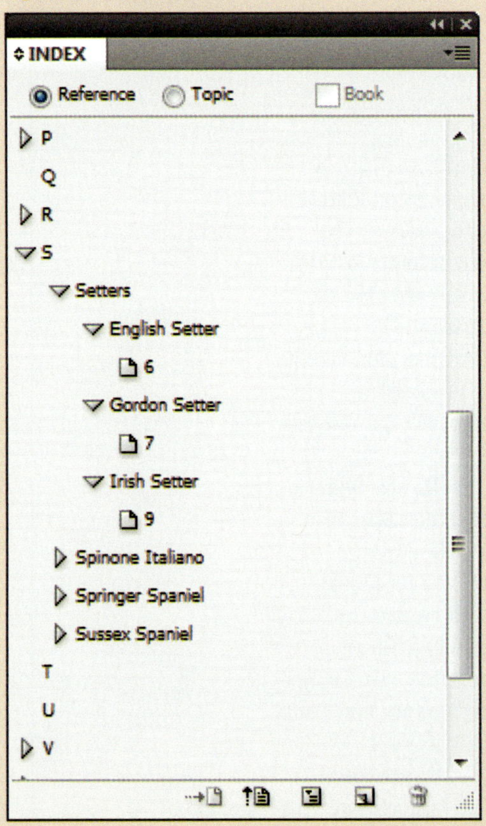

You work for a publishing company, and you have created an index for a book on dog breeds. Your boss comes to you and tells you that the index is not complete as is; he wants you to create a cross-reference entry titled "Red Setter" that points to the Irish Setter page.

1. Open ID 10-15.indd, then save it as **Cross-reference Setters**.
2. Verify that the Selection tool is selected.
3. Click the Index panel options button, then click New Cross-reference.
4. In the Topic Levels section, type **Red Setter** in the number 1 text box.
5. Click the Type list arrow, then click See.
6. In the large box at the bottom, scroll to the "I" section, then click the triangle to expose the "I" index entries.
7. Drag Irish Setter into the Referenced text box, then release the mouse button when the plus sign appears in the pointer.
8. Click OK.
9. Scroll to the R section of the Index panel to view the cross-reference, then compare your Index panel to Figure 50.
10. Save your work, then close Cross-reference Setters.

Figure 50 *Completed Project Builder 2*

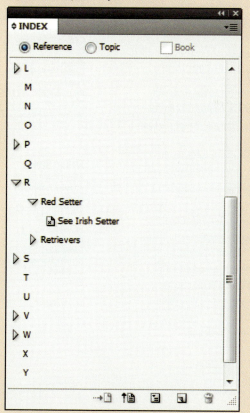

You are a graphic designer at a publishing company. One of your clients comes to you with an InDesign file and says he needs your help. He generated a table of contents from a book file, and he was surprised that the paragraph styles used to create the book did not work for the layout of the TOC. He gives you the file on disk, and you note that he didn't include the book file. This means that you can't regenerate a new TOC file. Therefore, you decide to reformat the layout directly in the InDesign document.

1. Open ID 10-16.indd, then save it as **TOC Redesign**.
2. On the Paragraph Styles panel, double-click Breed Name, click Basic Character Formats, change the Font size to 10, then click OK.
3. Double-click Section Name, click Basic Character Formats, change the Font size to 16, click Advanced Character Formats, change the Horizontal Scale to 72%, then click OK.
4. Select the text frame, open the Text Frame Options dialog box, change the number of columns to 4, then click OK.
5. Triple-click the word Contents, then delete it.
6. Delete any extra space at the top of the column, deselect all, press [W] to hide guides, then compare your page to Figure 51.
7. Save your work, then close TOC Redesign.

Figure 51 *Completed Design Project*

Herding Breeds

Australian Cattle Dog..........5
Australian Shepherd..........7
Bearded Collie..........6
Belgian Malinois..........8
Belgian Sheepdog..........9
Belgian Tervuren..........10
Border Collie..........13
Briard..........14
Canaan Dog..........11
Cardigan Welsh Corgi..........12
Collie..........15
English Sheepdog..........3
German Shepherd..........16
Pembroke Welsh Corgi..........4
Polish Sheepdog..........17
Puli..........18
Shetland Sheepdog..........19

Hound Breeds

Afghan Hound..........35
American Foxhound..........36
Basenji..........21
Basset Hound..........22
Beagle..........23
Bloodhound..........24
Borzoi..........25
Dachshund..........26
English Foxhound..........31
Greyhound..........32
Harrier..........33
Ibizan Hound..........34
Irish Wolfhound..........37

Norwegian Elkhound..........38
Otterhound..........27
Pharaoh Hound..........28
Rhodesian Ridgeback..........29
Saluki..........30
Scottish Deerhound..........39

Sport Breeds

American Spaniel..........49
Brittany..........41
Chesapeake Retriever..........44
Clumber Spaniel..........50
Cocker Spaniel..........51
Curly Retriever..........47
English Setter..........45
English Spaniel..........53
Field Spaniel..........56
German Pointer..........43
Golden Retriever..........52
Gordon Setter..........46
Irish Setter..........48
Irish Water Spaniel..........57
Labrador Retriever..........55
Pointer..........42
Pointing Griffon..........63
Spinone Italiano..........58
Springer Spaniel..........54
Sussex Spaniel..........59
Vizsla..........61
Weimaraner..........62
Welsh Spaniel..........60

Terrier Breeds

Airedale Terrier..........65
Australian Terrier..........67
Bedlington Terrier..........68
Border Terrier..........69
Bull Terrier..........70
Cairn Terrier..........71
Dinmont Terrier..........72
Irish Terrier..........73
Jack Russell Terrier..........81
Kerry Blue Terrier..........74
Lakeland Terrier..........75
Manchester Terrier..........76
Miniature Bull Terrier..........77
Miniature Schnauzer..........78
Norfolk Terrier..........79
Norwich Terrier..........80
Scottish Terrier..........82
Sealyham Terrier..........83
Skye Terrier..........84
Smooth Fox Terrier..........85
Staffordshire Terrier..........66
Welsh Terrier..........87
West Highland Terrier..........88
Wheaten Terrier..........86
Wire Fox Terrier..........89

Toy Breeds

Affenpinscher..........93
Brussels Griffon..........94
Chihuahua..........100
Chinese Crested..........103
English Toy Spaniel..........104

Havanese..........97
Italian Greyhound..........98
Japanese Chin..........101
King Charles Spaniel..........99
Maltese..........102
Miniature Pinscher..........105
Papillon..........106
Pug..........95
Shih Tzu..........96
Silky Terrier..........91
Toy Fox Terrier..........92
Yorkshire Terrier..........107

This portfolio project is designed to show you the type of thinking that must go into creating an index. You will open a single InDesign document that contains 17 pages, each featuring one dish. An index entry has been made for all 17 dishes. An additional index entry has been made for "Marsala Dishes," under which three Marsala dishes have been sorted.

This project is not about generating an index; it's about looking at data and deciding how an index can best refer to that data. You should think about which dishes might require a cross-reference. You should also consider different ways the dishes can be sorted.

This project does not have a specific solution. Instead, you should decide when the index has been thoroughly cross-referenced and sorted.

Discussion

1. Open ID 10-17.indd, then save it as **Portfolio Project**.
2. Scroll through the pages and note the names of the dishes.
3. Can any of the dishes be referred to by a different name? If so, which dishes?
4. Create cross-reference index entries for dishes that can be referred to by a different name.

5. Which of the 17 dishes are similar enough that they can be sorted together?
6. Do you think it is necessary to sort the two chicken dishes under a new entry named Chicken Dishes? Why or why not?

7. Create new index entries that are appropriate for sorting groups of dishes.
8. Save your work, compare your index to the sample shown in Figure 52, then close Portfolio Project.

Figure 52 *Completed Portfolio Project*

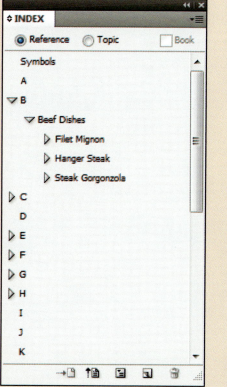

CHAPTER

PREPARING, PACKAGING, AND
EXPORTING DOCUMENTS
FOR PRINT

1. Create bleeds, slugs, and printer's marks

2. Use the Ink Manager and preview color separations

3. Preflight and package a document

4. Export a document

11

PREPARING, PACKAGING, AND EXPORTING DOCUMENTS FOR PRINT

When it comes time to output a document, you will be impressed with the many well considered options InDesign makes available for printing, exporting, and sending to a service bureau.

InDesign comes complete with all the industry-standard printer's marks that you would expect from a professional layout application. Crop marks, bleed marks, color bars, and registration marks are all available in the Print dialog box. Additionally, you can create bleed and slug areas in the Document Setup dialog box, which offers input options for these important components of a layout.

The Ink Manager makes it easy to specify how the document will color separate and allows you to convert spot inks to process inks with a simple click of the mouse. The Separations Preview panel is a great resource for the designer and the print professional to see at a glance how a document will color separate and to inspect each plate quickly.

If the document is going to be shipped to a printer or service bureau, the Preflight and Package commands automate these all-important steps in the production process.

Rather than print, you might want to export a document. You'll find that InDesign offers all of the file formats that you need and expect. You can export a document as a PDF, which opens easily in Adobe Acrobat. You can export a selected item or the whole layout as a JPEG image, handy for web viewing or emailing to a client as a sample of what the final product will look like. If you want to manipulate a layout in Photoshop or Illustrator, choose the EPS format in the Export dialog box.

Document Setup

Intent: Print

Number of Pages: 5 ☑ Facing Pages

Start Page #: 1 ☐ Master Text Frame

OK
Cancel
Fewer Options

Page Size: [Custom]

Width: 6 in   Orientation: ▣ ▣
Height: 3 in

Bleed and Slug

	Top	Bottom	Inside	Outside
Bleed:	0.125 in	0.125 in	0.125 in	0.125 in
Slug:	0 in	0 in	0 in	0 in

Print

Print Preset: [Custom]
Printer: Adobe PDF
PPD: AdobePDF 8.0

General
Setup
Marks and Bleed
Output
Graphics
Color Management
Advanced
Summary

Marks and Bleed

Marks
☑ All Printer's Marks   Type: Default
☑ Crop Marks   Weight: 0.25 pt
☑ Bleed Marks   Offset: 0.0833 in
☑ Registration Marks
☑ Color Bars
☑ Page Information

Bleed and Slug
☑ Use Document Bleed Settings
Bleed:
Top: 0 in   Inside: 0 in
Bottom: 0 in   Outside: 0 in

☐ Include Slug Area

Save Preset...   Setup...   Print   Cancel

CONDITIONAL **PREFLIGHT** LINKS PAGE TRANSI

☑ On   Profile: [Basic] (working)

Error	Page

▷ Info

● No errors   Pages: ◉ All   ○ 1

SEPARATIONS PREVI...

View: Separations   300%

👁	✕	CMYK	0%
👁	▪	Cyan	0%
👁	▪	Magenta	0%
👁	▪	Yellow	0%
👁	▪	Black	0%
👁	▪	PANTONE 2925 C	0%

File name: OAHU to Print
Save as type: InDesign CS3 Interchange (INX)

Save
Cancel

Adobe Flash CS4 Pro (XFL)
Adobe PDF
EPS
InCopy CS3 Interchange
InCopy Document
InDesign CS3 Interchange (INX)
InDesign Markup (IDML)
InDesign Snippet
JPEG
SWF
XML

Create Bleeds, Slugs,
AND PRINTER'S MARKS

What You'll Do

▶ *In this lesson, you will create bleed and slug areas, and then you will output a document with printer's marks.*

Understanding Bleeds

Before discussing bleeds, it's important to define trim size. **Trim size** is the size to which a printed document will be cut, or, trimmed, when it clears the printing press. For example, an 8"× 10" magazine may be printed on a page that is 12" × 14", but it will be trimmed to 8" × 10".

Professionally printed documents are printed on paper, or, a "sheet," that is larger than the document's trim size. The extra space is used to accommodate bleeds, crops, and other printer's marks. **Bleeds** are areas of the layout that extend to the trim size. In Figure 1, the green background extends to the trim on all four sides; the yellow strip extends to the trim on the left and the right. Both are said to "bleed" off of the edge.

It's important to understand that areas of the layout that extend to the trim—areas that are meant to bleed—must actually go beyond the trim size when the document is prepared for printing. Why? To accommodate for the margin of error in trimming.

Nothing or nobody is perfect, and this includes the cutting device that is used to trim printed pieces when they clear the

printing press. You can target the cutting device to slice the paper exactly at the trim size, but you can never expect it to be dead-on every time. There is a margin of error, usually 1/32"–1/16".

To accommodate for this margin of error, any item that bleeds—any item that extends to the trim size—must actually extend *beyond* the trim size in your final layout. The standard measurement that a bleed item must extend beyond the trim size is .125".

Creating Bleeds

You define a bleed area for a document in the Bleed and Slug section of the New Document dialog box when you're creating a document. Or, if you want to define a bleed area after the document has been created, you can do this in the Document Setup dialog box, shown in Figure 2.

QUICK TIP

Most designers prefer to address the issues with items that bleed after they've designed the layout.

Figure 2 shows that the trim size for the document is 6" wide by 3" in height and that a .125" bleed area is to be added outside the trim size. This bleed area is reflected in the document by a red guide, shown in Figure 3. You use this guide when you extend areas that bleed beyond the trim size.

As shown in Figure 4, the green background has been extended to the bleed guide on all four sides, and the yellow strip has been extended on the left and the right. If the

trimmer trims slightly outside of the trim size (the black line), the extra bleed material provides the room for that error.

Figure 1 *Identifying areas that will bleed*

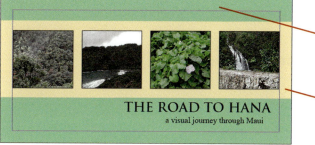

Green extends to the trim size on all four sides

Yellow extends to the trim size on two sides

Figure 2 *New Document dialog box*

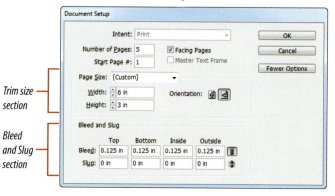

Trim size section

Bleed and Slug section

Figure 3 *Identifying the bleed guide*

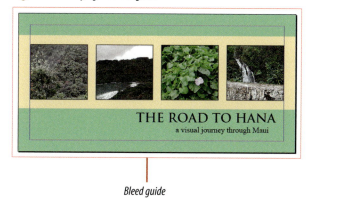

Bleed guide

Figure 4 *Extending bleed items to the bleed guide*

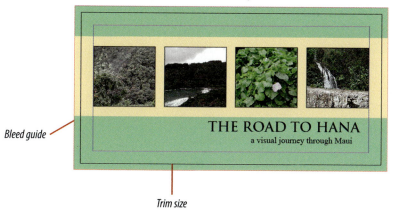

Bleed guide

Trim size

Creating Slugs

When you output a document, often you'll want to include a note on the output. Printers refer to that note as a **slug**. Slugs are often notes to the printer, phone numbers to call if there are any problems, or other information related to the file.

Obviously, slugs are not meant to be part of the final trimmed document. They must be positioned outside the trim size and outside the bleed area so that they will be discarded when the document is trimmed. InDesign allows you to create a **slug area** in the Bleed and Slug section of the Document Setup dialog box or the New Document dialog box, shown in Figure 5. In this figure, .5" has been specified for a slug area on all four sides of the document. The slug area is identified by a blue guide, shown in Figure 6. Create a text frame, position it in the slug area, then type whatever information you want to keep with the file, as shown in Figure 7.

When you create a slug, use the **Registration swatch** on the Swatches panel as the fill color for the text. When the document is color separated, anything filled with Registration appears on all printing plates.

Figure 5 *Defining the slug area*

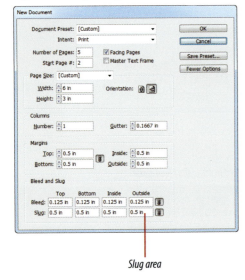

Slug area

Figure 6 *Identifying the slug area*

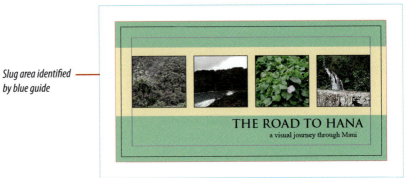

Slug area identified by blue guide

THE ROAD TO HANA
a visual journey through Maui

Figure 7 *Adding a slug*

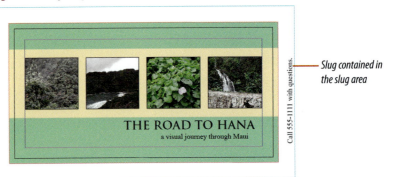

Slug contained in the slug area

Call 555-1111 with questions.

THE ROAD TO HANA
a visual journey through Maui

Previewing Bleeds and Slugs

The bleed and slug areas are not visible in Preview mode. If you want to see a preview of the page with those areas visible, press and hold the Preview button at the bottom of the Tools panel to reveal the Bleed and Slug buttons, as shown in Figure 8. Bleed mode will show you a preview with the bleed area included, and Slug mode will show you a preview with both the bleed and slug areas included.

Printing Bleeds, Slugs, and Printer's Marks

When you output a document, you can choose whether or not the bleed and slug

areas will print; usually they are printed along with printer's marks. You specify these items to print in the Marks and Bleed section of the Print dialog box, shown in Figure 9. **Printer's marks** include **crop marks**, which are guide lines that define the trim size. **Bleed marks** define the bleed size. Printers use **registration marks** to align the color-separated output. **Color bars** are used to maintain consistent color on press, and **page information** includes the title of the InDesign document.

Figure 10 shows a printed document output with a bleed area and a slug area, and identifies all five printer's marks.

Figure 8 *View mode buttons*

Figure 9 *Print dialog box*

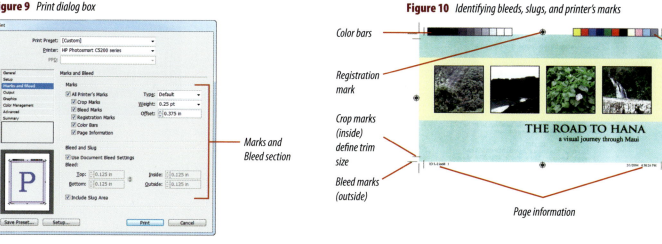

Figure 10 *Identifying bleeds, slugs, and printer's marks*

Create a bleed

1. Open ID 11-1.indd, then save it as **OAHU to Print**.

2. Verify that you are in Normal view so that guides are visible.

3. Click **File** on the Application bar, then click **Document Setup**.

4. Click **More Options** to display the Bleed and Slug section if it is not showing, as shown in Figure 11.

   The document's size, or, the trim size, is 6" × 7.5".

5. Type **.125** in the Top, Bottom, Inside, and Outside Bleed text boxes, click **OK**, then compare your page to Figure 12.

TIP Rather than enter .125 four times, click the Make all settings the same button, type .125 once, press [Tab] and the other three text boxes will automatically update.

A bleed guide appears defining the bleed area, which is .125" outside the trim size on all four sides.

6. Click the **Selection tool** ▶, select the blue frame, then drag the frame corners to the bleed guide so that your document resembles Figure 13.

You specified the bleed area in the Document Setup dialog box, then you modified an object on the page so that it will bleed on all four sides.

Figure 11 *Document Setup dialog box*

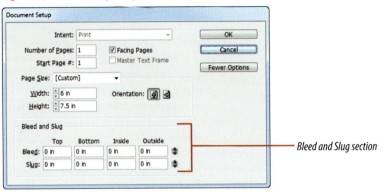

Bleed and Slug section

Figure 12 *Bleed area*

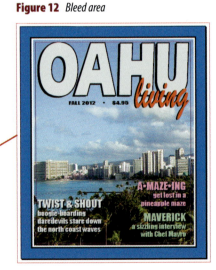

Bleed guide

Figure 13 *Modifying an object's size to bleed*

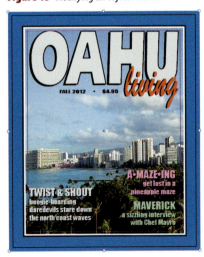

Preparing, Packaging, and Exporting Documents for Print

Figure 14 *Slug area*

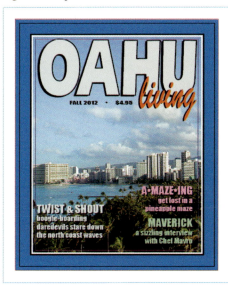

Slug guide

Figure 15 *Typing a message in the slug area*

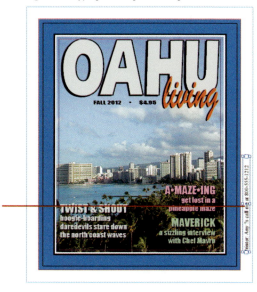

Message to printer

Create a slug

1. Click **File** on the Application bar, then click **Document Setup**.

2. Type **.5** in the Top, Bottom, Inside, and Outside Slug text boxes, click **OK**, then compare your page to Figure 14.

   A slug guide appears, defining the slug area, which is .5" outside the trim size on all four sides.

3. Drag the **text frame** from the pasteboard into the slug area at the right of the document, then change the stroke color of the text frame to None.

4. Click the **Type tool** T, then type the following in the text frame: **Printer: Any ?s call me at 800-555-1212**.

5. Click the **Selection tool** ▶, then position the text frame in the same location shown in Figure 15.

6. Verify that the text frame is still selected, then click the **Formatting affects text button** T on the Swatches panel.

7. Change the fill color of the text to **[Registration]**, then deselect the text frame.

   With a Registration fill, the slug text will appear on all printing plates if the document is color separated.

You specified a slug area in the Document Setup dialog box, you typed a message for the printer in the slug area, then you filled the text with the Registration swatch.

Preview bleeds and slugs

1. Click the **Preview button** ⬛ at the bottom of the Tools panel.

   In Preview mode, neither the bleed nor the slug area is visible.

2. Press and hold the **Preview button** ⬛ until you see the Bleed and Slug buttons, then click the **Bleed button** ⬛.

   Bleed mode shows the document and the bleed area.

3. Press and hold the **Bleed button** ⬛, then click the **Slug button** ⬛.

   As shown in Figure 16, in Slug mode, the bleed and slug areas are previewed along with the document.

4. Click the **Normal button** ⬛.

You viewed the layout in Preview, Bleed, Slug, and Normal modes.

Print bleeds, slugs, and printer's marks

1. Click **File** on the Application bar, then click **Print**.

2. Verify that Copies is set to 1 and Pages is set to All, then click **Setup category** in the box on the left.

   TIP Don't click the Setup (Win) or Page Setup (Mac) button at the bottom of the dialog box.

3. Click the **Paper Size list arrow**, click **Letter**, click the **Page Position list arrow**, then click **Centered**.

   Your dialog box should resemble Figure 17.

(continued)

Figure 16 *Viewing the layout in Slug mode*

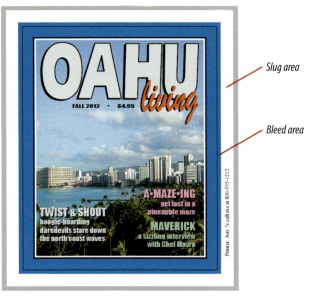

Slug area

Bleed area

Figure 17 *Setup category in the Print dialog box*

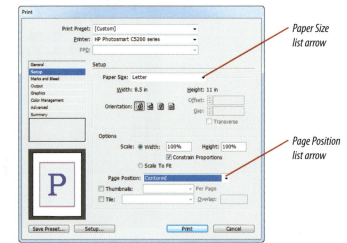

Paper Size list arrow

Page Position list arrow

Figure 18 *Activating printer's marks*

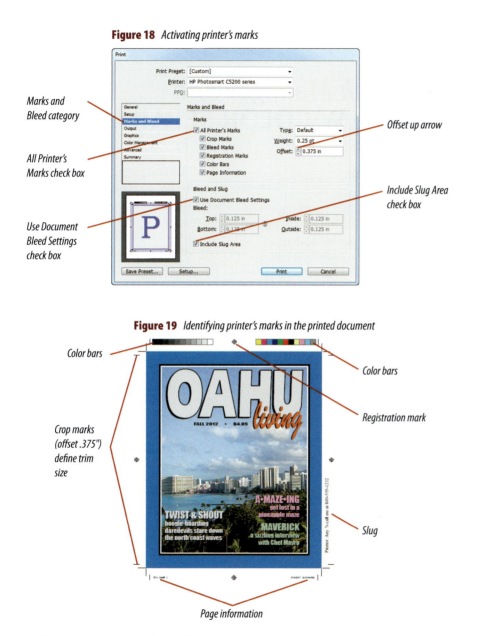

Marks and
Bleed category

All Printer's
Marks check box

Use Document
Bleed Settings
check box

Offset up arrow

Include Slug Area
check box

Figure 19 *Identifying printer's marks in the printed document*

Color bars

Crop marks
(offset .375")
define trim
size

Color bars

Registration mark

Slug

Page information

TIP Your letter choice may be Letter (8.5 × 11 in), US Letter, or another variation of an 8.5 x 11 in document, depending on your printer type.

4. Click the **Marks and Bleed category** in the box on the left.

5. In the Marks section, click the **All Printer's Marks check box**, then click the **Offset up arrow** until the value reads .375 in.

  The Offset value specifies how far outside the trim that the crop and bleed marks will be positioned. This is something to consider if you have bleed elements. Let's say your bleed is .125" which is standard. Since you don't want your crop marks *inside* the bleed element, you'd set the Offset value to .25" or greater. That way, the crop marks are positioned outside the bleed.

6. In the Bleed and Slug section, verify that the Use Document Bleed Settings check box is checked, then click the **Include Slug Area check box**.

  Your dialog box should resemble Figure 18.

7. Click **Print**.

  Compare the printer's marks in Figure 19 to your own output.

8. Save your work.

You opened the Print dialog box, set the paper size and page position, and activated all printer's marks, the document's bleed settings, and the slug area. You then printed the document.

Use the Ink Manager and
PREVIEW COLOR SEPARATIONS

What You'll Do

In this lesson, you will use the Ink Manager to specify swatches as process or spot colors, and then you'll preview separations on the Separations Preview panel.

Using the Ink Manager

The Ink Manager dialog box, shown in Figure 20, gives you control over the inks that you create on the Swatches panel. One important function that the Ink Manager provides is the ability to convert spot colors easily to process inks if you should want to do so.

QUICK **TIP**

You can access the Ink Manager from the Swatches panel menu.

You may ask, "Why would you create a swatch as a spot color if you intend to output it as a process color?" Good question. You should know that many designers choose not to be too meticulous when creating swatches. Often, they will use the PANTONE panel to create swatches without a care as to whether they are defined as spot or process. That's why many printers are seldom surprised when they open a client's document for a standard 4-Color print job and find that it has been saved with 22 spot inks!

The Ink Manager makes it easy to specify how the document will color separate. It is important to remember that using the Ink Manager is a function of output. The changes that you make to inks in the Ink Manager only affect the output of the document, not the inks in the document. For example, you might convert a swatch from a spot ink to a process ink in the Ink Manager, but the swatch will continue to be defined as a spot ink on the Swatches panel.

Using the Separations Preview Panel

The Separations Preview panel, shown in Figure 21, is another panel that allows you to see at a glance the number of inks available for printing the document. The Separations Preview panel lists only the four process inks and any swatches that are defined as spot inks.

The Separations Preview panel is interactive. Click on an ink, and the areas of the document that use that ink will appear black. The areas that don't use that ink will disappear. Figure 22 shows Black selected in the panel and only the areas of the document that contain black ink being previewed in the document.

Why is this useful? It's important to note that the Separations Preview panel comes into play in the output stages, not in the design stages. But at the output stage, it is a great resource for the print professional to see at a glance how a document will color separate and to inspect each plate quickly.

Figure 20 *Ink Manager dialog box*

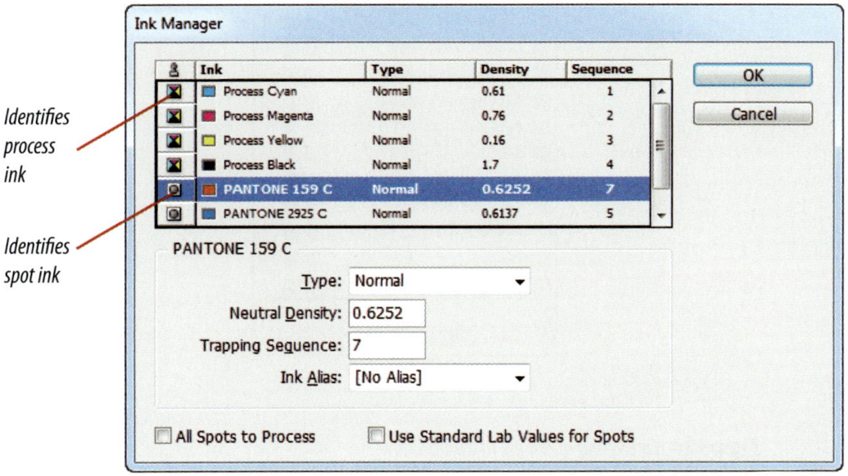

Identifies process ink

Identifies spot ink

Figure 21 *Separations Preview panel*

Figure 22 *Viewing the Black ink in the document*

Use the Ink Manager

1. Open the Swatches panel, then note the three PANTONE spot ink swatches, as shown in Figure 23.

2. Click the **Swatches panel options button** ▾☰, then click **Ink Manager**.

3. Scroll in the Ink Manager dialog box and note the inks listed.

   The list of inks in the Ink Manager window is different from the list on the Swatches panel. The Ink Manager lists the four process inks (CMYK) and the three swatches specified as spot inks. Any other process swatches are not listed because they are composed of the four process inks.

4. Click **PANTONE 427 C**, then click the **spot ink icon** ◉ to the left of PANTONE 427 C to convert it from a spot ink to a process ink, as shown in Figure 24.

   You have converted PANTONE 427 C from a spot ink to a process ink.

5. Click **PANTONE 159 C**, then click the **spot ink icon** ◉ to the left of PANTONE 159 C.

   The document will now output four process inks and one spot ink, for a total of five inks.

6. Click **OK**.

(continued)

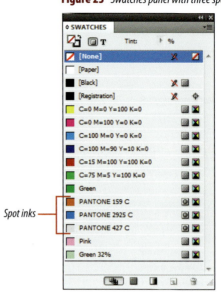

Figure 23 *Swatches panel with three spot inks*

Spot inks

Figure 24 *Converting a spot ink to a process ink*

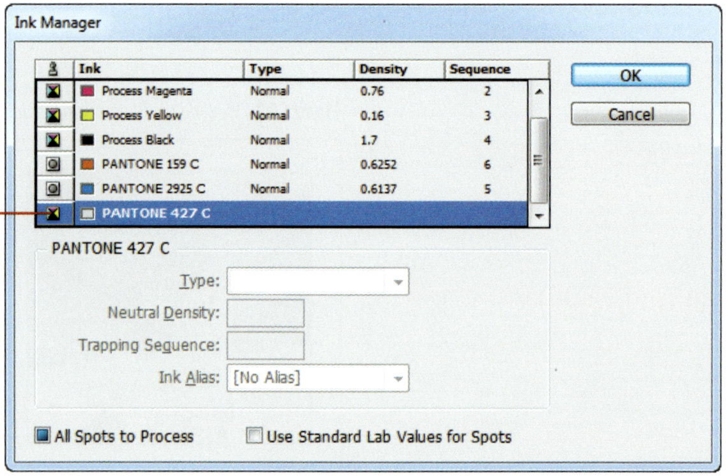

Spot ink icon changes to process ink icon

Preparing, Packaging, and Exporting Documents for Print

Figure 25 *Viewing the Inks section in the Print dialog box*

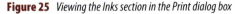

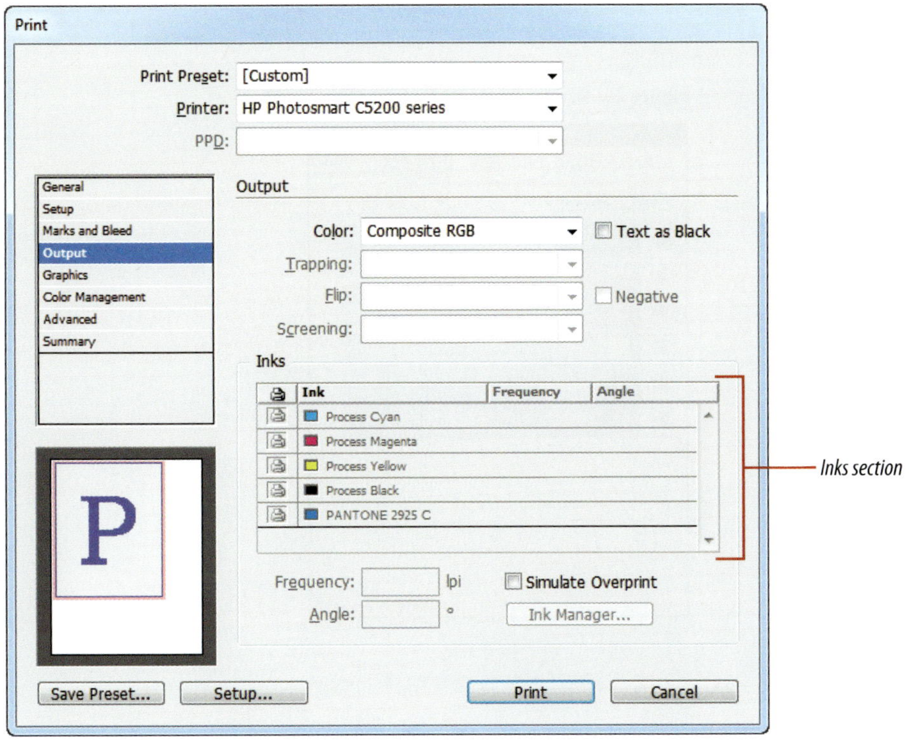

Inks section

7. Note the inks on the Swatches panel.

Changes you make using the Ink Manager affect only the output; they do not reflect how colors are defined in the document. Though PANTONE 427 and 159 will be output as process inks, the Swatches panel continues to show a spot ink icon beside them, because that is how they were specified when created.

8. Click **File** on the Application bar, click **Print**, then click the **Output category** on the left.

As shown in Figure 25, the Inks section of the Print dialog box specifies that the document will separate into five inks.

9. Click **Cancel**.

You used the Ink Manager to convert two spot inks to process inks. You then switched to the Output category of the Print dialog box to verify that the document would separate into five inks, as shown in the Ink Manager dialog box.

Use the Separations Preview panel

1. Click **Window** on the Application bar, point to **Output**, then click **Separations Preview**.

2. Click the **View list arrow** on the Separations Preview panel, then click **Separations**.

    As shown in Figure 26, the document is specified to color separate into five inks—the four process inks plus PANTONE 2925 C, which has been specified as a spot ink in the Ink Manager dialog box.

3. Move the Separations Preview panel to the side so that you can see the entire document.

4. Click **PANTONE 2925 C** on the Separations Preview panel.

    The areas of the document that have PANTONE 2925 C applied appear as black. Other areas are invisible.

5. Position the pointer over the black border in the document.

    100% appears beside the ink listed on the panel, indicating that this area is to be printed with 100% PANTONE 2925 C.

    (continued)

Figure 26 *Viewing five inks on the Separations Preview panel*

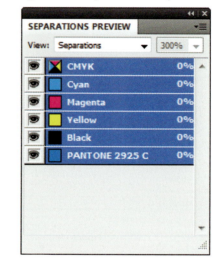

Figure 27 *Viewing a single ink on the Separations Preview panel*

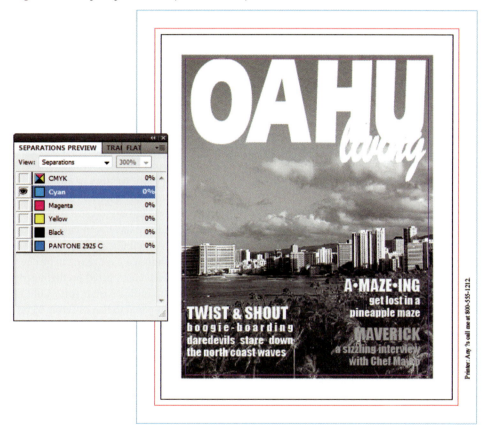

6. Click **Cyan** on the Separations Preview panel.

   As shown in Figure 27, the areas of the document that have Cyan applied appear as black. Note that the slug message is showing because it is filled with Registration and thus is on every separation.

7. Move the pointer over the document and note the percentages of cyan and the other inks.

   There is 0% cyan in the title OAHU and 0% PANTONE 2925 C anywhere except in the border.

8. Click **Magenta**, then click **Yellow**, then click **Black** to preview those inks.

   Note that the slug appears on all plates because it's filled with the Registration ink, which appears on every printing plate.

9. Click **CMYK** to preview only the areas of the document that will be printed with process inks.

10. Click the **empty gray square** beside the PANTONE 2925 C ink to make the ink visible in the preview.

11. Click the **View list arrow** in the Separations Preview panel, click **Off**, then close the Separations Preview panel.

You used the Separations Preview panel to preview how the document will be color separated into five inks.

Preflight and Package
A DOCUMENT

What You'll Do

Name	Type	Size	Tags
Fonts	File Folder		
Links	File Folder		
Instructions	Text Document	2 KB	
OAHU to Print	InDesign Document	1,656 KB	

In this lesson, you will explore options for preflighting and packaging a document.

Preflighting a Document

Before an airplane takes off, the pilots perform a preflight check. Running down a checklist, they verify that the many controls necessary to fly a plane safely are all working properly.

In the print world, designers and printers have co-opted the term "preflight" to refer to checking out a document before it's released from the designer to the printer or service bureau, or before it's actually downloaded to an output device.

When you complete a document, it is important to find and correct any errors in the document to ensure that it prints correctly. The Preflight feature is an InDesign utility that you can use to check an open document for errors such as missing fonts, missing or modified links, and overset text. Any errors that are found are listed on the Preflight panel; you can use this list to fix any problems by substituting fonts, fixing overset text issues and/or updating missing and modified files. A green circle on the left side of the status bar, also known as Live Preflight, indicates that there are no preflight errors in a document; when the circle is red, there are errors. The Preflight panel is shown in Figure 28. The On check box is checked because Preflight is on. The [Basic] Preflight profile, which, by default, checks for missing fonts, missing or modified links, and overset text, is selected. The Preflight all pages option button indicates that all pages in the document have been checked. You can click the Preflight specified pages option button to choose a page range to be checked. You can create customized preflight profiles in which you indicate what you would like the Preflight panel to flag as errors to be fixed. For example, you may want InDesign to flag font sizes under 12 points as an error because your document cannot have them for one reason or another. To create a custom preflight profile, click the Preflight panel options button, then click Define Profiles. Click the New preflight profile button (plus sign) on the left, name the profile, pick and choose settings in the right pane, then click OK. Custom preflight profiles can be accessed by clicking the Profile list arrow on the Preflight panel.

Packaging a Document

Once a document has been preflighted, it's ready to be packaged. Packaging a document means getting it ready to send to a printer, a composition house, or a client for printing or archiving. Remember, a complete InDesign document is the document itself plus any and all placed graphics and any fonts that are used. All of the components are required in order to output the document successfully.

When you use the Package command, InDesign automatically creates a folder and packages a copy of the InDesign document, copies of all the placed graphics, and copies of all the fonts used. It also offers the Printing Instructions dialog box, shown in Figure 29, which generates a report based on the information you enter. By automating the process, the Package command removes much of the potential for human error.

Figure 28 *Preflight panel*

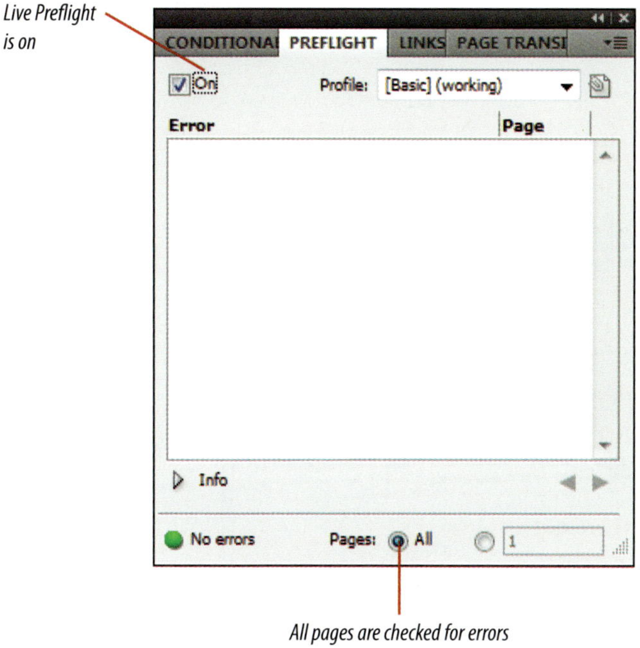

Live Preflight is on

All pages are checked for errors

Figure 29 *Printing Instructions dialog box*

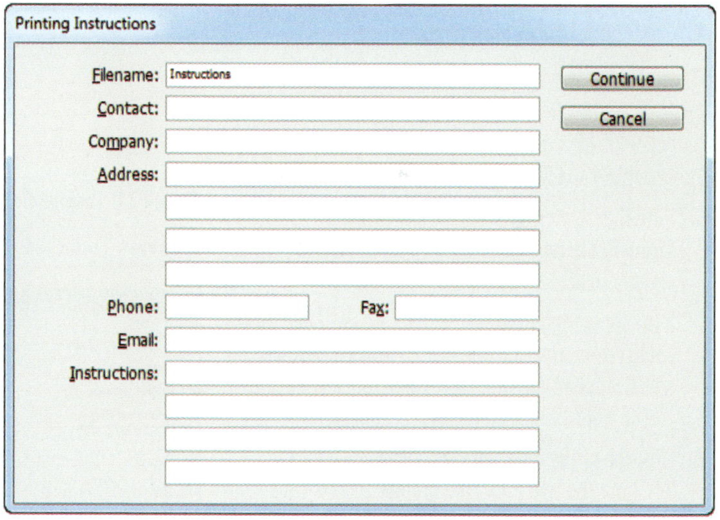

Preflight and package a document

1. Click the **Preflight menu arrow** on the status bar, then click **Preflight Panel**, as shown in Figure 30.

   The Preflight panel opens, showing no errors.

   TIP You can also open the Preflight panel using the Window menu.

2. Close the Preflight panel.

3. Click **File** on the Application bar, then click **Save**.

   A file must be saved before it can be packaged.

4. Click **File** on the Application bar, then click **Package**.

   The Package dialog box opens, as shown in Figure 31.

5. Click the **Fonts category** in the box on the left.

6. Note the two fonts listed, then click the **Show Problems Only check box** if it is not already selected.

   If the fonts used in the document are available on your system, the two fonts listed in the window will disappear. You may have more fonts listed if you do not have the same fonts installed.

7. Click the **Links and Images category** on the left, note the two imported graphics listed, then note the information below the window for each selected graphic.

8. Click the **Show Problems Only check box** if it is not already selected.

   If the links to the two imported graphics have been updated, they should disappear from the window.

   (continued)

Figure 30 *Opening the Preflight panel*

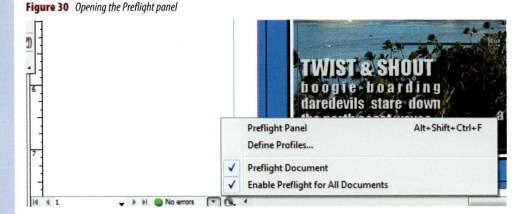

Figure 31 *Package dialog box*

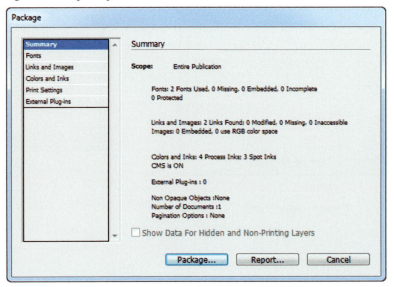

Preparing, Packaging, and Exporting Documents for Print

Figure 32 *Package Publication dialog box*

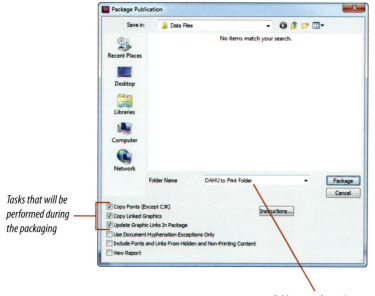

Tasks that will be performed during the packaging

Folder name for package

Figure 33 *Contents of the OAHU to Print Folder*

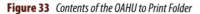

Name	Type	Size	Tags
Fonts	File Folder		
Links	File Folder		
Instructions	Text Document	2 KB	
OAHU to Print	InDesign Document	1,656 KB	

9. Click the **Colors and Inks category** on the left.

   Because three swatches are specified as spot inks on the Swatches panel, all three are listed here as spot inks. However, two of them have been converted to process inks using the Ink Manager dialog box, which overrides the information in this window.

10. Click **Report**, then click **Save** in the Save As dialog box.

11. Click **Package**, type **Instructions** in the Filename text box of the Printing Instructions dialog box, then click **Continue** to open the Package Publication dialog box (Win) or the Create Package Folder dialog box (Mac), shown in Figure 32.

   A folder is automatically supplied for you, and the three checked items in the lower-left corner are the tasks that will be performed during the packaging.

12. Click **Package,** then click **OK** if the Font Alert dialog box appears.

13. Open the OAHU to Print Folder, then compare its contents to Figure 33.

   The folder contains the InDesign document, the .txt instructions document, a Fonts folder, and a Links folder.

TIP If your list of files does not show the Instructions text file, click the Files of type list arrow in the bottom of the Open a File dialog box, then click All Files.

14. Click **Cancel** to close the dialog box, then return to the OAHU to Print document in InDesign.

You preflighted a document, then packaged a document, noting that copies of fonts and linked graphics were stored in the delivery folder.

Export A DOCUMENT

What You'll Do

In this lesson, you will explore four options for exporting a document.

Exporting a Document

Exporting a document is a different function than saving a document or printing a document. When you export a document, the document that you create is your InDesign file saved in a different file format. Figure 34 shows the Export dialog box and the available file formats for exporting.

"Why would I do this?" you may be asking. The Export command is used most often to translate a document into another format so that it can be used in another application or uploaded to the World Wide Web.

Common exports of InDesign documents include:

EPS An EPS or encapsulated PostScript file can be placed as a bitmap graphic in Adobe Photoshop or Adobe Illustrator.

PDF Portable document format, or PDF, is the file format used in Adobe Reader, a free software program that allows you to view documents created from other software programs without having to have those programs installed on your computer. When an InDesign document is exported as a PDF, all fonts and placed graphics are embedded in the PDF. Thus, the PDF is a complete and self-contained export of the entire document. In CS5, you have a print and an interactive PDF export option.

JPEG A JPEG is a compressed graphic file format which has a smaller file size than other graphic formats and is ideal for use on the web. You can export an object or objects on an InDesign document page as JPEG files. Or you can export one page, a range of pages, or an entire InDesign document as a JPEG. Exporting InDesign objects or document pages as JPEG files is useful when you want to post a selection, page, or pages as an image on the web. To export a selected object, page, or document as a JPEG file, choose JPEG in the Save as type box in the Export dialog box.

Dreamweaver Adobe Dreamweaver CS5 is a web development program that lets you create web pages containing text, images, hyperlinks, animation, sounds, and video. You can use Dreamweaver to create complex websites or individual web pages. To export an InDesign document as a Dreamweaver file, click File on the Application bar, then click Export for Dreamweaver. In the XHTML Export Options dialog box that opens, you can choose options for exporting a selection or the entire document, image quality options, color palette options, and options for dealing with CSS (Cascading Style Sheets) and JavaScript. When you export an InDesign document for Dreamweaver, you create an HTML file of the document and a folder containing all of the optimized images.

SWF (Shockwave Flash) Shockwave Flash format is a very popular format for online animations and online games. SWF files (referred to as "swiff" files) are scalable and compact which makes them perfect for the web. SWF files can be viewed by anyone with Flash Player installed on his or her computer. To export an InDesign document as an SWF file, choose SWF in the Save as type

box in the Export dialog box. If you wish to preview your SWF file in a browser window quickly after exporting, be sure to click the Generate HTML File check box and the View SWF After Exporting check box in the Export SWF dialog box that opens before the file export is complete. All hyperlinks and buttons are active in the exported SWF file.

Figure 34 *Export dialog box*

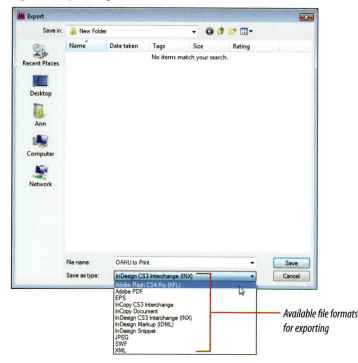

Available file formats for exporting

Digital Editions Adobe Digital Editions is a new reader software program. You can export a document or a book as a reflowable eBook (electronic book). To export an InDesign document to Digital Editions, click File on the Application bar, then click Export for Digital Editions.

Exporting a PDF for Print and for Email

PDF is one of the most common export formats for InDesign documents. The key to the relationship between InDesign and PDF is that, as a PDF, the InDesign document is complete and self-contained. Issues with imported graphics and fonts become non-issues. The PDF file includes all imported graphics and fonts. The recipient of the file does not need to have the document fonts loaded to view the file correctly.

The self-contained nature of PDFs, and the issues that it solves, makes PDF the format of choice for both professional printing and for emailing documents. In advertising and design agencies, it's standard procedure to export an InDesign document as a PDF to email to the client for approval. For professional printing, it's becoming more and more the case that, rather than package an InDesign document with all supporting graphics and fonts, printers ask for a single "high-res" PDF.

Understanding InDesign Compatibility

One of the most important features of Adobe InDesign is that it interfaces effectively with other Adobe products. An InDesign layout can be exported as a PDF, which means that the layout can be opened in both Adobe Photoshop and Adobe Acrobat. You can export the layout as an EPS, so it can be placed in both Adobe Photoshop and Adobe Illustrator. Adobe InDesign documents can also be exported to Adobe Flash. The relationship between the Adobe products also works when importing files into an InDesign layout. If you have a Photoshop file with many layers, you don't need to save a flattened copy for use in InDesign—InDesign will place a layered Photoshop document without any problems. Similarly, you can place Illustrator files in InDesign without saving it in the EPS format.

The two examples above convey the "low-end" and "high-end" roles of the InDesign-PDF relationship. When a layout includes placed graphics, especially high-resolution, large-file-size Photoshop images, how you export the PDF affects how the document is compressed to reduce the resulting file size.

When emailing a layout as a PDF, you will export the document with compression utilities activated to reduce the file size for email. These compression utilities will compress the file size of placed images.

When sending a layout to a printer for professional printing, you won't want the placed graphics to be compressed. In this case, you'll export the PDF with compression utilities turned off. The resulting PDF will likely be too large to email, but it will remain high quality for printing.

Using the Flattener Preview Panel

If you prepare InDesign documents for output or prepress, you will be interested in the Flattener Preview panel. It's important to remember that InDesign is a graphic design application as well as a layout program. Designers typically create layered documents, often with blending modes between the layers to create special effects. Complex documents like these can be a challenge to print—a layered document sometimes appears differently as output than it does on the screen. The Flattener Preview panel allows you to preview how specific areas of a layout will appear when output. This panel is especially useful for previewing transparent drop shadows, objects with a feathered edge, transparent placed graphics from Illustrator or Photoshop, and the graphics that interact with the types of objects listed previously.

Understanding Text Variables

Text variables are preset bits of information that you can automatically insert into your InDesign documents. Text variables, such as Running Header, Modification Date, and Chapter Number, go hand in hand with using master pages on multipage documents as well as with headers and footers. You can define a text variable by telling exactly where it should go (before an em dash, after punctuation, and so on) and then insert it on the page. To work with text variables, click Type on the Application bar, point to Text Variable, then click Define or Insert Variable. You can also create new text variables by clicking the New button in the Text Variables dialog box. Like all master page items, text variables work to ensure consistency across your publication.

Export a page to EPS format

1. Click **File** on the Application bar, then click **Export**.

2. In the Export dialog box, click the **Save as type list arrow** (Win) or the **Format list arrow** (Mac), click **EPS**, as shown in Figure 35, then click **Save**.

3. In the Export EPS dialog box, note that you can choose which pages you want to export.

   Because this document is a single page, you will accept the default in the Ranges text box.

4. Click the **Color list arrow** to select CMYK if it is not already selected, then click **Export**.

5. Open Photoshop, click **File** on the Application bar, click **Open**, then open OAHU to Print.eps.

   The Rasterize EPS Format dialog box opens which gives you options for converting the EPS to a bitmap image.

6. Accept the settings in the Rasterize EPS Format dialog box, then click **OK**.

   (continued)

Figure 35 *Exporting a page as an EPS file*

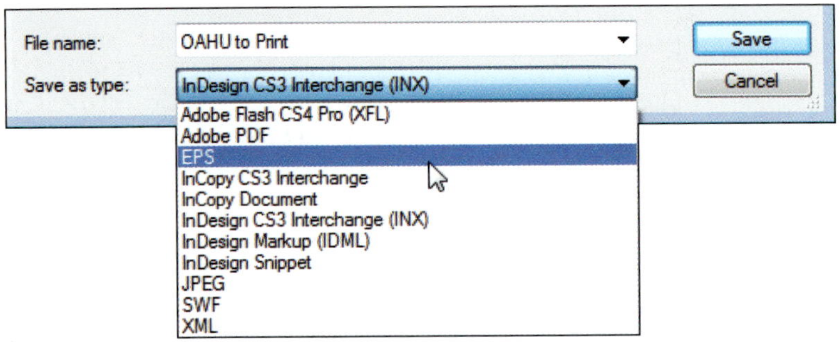

| File name: | OAHU to Print | | Save |
| Save as type: | InDesign CS3 Interchange (INX) | | Cancel |

Adobe Flash CS4 Pro (XFL)
Adobe PDF
EPS
InCopy CS3 Interchange
InCopy Document
InDesign CS3 Interchange (INX)
InDesign Markup (IDML)
InDesign Snippet
JPEG
SWF
XML

Using CS Review

Many publishing scenarios involve a team of people working together to produce a document. For example, if you were using InDesign to layout your company's monthly newsletter, the designer, copy editor, project manager, and probably the boss would all need to see the document, make changes and ultimately sign off on it. CS Review lets you share your InDesign layouts as PDFs over the web so that other members of your team can view them and provide feedback. Create a "review" by using the CS Review panel in the Window/Extensions menu. Invite reviewers to view and comment on your layout using just a web browser. CS Review is an online subscription service. Go to https://acrobat.com/csrlive_learnmore.html to learn more or to register.

Preparing, Packaging, and Exporting Documents for Print

Figure 36 *Viewing the InDesign page as a bitmap graphic in Photoshop*

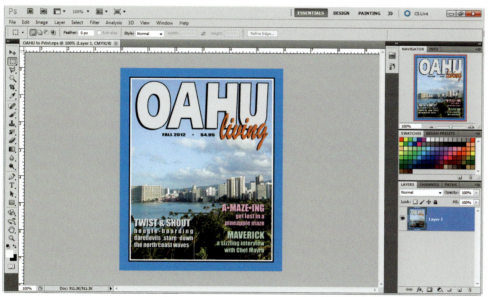

7. As shown in Figure 36, the page from InDesign opens in Photoshop as a bitmap graphic.

   Like all bitmap graphics, this graphic can be edited in Photoshop.

8. Exit Photoshop without saving changes to the file, then return to the OAHU to Print document in InDesign.

Using the Export as EPS option, you were able to open an InDesign page in Photoshop as a bitmap graphic.

Export a compressed PDF for email

1. Click **File** on the Application bar, then click **Export**.

2. In the Export dialog box, name the file OAHU to Print Compressed.

3. Click the **Save as type list arrow** (Win) or the **Format list arrow** (Mac), click **Adobe PDF (Print)**, then click **Save**.

4. In the Export Adobe PDF dialog box, click the **Adobe PDF Preset list arrow**, then click **[Smallest File Size]**.

   The presets in the list are standard settings that you can use as a starting point for exporting a PDF. For example, Smallest File Size is preset with compression settings that will reduce the size of any and all placed graphics.

   (continued)

5. Verify that View PDF after Exporting is checked.

6. Click **Compression** in the box on the left side of the dialog box.

   The settings in this dialog box have been input and saved with the Smallest File Size preset.

7. Enter the settings shown in Figure 37.

   The settings indicate that for both color and grayscale images, InDesign will use JPEG compression with Medium image quality to reduce the file size. The settings also indicate that InDesign will use Bicubic Downsampling (standard pixel interpolation) to reduce to 72 pixels per inch any color or grayscale graphics that are over 72 pixels per inch. Downsampling refers to reducing the resolution of a bitmap image. Thus, a 300 pixel per inch PSD graphic in the layout will be reduced to a 72 pixel per inch JPEG with Medium quality in the PDF.

8. Click **Marks and Bleeds** in the box on the left side of the dialog box and verify that nothing is checked.

9. Note that the word (modified) now appears beside Smallest File Size at the top of the dialog box.

   This indicates that the Smallest File Size preset has been modified, because you changed the compression settings.

10. Click the **Save Preset button** in the lower-left corner, type **My Email Export** in the Save Preset dialog box, then click **OK**.

    These new settings are now saved and will be available in the Preset list for any future PDFs that you want to email.

(continued)

Figure 37 *Compression settings for the PDF*

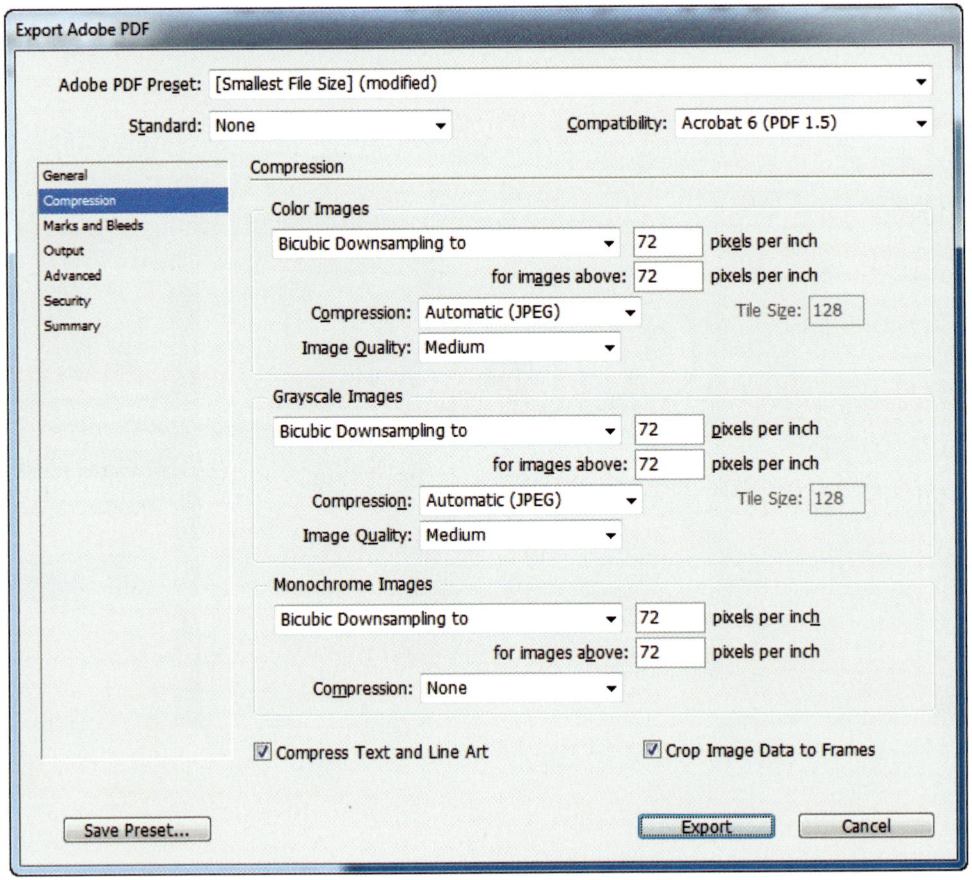

Preparing, Packaging, and Exporting Documents for Print

Figure 38 *Compression and downsampling deactivated*

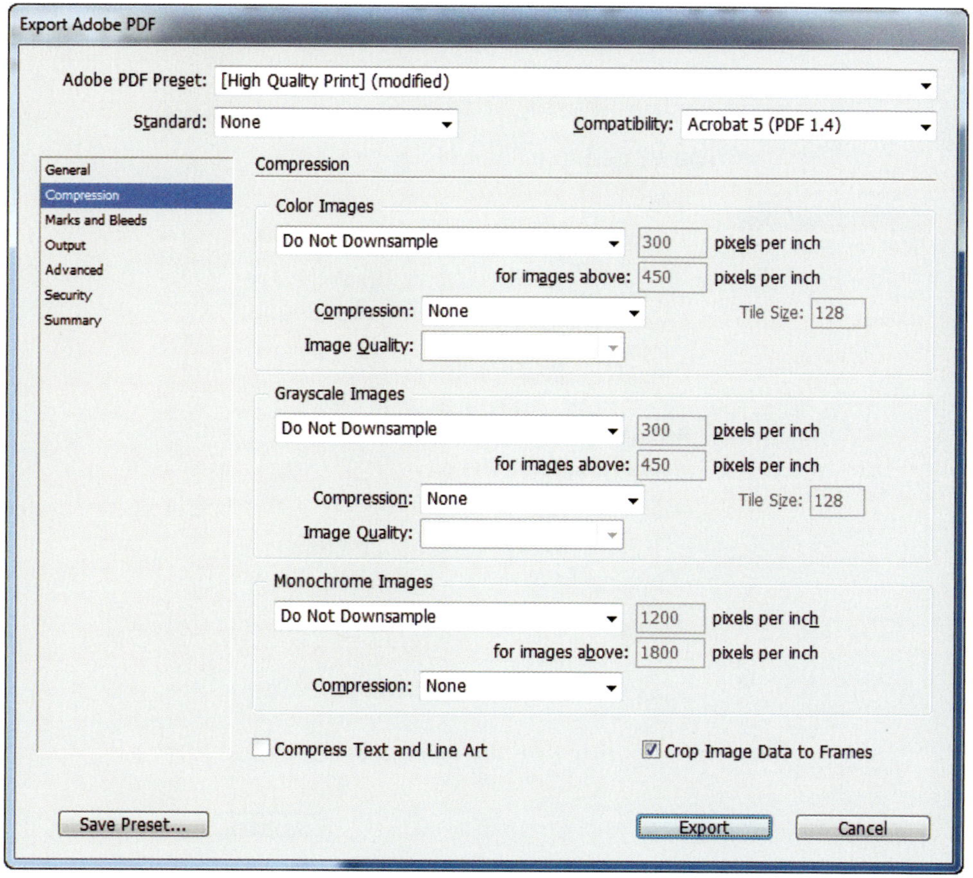

Export Adobe PDF

Adobe PDF Preset: [High Quality Print] (modified)

Standard: None   Compatibility: Acrobat 5 (PDF 1.4)

General
Compression
Marks and Bleeds
Output
Advanced
Security
Summary

Compression

Color Images

Do Not Downsample   300   pixels per inch

for images above: 450   pixels per inch

Compression: None   Tile Size: 128

Image Quality:

Grayscale Images

Do Not Downsample   300   pixels per inch

for images above: 450   pixels per inch

Compression: None   Tile Size: 128

Image Quality:

Monochrome Images

Do Not Downsample   1200   pixels per inch

for images above: 1800   pixels per inch

Compression: None

☐ Compress Text and Line Art   ☑ Crop Image Data to Frames

Save Preset...   Export   Cancel

---

11. Click **Export**.

The PDF will open in Acrobat for you to view. The exported PDF file size is less than 1 MB.

You exported the OAHU to Print document as an Adobe PDF file with a file size small enough to email. You entered settings for JPEG compression and for reducing the resolution of placed images. You then saved a preset for the settings you entered.

Export an uncompressed PDF

1. Click **File** on the Application bar, then click **Export**.

2. In the Export dialog box, name the file **OAHU to Print Uncompressed**.

3. Click the **Save as type list arrow** (Win) or the **Format list arrow** (Mac) to select Adobe PDF (Print) if it is not already then click **Save**.

4. In the Export Adobe PDF dialog box, click the **Adobe PDF Preset list arrow**, then click **[High Quality Print]**.

Note that My Email Export is listed as a preset.

5. Verify that View PDF after Exporting is checked.

6. Click **Compression** on the left side of the dialog box.

7. Enter the settings shown in Figure 38.

The settings indicate that no compression or downsampling will be applied to any of the images in the layout. Thus, if this document were built for professional printing, with high resolution images, the images would not be affected.

(continued)

8. Click **Marks and Bleeds** in the box on the left side of the dialog box, then enter the settings shown in Figure 39.

   Printer's marks include crop marks and color bars. Note that the Use Document Bleed Settings and Include Slug Area are checked. All of these settings will be represented in the final PDF.

9. Note that the word (modified) now appears beside High Quality Print at the top of the dialog box.

10. Click the **Save Preset button** in the lower-left corner, type **My Zero Compression** in the Save Preset As dialog box, then click **OK**.

    These new settings are now saved and will be available in the Preset list for any future PDFs that you want to export with no compression.

    (continued)

Figure 39 *Marks and Bleeds*

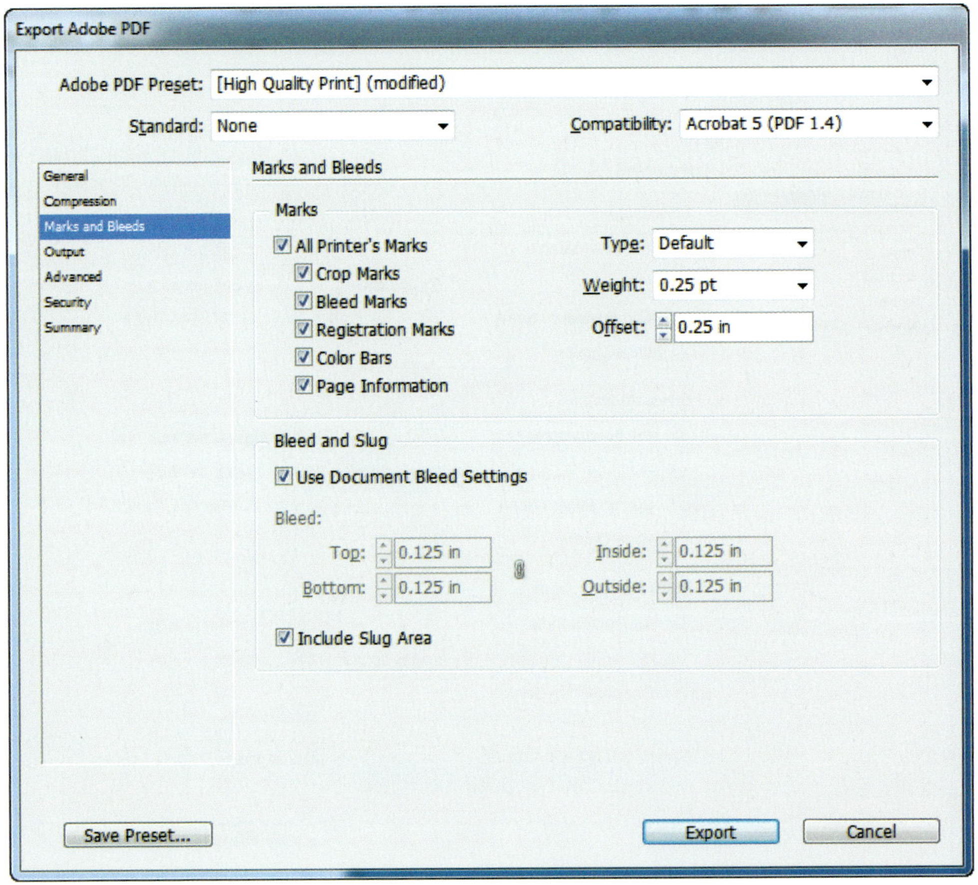

11. Click **Export**.

The PDF will open in Acrobat as shown in Figure 40. The OAHU image has not been affected in any way since being placed in InDesign.

12. Save your work, then close OAHU to Print.

You exported the OAHU to Print document as an Adobe PDF file with no compression.

Figure 40 *Exported PDF with no compression and with printer's marks and bleed and slug*

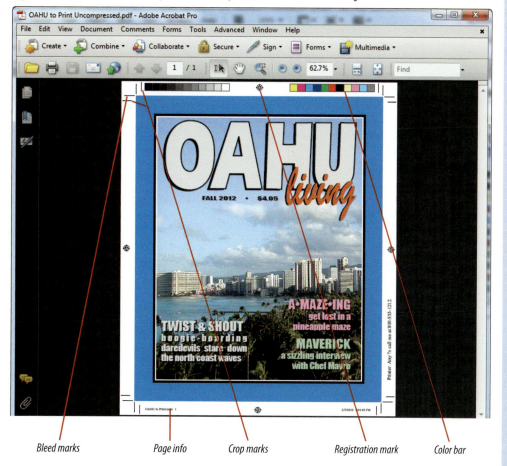

Bleed marks   Page info   Crop marks   Registration mark   Color bar

Create bleeds, slugs, and printer's marks.

1. Open ID 11-2.indd, then save it as **Hana**.
2. Verify that guides are showing.
3. Click File on the Application bar, then click Document Setup.
4. Click the More Options button if necessary to display the Bleed and Slug section of the dialog box.
5. Type **.125** in the Top, Bottom, Left, and Right Bleed text boxes, then click OK.
6. Click the Selection tool, select the green frame on Page 1, then drag the frame's corners to the bleed guide on all four sides.
7. Select the yellow frame on page 1, then drag the left and right sides of the frame to the left and right edges of the bleed guide.
8. Using the same methodology, create bleeds for the green and yellow frames on pages 2–5.
9. Press and hold the Normal button on the Tools panel, then click the Preview button.
10. Press and hold the Preview button, then click the Bleed button.
11. Click the Normal button.
12. Click File on the Application bar, then click Print.
13. Verify that Copies is set to 1 and Pages is set to All, then click the Setup category in the box on the left.
14. Verify that Paper Size is set to Letter, click the leftmost Orientation icon, click the Page Position list arrow, then click Centered.
15. Click the Marks and Bleed category on the left.
16. In the Marks section, click the All Printer's Marks check box, then set the Offset value to .385 in.
17. In the Bleed and Slug section, verify that the Use Document Bleed Settings check box is checked.
18. Click Print.

Use the Ink Manager and preview color separations.

1. On the Swatches panel, note that three swatches are specified as spot inks.
2. Click the Swatches panel options button, then click Ink Manager.
3. Scroll in the Ink Manager and note the inks listed.
4. Click Royal, then click the spot ink icon to the left of Royal to convert it to a process ink.
5. Click PANTONE 1205 C, then click the spot ink icon to the left of PANTONE 1205 C to convert it to a process ink.
6. Click OK.
7. Click Window on the Application bar, point to Output, then click Separations Preview.
8. Click the View list arrow on the Separations Preview panel, then click Separations.
9. Move the Separations Preview panel to the side so that you can see the entire document.
10. Click PANTONE 353 C on the Separations Preview panel.
11. Click Cyan on the Separations Preview panel.
12. Move the pointer over the document and note the percentages of cyan and the other inks.
13. Click Magenta, then click Yellow, then click Black to preview those inks.
14. Click CMYK to preview only the areas of the document that will be printed with process inks.
15. Click the empty gray square beside the PANTONE 353 C ink to make the ink visible in the preview.
16. Click the View list arrow, click Off, then close the Separations Preview panel.

Preflight and package a document.

1. Click the Preflight menu arrow on the status bar, then click Preflight Panel.
2. Close the Preflight panel.
3. Click File on the Application bar, then click Package.
4. Click the Fonts category on the left.
5. Verify that the Show Problems Only check box is not checked.
6. Note the font listed.
7. Click the Links and Images category on the left, verify that the Show Problems Only check box is not checked, note the imported graphics listed, then note the information below the window for each selected graphic.
8. Click the Show Problems Only check box.
9. Click Report, use the filename given, then click Save.
10. Click Package, then click Save.
11. Type Instructions in the File name text box, if the filename is not already there.
12. Click Continue to open the Package Publication dialog box (Win) or the Create Package Folder dialog box (Mac).

13. Note that a folder name has been supplied for you, then note the three checked items to the left.
14. Click Package.
15. Click OK in the Font Alert dialog box that follows.
16. Minimize InDesign, go to where you saved your Hana Folder, then open it.
17. Open the Links folder to view its contents.
18. Return to the Hana document in InDesign.

Export a document.

1. Click File on the Application bar, then click Export.
2. In the Export dialog box, name the file **Hana to Print Compressed**.
3. Click the Save as type list arrow (Win) or the Format list arrow (Mac), click Adobe PDF (Print), then click Save.
4. In the Export Adobe PDF dialog box, click the Adobe PDF Preset list arrow, then click [Smallest File Size].
5. Verify that All is selected in the Pages section and that View PDF after Exporting is checked.
6. Click Compression in the box on the left side of the dialog box.
7. Enter the settings shown in Figure 41.
8. Click Marks and Bleeds in the box on the left side of the dialog box and verify that nothing is checked.
9. Note that the word (modified) now appears beside Smallest File Size at the top of the dialog box.

Figure 41 *Compression settings for the PDF*

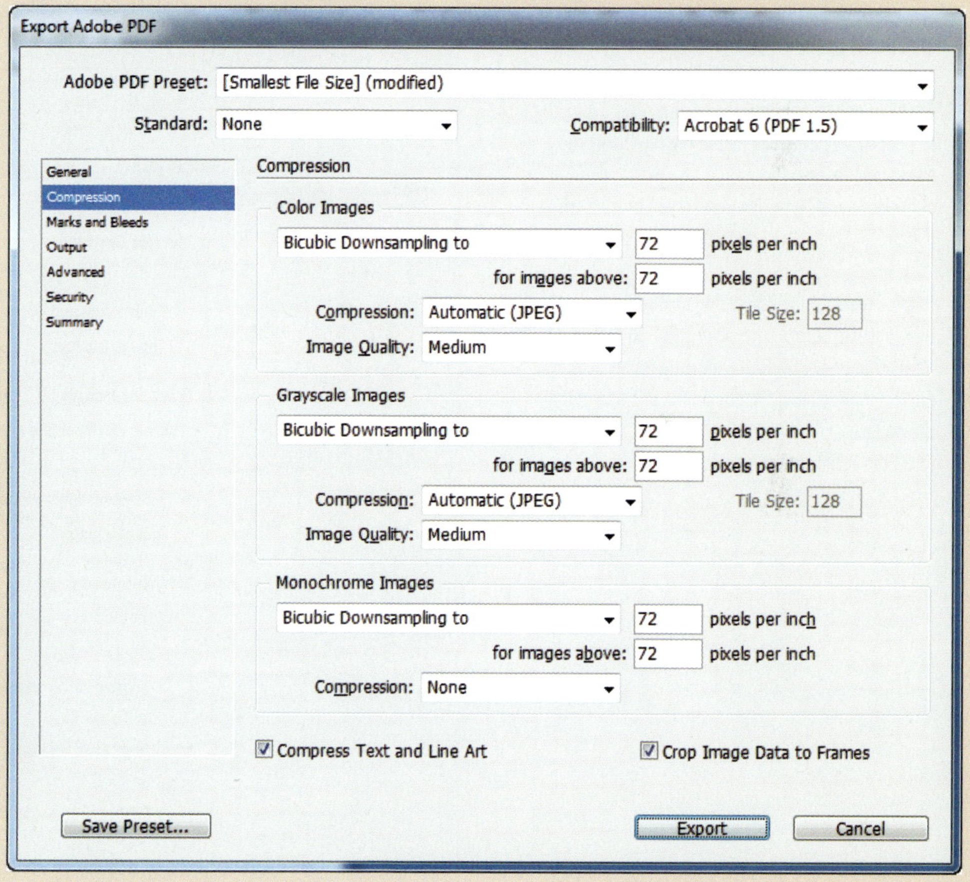

Export Adobe PDF

Adobe PDF Preset: [Smallest File Size] (modified)

Standard: None   Compatibility: Acrobat 6 (PDF 1.5)

General
Compression
Marks and Bleeds
Output
Advanced
Security
Summary

Compression

Color Images

Bicubic Downsampling to   72   pixels per inch
for images above: 72   pixels per inch
Compression: Automatic (JPEG)   Tile Size: 128
Image Quality: Medium

Grayscale Images

Bicubic Downsampling to   72   pixels per inch
for images above: 72   pixels per inch
Compression: Automatic (JPEG)   Tile Size: 128
Image Quality: Medium

Monochrome Images

Bicubic Downsampling to   72   pixels per inch
for images above: 72   pixels per inch
Compression: None

☑ Compress Text and Line Art   ☑ Crop Image Data to Frames

Save Preset...   Export   Cancel

SKILLS REVIEW
(CONTINUED)

10. Click the Save Preset button in the lower-left corner, type **Hana Email Export** in the Save Preset As dialog box, then click OK.
11. Click Export.
12. Click File on the Application bar, then click Export.
13. In the Export dialog box, name the file **Hana to Print Uncompressed**.
14. Click the Save as type list arrow (Win) or the Format list arrow (Mac), click Adobe PDF (Print), then click Save.
15. In the Export Adobe PDF dialog box, click the Adobe PDF Preset list arrow, then click [High Quality Print].
16. Verify that View PDF after Exporting is checked.
17. Click Compression in the box on the left side of the dialog box.
18. Enter the settings shown in Figure 42.

Figure 42 *No compression or downsampling applied to the PDF*

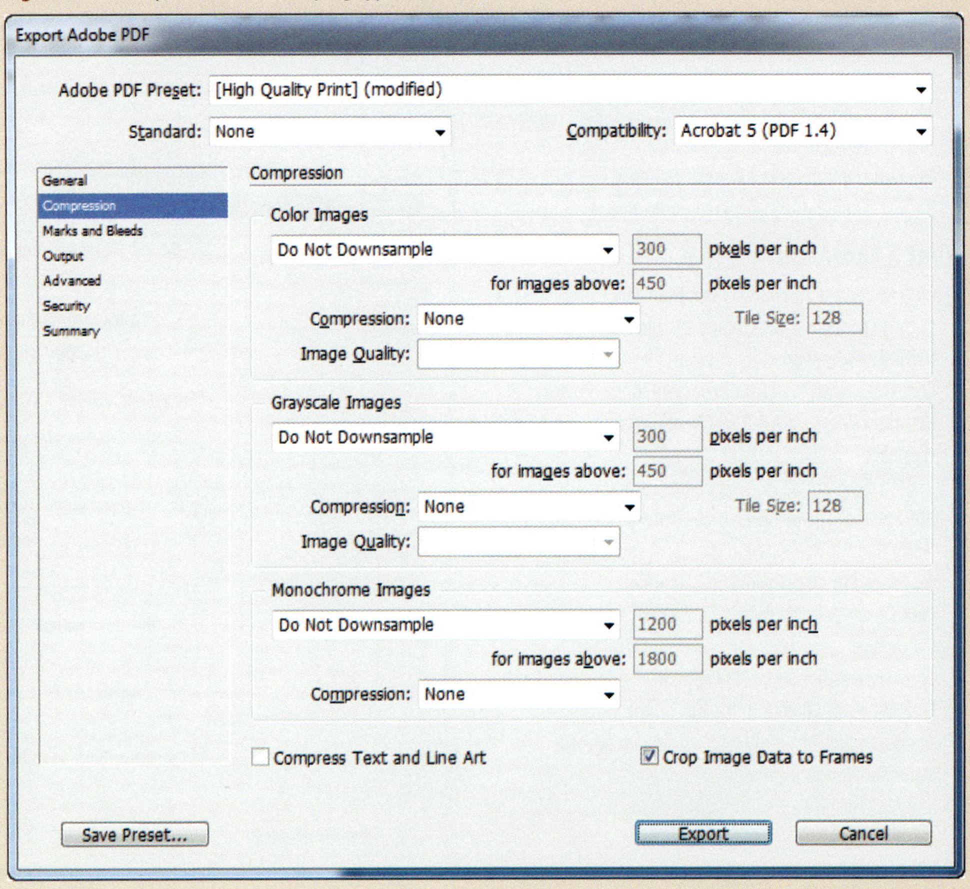

19. Click Marks and Bleeds in the box on the left of the dialog box, then enter the settings shown in Figure 43.

20. Note that the word (modified) now appears beside High Quality Print at the top of the dialog box.

21. Click the Save Preset button in the lower-left corner, type **My No Compression** in the Save Preset As dialog box, then click OK.

22. Click Export, then compare the first page of your PDF file to Figure 44.

23. Save the file, then close Hana.indd.

Figure 43 *Marks and Bleeds*

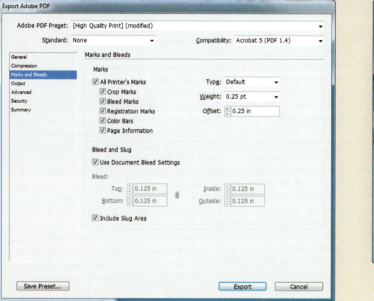

Figure 44 *Completed Skills Review*

As part of your job at a prepress service company, you open customers' documents, preflight them, then output them. Starting on a new project, you open the customer's InDesign layout and note that the job ticket says that this page is to be printed at letter size. You notice immediately that the document has been built to letter size, but the customer failed to create bleeds.

1. Open ID 11-3.indd, then save it as **Multiple Bleeds**.
2. Verify that guides are showing.
3. Open the Document Setup dialog box.
4. Type .125 in all four Bleed text boxes, then click OK.
5. Click the Selection tool, select the large background graphic, then drag the frame's four corners to the bleed guide on all four sides.
6. Click Object on the Application bar, point to Fitting, then click Fit Content to Frame.
7. Select the Windmill Silhouette graphic in the bottom-left corner, then drag the left and bottom sides of the frame to the left and bottom sides of the bleed guide.
8. Select the Windmills Color graphic on the right side of the layout, then drag the right side of the frame to the right side of the bleed guide.
9. Deselect all, compare your work to Figure 45, save your work, then close Multiple Bleeds.

Figure 45 *Completed Project Builder 1*

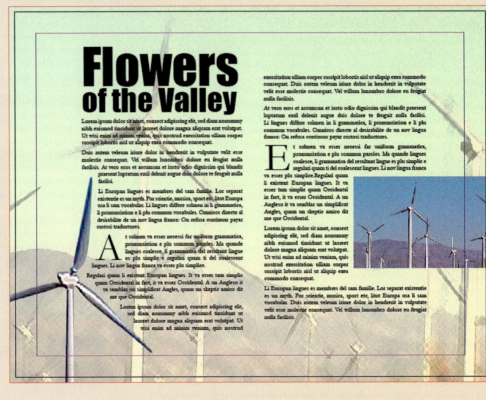

You work for a prepress service bureau, opening customers' documents, preflighting them, then outputting them to film. You've just opened the file for the cover of a monthly dog magazine. The job ticket says that it will print with five colors—CMYK + PANTONE 117 C. You decide to check that the customer specified inks properly.

1. Open ID 11-4.indd, then save it as **Lab Separations**.
2. Open the Separations Preview panel, turn separations on, then note that the document is currently specified to separate into seven colors.
3. Click the Swatches panel options button, then click Ink Manager.
4. Convert PANTONE 183 C and PANTONE 2706 C to process inks, then click OK.
5. On the Separations Preview panel, verify that the document will now separate into five colors.
6. Click PANTONE 117 C on the Separations Preview panel to preview where the spot ink will print, then compare your screen to Figure 46.
7. Turn separations off on the Separations Preview panel, then close the Separations Preview panel.
8. Save your work, then close Lab Separations.indd.

Figure 46 *Completed Project Builder 2*

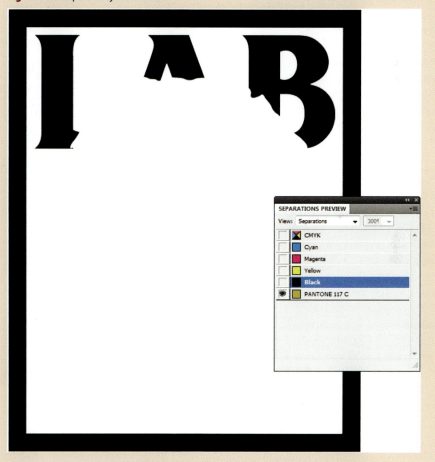

You are the webmaster at LAB magazine. Every month, you update the website with the contents from the current issue. The art director from the print department has sent you the InDesign layout for this month's cover. You will need to resize it to 50% of its original size, then upload it to the website. But first, you need to export it from InDesign so that you can manipulate it in Photoshop. Note: If you do not have Photoshop, end the exercise after Step 5.

1. Open ID 11-5.indd, then save it as **Lab Web Cover**.
2. Click File on the Application bar, then click Export.
3. Export the file in EPS format, then click Save.
4. In the Export EPS dialog box, click the Color list arrow, then click RGB. (**Hint**: Color bitmap graphics for the web are saved in RGB mode.)
5. Click Export.
6. Open Photoshop, click File on the Application bar, click Open, then open Lab Web Cover.eps.
7. In the Rasterize EPS Format dialog box, verify that the Mode text box reads RGB Color, then click OK.
8. Compare your Photoshop file to Figure 47.
9. Close the Photoshop file without saving changes, then close Photoshop.
10. Return to InDesign, then close Lab Web Cover.indd.

Figure 47 *Completed Design Project*

Preparing, Packaging, and Exporting Documents for Print

This project is designed to challenge you to figure out how to create a bleed for a tricky document. Finch Design has sent an InDesign file to be printed as a business card. Its main graphic is a large letter F, which has been specified in the Impact font. The top and bottom of the letter F must bleed. Enlarging the letter F to create the bleed is not an option; the client has noted that the relationship between the letter F and the company name (finch design) must not be altered in any way.

The challenge is to figure out the best way to create the bleed at the top and bottom.

1. Open ID 11-6.indd, then save it as **Finch Bleed**.
2. Verify that guides are visible.
3. Open the Document Setup dialog box.
4. Type **.125** in the Top and Bottom Bleed text boxes, then click OK.
5. Click the Selection tool, then select the letter F text frame.
6. Create outlines.
7. Click the Direct Selection tool, then select the top two anchor points of the letter F.
8. Move the top line of the letter F up to the bleed guide.
9. Select the bottom two anchor points of the letter F, then move the bottom line of the letter down to the bleed guide.
10. Deselect, compare your work to Figure 48, save your work, then close Finch Bleed.

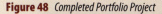
Figure 48 *Completed Portfolio Project*

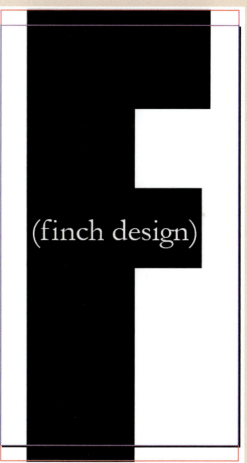

CHAPTER 12 CREATING AN INTERACTIVE DOCUMENT

1. Explore interactive documents

2. Set up interactive documents

3. Incorporate hyperlinks and buttons

4. Apply and view page transitions

5. Add animation

CHAPTER 12

CREATING AN
INTERACTIVE DOCUMENT

In the last few years, InDesign has established itself as the preeminent software package for print layout and design. With the advent of "new media," however, we're seeing an evolution—a rethinking—of InDesign's role for both print and "interactive" layouts. With CS5, you will notice that Adobe has made a large investment to enhance the interactive design capabilities of InDesign.

The whole concept of "media" has changed; we all know that. And with the changing of media comes the changing of the medium itself. InDesign is recognized as the best medium for producing a print document, but print is no longer the only medium out there. Today's publishers have all kinds of venues to deliver their content. Print will always be one of those venues, but suddenly we have the Internet, smart phones, tablet readers, and other types of "electronic communication" thrown into the mix. Adobe is savvy enough to see clearly that it's no longer enough for InDesign to do just print.

It helps to define the parameters here: all "new media" is essentially "on screen" presentation, whether that media is a web site, slide show, or animation displayed on a smart phone or tablet reader. That's the fork in the road for InDesign: to maintain its status as the best software package for print design and to emerge as the top choice for a graphic designer—not a Flash programmer, but a *graphic designer*—creating on-screen presentations.

HYPERLINKS

Hyperlinks

URL: http://www.lecinqueterre.org/eng/

Email Address

Go to Page 2

Official Home Page

Cross-References

BUTTONS

Name: Button 3

Event: On Release

Actions:

[No Actions Added]

Appearance

[Normal]

[Rollover]

[Click]

Hidden Until Triggered

PAGE TRANSITIONS

Transition: Wipe

Direction: Left

Speed: Medium

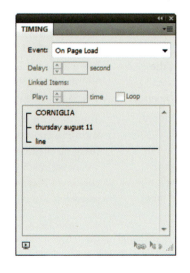

TIMING

Event: On Page Load

Delay: second

Linked Items:

Play: time   Loop

CORNIGLIA

thursday august 11

line

ANIMATION

Name:

Preset: Custom (Grow Large)

Event(s): On Roll Over (Self)

Reverse on Roll Off

Duration: 1 second

Play: 1 time   Loop

Speed: None

Properties

Animate: From Current Appearance

Animate To

Rotate: 0°

Scale W: 200%   H: 200%

Opacity: None

Visibility: Hide Until Animated
Hide After Animating

Explore Interactive
DOCUMENTS

What You'll Do

In this lesson, you will read through an overview of interactive InDesign documents and how to create, save, and view them.

Defining an Interative InDesign Document

To define an interactive document, let's start with a "classic" non-interactive print document. Traditionally, an InDesign document is a layout for print, containing the four basic elements of text, color tints, illustrations, and imagery. Generally speaking, in a traditional document, text and color tints are created in InDesign, vector illustrations are imported from Adobe Illustrator, and bitmap imagery is imported from Photoshop.

An interactive InDesign document is everything that a traditional InDesign document is, with additional "interactive" features. An interactive document often features the same basic elements, such as text and images, but in an interactive document, the interactive component allows you, literally, to interact with the document. For example, clicking an element on the page will take you to another page. Clicking a line of text might open a new window and take you online to a Web site.

What's more, interactive InDesign documents offer exciting features that you never saw in a print document. For example, you can animate objects on the page. Headlines might "fly in" from off the page. Images might fade in or fade out—or they too might fly in and out of the page, rotating while they do so. Text balloons might "pop up," appearing from nowhere and disappearing when you click them.

You can make transitions between pages, so that when you move from page to page, an animation occurs. Maybe one page dissolves into another, or maybe a page "curls" to reveal the next page "beneath" it. Figure 1 shows a page curl transition available in Adobe InDesign.

You can even incorporate movies and sound in an interactive InDesign document. Imagine clicking a text box and hearing a voiceover reading the text on the page or clicking a Play button and wow—you're watching a movie!

Creating an Interactive Document

Creating a Destination for an Interactive InDesign Document

First of all, let's be clear that the InDesign document itself is a means to an end. In other words, the interactive InDesign document is not the end product. It's the layout for the end product.

Secondly, let's clarify that the *medium* for an interactive document is a screen—usually a computer screen.

There are three basic types of output for interactive documents:

- An interactive document for the Web
- An interactive on-screen presentation
- An interactive document for Adobe Flash

When you think about it, all three are really the same thing; they are interactive, on-screen presentations. If you export one InDesign layout to be presented on the Web and another to be presented only on your laptop screen, there's really no difference between the two, except that the Web document is accessible to a larger audience. Exporting a document to Adobe Flash is merely an interim step towards the same goal;

Flash will create an interactive presentation for the Web or for an individual computer.

Understanding the Relationship Between InDesign and Flash

Adobe Flash is itself an interactive layout "authoring" software package, and a very powerful software package at that. The interactive layouts you create in Adobe Flash can be as complex as any of the eye-popping Web sites you see on the Internet. In fact, Flash is the established software package for creating professional-level Web sites.

Figure 1 *Page curl transition*

In addition to its layout utilities, Flash offers high-level ActionScript coding to create dramatic animation and complex interactivity with buttons, bells, and whistles.

Flash and InDesign are, of course, both Adobe products, and what you're seeing here with interactive InDesign documents is an overlap between InDesign and Flash. Some designers design a layout from scratch in Flash. Other designers are more comfortable in InDesign. For these latter designers, Adobe offers the ability to create a layout in InDesign and export it to Flash for further scripting and interactivity.

In this scenario, the InDesign layout is truly a means to an end. One of the inherent issues in this method involves how much interactivity you create in InDesign before exporting to Flash. While Flash does support some of InDesign's interactive elements, the best methodology is to do all the interactive work, such as animations, buttons, and hyperlinks, in Flash. In other words, if the destination is Flash, use Flash to do what Flash does best. Use InDesign to create the layout, but use Flash to add the interactivity. This is, in most cases, the *only* choice, because Flash offers limited support to interactive elements created in InDesign.

Exporting InDesign Documents to Adobe Flash

You export your InDesign document to Flash using the FLA file format. When you do so, you can then open the document in

Adobe Flash to edit its contents and use the Flash authoring environment to add such elements as animation, sound, complex interactivity, and video. Figure 2 shows the export dialog box in InDesign for FLA.

Understand that the FLA format is "proprietary" to Adobe Flash. In other words, an FLA file is itself a Flash file. An FLA file cannot be opened or viewed directly in a Web browser. It must first be exported from Flash to be viewed or otherwise presented.

Exporting a "Presentation-Ready" Interactive Document

If you're not a Flash designer or a Flash programmer, what you really want is to build the interactive presentation exclusively in InDesign then export a file that's complete and ready for viewing. The fact that you can create an interactive presentation in InDesign, complete with elements such as animations, hyperlinks, and buttons, and export a file ready for viewing, is the dramatic interactive upgrade that is InDesign CS5.

Figure 2 *Export FLA dialog box*

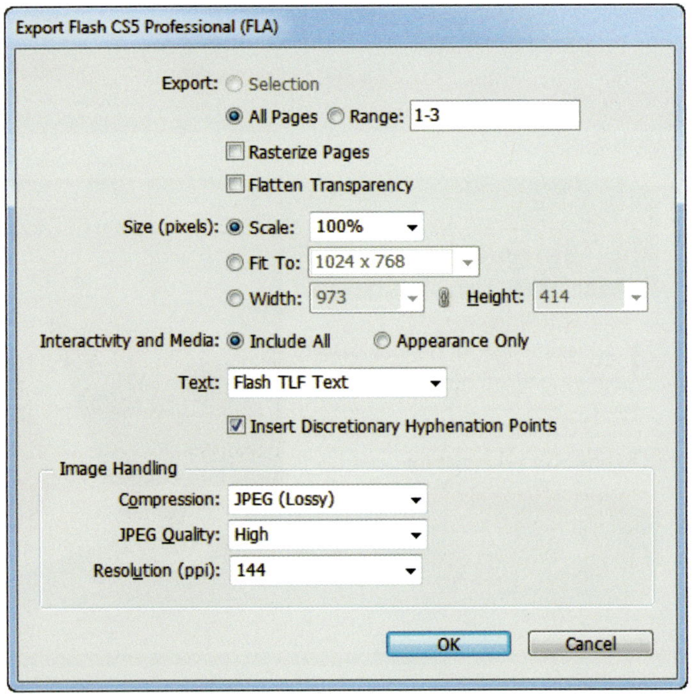

Creating an Interactive Document

When you're finished designing your interactive document in InDesign, or if you're just at a stage where you want to test it out, export the file as an SWF or an interactive PDF. These are "presentation-ready" formats; when you open the document to view it, the entire layout, all its pages, and all its interactivity is visible and ready to go.

PDF, an acronym for portable document format, is a great format for creating a presentation complete with interactive components like buttons, movies, sound clips, hyperlinks, and page transitions. But you should note an important disclaimer: InDesign animations are not supported by the PDF format. PDF is a great choice for emailing an interactive InDesign presentation that can be viewed by anybody with Acrobat Reader.

SWF is an acronym for Shockwave Flash, though it's also been known offhand as "small Web format." SWF supports all InDesign interactivity, including animation. You can open and interact with your SWF presentation in Adobe Flash Player or in common browsers such as Internet Explorer and Firefox.

Figure 3 shows the Export SWF dialog box in InDesign. Note the Interactive Page Curl option: this great effect is available with export to the SWF format, not the PDF format.

Your SWF file can be used as a presentation on your own computer. If you have an overhead display connected to your computer, an interactive InDesign document exported as an SWF file can make for a spectacular slideshow. You could distribute your SWF presentation to multiple computers for an interactive learning experience, or you could upload your SWF as content on your own Web site.

Figure 3 *Export SWF dialog box*

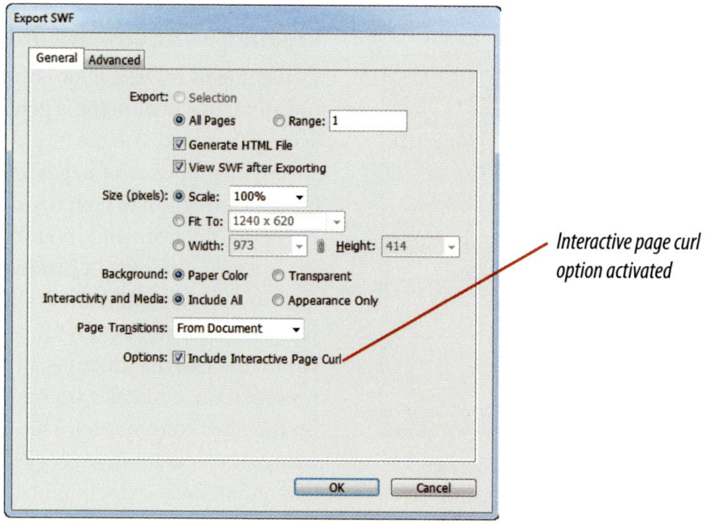

Interactive page curl option activated

Creating Interactive Forms with the PDF Format

To understand interactive forms, think of an application that you might fill out online on a Web site, like an online driver's license renewal, an IQ test, or an insurance application form. Any form that you can fill out on your computer is an interactive form. InDesign does not provide tools for creating interactive form fields, but allows you to create a sophisticated layout for the form, using tables, charts, radio buttons, text fields, and check boxes. Once you're done creating the layout, you can then export the file as a PDF. Adobe Acrobat is Adobe's long-standing software package for working with PDFs. Acrobat will open the PDF and convert the placeholders into form fields.

Set Up
INTERACTIVE DOCUMENTS

What You'll Do

In this lesson, you will set up an interactive document from scratch and you will modify an existing layout to be an interactive document.

Creating an Interactive Document

Designing in InDesign for either a print or interactive document is generally the same procedure; you create a document, specify the number of pages, and then create design elements like text, tints, and images. However, the print and interactive mediums are innately different. A printed document is a tangible item, and any color in a printed piece is based on the CMYK color model. An interactive document is an on-screen presentation, and color on screen is based on the RGB color model. This is just one of many significant differences between a print and an interactive document.

When you set up a new interactive document, you must consider that the settings you enter are specific for on-screen presentations. For example, the page size of the presentation will be related to the size of a computer monitor, and you'll need to specify the color setting for the document to be in the RGB color space.

Figure 4 shows the New Document dialog box in InDesign set up for an interactive document. Note that the Intent option is set to Web. (The two choices available for Intent are Print or Web.) Note that this option

doesn't necessarily mean that the document must be used on the World Wide Web, but, rather, indicates that the document will be set up for an on-screen presentation. When you choose Web as the Intent, the document's color space is automatically set to RGB.

Note that the document is set up with multiple pages, and, in this case, three. You might at first think of a Web site as being a single page, but on further consideration, it's apparent that they are multiple pages. For example, when you click a link on a Web page and that takes you to a different page, you have, at that point, seen two pages. This scenario is represented in InDesign by multiple pages.

The Page Size menu offers standard document sizes for on-screen presentations. 1024 x 768 is an oft-chosen size because it is the dimension of a standard 17-inch computer monitor.

Note that these page sizes are measured in pixels. Pixels are the smallest increment of an on-screen display, and they are the means by which monitors display color. The standard measurement for monitors (sometimes referred to as monitor resolution) is 72 pixels per inch.

You don't necessarily need to use the standard page sizes in the New dialog box when setting up an interactive document. You do, however, want to be sure that the document is sized so that it fits on a standard-sized screen. If your document is larger than the screen upon which it's being displayed, you'll need to scroll to see parts of the layout that are off screen, which will greatly diminish the impact of your presentation. Alternately, you could apply settings that would scale the document to fit on the screen, but scaling a document can have adverse effects on color quality and image quality. In a nutshell, it's best to build your document to a size—especially a width—that fits on the screen.

Redefining a Traditional Document as an Interactive Document

There's no line in the sand between a print InDesign document and an interactive InDesign document; they're both InDesign documents. It's the output method that determines its function.

In fact, you can have a single InDesign document doing "double duty" as a document that you print and present on screen with animation. This is worth exploring. Let's say you had an 8.5" x 11" document with multiple images placed from Photoshop. In Photoshop, those images were saved in the CMYK color space to print. In InDesign, you've added a number of interactive aspects to the layout, such as objects that function as buttons, text elements

Figure 4 *New Document dialog box set up for an on-screen (Web) document*

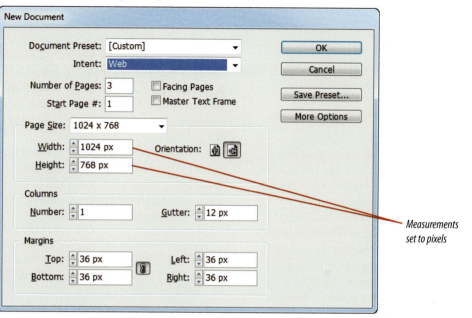

Measurements set to pixels

The Problem with Pixels

If I told you that a picture frame in your layout was 720 pixels by 360 pixels, would that mean anything to you? At 72 pixels per inch, the frame would be 10" x 5." But even that relatively easy math requires that you run the numbers in your head. Imagine if I told you that a frame was 672.3 pixels by 123.7 pixels. Would you have any sense at all how big the frame is?

Some Web designers feel comfortable working exclusively with pixels as their basis for measurments. The rest of us, however, might feel comfortable sticking to good old inches or maybe picas and points. When you create a new document and specify it as a Web document, by default, your ruler units are specified as pixels. That means every frame you create and all the positioning information for objects on the page will be specified in pixels. If you don't like that, don't feel that you have to live with it. Simply change your Units & Increments preferences to Inches. It will still be a "Web" document.

that function as hyperlinks, and images that have animation settings applied to them.

You could print this document on your own color printer or even have it printed professionally in mass quantities, just like any other printed piece. The interactive settings you applied simply would be inconsequential and wouldn't disrupt the printing process.

On the other hand, you could export the same document as an SWF and produce for yourself an on-screen presentation, complete with all the interactive elements you specified. All color on screen is presented in RGB, because monitors display color in RGB. So the fact that the files were saved in CMYK in Photoshop has no impact on the ability to present the layout on screen. In fact, the presentation is already being displayed on screen as you work on it in InDesign, right?

Once you start working with InDesign's interactive features, you'll find that you want to try out some existing layouts as interactive, on-screen presentations. When you do this, you'll need to consider document size and transparency blend space.

As stated previously, you want your presentation documents, especially the width, to fit on the screen upon which it's being presented. The width is most critical, because it's standard to scroll down a page on a Web site, but rare and undesirable to scroll horizontally.

When repurposing an existing layout as an interactive layout, verify that the width is small enough to fit on a standard screen. A standard 17" monitor has a screen width of 1024 pixels at 72 pixels per inch. Thus, ideally, you want your InDesign document to be no larger than 14.2 inches wide (1024 divided by 72 = 14.2). It's often a smart choice to convert your Units & Increments preferences from Inches to Pixels when repurposing a print document. In doing so, you'll get the exact number of pixels that make up the document's width and height. Figure 5 shows the Units & Increments preferences dialog box set to Pixels.

The transparency blend space setting is a color setting that applies to transparency in your InDesign layout. When output—either as a print or an on-screen document—InDesign must define the colors of all overlapping transparent areas in the document. For example, it must say, "Where this pink circle overlaps the yellow square, the overlapping color is X." To define that color, InDesign must refer to a color model or a color "space." To avoid unexpected shifts in color, for on-screen documents, switch the transparency blend space from the default CMYK space to RGB. To do so, click Edit/ Transparency Blend Space/Document RGB.

Figure 5 *Units & Increments ruler units set to pixels*

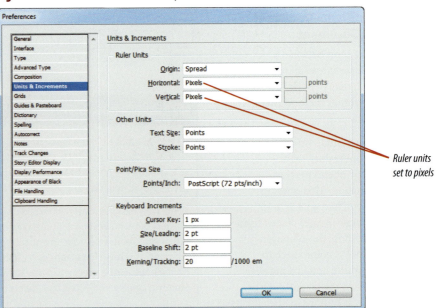

Figure 6 *Setting up a new interactive document*

New Document

Document Preset: [Custom] ▼	OK
Intent: Web ▼	Cancel
Number of Pages: 3 ☐ Facing Pages	Save Preset...
Start Page #: 1 ☐ Master Text Frame	More Options

Page Size: 1024 x 768 ▼

Width: 1024 px   Orientation: [icon] [icon]
Height: 768 px

Columns

Number: 1   Gutter: 12 px

Margins

Top: 36 px   Left: 36 px
Bottom: 36 px   Right: 36 px

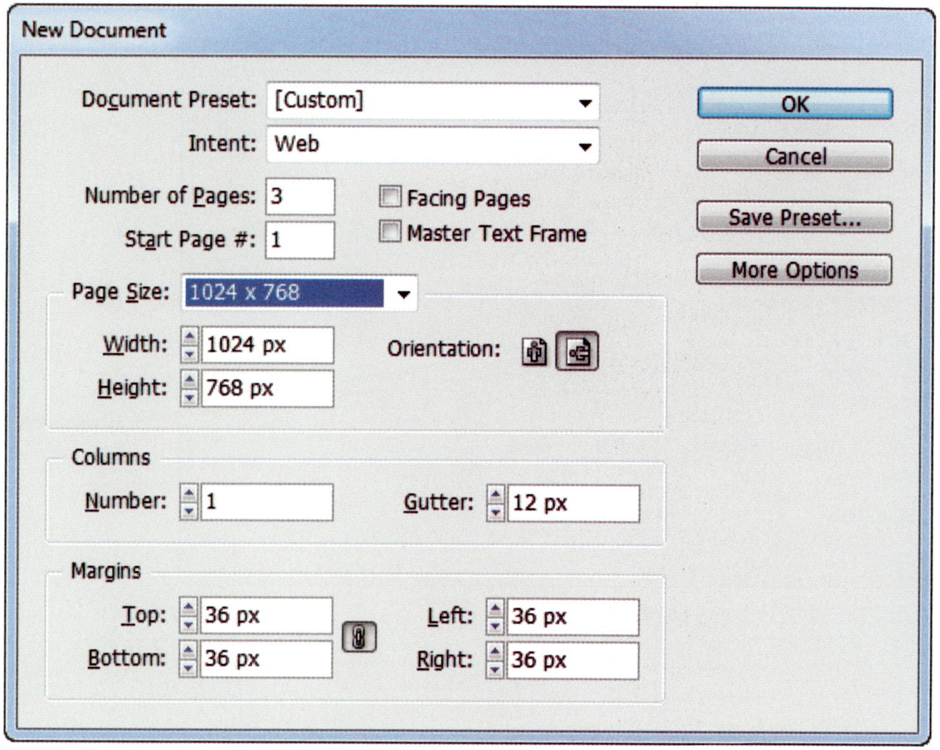

Create a new interactive document

1. Verify that no other documents are open.
2. Click **File** on the Application bar, point to **New**, then click **Document**.

   The New dialog box opens.
3. Click the **Intent list arrow**, then click **Web**.
4. Enter **3** for the number of pages.
5. Verify that Facing Pages is not checked.

   Generally speaking, you'll never use Facing Pages for an on-screen presentation.
6. Click the **Page Size list arrow**, then click **1024 x 768**.

   Your New Document dialog box should resemble Figure 6.
7. Click **OK**.
8. Click **Edit** on the Application bar, then point to **Transparency Blend Space**.

   Because the document was set up as a "Web" document, the Transparency Blend Space is automatically set to Document RGB.
9. Click **Edit** (Win) or **InDesign** (Mac) on the Application bar, point to **Preferences**, then click **Units & Increments**.

   The document is automatically set up with Ruler Units set to Pixels.
10. Click the **Cancel button**.
11. Save the file as **Presentation Document**.
12. Close the file.

You created a new presentation document from scratch. In the New Document dialog box, you specified the intent, the number of pages, and the page size for the document. Once the document was created, you noted the default transparency blend space and ruler units.

Redefine an existing document as an interactive document

1. Open ID 12-1.indd, then save it as **Italy Presentation**.

   This file is the same file with which you worked throughout the book, especially in Chapter 8. The file was originally conceived as a print document, with no thought given to any on-screen settings or interactive components.

2. Click **File** on the Application bar, then click **Document Setup**.

   The Document Setup dialog box opens. The document dimensions are specified as inches.

3. Click **Cancel**.

4. Click **Edit** (Win) or **InDesign** (Mac) on the Application bar, point to **Preferences**, then click **Units & Increments**.

5. In the Ruler Units section, set the Horizontal and Vertical units to Pixels, then click **OK**.

6. Open the Document Setup dialog box again, then compare your screen to Figure 7.

   TIP You may have to click the More Options button to display the full dialog box.

   At 972 pixels, the document's width is less than 1024, meaning it will fit on most computer screens, including most laptop computers. At 414 pixels, the document's height will fit easily on most computer screens.

7. Click **Cancel**.

(continued)

Figure 7 *Document Setup dialog box displaying dimensions in pixels*

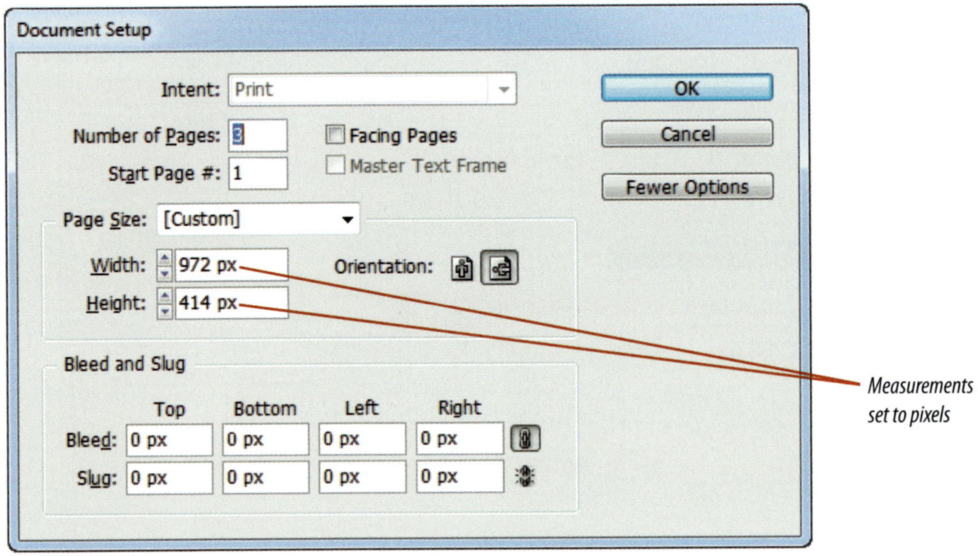

Measurements set to pixels

Figure 8

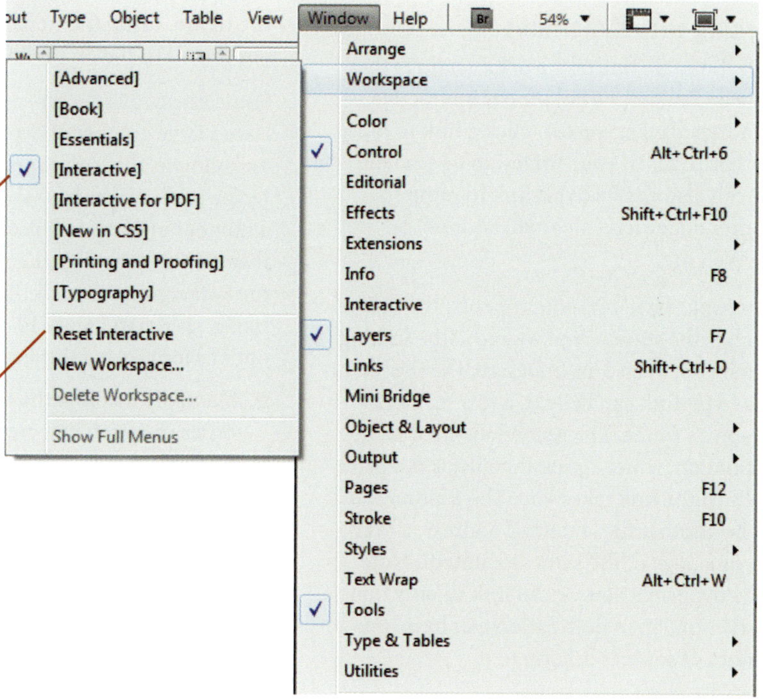

Click to switch to the [Interactive] Workspace

Click to reset Interactive Workspace

8. Open the Units & Increments dialog box again, then set the Horizontal and Vertical ruler units back to Inches.

   The ruler units are set to pixels only so that the Document Setup dialog box will provide the document dimensions in pixels. For working in the document, however, it is easier to work in inches. At 72 pixels per inch, the 1024 width ppi equals approximately 14.2 inches. In the future, you don't need to convert your units to pixels—just verify that the document's width is less than 14.2 inches.

9. Click **Edit** on the Application bar, point to **Transparency Blend Space**, then click **Document RGB**.

10. Click **Window** on the Application bar, point to **Workspace**, then click **[Interactive]**, as shown in Figure 8.

TIP You might need to click Window again, point to Workspace, then click [Reset Interactive] if you do not see any change in your Workspace. See Figure 8..

11. Save the file.

You opened an existing layout, then changed the ruler units to pixels to check the dimensions of the document in pixels, verifying that the width was less than 1024 pixels. You changed the ruler units back to inches. You then changed the Transparency Blend Space to Document RGB and set the workspace to the Interactive workspace.

Incorporate Hyperlinks
AND BUTTONS

What You'll Do

In this lesson, you will incorporate hyperlinks and buttons to navigate around the document and to link to an online Web page.

Working with Hyperlinks

Hyperlinks are one of the great features that make an interactive document interactive. With hyperlinks, you can click a link to jump to other pages in your InDesign document. You can also click a hyperlink to jump to another document, an email address, or to a Web site.

Hyperlinks have two components, the first of which is the **source**. The source is the linking element itself, and, in InDesign, the source for a hyperlink can be text, a text frame, or a graphics frame. The second element is the **destination**, which, quite literally, is the place to which the link takes you. The destination can be another file, an email address, a Web site, or a page in the same document. Note that a hyperlink source can link to only one destination, but a destination can have any number of sources linking to it.

Hyperlinks in InDesign are created in the Hyperlinks panel, shown in Figure 9. When you create a hyperlink, it appears in the panel with a name automatically given in the panel, usually Hyperlink 1, Hyperlink 2, and so on. You can apply a more descriptive name to the hyperlink, as shown in

the figure, using the Rename Hyperlink command in the Hyperlink panel menu.

Some interactive documents you create might have a large number of hyperlinks. Imagine, for example, that you've produced an online recipe book. You might want to hyperlink a number of terms to link to other recipes that use the same ingredients. In any case, the Sort command in the Hyperlinks panel menu, shown in Figure 10, offers the following options for viewing the links listed in the panel:

- **Manually** displays the hyperlinks in the order in which you created them.
- **By Name** displays the hyperlinks in alphabetical order.
- **By Type** displays the hyperlinks in groups of similar type, such as page links and URL links.

Creating Buttons

Buttons perform actions when clicked in an InDesign document exported to SWF or PDF formats. Clicking a button could take you to a different page in the document, or it could open a Web site, or it could play a movie, a sound, or an animation. Buttons you create are listed and formatted in the Buttons panel, shown in Figure 11.

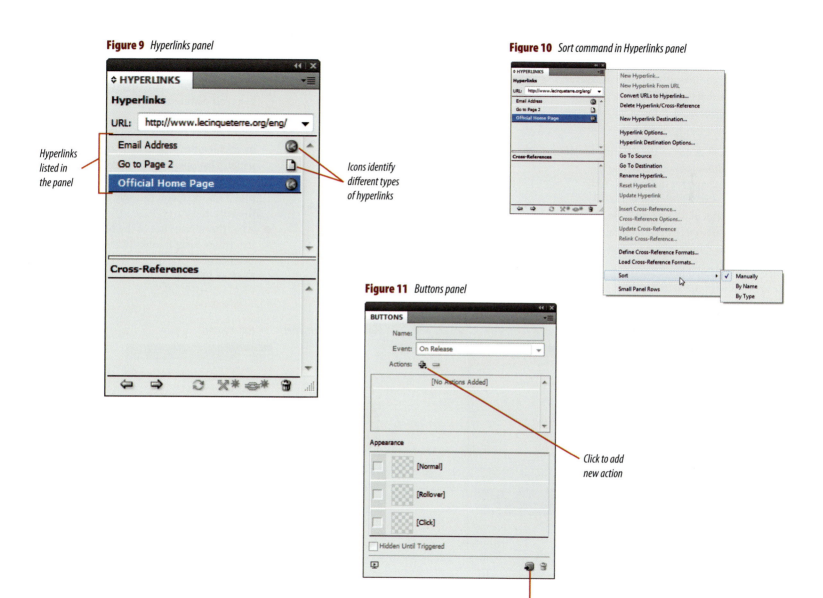

Figure 9 *Hyperlinks panel*

Hyperlinks listed in the panel

Icons identify different types of hyperlinks

Figure 10 *Sort command in Hyperlinks panel*

Figure 11 *Buttons panel*

Click to add new action

Convert Object to a Button

You might be thinking that buttons sound a lot like hyperlinks. To a degree that's true, though buttons and hyperlinks are mutually exclusive in some things that they do. To make a clearer distinction in your head, think of buttons as *artwork* to which you apply an action.

Use the Pen tool or any of the drawing tools such as the Ellipse tool or the Rectangle tool to draw a shape for the button. You can design to your heart's content. Add fills, strokes, text, gradients, and effects. Or don't. Button artwork can be as simple as a rectangle or an ellipse with a fill.

Once you've created button artwork, select the artwork with the Selection tool. If the button artwork is created from multiple objects, group the objects. With the artwork selected, convert it to a button in either of the following two ways:

- Click the Convert Object to a Button icon on the bottom of the Buttons panel.
- Click Object on the Application bar, point to Interactive, then click Convert to Button.

The artwork will be converted to a button. A dotted line will appear around the artwork, and a small button icon will be positioned within the dotted line. The artwork will appear in the Normal section at the bottom of the Buttons panel, as shown in Figure 12.

Once you've converted artwork to a button, you format the button in the Buttons panel:

- Give the button a descriptive name to help you distinguish it from other buttons you create.
- Apply one or more actions to the button by clicking the plus icon on the Buttons panel. That opens the buttons action presets menu shown in Figure 13. Click a preset on the menu to apply an action to the button.
- Alter the appearance of the button to determine what it looks like when you "mouse over" the button or click it in the SWF or PDF file.

Figure 12 *Converting artwork to a button*

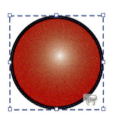

Figure 13 *Action presets in the Buttons panel*

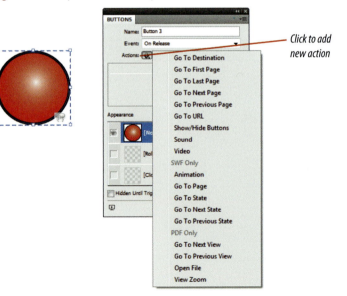

Click to add new action

At any time, you can convert button artwork back to regular artwork. Select the button artwork, click Object on the Application bar, point to Interactive, then click Convert to Object.

Changing Button Appearances for Rollover and Clicking

Once you convert artwork to a button, you can format it with as many as three appearances, which are referred to as **states**. These states are Normal, Rollover, and Click.

By default, the button you create is defined as the Normal appearance of the button. In the exported file, the Normal appearance is used until the mouse pointer moves over the button, which triggers the Rollover appearance, or it is used until you click the button, which triggers the Click appearance.

You don't have to assign different appearances to the three different states, but you'll find that having these visual cues in place enhances the interactive experience with the buttons.

To define the appearance for a given state, select the button on the page, then click the state in the Buttons panel. You then modify the button directly, typically modifying the fill color for each state.

Figure 14 shows the red button in its Normal state. In Figure 15, the Rollover state is targeted in the Buttons panel, and a green gradient has been applied to the button. Therefore, when you load the page, the button will appear as red, but when you position the mouse pointer over it, the button's appearance will change to green.

Figure 14 *Normal state in the Buttons panel*

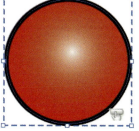

Figure 15 *Rollover state in the Buttons panel*

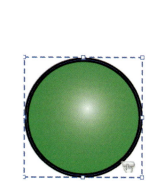

In Figure 16, the Click state is targeted in the Buttons panel, and a blue gradient has been applied to the button. The button will appear blue when clicked in the exported document.

Note that the Click state color changes have very little visual impact because the jump to the other page happens so quickly that the visual change on the click is negligible. On the other hand, for buttons that don't change the page view, applying a color change to the Click state can be visually effective. For example, if you create a button that pauses a video on the page, having

that button change color when it's clicked and the video is paused can make for an important visual cue.

Some changes, like color changes, affect only the selected appearance. For another example, let's say you had a button that incorporated text. You could change the text in each appearance so that the text would be different in the Normal, Rollover, and Click states. Other changes you make affect all active states. For example, if you use the Selection tool to move or scale the button, the change can't be applied to a single state and will affect all three.

Adding Actions to Buttons

You use the Buttons panel to create, edit, and manage actions that you want to apply to buttons. Actions you apply to buttons are interactive and occur when you click a button. Clicking the button is the interactive component; you interact with the button and an action happens.

The Buttons panel lists six events, as shown in Figure 17. An **Event** is the specific interactive occurance that triggers the action of a button. In other words, they're what the user of the exported document does to interact with

Figure 16 *Click state in the Buttons panel*

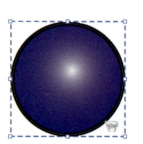

Figure 17 *Event list in the Buttons panel*

Six Event choices

Creating an Interactive Document

the button and trigger an action. Of the six events, four are standard, and are grouped separately in the Event menu. They are:

- **On Release** This is the default event. When the mouse button is released after a click, the action or actions applied to a button are triggered. This is the most commonly used event because it gives the user a last chance to not execute the action by not releasing the mouse button after clicking.
- **On Click** When the mouse button is pressed down, the action is triggered. Unless you have a specific reason for using this event, use On Release for the reason stated above.
- **On Roll Over** When the mouse pointer enters the area defined by the button's bounding box, the action is triggered.
- **On Roll Off** When the mouse pointer leaves the area defined by the button's bounding box, the action is triggered.

Actions indicate what happens when the specific event occurs—usually when someone clicks a button. It's important to note that you can apply multiple actions to a single button. For example, you could specify that On Release, a sound is generated and the document moves to the next page.

To apply an action to a button, click the plus icon in the Buttons panel to expose the list of preset actions, shown in Figure 18. Note that some actions can be applied for SWF output only, and others for PDF output only. Following is a list of the more commonly used actions:

- **Go To First/Last/Next/Previous Page** Jumps to the specified page. Select an option from the Zoom menu on the Buttons panel to specify the magnification at which the page will be displayed.
- **Go to URL** Opens the Web page of the specified URL.
- **Video** Lets you assign actions to buttons that allow you to play, pause, stop, or resume a selected movie. Only movie files that have been placed in the document appear in the Video menu in the Buttons panel.
- **Sound** Lets you assign actions to buttons that allow you to play, pause, stop or resume a selected sound clip. Also let's you apply a sound to an event, like clicking a button. Only sound files that have been placed in the document appear in the Video menu in the Buttons panel.

Figure 18 *Actions list in the Buttons panel*

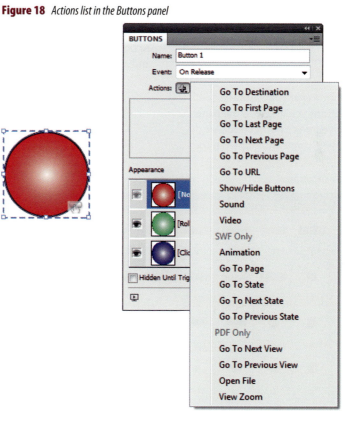

Using the Sample Buttons Panel

As shown in Figure 19, the Sample Buttons panel is a great resource for quickly adding buttons to your presentation without having to design them yourself. The Sample Buttons panel contains dozens of buttons and arrows that are already formatted as buttons. Visually, they include effects such as gradient feathers and drop shadows, and each has a slightly different appearance pre-loaded for the [Rollover] appearance. The sample buttons also have actions already assigned to them. For example, the arrow buttons already have Go To Next Page and Go To Previous Page actions. You can edit or delete these pre-assigned actions as you have need.

The Sample Buttons panel is a library. You can add the buttons you create to the panel and delete any you don't want. To access the panel, choose Sample Buttons from the Buttons panel menu. Simply drag buttons from the panel to the document. If you want to use a button on every page, drag it to a master page.

Assigning a Sound to a Button

Sounds and buttons are a match made in interactive heaven. Click a button, hear a sound. Sounds, in general, add a whole new layer of interativity to a presentation.

Sounds are applied to buttons as actions in the Buttons panel. Click a button with the Selection tool, then choose Sound from the Actions list. In order for a sound to be listed and available in the Buttons panel, the sound file itself must be placed in InDesign. You place sound files like you would any other file, using the Place command on the File menu.

When you place a sound file, it is a non-printing, invisible component of your presentation. A sound file is placed in an InDesign frame, so you can select and move the frame. But the frame will appear as an empty square unless you've chosen Show Edges on the View menu. In that case, a sound file will show an icon, as shown in Figure 20.

Most designers position the file on a master page so that it is available for animations on every page of the document.

Figure 20 *Sound file icon appears when Frame Edges are showing*

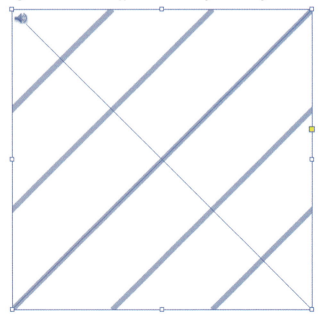

Figure 19 *Sample Buttons panel*

Figure 21 *Selecting text to hyperlink*

Selected text

*Create new
hyperlink button*

Figure 22 *New Hyperlink dialog box*

Create hyperlinks between pages in a document

1. If guides are showing, hide them.
2. Scroll through the three pages of the document to see the content on all three pages, then return to page 1.
3. Expand the Hyperlinks panel.
4. Click the **Type tool** T, then select only the word **Manarola** in the left column, as shown in Figure 21.
5. Click the **Create new hyperlink button** at the bottom of the Hyperlinks panel.

   The New Hyperlink dialog box opens.
6. Click the **Link To menu list arrow**, then click **Page**.
7. Set the destination page to **3**.
8. Click the **Zoom Setting menu list arrow**, then click **Fit in Window**.
9. In the Character Style section, click the **Style menu list arrow**, then click **Blue Text Links**.

   Your New Hyperlink dialog box should resemble Figure 22.

(continued)

10. Click **OK**, then deselect the text.

Because you applied the Blue Text Links character style as part of the formatting for the hyperlink, the Manarola text is now blue and underlined. The hyperlink was named automatically and is now listed in the Hyperlinks panel, as shown in Figure 23. You can always change the name of a hyperlink with the Rename Hyperlink command on the Hyperlinks panel menu.

11. Using the same methodology, hyperlink the word Firenze on page 1 to page 2 in the document.

12. Save your work.

You created a hyperlink from the word "Manarola" on page 1 to the Manarola feature on Page 3. You then hyperlinked the word "Firenze" on page 1 to the Firenze feature on Page 2.

Create a hyperlink to a Web page

1. Scroll to page 1 in the document, then select the text frame shown in Figure 24.

2. Click the **Create new hyperlink icon** on the Hyperlinks panel.

3. In the New Hyperlink dialog box, click the **Link To menu list arrow**, then click **URL**.

(continued)

Figure 23 *Manarola hyperlink in Hyperlinks panel*

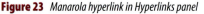

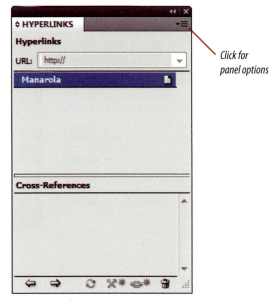

Click for
panel options

Figure 24 *Selecting the text frame to hyperlink*

Selected text frame

Creating an Interactive Document

Figure 25 *Specifying the URL for the Web site*

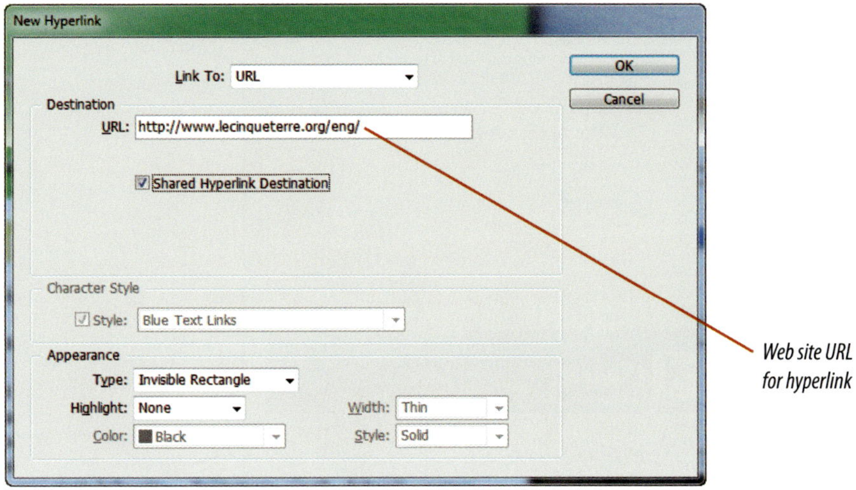

Web site URL
for hyperlink

4. In the URL text box, click after http://, type
   www.lecinqueterre.org/eng/ so that your
   dialog box resembles Figure 25, then click **OK**.

   The word Hyperlink appears and is selected in the
   Hyperlinks panel.

5. Open the Hyperlinks panel menu, then click
   Rename Hyperlink.

6. Rename the link as **Official Home Page**, then
   click **OK**.

   At this point in the project, you would likely
   export the file as an SWF to test the hyperlinks.
   For the purposes of working with these lessons,
   we will export the document at the very end of
   Lesson 3, when we view page transitions.

7. Save your work.

*You created a hyperlink from a text frame to a Web page. You
renamed the hyperlink with a more descriptive name in the
Hyperlinks panel.*

Convert artwork to buttons

1. Expand the Buttons panel.

2. Select the left triangle artwork on Page 1.

3. Click **Object** on the Application bar, point to **Interactive**, then click **Convert to Button**.

   The artwork appears as the Normal state in the Appearance section at the bottom of the Buttons panel.

4. Enter **P1L** in the Name text box in the Buttons panel.

   Your Buttons panel should resemble Figure 26. P1L stands for Page 1 Left.

5. Select the right triangle artwork on Page 1.

6. Click the **Convert Object to a Button icon** at the bottom of the Buttons panel.

7. Enter **P1R** in the Name text box in the Buttons panel.

8. Go to page 2 in the document.

9. Select both triangles on the page, then click the **Convert Object to a Button icon**.

   There's no relationship created just because both are converted simultaneously; they will still be separate buttons.

10. Deselect, select only the left button, then name it **P2L**.

11. Name the right button **P2R**.

12. Convert both triangles on page 3 to buttons, then name them **P3L** and **P3R** respectively.

13. Save the file.

You converted six objects to buttons and gave them descriptive names.

Figure 26 *New button added to Buttons panel*

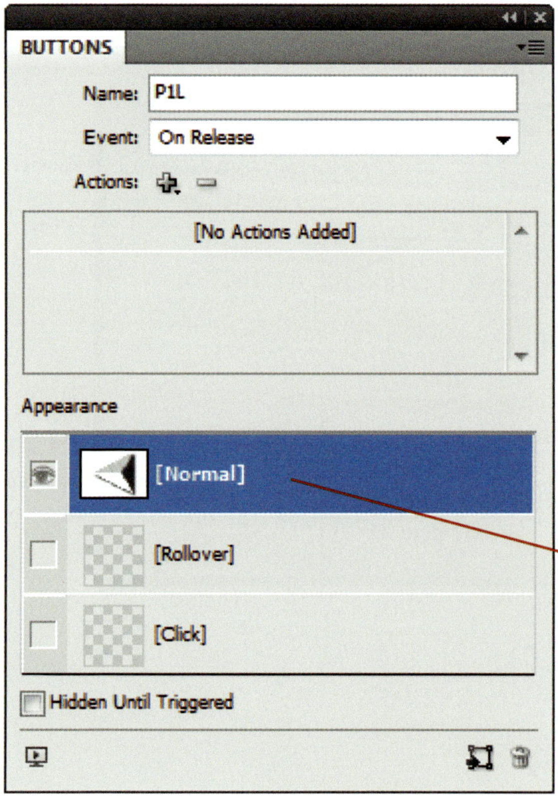

Button automatically appears as the [Normal] appearance

Creating an Interactive Document

Figure 27 *Changing the [Rollover] status fill color*

Gold button appearance in the
Buttons panel and on the page

Figure 28 *Changing the [Click] status fill color*

Modify button appearances

1. Verify that the Swatches panel is expanded and available.

2. Scroll to Page 1, then select the left button.

3. Click the grayed-out **[Rollover] status** at the bottom of the Buttons panel.

   The status is enabled and the triangle button appears as an icon.

4. Use the Swatches panel to change the fill color of the button to **Gold** so that your screen resembles Figure 27.

   In the exported file, when the mouse pointer is positioned over the button, the button will change from silver to gold.

5. Click the **[Click] status** at the bottom of the Buttons panel to activate it.

   The button on the page reverts back to its original silver color.

6. Change the fill color of the button to **Good Green** so that your screen resembles Figure 28.

   In the exported file, when you click the button, it should change from gold to green. Note, however, that the jump to the other page will happen so quickly that the visual change on the click will be negligible.

7. For the right button on Page 1, change the [Rollover] status fill color to **Gold**, then change the [Click] status fill color to **Good Green**.

8. For the two buttons on pages 2 and 3, change the [Rollover] status fill color to **Gold**.

(continued)

9. For the two buttons on page 3, change the [Click] status fill color to **Good Green**.

10. For the two buttons on page 2, change the [Click] status fill color to **Real Red**.

    Save your work.

    When creating buttons and specifying their appearances, use all the skills you've learned throughout the book. In the example in this lesson, you could have created the buttons on a master page and applied their appearance colors on the master page. You will apply this alternative method in the Skills Review at the end of this chapter.

    You converted six objects to buttons and gave them descriptive names.

Apply actions to buttons

1. Scroll to Page 1, click the **Selection tool** 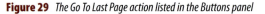, then select the left button on the page.

2. Click the **plus icon** in the top section of the Buttons panel to reveal the Actions menu.

3. Click **Go To Last Page**, then compare your Buttons panel to Figure 29.

    The Go To Last Page action is listed in the panel and is checked. Note that, by default, the Event is listed as On Release. In the exported document, upon releasing the mouse pointer, the button will take you to the last page of the document.

TIP You may have a different status highlighted at the bottom of your Buttons panel. The highlighted status is irrelevant when you're applying an action to a button.

(continued)

Figure 29 *The Go To Last Page action listed in the Buttons panel*

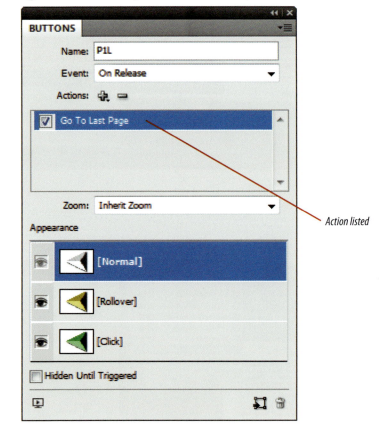

Action listed

Figure 30 *Sound files on the master page*

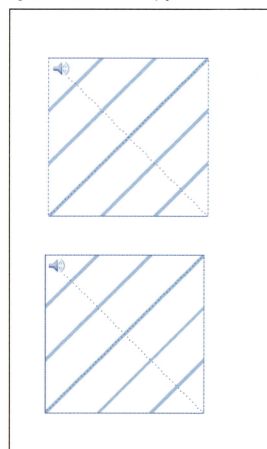

4. Click the **Event menu list arrow** on the Buttons panel to see the other options, but keep the On Release option.

5. Click the **Zoom list arrow** to see the other options, then verify that Inherit Zoom is chosen.

   Inherit Zoom specifies that when the button takes you to the specified page, the new page will be displayed with the same magnification as the current page. In other words, it will "inherit" the zoom from the current page.

6. Click the **P1R button** (right button) on the page, then click the **plus icon** on the Buttons panel.

7. Click **Go To Next Page** on the Actions menu.

8. Apply the Go To Next Page action to button **P2R**.

9. Apply the Go To Previous Page action to buttons **P2L** and **P3L**.

10. Apply the Go To First Page action to button **P3R**.

11. Save your work.

You applied actions individually to each of six buttons, actions that will control how clicking each button moves the reader through the pages in the document.

Apply sounds to buttons

1. Scroll to page 1, then show frame edges using Extras on the View menu.

2. In the Pages panel, double-click **A-Master**.

   As shown in Figure 30, two sound files have been placed on the master page. The source files are located in your Chapter 12 Data Files folder, and their format is MP3, a standard format for sound files. Their names are Click and Squeak.

   (continued)

3. Hide frame edges.

4. Double-click **page 1** in the Pages panel, click **View** on the Application bar, then click **Fit Page in Window**.

5. Click the **Selection tool**, then click the **right button** on the page to select it.

6. In the Buttons panel, click the **plus icon**, then click **Sound**.

7. Click the **Sound menu list arrow**, then click **Click.mp3**.

   Your Buttons panel should resemble Figure 31. Remember that the sound, like any action, is tied to the event. In this case, the Click.mp3 sound will play On Release.

8. Using the same method, apply the **Click.mp3** sound to the right button on page 2 and the right button on page 3.

9. Click the **left button** on page 1 to select it.

10. In the Buttons panel, click the **plus icon**, then click **Sound**.

(continued)

Figure 31 *Click.mp3 sound clip in the Buttons panel*

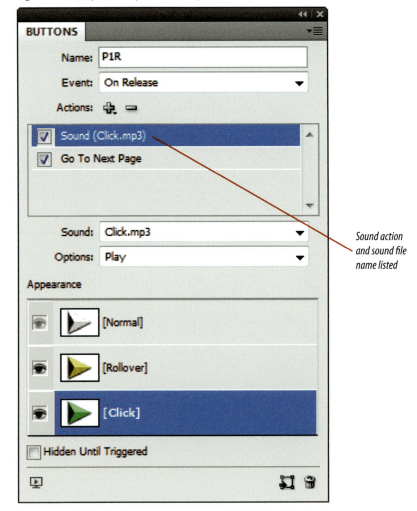

Sound action and sound file name listed

Creating an Interactive Document

Figure 32 *Squeak.mp3 sound clip in the Buttons panel*

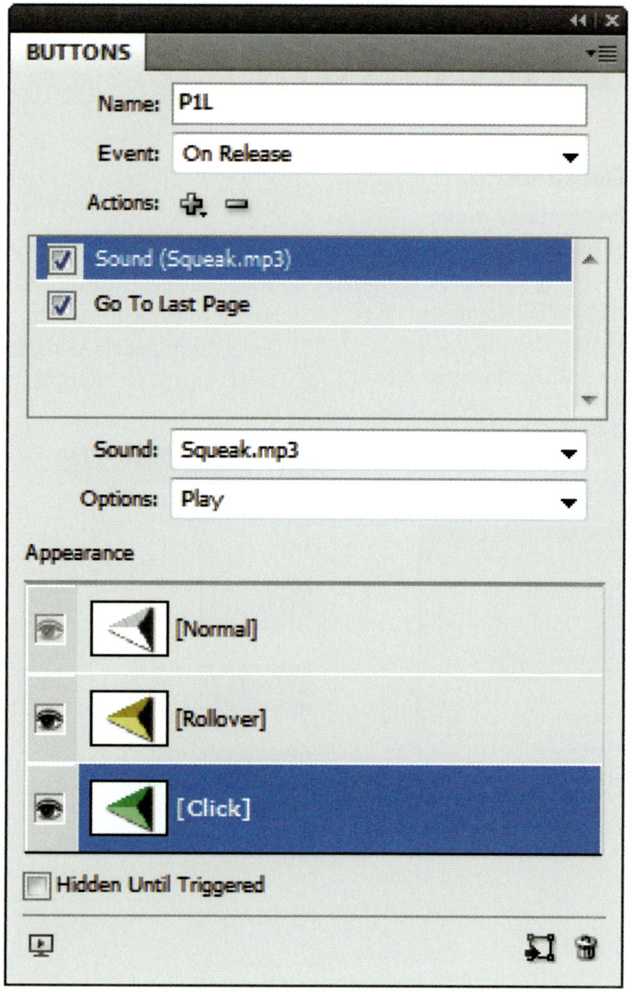

11. Click the **Sound menu list arrow**, then click **Squeak.mp3**.

    Your Buttons panel should resemble Figure 32. It doesn't matter what appearance is targeted when you apply a sound or any action, because actions are tied to events, not appearances.

12. Using the same method, apply the Squeak.mp3 sound to the left button on page 2 and the left button on page 3.

13. Save your work.

You viewed two sound files placed on the master page. You applied the two sound files to buttons in the document.

Apply and View
PAGE TRANSITIONS

What You'll Do

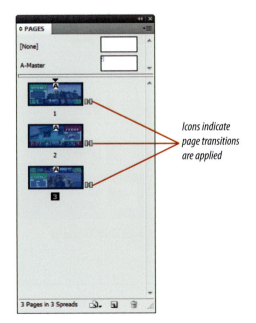

In this lesson, you will apply page transition effects and export an SWF file to view them.

Applying Page Transitions

Page transitions display classic video transition effects, such as dissolve, push, or wipe, when you're moving from page to page in an exported SWF or PDF document. You can apply different page transition effects to different pages in a single document, or you can apply a single transition to all the pages. You cannot apply page transitions to master pages.

You apply page transitions with the Pages panel, working in tandem with the Page Transitions panel. As shown in Figure 33, you target a page or multiple pages in the Pages

Figure 33 *Applying page transitions*

Icons indicate page transitions are applied

Creating an Interactive Document

panel, then choose, in the Page Transitions panel, the transition you want to apply. When you do, a Page Transition icon appears beside the page thumbnail in the Pages panel.

QUICK TIP

If you want to hide the Page Transition icon, deselect the Page Transitions option in the Panel Options dialog box.

The Page Transitions panel offers previews of how the transition behaves when applied. You can customize the transition to your liking by choosing options from the Direction and Speed menus.

If you select multiple page thumbnails in the Pages panel, the transition you choose will be applied to the selected pages. In many cases, you'll want to apply the same transition to all pages in a document. For example, if you're producing a slideshow, for visual consistency, you'll likely want the same transition between each "slide." To apply a selected transition quickly to all spreads currently in the document, click the Apply To All Spreads icon on the Page Transitions panel, or choose Apply To All Spreads from the Page Transitions panel options.

Exporting an SWF file

While you're working on your interactive document, you'll find yourself regularly exporting the document as an SWF and opening the exported file in your Web browser software to test the interactivity.

Exporting to SWF is a smart, simple option because it supports all InDesign interactivity, including animation, and is opened quickly and easily by Internet Explorer or Firefox on both the Windows and Mac platforms.

In InDesign, you don't save an file as an SWF, you export it. To do so, click the

Export command on the File menu. Choose Flash Player (SWF) from the Save As Type menu (Win) or Format menu (Mac) then click Save.

When you export the document, the Export SWF dialog box opens, as shown in Figure 34. The dialog box has two

Figure 34 *General options in Export SWF dialog box*

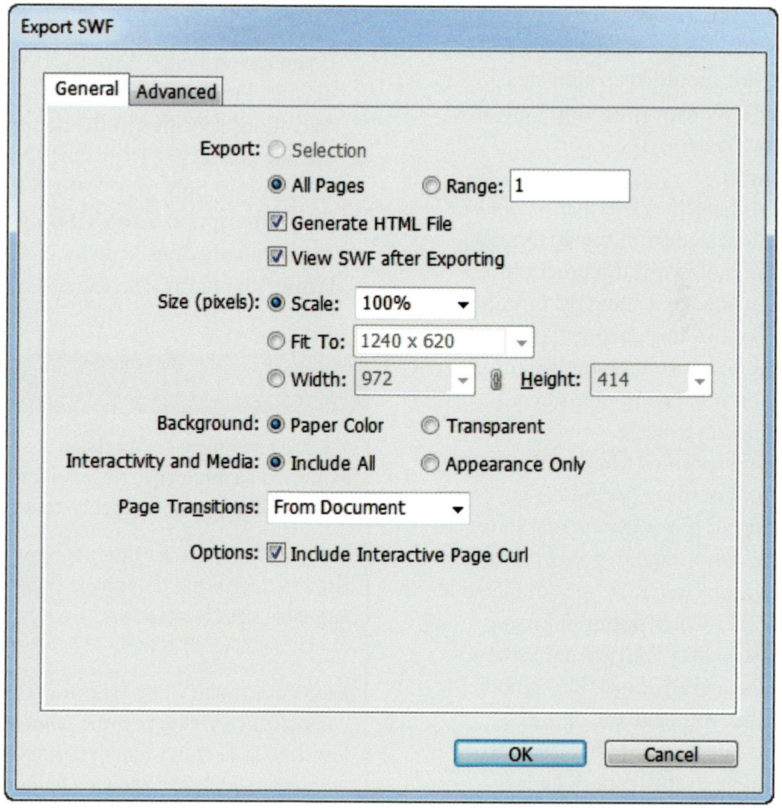

tabs—General and Advanced. The following options are available to you on the General tab:

- **Export** allows you to determine whether to export the current selection, all pages in the document, or a page range. Choosing a specific page or page range can be a good idea in long documents when you are exporting only to test out interactivity on a specific page or area of the document.
- **Generate HTML File** generates an HTML page that plays back the SWF file and is one that you should keep activated.
- **View SWF after Exporting** automatically opens the SWF for viewing in your browser.
- **Size (pixels)** specifies whether or not the SWF is scaled from the document size. If you build your document to a standard width for a standard monitor (see Lesson 1 in this chapter), you can feel comfortable that your layout will display properly on most computer screens without having to scale.
- **Background** specifies whether the background of the exported file is transparent or if it is the current Paper color from the Swatches panel (almost always white). Generally speaking, you'll use the Paper Color option for most layouts, because a Transparent setting disables Page Transitions. Remember, though, that you have the option of specifying a transparent background. This could be useful, especially for

some object-level animations that aren't necessarily meant to be part of a layout or appear on a page.

- **Interactivity and Media** has a default "Include All" setting that you should keep activated to allow movies, sounds, buttons, and animations to be interactive in the exported SWF file.
- **Page Transitions** allows you to apply one page transition to all pages in the export document if you haven't already applied them to individual pages in the document. If you have already, leave the option as the default "From Document" to use the page transitions specified in the document.
- **Include Interactive Page Curl** applies to SWF output only (not PDF). When you select this option, users viewing the SWF can manually drag a corner of the page layout, giving the effect that the page is

turning like a page in a book. Think of this effect as being independent from the page transitions you set up in the book. For example, if you set a Wipe page transition for every page in the document, you could still implement the Include Interactive Page Curl option. In the exported document, the Wipe transition would execute when you navigate from page to page, but you'd have the alternate option of manually dragging pages with the Page Curl effect.

The following options are available to you on the Advanced tab shown in Figure 35.

- **Frame Rate** directly affects the smoothness of animations. A higher number of frames per second creates smoother animations but can also increase the file size. The default 24

Too Big to Mail?

File size and image compression are always a consideration when exporting a document. When exporting an interactive document that will be emailed or presented online, you'll need to consider compressing bitmap images so that the overall file size won't be too large for email or for download.

In the early days of the Internet, slow download speeds made file size and image compression big issues to tackle. But times have changed. Today's robust Internet connections allow for relatively larger file sizes to download in a jiffy. Even mass market email services like Yahoo! mail allow for email attachments up to 10MB.

Keep this in mind when exporting your interactive presentations. Don't feel that you need to compress everything past the point of quality to get your export file size under one megabyte. That's just overkill. Keeping your export file size under 5MB will allow you to maintain quality images and animations while still allowing for quick downloads and the ability to email the presentation.

frames per second is usually satisfactory, especially for the animation presets in the Animation panel.

- **Text** specifies how InDesign text is output. Use the default Flash Classic Text to output searchable text that results in the smallest file size.
- **Rasterize Pages** converts all InDesign page elements into bitmaps. Unless you have a specific reason, keep this option in its default inactive state.
- **Flatten Transparency** removes transparent effects from the SWF document and preserves their appearance. However, it also removes all interactivity from the exported file, so keep this option in its default inactive state unless you have a specific reason for activating it.
- **Compression** determines how grayscale and color images will be compressed for quicker downloads. Compression is always a tug-of-war between download speed and image quality. JPEG (lossy) is the default compression algorithm and is generally suitable for grayscale or color images. The term "lossy" refers to the fact that JPEG compression always removes image data to reduce file space. Sometimes that removal results in a degradation of image quality. Usually, JPEG compression works well, but if you notice an unacceptable reduction in image quality, use PNG ('ping'), which is a "lossless" compression algorithm.
- **JPEG Quality** specifies the amount of detail in exported images. The higher the quality, the larger the file size. Given

today's robust Internet connections, you can feel free to choose High or even Maximum.

- **Resolution** is the number of pixels per inch in a bitmap image. The more pixels per inch, the more detail in the image, and the higher the image quality. 72 pixels per inch (ppi) is the standard resolution for images presented on a monitor or screen. This setting in the Export SWF dialog box overrules the native resolution of placed images. In other words, if

you place an image that has a 150ppi resolution and export it at this setting, the image in the exported document will have a 72ppi resolution. 72ppi is usually high enough resolution for all images. However, some animation presets allow you to zoom in on an image on the page, enlarging them substantially. Choosing a higher resolution is important for allowing viewers to zoom-in on images, but can increase the file size significantly.

Figure 35 *Advanced options in Export SWF dialog box*

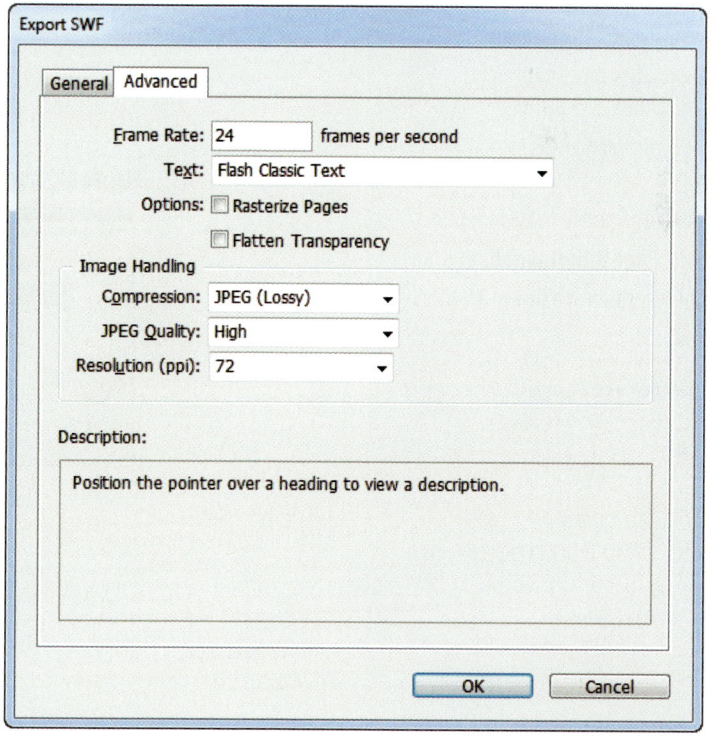

Add page transitions

1. Expand the Pages panel.

2. Verify that the Page Transitions panel is expanded.

3. Double-click the **Page 1 thumbnail** in the Pages panel.

4. Click the **Transition menu list arrow** on the Page Transitions panel, then click **Blinds**.

5. Click the **Direction menu**, then click **Vertical**.

   Your panels should resemble those in Figure 36. Note the Page Transitions icon beside the page thumbnail in the Pages panel.

6. Double-click the **Page 2 thumbnail**.

7. Click the **Transition menu** on the Page Transitions panel, then click **Split**.

8. Verify that the Direction menu is set to Horizontal In.

   Your panels should resemble those in Figure 37.

9. Double-click the **Page 3 thumbnail**.

10. Apply the Wipe transition in a Down direction.

11. Save your work.

You applied three different transitions to pages in the document.

Figure 36 *Blinds transition in the Page Transitions panel*

Page transition applied icon

Figure 37 *Split transition in the Page Transitions panel*

Creating an Interactive Document

Figure 38 *General settings for exporting an SWF file*

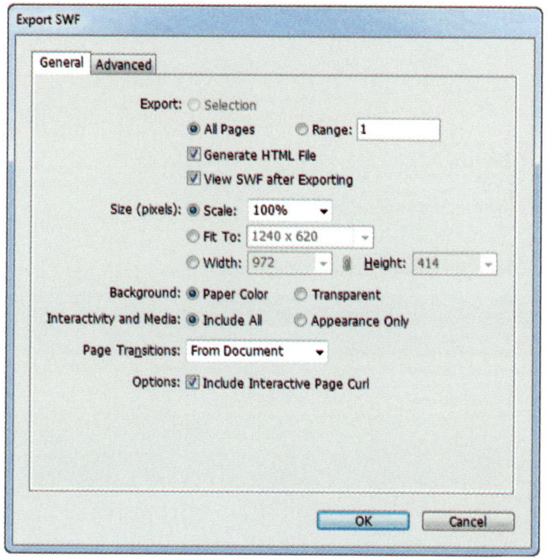

Figure 39 *Advanced settings for exporting an SWF file*

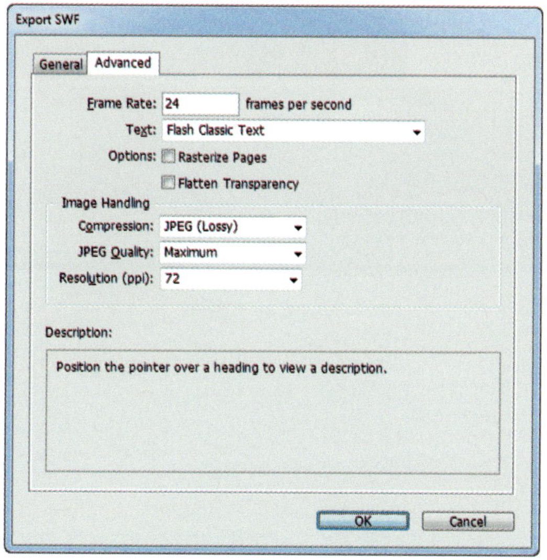

Export an SWF file

1. Click **File** on the Application bar, then click **Export**.

2. Navigate to the folder on your computer in which you want to save the exported file.

3. Choose Flash Player (SWF) from the Save As Type menu (Win) or Format menu (Mac), then click **Save**.

   The Export SWF dialog box opens.

4. Enter General export settings to match those in Figure 38.

   Note that Include Interactive Page Curl is checked. Note too that View SWF after Exporting is checked. The file will open automatically in your browser software after exporting.

5. Click the **Advanced** tab, then enter settings that match those in Figure 39.

   (continued)

6. Click **OK**.

   As shown in Figure 40, the document opens in your browser software. If your document doesn't open automatically, launch Internet Explorer or Firefox on the Windows or Mac platform, then open the SWF file that you exported.

TIP If you get a warning dialog box saying that pages in the document have overset text you should ignore it by clicking Don't show again.

You applied three different transitions to pages in the document.

Test interactive settings in an SWF file

1. Position your mouse pointer over the **right triangle button on page 1**.

   As shown in Figure 41, the button appearance changes to gold.

2. Click the **right triangle button**.

   The Click sound activates, and the page changes to page 2 via the Split page transition. The page transition is always that which has been applied to the *destination* page, and the Split page transition was applied to page 2.

3. Click the **left triangle button on page 2**.

   The Squeak sound activates, and the page changes to page 1 via the vertical Blinds page transition.

4. Click the blue underlined word **Manarola** on page 1.

   The hyperlinked text takes you to page 3, the Manarola page, via the Wipe Down page transition.

   (continued)

Figure 40 *SWF document displayed in Internet Explorer browser*

Creating an Interactive Document

Figure 41 *Viewing the Rollover appearance on the right button*

Button changes to gold
on mouse rollover

5. Click the **right triangle button on the page**.

   The button, formatted with the Go To First Page action, takes you to Page 1 via the Blinds vertical page transition.

6. Click the **visit the official home page link**.

   A new browser window is "spawned" displaying the Web page.

   It is possible that the security settings in your browser or Adobe Flash Player will block the pop-up of the Web page. If that occurs, follow the browser's suggested steps to change your security settings and allow the Web site to launch.

7. In your browser, close the new window and return to the window for the exported SWF file.

   (continued)

8. Float your mouse pointer over the bottom-right corner, then click and drag to turn the page manually, as shown in Figure 42.

9. Turn pages to move back and forth through the document.

10. Close the browser window, then return to the Italy Presentation.indd InDesign document.

You applied three different transitions to pages in the document.

Remove page transitions and apply a page transition to all pages in a document

1. Shift-click to select the three page thumbnails in the Pages panel.

2. In the Page Transitions panel, click the **Transition menu list arrow**, then click **None** (Win) or **Clear All** (Mac).

   The transitions are removed from all pages, and the Page Transitions icons disappear from the Pages panel.

3. Click the **background area of the Pages panel** to deselect all page thumbnails.

(continued)

Figure 42 *"Turning the page" with the Interactive Page Curl option*

Creating an Interactive Document

Figure 43 *Specifying settings for the transition*

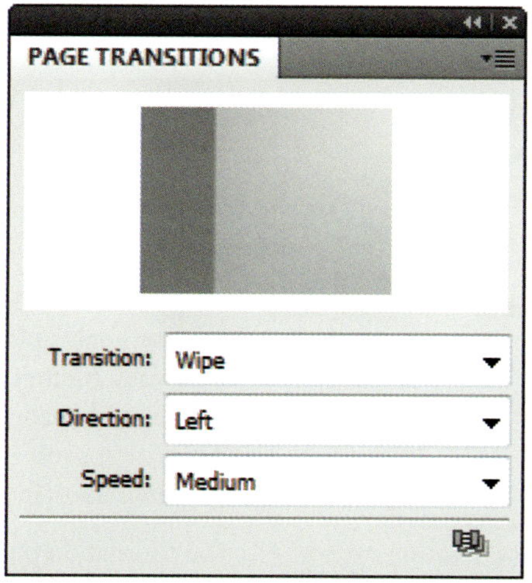

Exporting XHTML for Dreamweaver

InDesign is not just for print. In many cases, you'll want to use your InDesign layout or content on the Web. In that case, you can export to the XHTML file format, which can be read and imported by Dreamweaver, which is Adobe's web page layout authoring software. Click the File menu, point to Export for, then click Dreamweaver. Your layout, or the selected frame or story in your layout, will be exported in the XHTML format.

XHTML preserves the names of paragraph styles, character styles, object styles, and table and cell styles, making them all available in the Dreamweaver document. Using Adobe Dreamweaver you can quickly format the contents for the web. XHTML exports most essential InDesign layout components, including stories, placed graphics, SWF movie files, bulleted and numbered lists, internal cross-references, and hyperlinks that jump to text or web pages. Note, too, that you can export InDesign tables to Dreamweaver, though some formatting like cell and stroke color won't be exported.

You might ask, "Why not just create the contents in Dreamweaver in the first place?" That's a good question, and Dreamweaver offers a lot of great layout options. However, there are just some things that InDesign does so well, and some designers are just more comfortable working in InDesign. For example, rather than design a complex table in Dreamweaver, you might want to use InDesign's easy to use Table feature and export the table as XHTML to Dreamweaver.

4. In the Page Transitions panel, click the **Transition menu list arrow**, then click **Wipe**.

5. Click the **Direction menu list arrow**, then click **Left**.

   Your Page Transitions panel should resemble Figure 43.

6. Click the **Apply to All Spreads button** on the Page Transitions panel.

   The transition is applied to all pages, and the Page Transition Applied icons appear beside the thumbnails in the Pages panel. When using this method, page thumbnails do not need to be selected in the Pages panel for the transition to be applied.

7. Save your work.

You applied a single transition to all pages using the Apply to All Spreads button in the Page Transitions panel.

Add ANIMATION

What You'll Do

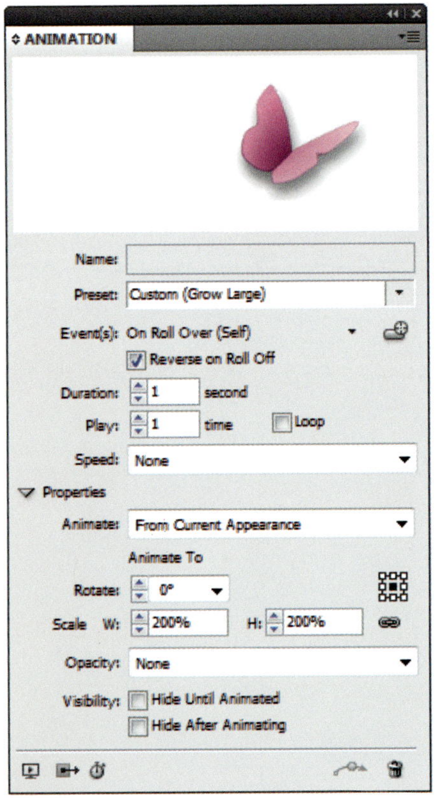

In this lesson, you will incorporate various motion presets to make objects in the layout move.

NEW Using the Animation Panel

Animation effects let you make objects move and fade, appear and disappear in your exported layout. For example, you can apply a **motion preset** to make an object appear to "fly in" from the left side of the screen, or you can make another object fade in or out when the exported page is loaded.

Motion presets are pre-defined animations that you can apply quickly and easily to objects in your layout. Motion presets are accessible in the Animation panel shown in Figure 44. The Animation panel is command central for applying animation in InDesign CS5.

Use the Animation panel to apply motion presets to objects, to change animation

Figure 44 *Animation panel*

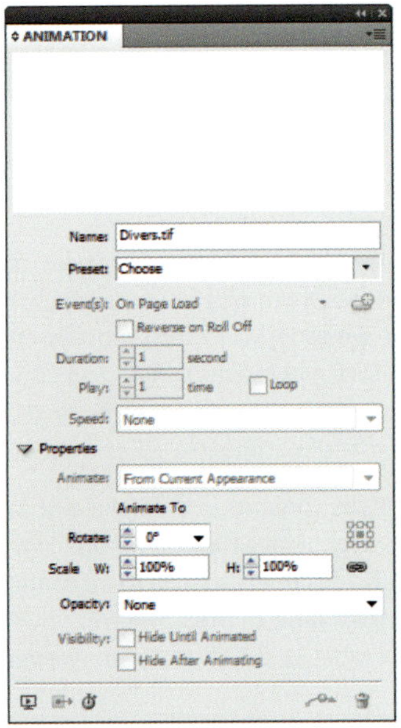

settings such as speed and duration, and to specify when an animation occurs.

The Animation panel contains many fun and useful animations. Most are self-explanatory, just by their names. For example, the Fade animation expresses quite clearly what the preset does to an object. You'll find that working with motion presets in the Animation panel is intuitive, and a learn-as-you-go approach is effective for incorporating the various options you have with different animations. Sometimes the animation will behave exactly as you expect it to, sometimes it will surprise you, and sometimes you'll find that you'll need to be strategic in duplicating objects and applying various motion presets to get the more complex animation effects you are seeking.

Previewing Animations

Applying animations can be simple or complex, depending on the goal toward which you are striving. As you work, you'll want to test out the animations you're applying to see if you like the motion effects. Rather than export the file over and over again, you can use the Preview panel, shown in Figure 45, for a quick preview of your work.

When you press the Play button on the Preview panel, the page is reloaded in the panel, just as it would be in your browser window. The Preview panel then "plays" the presentation, showing animations as they would occur in the exported file.

The Preview panel shows only the current page in the layout. It doesn't link from page to page, so it, therefore, doesn't preview page transitions. But those limitations don't detract much from the usefulness of the Preview panel. You can resize the panel by dragging its lower corner, making all of the objects on the page large enough to test.

In addition to showing all animations, the Preview panel will show button appearances and play any sounds that you've ascribed to buttons. This is just one example of the important role the panel plays.

The Preview panel will show you if a hyperlink is live; the mouse pointer will turn to the classic finger-point hand icon when floated over a hyperlink. The panel will not show a destination page within the document if you click such a hyperlink, but it will spawn a browser page if you click a hyperlink to a URL.

Figure 45 *Preview panel*

Click Play every time you make a change to preview the change

Figure 46 shows an enlarged Preview panel displaying the [Rollover] appearance of the right button.

Using the Timing Panel

To work with animation, you need to think of the exported document as being a presentation displayed in a linear timeline. This is just a concept; there's no actual timeline in InDesign. But you can think of the moment when the exported page loads in the browser window as starting the timeline for the presentation. For example, if you set an animation to occur when the page is loaded, and you set the duration for the animation to be five seconds, you can think of the animation as playing for the first five seconds of the presentation.

This implies the question, "Then what happens?" The answer could be, "Nothing more happens." In some presentations, animations occur when the page is loaded, and that's it—after that, there are no more animations. You're left to read the page, view items on the page, or click links or buttons that take you to another page. But when you think of a presentation as occurring on a timeline, it opens the possibility of sequential animation. In other words, first this happens, *then* this

Figure 46 *Enlarged Preview panel showing [Rollover] status of right button*

Drag corner to enlarge Preview window

happens, *and then*, when I click this, this happens.

The Timing panel, shown in Figure 47, is command central for controlling when animated objects play. The Timing panel lists all the animations on a current spread, specifying the page event assigned to each animation. For example, some animations are set up to occur when the page is loaded, while other animations occur when an object is clicked.

One useful event is Page Click. Rather than clicking a specific button or link on the page, you can simply click any area of the page to execute animations set up as Page Click events. This can be useful with slide presentations and creating "invisible" launch events. In other words, rather than clicking a button, which is an obvious move to launch an animation, you can unobtrusively click anywhere on the page, making animations happen under your control but to your audience, seemingly at your will while you're presenting.

By default, animated objects are listed in the Timing panel in the order they were created. Similarly, by default, animations listed for the Page Load event occur sequentially in the order they were created, one after the other with no pause in between. Animations specified for the Page Click event occur sequentially every time the page is clicked.

This is a powerful option, since you can control when each one is played.

The Timing panel does more than just order animations. You can use the panel to change the order of animations, have animations play at the same time, and delay the start of animations.

Figure 47 *Timing panel*

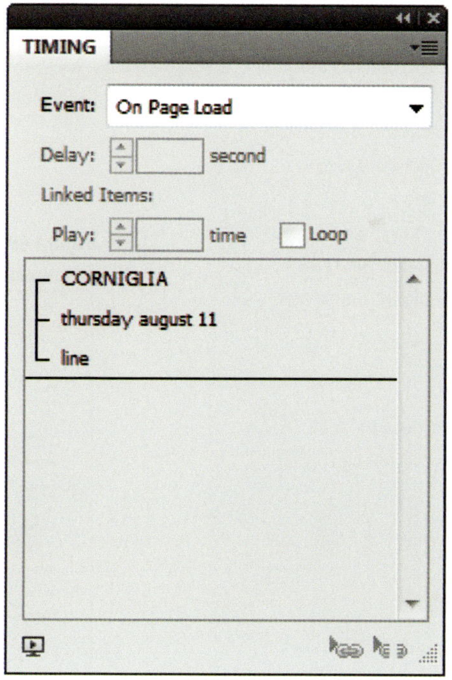

NEW Apply fly-in animations

1. Verify that you are on page 1 of the InDesign document.

2. Click the **Selection tool**, then select the text frame for the thursday august 11 text.

   In the Animation panel, the words thursday august 11 automatically appear in the Name text box.

3. Click the **Preset menu list arrow**, then click **Fly in from Left**.

   As shown in Figure 48, the options on the Animation panel are activated, and the motion path attached to the text frame becomes visible. The editable motion path indicates the default path and distance the animated object will move along.

4. Click the **Event(s) menu list arrow** to expose the menu of options, as shown in Figure 49, making sure to leave the choice at the default On Page Load.

5. Set the duration to 2 seconds.

   TIP When you alter the default options, the word Custom appears in the Name text box preceding the animation name.

6. Click the **Properties arrow** on the Animations panel to display Properties options if necessary, then note the Location text box.

   The default To Current Location specifies that when the animation is completed, the frame's position will be the current location.

   (continued)

Figure 48 *Animation panel and motion path*

Motion path

Figure 49 *Event(s) menu in Animation panel*

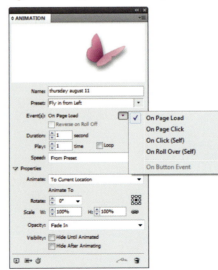

Figure 50 *Settings for Fly in from Left animation*

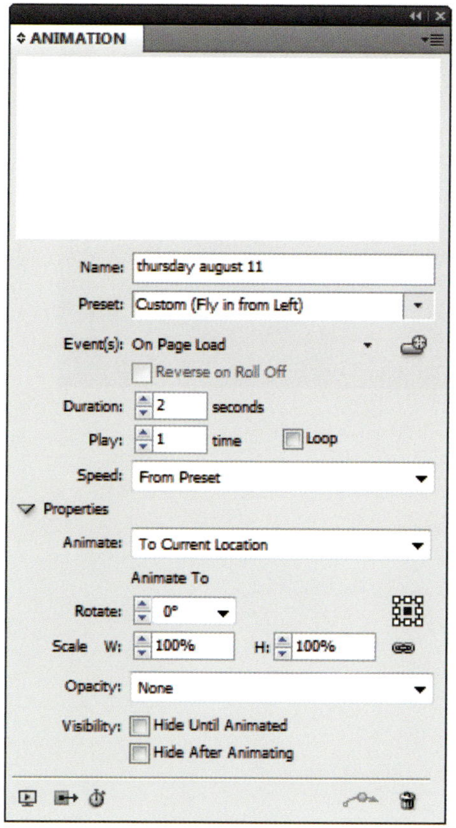

Figure 51 *Settings for Fly in from Top animation*

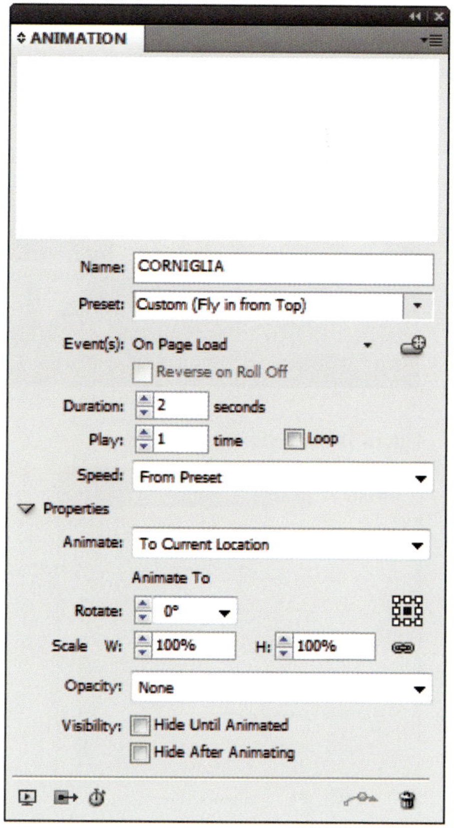

7. Click the **Opacity menu list arrow**, then click **None**.

   Your animation panel should resemble Figure 50.

8. Select the text frame for the CORNIGLIA text.

9. Click the **Preset menu list arrow**, then click **Fly in from Top**.

10. Set your other Animation options to match Figure 51.

11. Save your work.

You applied two different "fly in" animations to two different text frames.

Apply a Fade animation

1. Use the Selection tool to select the large "Corniglia" image on the page.

2. Click **Edit** on the Application bar, click **Copy**, click **Edit** on the Application bar again, then click **Paste in Place**.

   (continued)

3. Click **File** on the Application bar, click **Place**, navigate to where your Chapter 12 Data Files are stored, navigate to the Links folder, then place the image **Corniglia BW.tif**.

   Your page should resemble Figure 52. Because the two images are exactly the same size and have the same number of pixels, the black and white version aligns perfectly with the color image beneath it.

4. With the frame still selected, click the **Preset menu list arrow** on the Animation panel, then click **Fade Out**.

5. Change the Name text box to read **Corniglia BW**.

6. Set the duration to 8 seconds.

7. Click the **Event(s) menu list arrow**, then click **On Page Click**.

   On Page Click is added to the On Page Load. This means the animation would happen on two events: when the page is loaded and when the page is clicked.

8. Click the **Event(s) menu list arrow again**, then click to uncheck **On Page Load**.

   Your Animation panel should resemble Figure 53. When you click the black and white image, it will slowly fade out to reveal the color image beneath it, creating the effect that the black and white image is "becoming" a color image.

9. Save your work.

You placed a grayscale copy of an image, then set the grayscale image to fade with the Fade Out animation preset.

Figure 52 *Placing the grayscale copy of the main image*

Figure 53 *Animation settings for fade*

Creating an Interactive Document

Figure 54 *Gold line on page*

CORNIGLIA

thursday august 11

Gold stroke

Figure 55 *Shrink animation settings for the gold line*

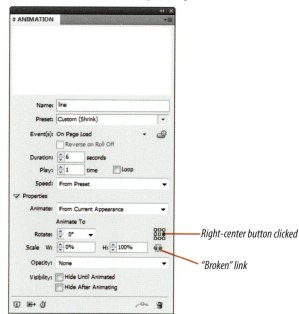

Right-center button clicked

"Broken" link

1. Use the Selection tool to select the red horizontal line on the page.

2. Click **Edit** on the Application bar, click **Copy**, click **Edit** on the Application bar again, then click **Paste in Place**.

3. Use the Swatches panel to change the stroke color to Gold.

   Your page should resemble Figure 54.

4. With the line still selected, click the **Preset menu** on the Animation panel, then click **Shrink**.

5. Set the duration to **6** seconds.

6. Verify that the Event(s) menu reads On Page Load.

7. In the Properties section, click the **Constrain the scale value (link) icon** if necessary so that it appears unlinked, or broken.

8. Verify that the Opacity menu reads None.

9. Set the W (width) value to **0**, then set the H (height) value to **100%**.

10. Click the **right-center button** on the origin chart.

    Your Animation panel should resemble Figure 55. On page load, the horizontal size of the line will shrink to 0%, using the right edge of the line as the point of origin for the transformation. The height of the line will not change.

11. Save your work.

You copied a line, changed its stroke color, then applied the Shrink animation to it.

Use the Preview and Timing panels

1. Verify that page 1 is targeted in the Pages panel.

2. Expand the Preview panel, then drag the **lower-right corner** and the **left edge** to enlarge the panel.

3. Click the **Play button**.

   Three animations occur sequentially in the order they were applied: Fly in from Left, then Fly in from Top, then Shrink. By default, animations are played in the order they were applied. The Fade animation doesn't play automatically because it is set to play when clicked, not on page load.

4. Click the **main image in the Preview window**.

   The black and white image fades away, revealing the color image beneath it. You can click anywhere on the page to launch this animation.

5. Click **either of the two triangle buttons**.

   The [Rollover] appearance shows when you float over the button in the Preview panel, and, when you click, the associated sound clip plays.

6. Expand the Timing panel, then click the **thursday august 11** item in the list.

   As shown in Figure 56, three animations are listed in the Timing panel in the order that they were applied and the order in which they will play. The Fade animation is not listed, because it doesn't occur automatically. With the **thursday august 11** animation selection, the Event you specified—On Page Load—is displayed, and the Delay text box becomes available.

7. Click the **up triangle** to set the Delay to 6 seconds.

   (continued)

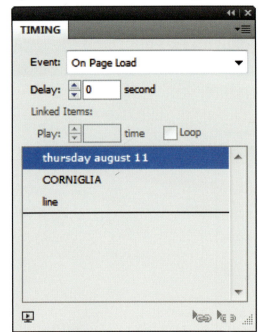

Figure 56 *Three animations listed in the Timing panel*

Figure 57 *CORNIGLIA animation moved to the first in the list*

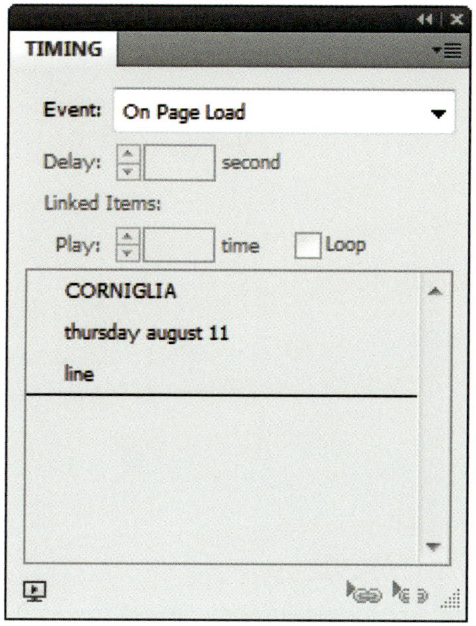

Figure 58 *Setting animations to play simultaneously*

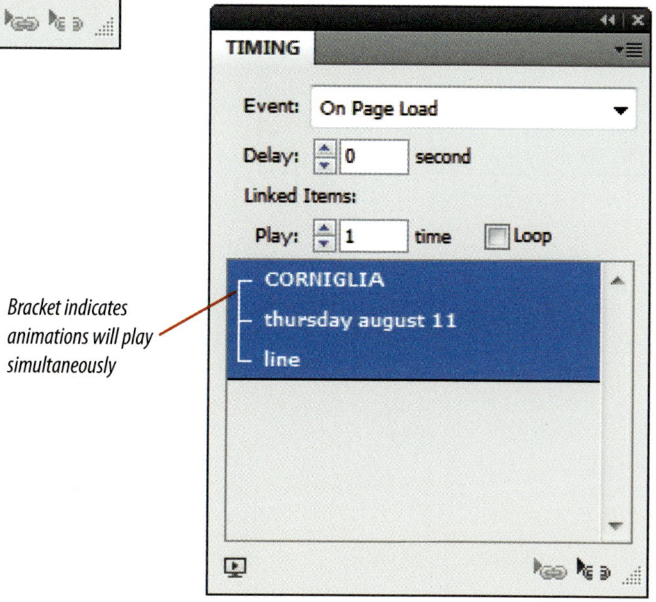

Bracket indicates animations will play simultaneously

8. Click the **Play button** on the Preview panel.

   The animation is delayed for six seconds. The two subsequent animations are therefore also delayed.

9. In the Timing panel, set the Delay for the "thursday" animation back to zero.

10. Click and drag the **CORNIGLIA animation** to the top of the Timing panel, as shown in Figure 57.

    A horizontal black bar appears as you drag the animation in the panel.

11. Click the **Play button** on the Preview panel.

    The CORNIGLIA animation plays first, and the "thursday" animation is no longer delayed.

12. Shift-click to select all three animations in the Timing panel.

13. Click the **Play together button** at the bottom of the Timing panel.

    As shown in Figure 58, a bracket indicates that the animations are "linked" to play together. The Play separately button becomes available at the bottom of the panel.

14. Click the **Play button** on the Preview panel.

    The three animations play simultaneously.

15. Save your work.

You used the Preview panel to preview animations as you altered the document. You used the Timing panel to add a delay to an animation, to reorder animation, and to make three animations play simultaneously.

Apply a Grow Large animation

1. Use the Selection tool to select the five small images at the bottom of the page.

(continued)

2. Click the **Preset menu list arrow** on the Animation panel, then click **Grow Large**.

3. Click the **Event(s) menu list arrow**, then click **On Roll Over (Self)**.

4. Click the **Event(s) menu list arrow** again, then click **On Page Load** to deselect it.

5. Click to activate Reverse on Roll Off.

6. In the Scale text boxes, set the W and H to **200%**.

Your Animation panel should resemble Figure 59. In the exported file, when you position your mouse pointer over any of the images, it will increase to 200%. When you remove the pointer from the image, the animation will reverse.

7. Save your work.

You applied a Grow Large animation simultaneously to five images. You specified that the images would enlarge to 200% when rolled over in the exported document, and that the animation would reverse when "rolled off."

Export an animated document as an SWF

1. Click **File** on the Application bar, then click **Export**.

2. Navigate to the folder on your computer in which you want to save the exported file.

TIP If you're asked at any point in this lesson to replace the SWF you exported earlier in this chapter, click OK.

3. Choose Flash Player (SWF) from the Save As Type menu (Win) or Format menu (Mac), then click Save.

The Export SWF dialog box opens.

4. Verify that your General export settings match Figure 60.

(continued)

Figure 59 *Settings for the Grow Large animation in the Animation panel*

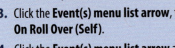

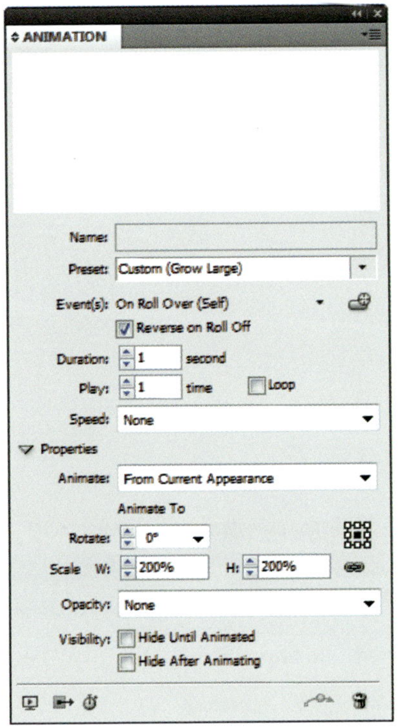

Figure 60 *General settings in the Export SWF dialog box*

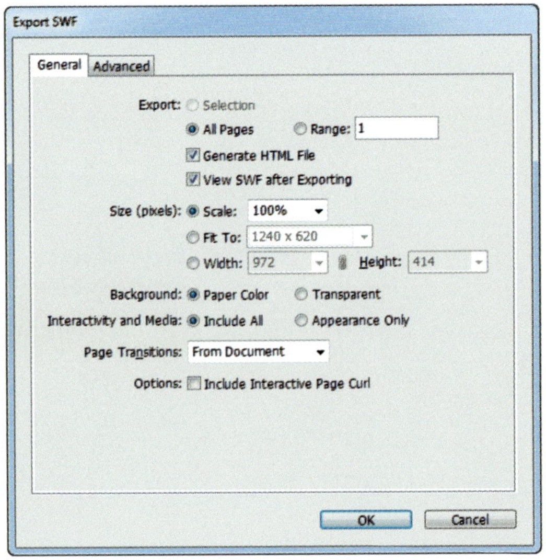

Figure 61 *Advanced settings for exporting an SWF file*

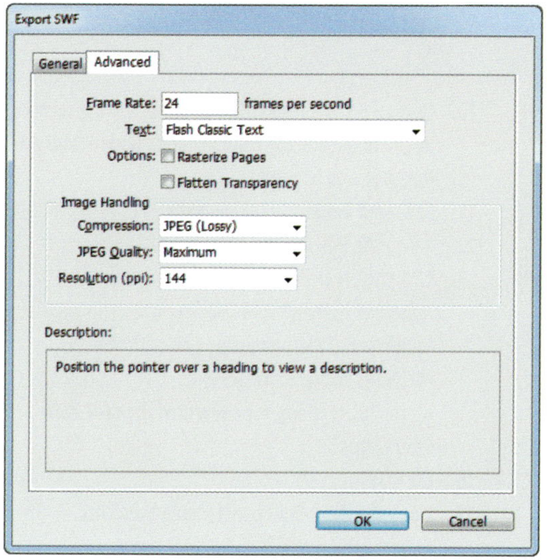

Export SWF

General | Advanced

Frame Rate: 24 frames per second

Text: Flash Classic Text

Options: ☐ Rasterize Pages
☐ Flatten Transparency

Image Handling

Compression: JPEG (Lossy)

JPEG Quality: Maximum

Resolution (ppi): 144

Description:

Position the pointer over a heading to view a description.

OK   Cancel

Figure 62 *Testing the Grow Large animation in the exported document*

Note that Include Interactive Page Curl is not checked for this export. Sometimes the interactive page curl effect can interfere with some animations, so, to rule that out for this lesson, deselect the option.

5. Click the **Advanced tab**, then verify that your Advanced export settings match Figure 61.

Note that for this export, the Resolution for the file is set to 144, double the default standard 72. Do this because the five small images at the bottom of the page are set to grow 200%. We want the image resolution in the exported document to be high enough that the enlarged images look good.

6. Click **OK**.

The SWF file opens automatically. Three animations occur simultaneously upon page load.

7. Click the main image.

The main image fades slowly from black and white to color.

8. Position your mouse pointer over the leftmost image at the bottom of the page.

As shown in Figure 62, the image size is doubled.

9. Remove the mouse pointer from the image, and mouse over the other four images.

The image returns to the small size.

10. Return to the InDesign file and save your work.

11. Close Italy Presentation.

You exported an animated document with no interactive page curl and with resolution set to 144. You then clicked in the SWF to test animations.

Set up interactive documents.

1. Verify that no other documents are open.
2. Click File on the Application bar, point to New, then click Document.
3. Click the Intent list arrow, then choose Web.
4. Enter **3** for the number of pages.
5. Verify that Facing Pages is not checked.
6. Click the Page Size list arrow, then click 1024 x 768.
7. Click OK.
8. Click Edit on the Application bar, then point to Transparency Blend Space, noting that because the document was set up as a "Web" document, the Transparency Blend Space is automatically set to Document RGB.
9. Click Edit (Win) or InDesign (Mac) on the Application bar, point to Preferences, then click Units & Increments, noting that the Web document is automatically set up with Ruler Units set to Pixels.
10. Click Cancel.
11. Save the file as **Skills Presentation Document**.
12. Close the file.
13. Open ID 12-2.indd, then save it as **Maui Presentation**.
14. Click Edit (Win) or InDesign (Mac) on the Application bar, point to Preferences, then click Units & Increments.
15. In the Ruler Units section, set the Horizontal and Vertical units to Pixels, then click OK.
16. Open the Document Setup dialog box again. At 864 pixels, the document's width is less than 1024, meaning it will fit on most computer screens, including most laptop computers.
17. Click Cancel.
18. Open the Units & Increments dialog box again, then set the Horizontal and Vertical ruler units back to Inches.
19. Click Edit on the Application bar, point to Transparency Blend Space, then click Document RGB.
20. Click the Window menu, point to Workspace, then click [Interactive]. If the workspace does not appear to change, click Window again, point to Workspace, then click [Reset Interactive].
21. Save the file.

Incorporate hyperlinks and buttons.

1. If guides are showing, hide them.
2. Scroll through the five pages of the document to see the content on all five pages, then return to page 1.
3. Expand the Hyperlinks panel.
4. Click the Selection tool, then select the first image on page 1.
5. Click the Create new hyperlink icon at the bottom of the Hyperlinks panel.
6. In the New Hyperlink dialog box, click the Link To menu list arrow, then click Page.
7. Set the destination page to 2.
8. Click the Zoom Setting menu list arrow, click Fit in Window, then click OK.
9. Note that a hyperlink named **Hyperlink** is now listed in the Hyperlinks panel.
10. Using the same methodology, hyperlink the second image to page 3, the third image to page 4, and the fourth image to page 5.
11. Save your work.
12. Select the Road to Hana text frame.
13. Click the Create new hyperlink icon on the Hyperlinks panel.
14. In the New Hyperlink dialog box, click the Link To menu list arrow, then click URL.
15. In the URL text box, type **www.visitmaui.com** after http://.
16. Click OK.
17. Open the Hyperlinks panel menu, then click Rename Hyperlink.
18. Rename the link as **Visit Maui**, then click OK.
19. Save your work.
20. In the Pages panel, double-click B-Master thumbnail to go to the B master page.
21. Expand the Buttons panel.
22. Click the Selection tool, then select the left arrow artwork.
23. Click Object on the Application bar, point to Interactive, then click Convert to Button.
24. Type **LEFT** in the Name text box in the Buttons panel.
25. Select the right arrow artwork.
26. Click the Convert Object to a Button icon at the bottom of the Buttons panel.
27. Type **RIGHT** in the Name text box in the Buttons panel.
28. Select the green circle artwork.

29. Click the Convert Object to a Button icon at the bottom of the Buttons panel.
30. Type **HOME** in the Name text box in the Buttons panel.
31. Save the file.
32. Verify that the Swatches panel is expanded and available.
33. Select the left button.
34. Click the grayed-out [Rollover] status in the lower part of the Buttons panel.
35. Use the Swatches panel to change the fill color of the left arrow to Green.
36. For the right arrow, change the [Rollover] status fill color to Green so that your screen resembles Figure 63.
37. Select the left arrow on the page.
38. Click the plus icon on the Buttons panel to reveal the Actions menu.
39. Click Go To Previous Page.
40. Click the right arrow, then click the plus icon on the Buttons panel.
41. Click Go To Next Page on the Actions menu.
42. Click the green circle, then click the plus icon on the Buttons panel.
43. Click Go To First Page on the Actions menu.
44. Save your work.
45. Show Frame Edges.

Figure 63 *Changing the [Rollover] status color*

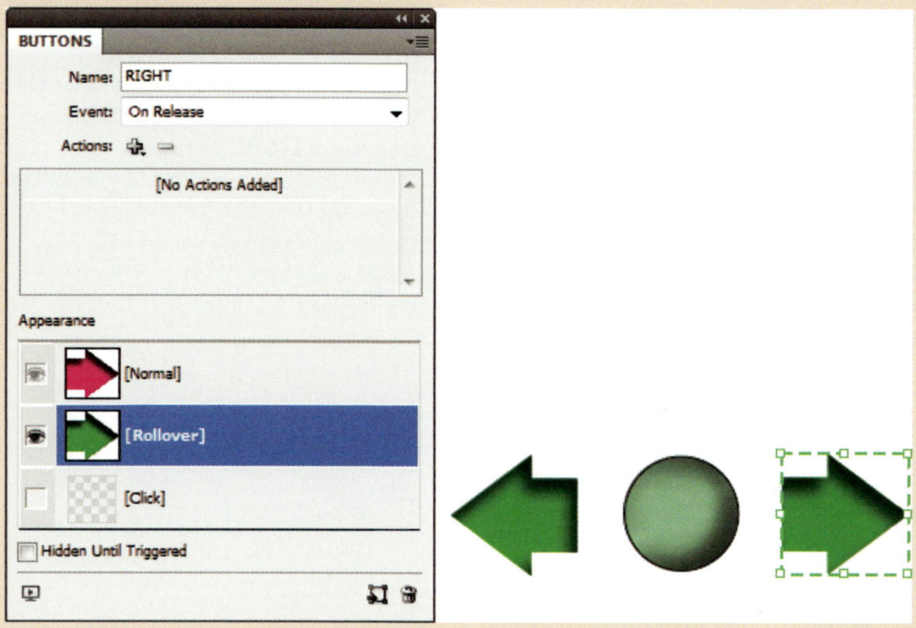

46. As shown in Figure 64, two sound files have been placed on the master page.
47. Hide Frame Edges.
48. Click the Selection tool, then select the left arrow on the page to select it.
49. In the Buttons panel, click the plus icon, then click Sound.
50. Click the Sound menu list arrow, then click Click.mp3.
51. Using the same method, apply the Click.mp3 sound to the right arrow.
52. Save your work.

Apply page transitions.

1. Verify that the Page Transitions panel is expanded.
2. Double-click the Page 1 thumbnail in the Pages panel.
3. Click the Transition menu on the Page Transitions panel, then click Blinds.
4. Click the Direction menu, click Vertical, then verify the Speed is set to Medium.
5. Click the Apply to All Spreads button on the Page Transitions panel.
6. Save your work.

Add animation and view page transitions.

1. Verify that you are on page 1 of the InDesign document.
2. Click the Selection tool, then select the two middle images.
3. In the Animation panel, click the Preset menu list arrow, then click Fly in from Top.
4. Click the Event(s) menu list arrow to expose the menu of options, but be sure to leave the choice at the default On Page Load.
5. Set the duration to **3** seconds.

Figure 64 *Sound files on the master page*

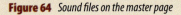

6. Verify the Opacity is set to Fade In, then compare the settings on your Animation panel to those in Figure 65.

7. Click the Selection tool, then select the leftmost image.

8. In the Animation panel, click the Preset menu list arrow, then click Fly in from Left.

9. Set the duration to **3** seconds, then verify that the Opacity reads Fade In.

10. Click the Selection tool, then select the rightmost image.

11. In the Animation panel, click the Preset menu list arrow, then click Fly in from Right.

12. Set the duration to **3** seconds, then verify that the Opacity reads Fade In.

13. Expand the Preview panel, then drag the lower-right corner and the left edge to enlarge the panel.

14. Click the Play button to view the four animations, which occur sequentially in the order they were applied.

15. Click either of the two triangle buttons to view the [Rollover] appearance.

16. Expand the Timing panel to view the sequentially order of the animations.

17. In the Timing panel, select the first two animations to play: Flower and Lagoon, as shown in Figure 66.

18. Click the Play together button at the bottom of the Timing panel.

19. In the Timing panel, select Tree coverage and Waterfall.

20. Click the Play together button at the bottom of the Timing panel.

21. Click the Play button on the Preview panel to view the altered timings of the animations, with the two outside images flying in simultaneously after the middle two fly in simultaneously.

22. Save your work.

23. Click File on the Application bar, then click Export.

24. Navigate to the folder on your computer to which you want to save the exported file.

25. Choose Flash Player (SWF) from the Save As Type menu (Win) or Format menu (Mac) then click Save. The Export SWF dialog box opens.

Figure 65 *Animation panel*

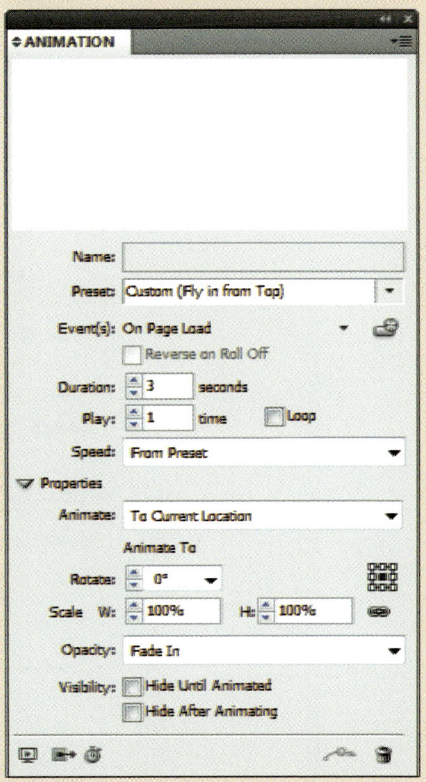

Figure 66 *Selecting the first two animations to play simultaneously*

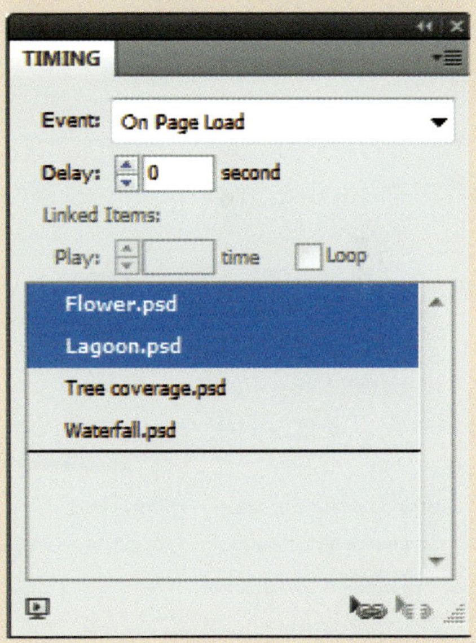

SKILLS REVIEW
(CONTINUED)

26. Verify that your General export settings match Figure 67.
27. Click the Advanced tab, then verify that your Advanced export settings match Figure 68.
28. Click OK, then watch as the SWF opens automatically and the animations play.
29. Click the leftmost image.
30. Click and drag to turn pages with the Interactive Curl effect.
31. Click the arrow buttons to move back and forth through the document.
32. Click the center button to go to the home page.
33. Return to the InDesign file and save your work.
34. Close Maui Presentation.

Figure 67 *General settings in the Export SWF dialog box*

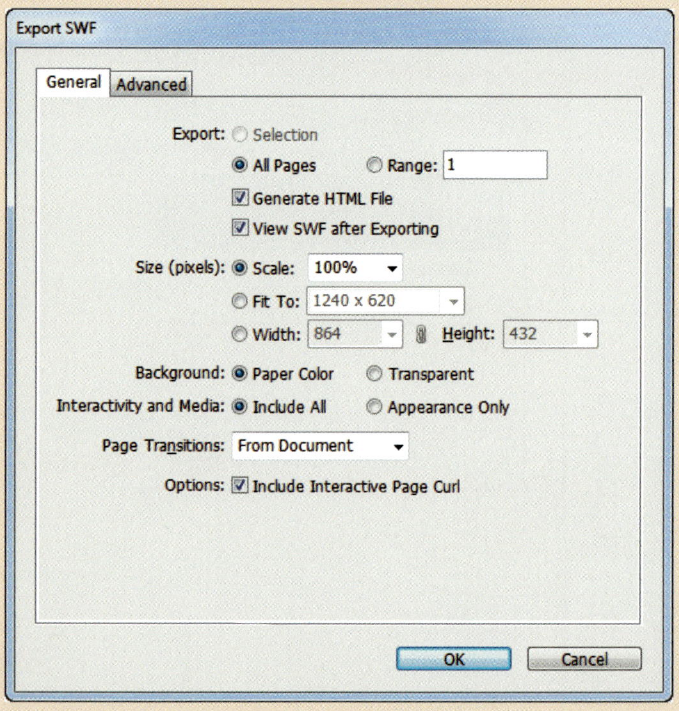

Figure 68 *Advanced settings in the Export SWF dialog box*

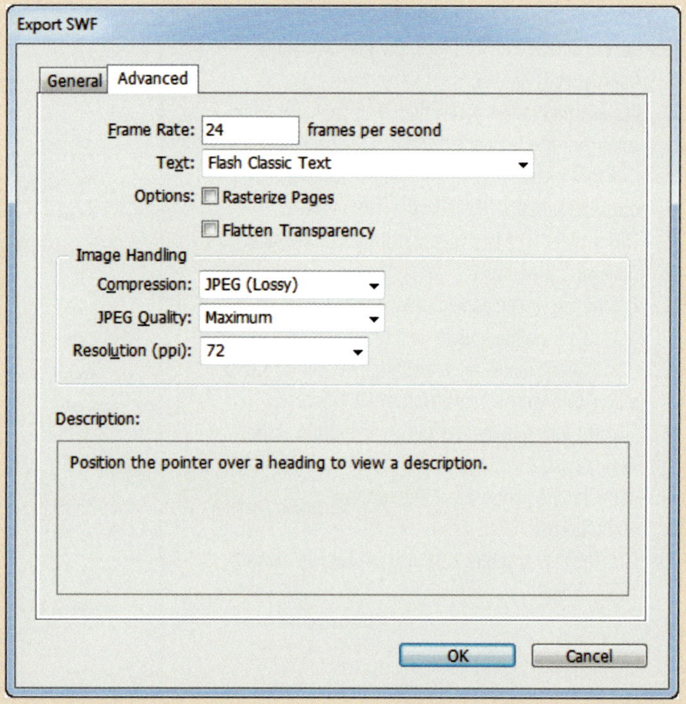

You're working on an interactive InDesign layout that has some animations already applied. Your creative director asks you to add some navigation buttons to the pages quickly. She tells you they should be in the same location on every page. Since you don't have time to design buttons, you decide to use the Sample Buttons panel.

1. Open ID 12-3.indd, then save it as **Sample Buttons**.
2. Click the Play button in the Preview panel to see the existing animations.

3. Open the Layers panel, then click the Buttons layer to target it.
   The buttons you create will be positioned on the Buttons layer.
4. Open the Buttons panel, display the panel options then click Sample Buttons.
5. Drag button #14 onto page 1, then drag another copy of button #14 onto page 1.
6. Align the buttons and position them centered relative to the headline as shown in Figure 69.
7. Select both buttons, then cut them.
8. Navigate to the B-Master page.

9. Click Edit, then click Paste in Place.
10. Click the Convert Button to an Object button at the bottom of the Buttons panel, then click OK in the warning dialog box.
11. Click the NEXT button in the pasteboard, click Object on the Application bar, point to Arrange, then click Bring to Front.
12. Move the NEXT text frame from the pasteboard so that it is positioned over the right button.
13. Drag and drop a copy over the left button, then change the text to read PREV.
14. Group the right button and the NEXT text frame.

Figure 69 *Positioning sample buttons*

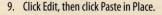

Creating an Interactive Document

15. Group the left button and the PREV text frame.
16. Click the NEXT group, then click the Convert Object to Button button on the Buttons panel.
17. Click the plus icon on the Buttons panel, then click Go To Next Page.
18. Click the PREV group, then click the Convert Object to Button icon on the Buttons panel.
19. Click the plus icon on the Buttons panel, then click Go To Previous Page.
20. Double-click Page 1 in the Pages panel. The buttons appear on all pages, as shown in Figure 70.
21. Export an SWF file, and test out the buttons.
22. Save your InDesign work, then close the file.

Figure 70 *Completed Project Builder 1*

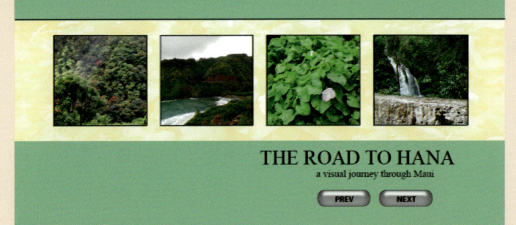

You're working on an interactive InDesign document and have two images that work well with a given set of text. You can't decide which to use, so you ask your creative director. She tells you, "Use both."

1. Open ID 12-4.indd, then save it as **Fly Out**.
2. Use the Selection tool to select the large image on the page.

3. Click Edit on the Application bar, click Copy, click Edit on the Application bar again, then click Paste in Place.
4. Click File on the Application bar, click Place, navigate to where your Chapter 12 Data Files are stored, navigate to the Links folder, then place the image named **Lagoon**.

5. With the frame still selected, click the Preset menu on the Animation panel, point to Fly out, then click Fly out Left.
6. Enter the animation settings shown in Figure 71.
7. Open the Timing panel, then click Lagoon.psd.
8. Set the Delay to 5 seconds, then press [Enter].
9. Export an SWF file to preview the effect, then compare your results to Figure 72.
10. Save your InDesign work, then close the file.

Figure 71 *Animation settings for Project Builder 2*

Figure 72 *Fly out Left animation in Project Builder 2*

Your creative director likes the animations you've applied to a splash page, but asks that you use additional animation to apply a "subtle grace note."

1. Open ID 12-5.indd, then save it as **Shrink to Center**.
2. Use the Selection tool to select the black horizontal line on the page.
3. Click Edit on the Application bar, click Copy, click Edit on the Application bar again, then click Paste in Place.
4. In the Swatches panel, click the Magenta swatch to change the stroke color to Magenta.
5. With the line still selected, click the Preset menu on the Animation panel, then click Shrink.
6. Set the duration to 6 seconds.
7. Verify that the Event(s) menu reads On Page Load.
8. In the Properties section, click the Constrain the scale value (link) icon so that it appears broken.
9. Verify that the Opacity menu reads None.
10. Set the W (width) value to 0, then set the H (height) value to 100%.
11. Click the center button on the origin chart, then enter the Animation panel settings to shown in Figure 73.
12. Deselect the line.
13. Press Play in the Preview panel to see the animation.
14. Save your work, then close the file.

Figure 73 *Animation settings for Design Project*

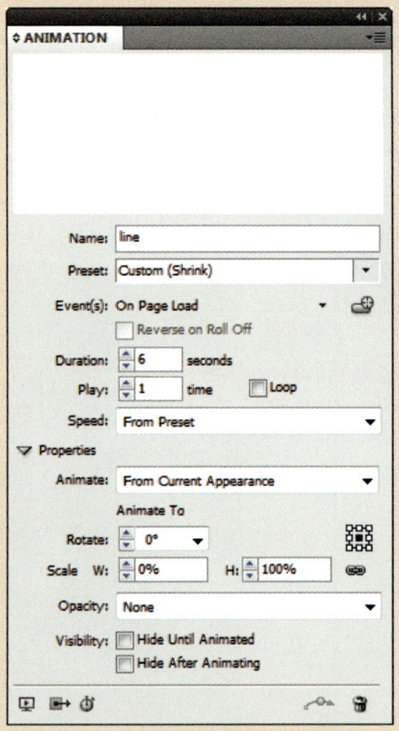

Creating an Interactive Document

Your creative director is impressed with the work you have done so far and asks you to take on the challenge of creating a complex animation, making it appear that two animations are applied to single objects. The animations already in this Data File are set up so that four black and white images fly in from the top. She would like you to make those four images gradually become colorized, which will require a second animation.

1. Open ID 12-6.indd, then save it as **Multiple Color Fade In**.
2. Click Play in the Preview panel to see the animations already applied.
3. Use the Selection tool to select any one of the four black and white images on the document page.
4. In the Animation panel, note the duration of the Fly in From Top animation.
   The duration of the animation is 3 seconds.
5. Show the Layers panel, then make the Page 1 Color Pics layer visible.
6. Use the Selection Tool to select all four color pictures.
7. Click the Preset menu on the Animation panel, then click Fade In.
8. Set the duration to 4 seconds.
9. Verify that the Event(s) menu reads On Page Load.
10. Click the Show Timing Panel button at the bottom of the Animation panel.
11. Select the bottom four animations in the Timing panel, set them to play together, then compare your Timing panel settings to those in Figure 74.
12. Minimize the Timing panel.
13. Export an SWF file to preview the animation.
14. Save your InDesign work, then close the file.

Figure 74 *Timing panel settings for Portfolio Project*

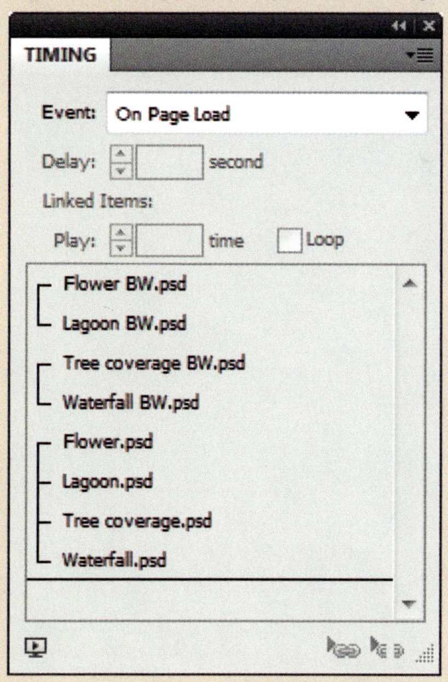

ACE CERTIFICATION GRID FOR ADOBE INDESIGN CS5

Topic Area	Objectives	Chapter(s)
1.0 Laying out a document	1.1 Create a new document with settings appropriate for print or onscreen display.	3 (p. 4)
	1.2 Adjust the size and position of one or more pages in a document with the Page tool.	8 (p. 15)
	1.3 Given a scenario, work with master pages (scenarios include: locking master page items; loading, creating, and applying master pages; based-on master pages; overriding master page items; text wrap).	3 (p. 4-43)
	1.4 Create a grid of objects while using the Place cursor, the Frame tools, or Selection tool.	8 (p. 16-21)
	1.5 Use the Gap tool to change the size or position of gaps and frames.	4 (p. 11-17)
	1.6 Use Layers to organize the structure of a document (scenarios include naming, arranging, and managing objects and groups).	4 (p. 20-31)
	1.7 Explain the process of using Data Merge to build a template and import data into a final InDesign or PDF document.	2 (p. 22)
	1.8 Modify and transform objects by using the transformation tools and the Control panel (including scaling, rotating, and resizing).	3 (p. 8-11, 22-23)
	1.9 Create, apply, and modify an object style.	8 (p. 38-51)
	1.10 Create, edit, and manipulate text on a path.	2 (p. 15)
	1.11 Describe the use of Smart Guides and the Smart Cursor (including their preferences).	1 (p. 35)
	1.12 Rotate page spreads and, when required, clear the rotation.	3 (p. 26)
	1.13 Use the CS Review panel to start a review, invite participants, and manage comments.	11 (p. 26)

CERTIFICATION GRID

(CONTINUED)

ACE CERTIFICATION GRID FOR ADOBE INDESIGN CS5		
Topic Area	**Objectives**	**Chapter(s)**
2.0 Working with text	2.1 Insert special characters by using the Type menu, Glyph panel, or context menu.	2 (p. 21) 3 (p. 25-27, 29)
	2.2 Given an option, edit text (options include: Story Editor, Drag and Drop text, Autocorrect).	2 (p. 27,28)
	2.3 Adjust the look of text inside a text frame by using Text Frame Options (including columns, inset spacing, first baseline offset, balanced columns, and vertical justification).	9 (p. 7)
	2.4 Given a scenario, set a paragraph to span across more than one text column or split into multiple sub-columns.	4 (p. 48)
	2.5 Manipulate text flow by using text threading, smart text reflow, resizing, and text wrap (including ignore text wrap).	3 (p. 44-55)
	2.6 Given a scenario, create and apply styles in an automated fashion (scenarios include next paragraph, nested styles, grep styles).	8 (p. 26-31)
	2.7 Manage review and editing using Track Changes.	2 (p. 31)
	2.8 Create a user dictionary and populate it with custom words.	2 (p. 27)
	2.9 Import an RTF or Word file and map style names to styles in the current document.	3 (p. 50)
	2.10 Assign and format automatic bullets or numbering to paragraphs (including numbering across multiple non-threaded frames).	2 (p. 30-33)
	2.11 Given a scenario, set up a document or frame-based baseline grid.	1 (p. 21)
	2.12 Make a dynamically changing running head (options include: text variables, section marker).	11 (p. 25)
	2.13 Create and apply text conditions and condition sets, including synchronizing across documents in a book.	3 (p. 16)
	2.14 Given a feature, avoid widows, orphans, and other typographic problems (using features such as Keep Options, Justification, Hyphenation).	2 (p. 14)

Topic Area	Objectives	Chapter(s)
ACE CERTIFICATION GRID FOR ADOBE INDESIGN CS5		
3.0 Working with tables	3.1 Modify tables (options include: adding or removing columns/rows, merging cells, splitting cells, selecting cells).	9 (p. 14-33)
	3.2 Edit and format a table (options include: formatting text, editing tables in the Story Editor, adding Notes, strokes and fills, text alignment).	9 (p. 14-33)
	3.3 Create, apply, import, modify, and organize cell and table styles.	9 (p. 14-33)
	3.4 Update the information in a table when the original data has changed (via linking or copy/paste).	9 (p. 14-33)
4.0 Managing graphics	4.1 Given a scenario, determine the best settings for choosing and placing an image (options include import options, Illustrator artboards, choice of file format, resolution, ICC color profiles, layers, and transparency).	4 (p. 32) 6 (p. 22-25)
	4.2 Given a scenario, configure the Links panel to reveal metadata and attributes such as current image resolution.	6 (p. 14-27)
	4.3 Create a graphic frame that resizes its content automatically.	6 (p. 5)
	4.4 Hide or show layers in placed PSD, AI, INDD, and PDF files, and discuss how image transparency is handled.	6 (p. 34-43)
	4.5 Manage placed files by using the Links panel (including revealing metadata and attributes in Link Info, editing the original, relinking to new files, and updating modified files).	6 (p. 14-21)
	4.6 Create a caption for a graphic based on the image's metadata.	4 (p. 44)
5.0 Understanding color and transparency	5.1 Explain the use of named swatches versus unnamed colors.	5 (p. 6-7, 11)
	5.2 Given a scenario, create, modify, and apply gradients to objects or text using the appropriate panels and tools.	5 (p. 30-37)
	5.3 Describe how and why to create mixed inks.	5 (p. 28)
	5.4 Assign transparency effects to stroke, fill, and image/text individually (options include opacity, blending modes, drop shadows, feathering, and other effects).	8 (p. 38-53)
	5.5 Given a scenario, choose the best course of action to manage color (options include Transparency Blend Space, Color Settings, Overprint Preview, ICC profiles, mixed RGB and CMYK).	8 (p. 51)

	ACE CERTIFICATION GRID FOR ADOBE INDESIGN CS5	
Topic Area	**Objectives**	**Chapter(s)**
6.0 Creating and working with long documents	6.1 Insert and format footnotes in a document.	2 (p. 10-11)
	6.2 Create a book in a book panel and paginate the documents.	10 (p. 4-15)
	6.3 Create a table of contents across one or more documents.	10 (p. 6-21)
	6.4 Synchronize master pages, styles, and swatches in a book.	10 (p. 17-20)
	6.5 Define and insert text variables.	11 (p. 25)
	6.6 Create and apply cross-references, edit cross-reference format.	10 (p. 28-30)
7.0 Building interactive documents	7.1 Create interactivity for an InDesign document that will be exported as a PDF or SWF document (including adding movies, animations, sounds, multistate objects, and buttons).	12 (entire chapter)
	7.2 Describe how to view, import, and control video and sound files, and to preview interactive document elements inside InDesign.	12 (p. 20, 27-29, 41,48-49)
	7.3 Create functional hyperlinks in exported PDF documents or SWF files (options include Hyperlinks panel, Table of Contents, Cross-References, and Buttons).	12 (p. 14, 21-23) (entire lesson 14-29 covers hyperlinks and buttons) 10 (p. 6-21, 28-30)
8.0 Importing and exporting for cross-media	8.1 Given a scenario, choose the correct options to export document content to Flash Professional CS5.	12 (p. 4-13, 31-33, 35-36)
	8.2 Given a scenario, choose the correct options to export a story or document to the ePub or XHTML format.	12 (p. 39)
	8.3 Given a scenario, choose the correct features and settings to create an interactive PDF file.	12 (p. 6-7)
	8.4 Define and assign XML tags, and export an XML file.	6 (p. 18)
	8.5 Map styles to tags and XML tags to styles using the Tags panel and the Structure view.	6 (p. 18)
9.0 Managing prepress and printing	9.1 Troubleshoot common printing issues by using Live Preflight (options include using Basic profile to locate and correct errors, create custom profile, create a Preflight report, share profiles).	11 (p. 18-21)
	9.2 Troubleshoot common printing issues by using the Separations Preview panel (options include process inks, spot colors, ink density, and the Ink Manager).	11 (p. 12-17)
	9.3 Given a scenario, choose the appropriate Print dialog box options (options include Printers Marks, Bleeds, Output Space, PPD fonts).	11 (p. 7, 10-11)
	9.4 Given a scenario, choose the appropriate PDF Preset or PDF Export settings.	11 (p. 27-31)

ADOBE INDESIGN CS5			
Chapter	**Data File Supplied***	**Student Creates File**	**Used In**
Chapter 1	ID 1-1.indd		Lesson 1
	ID 1-2.indd		Lesson 2, 3, 4, Skills Review
	ID 1-3.indd		Skills Review
	ID 1-4.indd		Skills Review
	None	Student creates file, explores interface, no solution file	Project Builder 1
	ID 1-5.indd		Project Builder 2
	ID 1-6.indd		Design Project
	ID 1-7.indd		Portfolio Project
Chapter 2	ID 2-1.indd		Lesson 1 & 2
	ID 2-2.indd		Lesson 3
	ID 2-3.indd		Lesson 4
	ID 2-4.indd		Lesson 5
	ID 2-5.indd		Skills Review
	ID 2-6.indd		Skills Review
	ID 2-7.indd		Skills Review
	ID 2-8.indd		Skills Review
	ID 2-9.indd		Project Builder 1
	ID 2-10.indd		Project Builder 2
	ID 2-11.indd		Design Project
	ID 2-12.indd		Portfolio Project

*See Support Files List at end of table for a list of files students do not open, but need in order to work with the Data Files.

DATA FILES LIST

(CONTINUED)

ADOBE INDESIGN CS5			
Chapter	**Data File Supplied***	**Student Creates File**	**Used In**
Chapter 3	ID 3-1.indd		Lessons 1, 2, 3, 4
	ID 3-2.indd		Lesson 5, 6
	None	Skills Review	Skills Review
	ID 3-3.indd		Project Builder 1
	ID 3-4.indd		Project Builder 2
	ID 3-5.indd		Design Project
	ID 3-6.indd		Portfolio Project
Chapter 4	ID 4-1.indd		Lesson 1
	ID 4-2.indd		Lesson 1
	ID 4-3.indd		Lesson 1
	ID 4-4.indd		Lesson 2
	ID 4-5.indd		Lesson 2
	ID 4-6.indd		Lesson 3
	ID 4-7. indd		Lesson 4
	ID 4-8.indd		Skills Review
	ID 4-9.indd		Skills Review
	ID 4-10.indd		Project Builder 1
	ID 4-11.indd		Project Builder 2
	ID 4-12.indd		Design Project
	ID 4-13.indd		Portfolio Project

*See Support Files List at end of table for a list of files students do not open, but need in order to work with the Data Files.

ADOBE INDESIGN CS5			
Chapter	**Data File Supplied***	**Student Creates File**	**Used In**
Chapter 5	ID 5-1.indd		Lessons 1, 2, & 3
	ID 5-2.indd		Lesson 4
	ID 5-3.indd		Skills Review
	ID 5-4.indd		Skills Review
	ID 5-5.indd		Project Builder 1
	ID 5-6.indd		Project Builder 2
	ID 5-7.indd		Design Project
	ID 5-8.indd		Portfolio Project
Chapter 6	ID 6-1.indd		Lessons 1
	ID 6-2.indd		Lesson 2 & 3
	ID 6-3.indd		Lesson 4 & 5
	ID 6-4.indd		Lesson 6
	ID 6-5.indd		Skills Review
	ID 6-6.indd		Skills Review
	ID 6-7.indd		Project Builder 1
	ID 6-8.indd		Project Builder 2
	ID 6-9.indd		Design Project
	ID 6-10.psd		Portfolio Project
	ID 6-11.indd		Portfolio Project
Chapter 7	ID 7-1.indd		Lesson 1
	ID 7-2.indd		Lessons 2
	ID 7-3.indd		Skills Review
	ID 7-4.indd		Project Builder 1
	ID 7-5.indd		Project Builder 2
	ID 7-6.indd		Design Project
	ID 7-7.indd		Portfolio Project

ADOBE INDESIGN CS5			
Chapter	**Data File Supplied***	**Student Creates File**	**Used In**
Chapter 8	ID 8-1.indd		Lessons 1
	ID 8-2.indd		Lesson 1
	ID 8-3.indd		Lesson 2
	ID 8-4.indd		Lesson 3
	ID 8-5.indd		Lesson 3
	ID 8-6.indd		Lesson 3 & 4
	ID 8-7.indd		Lesson 5
	ID 8-8.indd		Lesson 6
	ID 8-9.indd		Skills Review
	ID 8-10.indd		Skills Review
	ID 8-11.indd		Skills Review
	ID 8-12.indd		Skills Review
	ID 8-13.indd		Skills Review
	ID 8-14.indd		Project Builder 1
	ID 8-15.indd		Project Builder 2
	ID 8-16.indd		Design Project
	ID 8-17.indd		Portfolio Project

*See Support Files List at end of table for a list of files students do not open, but need in order to work with the Data Files.

ADOBE INDESIGN CS5			
Chapter	**Data File Supplied***	**Student Creates File**	**Used In**
Chapter 9	ID 9-1.indd		Lesson 1
	ID 9-2.indd		Lessons 2 & 3
	ID 9-3.indd		Lessons 3 & 4
	ID 9-4.indd		Skills Review
	ID 9-5.indd		Skills Review
	ID 9-6.indd		Skills Review
	ID 9-7.indd		Project Builder 1
	ID 9-8.indd		Project Builder 2
	ID 9-9.indd		Design Project
	None	Holiday Chart	Portfolio Project
Chapter 10	ID 10-1.indd		Lessons 1, 2, 3, & 4
	ID 10-2.indd		Lessons 1, 2, 3, & 4
	ID 10-3.indd		Lessons 1, 2, 3, & 4
	ID 10-4.indd		Lessons 1, 2, 3, & 4
	ID 10-5.indd		Lessons 1, 2, 3, & 4
	ID 10-6.indd		Lesson 3
	ID 10-7.indd		Lesson 4
	ID 10-8.indd		Skills Review
	ID 10-9.indd		Skills Review
	ID 10-10.indd		Skills Review
	ID 10-11.indd		Skills Review
	ID 10-12.indd		Skills Review
	ID 10-13.indd		Skills Review
	ID 10-14.indd		Project Builder 1
	ID 10-15.indd		Project Builder 2
	ID 10-16.indd		Design Project
	ID 10-17.indd		Portfolio Project

DATA FILES LIST

(CONTINUED)

ADOBE INDESIGN CS5			
Chapter	**Data File Supplied***	**Student Creates File**	**Used In**
Chapter 11	ID 11-1.indd		Lesson 1, 2, 3, 4
	ID 11-2.indd		Skills Review
	ID 11-3.indd		Project Builder 1
	ID 11-4.indd		Project Builder 2
	ID 11-5.indd		Design Project
	ID 11-6.indd		Portfolio Project
Chapter 12	ID 12-1.indd		Lesson 1, 2, 3, 4, 5
	ID 12-2.indd		Skills Review
	ID 12-3.indd		Project Builder 1
	ID 12-4.indd		Project Builder 2
	ID 12-5.indd		Design Project
	ID 12-6.indd		Portfolio Project

*See Support Files List at end of table for a list of files students do not open, but need in order to work with the Data Files.

Chapter	Support Files Supplied
Chapter 1	AID Ambrosia, AID Apple Tart, AID Clio, AID Rhubarb Pie, AID Tea Cakes, AID Vacherin, Flower, Flower, Lagoon, Oualie Scarf, Tree coverage, Waterfall
Chapter 2	No support files
Chapter 3	Bulletin text, Chapter 1 text, Greek Text, Skills Review Text
Chapter 4	2 Windmills, AID Rhubarb Pie, Black 1, Black 2, Chapter 1 text.doc, Dog Silo, Flower, Flower Reduced, Lagoon, P8241449, P8241453, P8241476, P8241483, P8251520, P8251552, P8251555, Red 1, Red 2, Red Full Bleed, Red Silo, Sidebar copy, Skills Text, Test, Tree coverage, Vista, Waterfall, Windmill text, Windmills Color, Windmills Ghost, Windmills Silhouette, Windmills Spread
Chapter 5	BW Wally Head Silo, BW Wally Scarf, LAB, Living Graphic, OAHU graphic, Oahu, Wally Head Silo, Wally Scarf, White LAB
Chapter 6	Black 1, Black 2, Black Ghost, Black on Blue, Blake, Dog Layer, Dog Silo, Faces of the Min Pin, Final Logo, Flower, Logo, Greek Text, LAB, Lagoon, Logo with Shadow, Message from Montag Min Pin Text, Montag, Orange Dogs, Petey, Puppies, Red 1, Red 2, Red Full Bleed, Red Ghost, Red Silo, Red Silo with Alpha Channels, Skills Text, Snowball, Spotlight, Susan Headshot, Wally Head Silo, Wally Scarf, Waterfall

Chapter 6 Subfolders and Contents

- **EOU Moved**
  susan
- **Hidden Tree**
  Tree coverage
- **Moved Files**
  Corniglia, Duomo, Hat
- **Photography**
  Arno, Bicycle, Birdseye, Boats, Bus stop, Campanile, Cemetery, Child, Corniglia, David, Divers, Dusk, Fauna, Girls, HiFi, Launch, Leather, Man and Strega, Manarola, Michael Jackson, Monterossa, Mountain Path, Pisano, Sculler, Sheets, Shrine, Statue, Strega, Sunflowers, Three houses, Townsfolk, Window, Woman in Window

DATA FILES LIST

(CONTINUED)

Chapter	Support Files Supplied
Chapter 7	Atlas, Blue clouds, bullseye, Color Lagoon, Garden Party, Garden Party Screen, Gray Clouds, Orange Clouds, witch template
Chapter 8	Flower, Lagoon, Portrait, Tree Coverage, Waterfall
	Chapter 8 Subfolders and Contents
	■ **Florence**
	Arch, Bags, Bodega Statue, Campanile, Façade, Luigi, Manequins, Pay Phone, Pisano, Placard, Sabines, Soda, Strega and Man, Strega, Sunrise, Towels
	■ **Photography**
	Arno, Bicycle, Birdseye, Boats, Bus stop, Campanile, Cemetery, Child, Corniglia, David, Divers, Dusk, Fauna, Girls, HiFi, Launch, Leather, Man and Strega, Manarola, Michael Jackson, Monterossa, Mountain Path, Pisano, Sculler, Sheets, Shrine, Statue, Strega, Sunflowers, Three houses, Townsfolk, Window, Woman in Window
Chapter 9	Crab salad, CT State Flag, Gnocchi, Key, Kids.psd, Kids.tif, MA State Flag, masks, ME State Flag, Moon, Music, NH State Flag, RI State Flag, Sole, Striped bass, sun, Susans Logo, Take out, take out, tie, Tuna, Veal, VT State Flag
Chapter 10	Afghan, Appetizers, Beagle, Bull Terrier, Collie, Desserts, Entrees, Labrador, MinPin, Poodle, Soups
Chapter 11	Chapter 1 text, Flower.psd, LAB, Lagoon, Living Graphic, Oahu, Tree coverage, Wally Head Silo, Wally Scarf, Waterfall, Windmills Color, Windmills Ghost, Windmills Silhouette
Chapter 12	■ **Links**
	Bicycle, Birdseye, Boats, Bus stop, Corniglia, Corniglia BW, David, Divers, Duomo, Dusk, Fauna, Flower, Flower BW, Hat, Lagoon, Lagoon BW, Launch, Manarola, Manarola BW, Pisano, Sheets, Three houses, Tree coverage, Tree coverage BW, Waterfall, Waterfall BW, Window, Woman in Window, Woman in Window BW
	■ **Sounds**
	Click, Squeak

GLOSSARY

A

Actions
Indicate what happens when the specific interactive event occurs—usually when someone clicks a button.

Align
To position objects in specific relationship to each other on a given axis.

Alpha channel
Selections made in Photoshop that have been saved with a descriptive name, and which can be loaded into an InDesign document.

Anchored Objects
Objects created and used as text characters within a block of text.

Animation effects
Let you make objects move and fade, appear and disappear, in your exported layout.

Arrange
To adjust the position of an object in the stacking order.

Autoflow
The automatic threading of text through multiple text frames.

B

Baseline
The imaginary line on which a line of text sits.

Bitmap graphics
Images that are created by pixels in a program like Photoshop. Every digital image and scanned graphic is a bitmap graphic.

Bleed marks
Marks that define the bleed size.

Bleeds
Areas of the layout that extend to the trim size.

Blending modes
An InDesign feature that allows you to create different transparency and color effects where two or more objects overlap.

Bounding box
Always rectangular, the frame that defines the horizontal and vertical dimensions of the graphic.

Buttons
Perform actions when the InDesign document is exported to SWF or PDF formats. Clicking a button could take you to a different page in the document, or it could open a website, or it could play a movie, a sound, or an animation. Buttons you create are listed and formatted in the Buttons panel.

C

Caps
Define the appearance of end points when a stroke is added to a path. The Stroke panel offers three types of caps: butt, round, and projecting.

Cell
A rectangle in a table row or column.

Clipping path
A graphic you draw in Photoshop that outlines the areas of the image to be shown when the file is placed in a layout program like InDesign.

Closed path
Continuous lines that do not contain end points.

Color bars
Used to maintain consistent color on press.

Color stops
Colors added to a gradient located between the starting and ending colors.

Column break
A typographic command that forces text to the next column.

Columns
Vertical page guides often used to define the width of text frames and body copy. Also, in a table, the vertical arrangement of cells.

Compound paths
One or more closed paths joined using the Make Compound Path command to create one complete path. You create compound paths when you want to use one object to cut a hole in another object.

Condition set
A snapshot of the current visibility of applied conditions to text; Allows you to set multiple conditions simultaneously.

Content Management Application
A framework to organize and access electronic content, such as Adobe Bridge.

Corner points
Anchor points that create a corner between two line segments.

Crop marks
Guide lines that define the trim size.

D

Dashed strokes
Strokes that consist of a series of dashes and gaps, created and formatted using the Stroke panel.

Data merge
When a data source containing fields and records is merged with a target document to create personalized documents.

Direction handle
The round blue circle at the top of the direction line that you drag to modify a direction line.

Direction lines
Two lines attached to a smooth point. Direction lines determine the arc of the curved path, depending on their direction and length.

Distributing
Positioning objects on a page so that they are spaced evenly in relation to one another.

Dock
To connect the bottom edge of one panel to the top edge of another panel so that both move together.

Document grid
An alignment guide to which objects can be aligned and snapped.

Drop cap
A design element in which the first letter or letters of a paragraph are increased in size to create a visual effect.

Dynamic preview
An InDesign feature in which the entirety of a placed graphic, including areas outside a graphics frame, can be seen as the graphic is being moved.

E

Em space
A type of white space inserted into a text box. The width of an em space is equivalent to that of the lowercase letter m in the current typeface and type size.

En space
A type of white space inserted into a text box. The width of an en space is equivalent to that of the lowercase letter n in the current typeface and type size.

Effective resolution
The resolution of a placed image based on its size in the layout.

Ending color
The last color in a gradient.

Event
The specific interactive occurrence that triggers the action of a button.

F

FLA
File format used for exporting InDesign layouts to Adobe Flash.

Facing pages
Two pages in a layout that face each other, as in an open magazine, book, or newspaper.

Fields
Labels in a data source that categorize information in the records of a database, which are placed in a target document to specify how to do a data merge.

Fill
A color you apply to the inside of an object.

Flash
Adobe System's web authoring software.

Flattening
Merging all layers in a layered document.

Frames
Rectangular, oval, or polygonal shapes that you use for a variety of purposes, such as creating a colored area on the document or placing text and graphics.

Frame edges
Visible edges of frames; when frames are selected, edges are automatically highlighted.

G

Glyphs
Alternate versions of type characters; usually used for symbols like trademarks, etc.

Gradient
A graduated blend between two or more colors.

Graphic
An element on a page that is not text. In an InDesign document, refers to a bitmap or vector image.

Graphics frames
Rectangles in which you place imported artwork.

Grayscale image
A digital image reproduced using only one color. In most cases, that color is black.

GREP style
A style that is applied to patterns of text, such as a telephone number, based on code.

Gridify
To position frames into a grid pattern in one move, using tool and keypad combinations.

Gridify Behaviors
Various gridify moves accomplished using various tool and keypad combinations.

Guides
Horizontal or vertical lines that you position on a page. As their name suggests, guides are used to help guide you in aligning objects on the page.

Gutter
The space between two columns.

——————— **H** ———————

Hyperlinks
Interactive text that jumps to other pages in a document, another document, an email address or to a website.

——————— **I** ———————

In port
A small box in the upper-left corner of a text frame that you can click to flow text from another text frame.

Interpolation
The process by which Photoshop creates new pixels in a graphic to maintain an image's resolution.

——————— **J** ———————

Joins
Define the appearance of a corner point when a path has a stroke applied to it as miter, round, or bevel.

——————— **K** ———————

Kerning
The process of increasing or decreasing space between a pair of characters.

——————— **L** ———————

Leading
The vertical space between lines of text.

Libraries
Files you create that appear as a panel in your InDesign document for organizing and storing graphics. Also called Object Libraries.

Linear gradient
A series of straight lines that gradate from one color to another (or through multiple colors).

——————— **M** ———————

Margin Guides
Page guides that define the interior borders of a document.

Master items
All objects on the master page that function as a place where objects on the document pages are to be positioned.

Master pages
Templates that you create for a page layout or for the layout of an entire publication.

Merged document
A target document which has been merged with records from a data source.

Motion presets
Pre-defined animations that you can apply quickly and easily to objects in your layout.

Multiply
A practical and useful blending mode in which the object becomes transparent but retains its color.

——————— **N** ———————

Named color
Any color that you create in the New Color Swatch dialog box.

Nested styles
Paragraph styles that contain two or more character styles within the paragraph style.

Non-destructive effects
Applied effects such as glows, shadows, bevels, and embosses that do not permanently change the graphic to which they are applied.

Normal mode
Screen mode in which all page elements, including margin guides, ruler guides, frame edges and the pasteboard are visible.

——————— **O** ———————

Object Libraries
See *Libraries*

Objects
Text or graphic elements such as images, blocks of color and even simple lines that are placed in an InDesign document.

Offset
The distance that text is repelled from a frame. Also, the specified horizontal and vertical distance a copy of an object will be from the original.

Open path
A path whose end points are not connected.

Orphans
Words or single lines of text at the bottom of a column or page that become separated from the other lines in a paragraph.

Out port
A small box in the lower right corner of a text frame that flows text out to another text frame when clicked.

Override
To modify a master page item on a document page.

Overset text
Text that does not fit in a text frame.

P

Page information

A type of printer's marks that includes the title of the InDesign document.

Page size

See *Trim size.*

Page transitions

Display classic video transition effects, such as dissolve, push, or wipe, when you're moving from page to page in an exported SWF or PDF document.

Paragraph return

Inserted into the text formatting by pressing [Enter] (Win) or [return] (Mac). Also called a hard return.

Pasteboard

The area surrounding the document.

Paths

Straight or curved lines created with vector graphics.

Pixel

Nickname for picture element; a single-colored square that is the smallest component of a bitmap graphic.

Point

A unit used to measure page elements equal to 1/72 of an inch.

Point of origin

The location on the object from which a transform is executed.

Preflight

Refers to checking out a document before it's released to a printer or downloaded to an output device.

Presentation mode

A screen mode in which all non-printing elements, panels, and Application bar are invisible and the page is centered and sized against a black background so that the entire document fits in the monitor window.

Preview file

A low-resolution version of the placed graphic file. As such, its file size is substantially smaller than the average graphic file.

Preview mode

A screen mode in which all non-printing page elements are invisible.

Preview panel

Shows a preview of animations in your document.

Printer's marks

Include crop marks, bleed marks, registration marks, color bars, and page information.

Process colors

Colors you create (and eventually print) by mixing varying percentages of cyan, magenta, yellow, and black (CMYK) inks.

Process inks

Cyan, Magenta, Yellow, and Black ink; the fundamental inks used in printing.

Pull quote

A typographical design solution in which text is used at a larger point size and positioned prominently on the page.

R

Radial gradient

A series of concentric circles, in which the starting color appears at the center of the gradient, then radiates out to the ending color.

Records

Rows of information organized by fields in a data source file.

Registration marks

Marks that align color-separated output.

Registration swatch

The swatch you should use as the fill color for slug text so that it appears on all printing plates.

Resolution

The number of pixels in an inch in a bitmap graphic.

Resolution Independent

When an image has no pixels; usually refers to vector graphics.

Row

In a table, the horizontal arrangement of cells.

Ruler Guides

Horizontal and vertical rules that you can position anywhere in a layout as a reference for positioning elements.

Rulers

Measurement utilities positioned at the top and left side of the pasteboard to help you align objects.

Rules

Horizontal, vertical or diagonal lines on the page used as design elements or to underline text.

S

SWF

Acronym for Shockwave Flash. Supports all InDesign interactivity, including animation.

Screen Mode

Options for viewing documents, such as Preview, Normal, and Presentation mode

Sections

Pages in a document where page numbering changes.

Semi-autoflow
A method for manually threading text through multiple frames.

Silhouette
A selection you make in Photoshop using selection tools, such as the Pen tool.

Slug
A note you include on your document for a printer. A slug usually contains special instructions for outputting your document.

Slug area
The area for a slug, positioned outside of the document's trim size, so that it will be discarded when the document is trimmed.

Smart Guides
Guides that appear automatically when you move objects in a document that provide information to help position objects precisely in relation to the page or other objects.

Smooth points
Anchor points that connect curved segments.

Snippet
An XML file with an .inds file extension that contains complete representation of document elements, including all formatting tags and document structure.

Soft return
In typography, using the Shift key in addition to the Enter (Win) or [return] (Mac) key to move text onto the following line without creating a new paragraph.

Spot colors
Non-process inks that are manufactured by companies; special pre-mixed inks that are printed separately from process inks.

Spread
See Facing pages.

Square-up
The default placement of a Photoshop file in InDesign that includes the entire image with background.

Stacking order
Refers to the hierarchical order of objects on a level.

Starting color
The first color in a gradient.

Stroke
A color applied to the outline of an object.

Stroke weight
The thickness of a stroke, usually measured in points.

Style
A group of formatting attributes that can be applied to text or objects.

——————— **T** ———————

Tables
Rectangles in horizontal rows and vertical columns that organize information.

Tabs
A command that positions text at specific horizontal locations within a text frame.

Target document
An InDesign file containing text that will be seen by all recipients as well as placeholders representing fields in a data source with which it will be merged.

Target layer
The layer selected on the Layers panel.

Targeting
Clicking a layer on the Layers panel to select it.

Text frames
Boxes drawn with the Type tool in which you type or place text.

Text insets
In a text frame, the distance the text is from the frame edge.

Threading
Linking text from one text frame to another.

Timing panel
Command central for controlling when animated objects play.

Tint
In InDesign, a lighter version of a given color.

Tracking
Adjusting the spaces between letters in a word or paragraph.

Transform
The act of moving, scaling, skewing, or rotating an object.

Transparency blend space
Setting that applies to managing color for transparency in your InDesign layout.

Trim size
The size to which a printed document will be cut when it clears the printing press.

——————— **U** ———————

Unnamed colors
Any colors you create that aren't saved to the Swatches panel.

V

Vector graphics
Artwork created entirely by geometrically defined paths and curves. Usually created and imported from Adobe Illustrator.

Vectors
Straight or curved paths defined by geometrical characteristics, usually created and imported from a drawing program.

W

Widows
Words or single lines of text at the top of a column or page that become separated from the ther lines in a paragraph.

Workspace
The arrangement of windows and panels on your monitor.

Z

Zero point
By default, the upper-left corner of the document; the point from which the location of all objects on the page is measured.

ART CREDITS

INDESIGN ART CREDITS	
Chapter 1	©Neal Cooper | Dreamstime.com ©iStockphoto.com/ETIEN
Chapter 2	©Richard Carey | Dreamstime.com ©iStockphoto.com/Alex Bramwell
Chapter 3	©Chris Lorenz | Dreamstime.com ©Vladimir Sazonov | Shutterstock Images
Chapter 4	©Gkuna | Dreamstime.com ©Tony Emmett | Shutterstock Images
Chapter 5	©Morten Elm | Dreamstime.com ©Michael Zysman | Dreamstime.com
Chapter 6	©iStockphoto.com/Nico Smit Photography ©iStockphoto.com/Freder
Chapter 7	©iStockphoto.com/Malsbury Enterprises Ltd ©iStockphoto.com/charcoal design
Chapter 8	©Jemini Joseph | Dreamstime.com ©Janice McCafferty | Dreamstime.com
Chapter 9	©Christian Bech | Dreamstime.com ©iStockphoto.com/ThaiEagle
Chapter 10	©Jay Bo | Shutterstock Images ©123RF LIMITED | Kitch Bain
Chapter 11	©Kendrick Moholt Photography ©Creativemarc | Dreamstime.com
Chapter 12	©Davthy | Dreamstime.com ©Michael Zysman | Dreamstime.com
Data Files/Glossary/Index	©Dsmith123 | Dreamstime.com ©worldswildlifewonders | Shutterstock Images